BILL
CLINTON

BILL CLINTON

Mastering the Presidency

NIGEL HAMILTON

PublicAffairs
New York

Published in the United States by PublicAffairs™, a member of the Perseus Books Group.

Printed in the United States of America.

Library of Congress Cataloging-in-Publication Data
Hamilton, Nigel.
  Bill Clinton : mastering the presidency / Nigel Hamilton. — 1st ed.
     p. cm.
  Includes bibliographical references and index.
  ISBN-13: 978-1-58648-516-0 (hardcover)
  ISBN-10: 1-58648-516-4 (hardcover)
  1. Clinton, Bill, 1946- 2. Presidents—United States—Biography. 3. United States—Politics and government—1993–2001. 4. Political leadership—United States—Case studies. I. Title.

E886.H365 2007
973.929'092—dc22
[B]

2007014494

10 9 8 7 6 5 4 3 2 1

for Raynel

CONTENTS

PROLOGUE

B ILL CLINTON BECAME PRESIDENT OF THE UNITED STATES at a defining moment in its history, following the end of the Cold War: the flowering of a new era of communications, and a raft of new global challenges, from trade to terrorism. He was the first of his generation—the so-called "baby boomers"—to win the White House, and his period in office was marked by intense partisanship that reached its apogee in one of the most extraordinary scandals in American history. Many books have been written by participants, observers, and journalists since those momentous events, but no full-scale biography of the man at the center of this whirlwind: William Jefferson Clinton, née Blythe.

In *Bill Clinton: An American Journey* I first recounted the background and formation of Bill Clinton's *character*: not only as an Arkansas saga par excellence, but as the archetypal story of a baby boomer facing the multiplicity of opportunities, challenges, and seductions of his generation in America, from Vietnam to sex, drugs, and rock-and-roll. Predictably, although I interviewed as many witnesses of Clinton's early years and his rise to political triumph as I could, the book aroused the ire and even scorn of many readers still conflicted in the way they feel about the issues of the sixties and seventies, from feminism and fidelity to liberalism and the draft.

Bill Clinton: Mastering the Presidency is no longer about personality but about performance. How did the Man from Hope *do*, once he won the White House?

Over the years I have made the study of leadership—literary, military, and political—my particular biographical focus. In recounting the life and times of Bill Clinton as forty-second president I wanted to address something no previous writer—including the president himself, in his somewhat calendrical memoirs—has really tackled. I wished to penetrate the fog of political war and describe this man's faltering, at first disastrous, but ultimately successful attempt to become a truly modern president, in a modern world. It is, to my mind, one of the epic sagas of the 1990s.

In telling this story, I have concentrated my account on key episodes of Clinton's first term as president, beginning with the worst transition since presidential transitions began; the lamentable failure to appoint an effective chief of staff (which thereby compelled his unelected wife to perform part of that role); and the series of missteps and fiascoes that followed, at every level from domestic policy and congressional relations to international failures such as Somalia, the *Harlan County* episode, the genocide in Rwanda, and the failure to intercede in Bosnia. The disaster over Hillary Clinton's health care reform capped a litany of first-term errors—and when the Democratic majority in both houses of Congress was lost in the great midterm meltdown of November 1994 it looked as if President William Jefferson Clinton's days in office, for all his genius-level IQ, were numbered.

How Bill Clinton reinvented himself thereafter and came close to greatness as president of the United States in the final decade of the twentieth century is to my mind one of the most extraordinary reversals of fortune in modern American biography. Understandably it is not a story that President Clinton—who dislikes admitting to error or inconstancy—has been anxious to tell, yet it is one that, for his biographer, has a truly epic quality. As will be seen, I do not take the view held by his media director and later adviser George Stephanopoulos that, following the loss of Congress in 1994, Bill Clinton became a liberal turncoat. Nor do I subscribe to the president's own version of his presidency, in his memoirs, as a problem merely of communication with the public. Rather, I see his first term in office as an object lesson: an archetypal example of how *not* to conduct the presidency of the United States, followed by an extraordinary learning curve in which the young man from Hope—or better said, Hot Springs—faced up to his mistakes and *refashioned himself* as the undisputed leader of his country, at home and abroad. Aided by a new and effective chief of staff, his performance—from the Oklahoma City bombing to the bombing of the Serbs, the imposition of a peace in Bosnia that has held to the present day, and the bitter struggle to counter Newt Gingrich's shutdown of the U.S. government— became possibly the greatest example of self-reinvention as president in office in modern times, and, as such, contrasts vividly with its polar opposite, the promising start but disastrous performance of his successor, the forty-third president, in the White House.

At a time when the Bush administration has lost its way—internationally and domestically—it is, in my view, all the more important to look afresh at the experience of Bill Clinton in his first term of office, before another Democrat is elected president.

The world has changed a great deal since November 1992, when Governor Bill Clinton triumphed over President George H. W. Bush at the polls. Yet the *challenges* of presidential leadership remain the same, from the importance of the transition to the staffing and running of the White House in the first months of a new administration, and the tackling of domestic and international issues thereafter. Charting, in the context of Bill Clinton's character, the vicissitudes and disasters of his early presidency, followed by his belated epiphany when all seemed lost and he was widely seen as a lame duck, seems to me a very important journey to reconstruct. Once Bill Clinton finally figured out the way to be president as a Democrat, he became unbeatable—and thereafter he led his country not only into the longest sustained economic boom in its entire annals, but set American standing in the world higher than it has ever been since.

Much of the above became obscured, sadly, by the Lewinsky scandal and the impeachment of President Clinton, later in his second term. It was for that reason, among others, that I felt it vital to separate Bill Clinton's first term from his second—when the dogs of fanatical Republicanism finally brought a popularly elected serving president to the edge of resignation, with grave implications for America's role as a world leader; indeed, paved the way, as they had prayed, for a Republican incumbent who, they dreamed, would do better: be a more muscular, more ideological figure, less concerned with public opinion and America's standing in the outside world. Well, that alternative approach to leadership has been tried—and found deeply, deeply wanting.

Every president of the United States is the subject of retrospective judgment and assessment; this is mine—as Clinton's first full-scale biographer. I hope this account of Bill Clinton's epic first term as president will find favor, if not among all readers, then at least among those who favor a change in direction in American governance today. Most of all, however, I hope it will be read for what it is: the life story of one of the most extraordinary figures of our time.

BOOK ONE

PARADISE LOST

THE FRESHMAN

CHAPTER ONE

INAUGURATION

Washingstock

Driven from Monticello in a simple bus bearing the registration "Hope 1," President-elect William Jefferson Clinton and Mrs. Clinton arrived at the Lincoln Memorial, Washington, D.C., at 3 P.M. on the afternoon of January 17, 1993, where they were welcomed by a Quincy Jones-produced musical event, held before four hundred thousand supporters. After twelve years of Republican presidential rule there was palpable excitement on the Mall as the vast, outdoor extravaganza began, in bright winter sunshine, starring Diana Ross, Michael Jackson, and Bob Dylan. "Here at the feet of Mr. Lincoln, let us renew our pledge to the reunion of America in our time, a union not just in law but in fact, a union not simply physical but also spiritual," Clinton implored at the climax. "Let us build an American home for the twenty-first century, where everyone has a place at the table and not a single child is left behind." Thereafter, like the Pied Piper, he personally led the crowds across Memorial Bridge. The Clinton administration was about to begin.

Gazing at the "polycultural mass" of families and faces, taking in their decidedly Democratic attire, hearing Bob Dylan live from the stage below the Lincoln Memorial, the picture resembled "nothing less than Washingstock," a triad of *Village Voice* journalists recorded, noting the "palpable feeling of hope and optimism" as the crowds surged forward behind their new leader. Under the headline "SHOWTIME" the reporters considered that the "television inauguration of Bill Clinton" would finally complete the "transition of his 60s generation into the 90s."

How accurate was the comparison, though? "On the screen," the reporters warned, the "gathering on the Mall undoubtedly inspired a sense of budding empowerment," yet to "walk that crowd was to sense that we were there mostly as props for a show—and worse, most of us were comfortable with that passive role." The sixties might well be back in vogue, even in spirit—but sixties *activism* was not; indeed it was almost the reverse, as *anti*-sixties activists—religious fundamentalists, anti-abortion activists, gun lobbyists, and right-wing opponents of government—prepared to vent their frustrations against a largely passive majority.

Oblivious of this sullen, unseen intifada, President-elect Bill Clinton's fans meanwhile converged on the capital and the parties, some tickets to events costing as much as five hundred dollars per person. The black magazine *Jet* recorded that "they had a ball—eleven balls to be exact," on the eve of the inauguration itself, with some seventy thousand revelers forming seas of "happy humanity as they listened to rock n' roll, R&B, soul, funk and pop, and moved in waves of excitement on ballroom floors executing waltzes, conga-lines, the two-step, tangos, the electric slide and every dance in between—at eleven official balls!"

The repetition of the number was significant. For Eisenhower's 1953 inauguration, forty years before, the number of balls had been increased from one to two. "But Ike wasn't a Baby Boomer," *Jet*'s editors pointed out.

Aged forty-six, William Jefferson Clinton had become "a symbol of just how much things have changed since then." At the Arkansas Ball in the Washington Convention Center, for example, the president-elect took a saxophone from Ben E. King and played "Your Momma Don't Dance." In the Armory, at another ball, he played "Night Train." Thelonious Monk, Herbie Hancock, Grover Washington Jr., Wayne Shorter, and a host of other musicians and singers from Michael Jackson to Barbra Streisand played, crooned, and celebrated the arch-baby boomer's rise to supreme authority. What General Robert L. Stephens, chief of the inaugural festivities, had thought would be "a run-of-the-mill program" now "zoomed into a spectacle—the largest, most far-ranging and colorful presidential inauguration ever designed. The new team of President Bill Clinton and Vice President Al Gore has generated more enthusiasm, say insiders, than even the inaugural reception for President John F. Kennedy."

Younger people certainly seemed to enjoy the circus while remaining remarkably, indeed almost cynically, undeceived. "Dylan sounded terrible," wrote the rock critic Greil Marcus, "but his purple jacket with black appliqué was fabulous; he looked as if he'd bought a Nashville haberdashery." Nor was Marcus entirely convinced by the marriage of sixties folksong and, at last, a baby boomer president. The "We are the World" anthem "brought forth great good feeling," he acknowledged, "no matter that at the heart of the performance there was perhaps only a glamorous sheen of communal self-recognition disguising a new leader who may leave the country as he found it." Clinton's "demeanor" was full of promise, but had to be seen against "his political instinct to pull back at the first sign of trouble," Marcus warned. If there was to be change in America, it would be up to those who really wanted to make it happen, he said. "Desires have been loosed in the air, and there's no telling where they'll light"—though, as he added with prophetic caution, the grand wedding of Mr. Froggie and Miss Mousie had ended, in *Good as I Been to You*, with "the massacre of the bride, groom, and everyone else at the party."

In other words, many were celebrating, but few were holding their breath.

The Ship of the Sixties

An estimated 800,000 people—predominantly young, more ethnically diverse than ever before, and distinctly more casual in dress and demeanor— were in Washington to witness the inauguration of the first Democratic president in twelve years.

The casualness of dress worried those who stood by the dignity of the event—indeed, such observers were often outraged by the lack of respect for the emblems of tradition and patriotism beloved by hardcore Republicans. Donna Minkowitz, writing for the *Village Voice*, described how, at the Triangle Ball, "kicked-out marine Joe Steffan sang the national anthem while an honor guard of homosexuals purged from the military carried in the flag."

Older Washingtonians, recalling JFK's inauguration, were shocked, yet impressed, too, by the obvious and genuine public outpouring of hope and goodwill. To those who criticized Clinton for being ersatz Kennedy, the seventy-two-year-old millionairess Pamela Harriman, for example, gave short shrift. Bill Clinton, she reminded them, had "got there all by himself." (Ms. Harriman knew; she had taken Winston Churchill's son Randolph as her first husband, followed by a series of millionaires.)

Vice President Al Gore's mother, however, took a less enthusiastic view. "Bill came up in a *very* provincial atmosphere," she later sniffed at Bill Clinton's social credentials. "And even though he went to Yale, and he went to Oxford, you don't undo or move out of that provincial atmosphere that has influenced you in your early life."

Could he not? Certainly President and Mrs. George Bush were amazed when the president-elect, after returning to Blair House at 2 A.M. on January 20, 1993, in the wake of the eleven inaugural balls, and having worked till 4:30 A.M. on the hopefully final draft of his inaugural speech, and having then worshipped at the black Metropolitan AME church near the White House (the first time an incoming president and his vice president had ever chosen a black church to attend on inauguration morning) arrived at the White House a half hour late, accompanied by his wife—and two uninvited guests!

As a White House FBI agent recalled, one of the reasons for the tardiness "was because Vice President Gore had just found out that the West Wing office usually reserved for the vice president was instead going to be occupied by the first lady." The resultant uproar caused by this discovery had been witnessed by network television cameras "trained on Blair House." These had "recorded a glimpse of the president and first lady screaming at each other."

The FBI agent was not the only one to be amazed by the tempest. "A shocked park police guard later reported that Clinton had referred to his wife as a "fucking bitch," Hillary's biographer Joyce Milton recorded, "while she came charging out the front door calling him a 'stupid mother-fucker.' " "Sources I consider very reliable affirm that Clinton told Hillary that if she didn't back off from her plans to unseat Gore, Gore would go public with his anger and perhaps resign," the White House FBI agent recalled. Hillary merely shouted at her husband "that as far as she was concerned, they had a deal—a deal that dated back to the campaign, when Lloyd Cutler had convinced her to stand by Clinton despite the allegations that he'd had an affair with Gennifer Flowers. The matter had already been decided, she said, and she had no intention of backing off; Gore was bluffing."

The Kiss of Death

In a presidential partnership that was clearly going to break new ground in the history of the White House, such marital discord was amazing, especially to those supporters concerned lest Hillary blow her chance of preparing America for a more proactive first lady.

The columnist Sally Quinn had already noted that Hillary had become, in the lead-up to the inauguration, "Topic A" in the offices, in the drawing rooms, and at the dining tables of the capital. "At a Washington dinner recently she was heard to talk about the budget. She was impressive and knowledgeable. But her conversation was peppered with 'we,'" as in " 'We got our first look at the budget.' Those who've known Hillary for years say that she has always used 'we,' that the Clintons have always operated as a team. But Little Rock is not Washington. 'We' is the kiss of death in Washington," Ms. Quinn warned.

It was not that Hillary should confine herself to being but a conventional homemaker, Quinn wrote. It was simply that "Hillary Clinton was not elected president." It would, Quinn added, "be preferable for Hillary Clinton to get something outside government in her own field of child welfare, health and education." She should certainly "not attend her husband's meetings. Poor Rosalynn Carter, whose motives were pure and whose heart was in the right place, got killed for going to cabinet meetings. She had the right idea—to be informed—but she did it the wrong way. . . . She set herself up for criticism. Nancy Reagan operated 'behind the scenes': she called people up on the telephone and told them what to do. Never mind that sometimes she was right. People hated her for it, and in the end it destroyed her reputation."

Among Washington's professional women of Hillary's generation, Quinn pointed out, "women lawyers, lobbyists, reporters, producers, economists, environmentalists and health-care experts are watching with a mixture of pride and apprehension to see how she is going to handle the position. These are women who have worked their way up in Washington, which has always been and still is to a certain extent a man's town. Many of these women are worried that she has already made a few missteps that could get her off to a troubled start."

The caution was meant kindly. But would Hillary listen? Dick Morris, pollster-architect of Bill Clinton's gubernatorial comeback in 1982, knew Hillary much better than Quinn did—and knew that the argument over an office in the West Wing was par for the Clinton course. "From the very beginning of his time in politics, she has alternated between constructive periods of abstinence from direct political involvement," Morris later reflected, "and destructive phases when she assumes a greater role and more power than the public will tolerate." By saving her husband during the controversy over his relationship with Gennifer Flowers, Hillary had persuaded herself that Bill owed her one. "It always starts when Hillary has to rescue her husband from sexual accusations. But, after the rescue, Hillary assumes greater power over the rest of her husband's career than she should. Like the Russians," he noted, "she gets rid of the Germans for you, but then she sticks around."

At the White House, the two uninvited guests, Harry and Linda Bloodworth Thomason (the Hollywood-Arkansas couple who had made the *Man from Hope* movie for the Democratic convention), attempted to keep the peace between the president-elect and his consort as they met with the outgoing president and first lady.

In her memoirs Hillary would refer only to "coffee and small talk" in the Blue Room. Hillary's biographer Gail Sheehy described, however, a more dramatic rencontre. The Bushes, Sheehy wrote, "were startled. The Clintons wanted to show their friends the Lincoln Bedroom, where they would be spending the night, seemingly treating the White House as a group share."

The Bushes, unaware of the Thomasons' peace-keeping mission, certainly found themselves speechless—though Barbara Bush, looking out at the posse of cameramen and reporters camped outside the White House, found a common bond with Hillary when she remarked, "Avoid this crowd like the plague."

Hillary agreed. After her fight with Bill, she was tenser than anyone had ever seen her. The Thomasons, attempting to work with the official inaugural committee responsible for the day's events, had been concerned to make the inauguration as successful as the Democratic Party Convention in New York the previous July. To this end they'd arranged an unobtrusive footstand for Hillary to step onto as she moved forward to hold her husband's Bible, while he was sworn in as president of the United States by the Republican chief justice of the Supreme Court. Hillary had refused it. "I'm not getting on that riser," she said—and she didn't, spoiling the traditional official portrait, which to the chagrin of the Thomasons was obscured by the microphones. As Hillary's biographer recorded, "the word was already rippling through the members of the inaugural committee: *She's a pill.*"

Washington Inertia

Bill Clinton, by contrast, might be a philanderer in the same mold as his predecessor and hero John F. Kennedy, but he was not a pill. The question was, rather, would he be tough enough to tame "the woolly mammoth that is Washington?" as Jonathan Alter had pointedly asked in *Newsweek*. In the nation's capital there were now more lobbyists (eighty-eight thousand, Alter reckoned) than men, women, and children in Clinton's hometown, Hot Springs. "And every last one of them is waiting to chew off a piece of the president," Alter warned.

First and foremost there was Congress, which was beset by gridlock. "The biggest problem is just inertia," a Clinton aide, familiar with the ways of Congress, lamented. "Washington has atrophied in the last twelve years and doesn't remember how to move. Every time you mention a proposal, they say it can't get done—the lobbyists or the chairman or someone won't let it. It's as if members think they'd be doing their job wrong if they passed legislation." Still optimistic about the jobs/health-care/national-service/deficit-reduction agenda of the newly elected president, the aide had said that "the only thing that's changed about Washington is the president." But could a new president get Congress to cooperate? Alter was skeptical. "Let's face it: no Democrat in a quarter century has managed to bend Washington to his will. Clinton may still believe in a 'place called Hope,' but Washington believes more in a complacency called money and status. Why change when everyone in town is doing so well with the system the way it is? The lava of lawyer-lobbyists, who tell people at parties that they are in 'government affairs,' has cooled and solidified into an entrenched white, upper-middle-class subculture, complete with its own cozy and rationalizing journalists."

One way to free up congressional gridlock was to create a tide of public support for his agenda. Hillary might scorn the fourth estate, but the president-elect knew that, though he got mad at journalists on occasion, he lived and died by the sword of media coverage. For his inauguration, therefore, he had wanted especially good coverage—and an especially good speech.

To help craft his inaugural address the president-elect had called upon an army of literary contributors. "Whoever managed to wander in—friends, family, the caterer—could have his say on the new president's first words,"

Clinton's young director of communications, George Stephanopoulos, later recalled; the draft was kicked around between David Kusnet, Bruce Reed, Stephanopoulos, Tommy Caplan, Taylor Branch, Al Gore, and a host of others. The result had been dismayingly bad, and got even worse as the inauguration drew closer—indeed, the speechwriters were still working on it with the president-elect at three-thirty on the morning of the inauguration. Clinton had then tinkered for yet another hour with the draft—"another all-nighter," as Stephanopoulos remarked, adding: "Adrenaline and anxiety were fueling Clinton, but the rest of us were starting to sag."

As veteran Arkansas reporters knew best, this was the way big Bill Clinton had always operated. Despite his calls for change in America, the shaggy Clinton approach seemed something he himself was unable to improve—or its ripple-effect upon his staff. Beginning with the draft for the inaugural address, it now set the "pattern for his presidency," as political observer Elizabeth Drew noted, providing a veritable torment to those whose job it was to handle the mechanics of such events. The Clintons might profess concern for the "little people"—children and the disadvantaged in society—but they could be remarkably cavalier in their expectations of those mortals whose professional job it was to look after the nuts and bolts. "The teleprompter operators at the Capitol," Drew noted, for example, "were becoming highly anxious—they were accustomed to getting a major speech hours in advance, so they could test it on their machines. They didn't get Clinton's until 11:30 A.M., thirty minutes before the ceremonies were to begin."

Forcing the Spring

The inaugural speech—drafted and re-drafted, honed and re-honed, subjected to endless addition and subtraction—reflected its plethora of originators, including the caterer.

The truth was, the justifiable pride Clinton felt as the single-mothered boy from Hope, Arkansas, stepping forward to deliver his first address as president of the United States of America, could simply not be matched by the patchwork of speechwriters' competing rhetorics.

Father Tim Healy, former president of Georgetown University, had, for instance, been found on his recent death to have left in his typewriter a letter to Bill Clinton that was forwarded to the president-elect. This, too, was squeezed into the sprawling draft of the oration, punctuated with clichés and one-liners. Thus the speech was to kick off with a dubious assertion that would raise frowns rather than applause: that America could, in the cold of Washington, D.C., in mid-January, "force the spring," and that America was—Iceland, Britain, and other ancient polities notwithstanding—"the world's oldest democracy."

Yet between its questionable platitudes and mixed metaphors the address that was belatedly loaded onto the inaugural stand teleprompter contained moments of plain truth-telling that reflected the real Bill Clinton's real feelings about his real country—its economy and its social tapestry. It was deeply felt—and deeply American.

"On behalf of our nation, I salute my predecessor, President Bush, for his half-century of service to America," the new president said at midday, January 20, 1993, having sworn his oath of allegiance on his family Bible, before Chief Justice William Rehnquist. "And I thank the millions of men and women whose steadfastness and sacrifice triumphed over depression, fascism and communism."

Those days were over, however, the baby boomer now announced, his prose attempting to emulate Theodore Sorenson's famous 1961 cadences. "Today, a generation raised in the shadows of the Cold War assumes new responsibilities in a world warmed by the sunshine of freedom but threatened still by ancient hatreds and new plagues. Raised in unrivaled prosperity, we inherit an economy that is still the world's strongest, but is weakened by business failures, stagnant wages, increasing inequality, and deep divisions among our people."

This situation was, the new president stated, not the fault of his predecessor, who sat in the biting cold next to him on the stand, but the product of a new economic reality—one that affected every mortal on the globe. "When George Washington first took the oath I have just sworn to uphold," the former Arkansas governor pointed out, aligning himself neatly beside the first American president, "news traveled slowly across the land by horseback and across the ocean by boat. Now, the sights and sounds of this ceremony are broadcast instantaneously to billions around the world. Communications and commerce are global; investment is mobile; technology is almost magical; and ambition for a better life is now universal." However, there were both benefits and costs attached to this development, he warned. "We earn our livelihood in peaceful competition with people all across the earth. Profound and powerful forces are shaking and remaking our world, and the urgent question of our time is whether we can make change our friend and not our enemy."

The bewildering medley of cliché, Sorensonian turn of phrase, and intelligent comment was strangely arresting as the president went on to acknowledge how some Americans had already seen the modern economic light, and had profited from it. "This new world has already enriched the lives of millions of Americans who are able to compete and win in it. But when most people are working harder for less; when others cannot work at all; when the cost of health care devastates families and threatens to bankrupt many of our enterprises, great and small; when fear of crime robs law-abiding citizens of their freedom; and when millions of poor children cannot even imagine the lives we are calling them to lead," the forty-second president declared, "we have not made change our friend.

"From our Revolution, the Civil War, to the Great Depression to the civil rights movement, our people have always mustered the determination to construct from these crises the pillars of our history. Thomas Jefferson believed that to preserve the very foundations of our nation, we would need dramatic change from time to time. Well, my fellow citizens, this is our time. Let us embrace it.

"Our democracy must be not only the envy of the world but the engine of our own renewal. There is nothing wrong with America that cannot be cured by what is right with America.

"And so today, we pledge an end to the era of deadlock and drift; a new season of American renewal has begun. To renew America, we must be bold. We must do what no generation has had to do before. We must invest more in our own people, in their jobs, in their future, and at the same time cut our massive debt. And we must do so in a world in which we must compete for every opportunity. It will not be easy; it will require sacrifice. But it can be done, and done fairly, not choosing sacrifice for its own sake, but for our own sake. We must provide for our nation the way a family provides for its children."

The new president's inaugural speech ended with an outsider's appeal to the power players of Washington to help him bring the nation together, not split it further apart in bitter partisanship. "This beautiful capital, like every capital since the dawn of civilization, is often a place of intrigue and calculation. Powerful people maneuver for position and worry endlessly about who is in and who is out, who is up and who is down, forgetting those people whose toil and sweat sends us here and pays our way.

"Americans deserve better, and in this city today, there are people who want to do better. And so I say to all of us here, let us resolve to reform our politics, so that power and privilege no longer shout down the voice of the people. Let us put aside personal advantage so that we can feel the pain and see the promise of America. Let us resolve to make our government a place for what Franklin Roosevelt called 'bold, persistent experimentation,' a government for our tomorrows, not our yesterdays. Let us give this capital back to the people to whom it belongs."

The Pulse of a New Day

For those who knew Bill Clinton's reputation for prolixity, the 1993 inaugural address, at fourteen minutes in length, was considered to be unusual in its brevity. Certainly it was well-received by the crowd below the Capitol, the television commentators, and by the next day's press. Maya Angelou's long and rambling poem, with its own storybook mythology, was intended to be equally inspiring. It ended with the simplest of lines:

> *Here on the pulse of this new day*
> *You may have the grace to look up and out*
> *And into your sister's eyes, into*
> *Your brother's face, your country*
> *And say simply*
> *Very simply*
> *With hope*
> *Good morning.*

Not everyone quite followed Maya Angelou's references, though, or was won over by the president's homilies. However, as the former governor of a tiny state of 2.4 million inhabitants more than a thousand miles from Washington, D.C., would the new president ensure the Beltway transition from selfishness to social responsibility and compassion? This had nowhere been indicated in the president's speech, and would have to await his first State of the Union budget address. There was also the puzzle of a strange "mastodon" that was mentioned in Angelou's poem. The Asian, the

Hispanic, the Jew, the African, the Native American, the Catholic, the Muslim, the French, the Greek, the Irish, the rabbi, the priest, the sheikh, the gay, the straight, the preacher, the privileged, the homeless, and the teacher were all icons of diversity, but the prehistoric beast?

According to the dictionary, a mastodon was an elephant-like mammal, a figure of "immense size, power, influence." Was Maya Angelou's reference a metaphor for Bill Clinton himself, following an epithet that had been used of Alexander the Great, when the young Greek emperor was referred to as "one of the mastodons of the ancient world"? Only time would tell.

Immediately after the ceremonies, the senior White House FBI agent recorded, "Bill and Hillary Clinton were taken to a holding room in the Capitol," while the many dignitaries of the Senate and House of Representatives patiently marked time. When the couple did not emerge from the holding room, however, a policeman was sent to knock and inform the forty-second president (the third youngest in American history) and his first lady (the first to have a law degree) that "everyone was ready and waiting." Unwisely, the policeman opened the door. "You fucking asshole!" Hillary screamed—not at the policeman but at the president.

The innocent constable withdrew in confusion. "Apparently," the White House FBI agent noted, "the matter of office space was *not* settled."

CHAPTER TWO

INVESTMENT OR DEFICIT REDUCTION?

The Coded Message

Behind the plethora of inaugural assertions was, in truth, a coded message to the American public: that the nation must prepare itself for some bitter medicine.

Already, on January 7, 1993, a historic first struggle between deficit-reducers and public investment protagonists had taken place over six hours in Little Rock—debating an issue that threatened to split both the White House and the Democratic Party in two.

From the new labor secretary Robert Reich's perspective, the chips were stacked against public investment from the moment the president-elect announced his administration's economic team. For a start, Clinton had appointed as his Treasury secretary—ruling an empire of a hundred sixty thousand public servants—Senator Lloyd Bentsen, a stalwart proponent of Texas's oil and gas industry, who had made a fortune in financial services on Wall Street. Senator Bentsen had famously crushed Republican vice president-nominee Dan Quayle in the 1988 debates by telling him he was "no Jack Kennedy." But was Bentsen, either? When Clinton asked Reich his opinion of the possible choice of Bentsen as Treasury secretary, Reich had been appalled. "He'd be a valuable adviser," Reich had allowed. "But hell, he's not exactly committed to *your* agenda."

What *was* Bill Clinton's agenda, though? Unsure himself, but trusting his instincts, Clinton had ignored Reich and duly appointed the Texas senator—

turning Reich down not only for the new National Economic Council, or chief economic adviser to the president, but even for the post of chairman of the President's Council of Economic Advisers. Instead, Robert Rubin, a Goldman Sachs executive who had fund-raised for Clinton's campaign, took the NEC post, while Laura Tyson was appointed chair of the Council, and Reich was offered the consolation prize of Labor.

Reich had naturally been disappointed, but such feelings had paled beside his concerns about the direction in which the Democrats were headed.

The problem for Reich as a socio-economic engineer, intent upon righting the wrongs of twelve years of Republican presidential misrule, was the sheer magnitude of the national deficit—a figure far in excess of all economists' predictions. Alan Greenspan, responsible for interest rates for the nation as chairman of the Federal Reserve Board, had explained to the president-elect that the only way to bring down rates was to buck the old Keynesian notion of deficit spending. By robustly tackling the national deficit, the president would be able to bring down long-term interest levels, as investors—convinced that the government meant business—moved from bonds to stocks, thereby releasing more money into the economy as mortgage payments came down. While inflation was reduced, the stock market would soar.

Greenspan was rather pleased with his tutorial. Others, he knew, contested the notion that deficit reduction would, *per se*, lead to lower interest rates, for predicting bond trader responses was no less speculative than share trading. What was refreshing was to find a president-designate open to theoretical argument, rather than being *parti pris*, or worse, party pris. Greenspan recognized in Bill Clinton an "intellectual pragmatist," who could, if steered right, turn the Democrats away from their ideological commitment to FDR-style economic management and into the market-dominated world of 1990s capitalism. So pleased with himself, as he left, was Greenspan that he actually wondered if he had somehow deluded himself into thinking the Democratic president-elect was in agreement with him—that Clinton had been "pulling his leg."

Clinton hadn't been, however. "What?" Clinton had yelled when a few days later he learned the annual deficit was $60 billion worse than he'd been told. "I thought we'd been through all that!" With each new estimate of the nation's near bankruptcy, the task seemed more daunting—yet at the same time more urgent to tackle. By December 23, two weeks after the historic economic summit that Clinton was convening in Little Rock, the

Reich transition economic team's "Economic Overview" had spoken of the president-elect having "inherited a two-part challenge of historic proportions"—how to reduce the deficit while, at the same time, increasing it by the investment programs the Clinton campaign had promised.

The Turning Point

Could deficit and investment *both* be done, *simultaneously*, or should they start by massive investing, *then* the tackling of the deficit?

"Clearly, budget making is a balancing of spending priorities and the necessity of keeping the deficit under control. And at that moment," recalled Alice Rivlin, the new deputy director of the White House's Office of Budget and Management (OMB), "I felt strongly that we *had* to give high priority to getting the deficit down, or we couldn't do anything else. That the promises made in the campaign were not always very specific, but if you put the larger numbers with them, they could *not* be accommodated in a budget where you were trying to reduce the deficit." The meetings of the president's economic team thus went on ceaselessly until finally, on January 7, 1993, there had been in Little Rock the climax: a "very formal discussion, led by Bob, about how much deficit reduction there should be. What our goal should be."

The meeting was, in the view of Lawrence Summers, as number three in the new Treasury lineup under Bentsen and Roger Altman, the "turning point." Present were "all the principal political advisers, with the president, the vice president, Hillary," Robert Rubin later recalled.

"All" was a misnomer, given Reich's absence, but even Robert Reich, had he been able to be there, would have found himself powerless to turn the gathering tide of deficit-reduction enthusiasts. In the context of the latest deficit crisis figures, thirty-one-year-old George Stephanopoulos, as transition communications director, had been as concerned as Reich lest the president-elect be swept by panic from his election platform and promises. Certainly Rubin clearly recalled Stephanopoulos warning him, before going into the meeting: "You all are going to recommend very strong deficit reduction. But that means the president is going to have to defer doing a lot of other things that he thinks are extremely important. You can't possibly expect him to make that decision at this meeting."

Ignoring Stephanopoulos, Rubin called upon the different advisers, one by one, to lay out the competing urgencies of universal health insurance, welfare reform, the middle-class tax cut, education, and job training programs. In the end it became clear that without first tackling the national deficit, the nation would go deeper and deeper into a national debt from which it might never recover.

Alan Blinder, Laura Tyson's new deputy chair of the CEA, had pointed out that the success of a bold deficit-reduction plan hinged on the willingness of market traders to buy bonds, and thus reduce long-term interest rates, as well as the Federal Reserve's willingness to reduce the short-term interest rate. He frankly doubted whether bond traders would actually operate in the national interest, under a Democratic administration. The president-elect murmured audibly: "You mean to tell me that the success of the program and my re-election hinges on the Federal Reserve and a bunch of fucking bond traders?"

Put that way, it seemed risible. Yet somehow the president-elect *had* to take control of the economy, or Congress eventually would—for the nation was sliding towards economic disaster. "Alan Blinder and Laura Tyson were much more cautious about deficit reduction," Alice Rivlin recalled. "They thought there was a risk of reducing too much, and that if we did too steep a reduction, we would risk derailing the economic recovery." This was not something Dr. Rivlin or her transition team colleagues credited. "I did not think that. And Bentsen particularly didn't think that. Because he thought that if we did a very strong deficit reduction package, that interest rates would come down and send a signal to the markets—in fact interest rates were already coming down," Rivlin noted, in anticipation. "I was taking the hawk position—for larger deficit reduction. I sort of served the purpose of anchoring the hawk end."

Inevitable Is Inevitable

Thus lined up, the hawks of the impending Clinton administration team were implacable. Rubin recalled the president-elect saying, after only half an hour of discussion, "Look. There are a lot of things that I think we need to do, but the threshold issue is the deficit. Until we deal with that, nothing else is going to work, and we're not going to do the rest of what we want to do. So let's take that as our threshold issue and then, within that context, let's do as much else as we can."

Others, such as Congressman Leon Panetta, chairman of the House Budget Committee and now OMB director-designate, and Larry Summers, did not recall the president-elect being quite so decisive. Nevertheless, as the hours ticked away, there was a growing sense of the inescapable. "I think my view was, inevitable is inevitable: there really wasn't a choice," Summers remembered feeling. "You had to propose a responsible fiscal policy or the markets would go nuts."

"There were some strong personalities there," Panetta recalled—including Hillary Clinton. "I spoke for taking a strong stand on the deficit. Lloyd Bentsen spoke for that. Al Gore was very supportive of that kind of tough approach as well. And the economists. Bob Rubin. . . . And then there was a group of Clinton's aides—Stephanopoulos, Gene Sperling, people that had worked during the campaign, who were raising concerns about what would happen. On the grounds that: you've got an economy that's still coming out of a recession. You've got some key priorities that you said you wanted to achieve, in education and other things—and ultimately, you'll be judged, your legacy will be judged more by what you do in those areas than what you do with regards to the deficit."

Bill Clinton, who had the sharpest political antennae of all, listened to Al Gore's contention that boldness had been the essence of FDR's Hundred Days, and that the task of the new Clinton-Gore administration would be to prepare a new program, based on the critical situation they were inheriting. "Roosevelt was trying to help the American people," Clinton pointed out, however. "Here we help the bond market, and we hurt the people who voted us in."

It was a salutary caution, from a president-elect who might, Stephanopoulos warned, only last a single term if, as had happened with his predecessor, the economic medicine didn't work in time. But worse than the time factor was the likely response from Congress.

"The biggest problem that we always had," Panetta recalled, "was that the Democrats generally did not believe that confronting the deficit was the number one challenge. It was always how you *spent* the money, not so much how you *saved* money that drove a lot of Democrats. . . . Although, clearly the politics had changed a lot with third-party presidential candidate Ross Perot and others, who had raised it during the campaign."

Though Rubin recalled, in retirement, his former president's decisiveness on the issue, Panetta did not. Nor did he blame the president-elect at that moment in time. "I think what happened at that meeting was that, for the first time, Clinton was . . ." Panetta's voice faltered. "He was concerned about the fact that, 'if we make these tough choices, if we raise taxes, if we cut the entitlement programs, if we make the very tough cuts that are necessary [to reduce the deficit], am I going to undermine the politics for Democrats—for myself, for the Congress—in that process? Are we going to pay a heavy price, politically, for doing that? And will there be enough time to reap the rewards?' "

If the new president truly wished to force the spring and carry out an ambitious investment agenda—especially one that would have to take place alongside his major deficit-reduction program—he would need the support of Congress and the power brokers of Washington. To merit that support he must project leadership not only in terms of ideas and personality, but of effective governance.

"If the transition has gone well," a Reagan aide noted, its energy and decisiveness carry over into the presidency, creating a sense among the people and the press that "this is a president who knows what he's doing. And so it supports the impression the people have of the president's ability to govern." In sum the transition process was "absolutely critical to doing a good job of governing. It's important for the impression the people have of the ability to govern."

Unfortunately the Clinton transition had given the opposite impression. Though the president-elect had shown courage in facing up to the need to tackle the country's spiraling deficit, there had been no attempt to lay down, forcefully and decisively, a strategic plan. Instead, there would be many hundreds of competing objectives—and no effective chief of staff. Worse still, there was—apart from Congressman Leon Panetta—almost no relationship yet between the incoming White House staff and Congress. As a result, despite the most enthusiastic popular welcome for a new president in living memory, the Clinton administration would get off to a perilous start. Within hours of the president's swearing the oath of office, the Clinton White House would move into crisis mode over the woman Hillary had selected as the nation's new attorney general, Zoë Baird, and over an incendiary remark the president-elect had made on Memorial Day—that he would, on taking office, unilaterally permit gays to serve in the military.

CHAPTER THREE

A PERILOUS TRANSITION

"Where's My Vacation?"

Behind the scenes, unknown to the public, the Clinton transition had been a disaster. Not having quite dared dream victory would be won, Clinton's campaign press secretary, Dee Dee Myers, for example, later confessed to total exhaustion. "I mean," she recalled, "I was so used to losing campaigns at this point, that [I felt] like, 'Where's my vacation to the Bahamas?'"

In the opinion of close observers, a vacation in the Bahamas had been exactly what the victorious candidate should—like JFK in 1960—have taken. Henry Cisneros, the former mayor of San Antonio, had joined Clinton on the plane in Texas, and had flown with him to Dallas at midnight before polling day, then to Albuquerque at 2 A.M., then to Denver about 7 A.M., and finally to Little Rock around 9 A.M. "He just went all night!" Cisneros recalled, amazed. When he saw Clinton again, the morning after the election, he was appalled. "I frankly was worried," Cisneros remembered, aware that among the entire corpus of politicians in America, Bill Clinton had the blessing of a physiognomy that never seemed to show tiredness. "Whereas other people show absolute exhaustion on their face, become haggard and drawn and sunken-cheeked, and have dark circles under the eyes, he just had this sunny expression—normally. But that day, Wednesday, November 4, 1992, was different. "He had not one whit of energy left."

Understandably worn out, the president-elect should have delegated the running of the transition to the man he'd made his transition director-presumptive—his victorious campaign chairman, Mickey Kantor, and Kantor's team on the thirteenth floor of the downtown Worthen Building.

Instead, leaving his childhood friend Carolyn Staley's house after brunch and a group photograph, the president-elect returned with Hillary to chair Kantor's next meeting: his first meeting as president-elect of the United States. And the long-prepared switch from campaign to transition had fallen apart as Hillary took umbrage at the style of the transition director.

Jockeying for Position

Staffs, by tradition, abhor a vacuum. Aware of this, Mickey Kantor and his colleagues at CGPTF (the Clinton-Gore Pre-Transition Foundation) had drawn up a series of "plans for going forward," as Cisneros recalled. "And Mickey was pushing for decisions by the end of the week. This was Wednesday after the election, which had taken place on the Tuesday. Hillary was in the room. And it was like, 'You've got to name the secretary of state by the end of the week or—.' You know, it had to be done on Mickey's timetable. And the president-elect was exhausted. He had no voice. His posture was slumped in the chair—he might as well have been sleeping for the way his body looked. . . . But that was a Bill Clinton trait: to push himself to the point of exhaustion and beyond. And he did things in that campaign that nobody had ever done before. More cities in a single day . . ." Cisneros' voice trailed at the recollection. "And Hillary leveled that cold stare that she can, and her face was firm. She said to Mickey: 'Don't do that! You're not going to push him! Look how exhausted he is! We are not going to be pushed. *So back off!*' "

The "we" sent a chill through all those who were there.

Kantor was a fighter who never gave up, however. "Mickey just has a style—at least he did then, though he mellowed out later—that's a little bit too obsessively control-oriented. Just upsets people. Because he never stops pushing. And Clinton didn't want that. He wanted, kind of a mellower person."

The result was that, at the very cusp of transition, the structure that had carried the candidate to victory, against almost all expectations, had teetered—Hillary locking horns with the man charged with directing the transition, and who was expected by all to become the White House chief of staff in the mold of Jim Baker or John Sununu. With his authority thus challenged by Hillary, Kantor's emerging position had become untenable as every member of the victorious but leaderless campaign team had his or her say. "The confetti still lay in the streets of Little Rock," recalled Warren Christopher—the attorney who'd conducted the search for a Democratic vice-presidential nominee for Bill Clinton earlier that summer—"when the jockeying for position among Clinton's hard-charging campaign aides began."

The Naming of a Transition Director

Mickey Kantor, chairman of the Clinton election campaign, had been preparing the transition plan as far back as September, Warren Christopher recorded, installing Gerald Stern, a lawyer on leave from Occidental Petroleum, with a team of eleven people to "develop a transition plan. Gerry, an experienced Washington hand, generated a thick notebook, replete with elaborate diagrams, as a blueprint for organizing the incoming administration. By early November, the Kantor-Stern operation was ready to roll"—but neither Hillary nor the president-elect were.

As Dan Balz afterwards wrote, "the weary Clinton wasn't buying. It was all too tidy for a man who likes to mull his options and make his own decisions. He was in no rush, Clinton told the transition advisers, to do anything until he felt more rested. Whether the advisers realized it or not, that was a signal that Kantor's appointment was in big trouble, ambushed by an angry campaign team who had never worked well with him." Declining to officially appoint Kantor the transition director, Clinton had merely decided to keep the CGPTF going for the moment. Then in a move that suggested he was feeling unsure of himself, the president-elect added to the CGPTF committee an old kindergarten friend from Hope, Thomas F. "Mack" McLarty.

Poor Mickey Kantor, a fifty-three-year-old lawyer and political activist, had run Walter Mondale's 1984 losing presidential campaign and chaired Bill Clinton's winning one. He had also had the experience of working alongside Hillary on the board of the national Legal Services Corporation in 1978, but had fallen out with Hillary's friend and campaign scheduler during the '92 struggle, Susan Thomases.

The press, having seen little of Hillary during the election, had reported that the new first lady was "not expected to be appointed to the cabinet," and assumed blithely that "she will likely play a major role in advancing issues involving children." Little did such journalists know! Hillary and Susan were not, however, the only campaigners pushing to the front of the administration pack as the transition got under way. Concerned with his own political future, the ambitious George Stephanopoulos, as communications director, had been deeply jealous of Kantor, as was James Carville, Clinton's "ragin' Cajun" strategist. Researching the foreign policy ramifications of the election almost a decade later, David Halberstam recalled that "[t]he degree of squabbling in the early days of the transition—how poisonous it was and how far apart were the people who should have been on the same side—quite startled the president-elect."

It did—but lacking military command or even company management executive skills, Clinton had proved unwilling to empower Kantor and move on into the next stage of life: governing America through effective subordinates and a clear staff structure. Instead, as the hours and days had gone by, there had been ominous silence from the Governor's Mansion.

As the hiatus had continued, and the in-fighting had grown more savage, the president-elect had become more bewildered and uncertain. "Unlike President Bush, who four years ago announced key staff positions immediately after the election, Clinton was taking his time," newspapers had recorded—their correspondents amazed that, after Russian premier Boris Yeltsin telephoned Clinton and spoke with him for more than twenty minutes, there had been more news to be had from Moscow than from Little Rock. "But Clinton may announce his choice of a transition planning chief as soon as today in order to quell a dispute that has broken out among his top advisers about who will oversee the transfer of power from the Bush White House," it was reported. "Aides to Clinton said his closest advisers are badly split over whether Clinton campaign chairman Mickey Kantor should run the transition office. Officials familiar with Clinton's thinking said he has been urged to announce the decision, which he apparently already has made."

But had he?

The Worst Transition in U.S. History

Indecisiveness had always been Bill Clinton's Achilles heel, and it was never more so than in the days following his election. Flushed with the pride of populist victory, Bill Clinton had wanted understandably to take stock, rather than to rush forward. As he'd declared in his pre-dawn acceptance speech on the steps of the Old State House, in Little Rock—the very podium on which he had announced his candidacy in the fall of 1991— "We're all in this together, and we'll rise and fall together. If we have learned anything in this world today, it is that we accomplish more by team-work, by working together, by bringing out the best in all the people we see. And we will seek the best and most able and most committed people throughout this country to be a part of our team."

Democratic Party chairman Ron Brown had seconded the notion of a new kind of Democratic team—men and women committed not to an old-fashioned ideological agenda but to a centrist, pragmatic, multilateral, *bipartisan* approach. "We're a new and different party. You've got to be able to respond to the times in which you live. If you don't change, you don't deserve the opportunity to lead America. This is a new world. It's a new country."

In that centrist spirit the president-elect had sounded hoarse but magnanimous. "We will ask the Democrats who believe in our cause to come forward—but we will look too among the ranks of independents and Republicans who are willing to roll up their sleeves . . . and get on with the business of dealing with the nation's problems." Appointments in the new administration would be made "to heal the wounds of political division in America," indeed to create a "Re-United States."

With those noble words, as one staff member admitted to a *New York Times* reporter, the transition had then fractured into "a bloody, ugly mess."

With his staff squabbling bitterly, the pressure had been on Clinton to decide on his transition director, who could then become his White House chief of staff. But did he really *want* a chief of staff who might upset people yet would get things done—or was that the wrong model? True to his academic training, Clinton had asked Bill Galston, a former Mondale adviser now teaching public policy at the University of Maryland, to put together a history of transitions.

In the meantime, others had felt it vital not to lose the magical link with the electorate. "My view was that the campaign had been a sacred thing," Paul Begala, his campaign consultant, later noted, "because I was there and I saw the connection that Clinton made with people, and the connection they made with him. And I felt this very personally, and I know the president[-elect] did too."

Begala was correct. Governor Clinton had felt he owed his victory, in the end, to the "little people": the voters who had turned out in record numbers (since 1972, at least), *and he wanted to keep faith with them*—a compact he feared would be compromised, even vitiated, if he appointed a hierarchical staff structure, under a strong chief of staff. As David Matthews, an Arkansas state legislator and Clinton confidant, put it, "he doesn't want to be protected, he doesn't want to be insulated. He likes to hear all sides. I think you'll find the role of chief of staff very different under Bill Clinton."

It would be—unfortunately. In the opinion of Stephen Hess, who had held White House positions in the Eisenhower and Nixon administrations, and was a fellow at the Brookings Institution, the manner in which the victorious campaign turned into an inglorious mess was almost incredible. Hess had witnessed every postwar transition. "I had written a little book called *Organizing the Presidency*. And I just couldn't believe what was happening! I mean, when very smart people continue to do very dumb things. And listen: these aren't very complicated things! You don't have to go to Oxford or anything to do them."

Reflecting on the way Clinton had shot himself in the foot after such a brilliant campaign, Hess sought to compare 1992–3 to previous transitions. "It was," he sputtered in disgust, "*the worst transition in modern American history.*" In fact it was even worse than that, he reflected as the memory of it returned. In his opinion, the nearest parallel to Clinton's had been that of Ronald Reagan—"similar even to the degree that a sitting president (Jimmy Carter) had been defeated. So to that degree they were exact parallels. And the Reagan transition of 1980 was the *best* transition in American history! So all Clinton had to do was turn around and look at how the thing was done. It wasn't really very difficult."

Instead, Hess enlarged his judgment: Clinton's proved to be "the worst transition in *all* American history! And it needn't have been!"

A Palace Coup

Unlike the campaign of Ronald Reagan, "who was an ideologue," Clinton's campaign had been one of opposition to the sitting president, and therefore critical of President Bush's policies in the abstract, rather than presenting a clearly worked-out, realistic agenda, honed by experienced advisers. It had therefore been vital to have from the beginning a chief of staff who would structure the transition, while building up a White House staff—a staff whose role reflected, more and more in the history of American government, the flow of power from the cabinet to the White House. Far from appointing a White House chief of staff, however, Bill Clinton had failed even to appoint a transition director!

"Clinton so far has resisted entreaties by his advisers to quickly name a transition director," the *Washington Post* had reported on Friday, November

6, "and a source said the fact that Clinton has decided to hold off for a few days may be an indication he is troubled by the complaints of some top campaign aides critical of Mickey Kantor, his campaign chairman, who until this week has been considered the most likely candidate for the job."

Flying back to Little Rock from a Park-O-Meter lawsuit hearing in Washington, D.C., on November 7, Webb Hubbell, Hillary's law firm colleague and Bill Clinton's golfing partner, vividly recalled the disintegration of group loyalty that had by then gripped the once remarkably cohesive, innovative, and energetic Clinton transition staff—leading to "a palace coup."

"The campaign team got to Clinton first," the *Washington Post* had reported, having got hold of the inside story. Nervous about their own futures, the staff had begun to spread sly rumors and badmouth Kantor to the president-elect. "They were hot," Dan Balz had quoted a witness. "They just chopped his legs off."

Kantor, at the urging of Hillary and others, was thus dismissed. Webb Hubbell drove the bitterly hurt Kantor to the airport, east of downtown Little Rock. Kantor was "devastated," Hubbell remembered. "He felt betrayed"—for many of the negative stories about him in the press, he felt, "had been planted by people in the [Clinton] campaign. He suspected George Stephanopoulos was behind it."

If such aides had hoped to get good White House jobs more swiftly as a result, they had been bitterly disappointed. Clinton's campaign press secretary, Dee Dee Myers, whom Kantor had brought into the team the previous year, summed up the situation. The "transition was the worst part of my entire association with the campaign and the presidency," she later lamented. There was "tremendous uncertainty about our own jobs. You know, nobody told us the day after the election, 'Hey, yeah, you're going to the White House,' or 'You're not.'" Beyond the gates, outside, a veritable army of journalists had assembled "with nothing to do," since no cabinet, sub-cabinet, or White House staff announcements were being made; inside there was a "young and insecure staff, and a president-elect who is taking his time making really big decisions. So it really stank. Everybody was miserable."

Flying away to exile in California, Kantor had understandably been mortified. Hubbell recalled sadly, "Since 1987 he had worked diligently to get Bill Clinton elected president. Now, the day after Mickey achieved that goal he was forced out."

Hubbell blamed the looming shadow of Washington. But the shadow lay within Hubbell's brilliant but undependable golfing partner. Hillary's wishes, now that she was licensed to step out from the campaign shadows and prepare to become first lady, would also have to be respected.

Starting from Scratch

With Kantor banished to calm the baying wolves, who would take charge of the immediate and urgent transition process? At the week's end transition reporters had their answer: a sixty-seven-year-old corporate lawyer from outside the campaign, who had helped Clinton select his running mate earlier that year, and who had been summoned again to offer outside advice: Warren M. Christopher.

As even Warren Christopher himself later acknowledged, "We were starting from scratch," thanks to the ouster of Kantor. Moreover the president-elect should first and foremost have chosen a White House chief of staff, indeed the key members of the White House staff. Christopher, however, was not one to contradict his boss, let alone guide him. "Christopher's not that kind of guy," Congressman Leon Panetta, a fellow Californian, expostulated candidly. "Christopher's not a 'Look, you've gotta do this!' kind of person! He's a facilitator, he's someone who will work with you and try and sense what you're thinking, try to get it done—but he's not someone who will say: 'Look, you son of a bitch, *do* this!' He's not a Jim Baker-type."

Mickey Kantor would have been that type, in Panetta's view. "He would have been better—he's much more forceful at saying 'Don't do that, do this'-kind of approach"—a role that Betsey Wright had performed relentlessly in Arkansas as Clinton's chief of staff, but which Clinton now balked at recreating, on the cusp of supreme power. Thus, instead, the president-elect had reversed engines and had made do for the moment with a gentle facilitator.

Sentimentality had meanwhile mixed with exhaustion, as waves of goodwill, gratitude, and disorientation had blurred Clinton's tactical vision. He had simply not had, nor taken, the time to think about the people he wanted in his administration. "What they focused on, and again, it was typical Bill Clinton fashion—he focused long and hard on the cabinet," Panetta recalled. "He wanted to have superb people in the cabinet, he wanted to have this 'rainbow' appearance in the cabinet." Thus, instead of preparing *himself* for the role of the nation's new commander-in-chief and chief executive in the White House, the president-elect had immersed himself in the cosmetics rather than substance of his future government.

Even in later years Bill Clinton found it hard to discern the lesson here for all incoming presidents. Although he did acknowledge that he'd spent "so much time on the cabinet that I hardly spent any time on the White House staff," he seemed unable, even in retirement, to distinguish the relative importance of the two. Over recent decades the White House had become the real engine of American government—yet Bill Clinton, voracious reader of political theory and praxis, seemed to have no grasp of this evolution. In a later Brookings Institute survey, presidential scholar Charles O. Jones interviewed a veritable army of Clinton aides and advisers who recorded their disappointment, frustration, and near despair at Clinton's "biggest mistake" in the final months of 1992—for the failure to lead a clear, capable, focused, and consistent transition had, many of them felt, doomed Bill Clinton's entire first year in office. Warren Christopher was charged with helping the president-elect choose only a cabinet and sub-cabinet. Why was it more important for the president to personally select the first black to be secretary of agriculture—Congressman Mike Espy—than a transition director or a chief of staff? observers wondered. Because there was no White House staff appointed, and no one with real experience of transition to advise the president-elect, there arose a sense that the new president was making it up as he went along—anxious not to commit mistakes or appear amateur, yet without any real notion of the importance of strong management in sending the right signals to those who would make or break the looming presidency.

And in his exhaustion, the president-elect had simply not been able to open his eyes to the way he was failing. On the night before the election, campaign aide Paul Begala had asked David Gergen, a communications guru to three past American presidents and an editor-at-large of *U.S. News & World Report,* his opinion. "I said, I want to have a confidential off-the-record conversation with you, David. How did Reagan keep the focus on the economy when he got started?" Gergen had obliged with "this wonderful story about how Al Haig, as secretary of state in the Reagan administration, at the beginning had come up with some new anti-drug strategy. Jim Baker, the chief of staff under Reagan, was not, however, amused by Haig's grandiose scheme. He called him in and said, "If I see any more of your drug stories in the paper, I'm going to fire you." "Because," Begala noted,

"Baker understood that the one job they had at the start was passing the Reagan economic plan.

"Well, that was like turning on a light!" Begala recalled. "I am a person who craves clarity. I am a reductionist. I want to do one thing. I loved hearing that story, and I related it back to the governor that night. 'This is what you need to do. This is how Gergen said Reagan did it.'"

The story had simply gotten filed in Bill Clinton's capacious brain, but not in his tired head. As Begala lamented, "Getting off that focus was an enormous mistake." He did not blame the president-elect, given the thousand pressures weighing on him; but it was, Begala felt, a fatal, collective "lack of focus, and I think everybody who was around that has to share some of the responsibility."

All too soon, then, an atmosphere of confusion, not focus, had thus engulfed the proto-presidency—a nascent institution that still lacked a staff—with serious side-effects, "The biggest mistake that can be made is to portray a sense of confusion, chaos," one transition aide bewailed—for this was something that "shows the president is not in charge and does not have good leadership skills. Then that creates an impression that carries over into his governing."

For Panetta the Clinton transition had been "absurd"—the president-elect somehow trusting his own ability to create a coherent administrative set-up by sheer force of personality, optimism, idealism, and goodwill. "To a great extent I really think he thought he could basically run the show the way you could be governor of Arkansas, and that he had enough handles on what was going on that, in the end, he felt like he would be able to shape the future . . ." Though this might smack of hubris, it was probably closer to naïveté—the sudden fantasy of a government of equals. "It may be that he thought this could be very much a 'team approach,' that it wouldn't have to be, you know, 'military style'!"

Employing a real chief of staff implied *giving and handing down orders*—and in the euphoria of victory, this aspect of leadership had proven simply beyond the Arkansan. "It's probably his lack of having had a military background," Panetta reflected, "but it was a sense that if you bring enough good people on board, that ultimately the right things will happen, and you don't have to issue orders, you don't have to establish discipline, you don't have to have this kind of military approach."

To Panetta—trained in the U.S. Army, a veteran of the civil rights division in the Justice Department, and about to start his ninth elected term of office as a congressman from California—there was something oddly, almost charmingly innocent about a newly-elected president so utterly unaware of the requirements of command, or the *challenges*—especially in dealing with personalities on the Hill. "Pretty naïve? But there *is* a certain kind of naiveté to Bill Clinton! Even though he's a political realist, even though he understands politics, there's a certain part of him that just tends to underestimate people. . . . There's a part of Bill Clinton that thinks: 'There's good in people and I can bring it out of them, so I don't have to worry about their dark side.' "

For a man as intelligent as Bill Clinton, this naiveté was, and remained, to Panetta "a paradox. I think you'd probably need to speak to a shrink at some point to know what all this was about, but I think that he was smart enough to know that he needed to have discipline, because that was a weak side. Clearly he wanted to do everything—he wanted to *please* everybody. He knew the problems that he had and that he needed discipline. But at the same time he resisted that—he didn't want it to consume his ability to be creative. And I think that's the conflict that went on. And I think whatever happened previously, he thought: 'I can handle this a lot more creatively, because I've just become president of the United States. I don't want somebody [as chief of staff] who's going to try to shackle me.'"

The result had been the choice of perhaps the most ineffective initial chief of staff in modern American history—chosen deliberately.

Secrets d'alcôve

Part of the paradox in Bill Clinton was that, side by side with his innocent idealism about getting the best out of people, there was a deep lack of ultimate *trust* in others, too, which made it even more difficult for him to imagine handing power to an effective chief of staff. Betsey Wright, after all, had become privy to his secrets—and had stopped him from running for the presidency in 1988, lest his *secrets d'alcôve* be exposed and destroy them all.

Watching the squabbling among his courtiers ("many of whom were beginning to show predictable and understandable signs of exhaustion, irritability, and anxiety about the future," Clinton himself recalled), something deep inside the president-elect had urged personal caution—a sort of concern, in the midst of so much jubilation, that stories might yet emerge and things still go wrong, so that he would have need not of a tough enforcer but of a loyal *friend*: one who could be relied upon to offer no criticism, and who would back his judgments as president, not contest them. The governor had thus whispered to his childhood friend Mack McLarty that he would like to consider him for the eventual position of White House chief of staff—despite McLarty's complete lack of experience in such a role and his absolute lack of knowledge of Washington or Congress.

Warren Christopher, as the suddenly promoted transition director, was amazed, but too courteous to protest. He later acknowledged that "no presidential appointment is more important" than that of chief of staff, who was expected to drive "the president's policy throughout the executive branch as well as on Capitol Hill." Indeed the very "success or failure of the presidency," Christopher later quoted James Baker, "depends in large measure on the skills of the chief of staff." Nevertheless Christopher declined to interfere. Ambitious and obsequious, the wizened lawyer resembled King Henry VIII's vizier, Thomas Cromwell, taking over the direction of state affairs after the dismissals of Cardinal Wolsey and Sir Thomas More. Not only did Christopher not remonstrate or advise the president-elect to think again regarding the appointment of a tough chief of staff or even the all-important members of the future White House staff, but—having declared his own and Vernon Jordan's ethical status as transition directors who were not going to be officeholders in the Clinton cabinet—Christopher had quietly left his *own* name in play as possible chief of staff. Failing that, Christopher had coveted the position of secretary of state that had been denied him under President Carter—the post to which the president-elect duly appointed him on Christmas Eve, 1992.

The utter chaos of the nascent Clinton administration was then felt by all who were involved in the transition. Without an enforcer Bill Clinton had been left, as underneath was his wish, to oversee his *own* transition, using Christopher as his courtly, temporary amanuensis: a president-elect of the United States running a literal "kitchen cabinet," side by side with his wife, Hillary, in the galley of the Governor's Mansion in Little Rock. The "kitchen table" in the Governor's Mansion had become "the nerve center of the Clinton transition," Hillary herself later described; "potential cabinet nominees came in and out, phones rang around the clock, piles of food were consumed." The result, as David Gergen later commented, had unfortunately been that the president-elect "put his White House team together at the last minute. People didn't know where they would be sitting until the last minute, didn't know what their jobs would be."

Recovering his energy, the president-elect had thrown himself into the "rainbow" cabinet selection process. It was like judging Miss America. "You know, all of this time that he spent putting together those fourteen people for the cabinet, of which only four were of any importance," Stephen Hess expostulated, "shows that even, with everything he's supposed to know, he didn't know anything. He had it all wrong. Why was he spending all this time choosing who was going to be Secretary of HUD? Of Labor? But he did. He loved it. 'Being president is picking the cabinet.' And so he spent all of his time picking a cabinet, when in fact, with the exception of State, Treasury, Defense, and Justice, it didn't make any difference. And he certainly screwed it up with Justice. And it turned out, he was wrong with Defense, too. . . . "

An Off-the-Cuff Remark

Eight long days after the election, the president-elect had then given his first public address—without a chief of staff. It had been a simple address to celebrate Veteran's Day, delivered in Little Rock's State Capitol Rotunda. It would result in catastrophe.

Clinton had meant well: to give a pledge to ease the transition from Cold War security considerations and claim the "peace dividend"—slimming the armed services of the United States by providing incentives for early military retirement and better, more accessible health care. Meanwhile, as commander-in-chief of the remaining U.S. military, he had vowed to "keep this country the strongest in the world" by maintaining the "strongest and most appropriate defense forces" with the "best possible technology," emphasizing air and sea mobility.

Certainly the president-elect had looked and sounded full of renewed energy. "Clinton has remained largely out of sight, closeted with advisers, since the election," the *Washington Post* reported. "But today's appearance signaled the beginning of an apparently more activist phase, with his first news conference scheduled for Thursday, and a meeting here Sunday with Senate Majority Leader George J. Mitchell, House Speaker Thomas S. Foley and House Majority Leader Richard A. Gephardt."

All this had sounded good—but without a White House chief of staff appointed, indeed any White House staff *at all*, the speech had quickly given rise to one of the first nightmares of his looming administration.

Paul Begala could only watch in anguish. "It was Veteran's Day, and he had laid a wreath on a veteran's memorial in Little Rock. As he was walking away, Andrea Mitchell, is my recollection, shouted out to him, 'Are you going to keep your promise to put gays in the military?'"

Given the week of silence from his transition headquarters, "people in the press were starting to say, 'Clinton is going to break all of his many campaign promises,' and so he flashed on it," Begala recalled. Instead of saying what he'd told Ted Koppel the day after the election, namely: "No, I'm going to focus like a laser beam on the economy. Once we get this economy growing, I will address other pressing needs," the president-elect had uttered the first fatal words for Phase One of his administration: "You bet. I'm going to keep that promise and all of them right away."

Begala's memory was all too accurate. Soon, every newspaper in the land had focused on the subject. "The incoming administration has made it clear: An end to the Pentagon's ban on homosexuals is all but inevitable. But this about-face may not be crisply executed," the *New York Times* reported—quoting one sociologist who warned: "This is causing more heartburning in the military than women in combat."

The president-elect's off-the-cuff remark, once printed, had enraged senior officers, senators, congressmen, and an army of conservatives across the land. Worse still, the gay and lesbian world began to mass ranks behind the president-elect—preparing for a fight over a subsidiary issue that had hardly figured in the election.

Surveys had shown that almost 60 percent of people polled were, in theory, in favor of relaxing the ban on gays in the armed services; moreover the navy had just had to reinstate a homosexual petty officer, who had successfully appealed his dismissal. But Washington was Washington, the Hill was the Hill, and the military was the military. To try and bite the gay military bullet prematurely was to risk an early politico-military battle, over a tangential issue: something no one was empowered or willing or experienced enough to tell the new president, save his wife—who was known to be gay friendly.

"Gays in the military?" Stephen Hess later shook his head. "It wasn't his issue. It wasn't even a major issue for *gays*! I mean, gays had a very *good* agenda—this wasn't particularly *on* it. It really was a mess, in my judgment."

And then, on top of that, there'd been the matter of Hillary's role.

Title 5

As first lady-in-literal-waiting, according to her biographer Gail Sheehy, Hillary coveted the job of attorney general—a job for which she would have been well-suited. Had she taken that post while remaining her husband's most loyal assistant and adviser, the parallel with Bobby Kennedy and President Kennedy might have been remarkable. Robert F. Kennedy had, after all, performed the role of tough, no nonsense, ass-kicking confidant to Senator John F. Kennedy in his 1960 campaign for the presidency. Thereafter, at his father's insistence and with the confirmation of Congress, Robert F. Kennedy had become attorney general of the United States, while also working at his brother's right hand during emergencies such as civil rights clashes and the Cuban Missile Crisis.

Such a historic role would, however, be denied Hillary. Once Bobby Kennedy left the Justice Department, in 1964, Congress had introduced new legislation barring spouses or relatives from ever again being appointed to any government-funded office by a "public official"—nomenclature that incorporated any job-giving officer of the U.S. government, *"including the President. . . . "*

Title 5 of the U.S. Code—originally enacted in 1967, and amended in 1978—was unmistakably explicit. From the president downwards, no public official was permitted to even advocate the appointment of a relative. The term "relative," moreover, was more restrictive than for marriage! As Title 5 stated unequivocally, the word "relative" embraced any "individual who is related to the public official as father, mother, son, daughter, brother, sister, uncle, aunt, first cousin, nephew, niece, husband, wife, father-in-law, mother-in-law, brother-in-law, sister-in-law, stepfather, stepmother, stepson, stepdaughter, stepbrother, stepsister, half brother, or half sister."

So there it had been, in black and white: staring back at the Rose Law Firm partner and *her* partner—the former University of Arkansas law professor, now president-elect.

By legislative decree Hillary Rodham Clinton had thus been denied the chance to become a Bobby Kennedy or Sargent Shriver in the new Clinton administration. Stymied—boxed in by marriage, boxed out by federal law. From that sad fact many malevolencies, indeed jinxes, would flow.

Without a federal job, or the hope of one, Hillary and the people she gathered around her in the hope of advancement posed a problem. Hillary's intellect was powerful, but her knowledge of Washington was limited and her political touch far from lucky. Like apostate Bobby Kennedy (who had moved from Joe Kennedy/Joe McCarthyite conservatism to compassionate liberalism, but had never changed in his essentially besieged, aggressive-defensive nature), Hillary was a Republican convert to the Democratic cause. Like Bobby she was also, when crossed, a distruster by nature. After years in a southern state in which she had always been an outsider and a threat to the "good ol' boys," Hillary Clinton had come to distrust people more than ever. Anyone she didn't know personally was suspect until proved otherwise. Even those she *did* know, she only really trusted when they were self-effacingly loyal or uncritical of Bill—and of her.

Given the absolute need for a White House presidential staff that would be in place in good time, as well as Washington-savvy—men and women of national political experience, who would have the courage to criticize and guide the "outsider" president —this had been unfortunate, to say the least. Hillary loved and admired her husband, but she had already, in exiling Kantor and scrapping his preparations for transition and a functioning White House staff, unwittingly destroyed her husband's chances of an easy launch as forty-second president.

In the looming saga of postmodern American presidential politics *qua* performance art, the performance of "Lady Macbeth of Little Rock," as the *Washington Post* soon referred to her, would, on transfer to the boards of Washington, D.C., become both comic and a calamity. For the sad fact was that President Bill Clinton *already had* a popularly validated co-president—a man who possessed not only Hillary's virtues of intellectual clarity, doggedness, focus, and decisiveness, but long experience of Congress—Senator and soon-to-be Vice President Al Gore.

Pulling the Trigger

The collision between the elected vice president-elect and the first lady *un*-elect had become a sad and wholly unnecessary train wreck. Without Hillary in the kitchen cabinet, the Clinton-Gore leadership could have proceeded without upset—as, after all, had happened after the Democratic Party's rapturous nomination of the two candidates at its national convention in New York in July 1992, and the tightly marshaled campaign that followed it.

Gore's biographer, Bill Turque, later described the Tennessee senator's genuine admiration for Bill Clinton. Gore, Turque recorded, "respected Clinton's intellect"—adding, however, that it was also difficult to ignore Clinton's lack of discipline and resolve, as a result of which Senator Gore felt he could, "in essence, be the steel in Clinton's spine." At the same time Gore could, Turque noted, "move some of his [own environmental] agenda in the bargain."

This was a noble vice presidential endeavor, indeed an important one in the history of the American vice presidency: balancing Bill Clinton's popularity and charisma with his own decisiveness and environmental concerns as vice president. Unfortunately it was a co-presidential role that the president's wife *also* coveted! The stage had thus been set, after the Kantor demise, for a struggle of Othello-like proportions, involving suspicion, rivalry, and downright skullduggery—fought out between two characters, of the same age, who were individually among the most upright, honest, and noble souls of their generation. Like Hillary before him, Al Gore was drawn to what he could do for, and through, Bill Clinton. "He may have sensed it pretty early. Taken a measure of the guy," one of Gore's intimate colleagues reflected of the relationship between the two baby boomers, "and said 'You know, I can say no, he can't. I can pull the trigger, he can't.'"

Voters, viewing this spine-steeling, trigger-pulling relationship between the nominee and vice-nominee on the electoral stump, had validated it by their ballots on November 2, 1992. "Clinton received from Gore a dowry, not of geographical balance or political supporters, but of image," White House correspondents Maureen Dowd and Michael Kelly had noted. "With the square-jawed Dudley Doright from Tennessee by his side, Slick Willie from Arkansas did not seem quite so slippery. Having a Vietnam veteran as his running mate helped shield Clinton as he defended his own troubled war history. And with the openly affectionate Gores holding hands beside them, the Clintons were able to sidestep some old baggage, the appearance that their union was less a romance than an arrangement between two calculating souls."

Unfortunately this "good cop/bad cop" relationship with the nation's chief executive, was, in Hillary's mind, pre-assigned to her. She'd selflessly kept her feminist head veiled after the electoral trials of New Hampshire—especially after the "Los Alamos Experiment," when voters gave the thumbs down the moment Hillary appeared on their screens. Raising her head after the election, however, she'd found herself in a double bind, observers felt. She'd helped behind the scenes to make her husband president-elect of the United States; she'd then moved to get rid of Kantor as rival—her aides willfully circulating stories of Kantor as "a greedy, avaricious, corporate lobbyist thirsting for power." But thanks to Title 5 of the U.S. Code, she'd had no license to wear a federal badge or brandish her authority as a White House marshal, beyond her duties as first lady in a frock. Deputy Al Gore, elected by the people of the United States, did.

Matters were complicated for the president-elect, too; Bill Clinton *feared* Hillary's legendary wrath—something that was not the case with Al Gore, whom Bill merely liked and respected. It had thus been, such observers mused, an extraordinary situation—the president-elect faced with a power choice: the choice between his vice president and his wife, whose insistence on naming the attorney general would now spoil the long-awaited, much heralded Act One, Scene One of the Clinton administration.

CHAPTER FOUR

ATTORNEY GENERAL

Zoë Baird

Zoë Baird, a corporate lawyer with almost no bar experience, had been one of a number of virtually unknown female candidates for the top Justice Department post in the United States. (Brooksley Born, an equally unknown Washington, D.C., lawyer involved in women's issues, had been another. Summoned to Little Rock, Ms. Born had found herself interviewed not by the president but by Hillary, who spoke with her at length. It was clear who was making the appointment, Born realized. When Born had returned home in December, she'd boasted to her company colleagues that she had been chosen by Hillary to become the new attorney general. A few hours before Christmas she had found, to her chagrin, she had not! Nor had a succession of other wannabees, who failed to impress Hillary or her female cohort sufficiently.)

A friend of Susan Thomases, Zoë Baird was a regular attendee at the New Year Renaissance Weekend for high-fliers at Hilton Head, South Carolina—which had been attended by the president-elect and the new first lady, once again, over New Year 1993. Baird had once worked for the transition director, Warren Christopher, and now was employed as general counsel for Aetna Life and Casualty Company, one of America's leading insurance companies. She was earning a salary of more than half a million dollars a year, but her qualifications for the attorney generalship, beyond Christopher's recommendation, her gender, and Hillary's imprimatur, seemed insubstantial (in her twenties she had worked for two years in the Justice Department as a young assistant).

Neither the president nor the vice president had been permitted any input into the appointment—indeed the vice president had had to struggle to keep an office in the West Wing once Hillary had set her sights on it. Hillary's *eminence grise*, Susan Thomases, had actually gone to Washington to get architect's floor plans of the West Wing building, to ensure that the first lady—for the first time in history—would have her own office there, in addition to the traditional first lady's office in the East Wing. Such determination to have her own office in the West Wing had "sent a chill through everyone," one transition adviser had confided, for whoever was closest to the emperor, it was reckoned, would have most chance of bending the presidential ear. "Al Gore hasn't yet realized there is going to be a copresidency," one lobbyist had quipped, shortly before the inauguration, "but he's not going to be part of the *co.*"

Only one brave soul, Harold Ickes—son of FDR's famous secretary of the interior, who had been turned down as too feisty for deputy chief of staff to President Clinton—had meanwhile dared contest Hillary's choice for attorney general. He warned that Baird's known employment of illegal Peruvian immigrants as nanny and chauffeur, while withholding social security payments for them, could prejudice her nomination before the all-important Senate Judiciary Committee. Obsessed with ethnic and gender inclusiveness, the Clintons, fired up by their Renaissance Weekend, had not heeded Ickes, however. "Ultimately, with our help," Warren Christopher prided himself, "Bill Clinton fashioned the most diverse cabinet in American history:" three white women, six white men, one black woman, three black men, and two Hispanics.

Controlled by Democrats, Congress welcomed the rationale but, wary of the competence of such a "rainbow" list, insisted on carrying out its constitutional obligation to vet the president's choices—and in the case of Zoë Baird the Senate Judiciary Committee simply balked. With insufficient credentials for such a high cabinet post, and rumors that she was the choice not of the president but of the unelected first lady, Baird was quickly confronted by the same phalanx of senators who had so recently had to confirm, or not confirm, President Bush's nomination of Clarence Thomas as a justice of the Supreme Court barely a year before. As in that case, the senators zeroed in on Ms. Baird's weakest link: her employment of the illegal immigrants, and her failure to pay taxes on such personal servants. As the graybeards tortured the nominee, it became clear that this, not the all-important budget, would become the forty-second president's first challenge.

Culture Wars

"The nominee's style and situation triggered some deep seated anti-yuppie animosity that brought Middle America to attention," Warren Christopher later reflected—ignoring his own feebleness in having deferred to Hillary and Thomases' choice in the transition. Nevertheless, in his retrospective assertion Christopher was certainly right.

The Clintons, as quintessential baby boomers who had led their joyous supporters across Memorial Bridge, were almost inevitably going to face cultural opposition on the other side—and in their selection of attorney general they brought down a barrage of enemy artillery. Civility in the media had been declining for years. Now, in the transitional post-Cold War age, labels would be traded like comic books, as conservatives faced a rising tide of yuppies reaching the pinnacles of their professions in their forties (Zoë Baird was forty-one).

Was it innocence, then, on the part of Hillary Clinton to have chosen such a proxy—or arrogance? Had Baird possessed other, more traditional, demonstrable talents for the nation's top justice official—a cabinet officer responsible for the FBI, the Bureau of Prisons, the U.S. Marshals Service, immigration, civil rights, and federal pardons—the matter of nannies might have gained less purchase on the Senate Judiciary Committee's attention. But Baird had no such qualifications, and this was the United States: for centuries a melting pot of competing cultural groups, whose views were free and whose votes were counted every two years for congressmen, and six for senators. Once the *New York Times* article was published, calling attention to Baird's "nanny problem," senators and congressmen received a "stunning barrage of public and private calls opposing the nomination," the *St. Louis Post-Dispatch* soon recorded—indeed, phone calls to the Hill ran over three hundred to one against her. "Majorities of men and women, Republicans and Democrats, and people of all ages, incomes and educational levels, said the Senate should reject her nomination," said *USA Today*'s own poll, taken the night after the inauguration, which showed that 54 percent indicated "she felt she was above the law," 59 percent that her violation of the law "undermines her ability to enforce the country's laws as attorney general"—and 42 percent that the nomination of Baird decreased their confidence in President Clinton's ability to make good appointments.

This latter poll result was the most worrying. The next day the negative figures had risen to the sixties—with Rush Limbaugh, the unashamedly male-chauvinist right-wing Republican talk-show host, having a field day.

In the context of a fresh administration falling in, but a cultural backlash already fermenting, indeed foaming, few politicians dared overlook the nominee's lack of credentials to be made the nation's top law enforcement officer, however much the first lady might want her. Instead, even Democratic senators now acted out their supervisory roles with almost Victorian earnestness—challenging big Bill Clinton, the new president of the United States, head-on, during his first day in office.

The president was shocked by the volume of fire. Summoning Hillary's former boss Bernie Nussbaum, his new chief White House legal counsel (and another Hillary appointment), from his lunch in the White House, the forty-second president asked what he should do, given the darkening prospects for Baird's confirmation. "Fight!" Nussbaum advised (or misadvised) the young president—Nussbaum still ignorant of the fact that he was addressing a man who was not a born fighter.

Neither was the new president a coward. It was simply that he felt no desire to expend his initial political capital on defending a woman he did not know, whom his wife had chosen, and in a fight that was not central to his agenda. If he were to allow Baird's nomination to fail, however, would his new administration be viewed as weak?

Disconcerted at being put in this position by Hillary and her gray eminence, the president swallowed his irritation. He backed Baird—but only half-heartedly, waiting to see how, in fact, the wind would blow. This forced the newly appointed White House communications director, the even younger yuppie George Stephanopoulos, to have to prevaricate on his first day's briefing of the press, when responding to a reporter's question whether the president would like Baird to withdraw her nomination. *"Well, dub. Of course he would, wouldn't you?"* he later remembered thinking. *"We're sucking wind on our first day with a candidate for attorney general who broke the law. But she says she told Warren Christopher about it before Clinton chose her, so it's our fault—and she doesn't want to quit before clearing her name. So we're stuck."* Instead he pretended to be emphatic, saying: "No, he thinks she'll make an excellent attorney general. . . . "

The first full day of the Clinton presidency had come, meanwhile, to a convivial end. Hillary's parents and brothers, Clinton's brother Roger, their mother and stepfather, Jim Blair and his wife Diane, the Thomasons, and friends of Bill and Hillary's daughter, Chelsea, were all staying over at the White House. Vodka and goodwill were shared in the private quarters, Hillary later chronicled—but she omitted mentioning a message that came from Senator Joe Biden, to alert the new president of the United States to the sad news: that even moderate Democratic members of his Judiciary Committee, responding to voter venom, were now going to turn down Baird's appointment, if he went ahead with it.

"My job that day was to act like one of his henchmen—to hang Zoë out to dry," Stephanopoulos later recalled. "She didn't know it yet, but she was toast." Through an exchange of letters Baird would have to face the fact—Stephanopoulos was bringing in his young deputy communications director, David Dreyer, to write her official suicide note.

Unfortunately, Zoë Baird wouldn't sign. "It took her a long time, I think, to accept that this was the decision," the diminutive Dreyer recalled, "and to rewrite my letter in a way that was comfortable to her, to edit it." Eventually it was only in the early hours of the second morning of Clinton's presidency that Baird accepted not only her fate but its wording.

Dreyer would never forget the moment, as the president arrived in Stephanopoulos's crowded office "wearing a sweatsuit and a baseball cap with an insignia—the Arkansas Razorbacks or whatever—pulled over his eyes, and in his hand an apple that is absolutely slathered with peanut butter." As the six-foot-three president sank down into a vacated seat, Stephanopoulos introduced his new deputy. "The president smiled and said, 'Hi,'" Dreyer remembered, "and asked, 'When did you get here?' 'Yesterday afternoon, Mr. President,' I answered. 'Well,' he said, 'it sure didn't take you long to screw up, now did it?'"

CHAPTER FIVE

GAYS IN THE MILITARY

No Harry Truman

At his first press briefing, Stephanopoulos had assured newspaper and television reporters that the president not only was serious about appointing Zoë Baird to be attorney general of the United States, but was determined to remove the ban on gays in the military by issuing an executive order, which would be signed "very soon—probably within the next week, but not today."

The next *week*? This was holding yet another red rag before the bulls of the press, the Congress, and the public. And the Pentagon. It was an act of sheer madness unless Clinton *truly* intended to go ahead with the decision by executive order, and thus, by a contest of wills, to stamp his authority on the armed services of the world's mightiest nation.

Stephanopoulos had been a crucial adviser reflecting the opinions of young people during the campaign, but this was now the presidency—"the big leagues," as Stephanopoulos himself called it. "I found George damned smart," Webb Hubbell later recalled, "but he was a bit cocky for my southern sensibilities." Worse, Stephanopoulos's smartness forbade him to admit he did not know the answer to something, or when to hold back information. "In front of the White House press corps, George Stephanopoulos time and again seemed unable to utter the simple words, 'I don't know'—even when those words described the truth," Hubbell recounted. Instead "'information' was shoveled in to fill the vacuum"—something that was anathema to Hubbell as a trained lawyer, and was ultimately counterproductive with journalists.

Why, journalists wondered, the urgency of an executive order, rather than a Pentagon study, following the inauguration? Randy Shilts's historical masterpiece, *Conduct Unbecoming*, had not yet been published (it was brought out in May 1993), and the subject had received very little public attention. "Anyone with an ounce of experience in Washington knew that you certainly don't want to take on the gays in the military issue as one of the first ones after going into office," Leon Panetta, as a nine-times elected congressman, felt—but he was not asked. Nor was there anyone of Panetta's experience to ask, given Clinton's failure to appoint his White House staff until the final days of the transition—and even then, to exclude anyone with previous Washington experience.

Michael Waldman, one of the president's young speechwriters, would later regret this. "You know, the thing with the White House that was probably different from what it should have been, it's not that there were too many kids in the White House," he maintained. "There are always thirty-two-year-olds in the White House. Bill Moyers, Ted Sorenson were that age." Rather, it was the lack of balancing people—people "with the long-time experience to say, 'Let's not do it that way.' " With the president having publicly committed his administration to carry out the promise over gays in the military, however, Rahm Emanuel, another young aide, lamented, "it became our priority"—with disastrous consequences for the shaky first footing of the new administration. "It totally threw it off. If you're trying to keep a rhythm and a tempo, it totally threw it off. There's no doubt about it. And it was costly."

Others, however, kept arguing that President Truman's executive order desegregating the military in 1948 had been a defining, indeed pioneering, act in the history of civil rights in America—an act Bill Clinton could follow with a simple, firm instruction.

Unfortunately, Bill Clinton was no Harry Truman—at least, not yet.

No one quite knew why a hitherto supercautious politician should have made such a monumental misjudgment in his first days in office—and in his memoirs President Clinton declined to explain his misstep, beyond recalling the hypocrisy behind the controversy. During the recent Gulf War the Pentagon had "knowingly allowed more than one hundred gays to serve, dismissing them only after the conflict," he pointed out. But such military two-facedness could not explain his own tactical gaffe in permitting the issue to take center stage on the first day of his new administration. Compared with health care, education, the environment, voluntary public service, reduction of the national deficit, and welfare reform, was this a battle worth fighting at the very outset of his presidency?

Having the authority to issue an executive order as president and commander-in-chief was, despite the example of President Truman, a dubious power, since if the matter became too contentious, Congress could subsequently overrule him—something that would distract from the president's major legislative programs, tying up his staff's time and effort. *And for what purpose*?

The vice president, Al Gore, urged the president, if he really intended to pursue the issue, to be firm and make the military recognize its subordinate role in American democracy. There were already gays serving honorably in the military, but they were not being allowed to openly acknowledge—or make others acknowledge—their sexuality. A bill to overturn an executive order would take time for legislators to mount, Gore reasoned, and public opinion might not necessarily favor such a hard-line military campaign directed at the elected leader of the nation, at a time when the Cold War was over, and international peacemaking, not warmaking, was likely to be the lot of U.S. combat forces. The gay cause might not necessarily be one that had engaged the larger public during the election, but it could certainly *become* a symbolic one in America, which in a way was more important— *doing what was right*, not necessarily politic. The new administration would occupy the moral high ground, however slight its forces—a crucial, Gandhi-esque factor in fighting any battle.

As word of Stephanopoulos's assurance spread, an urgent meeting with the president was requested by the Joint Chiefs of Staff—and the president had no option but to acquiesce. "I'm going to meet with them and discuss it this afternoon," the president told reporters on Monday, January 25, 1993, five days after the inauguration. "But I intend," he added obstinately, "to keep my commitment."

Blood in the Water

General Gordon Sullivan, chief of staff of the U.S. Army, was one of the Joint Chiefs who attended the meeting. "It was the very first time that I met Mr. Clinton: that day, the twenty-fifth of January, 1993," the general recalled, picturing the situation in the White House as the leaders of two armies—one political, the other military—approached each other in the

Roosevelt Room like opposing chieftains before a battle. "He was sick. He had a bad cold. That was apparent, that he was sick. It was late in the day, around four o'clock in the afternoon. He had told us, through Colin Powell [the chairman of the Joint Chiefs], at a meeting during the transition, that before he did anything on this issue he would meet with the chiefs. Well, that morning we woke up and we read the newspaper and it was announced by Congressman Barney Frank at a gathering that the president was about to sign an executive order, similar to what Harry Truman signed on blacks in the military—and that would be the end of it. So we felt as a group, if he did elect to do that, that we would at least have to have the benefit of being able to say, 'I told the president how I felt about it and what my recommendation was!' Unless I did that, I would be seen as a less than viable leader. So one thing led to another, and we went over to the White House.

"Each of us spoke. Each of us. He listened."

Tony Lake, as the new national security adviser to the president, cringed at the memory. "Well, he certainly had a lot of support from the gay community, in the campaign, and from gay friends, and lifting the ban is an enlightened view. But yes, he got entrapped, I'm sure of that. I wouldn't say he got entrapped into something he didn't believe—he just got entrapped into something he hadn't thought through." Tasked with addressing a series of major national security problems across the world, Lake had asked his friend John Holum to look at the options the president would have in lifting the gay ban, only to find that the issue was being seized upon by congressmen and senators—"especially the Republicans"—who were "not going to let go. And we're looking for help from Senator Sam Nunn, for example, and we're not getting it." "If there's a strategy there, it hasn't been explained to me," Senator Nunn (whom Clinton had failed to choose as his defense secretary) was heard to say—a covert invitation to Republican senators to combine with him in defeating any executive order.

For Lake, gays in the military was the last thing he wanted on his plate, as his first task in the new administration. "I did *not* welcome it as an issue," he acknowledged wryly, a decade later. "Which is not to say it's wrong. But when you're trying to deal with Bosnia and a lot of issues which are going to require convincing our military leaders that whatever it is we decide to go forward with, we shall do, you *don't* need this. Secondly, in terms of Clinton's personal relationship with the Joint Chiefs, it certainly made it very difficult. Because this is one of the first issues when they're just getting to know each other."

Whether because of his illness, allergies, or embarrassment at being lectured on the inadvisability of issuing an executive order, the president looked pale and downcast. As the president himself recalled, "When I raised the fact that it apparently had cost the military $500 million to kick seventeen thousand homosexuals out of the service in the previous decade, despite a government report saying there was no reason to believe they could not serve effectively, the chiefs replied that it was worth it to preserve unit cohesion and morale."

The president had never served in the military, and knew nothing of unit cohesion or morale; he therefore caved in—immediately. The chiefs had expected a fight, and were somewhat surprised. "There was not," General Sullivan recalled, "a lot of arguing back and forth. It was: 'Well, O.K., that's the way you feel,' as each of us told him in turn." Sullivan was unrepentant. "My view is that what you pay people like me for—or what you *appoint* people like me or [Marine General] Carl Mundy, or [Air Force General] Tony McPeak or Admiral Frank Kelsoe for—is to give their honest opinion on an issue. And then, if we're told to do it, we do it!"

Clearly the president was in no condition to tell the chiefs to "do it." "And then Colin [Powell] said—he didn't say 'Don't ask, Don't tell,' but he said: 'Mr. President, what if we just don't ask 'em at the recruiting station, and we just don't know?'—which is what goes on now," Sullivan remarked twelve years later. "We don't have a clue who sleeps with who. And as long as it doesn't become apparent to us, we *don't* know. So that's kind of how it went."

Badly burned, Clinton took a deep breath and, brightening up, said, as General Sullivan recalled, "'O.K. That's fine. Well then, let's study it.' He told Secretary Aspin [the new defense secretary] 'OK, let's get on with this and let's work it with the Department of Justice and with others, and let's get back together, and we'll see.' And that's how the meeting ended."

It was not, as General Sullivan put it, "necessarily how you'd prefer to start a relationship with the president," but it was "not confrontational," and the chiefs were satisfied. The notion of an executive order was dropped, while the matter of a compromise was studied.

If presidential leadership, as commander in chief, consists in giving orders, however, it was a presidential defeat, and news of defeat in the modern world traveled as swiftly as that of victory, perhaps more so. As the thirty-one-year-old Stephanopoulos witnessed the confrontation, his heart sank. It was like Inchon. They would have to retreat, while finding words to gloss over the withdrawal that he could use at his next, excoriated press briefing. *Why, oh why, had he announced its imminent enactment to the press*? And why had the president listened to such naïve urging?

Instead of emerging as a determined, honorable president who knew his own mind, and was willing to use his special executive power as president to take action—circumventing Congress, but for a noble cause—Clinton had made the motions of doing so, and then backed off! He was, the chiefs now knew, not only a Vietnam draft-avoider, but battle-shy: a commander in chief of little mettle, though very personable and intelligent. His nominee for defense secretary, Les Aspin, was equally smart but weak: a former congressman known for his long-windedness and conference style, not clarity of command leadership.

"So it gets the whole thing off to a *terribly* shaky start," Stephen Hess recalled. "And some of these decisions . . ." He paused, shaking his white-haired head, "they were so *unnecessary!*"

Leon Panetta, as the new director of OMB, was certainly appalled, anxious lest it have an adverse effect on members of Congress. "I think anytime the White House starts to make mistakes . . ." He paused. "Once there's some blood in the water, the Hill begins to tighten up a little bit, in terms of 'What's coming next?' and 'Where are we headed?'"

Spinning Out of Control

Why had the president's new chief of staff, Mack McLarty, *allowed* such a fiasco to arise? Why had there been so many leaks—giving rise to speculation, concern, public anxiety, and premature contention over an issue that was not central to Bill Clinton's new presidency? And why was the press, which had been so supportive of his candidacy the previous year, so unsympathetic?

One reason was that Hillary, in a moment of renewed madness, had locked the White House door that allowed correspondents, in the basement, access to the White House press office. As White House communications director, Stephanopoulos was all too aware of the blunder, which turned a largely sympathetic press corps against the new president. "They were confined to the basement, and they were pissed," he recalled—especially when they learned the first lady's actual intention had been to exclude them from the West Wing completely, in order that Hillary could re-commission an indoor swimming pool.

Once before, Hillary had outraged gubernatorial staff and advisers in Arkansas by insisting on the building of a swimming pool for herself and her friends at the Governor's Mansion in Little Rock. That notion, though squelched, had involved only an *outdoor* pool. As Stephanopoulos later described his thoughts on the subject, when reporters remonstrated: "*I'm not your problem; Hillary is. She and Susan Thomases cooked up this plan to move you to the Old Executive Office Building so we could reopen the indoor pool that used to be right below your feet before Nixon made this the press room. Barbara Bush told her we should show you guys who's boss right from the start. Easy for her to say; she doesn't have to deal with you anymore. Closing the door was our fallback position.*"

President Clinton, Stephanopoulos recalled, was nonplussed both by Hillary and Susan's proposed re-opening of the pool (which was never done) and the fall-back decision. Stephanopoulos recalled that when the president asked him about the closing of the door, his silent reaction was, "Um, have you talked to your wife about this, Mr. President?"

Closing the door on the White House correspondents proved an act of utter folly. Moreover, the mistake could not simply be attributed to Hillary or to the president's marital deference. The president himself seemed ignorant of the purpose and value of the White House press correspondents. Tom Lippman, a senior reporter for the *Washington Post*, later recalled his amazement at such a misunderstanding, one that he discussed with his equally surprised colleague David Broder. "Clinton had an idea that the press writ large had become an unnecessary middle man in the process of communicating with the American people," Lippman recalled their thinking. "That he didn't need to talk with us because he was going to talk to the masses. And so the Clintons tried that, through personal connections from television. So there was some apprehension in the Washington press corps: that Clinton was going to go right around us or over our heads, to the 250 million people out there."

What Stephanopoulos had failed to make clear to the new president was the difference between newspaper correspondents who virtually lived at the White House and reported on it, hour by hour, day by day, week by week, month by month, on the one hand, and television hosts on the other. Certainly neither Stephanopoulos nor the president seemed aware of the reality of the Washington media machine process. By befriending TV talk-show impresarios but failing to court the all-important White House newspaper correspondents—as JFK had done so brilliantly—Clinton did himself a serious disservice.

The closed door to serious White House correspondents, whose sympathy and understanding the new president would crucially need in his first few months in office, thus became a metaphor for arrogance and ignorance, which neither Hillary nor Bill Clinton would acknowledge, even a decade later, as the disaster of their first months in the White House receded into "living" history.

The door remained locked—for the next disastrous six months.

CHAPTER SIX

CAMP DAVID I

Camp David

In the wake of the gays in the military fiasco it dawned on seasoned insiders that President Bush might have been right: Bill Clinton had the brains but might not have the character yet to run America, Inc.

Clinton "was not well served by the wandering deliberations he permitted," Colin Powell lamented—an approach to leadership that led to comic opera the next weekend, when the top personnel of the Clinton administration assembled for the first time at Camp David, in the Catoctin Mountains of Maryland, a place Clinton would come to hate, owing to its effect on his allergies. There, each invitee was pressed to reveal a personal secret to fellow attendees. To give legitimacy to such a bonding strategy, moreover, the president himself, who loved Baptist church services where he could sing along lustily, was persuaded to take part. To the considerable embarrassment of his subordinates, the commander in chief of the United States announced, as his *secret d'alcôve*, that he had been humiliated as a child by being called "Fatso."

"Fatso"? Was such a confession before his new senior staff the right way for a tentative new president to imprint his leadership on the nation's top leadership team? Men like Lloyd Bentsen, the new Treasury secretary, simply boycotted the confessional by departing. Others, like Robert Rubin, refused to contribute their personal secrets. Madeleine Albright, the new ambassador to the UN, called it "a bizarre event, with barely acquainted people crowded into cabins and force-fed a dose of New Age relationship building." This was taking the approach of the "New Democrats" (the moniker given to centrist Democrats breaking away in the 1980s from the old party orthodoxies) to an extreme. The situation would have been laughable had it not, at the same time, been so serious. Here was the world's last remaining superpower, at the end of the Cold War, under the stewardship of a brilliant young man: charming, well-meaning, empathetic, hard-working, multi-tasking, multi-faceted, full of good intentions—yet in many ways still an ingénue.

Some years later, a television soap dedicated to the highly professional dramas of the White House would be produced, to high acclaim: *The West Wing*. But *this* soap, for all its amateurism, was real; the Camp David meeting of the cabinet and sous-cabinet resembled a pilot for a forthcoming comedy series, once Hillary Clinton rose and as co-president suddenly stole the show. Before the astonished audience she ridiculed the script of their proposed next episode and demanded a complete rewrite—replete with what she called "heroes and villains."

Putting People Last

Unknown to the public, a genuine crisis of an economic kind had been brewing for weeks. Two days before the Camp David bonding weekend, on January 28, 1993, the chairman of the Federal Reserve Board, Alan Greenspan, had come to the White House and warned of "financial catastrophe" unless the full-scale deficit reduction plan was put into effect forthwith. The secretary of the Treasury, Lloyd Bentsen, agreed. After all, had not the priority of deficit reduction been established at the January 7 meeting in Little Rock?

Had it, though? Robert Reich, Clinton's old Rhodes scholar friend and social policy guru, was devastated by the prospect of going back on their campaign promise to introduce an economic stimulus package immediately. How could the new administration shelve the raft of social and economic agendas that had already been shelved for the past *twelve* years of Republican presidential rule? "If Bill and Hillary are seriously considering Bentsen for this role, how committed can they be to raising the prospects of the working class and the poor?" Reich had already noted in his diary the previous November—and nothing in the intervening weeks had given him confidence that Clinton was going to make good on his promises. Unemployment was reaching almost 8 percent, but any attempt to reduce that number by pushing federally funded retraining programs would, Reich accepted, only further increase a national debt that was $125 billion worse than even Ross Perot, the third-party candidate, had pictured in the election. The nation's long-term debt would have to be tackled. It was a just a question of when. Should deficit reduction come *before* stimulus and investment programs? *Alongside* them? Or—if, per Richard Neustadt, presidents only have a brief window of legislative opportunity—*after* them?

Secretary Bentsen, backed by Robert Rubin, was all for deficit reduction as the first priority of the new administration—and assumed he had the president's backing. Others remained appalled by the prospect. The Camp David bonding weekend that began on January 30, 1993, therefore now turned into the opposite: a bifurcating event. Traditional party Democrats were chafing at the bit—ready to rise in uproar at what they perceived to be a "sell-out" of the election promises in *Putting People First*, Clinton's 1992 campaign book. "Putting people last," such Democrats now snarled at the president—who failed to mention, in his enthusiastic response to the initiatives proposed at Camp David, "the central importance of helping those in the bottom half of our society get a foothold in the new high-technology, global economy," as Reich noted in his diary.

Nor was Reich alone in such despairing concern: '92 election campaign staffers such as Mandy Grunwald, Stan Greenberg, and Paul Begala were already whispering in the first lady's ear the reason the administration was getting such bad press: not because of her closed-door policy, but because the president had become, overnight, a Republican!

Hillary had listened to such criticism with mounting concern. She'd been stymied in her earlier hopes of heading up her own government department, or even obtaining an official White House job such as domestic policy adviser to the president, but since the previous Monday, she did have a proud new and formal role in the administration—she had proposed that she take responsibility for health care reform.

Hillary Leads the President's Task Force

"President Clinton yesterday named his wife, Hillary Rodham Clinton, to lead six cabinet secretaries and a handful of senior White House advisers in tackling what is expected to be the most difficult domestic issue of his presidency: national health care overhaul," the *Washington Post* had reported on Tuesday, January 26. The first lady was to chair what would be called the "President's Task Force on National Health Care Reform." And the newspaper quoted the president's proud words: "This is going to be an unprecedented effort."

It would be—not least because, notwithstanding the bruising the first lady was receiving over the failed appointment of Zoë Baird, and the hammering the president was getting over gays in the military, Bill Clinton was now asking the impossible: that the task force "work constantly day and night until we have a health care plan" ready to submit to Congress within 131 days! Hillary's declared remit would be to cover the 37 million Americans without medical insurance, and to control health care costs, which had doubled in five years and were rising at four times the rate of inflation. She was also charged with the task of building public support and "consensus" for the plan, "which is expected to be highly controversial on Capitol Hill and among the interest groups concerned with health care," the *Washington Post* warned. "Administration officials are considering town hall meetings or other forums across the country."

Why *Hillary,* for such a crucial and difficult assignment? observers at the time—and health historians later—asked. Were there no other, more experienced national figures who could lead the search for a workable solution? Unfortunately, Al Gore had turned down the appointment, and Senator George Mitchell, in a moment of unusual obtuseness, had advised against the appointment of a U.S. senator, such as John D. Rockefeller of West Virginia, to take the job. Nor had anyone advanced the cause of the outgoing, highly respected surgeon general, Dr. C. Everett Koop.

Whatever the truth, the nation now had to confront the news that the president had asked his own wife to take on what Dick Gephardt, the House majority leader, called "the toughest bill since the Social Security Act of 1936." *How*, serious commentators asked, could such a task be achieved? Who would *pay* for such a massive reform—especially in a period of recession, with a president committed to deep deficit reduction on behalf of future generations of Americans?

No one really knew or could later explain how the president's decision to appoint his wife to lead health care reform came about. In her memoirs Hillary confessed that "few on the White House staff knew that Bill had asked me to chair the task force, or that Ira [Magaziner] would manage the day-to-day operations." Indeed, she admitted, Magaziner himself had "learned about his new job only ten days before the inauguration." This implied that the secretive decision was made around January 10—three days *after* the six-hour deficit-reduction meeting in Little Rock.

Had the president-elect gone out of his mind, historians wondered—setting up an atomic bomb-like project that would consume vast amounts of energy, resources, money, people, and political capital, in the very aftermath of a major meeting at which the president had seemingly definitively decided to go with deficit reduction as his number one target? Certainly there was no secrecy or ignorance about the magnitude of the task at the time, nor the painful options if it was to be achieved. "Clinton's advisers recently told him that providing coverage for all by the year 2000 would cost about $230 billion over five years," a nationally syndicated reporter noted the day after the announcement. "What's more, they said, the 'savings' from controlling costs just aren't enough. He would have to raise taxes, or watch the deficit soar."

Since these uncomfortable facts were known, and since the president himself was now committed to tackling the deficit, why had he ignored the very people he had, in the transition, appointed to draw up the costs of such a health plan? Judy Feder, his health care transition director, recalled how Larry Summers, for one, "read me the riot act" over the likely cost of the Clinton plan during transition planning—even her "low-ball estimates." So also had Senator Bentsen and Congressman Leon Panetta, for such expenditure would wreck their attempts at deficit reduction. When Dr. Feder informed the president-elect of this, he'd become equally furious—simply refusing to believe her, and insisting that savings in the health care system could be made to fund the cost of universal coverage *without* raising taxes, or affecting his deficit reduction plans.

Was there an evil genius whispering in Clinton's ear at the time, such participants wondered?

Was it Ira Magaziner, Clinton's old Rhodie colleague and a management consultant with a challenging, arrogant manner? No one knew for sure, other than that Bill Clinton also had, as he himself later confessed, a love of secrets that went back to his childhood: a reliance on shady characters to help him gain the advantage over opponents, when necessary, in the tough struggle to survive, whether in local or national politics. Dick Morris had performed that role in helping plot his comeback as defeated governor of

Arkansas in 1981–1982—but Morris had sat out the 1992 presidential campaign because he hadn't thought "much of his chances of winning," and was currently eating his hat. When asked about the appointment of Hillary, Morris agreed with other Clinton advisers, however. Even if Hillary managed to find a way round U.S. Code Title 5, "a president had to be able to fire his chief of staff if the occasion arose," Morris pointed out, "and it was difficult to imagine the first lady being fired."

The president-elect had ignored Morris' caution, though, just as he'd ignored Dr. Feder's warning over costs. "Bill wanted to approach health care from a new angle," Hillary later recalled, "and Ira [Magaziner], with his brilliant and creative mind, had a knack for coming up with inventive ways for looking at issues." After all, she pointed out, Magaziner owned a consulting business in Rhode Island that "advised multinational companies on how to become more productive and efficient."

Advising companies was not the same, though, as pushing the most controversial issue of the age through Congress—as even Hillary later acknowledged. Who, then, persuaded whom to press ahead with such a madcap scheme, on such a madcap timetable? As Hillary admitted, even Magaziner was daunted by the task. "Capitol Hill veterans were warning him that our timetable for delivering a health care reform bill in one hundred days was unrealistic," she recalled—indeed she described a panicky Magaziner ignoring his sandwich lunch and telling her, and the president, the latest warning from the Hill: "They think we're gonna get killed. We'll need at least four to five years to put together a package that will pass Congress."

Hillary later blamed Bill—for his response had been, she recalled, "I'm hearing the same thing. But we have to try. We just have to make it work."

Furthermore, why had the president so secretly—i.e., without reference or discussion with any member of his administration—appointed a fellow Rhodes scholar with as little Washington experience as Hillary had, to be her deputy and enforcer?

Judy Feder, as transition health director, had been mortified by the decision, about which—like the decision to appoint Hillary's friend Donna Shalala as secretary of Health and Human Services—she was not consulted. Nor was, incredibly, Donna Shalala.

Dr. Feder had never contemplated the post of Secretary of HHS, but she had hoped to be asked to take the post of health care adviser to the president, a position that President Bush had created. To her consternation, shortly after the inauguration, she found that it was to be given to Ira Magaziner, who had not even been on her transition health team, but who had "lurked" in the background.

Swallowing her pride, and taking the job of deputy assistant secretary of HHS under Donna Shalala but charged with helping the first lady's revolutionary health care reform agenda under Ira Magaziner, Dr. Feder would be asked to help prepare a plan that she had not envisaged during her role as adviser to the president-elect during the transition—a plan she felt from her long experience of Congress had no hope of succeeding!

Years later, Bill Clinton could shed no light on his decision—for by 2004 his first year's agenda, as freshman president in 1993, had become the memory of a seamless flow of noble decisions. "On January 25, Chelsea's first day at her new school, I announced Hillary would head a task force," he recorded in his memoirs. "I was pleased that Ira had agreed with Hillary. . . . I knew he would give Hillary the kind of support she needed. . . . I decided Hillary should lead the health-care effort because she cared and knew a lot about the issue. . . . I knew the whole enterprise was risky. . . . Nevertheless I thought we should try for universal coverage, which every other wealthy nation had long enjoyed. . . ."

Thus the key player, in a monumentally bad decision that would help lose both houses of Congress for the Democrats for the first time in four decades, simply drew a retrospective veil over his decision—its timing, the staffing, the time frame for completion, and the bitter, bitter lesson: that for a new president to tackle simultaneously two major domestic issues he not only risked mixing his message, after inauguration, but risked failing in both.

A Thankless Task

Hillary herself was unclear later as to why she proposed that she take the task force appointment, beyond the fact that Bill was persuasive about its importance (it had polled well in the final months of the election campaign) and that she wanted a major position in the new administration.

Though she admitted she knew very little about health care in the national policy arena, Hillary did have elderly parents and, as in education in Arkansas, where she had headed up a governor's committee on education reform, had the same concerns as most citizens: the desire to see a simpler, more affordable system of health care, as well as one that did not unfairly exclude many of the poorly paid, the unemployed, and the self-employed. But public education in Arkansas had been an issue on a minuscule scale, and even that had taken years to reform. How then did Hillary imagine that in a mere 131 days she could defy the gods and not only dream up a solution that involved no new monies or taxes but could also present it in a tailor-made health reform bill that Congress would pass?

In retrospect the task was not simply daunting, it was thoughtlessly, even cruelly, assigned—as Hillary recalled the governor of New York, Mario Cuomo, telling her when he heard of it: "What did you do to make your husband so mad at you?" sympathizing with what he saw as "a thankless task."

Hillary's friends, however, were proud of her. "This is an absolutely fabulous image for women in general," Boston lawyer Nancy Gertner said of the first lady's appointment to lead national health care reform. "What is happening now is people are getting used to seeing her as an extremely talented, competent woman, and understand that the Clintons' marriage is a partnership. These are not showy or hollow gestures."

More seasoned political veterans were appalled. "How does a secretary of health and human services or a budget director tell a president that his wife's idea is half-baked?" Gary Bauer, a domestic policy adviser under Ronald Reagan, asked. "They'll be sorry. It creates incredible accountability problems," remarked Sheila Tate, spokeswoman for Nancy Reagan—who had reason to know. And an editorial in the *St. Petersburg Times* warned that Hillary's "obvious influence with the president could inhibit candid debate within the administration on issues for which she is responsible. After all, how many White House officials who value their jobs are going to disagree with the president's live-in domestic policy adviser once she stakes out a public position on an issue?" Nevertheless, the editor was not, in the final analysis, astonished. "It was obvious from the start that Mrs. Clinton would play an important role in the new administration, whether or not it came with a formal title. Anyone who is truly surprised by her unique influence doesn't know much about politics. Or marriage."

Judy Feder bravely accepted her subordinate position with resignation—and foreboding. She had been a mere "placeholder" during the transition as its health division director, she realized in retrospect; now she was being asked to swallow a proposed medicine that, as national policy, she knew had little or no chance of being enacted. Health care reform might poll well, as a campaign issue, but "there's a long distance between a campaign proposal and a piece of legislative action," she later pointed out. "Health care is a very good electoral political issue. It's a lousy legislative issue. So I didn't have tremendous confidence."

Neither, in all truth, did her new boss, the secretary of HHS, Donna Shalala, who despite her friendship with Hillary later admitted her dismay over the time frame for the plan's presentation, the appointment of Hillary—and the lack of consultation. "Was it a bad political judgment to have her? We wouldn't be having this discussion if we were successful," she accepted, ruefully. Would she have advised the president to appoint Hillary? "He didn't ask me at the time."

Didn't ask his own senior cabinet officer, the secretary of Health and Human Services? Perhaps this was the most surprising facet of all—that in making a crucial decision affecting the nation's entire health care system, an $840 billion annual area of the economy representing 14 percent of the GDP, the president had not even asked the advice of his transition health care director or his cabinet-rank new HHS secretary.

Behind the mask of public accountability, openness, and access, the Clintons were behaving, in some respects, in an unaccountable way, for inscrutable reasons—and with untold consequences.

Confronting Bill

In her new role as health care reform czarina, at the Camp David meeting on January 30, the first lady thus listened to the objections to deficit reduction as the president's number one agenda with unusually open ears. She had never studied economics nor, as would become clear all too soon in the Whitewater investigation, did she possess a green thumb as far as financial management went. She'd stuck obstinately with her investment in Jim and Susan McDougal's 1978 real estate venture in the picturesque Ozarks, the Whitewater Development Corporation, long after it failed utterly to produce the profit with which she hoped to send Chelsea, one day, to college. Conversely, when she did make a windfall profit on an investment, as in her trades in cattle futures that netted her an astonishing hundred thousand dollars for a thousand-dollar stake in the early eighties, her gains proved highly contentious, indeed resulted in part in the arraignment of her broker. Certainly she had never made such a profit again.

What would the Clinton administration's program amount to, Hillary wondered, if Greenspan and Bentsen, supported by Panetta and Rivlin, were urging the president to hit the deficit from the right (as JFK had once done over defense), not the left? Aware that her proposals for health care reform were being unfairly dissed by the economists, she now took up the complaints of the former campaign team. Confronting her husband, she told him his problem: namely that, in bowing to pressure from his new economics team, he was losing faith with the people who had put him in office.

The president listened to his wife and to his political PR and marketing staff, aware that Hillary was, in terms of liberal idealism, correct: a huge swath of voters had helped make him president because they believed his impassioned talk of jobs, retirement, education, homes—and health care. Among voters whom Greenberg had polled there had been no mention of deficit reduction—a word that ordinary people, when they heard it, translated as private debt, hardship, and economic depression. "We've lost track of why we ran," Clinton now declared, after only ten days as president—passing the message of Greenberg's poll on to others at the Camp David gathering as if it were a divine revelation.

Hillary, frustrated and impatient, attempted to short-circuit the endless talk and interplay of ideas. In Madeleine Albright's view as a fellow feminist, she was "pure oxygen. Excited by the promise of what lay ahead, she was on top of all the issues and a persuasive participant in discussions." Before the most senior figures of the new administration Hillary therefore called attention to what she claimed was, for her, the single most significant event of the inauguration celebration: namely the opening of the White House on the first official morning of the new presidency, when she and Bill had, for six hours of hand-wringing, personally greeted the day's tourists. The tourists were, she was convinced, impressed that the White House now had occupants more "like" themselves—"little people," rather than dynastic family aristocrats. Such people needed to feel their new president and his administration were in touch with them and with their concerns, such as jobs and health care, she emphasized. They, not Congress, were the true Democratic constituency.

Given Hillary's personal inability to show easy empathy for ordinary people, indeed her reputation for arrogance when under pressure ("I want to get this shit over with and get these damned people out of here," she'd been heard to say after one event, involving her pet project, HIPPY, for preschool youngster tutoring), this was a strange exhortation. But, fearing that Hillary might upset the administration's applecart as the leader of the president's health care task force, the assembled cabinet and other dignitaries listened to her at Camp David, nodded politely—and kept their counsel.

A Hell of a Risk

Lloyd Bentsen was concerned at the president's wavering, which seemed ominously to reflect the first lady's stance. Why upset a deficit-cutting program that was already showing signs of success?

Bentsen's own first television interview as Treasury secretary had taken place the previous Sunday, and the markets had reacted very favorably to his comments about the administration's budding economic plan to deal with the deficit—so well, in fact, that the U.S. government's long-term interest rate had fallen to a six-year low. The national deficit could, Bentsen and Alan Greenspan were convinced, now be tamed, involving a judicious trimming of the federal budget, while leaving room, later, for new programs and, ultimately, promised tax cuts for the middle class. But the president's announcement of Hillary's new role, at 2 P.M. the next day, had caused the seventy-one-year-old secretary to bite his lip. "Bentsen thought the president was taking a hell of a risk appointing his wife," Bob Woodward recorded, "but he didn't feel he knew Clinton well enough to tell him."

Nor did anyone else. Larry Summers, as Bentsen's number three at Treasury, "got on well with Hillary, but not close." Summers felt the appointment was "a disaster. Who knows what he owed her? I mean, she put up with a lot, right? Who knows what he had to do? Who knows what he wanted to do? Who knows what he *had* to do! What the deal was between them was always a mystery. Somebody said, at a dark moment in the first year: 'There are three presidents—and two of them know what they want to do! The three being Bill, Al, and Hillary. Al had his agenda. And Hillary had her agenda. And Bill had *every* agenda!'"

Those who, like Summers, had attended the January 7 meeting in Little Rock found that at the bonding weekend at Camp David the tables had, in some respects, been turned. Hillary, with the best of intentions, was putting her spoke into the deficit reduction works. "She's moderated in recent years," Summers reflected, a decade afterwards, "but she was always quite to the left. And I don't think she much liked economists. I think she saw me as a bit, you know, with the economic conservative 'You-gotta-deal-with-the-deficit, the-health care-plan-doesn't-score' brigade, so economists are sort of negative people to her."

This was a problem not only for Secretary Bentsen but for the entire inner cabinet and senior White House staff. A *Boston Globe* poll in the second week of January had recorded 48 percent of respondents comfortable with Hillary sitting in on cabinet meetings, but New England was traditionally more liberal than much of the rest of the United States—and even in the Northeast, 43 percent were *against* such spousal involvement, even as a listener. In an editorial the *Washington Post* had referred to the "three decades or so" of argument about the roles of men and women, husbands and wives, fathers and mothers—adding that, although America's attitudes had changed since the sixties, "the country is still uncertain about many of the questions at stake. Will members of Congress master the art of mixing respect for the first lady with candor about the matter at hand? Will it be possible for other aides and subordinates of the president to stand up to his wife, or even to challenge her work to him, if they think they should (and as they would with any other person in her job)?" It was, the newspaper stressed, a "hazard both Clintons should be mindful of."

If the Clintons said they were mindful, it was only rhetoric. Thanks to Hillary's fighting spirit, they seemed, rather, to be energized by the very challenge of doing what no previous U.S. administration had ever managed.

"Powerful lobbies of special interests may seek to derail our efforts, and we may make some people angry, but we are determined to come up with the best solution," the president had declared when announcing his health care task force, the woman who would chair it, and its 131-day deadline. He was justly proud of his choice—"a first lady of many talents," he had extolled her before the cameras and press. Hillary would be "sharing some of the heat" that reform would doubtless generate, but she'd done a similar job over education in Arkansas, he had reminded reporters. "We are going to have to make some tough choices," he had accepted, but Hillary was "better at organizing and leading people from a complex beginning to a certain end," the president had declared on her behalf, "than anybody I've ever met in my life."

Tough choices? When had Bill Clinton ever liked to make those, journalists had wondered—at least, without tortuous, agonizing, and tormenting indecision? Was that why he was putting Hillary in charge of health care reform—so that *she* could make the tough choices necessary to produce a workable plan, that would be acceptable to Congress, in a mere 131 days? But what if she took his commission too zealously, and could not be reined in—thus prejudicing the success of the president's deficit-reduction economic plan?

Either way, it was too late. The die was cast: the Clintons were now joined at the hip politically, as the first couple—with the whole world watching.

CHAPTER SEVEN

CAMP DAVID II

A Latter-day Eleanor

That Hillary *meant* well was incontestable.

If she'd proposed that a swimming pool be installed at the Governor's Mansion in Little Rock, it was because the business of governing even such a small state as Arkansas was demanding, and a pool for Chelsea, herself, Bill, and their many friends would be healthy—certainly healthier than Bill's notorious jogging runs around the neighborhood. If she'd claimed, despite Morris's head-shaking, a partner's share of the proceeds from state government and government-client work at the Rose Law Firm, it was because she considered herself, a woman, just as smart and as hard-working a lawyer as any other partner, and that, despite her husband being governor, there was no conflict of interest that she could see. And if she insisted that so many of her law firm colleagues be given jobs in the new administration in Washington, indeed that so many of her friends as well as F.O.B.s (friends of Bill) be found positions at the White House and in various government departments, it was because she felt herself to be a sort of modern version of Franklin D. Roosevelt's spouse: a crusading woman with a genuine care for children and the underprivileged, and a retinue of loyal staffers and subordinates who could help her to achieve her mission.

That was it, Hillary began to feel: she *was* a latter-day Eleanor—whose bust she would soon order to be mounted in the Roosevelt Room.

Passion Play

Thus empowered by her new title—and ignoring the way others might see her, as well as the problems Eleanor Roosevelt had encountered in Washington—the forty-six-year-old first lady challenged head-on the get-together of the cabinet, sous-cabinet, and advisers at Camp David. "Hillary spoke to this group in a way no previous president's wife, however influential through her husband, would have found imaginable," Elizabeth Drew recounted. "It made clear the strong and central role she was playing."

To the consternation of the older participants, Hillary visualized the president's new administration as a sort of political passion play like the one she had already directed and acted in while in Arkansas, during the years after her husband's ignominious defeat by Frank White. In his first term in Little Rock, she explained, Bill had tried to do too much, as the "darling of the reform-minded-liberal press," as Bob Woodward afterwards reported her Periclean oration. But Governor Clinton hadn't communicated a vision or described "the journey he intended," the first lady told the president's audience—and thus had disconnected himself "from the people he was trying to help." As a result, he had been crucified, and beaten by a Republican businessman.

This was certainly true, if only a thumbnail version of the saga—leaving out Bill's "bearded troika" of deputies, his executive weakness, his raising of Arkansas car tag taxes, which ended up punishing ordinary people (especially the poor), his ineffective handling of the riots by Mariel boatlift refugees who were being held at Fort Chaffee, even the problem of her own insistence upon using her maiden name rather than her married name in Arkansas, as a feminist. . . .

Hillary, however, was not a historian but an advocate—with a gospel to present to the Camp David meeting. "In 1983, when he came back, they had devised a simple story," ran her new presentation, "with characters, with an objective, with a beginning, middle, and end. And it all had come from a moral point of view."

What of Betsey Wright, though? What of the painful struggle to make Bill Clinton a more effective executive leader, or manager, of the state of Arkansas? Hillary had forgotten that, or she had never really understood the transformation that Wright, as a brilliant new and tough chief of staff, had wrought in Bill Clinton's career. Paul Begala, ignorant of the truth, however, almost kissed Hillary on the spot, he was so impressed by her New Testament.

Hillary's Camp David intervention would be a landmark in the initial failure of the Clinton administration. By traducing Bill Clinton's real story—particularly Bill's need for a tough chief of staff and an efficient managerial system—Hillary was now setting up her husband for disaster. The president-elect had gathered perhaps the best economic team in modern memory but, thanks to the inexperience and loyalty-through-nepotism of so many other administration appointees (many of them Hillary's choices) there was, with no effective chief of staff, simply no one to contradict her childlike version of their political history—at least not in front of her husband, the president of the United States. Thus Hillary was permitted to recount her rose-tinted fable, and all were compelled to listen.

Together, the first lady explained, she and Bill had "taken on education reform" in Arkansas, recognizing, she went on to say, "the need for a story, complete with enemies and villains." They had even "villainized the teachers' union," which had for years been their ally—since, as she explained, "You show people what you're willing to fight for when you fight your friends." It had taken years to push the reforms through and see results, but people had learned that the Clintons' commitment to education was "genuine." Isolated initiatives, she maintained, "worked less well"—the moral being that politics was a matter of symbolic fights and signposting. "People have got to understand where he [the president] wants to take the country," she declared. "Telling a story to voters," she maintained, was what the new administration was all about.

To skeptics Hillary came across almost as a child. That a mature woman, at the height of her legal career, married to the most powerful man in the world, could have advanced such a simple fable, based on such a misrepresentation of the past and of the reality of his grave problems as an administrator, not as a policy wonk, in front of forty of the most senior government officials of the United States in the year 1993, seemed to skeptics an affront to the intelligence and experience of her listeners.

The real truth was that, with Betsey Wright and Dick Morris's help, the defeated governor of Arkansas had had to apologize to the electorate in special TV ads for raising car tag taxes. He had had to persuade Hillary to change her name, and, with Betsey's tough discipline as his chief of staff and enforcer, and Dick Morris's help in devising negative ads, had then worked to destroy his opponent for the Democratic nomination, and after that, his Republican opponent, Governor White. In the prolonged fight with the teachers' union over teacher-testing, the Clintons had indeed scored a popular victory. However this had *never* been a story-board plan with heroes and villains, but had evolved over time—thanks to the surprising hostility of the teacher's union—and had been combined with economic cheerleading, as the two areas in which Clinton could make most headway in Arkansas, leaving other, less malleable struggles, such as clearcut timber-felling, to be lost by the wayside. Now Hillary was suggesting it had all been carefully scripted in advance, and was proposing that they should plan and run the United States government in the same way, ten days into the presidency, with a 131-day timetable for health care reform, ignoring the problem of trying to address deficit reduction simultaneously—and all this without a tough chief of staff!

Begala, never having worked with Bill Clinton in Arkansas, was bewitched. He congratulated Hillary afterwards, as did Mandy Grunwald, who was also ignorant of the true Arkansas story and the crucial part that the *chief of staff* had played in imposing order on Bill's endless chaos. When the president walked up to them, they thus complained that his presidency was being compromised, indeed ruined, by argument over minutiae and the lack of *vision*. The president needed, they re-emphasized, "a story," with heroes and villains—not a new chief of staff.

"Why don't you do it?" the president responded, pressing them to script such a story. Thus deputized, Begala and Grunwald were instructed to write "the communications plan"—Hillary telling them to commandeer a navy truck to hightail back to Washington, see colleagues such as Stan Greenberg and David Dreyer, and get back to her ASAP with the storyboard so she could present it to her colleagues.

"Can you fax it up to me tonight?" Hillary asked Begala.

Begala beamed.

"General" Rodham had taken charge, he felt, while for her part, "Grunwald was delighted to see the first lady moving things," Bob Woodward recounted, since Hillary was "a great planner."

"The Plan," faxed to Hillary rather than to the president himself, said it all. It was as if the students of Clinton Junior High had taken over the controls of the world's most powerful nation, and the president—an adolescent himself—was powerless to stop them. Heralding this heroic new storybook saga, the first lady would lead the forces of health care reform, as she had once headed the governor's committee on educational reform in Arkansas, making it the defining story of her husband's presidency.

Unfortunately, however, what it would define would be failure, not victory.

CHAPTER EIGHT

HILLARY'S MESS

The Story

Had Hillary simply supported her husband, had she simply become cheer-leader for deficit reduction as the first chapter of the Bill Clinton Story, and had she encouraged the president to stay close to that script, with a staff worthy of the terrific cast Bill had chosen as his economic team, history might have been different. But, at that moment in her life, this was not a role worthy of Hillary's self-image.

Faxing Hillary the plot of the new school play, Begala was certainly overcome with admiration for the first lady and co-president. "At times he thought that without Hillary," Woodward recorded Begala's thoughts, "Clinton would have wound up as merely the most popular law professor at the University of Arkansas."

Begala's faxed text mapped out "The Story" to be put across to "the American people"—"The Story" being that of "villain" Bush and his be-trayal of the American people, supplanted by a heroic new president now at the helm. Every day "between now and the address to the Joint Session [of Congress]," set for February 17, 1993, "the president should be in the me-dia with an economic event stressing cuts in government and taxes on the rich," with health care reform in the works—which would make him a hero to the masses.

"The Story" would of course require mobilization of the White House and of government departments to "sell" the new potion, and a "campaign manager to coordinate its efforts." The fax, naturally, recommended Paul Begala for the job.

With the president's approval, the first lady immediately appointed Begala (who hitherto had had no formal White House job) as story co-ordinator, and Begala began work (without pay) the next day. "Time is extraordinarily limited," the fax had declared—and in this atmosphere of high-octane activity "The Story" was fleshed out.

Winston Churchill, as prime minister of Great Britain, had demanded "action this day" on his assumption of the prime ministership on May 10, 1940, but not even Churchill had been able to avoid Dunkirk, soon after, or the overrunning of most of Western Europe by Hitler between 1940 and 1942. Though Hillary, at Camp David, did point out the danger of promising too much too early, and acknowledged that "the journey" of education reform in Arkansas had been a long one, indeed had taken years to push through, a kind of mad hubris seemed now to take over. Ignoring her own warning, she became convinced that the administration had but a small window of opportunity to squeeze through Congress whatever economic and health program it devised. To the astonishment of the Camp David camp followers, she announced, as the new "czarina" of health care reform, that she intended to attach her health care reform program to the president's upcoming budget resolution—however indigestible it might make the overall outline package—so that it would require only fifty-one votes in the Senate, not the sixty votes necessary to avoid filibuster if the White House opted for a separate health care plan.

The economic members of the new Clinton cabinet, with no previous warning of such a plan, rubbed their eyes in disbelief.

Had Bill Clinton possessed, in an ideal world, an already formulated economic plan that incorporated a carefully worked-out answer to the health care problem in America—a workable solution to the escalating costs and escalating numbers of people without medical insurance—he might, with a well-tuned staff, friends on the Hill (where he'd once worked in Senator J. William Fulbright's office), and above all an effective chief of staff, had a slim but possible chance of railroading his double-barrelled shotgun proposals through the notoriously gridlocked Congress, aided by a sympathetic press, during the traditional presidential "honeymoon" that follows an inauguration.

Unfortunately, Bill Clinton had none of these assets.

The White House staff had only been appointed a few days before the inauguration, were almost all inexperienced, and had for the most part not even been through their FBI background checks. Moreover, many positions were still unfilled. Those that were reflected personal loyalty to the Clintons rather than intrinsic merit and government experience—intensifying the spotlight on the president and first lady rather than on the rainbow cabinet. In this way, the nation was deliberately set up for a charismatic rather than an executive presidency—in fact a charismatic *co-presidency*.

Thus, at Begala's and Grunwald's urging, the president ignored his real administrative problem, and sought to use his greatest asset—his communication skills—to make a new appeal not to Congress, in the first instance, but to the nation. With that in mind he sent Begala and David Dreyer, as his speechwriters, to see Alice Rivlin, Panetta's new deputy in the Office of Management and Budget in the Old Executive Office Building next door to the White House on Pennsylvania Avenue. Begala's fairy tale was to be transposed into presidential rhetoric.

Where, historians of the presidency asked in retrospect, was Mack McLarty, chief of staff to the president of the United States, in all this? McLarty's failure to bring order to the chaos and divisiveness that arose in the new co-presidency would have tragic consequences, yet he was himself such a genuinely nice man that no one dared tell the new president he had made a terrible error in making the appointment and must quickly dismiss him, before there were more disasters. "Bill Clinton has a problem firing people—definitely," Alice Rivlin later reflected, with sadness. "He and Mack had been friends since kindergarten. Mack is a wonderful man. He's intelligent, he's nice, he's everything. But he's not tough enough to be chief of staff. And yes, there was [in the White House] a lot of mess."

Mess was an understatement. The visit from the president's speechwriters, with McLarty exercising no control or direction, indeed submitting supinely to Hillary's imperative to include her new high-speed crusade on health care reform in the budget, said it all. "Oh, the White House process was chaotic," Rivlin recalled. "You had to have a lot of stamina to deal with it."

Dreyer, by contrast, thought McLarty's tolerant style delightful. "I love Mack—I'm a pro-Mack guy!" he later said, while conceding the mess at 1600 Pennsylvania Avenue. "Presidents in their first term have a window that closes after the first year," he went on, paraphrasing the historian Richard Neustadt. "And so we were constantly setting things in motion, getting initiatives out the door, not simply for the purposes of announcing initiatives, but to start the legislative process so that, if we announced

AmeriCorps, say, on the first of March, you'd have a chance of getting it through. So, because we were ambitious and wanted to accomplish a lot, we did a lot. And," he conceded, "ended up stepping on our message."

Kicking Out the Elves

Bob Woodward later described Rivlin as a "small, elfin woman." If she was, she was unimpressed by the visiting elves. "So what do you guys want?" she demanded when the speechwriters arrived at her office.

They wanted, they explained, to create a story in which an innocent new shoemaker must make a pair of new shoes by morning—for the president's first television address to the nation, in which he would explain the spiraling deficit and his plethora of plans, including health care, that would require new taxes, and, probably, mean the abandonment of promised tax cuts. "We have to walk people through the journey the president has gone from November to February," the speechwriters explained. "We have to explain why the deficit got worse and how it got worse"—villainizing former President Bush as they did so.

Dr. Rivlin, with a degree from Bryn Mawr and a Ph.D from Radcliffe, eyed the elves mercilessly. "That's nonsense," she snorted. "Bill Clinton knew where this deficit was going," she pointed out, having sounded him out on the subject in her very first interview in Little Rock.

Years later Rivlin reflected on the pretenses that were manufactured to fit the Hillary-Begala story. "In order to square what we were doing with what had been said in the campaign"—tax hikes instead of cuts—"there was a lot more emphasis on new information than was actually justified," she reflected. It was the campaign rhetoric that had been at fault, not the former president's concealment of statistics, she made clear to the elves—and kicked them out.

There would be, they realized, no new shoes at OMB.

CHAPTER NINE

ADDRESSING THE NATION

Home Alone 3

Two weeks later, the president gave Begala's "story" as a special television address to the nation. Behind JFK's massive desk—which he had ordered up from storage—Clinton looked "small, boyish, and uncomfortable, with his suit coat appearing oversized and bunched up in the back," as the journalist John Brummett recalled—a picture that led Tom Shales, television critic for the *Washington Post*, to comment that the president appeared to be in a still from *Home Alone 3* instead of the Oval Office.

Without a coherent staff structure, the argument over deficit reduction versus economic stimulus and investment had, in the six weeks since the historic six-hour meeting in Little Rock, become ever more bitter and contested. Begala, after a searing argument over the deficit with Dr. Rivlin, had descended into a kind of sixties class-warfare world, determined to follow Hillary's prescription of "heroes and villains" by urging the president to picture himself as a warrior against the rich. "I ask you that you join me in fighting them," he'd pressed Clinton to say—a combative tone that colored the uneasy speech Clinton read off the scrolling teleprompter, while pretending to speak extemporaneously.

Once again, as in Arkansas in his first term, when pushed and pulled in different directions by competing staffers, he gave an address that seemed more *mess*-age than message. Moreover, although the president explained that the "Federal deficit has roared out of control," thanks to "the big tax cuts for the wealthy, the growth in government spending, and soaring health care costs," Brummet recounted, "his listeners seemed to hear only one word: 'taxes.'"

Begala's rhetoric of "Let's punish the rich with higher taxes because they made out like bandits during the Reagan-Bush years" sounded punitive—followed by an apology that there would be no promised middle-class tax cut in the budget, only tax hikes. "I had hoped to invest in your future by creating jobs, expanding education, reforming health care, and reducing the debt [deficit] without asking more of you."

The president attempted to explain in mock-paternal, personal language. "But I can't, because the deficit has increased so much beyond my earlier estimates and beyond the worst official government estimates from last year. We just have to face the fact that to make the changes our country needs, more Americans must contribute today so that all Americans can do better tomorrow. . . . When I was a boy, we had a name for the belief that we should all pull together to build a better, stronger nation. We called it patriotism. And we still do. Good night, and God bless America."

The Dow Falls

Had the president been General de Gaulle, or Ed Murrow, such mock-paternalism might have been more palatable, but he wasn't—yet.

Begala's suggested use of the word "patriotism" in Clinton's teleprompter speech puzzled even sympathetic viewers. The president hadn't prepared the public in any way for such a grave appeal. The entire "story" of "crisis" and "wealthiest Americans" having to "pay their fair share," and "cuts" involving "billions of dollars," and predictions that within "minutes" of his State of the Union speech "the special interests will be out in force," flining the "corridors of power with high-priced lobbyists," sounded confusing, and somehow false. Sacrifice was one thing—indeed Greenberg's latest voter-surveys showed most Americans *were* prepared to make sacrifices, if they could see what they were sacrificing for—but invoking a word that was traditionally used for military service was inappropriate for a former university professor and draft avoider. As Brummett wrote: "Waving the old red-white-and-blue to rally support for paying higher taxes? It wasn't one of the talented Begala's better ideas."

Alarmed that the "New Democrat" had changed into an Old Democrat overnight, there was a palace protest—indeed the new national economic adviser, Robert Rubin, was beside himself. Hillary's Camp David "story" had morphed into a Begala fantasy, foisted onto an American public that had not voted for higher taxes, though it had wanted to see positive steps taken towards increased employment, reduction of the deficit, the ending of the recession, and movement towards a nationally sustainable health care plan sometime in the future. The next day, February 16, the Dow fell eighty-three points.

Already some people were predicting a one-term presidency, just as, in 1980, Clinton had become a one-term governor. Experienced Democratic congressmen and senators were especially uneasy over the amateur theatrics on Pennsylvania Avenue. It was, therefore, essential that President Clinton assert his leadership and discipline if he was to bend Congress to his will.

With the relative failure of his televised address to his nation, there was now little time to be lost as, day and night, the staff worked on his next, more important performance: his first speech to the Hill as president, to be called "Address Before a Joint Session of Congress on Administration Goals," to be delivered on February 17, 1993.

With the president up at 6 A.M. to help Chelsea with her math homework (instead of sending their daughter to a public school like the one in which the Carters' daughter had been enrolled, the Clintons had chosen to send Chelsea, now in eighth grade, to Sidwell Friends, a private school boasting high academic standards and even higher expectations of parent involvement), the draft for the hour-long speech on the Hill was, as usual, a shambles—and the president knew it. Like his television performance from the Oval Office, it sounded all wrong. By 4 o'clock that afternoon Hillary was rumored to be "displeased," and demanded that Rubin revise certain passages. In the Roosevelt Room, the president tried to collate different pages and sections, slashing, rewriting, and adding new things. "Okay," he was heard to announce, "it's time to get serious. Page one."

The scene, in comparison with previous presidencies, was surreal—and yet, having forced his staff to work through the previous Saturday, at the end of a grueling week of drafting and redrafting, Clinton remarked at 6 P.M., as the others dropped with fatigue: "I love this stuff."

It was a singularly revealing comment.

The Art of the Possible

If the inexperienced, out-of-their-depth White House staff were being driven to exhaustion by such a seemingly chaotic presidency, the president himself appeared unalarmed.

He was, to be sure, undergoing a learning experience, as he had in every role he had assumed in his life. He never would be the sort of leader, he knew deep in his psyche, capable of giving orders and asserting his wishes by force of character—of earning the loyalty of men and women by his firmness, clarity, and steadfastness. He *was* a leader, nevertheless, he felt: a different kind of leader, a human being blessed with an extraordinarily high IQ, an amazing ability to empathize with ordinary people, and endless energy. Despite the chaos—indeed, perhaps by unconsciously *inducing* chaos—he could wow his colleagues and subordinates by his ability to pull things together at the last minute and produce an "A," just as he had at Georgetown and Yale.

Laboring over his speech to Congress, the policy wonk in Bill Clinton certainly saw a different scenario from that of Begala and Hillary: that it was not a question of imposing an arbitrary "story" at this stage, but of exploring the possibilities, charting the limitations, working out not only what might be best for America, but what also was *possible* in the circumstances—circumstances it was his job to articulate for the public. After all, was not politics the art of the possible?

It wasn't leadership of the old style; indeed, it looked like chaotic pragmatism. It drove many of his staff crazy with vexation. But in a strange way—in its relentless, patient quest for consensus and workable synthesis of conflicting views—it suggested a new kind of late twentieth-century postmodern president: one who might be indecisive and weak, incapable of appointing strong deputies and staff lest they outshine him, oppress him, or limit his creativity, yet a man who was listening to the heartbeat of a changing, transitional America.

As Dreyer put it, a tougher chief of staff than McLarty would have reduced the chaos that reigned in the White House following the inauguration. Such chaos represented, however, the very divisions and uncertainties in American society at large. "If you believe there are no provable certainties and that decisions are best made on the basis of weighing probabilities, then you ought to be sitting still and hearing the 180-degree case before you make a decision," Dreyer considered. "Now, what happened was, some of these things dragged on too long for people who had a different tempo for making decisions. And they yapped about it outside the room. And that became an issue. But the process that Clinton went through, which in fact was quite admirable, got discredited in a way that it should not have been. Just the fact that he didn't make up his mind till he was good and ready— this was, despite flaws, a good way to make decisions, not a bad one."

Seen in the context of some of the fatal decisions made by the forty-third president, in the next century, Dreyer's point had much validity. For her part, however, Hillary had wanted a do-or-die approach, with enemies, villains, and heroes. The president had been intrigued, and willing to try that approach—but he had quickly recognized, after his television flop, that it was not in his character. Or necessarily the best way forward. Somehow, he reckoned, there must be a "third way"—a slogan he had used throughout his presidential campaign, referring to hybrid solutions that went beyond ideology and were best for America.

Spellbound

To the astonishment of his speechwriters and advisors on financial, economic, social, and other policy matters, the president of the United States looked up at the teleprompter in the packed hall of Congress, where FDR had famously declared war on Japan on December 7, 1941, and, impromptu, ignoring the mish-mashed script produced by a hundred hands, allowed himself to address the nation's problems, sympathetically and honestly: holding his congressional audience, as well as millions of television viewers, spellbound for fifty-eight minutes.

No longer was the president the somewhat lonely young politician hiding behind JFK's desk in his office, looking like a *Saturday Night Live* comedian imitating the president. He *was* the president, standing big and broadshouldered before the assembled senators and congressmen of the nation, outlining his vision of America's future:

I believe we can do better, because we remain the greatest nation on Earth, the world's strongest economy, the world's only military superpower. If we have the vision, the will, and the heart to make the changes we must, we can still enter the 21st century with possibilities our parents could not even have imagined, and enter it having secured the American Dream for ourselves and for future generations.

I well remember twelve years ago President Reagan stood at this very podium and told you and the American people that if our national debt were stacked in thousand-dollar bills the stack would reach 67 miles into space. Well, today that stack would reach 267 miles. I tell you this not to assign blame for this problem. There is plenty of blame to go around in both branches of the government and both parties. The time has come for the blame to end. I did not seek this office to place blame. I come here tonight to accept responsibility and I want you to accept responsibility with me. And if we do right by this country, I do not care who gets the credit for it.

It was, amidst the self-inflicted chaos of his new presidency, a *tour de force*. "He's riffing. He's making it up!" Mandy Grunwald realized in horror, but Stan Greenberg, watching his viewers' approval-dials, beamed as they kept jumping towards the seventies. As even Bob Woodward acknowledged, it was "fabulous"—"interrupted constantly, it seemed, by standing ovations."

Seated by strategic design beside Hillary in the front row of the visitor balcony was Alan Greenspan, whose prominent presence and nodding bald head signaled the Federal Reserve's approval of Clinton's message: *deficit reduction*—beginning with 150 tough cuts. *Then* health care. And finally, if necessary, *stimulus*. In that order.

CNN and *USA Today*'s poll showed an almost 80 percent public approval for the plan. Within five days long-term interest rates had fallen to a sixteen-year low—with thirty-year bonds dropping below 7 percent for the first time since the bond market began issuing them.

Whatever disparaging remarks might be traded about the New Democrat in town, Wall Street was won over. Bond dealers seemed convinced the near-$4 trillion American deficit, spiraling further and further out of control under a succession of Republican presidents, *would* be whipped. And with its whipping, not only would the property-owning middle class receive the equivalent of a massive tax break—the opportunity to refinance their mortgages at lower rates—but the programs that liberals held dear to their vision of a better American society could thereafter be undertaken. Having "control, some control over the discipline and the direction of the economy" through tackling the deficit was, as Clinton himself later remarked, "going to be a precondition to making my investment programs work."

Robert Reich, the new labor secretary, might seethe with disappointment—but the rest of America felt reassured. President Clinton might be a chaotic, flip-flopping, almost adolescent leader, but in the matter of The Economy, Stupid, the new president was clearly a star.

If, that was, he could translate his rhetoric into reality.

THE CLASH
OF CIVILIZATIONS

CHAPTER TEN

THE WORLD TRADE CENTER IS BOMBED

A Huge Explosion

Nine days later, just after midday on Friday, February 26, 1993, as the president flew to Little Rock for the weekend, a huge explosion rocked the World Trade Center in New York. It left a crater some 150 feet in diameter, with its epicenter only eight feet below the south wall of 110-story Trade Tower Number One—one of the famed Twin Towers in Lower Manhattan.

Five underground levels of concrete and steel were blasted into smithereens; in an instant, fire was blown through the Port Authority commuter rail station, sending pillars of smoke up the stairwells. Without working elevators or lighting many thousands of office workers found themselves trapped by the fumes billowing up through the buildings. "It felt like an airplane hit the building," said Bruce Pomper, a thirty-four-year-old broker.

Desperate for air, and not knowing whether to stay in their offices or brave the journey down via the smoke-filled stairwells, some workers had smashed windows with office furniture. There was total pandemonium as rescuers struggled to get oxygen to those on the upper floors. About 100,000 people worked or visited the 1,700-foot towers every day; noon was the busiest time.

Thousands poured out of the building, gasping for air and covered in soot. Lewis Mumford, the notable architectural historian, had denounced the soaring buildings as an "example of the purposeless giantism and technological exhibitionism that are now eviscerating the living tissue of every great city." Indeed, for years after their construction in 1979 the towers had proven difficult to fill, as if tenants were anxious not to tempt fate by offering enemies of capitalism such a provocative target. But eventually, in the Reagan years, the office buildings had found occupants, and to most New Yorkers by 1993 they had become pillars of the modern Manhattan skyline—a symbol of the city's proud place in America's *fin de siècle* empire as distinctive as the Eiffel Tower had been in that of *la Belle Epoque* in France, a century before.

Though it threatened to asphyxiate thousands of people, in the end the explosion killed only five innocent civilians and injured over a thousand. Erupting beneath the building, the detonation was certainly no accident, police immediately recognized. Instead it confirmed the fears of those who had opposed American triumphalism: an outrage aimed deliberately at the symbolic as well as material foundations of the Trade Center, as the United States prepared itself for its role not only of the world's predominant military, but also economic, superpower. A shaken Mario Cuomo, New York State's governor, told journalists: "We all have that feeling of being violated. No foreign people or force has ever done this to us. Until now we were invulnerable."

A New Holy War

From the start, President Clinton urged Americans "not to jump to conclusions" about who was responsible for the World Trade Center bombing, or why they did it. "I think it is very important not to rush to judgment here, not to reach ahead of the facts which are known, to reach broad conclusions about who was behind this or what happened," he was quoted at a news conference. "When I know who was behind this and what happened, I will then determine what the appropriate course for the United States is, and I will say it."

President Clinton was speaking like a lawyer. It was thus left to President Hosni Mubarak of Egypt, slated to visit President Clinton in Washington, to "say it" for him, once he learned that the FBI had arrested Mohammed A. Salameh, a follower of the blind fanatic Sheik Omar Abdel-Rahman, who in Brooklyn and New Jersey mosques preached holy war against the United States and other "enemies" of Islam. "This proves that terrorism is becoming a plague spreading all over the world," Mubarak told the press, and he called for "international cooperation to resist this unhealthy phenomenon. For a period of time, it was thought it's some sort of local phenomenon concentrating in the Middle East. But now we believe this shows it's not a local phenomenon. It's spreading."

In the newspaper interview, President Mubarak defended his government's "very heavy hand" against Islamic extremists, and ruled out further political liberalization as a more effective way to combat Islamic political activism. Soon afterwards, having ordered the torture of one of the World Trade Center bombing suspects who had fled back to Egypt with his German wife and four children, Mubarak announced in the London-based *Al-Hayat* newspaper "sensational confessions" made by the mass-murderer Mahmud Abouhalima, prior to his handover back to U.S. authorities. Abouhalima had revealed the whole plot against America. "During his interrogation he gave plenty of information, which I do not wish to discuss in the press," President Mubarak announced, explaining that "he has described how the operation was carried out and who participated in it"—a group that included Muslim fundamentalists linked to Sheik Omar Abdel-Rahman.

With sickening hearts, security forces in America had to face up to the possibility that the culprits were not the agents of a hostile *power*, but religious individuals, akin to anarchists. These anarchists believed in Islamic theocracy—implying the start of a new holy war between the dominant nation of the West, "The Great Satan," on the one hand, and "pure" Islam on the other. Sheik Rahman had got into the United States on a tourist visa, using a phony name on his application; he had then been given residency as a cleric by President Bush's administration—permission that was subsequently revoked. Informed that he would be deported, he had gotten an army of lawyers to fight for his right to remain in America and sew hatred. Hundreds of Muslims had protested in New Jersey at the accusations against him, which they took as an indictment of their faith. He was eventually sentenced to life in prison.

Mubarak was the first Arab leader to visit President Clinton. His message was stark in its implications. "It seems it's a phenomenon, something all over the world," he stated. Most of the media "is concentrating on Egypt, or on the Islamic people," he noted, but the phenomenon was, he claimed, part of a global phenomenon of religious-inspired extremism. "I tell you something," he cautioned. "Even the Copts and the Christians, they have fundamentalists."

A New Phase

In two interviews later broadcast on U.S. television, Osama bin Laden, founder of Al Qaeda ("The Base"), would refer to the terrorists who carried out the attack on the World Trade Center in 1993 as "role models" for Islamic terrorism across the world, and would exhort yet more of his followers "to take the fighting to America."

For those who had assumed the ending of the Cold War might lead to a less dangerous world, the switch from inter-national to inter-faith hostilities boded ill. "World politics is entering a new phase," Samuel Huntington warned that spring, "in which the great divisions among humankind and the dominating source of international conflict will be cultural." Instead of political ideology dividing nations, the new incubus of conflict, Huntington predicted, would center especially on religious differences—differences accentuated by widening disparities in a global economy. The resultant cultural conflicts would not necessarily take the form of traditional rivalries between nation states, he predicted, but would increasingly be between groups that Huntington termed, for want of a better word, "civilizations." Postcolonial tensions would make the clash even worse. "With the end of the Cold War, international politics moves out of its Western phase, and its centerpiece becomes the interaction between the West and non-Western civilizations," Huntington wrote. "In the politics of civilizations, the peoples and governments of non-Western civilizations no longer remain the objects of history as targets of Western colonialism but join the West as movers and shapers of history.

"From Yugoslavia to the Middle East to Central Asia," Huntington predicted, "the fault lines of civilizations are the battle lines of the future." If the millennium was ever to be reached in such a "world of different civilizations," he warned, each "will have to learn to coexist with the others."

Huntington's thesis, published in *Foreign Affairs*, was promptly ridiculed by traditional nation-state historians, but Huntington—who had served on President Carter's National Security Council during the Iran hostage crisis—responded by pointing out that "in the modern world, religion is a central, perhaps the central, force that motivates and mobilizes people. It is sheer hubris to think that because Soviet communism has collapsed the West has won the world for all time." Within Islam there were a thousand disputations and factions—as there were in "the West"—especially between religious zealots. The West too, he prophesied, would suffer its own internal clashes of civilizations or cultural groups, in the same manner as Islamic communities were, ranging from the former Yugoslavia to the Sudan and Pakistan, since "the assumption that increased interaction—greater communication and transportation—produces a common culture" was misguided. "In some circumstances this may be the case," he allowed. But wars "occur most frequently between societies with high levels of interaction, and interaction frequently reinforces existing identities and produces resistance, reaction and confrontation."

The bombing of the World Trade Center, as uncovered in the court trial that would begin in September 1993, amply demonstrated Huntington's thesis. Fanatics of Islamic "civilization" had declared mass-murdering jihad against unspecified Judeo-Christian infidels—and only luck had saved the World Trade Center from collapsing as the murderers had intended.

Meanwhile, even as Huntington's article went to press, President Mubarak's warnings were proving remarkably prescient. Only two days after the terrorist attack on the Twin Towers there began in Waco, Texas, a battle that would soon prove a model of the Huntington thesis, unfolding day by day before the world's television cameras: a messianic priest, Vernon Howell, calling himself David Koresh, was challenging local police, drug enforcement authorities, and the FBI to seize him. Four officers from the Bureau of Alcohol, Tobacco, Firearms, and Explosives (ATF) had already been killed, along with seven of Koresh's "dogs," or acolytes. An unknown number of women and children were in the compound of Koresh's religious group, which was called the Branch Davidians.

CHAPTER ELEVEN

WACO

Unwilling to Take Responsibility

Fifty-one days went by after the first, failed attempt to storm Koresh's heavily armed compound (containing submachine guns, hand grenades, sniper rifles, rockets, rocket launchers, automatic weapons, gas masks, helmets, gas cans, torches, twenty-two IMI Galil, Ruger, and FAL assault rifles, over fifty AK assault rifles, and a dozen shotguns). Sixty Branch Davidian members had managed to leave or flee the commune during the standoff—but left behind were some twenty-five children, who were considered by the FBI to be "hostages," many of them British, held by Howell in his Armageddon war with the U.S. government.

It was in this delicate situation that Janet Reno, the new attorney general, called the president to ensure she had his approval for a major raid that the FBI was urging to break the deadlock. Reno, a former Dade County, Florida, prosecutor, was ten years older than the president and "displayed the kind of straightforward talk and unassuming manner that have become her signature," as the *Chicago Sun-Times* had applauded after her appointment. At home in Florida she had no air conditioning, no television, no fans, not even a washer or dryer. When asked whether she would succumb to any modern conveniences if she moved to Washington, where winters could be brutal, the Floridian had quipped: "What about heat?"

"I went through it with him, told him why I decided that we should go ahead," Reno later said of her telephone conversation with the president on Sunday, April 18, 1993. "Are you sure you've had all your questions answered [about the FBI's plan]?" Clinton had asked her. Ms. Reno remembered that her most important concerns were that the FBI should not use any weapons that risked setting fire to the copious amounts of kerosene stored for lighting in the various rooms of the compound, now that the FBI had cut off electricity. "When I talked to him that Sunday afternoon, I advised him, we discussed it," Reno related, "and we went ahead."

The telephone call was Bill Clinton's first mortal test as president: the question of whether to use force, on a massive scale, that might, and probably would (given the fatalities resulting from the failed ATF raid in February), involve bloodshed. Unfortunately, it was not one for which he was subsequently willing to take responsibility.

On April 19, 1993, news of the FBI's assault was just emerging when CNN correspondent Wolf Blitzer asked, at the daily White House press conference, about the compound being on fire. Stephanopoulos later recalled, "I had no idea what he was talking about. Then someone handed me a note, and I left the podium to find out what was going on."

What the White House director of communications found out—that the Texas home of the Branch Davidians was now ablaze, possibly torching to death its inmates, including the children—was bad enough. Stephanopoulos compounded his ignorance, however, with advice to the president that he would later bitterly regret. He had already denied that the president had authorized the FBI operation. Now, in order to ensure that the president would not be retrospectively sued for "saying something that triggered Koresh to kill the kids who might still be alive," and/or to insulate the president from inevitable criticism for the operation, he advised President Clinton to remain silent. The president followed his advice and said nothing, even as seventy-eight Branch Davidians, most of them women and children, were found to have died in the flames, burned to cinders.

How an inexperienced young official could have been permitted to persuade the president of the United States to avoid his responsibility as president and commander-in-chief was incredible to seasoned reporters as they watched the Waco saga from the nation's capital—a seeming vindication of Ross Perot's widely publicized complaints that the president was turning out to be a straw man. In what was a true national crisis—a clear confrontation between a dangerous, heavily armed religious fanatic holding dozens of children hostage—the president had failed to establish and assert his authority or to take responsibility for the storming of the compound. It was left to Attorney General Janet Reno to take the rap for the bungled opera-tion—which, to her credit, Reno did.

As Stephanopoulos later reflected, "The first rule in a presidential crisis is to take responsibility fully and openly. Don't duck. That's the Bay of Pigs lesson that should have been burned in my bones." It was clear that the freshman president had a lot to learn.

CHAPTER TWELVE

EISENHOWER REPUBLICAN?

Deficit-itis

The Zoë Baird saga, gays in the military issue, World Trade Center bombing, and WACO—these were difficult enough for the new president. Finding his deficit reduction bill in danger of failing to pass Congress, however, was even more alarming.

At first, everything seemed to go smoothly. The House of Representatives had drawn up its resolution on the subject with only a few adjustments—but ominously, not a single Republican had voted for the resolution in the House Budget Committee, or on the floor. This had left Democrats to furnish all the votes themselves, which they'd done on April 1—having agreed to new taxes and major government cuts in order to shrink the deficit. On the other hand, the Democrats had refused to back a number of the president's stimulus proposals.

For the president, this was worrying—in fact, he exploded once the reality of his own party's rejection of his stimulus-investment plan, to accompany deficit reduction, was conveyed to him. "Where are all the Democrats?" the president had demanded later in the afternoon of April 7 in the Roosevelt Room, surrounded by his economic and health care advisers. "I hope you're all aware we're all Eisenhower Republicans," he said sarcastically—having been told the Republicans would filibuster in the Senate any attempt to raise the caps on investment spending, at a later stage. "We're Eisenhower Republicans here, and we are fighting the Reagan Republicans. We stand for lower deficits and free trade and the bond market," the president summarized. "Isn't that great?" he added, his high tenor voice dripping with sarcasm.

In the context of doing one thing at a time—first, ensuring that America emerged from the recession, then that it enjoyed a *sustained* period of growth, rather than boom-and-bust—his policies were working. But with the left wing of the West Wing protesting that the ideals and platform that had brought them victory in the presidential election were being abandoned, Bill Clinton was torn. "I don't have a God-damn Democratic budget until 1996," the president lamented, his voice becoming hysterical. "None of the investments [in training and social programs], none of the things I campaigned on." He paused. "At least we'll have health care to give them."

Paul Begala felt likewise—indeed, felt they should accelerate a health care reform bill, instead of delaying it. Those who could see the writing on the wall—especially the vice president, who had served many years in Congress—knew, however, that the more cautious economic mood among Democrats on the Hill should not be taken lightly. Prematurely presenting yet another huge package, on top of the economic plan, was to risk both of them being sundered. Hillary's health care reform plan must be postponed, Gore urged, not advanced.

Hillary was shocked, but bowed to the consensus of the meeting. "We've done the responsible good-government thing," she commented, sardonically, "which will get us beat."

Given the number of Senate seats up for reelection in 1994, this was realism, not pessimism—even the president himself accepted that the Democratic majority in the Senate might be lost in the midterm 1994 elections. Yet it was vital, he felt, for that very reason not to give hostage to fortune— or misfortune. The struggle for economic growth and security was not a quick-fix thing; even the prospects for ratifying President Bush's NAFTA treaty to open up trade with Canada and Mexico were looking dim. By convincing Americans that they were first righting the economy, in order to then tackle major social and health issues, from welfare to health, they would have their best chance of protecting their Democratic base.

The president's view, backed by the vice president, thus prevailed. It was crucial not to give the Republicans free meals. Yet, ironically, that was exactly what they were about to do.

Bill Clinton's economic plan was the largest federal budget-cutting plan in U.S. history: saving more than $700 billion in five years. Of that saving, some $200 billion was to be put back into the economy for job creation and long-term investment—leaving a net deficit reduction of almost $500 billion. Accordingly, the day after his meeting in the Roosevelt Room with his advisers, the president had sent up to the Hill his detailed $1.52 trillion proposal. The reconciliation part of the congressional budget process would now begin.

It was—on April 8, 1993—the start of a battle royal among Democrats that, over the next few months, would determine not simply the future of the Democratic Party but the future of the American economy for the remainder of the decade.

Journalists and political scientists were noting a general shift towards conservatism and Republicanism as a trend that the forty-second president—who had been elected by a plurality but not a complete majority of American voters—was bucking. The latest polls proved that, to a large extent, they were right—the country *was* moving right. The question, then, arose: how could a Democratic presidential trend-bucker prosper? By charisma? By dominating the national debate over critical national issues? By mastery of the mechanics of government—most especially relations with Congress?

Although President Clinton had thrown a tantrum over Congress' cap on his stimulus-investment package (cutting it by $60 billion), the congressional resolution had been only that: a piece of paper that the president was not required to sign, and could in fact ignore. The real test was coming up in the actual bill he was now sending to the Congress. Ross Perot had applauded the outline plan as "a good first step," but had warned that the "devil is in the details"—details that would now be fought over tooth and nail.

Panetta's Bad News

Leon Panetta brought the bad news to the White House. His tidings were frightening. Partisanship had, for some time, been increasing, but with the felling of their revered President Bush in mid-expected office, Republicans appeared to be, Panetta reported, in a meaner mood than ever. Far from the new president being able, as a centrist Democrat, to now move Congress out of gridlock and onto the sunny plains of bipartisan parliamentary progress, in the best interests of all Americans, Clinton would be confronted by two political armies, he explained, bent on mutual annihilation, as in World War I. From this point on, Panetta warned the president sadly, it was going to be a fight to the political death in Congress, with no quarter

given. The president had projected almost $500 billion in net deficit reduc-
tion over the next five years—the saved revenue split evenly between higher
taxes and spending cuts. Since Republicans had an ideological aversion to
higher taxes, they would, Panetta warned, continue to refuse to furnish a
single vote for the president's economic bill—in either the Senate or the
House. Moreover, in the Senate they would use their right to filibuster to
make passage of the bill—which by Senate rules could not be filibustered
during the resolution phase, but could be during the reconciliation
process—a nightmare, indeed impossible.

Panetta had at first been skeptical, yet the shift to the radical right was
unmistakable. In the House, Steve Gunderson of Wisconsin, the chief
deputy Republican whip who had supported Congressman Newt Gingrich
for the chief whip's role in 1989, had actually stepped down in January
1993, claiming the House Republican leadership had gone "hard right." In
the Senate, things were no better. As Panetta recalled, Senator Pete
Domenici "basically said: 'I have to tell you, [bipartisanship] is over.' Because, when Republicans had to walk the line on the Social Security vote
on the budget [in the 1980s] they had taken a tough decision [to rein in
Social Security cost-of-living increases], and the Democrats had just beat
the hell out of them. And they thought it probably cost them the Senate [in
1986]. So Pete was very frank with me. This was now *revenge*. It was that
simple: that because of what the Democrats had done to them, they were
going to stand on the sidelines, and let it happen."

"Don't look for any Republican support," Panetta thus warned the president. "They've pretty much made the decision that they're going to stand
on the sidelines. Democrats will have to carry this."

Looking back, Panetta saw this as the turning point in the history of *fin
de siècle* American politics. Domenici's warning "offended me in the sense
that these were generally good people who had worked with me in the past,
who were willing to work on good substance when it came to issues. But
here they clearly, because of political reasons, had drawn the line. It was
kind of the beginning of the arch-partisanship that has developed to the
present day."

Panetta shook his head at the recollection. Democrats had often opposed President Reagan in Congress, he allowed, though more recently
they had "cut the steel" with President Bush. Now, in a supreme irony—
since Democrats were regularly trashed by Republicans as being the party
of spend-spend-spend—it was becoming clear that Democrats would have

to push through the difficult deficit-reducing legislation on their own—and would need iron discipline. "So we knew that if we were going to get this package through, we were going to have to really have all the Democrats walking together."

None of this was the president's doing—but it did make it imperative that President Clinton and his White House staff rally and maintain the support of the entire Democratic membership on the Hill, if they were to push the deficit reduction bill through successfully, in the interests of the country. Without a single Republican daring to break ranks, the Republican leadership would, meanwhile, see how many Democrats they could pick off.

Unchanged since the previous congress, the 103rd Congress had fifty-seven Democratic senators facing forty-three Republicans—three short of the Democratic majority necessary to override filibusters. In the House, the Democratic majority was greater (258 to 176, with one Independent) and there was no threat of filibustering. Local concerns tended to be greater, however, and the split between old Democrats and centrist New Democrats was consequently larger.

Would the new president be up to the task of keeping discipline among the Democratic ranks of Congress? Panetta wondered.

A Very Personable Guy

"Bill Clinton, he's a very personable guy," Panetta said. "He has this charisma. He knows what to say. I mean, he can walk into any group, anywhere, any time. And for whatever it is, it's those magic antennae that go out: that can sense what an audience is about, who they are, are they conservative or liberal, or this or that—he can pick it up and he can speak to them, and have them in his pocket."

Dealing with congressmen and senators, though, demanded the most formidable presidential talent of all: the ability not just to wow an audience, but to gain and keep their *trust*, individual by individual, over a grueling period of time. It was here that Bill Clinton was, as yet, not so capable. "The part of Bill Clinton that was not so good was the ability to sit down, one on one, with a member of Congress and be able to listen to that person: I mean, to stop talking! And to just listen to that person, and their concerns and what they were saying, and to be able to stroke that person's ego in a way that would bring them on board. He was still somebody who wanted to do a lot of the talking and wanted to say, this is what I think needs to be done. And in Washington, particularly in dealing with the Hill and dealing with the egos on the Hill, you've got to let them basically feel like it's *their* show."

Bill Clinton had never in his life been good at this. Instead, he loved always to emerge as the likeable star of all proceedings, if he could—not the selfless facilitator of other stars. With only a part-time legislature in Arkansas, meeting once every two years, and with less than 10 percent of its members Republicans, he had had little trouble in maintaining his gubernatorial status. But Washington was not Arkansas, as his friend and new HUD secretary, Henry Cisneros, recalled. "It had nothing to do with his [young] age," Cisneros thought—"it was the lack of experience of Washington. I think he did not know the intensity of the Hill—the astuteness and skill level of the combatants were not what he was accustomed to in Arkansas." Indeed Clinton, he recalled, could not at first credit that Republican House members and senators would walk away from him completely—"they were more opposed to him than he expected, or had any reason to expect," Cisneros recalled. "First of all, [the Republicans] had this belief that they should be the governing party for this entire period—and they may have been right, in retrospect, when you look at this last [2004] election. The country is, essentially, Republican. And they questioned the legitimacy of his election. Not in a legal sense, but in a political sense. That it had been stolen from them. And secondly, I think that they regarded him as not fit to be president. Not fit by social standing, not fit by moral compass, not fit by preparation in the pecking order of American elites. . . ."

Such reflections by a close friend, a Hispanic, and a loyal political colleague, while they might explain Clinton's shock and concern at the white flight of congressional Republicans, did not, however, address the critical problem early in 1993: that of a president who had made a shaky transition start, but had then made an extraordinary comeback before Congress in his address to the joint session. Now, perforce, he must turn that enthusiasm into solid, loyal *Democratic* support in the Congress, without Republican help.

Could he do it?

CHAPTER THIRTEEN

REDUCING THE DEFICIT

A Crash Course in Governance

As the president sought to drive his huge, five-year economic plan through Congress, Hillary bulled ahead with her health care reform proposals. Indeed, as the president's plan became mired in new difficulties on the Hill, Hillary's response was not to go slower, but to redouble her own efforts and ratchet up her performance.

"I knew," the president said with pride, later, to Haynes Johnson and David Broder, who chronicled the demise of health care reform in America, "that she could manage a long, complex, highly contentious process." But was pride in his wife's abilities enough to excuse his error in tackling health care reform alongside his economic plan? Not since civil rights had there been anything as contentious as reform of America's entire medical insurance system; nor had anything as *complex* as such reform been promoted, right alongside a deficit reduction plan of historic proportions.

The truth was, health care reform was not simply an important area of domestic policy, it was a minefield: a problem so complex that it could not be reduced to simple solutions, unless one addressed the different problems separately, and in turn. Spiraling health care *costs* were one problem; health care *access*—for low-paid workers, the uninsurable, or impecunious—was another. Dreaming up, overnight, a wholesale fix that would reform both aspects of an almost intractable problem was to court disaster.

Most puzzling of all was that the first couple did not even try to court the press. Instead of seducing journalists, as Hillary and Bill had once done over education reform with critical newspaper commentators in Arkansas such as John Kenneth Starr, Hillary seemed to bow to her more instinctive, distrustful, secretive, and self-righteous self: developing an abrasive, hostile style that turned the serious press—which until the inauguration had been largely pro-Clinton—against them both. "I'm quite astonished," the *New York Times* Washington editor, Andrew Rosenthal, stated at the time. "Given the fact that this woman is one of the key policymakers in the United States of America, we're very interested in talking to her and we have almost no access to her." Such an attitude was profoundly dangerous in a first lady and her husband who did not really know Washington, and had political experience of only a tiny state in the South.

Don't Tread on Us

General Bernard Montgomery, the most famous British officer of World War II, warned in a seminal article before the war that the failure to prepare properly in advance for modern, fast-moving battle very often proves fatal, for it becomes almost impossible to regain the initiative once lost.

President Bill Clinton exemplified the danger of poor preparation for combat. By failing to prepare himself for his constitutional role as president, Bill Clinton now found he had created among senators and congressmen the impression that he could be "rolled." The case of Senator David Boren, five years older than Clinton and a centrist Democrat, was typical. Boren—who had been governor of Oklahoma before he'd won his Senate seat and an all-important place on the Senate Finance Committee—found himself in two minds about the new president. He'd admired Clinton's charismatic rhetoric before the joint session of Congress in February, but had become increasingly skeptical about the stimulus part of the president's huge deficit reduction bill, given that the economy was now reported to have grown as much as 5 percent in the final quarter of 1992. "People can't receive two messages at once," he warned Clinton. "You've gotten them all believing they've got to get the deficit down. This is mission one, and now you're confusing them by coming in with a spending program. That mixes the message."

Had Clinton been Gore, he might either have withdrawn his stimulus package until later, or simply have ignored Boren. In the latter case he would have bulled ahead with the dual package, including its controversial BTU energy tax: either winning Congress over, or failing to do so—in which case he would have covered Congress with gridlocked dishonor, fundamentally obstructive to the electoral wishes expressed by the American people and their president.

But Clinton was a consensus builder and *synthesizer*. At an earlier meeting with Boren at the White House over campaign finance reform, Boren had sensed the almost palpable challenge of the congressional Democratic leadership to the young president, and their unspoken injunction: *Don't tread on us or you'll be sorry*. Sympathetic to the new president, Senator Boren had pleaded aloud with Clinton to do just that, declaring: "Mr. President, I want you to step on our toes and make us mad. If you sit up here and you're going to be viewed as getting in bed with all the Washington insiders, the people that sent you here are going to feel you let them down." In other words: be presidential!

Sadly, in his early days in the White House Clinton failed to be presidential—indeed he seemed, in all the years of campaigning and running for the presidency, not to have thought about what the word "presidential," let alone the role of president, really meant. From his recent visit to former President Reagan he had brought back only Hollywood stories, and jellybeans. Thus, while others perceived in Reagan's assumption of the presidency in 1983 an awesome lesson in leadership, namely delegation and performance, Bill Clinton could see only the star. In his last television interview, with David Brinkley, Reagan was asked what had been the most important feature of his presidency—and had said, candidly: "Acting. If you can act, you've got it made." But by that, former CBS and NBC correspondent Marvin Kalb noted, Reagan had not meant pretense, but the "ability to rise to the expected stature of the presidency, and then to take a big idea and be able to sell it," largely through the media. In 1993, however, Bill Clinton seemed to have little or no idea of the image of strength and leadership he needed to project as president of the United States—from saluting to running the White House.

"The criticism of the salute was that he just didn't have a crisp enough salute," George Stephanopoulos later recalled. "I've looked back at some of those pictures. And it's kind of a tendentious charge—but it had become real. And it was, again, one of those moments: who could tell him?" If the vice president, who had served in Vietnam, was loathe to correct the commander-in-chief, then who was Stephanopoulos to do so? So the image of sloppy commander-in-chief became grafted onto the fiasco of gays in the military, thus further diminishing the authority of the White House, the

Oval Office, and its new occupant, especially after a young White House staffer, walking outside the building, had told a uniformed officer—Lt. General Barry McCaffrey, winner of two Silver Stars, four Bronze Stars, and three Purple Hearts in the service of his country—"I don't talk to the military," a phrase that spread like wildfire through the armed forces.

For all too many observers, this was a tragedy that should never have happened. "I've never forgotten my first impression of Clinton," Marvin Kalb recalled of meeting Governor Clinton in Georgetown. "This unbelievably young-looking politician arrives, and my first impression was that I couldn't take him seriously. He's too young! He's not been anywhere. Not done anything. Yes, he's the governor of Arkansas, but anyone could be the governor of Arkansas. The governor didn't have much to do there. And I felt this until he began to talk about policy. And then I realized that you were dealing with someone who was very special. Someone who had not only a deep grasp of issues but a quick, subtle awareness of where the mood in the room was shifting, of who was raising a tricky kind of question. A crafty politician: one to be admired.

"Based on that first impression I was quite impressed by some of the things that he was doing, and the way he won the '92 election. Overall I was more impressed than I was by any other incoming president since John Kennedy. The combination of obvious brain power, youth, and idealism—those three came together when Clinton came to Washington. And that is why I was so totally astonished and disappointed by stories that I heard from my colleagues when we learned that the White House was so badly run. For example, reporters would say that when they would call the press office to find out what was going to happen, they could get no reply. Not asking for any great secrets. Like: 'Is the president going to go to Camp David this weekend?' You never got an answer.

"You got an impression of either a screwed-up operation, or fear—staff not wanting to say anything without having explicit permission to say something." A response that, inevitably, gave rise to leaks and more speculation than was healthy for a new administration.

"Also, they were so young and inexperienced. The jokes and stories you've read about, such as offices filled with discarded boxes of [take-out] food—that story is true! I *saw* it. And it was rather revolting. You did not have to be a Republican to be offended by what the young people were doing with *our* White House."

As a result, the messages that came out of the White House became mixed, leading to sagging presidential performance polls. On his hundredth day in office Bill Clinton would be registering the lowest poll rating as president in recent history, way below that of presidents Kennedy, Reagan, or Carter at a similar stage in their presidencies—polls that would plummet still lower as the weeks went by.

We're Losing Our Soul

Frustrated, Bill Clinton's temper tantrums began to reach epic decibel levels, alarming those who heard, or overheard, them.

The president's outbursts—known as SMOs (Standard Morning Outbursts)—had been legendary during the election, as Carville and Stephanopoulos remembered. "It's just a physical force. It was just ferocious," Stephanopoulos once recalled. "And I never minded, because it wasn't personal and it wasn't particularly mean. . . . And it would just pass." Now, however, the outbursts were mean—and didn't pass so quickly. For a staffer, Stephanopoulos had claimed, "it's a kind of a source of power to be the one who gets the SMO. You're trusted enough, or you're important enough, to take the wrath and then try to fix it." Yet it was becoming increasingly obvious that Stephanopoulos *couldn't* "fix it"—frustrating the president still more.

"We've just gone too far. We're losing our soul," the president had declared in fury when he heard that Congress, in its initial resolution, had chopped the legs from under the stimulus part of his economic plan. But was such anger real—or feigned to impress the secretary of labor that he, the president, was being coerced by Congress against his conscience? "I wanted to keep as many of the promises as we could," Stephanopoulos recalled. "I was committed to the 'putting people first' agenda and actually saw my role, in many ways, as a defender of the promises"—promises that the president kept assuring him he wished to keep. But which ones—and when?

The chameleon in Bill Clinton meant that every individual who spoke to the chief executive saw a different president—when it was crucial, in the early months of his first term in office, to show clear, and clearly recognizable, leadership. As even his most admiring adviser, Robert Rubin, would later admit, President Clinton's ability to "captivate people" could "lead to a certain amount of misunderstanding"—imagining the president was on their side when he wasn't.

Rubin was perhaps the best adviser Clinton would ever have—for as a senior partner in Goldman Sachs, he was never in any awe of the man-orphan from Hope, Arkansas, who had enjoyed a meteoric political career, but had never made a penny. Rubin's advice to the president was thus clear, bold, and well taken—as advice. According to Bob Woodward, Clinton kept telling himself that "getting control of the deficit and the process would put him in a position of strength. Then, later, from that position of strength, he could move to what mattered." If the president did tell himself this at night, however, that mantra was not clearly communicated to his staff—who in turn were unable to put across this clear long-term goal to others, or to conceal the president's continual changes of view, mood, and mind. As Rubin himself recalled: "Clinton later said to me, this was a crucial tactical mistake. He should have been out talking about his economic recovery program every day. He told me he would never again attempt a major policy initiative without an integral communication and political strategy. He also said he should have made an intense effort to frame the debate from the very beginning."

To blame his communications team, in retrospect, was not simply hindsight, however, but blindsight. The problem of an unclear communications strategy derived not from a poor team but from the fact that the mixed messages emitted by the White House in the early months of 1993 reflected the president's own ambivalence about his agenda—even the advisability of tackling the national deficit head-on, ostensibly his main "story."

Rubin's team had pressed for deficit reduction as the administration's first priority. But might a too-massive deficit reduction actually strangle the economic recovery that was believed to be starting? Increasing taxation and cutting government programs to the tune of $500 billion threatened to drag down the very indicators of accelerating economic improvement. Thus advisers such as Nobel-Prize-winning economist Joseph Stiglitz warned that too much deficit cutting might well throttle the recovery—as had arguably happened to Clinton's predecessor, George H. W. Bush, a president who had also urged and obtained from Congress major government cuts, only to find recession and electoral defeat his reward.

"Unlike George Bush, he was and is capable of seeing many sides of the problem," Marvin Kalb observed. "Many, many sides. He was never absolutely convinced of anything he decided. And it's very difficult to run a country if you aren't convinced!"

Too Many Cooks

Prioritizing was not a concept in Bill Clinton's executive vocabulary; indeed in this sense Bill Clinton was, and always would be, a prisoner as well as beneficiary of his high intelligence—his very capaciousness of mind making it difficult, if not impossible, for him to hew consistently to one chosen line or strategy. As a result the White House became, each day, the veritable battleground of Bill Clinton's own free-ranging, endlessly curious and questing brain, as every adviser and every visitor was asked to contribute his or her opinion to help in the shaping of the president's view—a view that would then change with every subsequent idea or potential addition. "He could not let go of a problem," Marvin Kalb noted, "because he understood that decisions are only way stations. Decisions don't necessarily end the problem; it is merely a moment in the life of a process."

All intelligent ideas—even some unintelligent ones—were thus paraded and chewed over in the White House, the many cooks contributing to the presidential broth. This only confused Clinton's message to Congress and the public—and made the president look weak. Even his own polling consultant, Stan Greenberg, warned Clinton on April 20, 1993, as the Senate came to a complete standstill with a filibuster instead of approving the very modest, recently reduced White House stimulus package, that the "president had failed to communicate both the central values of his presidency and an organizing idea for his economic program."

If the stimulus package failed, Greenberg added, however, it was not the Congress that would be blamed but the president. Yet, instead of recommending that Clinton now concentrate entirely on pushing through a successful deficit reduction package, Greenberg advised Clinton to return to his election manifesto of the year before, *Putting People First*—thus confusing the public even more!

Greenberg spoke for Carville—who was now acting as an outside consultant—as well as Begala and Grunwald: the GCBG Group. It was the 1979–1980 "Bearded Troika" story of the governorship of Arkansas all over again—only a "Gang of Four" working for the president now, instead of Three. The GCBG group spoke for social change. Bentsen and Rubin spoke for Wall Street and the Federal Reserve under Alan Greenspan. Nobody seemed sensible enough, save Panetta and at times the increasingly panicky Stephanopoulos, to speak for Congress.

As a result, the phrase "forcing the spring" became more a question of delaying spring, at least in terms of health care reform, in the hope of passing the economic bill. Two Democratic senators had already jumped ship during the initial resolution stage—narrowing the Democratic majority in the Senate, before Congress even began its deliberations on the actual bill rather than the resolution. "We start shooting with real bullets from here on out," the minority leader in the Senate, Bob Dole, had then warned—and with a Democratic majority of only two in the all-important Senate Finance Committee, he wasn't joking. "It doesn't take many defections to turn things around in the Senate Finance Committee," Dole pointed out.

Warnings of failure now began to come in to the White House, thick and fast. "I know what's *wrong*!" Clinton screamed at his consultants, listening to the reports of his plunging polls and the tortuous passage of the bill through Congress. "Give me a strategy!"

Writing on the Wall

Had the president held to a strategy of "Germany First," as Roosevelt had done at Churchill's suggestion in World War II—by tackling the deficit first, and only then proposing a package of stimuli and investments—he would at least have conveyed presidential authority, tempered with realism and patience. Instead, true to his desire to accommodate all opinions and options, and still desperately naïve in his style of leadership in the White House, the president presented—and mirrored—a kaleidoscope of conflicting views.

With the Senate Republican filibuster on April 21, however, the writing was on the wall—and it was no longer in invisible ink. The president's much-vaunted economic plan looked in deep trouble, and the president himself began to look lost in the public's estimation, as Greenberg reported. Rather than flying to Camp David, however, to reconsider his leadership style and the restructuring of his White House organization, Bill Clinton merely tormented himself with yet more gnashing of teeth—even confiding to his staff that he personally agreed with the Senate filibuster: that the spending bill he'd sent up to Congress was ill-conceived and "had too much pork in it" for senators who were being asked to raise taxes and agree to major cuts in government spending.

This was a typical example of Clinton's forté—his ability to see the other man's point of view and his reasons for holding it. Yet it bespoke, too, his continuing lack of understanding of the art and skill of *command*. In a rage, he swore he would draw up the complicated legislative package himself, personally, next time.

Clinton's presidential performance became, if anything, more worrying thereafter. When on May 6, 1993, the entire eleven-man Democratic membership of the Senate Finance Committee came to see him in the Cabinet Room at the White House to discuss the reconciliation, or "real bill," process, the committee's chairman, Senator Daniel Patrick Moynihan, assured the president that, if they could only pass a budget that could reasonably be called "the president's plan," then the "presidency will be a success." So long as the eleven Democrats on the committee voted together, en bloc, the nine Republicans on the committee would be unable to stop it, Moynihan declared—whereas a single defection to the other side would produce a ten-ten tie.

The members thus looked to the president, in Woodward's words, to respond "with force, clarity, and warmth"—especially when the junior senator of North Dakota, Kent Conrad, voiced his reservations about the effects of the BTU tax in his own rural state.

Instead of giving the required forceful response, however, President Clinton turned to Senator Jay Rockefeller—and asked what *he* thought!

The senators were appalled. It was abundantly clear that Clinton, for all his brilliance, was still out of his depth as president of the most powerful nation in the world—a popular professor, as Paul Begala pictured him, rather than an effective leader.

The consequences, however, were dire. In evolutionary biology, weakness in human organisms invites predators and pathogens—and as President Carter had found, the same held true of presidential politics. In any event, having urged the president to be a commander-in-chief but sensing the chief executive's weakness, Senator Boren now decided himself to test the new holder of the highest office. He seconded Senator Conrad's concern about the BTU tax.

The president had assured Democratic leaders of the House of Representatives that he would stand or fall with them over the controversial, unpopular energy BTU tax—and believing him, they had bravely passed the bill with the new tax included. Now, Senator Boren was pouring cold water on the energy tax proposal—thus threatening the whole plan to drive, by a demonstration of ironclad Democratic solidarity, the president's bill through the Senate Finance Committee.

Boren's potential opposition triggered panic stations. When asked by Senator Moynihan if he hadn't said two months before, in February 1993, that he was unconditionally *for* the president's package, Boren responded that he'd been unconditionally in favor of the proposals in the president's address to the joint session, but that the bill being presented to Congress was different from the president's speech. To the consternation of Senator Moynihan and the other senators in the room, the Democratic senator now indicated that he wished to work with his Republican colleagues on the Finance Committee over the matter. The Democratic lock on the Senate would be broken—by a Democrat!

Senator Moynihan, a man of strong views but a somewhat ineffective committee chairman, turned to the president. The situation was critical, he warned. He and his ten colleagues controlled the future of the bill, the future of the country, and the future of the president himself. Clinton had only to help keep them together and he was assured of victory: "Mr. President, this is your presidency on the line. If you get this, you are a strong president. If this fails, you are a weak president."

It was meant as a clarion call, to ensure that the president recognized what he must do to ensure that he was seen as strong. But the president only nodded, without saying anything—and the meeting broke up in confusion.

Worse still, the next day, without consulting Senator Moynihan, the president arranged a secret meeting with Senator Boren, and undercut Moynihan's chairmanship by encouraging Boren to go ahead and work with Republican senators to see if *they* could do anything—despite the fact that no single Republican senator or congressman had yet voted for either the resolution or the reconciliation bill. "If you could help get bipartisan support for my plan, if you could help make my plan into a bipartisan proposal," Clinton urged him, lamely, "it'd be the best thing you could do for my presidency."

The president's chief of staff, Mack McLarty, was aghast. A tough chief of staff would have leaped into action. Yet McLarty was simply too pleasant—he was already nicknamed "Mack the Nice"—and too submissive either to head off such a preposterous proposition, or zap it before it became cancerous. In the ensuing weeks the tragi-comedy of the Clinton presidency, lurching from side to side, would be spectacularly demonstrated.

Swirl

"The key in Congress," Leon Panetta later tried to explain, "is that people change their minds, people change their positions, but the one thing they cannot do is change their word. If you tell somebody, 'This is going to happen,' you at least have to know that you will abide by that. People are respected if they stand by their word. And if they're gonna screw you, if they're gonna vote against you, at least you know where they stand. And with Bill Clinton, the Democrats were always very nervous; they never quite knew that he *would* stand by his position."

Unfortunately, Congressmen did not yet recognize that in Bill Clinton the country had elected not only a wholly new kind of Democrat, but a wholly new kind of *president*—one who ruled not by decisiveness but by a procedure unique in the annals of the White House: swirl.

"The way Clinton arrived at decisions," Leon Panetta explained, "was . . . he opened the door to *every* approach! His chemistry for coming to a decision was not to say, 'This is what my guts tell me is right, so therefore I'm going to do this.' It's not the way he operated. His chemistry was basically to say: 'O.K. I've got a problem. What are the ideas out there that confront that problem? I want to listen to everyone. I want to hear what they are.' And he would go through that process. You know, he would lean one way, lean the other way. . . . And then there was this mental process of evaluating all of these different ideas. And then, ultimately, trying to bring it together in a final answer that would not only bring the best ideas to bear, but would also come together in a way that would be politically sellable to everyone.

"And that's the way he operated," Panetta emphasized, torn between admiration for the president's high intellect and determination to find "the right decision, so that everyone would support him," on the one hand, and his knowledge that such a public approach, in real political life, is a recipe for chaotic management, on the other. "That's a very hard process to go through," Panetta commented, "because most decisions in the end are going to piss off people! And you have to kind of suck it up. But he, when he came to a decision that he knew might anger some people—he was always concerned it would anger people!"

He was not "confrontational"—and in this respect, the president's indecisive style became, perhaps by virtue of his position, infectious. "Neither was Al Gore, interestingly. They always found ways to be able to swing back and forth. So you never got a sense of boundary, or definition. Clinton never said to somebody, 'Look, you're crazy! That idea's nuts! There's no way we're gonna do that!' " Instead, there was a continuing Clinton see-saw—at the center of a White House going in circles.

"What happens in the White House is a reflection of the way he thinks," one cabinet officer explained to Elizabeth Drew at the time. "He doesn't want hierarchy. He doesn't want a strong chief of staff. He doesn't want a single economic adviser. He wants all kinds of advisers swirling around him constantly."

While "swirl" might reflect and suit Bill Clinton's mind, it did not necessarily suit the business of *leadership* as the leading of *others*, inside and outside the White House.

In Arkansas, Governor Clinton had had Betsey Wright to maintain order in such chaos. Now, in the White House, President Clinton had no tough chief of staff, only a tough wife, enmeshed in her own administration project, whispering in one ear, while his vice president, Al Gore, spoke into the other, and a dissonant chorus shouted in the background—each person, sensing the president's susceptibility to ideas, raising his or her own voice the louder, all crowding to get closer, since "those who have the most time with him have the most influence, so there's a great deal of stampeding around him."

Sarcastically Clinton had labeled himself early on as an "Eisenhower Republican," yet for all his biographical reading he seemed ignorant of Eisenhower's military genius: namely the general's ability, having collected ideas, to use a tough chief of staff and then mount the lonely stage of history to speak with a supreme commander's authority—as he had done when deciding to launch the weather-delayed D-Day landings in Normandy.

Even loyal Mack McLarty was rendered speechless at the extent of Bill Clinton's inability to exercise authority—indeed, in a light-hearted moment McLarty flattered his kindergarten companion-turned-boss. He was, he told Clinton, "convinced more than ever of your greatness," indeed was "more convinced than ever of your goodness. But what I'll never understand," McLarty added, shaking his head, "is how a man with such a genius of organizing his thoughts and articulating them could be so disorganized in managing himself."

By this McLarty meant the president's failure to discipline himself in order to better manage *others*. In a new administration, desperately lacking in experience after the Democrats had been out of office for twelve years, it was potentially catastrophic. In John Brummett's words, neither the new president nor the unfortunate White House staff he collected around him were "politically trained or Washington-seasoned or ready for prime time."

Thus ended the tragi-comedy of President Clinton's first one hundred days—a sorry performance when compared with those of Franklin Delano Roosevelt. As the clock started on the second hundred in April 1993, Senator Boren duly ditched his Democratic colleagues. From a brilliant, charismatic presentation in February before the joint session of Congress the forty-second president's deficit bill morphed into a wild summer session in which Senator Boren or indeed any senator who chose to do so was empowered to bring down the entire economic bill, and thus emasculate the Clinton presidency.

THE RED QUEEN

CHAPTER FOURTEEN

STAR WARS

"He Doesn't Seem to Be the President"

The irony of the Clinton Years, as they would become known, was twofold: first, that the American economy, under the stewardship of President Clinton, would eventually exceed the wildest dreams of the very opponents—conservatives and Republicans—who became most determined to bring the president down; second, that such opponents labored under a misapprehension.

This misapprehension, based on Clinton's poor initial performance in the White House, was that the president was by nature weak. Not only Republicans but even fellow Democrats in Congress became tempted, by virtue of the young president's chaotic governing style, to test the president's authority, from his immediate "gays in the military" blunder to the contested passage of his deficit reduction/stimulus bill.

Bill Clinton had, of course, been here before—indeed, the history of his governorship in Arkansas was as much a record of Clinton-testing as of teacher-testing. By presenting a picture of poor executive skills in the opening act of his presidential administration to Congress, to the military, and to the many factions in the nation, the forty-second president had only himself to blame. He had, ineluctably, lured adversaries, mercenaries—even those who just felt impelled to take advantage of perceived weakness—to attack, subvert, undermine, chip away at the seemingly slick body of the president and his White House, marred by its leaderless personnel structure, its endless dissension and procrastination, its flip-flopping president, its indiscipline and failures of command.

As Elizabeth Drew put it, "Very early, some saw that Clinton wasn't held in awe and inspired no fear, and they found this alarming." And she quoted Senator David Boren's ominous remark about Clinton, at the time: "He doesn't seem to be the president."

Health Wars

Two investigative accounts of what happened to Bill Clinton over the next eight years would use terms involving chase: the one entitled *Blood Sport*, the other *The Hunting of the President*. Both would be concerned to record, analyze, and report the systematic attempt—financed in large part by Republican and conservative opponents—to bring down the nation's chief executive. The authors of both books would understandably express abhorrence at one of the most disreputable, indeed quasi-treasonable, ad hominem anti-presidential linked campaigns of personal destruction ever seen in American history. Their narratives would make horrific reading— yet the authors seemed unable to accept that, in the modern world as in the ancient, a leader must lead and show powers of command, otherwise he or she sets him or herself up for mortal attack. In this sense, societies were like the human body, where health wars are in constant progress.

As the cell structures of the natural world had become, over eons of time, more complex, so too had their immunological systems. In human beings this involved, as Dr. Matt Ridley wrote in *The Red Queen*, an arsenal of about ten million different types of white blood cells, armed with their own antibody-making machinery, poised to pounce on any invading cell— viral, bacterial, or other—and destroy the infection. For their part, the pathogens "are continually changing" in order to gain an advantage over the host organism, developing not only new cell structures but new strategies and tactics, such as concealing themselves inside host cells—like the AIDS virus—or mutating so rapidly that the host's immunological response-time is tested to the point of breakdown, as in malaria.

In time, Bill Clinton's pathogenic opponents would use this tactic, testing the prodigiously gifted president's immunological system by ever-new mutations, and finally following a novel strategy in American anti-presidential history: piggy-backing on a host cell that could get past the guardroom—literally the White House gates. For the moment, however, the invaders merely tested the president's mettle, and took stock. As Elizabeth

Drew put it, "Congress takes its measure of every new president—the members watching and sniffing the air and feeling the pulse of their constituencies. It is constantly judging how strong a president is, as they make their calculations of how important it is to support him and the consequences of not doing so."

As Drew pithily remarked, "In Clinton's case, the first impressions weren't very good."

"Kick Me"

The president's Omnibus Budget Reconciliation Act (H.R. 2264), meantime, went before some thirteen tax-writing and authorizing committees in the House—whose deadline was May 14—and twelve in the Senate, with a deadline of June 18, 1993.

With the relatively small economic stimulus part of the resolution having been squashed by the Senate resolution bill in April, and Bob Dole threatening "real bullets" as the real plan now went up for real legislation, it was imperative the president show his mettle. House Democrats had been left "bruised and wary of again backing an unpopular measure only to see it unravel in the Senate," the *Congressional Quarterly* noted in its *1993 Almanac*. "If the president failed this time, he faced the prospect of losing control of the economic agenda and spending the rest of the year negotiating from weakness with a muscular Republican minority" or, worse still, "renegade blocs of his own party."

Nowhere was this dilemma more ruthlessly illustrated than among members of the media, whom Clinton had so brilliantly impressed and manipulated to his advantage during the election process when, as a young and little-known candidate, he needed them. Now, thinking he did not, he had invoked their resentment—and in the relentless manner of all evolution, the members of the media, he found, were mutating from parasites to piranhas.

To executive inadequacy and inexperience, moreover, had been added the simple fact of Bill Clinton's age. When set against the septuagarian George H. W. Bush during the election campaign, his youthfulness had been a plus. Once in office, however, it invited a certain lack of respect, particularly for a man who was so shamelessly friendly and open-hearted. Moreover, Clinton's "eagerness to please compounded the image of one not worthy of respect. It served to make critics feel powerful," John Brummett confessed on behalf of his brethren in the fourth estate. "It was as if Clinton, like an unpopular schoolchild, wore a sign on his backside that read: 'Kick me.'

"And kick him," Brummett added in considerable understatement, "we did"—especially when the president, lacking an effective chief of staff, supplied them with free material.

Clinton's first term was thus becoming less a presidency than a temporary residency.

Hairgate

While the president's omnibus budget bill made its tortuous way through the chain of House of Representatives committees, Hillary set off on a quick trip to New York on May 15, to take Chelsea and the president to see *Sleeping Beauty* at the American Ballet Theater. There Susan Thomases recommended a new French hair stylist, who was reputed to be pioneering a "thinking woman's approach to beauty," indeed talked "about higher aerodynamics" and had "extremely elaborate theories." He could even come to her hotel, he offered, to do the first lady's makeover.

The result was, as Hillary herself recalled, "International headlines." Under the title "White House cuts go to Hillary's head," the *South China Morning Post*, in Hong Kong, announced: "FORGET health-care reform. It is Hillary Rodham Clinton's stand on hair-care reform that is getting all the attention. She returned to Washington from a weekend trip to New York with her formerly shoulder-length hair cut to just below her ears. The new style is layered on the sides and swept away from her face." *USA Today* was equally bouleversé. "Hillary Rodham Clinton's new summer hairdo almost became 'Hair-gate' as the media feverishly tracked leads on her stylist—who turns out to be," the newspaper revealed, "Frederic Fekkai, with women's and men's salons at Bergdorf-Goodman in Manhattan."

Fekkai, who was of French origin and among his celebrity clients boasted Meryl Streep, John F. Kennedy Jr., and Sigourney Weaver, charged $275 a cut—though this was mild in comparison with the cost of taking Air Force One for the outing. As Hillary subsequently attempted to make light of the matter while giving the commencement address at the University of Pennsylvania (the president had only asked for 25 percent staffing cuts at the White House, she joked, but she had ordered a 50 percent cut), the president flew on to Los Alamos in New Mexico to inspect their new supercomputer, then to San Diego and, on May 18, to Los Angeles, where he played basketball with local community residents before flying home. Running late, as always, Clinton summoned his West Coast barber, Christophe of Beverly Hills, to his personal blue-and-white Boeing 747 on the LAX runway—thus forcing it and its accompanying airplane containing dozens of White House correspondents to wait on the tarmac at the busy commercial airport while the thick, fast-graying locks of the multi-tasking forty-second president were trimmed—and thousands of air passengers were stuck, unable to take off or land.

In itself, as historians later noted, the fiasco called "Hairgate" hardly merited a footnote. Nevertheless, it typified the problems of the White House under its new management, or mis-management. In its aftermath the president would claim he had twice asked to be assured that regular air traffic was not being held up, and the control tower had assured him, through his staff, that no air travelers were being inconvenienced. If so, the control tower or his staff were deceiving him, for the evidence, as Elizabeth Drew chronicled, "based on Federal Aviation Administration information," was that, instead of the customary twenty-minute moratorium, "other planes were delayed as two of LAX's four runways were shut down for over an hour."

Such an afternoon delay had seemed to Clinton and his aides relatively inconsequential in the frantic tapestry of presidential travel, but to those delayed in their travel plans, as well as those already worried by souring relations with the press, the enforced idleness of a planeload of discontented reporters on the runway for a presidential haircut had boded ill. Not only were the press still banished from access to the press office in the West Wing of the White House, but even the Secret Service and FBI officers had been told to leave the personal quarters of the wing whenever any single member of the "first family" was in residence, on Hillary's personal orders—directives that, as with the royal family in England, only made the royal personage more, not less, fascinating to reporters.

In the style section of the *Washington Post* the next day, the president's haircut, costing $200 (Christophe's normal fee to the glamorati of Beverly Hills) had been duly and appropriately reported. But at a moment when the White House was at pains to get Congress to pass a massive deficit reduction bill, involving the slashing not only of the federal budget but of many of the administration's most crucial social and economic programs, as well as the introduction of major tax hikes, the expensive haircut and the holding up of the nation's airways had been seen by reporters, still smarting at their exclusion from the West Wing and infuriated by the incompetence of Stephanopoulos's communications operation, as wasteful and symbolic: an act of arrogance, indeed presidential folly.

Gleefully the press took its revenge. "This is not good press for a president who proclaims to be a down-home boy and who spent much of his time on the campaign trail calling George Bush a preppy elitist," the *St. Petersburg Times* commented, calling it the First Hair Scandal. Hillary's makeover was one thing—but was the president, too, becoming swayed by the glitz of high office? "Clinton's choice of hairstylist has left some wondering what ever happened to the Razorback who loved smothered pork chops and McDonald's decaf? Where is the man who wore a baseball cap atop his puffy cloud of silver hair with all the style of an STP spokesperson? Where is Bubba? Ross Perot supporters noted that their man gets his weekly $10 haircut from the same North Dallas barber he has been using for 20 years."

Perot's remaining hair was, of course, a very different proposition than the president's. Nevertheless, the runaway runway story was easy to construe negatively, at a moment of national—even patriotic—belt-tightening to bring down the deficit.

USA Today was openly censorious. "It's not your hair," it fumed. "It's the economy, stupid. Are the Clintons really the Washington Hillbillies? Or are they glitzy Republicans in down home disguise? How could a woman who gets so irritated with the press's focus on her hair not know that going to an expensive famous hairdresser would set off alarms? And why would a president trying to balance the national budget book a costly Hollywood hairdresser?"

To add insult to injury, the White House communications staff seemed not to understand what was happening. Without thinking, Paul Begala went onto the counteroffensive. "It's stunning to me that on a day in which powerful forces are trying to cut Social Security, cut Medicare, cut tax burdens on the rich, that the great and powerful *Washington Post* wants to write about a damn haircut. That's pathetic. That's my response. Get a life." Nor did he stop there. Bill Clinton "has challenging hair to say the least," he said. "Even on a good day it sometimes looks like worn-out Brillo." How much he spends to fix it, Begala said, is "the last thing that anybody in America is worried about."

Begala, as became rapidly and embarrassingly clear, was plain wrong. Every newspaper in America from Tampa to Cleveland seized on the story of "the most expensive haircut in history," as it was quickly dubbed. "It smacks of being a little bit light, a little bit starstruck," a former White House pollster for President Carter was quoted—one of many hundreds of pundits all too keen now to toss in their penny-ha'pence worth. "By filing time the next day, we were in crisis mode," Stephanopoulos later confessed. "Aided by some inaccurate leaks from the Federal Aviation Administration, the press reported that thousands of air travelers had been delayed for the sake of the president's personal convenience."

As Elizabeth Drew noted, however, the press had been out to scalp not only the young president and his wife, but the White House's even younger, even hairier and yet more arrogant communications director—whose days in the job were numbered. "A lot of the press corps had been looking to put him in his place," Drew noted, since to many of them Stephanopoulos had seemed "flip, a bit of a smart-ass." At thirty-one and heading up a team of fifty incompetents, he had become "the embodiment of the 'kids,' and suddenly the kids weren't so cute anymore."

Travelgate

Hillary—tone deaf, as she herself acknowledged—seemed not to hear the drumming. Frustrated by the delay to her health care reform agenda owing to the prolonged struggle to get the president's economic bill through the thirteen House committees in Congress, she swung into personal action. On the spur of the moment she instructed Dee Dee Myers, through her staff, to announce the immediate firing of the entire seven-person White House travel staff.

Pandemonium ensued. On May 19, 1993, Stephanopoulos, still vainly attempting to explain to an angry press the reasons for the president's expensive haircut on a busy international runway, was brought rudely to his senses by Andrea Mitchell of NBC, the very television reporter who had once caused the president-elect to declare his determination to permit gays in the military. "George," the puzzled Andrea had asked him, "what are you guys doing firing the travel office?"

Stephanopoulos—having been personally assured by Hillary and her former Rose Law Firm partner, Vince Foster, that the entire White House travel office team was guilty of corruption—assured Mitchell, on Hillary's assurance, that she would be "embarrassed" if she started defending them. But Stephanopoulos would be proved wrong—for "we," Stephanopoulos lamented later, "were the ones who ended up with egg on our faces."

The egg smelled strangely bad as reporters listened to the cockeyed story of travel team embezzlement. "Charging gross financial mismanagement, the White House abruptly fired the seven longtime staff members at its travel office yesterday and replaced them with a team to be headed by President Clinton's cousin," the *Washington Post*'s Ann Devroy reported. "The seven fired workers were career government employees, with about 10 to 30 years' experience. Press secretary Dee Dee Myers said the White House held all seven responsible for the financial mismanagement, which she said had occurred 'for years and years' and that it was serious enough to ask the FBI to investigate. Catherine Cornelius, 25, who worked on travel during the Clinton campaign, will head the new office. Myers said replacing a career worker with a cousin of the president was not nepotism because 'she's a distant cousin.'"

Readers read over the report again in disbelief. It was, however, factually correct about the firings—none of the seven White House workers were being given a chance to respond to the accusations, which were based on a lightning, incomplete audit conducted the previous weekend for Hillary by KPMG management consultants, while Hillary was conveniently traveling to the ballet in New York. The workers were ordered to vacate their desks by noon. They were given two weeks' severance pay, and only a month's health benefits. So much for health care reform!

That Hillary—heading the health care reform task force—could imagine this to be an appropriate moment to take such unilateral, punitive action said little for her *savoir faire*, her timing, or her consistency. At the very moment when the president's economic bill was running towards a potential trainwreck in Congress, the summary firings—four months before Vice President Al Gore's "Reinventing Government" performance review was expected—proved the worst misjudgment of Hillary's entire career to date, as even she afterwards allowed. "I'm not sure I've ever learned so much so fast about the consequences of saying or doing anything," she later wrote, "before knowing exactly what's going on."

At the time, however, Hillary found herself utterly "surprised by the reaction in the press room." Given that individual American and international news organizations and agencies, not the U.S. government, had for decades happily paid the highly efficient White House press office staff to make all their reporters' travel arrangements—arrangements that had totaled at least $10 million over the past sixteen months alone—Hillary's declaration of "war on the press corps," as Stephanopoulos later put it, spoke volumes about her insensitivity.

The president, certainly, was completely blindsided by the new scandal, so soon after Hairgate. While Dee Dee Myers addressed the stunned press corps on Pennsylvania Avenue, the president was on Capitol Hill "trying to ward off a potentially disastrous rebellion against his economic plan next week by conservative and moderate Democrats, who believe he is seeking too many tax increases and too few spending cuts in his efforts to cut the deficit," the London *Times* reported. Congressional dissidents had seen public support for the plan fall, "and yesterday Ross Perot, who won 19 percent of last year's presidential vote, was in the same building as Mr. Clinton, telling Republicans the plan was 'tax-and-spend, and that's not what the American people want.'"

"Small-time Arkansas Self-dealing"

What the president wanted was an open question. Attempting to rescue his BTU energy tax, for example, the president had assured congressmen: "If you go out on a limb, I'll go with you." But could he really fulfill such a promise? Democrat leaders in the House had backed him, speaking of "strong support across the spectrum" and expressing confidence that the deficit reduction plan would pass. Six days later, on May 25, 1993, the House Budget Committee reported on the omnibus budget reconciliation, with the BTU tax proposal still in it. Senate acceptance, however, was another matter.

Democratic senators, noting recent events, were not impressed by the recklessness of the White House firings, and were alarmed by the negative press response—for, far from accepting Hillary's draconian dismissals at face value, journalists were spurred into doing their own investigations. Not only was the president's young "distant" cousin said to have been a poor travel staffer during the campaign, but two of the main characters driving Travelgate were once again the very couple who had made the party convention film, *The Man from Hope*—Harry and Linda Bloodworth Thomason. To the consternation of reporters, it was revealed that the Thomasons possessed White House passes permitting them unlimited access to the entire White House as consultants in charge of special appearances by the president—and rumor had it that Harry

Thomason, who had first recommended Christophe as hairdresser to the president, was behind the travel office firings on his own account. A charter airline had offered to provide low-cost charter air travel to White House officials, but when its offer was turned down by the permanent staff of the travel office, Harry—who had shares in the applicant company—had complained to his wife, Linda, a native Arkansan. Linda, in turn, had told David Watkins, another native Arkansan, who had charge of White House management and administration and had run an impeccable presidential campaign. Watkins had told twenty-five-year-old Catherine Cornelius, another native Arkansan, who worked under Watkins but had designs herself on the travel office. Catherine, in turn, had begun to steal documents from the travel office in an amateur version of the amateur sleuth Angela Lansbury—until the travel office had grown wise, had locked their files, and had prevented her from returning the documents she'd purloined. In this standoff, and with the approval of Mack McLarty, another Arkansan, and Bill Kennedy, Hillary's former Arkansas partner in the Rose Law Firm who was now working in the White House legal counsel's office, the FBI had then been brought in—without the knowledge or approval of the attorney general!

Kennedy had hoped that the name of the FBI would, when stitched into Stephanopoulos's and Dee Dee Myers's spin, make the accusations of corruption and dismissal look more authoritative. Instead, such machinations had backfired—making it look as if the White House was suborning the top federal law enforcement agency to achieve its tacky Arkansas-business ends. "The whole episode," as Stephanopoulos confessed afterwards, "looked like small-time Arkansas self-dealing."

Together with the visits of Hollywood stars like Barbra Streisand and Judy Collins to the White House, and the president's dinner with Sharon Stone in Vancouver, the image of Bill Clinton, the simple man from Hope with a mission to attack the deficit and to represent ordinary Americans, began to look insincere.

"President Clinton ended a calamitous week yesterday facing a barrage of charges of vanity, cronyism and nepotism," the London *Times* reported. "His claim to being a populist politician was undermined and he was accused of falling into the trap of being too star-struck by Hollywood. . . . There were also embarrassing new links between Mr. Clinton's friends and a rash of White House sackings, and fury on Capitol Hill. . . . As Washington ponders the morass of controversy, a persistent question is whether Mr.

Clinton has lost the common touch through arrogance or because there is no one senior enough to warn him about making mistakes."

This was the critical critique. As the journalist Ian Brodie noted, "at least during the campaign he had James Carville, the blunt-speaking Southerner known as the 'Ragin' Cajun,' to tell him candidly what he needed to hear. He coined the slogan 'It's the Economy, Stupid' to keep Mr. Clinton focused on the issue that won the election. Now Mr. Carville has gone to book-writing and lecturing and there seems no one else within earshot, not even Hillary Rodham Clinton, with enough political instincts and influence to extricate the president from blunders."

Foreign Affairs

International observers, watching the press eruption over Travelgate and Hairgate, became anxious lest the Clintons' *faux pas* spill over into foreign policy.

In February 1993, shortly after the inauguration, some nine thousand UN peacekeepers had been deployed to avoid a humanitarian catastrophe in Bosnia, where millions were starving. Food had had to be parachuted into Bosnian Muslim (Bosniak) enclaves by American planes, in order to overfly murderous Serbian roadblocks deliberately halting UN agency aid convoys that were traveling by road. On March 12 General Morillon, the UN commander in Bosnia, had bravely made his way through Serb lines and unilaterally declared besieged Srebrenica to be under "UN protection"—which, when ratified by UN Resolution 819 in April (declaring Srebrenica and its surroundings to be a "safe area," together with five other Muslim cities), doomed the UN to become a participant in the civil war, whether it wished to be or not.

UN-mandated forces could, and did, force the Muslim refugees and residents in the "safe areas" to disarm, and thus pose no threat to the Bosnian Serbs—but what would the lightly armed UN troops actually do if the Serbs renewed their assaults on the Muslim cities with heavy weapons? Despite his tough rhetoric in the 1992 campaign, President Bill Clinton had shown little stomach for a fight on the Adriatic peninsula. Nor—tragically—had he shown any enthusiasm for a negotiated solution presented by President Carter's former secretary of state, Cyrus Vance, who was working for the UN, and the former British Foreign Secretary David Owen, who represented the European Community.

In order to stop the Serbian leaders—who had already seized two-thirds of Bosnian territory by force, and "cleansed" it of non-Serbs—from simply rubbing out any chance of Bosnia's becoming a viable independent state similar to Slovenia and Croatia in the north of the former Yugoslavia, the Vance-Owen team had provisionally negotiated a ten-province Bosnian federation. Each of the demilitarized provinces would be almost completely autonomous. As part of this plan, however, the Serbs would have to give back more than 30 percent of the country they had captured and "cleansed" the year before—much as Israel had been asked to return to Muslim Palestinians territory it had overrun in 1948. Without the threat of international force, the Israelis had not done so. Nor was it any more likely the Serbs now would do so—leaving the Clinton administration in a quandary.

The president was as torn as his multiple advisers. Tony Lake, his national security adviser, had urged new, more robust American leadership after the Serb assault on Srebrenica in March—but this had merely led to a further month of endless meetings, without a presidential decision. As one official told Elizabeth Drew, "It wasn't policymaking. It was group therapy—an existential debate over what is the role of America."

For example, after a five-hour marathon principals meeting in the Situation Room of the White House on May 1, President Clinton had dispatched Secretary of State Warren Christopher to Europe to obtain agreement for a belated but supposedly muscular new American-led "lift and strike" option. "You've been a great lawyer and advocate all these years," Clinton had said to him—"now you've really got your work cut out for you."

In his entire life the secretary of state never proved, however, as uninspiring as on his May Day trip to Europe. In a mocking reference to the currently emerging gays in the military compromise resolution ("Don't ask, don't tell, don't pursue"), one official had coined the injunction for the secretary of state's mission: "Don't ask, tell!"—but it was cruelly misplaced. Not only did Christopher carry no big stick, but he was all too soon torpedoed—by the president. Hearing of the lukewarm European response to Christopher's lukewarm presentation, Clinton lost heart. He had just read Robert Kaplan's *Balkan Ghosts* and an op-ed piece in the *New York Times* by Arthur Schlesinger Jr. describing the Balkans as the black hole of history, a seething morass of centuries-old ethnic and religious hatred and hostilities. As such, it was a historical cesspit that was unlikely to be purified by allowing more weapons into Bosnia to protect Muslims, or by airstrikes without ground support. Reading this, the president had consequently given up any hope of interceding effectively. As Secretary Aspin memorably put it in a call to Christopher, "We have a serious problem. We're out there pushing a policy that the president's not comfortable with . . . [the president having now] gone south on us." The secretary of state duly returned from Europe, empty-handed.

The Only Game in Town Is Dead

America's NATO partners were aghast at the alternating signals coming from Washington. Lord Owen, however, was relieved. In Clinton's about-turn he recognized a belated realism on the part of the president: that "lift and strike" (lift embargo, strike if the Serbs moved) was not, at that point, a viable option, with so many vulnerable peacekeepers on the ground who could be taken hostage. Forceful negotiation had to be the way forward.

Unfortunately for Owen and for the Bosnian Muslims, the president's realization had come too late. It left the Great Powers without any leverage—and certainly without credible negotiating force. Without tough American backing, the Vance-Owen UN/EC Plan, approved by the Russians and accepted and signed by the leaders of the Bosnian-Serb, Bosnian-Muslim, and Bosnian-Croat provinces, and approved by the presidents of Serbia and Croatia, was not ratified by the Bosnian-Serb Assembly in Pale—which, thanks to the failure of Christopher's mission, saw no come-back if it resisted a settlement. The Pale assemblymen thus voted, instead, to put it to a popular Bosnian-Serb referendum—which decisively rejected it. The Vance-Owen peace deal—"the only game in town"—died. The Western allies, NATO, and the UN were all back to square one.

Warren Christopher's trip, David Halberstam later chronicled, had not only "turned into an absolute disaster" but had cemented Secretary Christopher's reputation as a "weak man personally, who was bearing a weak policy from a weak administration." Worst of all, it became abundantly clear that Christopher, like House Democrats, was promoting a policy when "the president himself was not entirely convinced of its validity, or that following through on it was worth the price it might extract from his presidency." Clinton "was on board, but then again, they might find out that he was not exactly on board. . . ."

Halberstam was stating no more than the truth. "The president's reputation for breaking promises has made him an object of cartoonists' ridicule," foreign correspondents reported dejectedly from Washington.

"Many interest groups, such as Irish Americans, who hailed Mr. Clinton as a hero, are now openly critical." The political consequences for Democrats were, Conor O'Clery noted, now serious. "The Clinton stumbles have rejuvenated the demoralized Republican opposition. Senator Dole organized a major psychological defeat of the administration by filibustering its $16.3 billion stimulus package out of existence." The fight for the Treasury secretary's vacated senate seat looked grim for Democrats—promising in Texas "two Republican senators for the first time in memory. Mr. Clinton will be blamed. Last week's performance by the White House has driven Mr. Clinton's supporters to despair. It 'crystalised everything that seemed to be wrong', exposing 'a White House that now seemed much closer to Hollywood than to a town called Hope,' the New York Times reported yesterday. The conservative columnist William Safire was more scathing. Mr. Clinton's 'image of manly informality had been blown away by a hairdryer,' he wrote. The president might get away with abandoning the Bosnians 'but he will pay for trying to swagger through his presidency with $200 haircuts from Christophe.' "

CHAPTER FIFTEEN

POLITICS AS
A SPECTATOR SPORT

Feet of Clay

"Whooosshhhh!!" David Gergen, the roving editor of *U.S. News & World Report*, had written even before Hairgate and Travelgate. "To paraphrase Ross Perot, that sucking sound you hear is the air rushing out of Bill Clinton's balloon as he ends his first 100 days in office. Over the past two weeks, in an orgy of harsh assessments, enemies and friends alike have been sticking in so many pins that his presidency is losing altitude at an alarming rate."

The president "has brought many of these troubles on himself," Gergen—who had been a presidential adviser to a series of Republican presidents in the past—considered. By pledging to have "the most productive 100-day period in modern history," he'd guaranteed a sense of letdown. "Clinton needs to refocus attention on his economic plan, especially on the creation of jobs, and postpone his health care proposals until fall. Otherwise, he risks loss of both."

As the article had progressed, however, its tenor had become less critical, for "something serious is at risk," Gergen pointed out. "Over the past 30 years, America has had a series of broken presidencies: Five of the past six occupants have been driven from the Oval Office in defeat or despair. Only Ronald Reagan survived for two terms, and he too was running out of steam before it was over. With so much to do at home, America cannot afford the destruction of another presidency," the veteran adviser warned. "But that is where we are headed unless we regain our sensibility. We are making politics a spectator sport in which our only duty is to vote somebody into office and then retire to the grandstands. When our hero first arrives, we stand and cheer. But when we see he has feet of clay—and they all do—it's 'Throw the bum out!' No democracy can succeed as an entertainment.

"We owe each other more," Gergen continued, rising to his theme. "The press should show us Clinton's warts, but what about the rest of him? Will his proposal for a national service corps—a fine idea that has been strengthened by his staff—receive as much attention this week as, say, Panetta's remarks last week ['ill-chosen words to the press that his boss was in trouble and Congress might reject his key proposals']? When Education Secretary Richard Riley issued a major initiative for overhauling schools recently, it wound up on page A–28 of the *Washington Post*. Is that balance?" Gergen asked, rhetorically. And he ended with a plea for media sanity: "Bill Clinton has had the courage to focus the nation on its major needs of better jobs, better education and better health care, and he is trying to fix them. If he doesn't have all the right answers, we should stop jeering, get off the sidelines and help him find them. For the next 1,300 days, he is the only president we have."

Looking for Leadership

For Bosnians, the president's irresolution was certainly becoming a matter of life and death. Since January 1993, Joe Klein wrote in *Newsweek*, the president had been unable to make any decision on the use of force in Bosnia, as there was no clear consensus among his military chiefs, or his national security advisers, or his political team.

Dr. Albright, the ambassador to the UN, later blamed General Powell, the chairman of the Joint Chiefs of Staff. "Time and time again he led us up the hill of possibilities and dropped us off on the other side with the practical equivalent of 'No can do.' After hearing this for the umpteenth time, I asked in exasperation, 'What are you saving this superb military for, Colin, if we can't use it?' "

Dr. Albright, however, had as little understanding of the Pentagon as the rest of Clinton's cabinet. In actuality the Pentagon was not only willing to move into Bosnia in force if the president so decided, but was ready to do so—as General Gordon Sullivan later revealed. Whatever Dr. Albright might later aver, the Pentagon had, in truth, been "planning and training" to go into the Balkans "as early as April of 1992," under President Bush. By December 1992 U.S. troops, under NATO command, were in Macedonia (to contain any possible expansion of the conflict), with preparations being made for a much larger force. "The army was planning to go to the Balkans in 1992 in one form or another," Sullivan confirmed. "We weren't sure what we would do, but we were actually planning. Then in May and June of 1993 I met with the V Corps commander on the subject of the U.S. Army Europe in the Balkans. Now, Colin felt, I think, that getting involved in this open-ended war was not the answer. But you're asking me, not Colin Powell," he responded to the question a decade later. "I thought it was worth it. Because I don't think instability in central Europe—you can argue that it's south-eastern Europe, but still, given the ties that exist, economically, culturally, between the Balkans and central Europe, it is the same thing—instability in the Balkans means instability in central Europe. Which impacts on the [Western] alliance, which I view as critical to the well-being of the United States of America. And by the way, if it's important to the United States of America, it's important to the Europeans. The Europeans were looking for leadership from the United States. With troops on the ground. And it was not forthcoming. Only air."

Only the president, as commander in chief, could decide—and he wouldn't. As Joe Klein put it in May 1993, Clinton "kept revisiting the problem, churning it over and over again, trying to find consensus among advisers with different points of view. Vice President Al Gore and national security adviser Tony Lake favored the use of force: 'There are people on his staff who just want to go ahead and bomb, and damn the consequences,' said one deputy. Secretary of State Warren Christopher was opposed, at least initially, to military action. Defense Secretary Les Aspin favored action, but only with a clear-cut objective he could sell the chiefs, especially Powell. But all three agreed on the importance of a brisk decision-making process."

In the case of Bosnia, however, the president's ability to "bend himself into a pretzel" could have its advantages. "Look, indecision is a lot better than plunging in and doing something stupid," Klein quoted a Pentagon Clintophile. "He kept postponing a choice because there were no good choices. His instincts prevented him from letting a bunch of op-ed columnists buffalo him into a decision that might have wrecked his presidency."

Such caution was perfectly sensible, Klein conceded, but it masked the real failure of the new president: his "muddy message." "Quiet agonizing and indecision is one thing, but that's not what Clinton did: he described the Bosnian conflict in a manner that implied a moral imperative (though he was careful never to use the term), then allowed the impression to be conveyed that he was ready to take action (U.S. DECIDES TO USE FORCE ON SERBS IN BOSIAN WAR was one *Washington Post* headline) . . . and then, unable to secure allied support, he put the action 'on hold.' The message—to the allies, to the Serbs, to every lobbyist and politician in Washington, and to troublemakers around the globe was irresolution. This may not be so damaging to a presidency as getting stuck in a quagmire, but it will make it harder next time for Clinton to convince friend and foe alike that he is serious."

Dismissing Stephanopoulos

In the atrocities and genocides to come, *Newsweek*'s warning would seem sadly prophetic. In the meantime, reorganizing his office, yet aware that the problem was still getting worse, not better, McLarty now hit upon yet another new staffing idea—a replacement for Stephanopoulos.

Inviting David Gergen, whom he had never met in his life, to lunch at the White House, McLarty made sure the president accidentally "dropped by to say hello," while the diminutive McLarty asked the six-foot-six Republican guru for his advice on what was wrong with the headquarters of world democracy.

There followed a flurry of phone calls, meetings, consultations with Hillary. . . . Then, on May 28, 1993, at 7:30 a.m., following near-midnight discussions to expedite the announcement, the president confirmed to reporters that, as rumored, the now thirty-two-year-old George Stephanopoulos had been removed as communications director (though given a consolation post as adviser) and Republican David Gergen, former communications director under President Reagan, and architect of the selling of Reaganomics, had been brought in, under the noble title of counselor, to take his place: a Republican serving a Democrat.

Stephanopoulos, naturally, was mortified—just as his own victim, Mickey Kantor, had been the previous November. "Not my happiest day in the White House," Stephanopoulos later confided. "And although it was, in part, well deserved," he admitted, "I took the fall for a lot of the problems in the first six months."

Not only did the firing seem "a betrayal of the things that we had fought for" in the campaign, in Stephanopoulos's view, but it was patently unfair. "I knew I couldn't show any unhappiness, or displeasure, or the blood would be in the water, and I would have no chance of keeping any job in the White House," Stephanopoulos recalled. "But there was this sense of the kids getting blamed for a lot of the things that weren't their fault. The kids didn't pick Zoë Baird. The kids didn't do the travel office. The kids didn't do gays in the military. . . ." And the "kids" didn't choose Lani Guinier— the next thorn in the administration's side.

CHAPTER SIXTEEN

LANI GUINIER

Using a Lot of Capital

While David Gergen, the new communications supremo, and his wife were completing their Bermuda vacation, Hillary and her cabal of female staffers and associates—Patsy Thomasson, Susan Thomases, Melanne Verveer, Eleanor Dean Acheson—added yet another obstacle to Bill Clinton's presidential coming of age: proudly picking Lani Guinier, who had attended Yale Law School with Hillary, to be the president's nominee as assistant attorney general in charge of civil rights.

Bill and Hillary had both attended Guinier's wedding on Martha's Vineyard in the mid-eighties. She was a woman. She was black. And she was a close friend. How Hillary failed to heed warnings—from Democrats like Senator Edward Kennedy, as well as Republicans—that Guinier's academic writings as a professor at the University of Pennsylvania Law School would make her too controversial as a civil rights nominee (rather than as a nominee for a normal post in the justice system) for a president with only a 43 percent popular mandate was, in retrospect, difficult to credit. Hillary's former boss and now White House counsel, Bernie Nussbaum, had yet again given poor advice, after having carefully read Guinier's articles: assuring the first lady that Guinier's controversial views on black minority rights, though clearly unconstitutional, would not be a negative in asking Congress to authorize her to take charge of the Civil Rights Division.

There had thus sometimes seemed, in the wake of gays in the military, Zoë Baird, Kimba Wood, Travelgate, Hairgate, and Hillary's secretive health care reform process (Hillary was soon sued for holding closed hearings), to be a kind of collective political doom wish among the friends, colleagues, and cronies who served the new king and his female co-president. It was as if, with a chief executive who had no ability to make clear decisions, and who refused to appoint an able chief of staff to help toughen his steel, there was no one who was clearly and irrevocably in charge. Stephanopoulos was right about the "kids" not being to blame for many of the early Clinton foul-ups—but Stephanopoulos overlooked the problem: that the task of the staff of a busy, activist president was as much to stop him doing unwise things as to help him do good ones. For this role, none of the president's in-house advisers save perhaps Robert Rubin had the maturity and toughness to stand up not only to the president but to the first lady.

"No matter how talented, two people cannot occupy that space, jointly making decisions," Gergen would later write. "There is no place for a co-presidency." This, however, Gergen wrote when he was a public service professor, in 20/20 hindsight. With the president of the United States begging him by telephone in the spring of 1993—"I'm in trouble. I need your help"—Gergen had been unable to say no: the very word he would have needed to be able to utter to be of any real use as counselor to Bill Clinton.

As usual, the president himself procrastinated: his big, loyal heart telling him to back his wife's choice of Guinier as part of the Clintons' contribution to gender and racial diversity, yet his seismically sensitive antennae telling him to be cautious, knowing Guinier's views were controversial and contentious, and that his deficit reduction and economic bill hung in the balance.

It was in this way that Bill Clinton had, once again, woken to find himself hoist by his own petard. If, encountering opposition in the Senate, he ditched the Guinier nomination—a prominent black woman with a Jewish mother—he might offend the Black Caucus in Congress at a crucial legislative moment. If he did not ditch her, however, he would, in order to secure her confirmation, have to back her with all his power and authority as president, if the Senate Judiciary Committee defied him.

The committee chairman, Senator Biden, had kindly warned Clinton in advance over Baird. Once again on May 27, a month after Clinton had announced Guinier's nomination, Biden again cautioned him. "Mr. President, I'll make you a deal. If you tell me," he assured the nation's chief executive, "or someone else calls me and says you have read the [controversial academic] articles [written by Guinier] and you stand by them and you'll stick with her, then I'll support her."

Asking that he stick with his nominee was, unfortunately, asking the impossible of Bill Clinton. Biden afterwards recalled how he had made himself crystal clear: "Mr. President, if you want to fight this I'll go to the wall with you, but I don't want to start down the road and then I get a call saying, 'We're withdrawing her.' " The president, Biden warned, must weigh carefully whom he wanted, in advance, and be prepared to fight for his nominee—knowing it wouldn't be easy, and he might make enemies. "Mr. President, you're going to have to use up a lot of capital."

This was precisely what President Clinton had not wished to hear and had not dared do, as June approached—in part because it was Hillary's staff who had proposed Guinier, not his own. Senator David Pryor, his Arkansas predecessor as governor, had put it bluntly to the president's consiglieri, Bruce Lindsey: "You don't have the capital in your bank account to do this, and you still have to get your economic program passed."

Typically, by shelving the problem for a month, in the hope that his economic bill would first pass and senators would grow weary of challenging his nominees, Bill Clinton had chosen his much vaunted "third way"—but, as so often in the freshman president's case, such postmodernism could easily be construed as a euphemism for indecision, or procrastination in the hope that a problem would somehow resolve itself. It hadn't, however. And now the day of reckoning came.

Two Minutes to Midnight

On Wednesday, June 2, 1993, with his economic bill still at issue in the Senate, and his health care reform therefore postponed until later in the year—possibly even the next year—President Clinton seemed ready to make a decision: Guinier's views were too "hot" for the senators; she would have to be dumped.

Such dilatoriness, in the train of such poor White House vetting and virtual cowardice by the chief of staff (who sent two emissaries to press Guinier to withdraw voluntarily, but did not empower them to order her to do so), now led to farce. "I'm not going to withdraw, and what I want is a hearing," Guinier had feistily countered—and she had gone on Ted Koppel's *Nightline* to get nationally heard, defending herself and her views in advance of a Senate hearing she still insisted upon.

The following morning the vice president tried to reason with the president to be firm, but still the president resisted, afraid to tell Guinier in person or on the telephone, and anxious, too, at the prospect of losing Guinier's many supporters in the civil rights movement—especially the Black Caucus in Congress.

As always, the president did not blame himself for giving his unelected wife the authority to nominate such a controversial figure—one whose views were well-known to Hillary and her associates. Instead he blamed others, telling Senator Biden he'd been assured by two constitutional law professors there was nothing to worry about in Guinier's views. "He was really angry about that," Biden recalled, the president's whole tone crying: " 'How the hell did this happen again?' "

It had happened because the former governor could not yet govern the United States—at least not without an effective Betsey Wright-style chief of staff. Even Paul Begala, whose views were out of sync with Congress, had been convinced that Guinier's withdrawal was a "no-brainer": a contentious nomination fight that would simply polarize people over an issue that, like gays in the military, was not even a central plank in the New Democrats' centrist agenda. Guinier's nomination had been, from the start, a dead end. Now, in terms of political strength, the president was hemorrhaging badly in polls, as well as in congressional support. He "doesn't have much blood left," was Begala's main concern.

The president's suave confidant and golf partner, Vernon Jordan, when summoned to the White House to give an impartial recommendation, had—as ever—been curt and to the point. "It's two minutes to midnight, Mr. President," Jordan had warned Bill Clinton as an African American, but most of all, as a loyal American who believed in the institution of the presidency. "It's time to decide."

Midnight had come, but still the forty-second president found himself unable to make up his mind.

Clinton's personal loyalty to Guinier as a friend told him to permit her, at least, her day in court: to be allowed to defend herself, lest her own career be destroyed; his loyalty to his office as president had, however, told him to be presidential—to make the tough decision to drop her immediately, before her appointment became more contentious in the nation, or his administration became further defined by his own indecisiveness.

Right-wing conservative moralists, like the former education secretary William Bennett (who had admired Bill Clinton as an education-minded governor and had appointed Hillary, whom he also admired, to an education commission), now began to see Clinton as the point man for "soft-core relativists": a president lacking in moral resolve; a prisoner not of his torn conscience, but of his lack of conscience; a man adrift in a moral-less, principle-less world in which, masked by the rhetoric of communitarianism and public duty, only personal ambition and survival really mattered.

Bill Clinton disputed that judgment. His spotless reputation as a student, indeed his whole adult career, was testament to his genuine communitarian idealism rather than his personal greed—something that his lack of a home he could call his own, after twenty years in politics, best demonstrated. What the followers of Ronald Reagan and Margaret Thatcher refused to see in their single-mindedness, Clinton felt, was that although ultimate victory in the Cold War seemed to have been achieved by bankrupting the Soviet Union—Reagan's "Evil Empire"—in a superpower arms race, the real victory of democracy and freedom over the ideology of communism had in fact been achieved by decades of patience and resilience: George Kennan's policy of containment and of talking, not conquest. Vietnam had achieved nothing—whereas firm containment, behind which free societies had been able to develop their modern economies without the stifling restrictions of communist bureaucracy, had.

Thus arose a tragic, indeed politically fatal, misconception, as men like Bennett misconstrued Bill Clinton's prevarications to be the result of lack of principle, whereas to a large extent Clinton's failure was that of too many principles—each one urging its competing merits on his receptive, compassionate mind.

Even the simplest decisions became torments for the president as he sought to choose between convictions. His agile brain took lightning stock of the ongoing, fast-moving drama of political life—a life in which every stance, once reached, seemed outdated or displaced by another, while the president sought to see each and every side and dimension of an issue before he could finally, wholeheartedly promote it. "He has not yet gotten it in his gut" was the way one aide described Clinton's intellectual process at the time—the president weighing his personal loyalty to Guinier as a dear friend against her chances of successful confirmation by the Senate; his own loss of authority and stature if she didn't get confirmed against the current damage he was suffering to his own agenda, Guinier publicly parading her contentious views on national television and implying that they reflected those of the president, who had in April nominated her. . . . Yet still the president could not utter the simple word: No.

The Squish Factor

As Joe Klein had written in *Newsweek*, Bill Clinton's prodigious ability to see every side of an argument, and even agree with it, inevitably led "to the question that every discussion of Bill Clinton always gets around to: does he have a larger sense of purpose? Is there a core—are there edges—to his marshmallowy, all-inclusive empathy? There have been endless debates over whether or not he is a 'new' Democrat. He is. He believes passionately in the agenda laid out by the moderate Democratic Leadership Council"— the group that Clinton helped found in 1985 to move the Democratic Party toward the center. "But he also believes, passionately, in the welfare-state liberal agenda espoused by Marian Wright Edelman's Children's Defense Fund. And he also believes in the industrial policy espoused by the Economic Policy Institute. Passionately," Klein mocked.

"He is a communitarian and a libertarian," the *Newsweek* guru summed up. "And he also believes in Ralph Nader-style litigation liberalism. You name it, if a Democratic faction believes in it, he does, too."

This was, ultimately, the Squish Factor, Clinton having by sheer force of personality and intelligence "neutered the eternal political question— what's he for?—and raised a darker, more perverse test of his leadership: What, if anything, is he against?"

Having at last read for himself Guinier's views, in her law journal articles, the president appeared to awake from a long sleep. Shaking his head, he declared that he did not, actually, concur with the views of his nominee.

Face to Face with Guinier

On June 3, 1993, the president held a pow-wow with his closest advisers at the White House—and from that emerged the decision to summon Lani Guinier for her first face-to-face meeting with the president for over a month, since he nominated her. Forty-five minutes late, the president asked his old friend to sit by him as he sank into his favorite yellow chair by the fireplace in the Oval Office.

With his deputy communications director, Ricki Seidman, as a witness, Bill Clinton nevertheless found it as hard as ever to carry out the political execution. Far from making it easy, moreover, Guinier urged him to go ahead with her Senate nomination hearings, believing senators would judge her as a whole person, not just by her writings, and would in the end confirm her.

Outside the Oval Office, the president's new counselor, David Gergen, was having a near seizure. Half an hour had passed without the door opening.

Gergen had already hinted to reporters that the president was dropping Guinier's nomination; he was thus forced to tell those who phoned him on deadline for the next morning's newspaper that "he could no longer say for sure what would happen." Would the president stand by her—or fire her? Nobody would hazard a guess.

"The president never explicitly told Guinier to withdraw," *Time* magazine recorded, and quoted "a source close to her. 'He went around it 25 different ways, and she never volunteered anything.'" Finally, plucking up his courage, the president did what he had to do. He did not agree with her published convictions, he explained to her, namely that blacks should be accorded special rights beyond those granted under the United States constitution: especially not exclusive rights to vote for their own local, state, and federal representatives in the legislatures of the nation. The cards might still be stacked against blacks, as a minority, almost a century and a half after the ending of slavery, he granted, but the United States Constitution was the Constitution. It was the basis of American law, whose terms were monitored, policed, and upheld by the Justice Department—a department in which she had declared her willingness to serve, not subvert. The weeks leading up to the Senate hearing would be "death by a thousand cuts," which "would not be good for you" and, worse still, "would not be good for the country. . . ."

"The trio at last emerged from the 75-minute session with reddened eyes," *Time* reported, "and 45 minutes later, the president mounted the podium in the press room to kill the nomination. Gripping the lectern and raising his fists, showing more emotion than he had expressed at any time since the dog days of New Hampshire, he said, 'I cannot fight a battle I know is divisive, that is an uphill battle, that is distracting to the country, if I do not believe in the ground of the battle.' He added, 'This has nothing to do with the political center. This has to do with my center.'"

The White House press correspondents, amazed at the president's mention of an actual center to his political beliefs, scurried away to file their delayed stories, but as Margaret Carlson and Michael Duffy learned for *Time*'s account, "As if that soul baring was not enough, Clinton continued the confessional at a White House dinner. 'It was the hardest decision I've had to make since I became president,' he told guests. 'I love her,' he said of Guinier, a 20-year friend of the Clintons. 'If she called me and told me she needed $5,000, I'd take it from my account and send it to her, no questions asked.'"

How, after the failed nominations of Zoë Baird and Kimba Wood, could the White House have got it wrong again? Gergen secretly wondered, as he vainly sought to mollify his former colleagues in the fourth estate. The president "suffered simultaneous public mockery of both his competence (one headline writer dubbed him 'Bumblin' Bill') and his conviction ('President Jell-O')," *Time* noted of the very individual it had made Man of the Year for 1992. "His downward spiral in popularity and his shift in positions are creating a sense of public vertigo. More than ever, Americans regard their new president with two nagging questions: Is he up to the job? and What does he stand for? Clinton must know that if he does not answer those questions soon, he may never be able to. One longtime friend who spoke with the president by telephone last week reported that he never sounded 'so sad in his life.'"

A Rolling Disaster

Finding a centrist core that would be clearly discernible to himself, to Congress, and to the nation was, in truth, only half Bill Clinton's battle. What the correspondents of *Time* magazine could not spotlight was the reality that their former colleague was now discovering on the inside: the power vacuum at the heart of the White House. Asked by Gergen to explain the management structure of the White House, McLarty had drawn two boxes, one on top of the other, and below them a horizontal line, from which dangled a plethora of further boxes. The chief of staff was represented by the lower of the top two boxes, with everyone else, represented in boxes, reporting to him. Who, then, was in the top box? Gergen asked innocently. If it was the president, where were the boxes of the vice president and first lady?

McLarty blushed. Every White House had its own unique patina, he explained as he shrugged. In the top box were Bill and Al. And Hillary. "All three of them sign off on big decisions."

Gergen frowned.

"You'll just have to get used to it," McLarty added.

Gergen swallowed, but was dumbfounded. The setup was, as he later put it, "a rolling disaster as far as I could tell," causing "untold delays, confusions, and divided loyalties." Yet neither he nor anyone else dared to tell this to the president. The merry-go-round of muddle, confusion, disagreement, and indecision was simply allowed to turn unabated—with each new convert expected just to "get used to it." "A member of the cabinet or staff might think that the president had decided something on Tuesday only to find that he was in a different place on Wednesday because," Gergen recalled, "he had since talked to his wife or the vice president."

Indecision had become Clinton's fourth name—a quality with distinctly negative appeal in a "can-do" nation, as his polls showed. Yet instead of getting better, it seemed doomed to get worse.

CHAPTER SEVENTEEN

A SHRINKING PRESIDENT

A Meandering Amble

The Guinier saga was, unfortunately, replicated in a raft of other early Clinton administration cases. For example, there was the president's dissatisfaction with the current director of the FBI, William Sessions—and his failure, even after seven months, to decide on a replacement, which resulted in the appointment of arguably the most disastrous FBI director in the history of the agency, Louis J. Freeh, who could not be removed for seven years.

Equally, there was a three-month procrastination over the choice of a new Supreme Court justice to replace the conservative justice Byron White—who had given ample notice of his impending retirement specifically to avoid a last-minute hiatus. With plenty of time to prepare for Justice White's successor, President Clinton had been given the first opportunity as a Democrat since President Lyndon Johnson to be able to select a Supreme Court justice—thus allowing him, if he wished, to reverse what was seen as the court's long march towards more conservative jurisprudence under the intellectual leadership of Justice Antonin Scalia.

Once again Clinton had held out a teasing carrot to Democratic governor Mario Cuomo—yet had declined to actually offer him the vacant seat on the bench, man-to-man or even telephone-to-telephone. No one knew why.

Diffidence? Uncertainty lest Republican members of the Senate take revenge for the Robert Bork and Douglas Ginsberg nominations in 1987, by savaging Cuomo's chances? Or was the new president—as in the case of his own chief of staff—simply psychologically incapable of appointing a candidate who would somehow, by his intelligence, competence, or renown, compete with, challenge, and perhaps upstage the still wobbly president?

Whatever the case, Clinton behaved less than honorably: because he was unable, when dangling the Supreme Court carrot via an aide, to reassure the skeptical New York governor that, as president, he would stand behind him, if the Republicans chose to contest his confirmation in the Senate, Cuomo withdrew his name from consideration.

As a consequence, no less than fifty alternative candidates for the Supreme Court had been considered over the spring and early summer of 1993, with the final choice narrowing down to Judge Stephen Breyer, chief judge in the U.S. Court of Appeals in Boston.

Loyal David Dreyer, running the communications team under Mark Gearan, was willing to go to the wall for his master, but even he allowed that "there were some episodes in the drama, like I guess consideration of who the Supreme Court nominee would be—where, in the eleventh hour and the fifty-ninth minute, a new name would pop up and all of a sudden for that minute that person would become the best possible choice. So there were flaws," he conceded. Overall, though, he still maintained that "this was a good way to make decisions, not a bad one." Better a meandering amble, Dreyer felt in the wake of Clinton's successor in the White House, than a rush to judgment. And Justice Breyer seemed an excellent choice.

The Ginsburg Nomination

Detailed vetting of the check stubs of the latest favorite by Vince Foster revealed, unfortunately, that Justice Breyer had a familiar case of Baird-itis: this time, trouble with his taxable payments to his domestic cleaner. . . .

In the end, with yet another major administration appointment fiasco brewing, Clinton met with a respected Jewish judge, Ruth Bader Ginsburg. Ginsburg was almost old enough to be his mother. Though she lacked Virginia Clinton Kelley's vivid personality, her long struggle against institutional prejudice against women fascinated the son of a nurse-anesthetist. She fit Hillary's feminist agenda and the president's diversity-in-government agenda. She was clean with regard to her employment of domestic servants. She offered no threat to Clinton's self-image—indeed was "charismatically challenged," as Al Gore, who had a certain lack of charisma himself, had put it.

Charisma was mercifully not essential on the Supreme Court, however, and at last, on June 14, 1993, Clinton publicly announced Ginsburg's nomination, weeping real tears as Ginsburg gave her carefully rehearsed life story to the assembled press.

The president's tears were those of a son honoring, symbolically, his own ailing mother and her generation—as well as tears of joy that he had finally found a nominee he could unashamedly stand behind: his own nominee, someone with whom he felt an emotional, even sentimental, connection.

Something, Anything, Must Be Done

Tears?

To Elizabeth Drew they seemed unseemly for a head of state who'd already heard Ginsburg's story first-hand, before they emerged before the cameras. "Partly this was a matter of generation," Drew allowed, "but others of his generation didn't feel so compelled to tell everyone their feelings. Its most serious effect was to eat away at the dignity of office a president needs if he wants people to follow him." Searching its library, a newspaper turned up at least a dozen recent cases of the president tearing-up in public. There were yet more tears, too, at the dedication of the U.S. Holocaust Memorial Museum—as well as shame, when Nobel laureate Elie Wiesel turned from his seat in the row in front. Wiesel there and then begged the president of the United States to do something to save the helpless Bosnians from Serbian "ethnic cleansing." "I cannot sleep since what I have seen. We must do something to stop the bloodshed," Wiesel—a Nazi death-camp survivor—pleaded with the president. "Something, anything, must be done." The president was known to "feel your pain." What use were tears of compassion, if the president of the United States *did* nothing?

With Senators Biden, Dole, and others pressing for a U.S. response to the killing in Bosnia, President Clinton had pledged at a news conference to announce "tougher steps" within days—but he hadn't, as usual, done anything. "We have no ability to close around here," one aide had lamented, while Vernon Jordan saw the lack of Washington experience among White House staffers as an almost insurmountable handicap: "There's nobody over there," Jordan said, "that's ever worked in the White House before." In a modern world where "personnel is policy," as Jordan aptly phrased it, such inexperience was a terrible mistake. *Time* magazine had openly mocked the chief executive on its cover as "THE INCREDIBLE SHRINKING PRESI-DENT"—yet still Clinton could not bring himself to dismiss members of his own staff. Even when he'd finally fired the struggling George Stephanopoulos as director of White House communications, it was only to compensate him by appointing him special counsel to the president, lest his feelings be hurt, or Clinton find himself as president pilloried by the "kids" for supplanting Stephanopoulos with a Republican like David Gergen. A party of sixty House Democrats, meeting Clinton in late May, had found the president "dispirited," and where they had expected "evangelism" they had gotten "a very rambling" address.

Clearly, the president needed help, and Christopher and Jordan, as his former directors of the transition, had nobly attempted to offer it. Late in May, the two disappointing co-directors of the Clinton transition team had sat with the president after dinner on the Truman balcony and had told him the bitter truth: that his administration was in trouble, and the trouble was with him. The president had to stop trying to be his own chief of staff, they argued.

Unfortunately they gave the wrong advice. Neither Jordan nor Christopher, as fat-cat lawyers, had any better notion of effective political command than their president. Having diagnosed the president's sickness, they had then recommended a medicine even worse than the disease: namely that Clinton now step back and empower his utterly ineffective chief of staff, Mack McLarty, to act for him!

Wearily, the president had shaken his head—knowing they were wrong, but not what would be right.

CHAPTER EIGHTEEN

VINCE FOSTER

Suicide

Hillary, so often a tower of strength when her husband was low, was beset by her own problems. Not only was she still chairing the president's Task Force on National Health Care Reform, which had run into legal difficulties (for holding secret meetings), but she was also attempting to carry out the traditional duties of first lady, to be mother to a teenage daughter in a new city and school, and to second-guess all her husband's major decisions and appointments. Such a responsibility—with Whitewater investigations in the background—was more than any normal person could be expected to bear, but Hillary was a fighter by nature and supported by a deeply loyal coterie of assistants and friends. Only when personal tragedies hit her did she show signs of collapsing under the strain.

Thus on April 7, when her beloved—yet also feared—father died in Little Rock, Hillary had gone into a sort of emotional rigor mortis, even giving way to dark thoughts and prognostications about the moral state of America. Then, with the economic bill still stalled in the Senate—forcing further postponement of her health bill—she heard of a further tragedy, affecting one of her closest colleagues from the Rose Law Firm, and number two on the White House legal team: Vince Foster.

The top graduate of his year at the University of Arkansas Law School, a father of three, upright and honest to a fault, Foster was not only deputy White House counsel, but the Clintons' personal lawyer for their financial affairs. He had thus kept their private and personal records safely locked in his office—records the Clintons had, naturally, been anxious to keep from prying eyes. Unknown to his colleagues, he had recently been seeking psychiatric help for depression—aggravated by the White House travel saga (which Foster's deputy, William Kennedy, had handled). This had then been followed by a lawsuit against Hillary for running the health care reform commission in closed meetings, without legal authority to do so. These problems had taken their toll. Hillary's snapped "Fix it, Vince!" had especially hurt him, as had accusations in the *Wall Street Journal* of cronyism in the White House. The Senate hearings worried him to the point of paranoia, certain that "'they' would use my hearings as a way to ask questions about Hillary," Webb Hubbell recalled him saying, as well as Foster's plaintive cry: "But Webb, they can destroy anybody if they want to—no matter how good a person you are. It can be vicious." Having eaten a hamburger at his desk—brought in a brown paper bag by his Arkansas colleague Marsha Scott—he had abruptly left the White House early on the afternoon of July 20, 1993, and did not return.

No one, surprisingly, had questioned the workaholic's unusual absence. At approximately six o'clock that evening, a body was found, after an anonymous tip-off, in a small park not far from Foster's house, across the Potomac, below a revetment near one of the cannons that had defended the capital in the Civil War.

The president was in the White House Library, appearing on *Larry King Live* after dismissing the FBI director, William Sessions (who had refused the attorney general's request that he resign). He was busy explaining his appointment of Judge Freeh as the new director of the FBI, and the announcement of his new "Don't ask, don't tell, don't pursue" sexuality policy for the military, which he'd made public at Fort McNair, across the Potomac—"not a perfect solution," as he'd explained to skeptical students at the National Defense University the day before, or "identical with some of my own goals. It is an honorable compromise."

President Clinton's performance was so good on Larry King's program, however, that he was asked on air by King—and agreed—to extend the hour-long live program by another half an hour, after the break for commercials. It was around 9:45 P.M. and the White House staff, watching the president perform so confidently, but having just heard a report that the body found in the park was that of Vince Foster, cringed. "So we're like, 'Oh, my God. We've got to put the kibosh on this extra time,'" recalled Dee Dee Myers, who had been concerned not to let word get out prematurely. "We're not sure who all's been notified," she was thinking. "I mean, your head starts working in strange ways. But we're afraid that somebody might pick it up on a police scanner in Virginia or something, and call the show and inform the president on the air."

Arranging with the producer to block any such calls, the president's staff, at the break, insisted it was a wrap. "At first I was irritated," Clinton later wrote, "thinking my staff was worried that I might make a mistake if I kept going, but the look in Mack's eyes told me something else was going on."

There was. Leading the president from the library up to the private quarters, McLarty broke the sad news. "Holding back tears, he told me Vince Foster was dead," Clinton later wrote. "Vince had left the Rose Garden after the ceremony for Louis Freeh, driven out to Fort Marcy Park, and shot himself with an old revolver that was a family heirloom. . . . Hillary called me from Little Rock. She already knew and was crying." As Hillary searched for an explanation and wondered what she might have done to avert such a terrible act, the president searched his own memory—recalling how, at the Rose Garden ceremony, he'd caught sight of Foster under an old magnolia tree, smiling. . . .

The president then "came back down," Dee Dee Myers recounted, "and did something—the only time in my tenure at the White House that I ever knew he did it—which was: left the building without the press. Just got into the limo with just a lead car and a tail service car and went over to the Fosters to try to console the family."

While the president offered his condolences, Hillary had other concerns. At the White House there followed a mad scramble of telephone calls from the first lady to her assistant, Maggie Williams, as well as to Susan Thomases, and to the White House counsel, Bernie Nussbaum, instructing her staff to remove sensitive private and privileged files from Foster's office in the West Wing—before the Park Police or the FBI could seal it.

Opening the Door to Suspicion

Foster's death was the first suicide in senior echelons of the American government since May 1949, when James Forrestal (whom President Truman had fired as secretary of defense) flung himself from a high window at Bethesda Naval Hospital, where he was being treated for depression.

Foster's death rocked the Washington establishment, stunning his friends and causing his enemies to wonder whether it could really have been self-injury. "The next day the press asked me, you know, well, 'Why,

why, why?'" Dee Dee Myers recalled. "And I said, 'It's unknowable. . . . Why does anyone take their life? You can never satisfactorily answer that question.' And of course, that just opened the door. 'What is it you're trying to hide? Why can't you answer that question?'"

Had Nussbaum and Hillary's staff not secretly searched the office and removed the files and hidden them in a private closet in the family quarters of the White House, or had Nussbaum, or the Park Police, or the FBI immediately found the quasi-suicide note—lying in pieces in Foster's briefcase in the White House office—and revealed it, much unfortunate speculation could have been avoided. Instead, a pattern of concealment was initiated that would lead, almost inevitably, to suspicion—and further Whitewater investigations.

"Hillary and I love his wife, Lisa, and their three children, and we want to draw them close to our hearts and keep them in our prayers in this painful moment of grief," the president stated meanwhile in an announcement at the White House. "His family has lost a loving husband and father, America has lost a gifted and loyal public servant, and Hillary and I have lost a true and trusted friend. My deepest hope is that whatever drew Vince away from us this evening, his soul will receive the grace and salvation that his good life and good works earned."

Such genuine thoughts, masking real grief and real tears, were exemplary, but as Dee Dee Myers admitted, "of course, once again, we didn't handle it as well as we could have."

This was an understatement. Was the secret removal of files from the dead man's office by Hillary's staff, in the hours after Foster's death, evidence of mere bungling—or something more sinister? Tongues quickly wagged—and in the end, a Park Police investigation, a Justice Department investigation by special counsel Robert Fiske, and, later, a Senate Banking Committee investigation would all be called for, and carried out—but with no indication of foul play. Even a private investigation by liberal criminal reporter Dan Moldea, sponsored by a right-wing publisher, turned up nothing save the sad reality of self-extermination.

The Rock of Gibraltar

In a way, the death of Vince Foster capped the whole sorry story of the Clinton White House in its first six months. It was, a Washington columnist wrote, "a cosmic kick in the stomach for an administration that started six months ago with such high energy and lofty aspirations, only to weather one strange and overwhelming calamity after another." "People are like zombies," a White House staff member said, describing the "funereal" atmosphere after Foster's death. "This will have affected the president more than anything else that has happened here in the last six months," another aide remarked. A senior Clinton adviser lamented: "The event was sad in and of itself, and sadder yet because the president doesn't deserve it. Everybody here grieves for Vince Foster, but it's just that the whole thing seems so unfair in so many different ways."

Pondering such a seemingly inexplicable death and its aftermath, "it has seemed that for every loud and confident expression of ambition, idealism and sometimes even hubris from Clinton & Co.," wrote Lloyd Grove in the *Washington Post*, "there has been an equal and opposite dose of harsh reality to subvert the intended message of accomplishment and hope: those early flaps over gays in the military and the misguided choices for attorney general; the stinging defeat of the economic stimulus package; Travelgate, Hairgate, the unpleasantly messy process of filling a Supreme Court seat. . . . "

"One of the things I'm glad to say has not materialized is a sense of bitterness about the culture here in Washington," a Clinton staffer maintained. "People seem to be treating it as very much a personalized, private matter. . . . I haven't found anyone who says, 'It's them—it's Washington that did it to him.' "

The president defiantly refused to see in the suicide either the signs of a "Gotcha!" Republican Washington culture, out to subvert his administration, or an implied, mortal critique of his stewardship. When a reporter suggested Foster's suicide might have been related to things that went wrong in the White House, the president shook his head. "I don't think so," he said. "I certainly don't think that can explain it, and I certainly don't think it's accurate."

But was it not? Clinton was tired and understandably upset. He'd been up till 2 A.M., his aides said, "perplexed like everyone else," asking himself why Foster—whom he'd telephoned the previous night, because, without Hillary in the White House, he simply felt "lonely"—could have done such a thing, without anyone save his doctor knowing he was suicidal, and without leaving a note.

Certainly Bill Clinton, unloading some of his own concerns, hadn't realized how near the edge of death his oldest friend from Hope had been. "I lived with my grandparents in a modest little house across from Vince

Foster's nice, big, white brick house," he recalled. "And our back yards touched. I just kept thinking in my mind of when we were so young, sitting on the ground in the back yard, throwing knives into the ground and seeing if we were adroit enough to make them stick. For more years than most of us like to admit, in times of difficulty, he was normally the Rock of Gibraltar while other people were having trouble. No one could ever remember the reverse being the case. So I don't know if we'll ever know." And he added: "It is very important that his life not be judged simply by how it ended, because Vince Foster was a wonderful man." None of it made any sense. "Even if you had a whole set of objective reasons, that wouldn't be why it happened, because you could get a different, bigger, more burdensome set of objective reasons. . . . So what happened was a mystery about something inside of him."

What became apparent to serious observers, however, was that, beyond the personal torment of a very buttoned-up individual, Foster's decision to take his own life, despite his responsibilities towards a wife and three children, did represent a sort of protest against the Washington vulture culture. Not even the good-natured president, straining to think the best of Foster and not to give in to victim-like thoughts, could ignore that aspect.

Others speculated openly. The *Wall Street Journal*'s allegations that Foster had behaved dishonestly over the travel office firings, in deference to the first lady, Foster had found especially hurtful—especially its pairing of Foster with Oliver North. "He may have felt hounded," Simon Tisdall, Washington correspondent of the London *Guardian*, wrote. "He may have been an honourable man who took such matters to heart. That, at least, would explain why Washington found him so unusual: for it was Washington that killed him."

Those who ridiculed such a suggestion by a foreign newspaper correspondent were brought rudely to their senses, however, a week later when the White House finally revealed the existence of the torn, handwritten piece of paper that "appeared to be a suicide note," Myers stated.

The document, ripped into twenty-seven pieces, turned out to be a list Foster had compiled, at his wife's suggestion, before going to see a psychiatrist, of the things that were bothering him—and as Dee Dee Myers now said, the text "did show him to be in a distressed state of mind or troubled state of mind per work. Maybe he just crawled into a space so dark he couldn't see his way out."

At first the document itself had been withheld for reasons of privacy. When the Justice Department finally released a copy, however, the hand-written note smacked of something worse than overwork. More than any document of the early Clinton administration it recorded the growing magnitude of the White House culture clash—the embattled "them and us" spirit coloring the corridors of the presidential palace, six months after the inauguration:

"I made mistakes from ignorance, inexperience and overwork," Foster acknowledged, but "I did not knowingly violate any law or standard of conduct." He accused the FBI of lying in its report to the attorney general, the press of covering up illegal benefits they'd received via the travel office, the Republican party of lying and misrepresentation—as well as covering up a prior investigation. He accused the White House ushers of profiting from redecoration of the private rooms of the White House. "The public will never believe the innocence of the Clintons and their loyal staff," his note ended ominously. "The WSJ [*Wall Street Journal*] editors lie without consequence." And then, hauntingly: "I was not meant for the job or the spotlight of public life in Washington. Here ruining people is considered sport."

Almost Paranoid Grief

Foster's suicide affected Hillary more deeply than anyone else at the White House—indeed she kept going, she later recorded, only by "sheer willpower."

Webb Hubbell found himself equally upset. He later recalled how, after Hillary telephoned from Little Rock to urge him to "hurry home" (to Arkansas), the two of them drove each other to near dementia in their grief. Foster had, it appeared, telephoned an old colleague at the Rose Law Firm in the days before his death to ask about Hillary Clinton's blind trust—anxious lest it become a target of investigation. To another colleague he was reported to have lamented, enigmatically, that it was "too late to save Bill and me, but maybe I can still protect Sheila [Foster's sister] and Webb." He had told both Hillary and Hubbell he was certain his telephone was bugged by an outside agency.

Such concerns raised inevitable doubts among survivors shocked by his death and unsure what to believe. When Webb Hubbell met Hillary again at the funeral service in Little Rock on July 23, Hillary even asked him, in his role as number three in the Department of Justice, to investigate whether Foster might have been the victim of an illegal navy hit squad!

Hubbell, who had secrets of his own and of the president to guard, was uncertain how to take Hillary's request. The hit squad was, the first lady explained, a secret U.S. government cell that Foster, as deputy White House counsel, might have stumbled upon; a team specializing in death-made-to-look-like-suicide, on supposed behalf of a military that had lost respect for the draft-dodging, pro-gays-in-the-military commander-in-chief.

Hillary had reason to be concerned. Aware that investigations into Jim and Susan McDougal's Whitewater realty company, as well as into Jim's client connection with the Rose Law Firm, the firm's client overbilling procedures, and even her own cattle-futures investments, might turn up embarrassing information in the wrong hands, Hillary had understandably been nervous about her personal tax files, hence anxious to retrieve them from Foster's office.

After the funeral, informed by her own squad that the files were in safe hands, Hillary had simply refused to return to Washington, sinking into a depressed state. "We shouldn't have asked him to come to Washington, Webb," she confided to Hubbell.

How times had changed! Only a few months before, in the wake of a triumphant election win, the idea of getting her Three Musketeer colleagues from the Rose Law Firm to move with her to the capital had seemed exciting. Vince and Webb were, after all, Hillary's "two best friends" in the world, the president himself mournfully remarked, and Bill Kennedy, Foster's deputy, also from the Rose Law Firm, was almost as close. Now, six months into the presidency, the appointment of such best friends looked to both Bill and Hillary outright folly, given the pressures of the Clinton White House and administration—with Webb Hubbell soon to be charged with mail fraud and tax evasion.

For Hillary this was the most "brutal" time of her life since the business of possible divorce in 1989. Her father had died. Bill's mother, Virginia, was suffering terminal cancer, as she finally confided. Another lost relative of Virginia's bigamous first husband had appeared out of the woodwork. With these and other dark clouds there was a tendency for both Hillary and her husband to see themselves at war on every front, personal as well as political, before being able to get into their stride. Responding to an SOS from Ira Magaziner at her health care task force headquarters in the East

Wing of the White House, a headquarters she herself had dubbed "the war room," Hillary threw herself back into battle over health care reform—but it was, she later recalled, a battle in danger of "being sidelined by budgetary battles."

No Time for Brooding

Had Bill Clinton dared ask his wife to withdraw from the health care task force, or to postpone her recommendations for six months—even make it the subject of a more comprehensive bipartisan commission—he might have bought himself time to grow as president, as every new occupant of the Oval Office must do.

There was, however, no tough chief of staff to dragoon him into such a masculine approach—indeed the White House staff seemed still ignorant of the ways of Washington, continuing to act, behind the gates of 1600 Pennsylvania Avenue, like castrati in the Golden Carriage Palace of the Forbidden City, intimidated into servility by an activist first lady who had not only cast herself as co-president, but had resorted to what she later called her typical response to "adversity: I threw myself into a schedule so hectic that there was no time for brooding."

It was in her deep state of mourning that Hillary now learned that the Secret Service, in response to Foster's concern that the White House was being bugged by a foreign power, had carried out a "sweep" of the entire building, including the private apartments, while Hillary was away at Foster's funeral—without her approval. Her fury, once she returned and found pieces of furniture had been moved, and documents possibly discovered or even copied, was tantamount to a volcanic eruption. In her memoirs she didn't deny she was "ready to explode." Indeed she felt violated and "undone by the invasion of our privacy," as she tore strips out of Mack McLarty, her husband's chief of staff, and David Watkins, the White House personnel director.

Hillary was, in fact, coming near to a breakdown. She later denied rumors that, in a fit of temper over the sleepover visit of singer Barbra Streisand at the White House while she was away, she'd thrown a lamp at Bill, but she did admit, "I probably should have taken more time to rest and let myself grieve."

Vince Foster's suicide thus capped a disastrous spring that President Clinton, per his inaugural address, had attempted but failed to force.

Hubbell's initial conviction that Foster had not committed suicide—"Don't believe a word you hear. It was not suicide. It could not have been," he'd claimed in telephone calls to friends (though later, he changed his view)—only made things worse.

Ordering her personal files to be removed from her dead lawyer's office, and those that remained to be carefully vetted via Bernie Nussbaum, seemed to the grieving, threatened first lady the most sensible, self-protective thing she could have done.

Meanwhile her husband, as president, would have to fend for himself.

MENDING
THE ECONOMY

CHAPTER NINETEEN

THE ECONOMIC BILL

Time to Deliver

The fate of the president's economic bill, meanwhile, also symbolized much that was going wrong in the White House. The president's staff was in a state close to pandemonium as the House of Representatives—having approved the president's economic budget plan by a substantial majority in April—had come within a hair's breadth of voting it down on May 27, 1993: a "near-death experience" in which, up to the final hour, the president had "worked the phones incessantly, calling one declared 'no' vote after another to make a personal plea."

"There is an incredible amount of nervousness about this bill," a Democratic aide had commented, for the president's BTU energy tax threatened to be a mark that would tar all those congressmen who voted for it—and who would be left stranded in their home constituencies if and when the president dropped it, once the measure went to the Senate. "We don't want to be in a position of walking the plank and then have them go over and make a compromise in the Senate," one congressman had warned.

The Speaker, Tom Foley, was aware that many representatives might lose their seats at the next year's election if they cast their votes for the measure. Yet with the president standing firm—seemingly—on the BTU tax, and claiming he would go down with the Democratic members of Congress rather than remove the tax from his bill, the House had listened as the Speaker pleaded. A defeat for the huge package would doom the Democratic presidency, Congressman Foley had warned. For the most part, he had not asked members of Congress to stand up and be publicly counted, at least on a domestic issue that might affect their chances of re-election. This was different. "This is a time," the Speaker had declared, "to stand and deliver; this is a time to justify your election."

Leon Panetta, the director of OMB, recalled the dilemma vividly. "BTU is one of those things where substantively it's the right thing to do," he later explained. "We'd been talking about doing that from a conservation point of view for a long time. But I also knew that it was politically one of those dynamite issues that could blow up on you, particularly for people from the oil belt. Gore thought this was just the perfect thing to do, it was the right thing to do, and Clinton kind of went along with it [assuring Democratic members of Congress the White House would make certain that the Senate also voted for a BTU tax]. But it didn't take very long before you suddenly realized that you make people walk that plank, it's gonna kill you! It's gonna kill your plan! And unfortunately we made the House walk that plank"—for, despite the defection of some thirty-eight Democrats, the House bill passed 219–213—"and then we pulled the plug [by failing to insist that the Senate follow suit]. It was just too bad."

It was. As expected, the Senate refused to stomach the BTU tax the House had just passed, and stripped it from the measures their committee approved, 11–9, after two weeks of tortuous negotiations before the Senate Finance Committee, on June 18. House Democrats were in an uproar when they heard what had happened—indeed some, especially those who later lost their seats as a result, would never have a good word to say for the president. Though the president claimed that House Democrats "didn't walk the line for nothing," since in "conference"—the merging of the Senate and House bills into a single measure—they would "get the best bill of all," this was small consolation to those who went down.

Nor did the abandonment of the BTU tax in favor of a small raise in gasoline fuel tax resolve the matter, for that too became deeply contentious for senators up for reelection in 1994. By June 25, when the full Senate voted on the president's $499 billion deficit-reduction plan, a plan that had now dropped the BTU energy tax, the eighteen-hour debate ended in a 49–49 tie—requiring the vice president to cast a tie-breaking vote for the first time since 1987 as ex officio president of the Senate. Meanwhile, though not permitted to filibuster over a budget bill, Republicans were encouraged by the minority leader, Bob Dole, to force floor votes on every specific feature of the package. This ensured that each Democratic senator's vote would be recorded—allowing Republicans to slay them in negative advertising at the next election.

President Clinton had won—but only just, only so far, and without an energy tax. There was worse to follow. The two hundred House and Senate conferees had but three weeks to cobble together a combined bill, before the summer recess—with waning enthusiasm and increasing fears of political and electoral backlash. Thus by late July, with yet another White House "war room" now operating in the Old Executive Building—this time under Roger Altman, deputy secretary of the Treasury, to ensure that the huge package got through—the prospects again began to look shaky.

The Honeymoon is Over

For President Clinton, the honeymoon was clearly over—indeed he would later complain that he had never been given one. His staff's fears of congressional defeat rose inexorably as Republicans denounced the plan—Senator Dole even appealing on prime-time TV to members of the public to call the White House, their congressmen, and their senators to complain about the profligate tax-and-spend measures on August 3. The result was a telephonic deluge: almost half a million calls coming in *per hour* at one point, most of them expressing objections to the bill.

Finally, on August 5, 1993, the House debated the conference-agreed plan. Not only was the president's twenty-five-man "war room" team pulling out every stop to marshall votes in Congress, but the president personally met with at least thirty groups, and telephoned three dozen more congressmen; the blitzkrieg even extended to an Oval Office telephone connection to the congressional bathroom that was kept open "so that Clinton could reach wavering lawmakers," as the *Washington Post* reported.

Still the numbers did not add up. As the economic debate came to an end, Tom Foley, the Speaker, implored his fellow Democrats to support their president, the Democratic Party, and the responsible way of tackling a national deficit that was out of control. "Tonight is the time for courage," he pleaded, in what the *Congressional Quarterly* called "a final appeal to Democrats, who had been bludgeoned by GOP attacks and pressured by constituent phone calls that were running, by most accounts, strongly against the plan." "Tonight is the time to put away the old, easy ways," Foley said. "Tonight is the time for responsibility. Tonight is the night to vote."

At the end of the mandatory fifteen-minute electronically tallied rollcall, the nays tied with the yeas, 210–210, after which only hand-signed votes on colored cards were permitted. "For several more moments, the tally seesawed back and forth, with Democrats winning one moment and losing next," the *Congressional Quarterly* recounted, bringing the score to 216–216. "House leaders agreed to keep the final tally open while a scrum of Democrats surrounded two undecided members, to derisive chants from Republicans of 'Let's make a deal,'" the London *Independent* reported afterwards.

Earlier, at 8:45 P.M., the office telephone of Mrs. Marjorie Margolies-Mezvinsky had lit up in the Longworth Building. It had been Roger Altman calling, to say that the Democrats were still short three votes; she might hear personally from the president.

She did—a freshman Democrat who had won her seat by less than 1 percent of the vote in her wealthy, largely Republican Pennsylvania district outside Philadelphia. A desperate president of the United States listened to her appeal for an entitlement conference, similar to the Little Rock economic summit that had been held the previous December, if she were to switch her vote and save his presidency. "You've got it!" Clinton assured her in desperation.

Even so, the fifty-one-year-old ex-television reporter balked, hoping against hope that she would not be required to vote for the bill, which she had opposed hitherto, lest she lose her own wafer-thin majority in Pennsylvania. "She let the fifteen minutes allotted for electronic voting expire before walking to the well, where she joined three other recalcitrant Democrats," *Newsweek* reported: Ray Thornton of Arkansas, Pat Williams of Montana, and Dave Minge of Minnesota. As the *Congressional Quarterly* described, "President Clinton's entire deficit-reduction package rested for a few tense, tumultuous moments at the end of the vote on Aug. 5 in the hands of a wide-eyed, terrified-looking freshman Democrat named Margolies-Mezvinsky."

Other Democrats, with safer seats, had already abandoned the president, and would thereby secure their own re-election in 1994, but at this point, the congresswoman—the first to win her district for a Democrat in over seventy years—was the president's last hope. Ray Thornton, the Arkansas Democratic representative for the central district in Arkansas—"who could not have been blown out of his seat with a stick of dynamite," as Bill Clinton later scaldingly remarked—duly cast his vote *against* the bill, tipping the scales of Congress against the president. All eyes now turned upon Mrs. Mezvinsky.

"That sealed it," the *Congressional Quarterly* reported. "Margolies-Mezvinsky had to vote for the conference report or it would go down. Rep[resentative] Sander M. Levin, D[emocrat]-Mich., held her arms with his hands and spoke to her for a few moments. 'Just do what's right,' he says he told her. Rep. Cardiss Collins, D-Ill., rubbed her back. Rep. Butler Derrick, D-S.C., gave her a green card. Hoping to spare her the burden of being the final vote, Rep. Pat Williams, D-Mont., says he told her, 'We have to vote together.' Williams then signed his card and handed it in, and, finally, agonizingly slowly, Margolies-Mezvinsky did the same. Cheers erupted. Republicans reportedly chanted, 'Goodbye Marjorie,' and waved at her. A few Democrats waved defiantly back. Levin kissed her on the cheek." She had been, as *Newsweek*'s reporters put it, "fed to the beast while senior men from safer districts walked."

"Back in the White House," Clinton recalled, "I let out a whoop of joy, and relief." Soon, before cameras and microphones, the president was declaring: "The margin was close, but the mandate is clear. What we heard tonight at the other end of Pennsylvania Avenue was the sound of gridlock breaking. This is just a beginning, just a first step toward seizing control of our economic destiny."

But the president was speaking too soon. Gridlock was by no means broken—especially in the Senate.

A New Democratic Gospel

Bill Clinton had been elected to the presidency of the United States by preaching a New Democratic gospel of bipartisanship—yet already, in August 1993, he was facing virtual civil war in Congress of historic dimensions. Senate historian Donald Ritchie, consulted by observers at the time, noted that no major piece of legislation since World War II in either house had ever been enacted without at least one vote from each major party. Even before World War II there were only two cases he could think of in American history where there were knife-edge outcomes for major issues in Congress: the bid to convict Andrew Johnson on impeachment charges in 1868, which failed in the Senate by one vote, and the extension of the military draft in 1941 on the cusp of World War II, which passed in the

House by one vote. Now Bill Clinton's economic bill was making history, for good or ill.

R. W. Apple of the *New York Times* felt that, for all that this might reflect the machinations, ambitions, and egoisms of congressmen and senators, it also mirrored the state of the nation. "One poll," he noted, "on the eve of the final vote showed that 43 percent of the electorate wanted the economic package passed and 44 percent did not. The country was right where the legislators were: split down the middle. It must not be as simple to fix this automobile as Ross Perot says it is."

Bill Clinton could not be faulted for this. In his memoirs he recalled how mightily he fought to get his bill passed, and the many individual promises, compromises, and deals he was compelled to make in transit. "Someone once said that the two things people should never watch being made," he wrote, "are sausages and laws." It was, he added, "ugly, and uncertain."

Uncertain was an understatement. On Thursday, August 5, the president had called Senator Bob Kerrey, the one-legged Nebraska maverick, to confirm that he would support the bill on Friday in the Senate. Clinton had just managed to persuade Senator Dennis DeConcini of Arizona to switch his vote to yea, so went white with anger when Kerrey told him that, having supported the president in the Senate over the bill in July, he was now going to vote no—as a Democrat.

Although he omitted the call from his later account, Bill Clinton was well aware at the time how significant was Kerrey's threatened defection. "Clinton exploded in anger," Dan Balz wrote in the *Washington Post*, "warning that his presidency was at stake and that Kerrey was threatening to punish him for trying to do what other presidents had avoided. 'He shouted at me,' Kerrey said. 'I shouted at him.'" The two men then hung up on each other.

Ego had confronted ego—and with the president aware he'd just kissed goodbye to secure passage of his bill in the Senate, it was left to the urbane, ever-calm new Republican counselor to the president, David Gergen, to do the job for which he was famous. Moments later "the telephone in Kerrey's office rang again," Balz recorded. "Would it help if we talked?" Gergen asked—and invited Kerrey to lunch at the American Café, where they were joined by Mack McLarty and Howard Paster, the president's unwearying liaison with Congress.

Lunch helped, but didn't alter Kerrey's indecision. He had always been a man of contradictions: the only holder in Congress of the Congressional Medal of Honor for his service as a U.S. Navy Seal in Vietnam; a divorcé who'd enjoyed a celebrated affair with the actress Debra Winger in the Governor's Mansion in Nebraska when running the state; a politician nicknamed "Cosmic Bob" for his unfathomable mind. He had traded bitter words with Governor Clinton when both men ran for the Democratic nomination the year before—and could not but be disappointed that Clinton had not chosen him as his vice presidential candidate.

"He listens to his own drummer," Bob Shrum, a political adviser to Kerrey, was quoted saying. "This is someone who doesn't fit the normal political categories. And that's what makes him fascinating and interesting and also makes him difficult at times for other people to deal with." Asked if he'd seen Kerrey on the Senate floor, Senator Trent Lott, a Mississippi Republican, remarked wittily, as he looked upward: "Oh, Kerrey, I saw him float over the chamber. He's communing."

In fact, to avoid further pressure from the president and his minions, the Nebraska senator decided to go that afternoon to a movie, and saw a biopic about Tina Turner, *What's Love Got to Do With It*. Leon Panetta remembered being charged with finding the errant war hero. "Oh, yeah," Panetta recalled, "it went right to the wire! We were on to the Senate, and Kerrey was at the movie theater, for Christ's sakes! I said: 'What the hell is he doing at the movie theater?'—because we were trying to find him, you know—figure out how he's going to vote. It was down to that."

Nobody, *en bref*, had any idea what the Nebraska senator would do.

Free Willy

The next day, when president-friendly reporters learned of the sanctuary Kerrey had sought, they had a movie suggestion for the Friday matinée, before the critical vote in the Senate: *Free Willy*.

The president, however, was not amused. He was taking no chances and, overcoming his fury at their telephone battle, had invited Kerrey to breakfast with him at the White House. Press secretary Myers had joked to correspondents that they would name a White House room after him if Kerrey agreed to support the bill, but the senator, even after ninety minutes with the nation's chief executive, was tight-lipped about his intentions.

Feelers were once again put out in the hope of tempting moderate Republicans with yet more concessions, but without much hope of success. The lines were drawn, everyone knew. The armies simply had to wait for nightfall, when the debate would come to a close.

"We've seen this before—smoke and mirrors—and here we are again. Step right up, ladies and gentlemen," Republican Senator Alfonse D'Amato shrieked like a barker in front of a blank chart representing insufficient deficit cuts in government spending. "Magical Bill and his band of liberal magicians," he sneered, "have a bag of tricks for you."

D'Amato was right in respect of one trick, at least—for President Clinton's breakfast magic had, in fact, worked. Though "war room" staffers trembled with anticipation during the ten-hour debate, the president was confident the maverick Vietnam veteran would not, in the end, bring down the government. Clinton had compromised again and again. He had now surrendered his BTU tax altogether, had had to cut down his alternative gasoline tax to a nominal 4.3 cents a gallon, had cut his proposed corporate income tax by half, had dumped his investment tax credit for business, blunted his tax breaks for business done overseas, narrowed his tax hike on Social Security benefits, got less money for social programs, and accepted deeper Medicare spending cuts than he wanted. But he *had* stuck with determination to his decision to raise personal income tax for the top 1.2 percent of taxpayers, *had* got a significant increase in corporate taxes, *had* expanded wage subsidies for the working poor, *had* increased funding for food stamps and childhood vaccinations, and *had* got tax incentives for business investment in empowerment zones. Above all, he *had* got a deficit reduction package of almost $500 billion that would—and did—send a message to bankers and markets both in America and abroad that the Clinton administration, after twelve years of Republican profligacy, was serious about setting the nation's fiscal house in order.

The tireless efforts of the president and his team were working. Towards eight o'clock there had been no change in expected positions adopted. Senator after senator pointed out the flaws in the bill, but a steady fifty percent praised its intent: to begin the process of national deficit reduction.

Dale Bumpers, the senator whose seat Bill Clinton had never quite dared contest while governor of Arkansas, pointed out that not only in their consciences but in their pockets the wealthy citizens of the nation— who had profited mightily during the Reagan years in comparison with others—had already swallowed the president's medicine. They would pay more income tax. "The markets, Wall Street, business in this country has already assumed that this is a done deal," Bumpers pointed out—proving his point by noting that "the market went up after the House passed it last night."

Aware that he could not change a single colleague's vote, Bumpers nevertheless made "a rather emotional appeal to the American people"—claiming that even the rich, who would pay higher taxes in the short term, had concerns that went deeper than the "Mercedes in their driveway." "Do you know what they talk about, I say to the senator?" he said, turning to the previous, Republican speaker. "They talk about their children. They talk about their children's future. That is what we all talk about. That is who we love most.

"I do not want to vote for this bill. It is not popular. You are not going to win anything. The Republicans can vote no, pat themselves on the back, and go home with their anti-tax awards.

"The truth of the matter is, we are trying to reverse twelve years of economic lunacy in this country. Do you know why? To keep faith with those parents who are sitting around the dinner table talking about their children's future. They deserve it. I intend to vote to give it to them."

Senator Paul Simon of Illinois, following Bumpers's lead, said the distinguished senator from Arkansas had "hit it right on the head." By claiming they could tackle the deficit merely by cutting more government programs and not raising taxes, Republicans were being deceitful. They might dragoon millions of callers to telephone the White House and thereby clog up the capital's telephone system, but despite such negative marketing powers Republicans had no real interest in cutting the deficit (as would be shown once the next Republican won the Oval Office).

"If I just wanted to do the popular thing it would be easy to vote against this," Senator Simon pointed out. "Cutting spending sounds great in the abstract. I notice our friends on the other side of the aisle kept it abstract. They have not pinpointed where they are going to do it. And raising revenue [taxes] obviously is unpopular." But, he warned, "we had better stop living on a national credit card." The invoice was arriving each year, in massive interest payable on money spent but not recouped. "This is the first generation of Americans to live on a national credit card saying, send the bill to our children and our grandchildren. We are finally starting to slow down and I hope we will take additional steps to move away from it. I am casting my aye vote, not with pleasure," he added, "because it is not pleasant to do what we are doing. But I am casting it knowing we are doing the right thing for the future of this country." And with that he yielded time back to the senator from Tennessee and chairman of the Senate Budget Committee, Jim Sasser.

"Mr. President, I see the distinguished senator from Nebraska has arrived in the chamber," Senator Sasser said, addressing the chair. "I ask the senator how much time he will require."

Kerrey, looking up, replied: "Fifteen minutes."

The chamber had filled, and the cameras and microphones of the nation's press—indeed the press of the world—were pointed at the highest-decorated veteran in their midst, as he moved to speak.

All were aware that Kerrey had the power, now, to humble or pay tribute to the president as sponsor of the bill: to wreak vengeance on the man who had beaten him for the Democratic presidential nomination, or to ennoble him and his efforts. To journalists who had asked him about the film he had seen the previous day, he had merely repeated, enigmatically, the title.

When Senator Kerrey began his speech, the chamber grew silent, and the significance of the movie's name became all too clear to the reporters, as well as the minority leader, Senator Dole, and other Republicans who were still begging him to join them in damning the president's bill for daring to raise taxes on the super-rich.

Voting Yes

Addressing the president of the Senate, Kerrey began apologetically. "Mr. President, I've taken too long, I'm afraid, to reach this decision," he started. "My head, I confess, aches with all the thinking. But my heart aches with the conclusion and that I will vote yes for a bill which challenges America too little because I do not trust what my colleagues on the other side of the aisle will do if I say no."

A ripple of relief followed by concern swept through the chamber as the senator tempered his accusation of untrustworthiness. "Individually, the Republicans in this body are fine and able people—patriots, parents, God-fearing citizens who came here to serve their country as every other member of this body. Collectively, however, you have locked yourselves together into the idea of opposition. Opposition not to an idea, but to a man."

That morning Kerrey had sat with the president, to test his beliefs, his values, his aspirations for America—and had been won over. The president had even reached him again in the Senate bathroom, later, to urge his case. "A man who came to this town green and inexperienced in our ways and who wants America to do better, to be better and to continue to believe in the invincibility of ideas of courage and action.

"Oh, you say this plan doesn't have enough cuts. You say it is too heavy on taxes. One by one you've approached, however, individuals and groups to tell them the price for this program is too high.

"Oh, how I wish this evening that I could trust you.

"But the truth, Mr. President, is in fact the price of this proposal is too *low*, it's too little to match the greatness needed from Americans now at this critical moment in this world's history.

"This is not to say we are free from blame on this side of the aisle. When the challenge came from someone who didn't want to pay or didn't want to accept less from their government we, unfortunately all too often, ran too. We ran when opposition arose to the BTU tax. We ran when some seniors said they didn't want to pay any higher taxes. We ran, Mr. President, when the program getters, the salary seekers, the pay-raise hunters, COLA receivers and other solicitors begged us to leave them alone.

"So I vote *yes*, Mr. President, and we pass a bill that seems to follow a perverse interpretation of the Sermon on the Mount: the meek shall inherit the earth."

Watching the television screens in the Old Executive Office building, overshadowing the White House next door, on Pennsylvania Avenue, under its late-nineteenth-century Parisian-style mansard roof and behind its imperial windows, junior staffers held their breath as the Nebraskan battle-hero now addressed a different president: the president of the United States of America.

"President Clinton, if you are watching now, as I suspect you are, I tell you this: I could not and should not cast a vote that brings down your presidency. You have made mistakes and know it far better than I. But you do not deserve, and America cannot afford, to have you spend the next sixty days quibbling over whether or not we should have this cut or this tax increase. America also cannot afford to have you take the low road of the too easy compromise, or the too early collapse. You have gotten where you are today because you are strong, not because you are weak. Get back on the high road, Mr. President, where you are at your best. On February 17 you told America the deficit reduction was a moral issue and that shared sacrifice was needed to put it behind us.

"Mr. President, you were right. . . . Shared sacrifice, Mr. President. It is our highest ideal, and the only way we will build the moral consensus needed to end this nightmare of borrowing from our children.

"Get back on the high road, Mr. President," the senator repeated. "You had the right idea, Mr. President, with the BTU tax. And when we came after you with both barrels blazing, threatening to walk if you did not yield, you should have let us walk," he declared. "You should have said to us that at least we would be exercising something other than our mouths.

"Instead, we find ourselves with a bill that asks Americans to pay 4.3 cents a gallon more. If they notice, they will be surprised. And if they complain, I will be ashamed. Instead of collecting $70 billion from consumption, we get it from incomes, personal and corporate. Instead of fairness we get retroactivity and surcharges. Instead of change we get the same old stuff.

"I am sympathetic, Mr. President. I know how loud our individual threats can be. But I implore you, Mr. President, say no to us. Get us back on the high ground, where we actually prefer to be. This legislation will now become law. As such, it represents a first step. But if it is to be a first step toward regaining the confidence of the American people and their Congress and their federal government, then we must tell Americans the truth. And the truth is, Mr. President, to spend less means someone must get less.

"And to control costs means someone must accept less. To save means I must spend less. And to grow, we must take the time and make the effort to build."

Senator Kerrey's homily was almost over, as he now addressed himself to his fellow patricians—mindful of their Roman forbears. "I began by saying that I do not trust forty-four Republicans enough to say no to this bill. I close by saying that I suspect the feeling is mutual. The challenge for us— and too much is at stake for us to even consider the possibility of failing— is for us to end this distrust and to put this too partisan debate behind us. For the sake of our place in history, rise to the high road that the occasion requires.

"Mr. President, I yield the floor."

Our Gettysburg

It was 8:30 P.M. on Friday, August 6, 1993—a day that certainly deserved to go down in history. The Senate chamber erupted with applause. Sometime later, when the vote was taken and produced a now predicted 50–50 deadlock, the vice president, Al Gore, was able to exercise his rare but constitutional tiebreaking privilege as president of the Senate. As he "loved to joke," Bill Clinton later wrote, "whenever he voted, we always won."

Outside of Congress there was as much jubilation as inside. "When the vote was announced on the Senate floor, about seventy-five Clinton aides who had gathered in the Roosevelt Room of the White House erupted in prolonged cheers, whoops, and applause," it was reported the next day. "The staff members greeted Lloyd Bentsen, the Treasury secretary, Leon E. Panetta, the budget director, and Roger C. Altman, the deputy secretary of the Treasury, by chanting their names as if they were rock stars. 'Leon, Leon!' they shouted. 'Roger, Roger!'"

Nor was the cheering confined to the White House, for the news soon spread around the world. As the London *Observer* noted, "President Clinton's battle of the budget has been won. If all goes according to plan the national deficit will be reduced by $496 billion (£330 billion) over the next five years. His victory may well be seen as a turning point in a presidency where the first six months have been dogged by irrelevant issues such as the status of homosexuals in the military. It was, as Wellington said of Waterloo, a near-run thing but the triumph will probably taste sweeter for it. 'This was our Gettysburg,' said one ecstatic White House aide on Friday evening. 'It's the turn of the tide. Now there's no looking back.'"

Whether that would be so remained to be seen. But in a post-Cold War world in which America's leadership was sorely needed—as in Bosnia, where Serbs were now shelling Sarajevo, or Somalia, where the warlord Mohamed Aideed was attacking UN humanitarian aid workers and the UN troops protecting them—the hope was, in getting through his domestic economic plan, President Clinton could at last attend to ills beyond American borders. He had, after all, not only shown courage but almost unbelievable patience in getting his plan through a partisan Congress in which, even in the Democratic Party, there were more fractious factions than a computer could calculate. "A lesser man might have ended up with nerves about as brittle as Melba toast, quite demoralised by the opposition from within his own ranks," the *Observer*'s Washington correspondent remarked. "But the Comeback Kid, as he likes to be known, appeared to emerge unscathed from his ordeal, apart from a touch of laryngitis apparently brought on by wheedling telephone conversations with the party faithless."

Republican Sour Grapes

"What we heard tonight at the other end of Pennsylvania Avenue was the sound of gridlock breaking," the president announced on the portico of the

North Entrance to the White House. "This is just a beginning, just a first step toward seizing control of our economic destiny. This was not easy, but change is never easy. We're determined to stop avoiding our problems and start facing them."

Senate Minority Leader Dole was crestfallen. He denounced the bill as "the largest tax increase in world history." Indeed, he and a host of fellow Republicans went on air to predict the downfall of the American—and world—economy, as a result, with worse unemployment and continued recession.

"It is a recipe for disaster," the deputy House minority whip, Dick Armey, warned. "This plan is not a recipe for more jobs. Taxes will go up. The economy will sputter along. Dreams will be put off, and all this for the hollow promise of deficit reduction, of lower interest rates."

Congressman Newt Gingrich, the minority whip and scourge of the Democrats, predicted the package would lead directly to "a job-killing recession." Congressman John Kasich, the ranking Republican on the House Budget Committee, claimed that "this plan puts the economy in the gutter."

They were all completely wrong, and the president was dead right, as time would prove.

Unfortunately, it would prove other things, too—including, despite Senator Kerrey's plea, the continuing failure of the greenhorn president to don the true mantle of the presidency, and to put his White House in order, before it became too late.

CHAPTER TWENTY

AN INDIAN SUMMER

Warning Waves

Returning to the White House on September 4 after his vacation on Martha's Vineyard, the president got his first real whiff of foreign danger when the CIA contacted him with an urgent memo. In defiance of the recent Governor's Island Accord, the supposedly outgoing military leaders of Haiti would *not* be leaving voluntarily, the CIA predicted.

The secretary of defense, Les Aspin, favored postponing the reinstatement of the deposed Haitian president, Jean-Bertrand Aristide, who was scheduled to be returned to the island aboard the USS *Harlan County*, backed by only two hundred lightly armed soldiers. Aspin, however, claimed he did not want to "box" President Clinton in, just as he was due to give a seminal address to the United Nations, setting out his Democratic administration's policy for the nineties. Thus he stopped his deputy undersecretary for policy from sending the president a letter urging him to convene a meeting of the National Security Council, and permitted the *Harlan County* to sail—with consequences that would be dire.

The president, Aspin knew, had other, seemingly more important challenges on his plate that fall. For a start, he had his wife's health care reform initiative to launch. Hillary and her six hundred twenty staff members were gearing up for the "grandmother of all political campaigns," in the words of the Democratic National Committee's project director: a grassroots crusade, costing $30 million and spread across all fifty states, with bumper stickers, T-shirts, toll-free numbers for donations, TV ads, and mailings. The climax would be a speech by the president to a specially convened joint meeting of Congress on September 22 to announce the overall thrust of the plan (similar in its way to the first Clinton budget and deficit reduction proposal in January) that had already been put before Congress in a 246-page draft document.

Observers were aware that an "earthquake" had beset the bloated medical insurance industry. Success would "assure Mr. Clinton's place in history," it was predicted. "Failure," however, would deal Bill Clinton, the Congress, and the presidency "immeasurable blows."

Climbing Polls

Ever the optimist, the president seemed a different man after his belated summer vacation on Martha's Vineyard—which helped distance both the president and the public from the many things that had gone wrong with the Clinton administration in the spring. Voters, taking stock, and viewing reports of the president relaxing in the summer sunshine with his wife and daughter, away from the tribulations of Washington, could see their president as a well-meaning paterfamilias, capable of making mistakes through inexperience, but usually with the best of intentions. His polls had begun to rise again, in consequence. From medical family leave to AmeriCorps (a domestic version of the Peace Corps), he did seem to have his heart in the right place, despite his errors. Perhaps, with his economic plan now passed into law, fortune would smile upon him. Certainly when, a few days after his return to the capital, he was presented with one of the great photoopportunities of the waning century, he seized it.

The Oslo Peace Accord

Throughout his childhood and youth Bill Clinton had been peacemaker in a troubled home. Standing six-three, on a world stage, he genuinely relished his chance to help overcome the bitterness between Jewish and Arab leaders. A Norwegian team in Oslo had brokered a new agreement, setting a timetable towards peaceful co-existence between Israelis and Palestinians, but, in asking for the signing to be done in Washington, the team had accepted that only the United States could guide, cajole, and even threaten a final resolution of the conflict—an agreement that would, it was hoped, ensure eventual peace in the Middle East in the twenty-first century.

In character, intelligence, religious faith, patience, and optimism big Bill Clinton seemed to be the perfect president, even hostile pundits allowed, to achieve such a resolution: an outcome that promised, too, security for the United States, which, by its very success as a capitalist democracy rather than a theocracy, was increasingly resented in the less affluent, post-communist Muslim world. The Palestine Liberation Organization's chairman, Yasser Arafat, had too much blood on his hands for the president to be willing to allow him a Middle Eastern kiss, so he had practiced an arm-blocking movement to stop Arafat. Thus, after shaking hands with Prime Minister Yitzhak Rabin and Chairman Arafat before the cameras, the big Arkansan "stepped back out of the space between them and spread my arms to bring them together," as he later recalled. "Arafat lifted his hand toward a still reluctant Rabin. When Rabin extended his hand, the crowd let out an audible gasp, followed by thunderous applause, as they completed the kissless handshake. All the world was cheering, except for diehard protesters in the Middle East who were inciting violence, and demonstrators in front of the White House claiming we were endangering Israel's security."

It was, in its way, the most hopeful moment of the 1990s: symbolic of goodwill rather than hate and revenge. Ignoring the protests, the president summed up the situation, after Rabin and Arafat had spoken. "Today," the president declared, "we bear witness to an extraordinary act in one of history's defining dramas, a drama that began in a time of our ancestors when the word went forth from a sliver of land between the River Jordan and the Mediterranean Sea. That hallowed piece of earth, and land of life and revelation is the home to the memories and dreams of Jews, Moslems and Christians throughout the world.

"As we all know, devotion to that land has also been the source of conflict and bloodshed for too long. Throughout this century, bitterness between the Palestinian and Jewish people has robbed the entire region of its resources, its potential and too many of its sons and daughters. The land has been so drenched in warfare and hatred, the conflicting claims of history etched so deeply in the souls of the combatants there, that many believed the past would always have the upper hand.

"Then, fourteen years ago, the past began to give way when at this place and upon this desk three men of great vision signed their names to the Camp David accords. Today we honor the memories of Menachem Begin and Anwar Sadat, and we salute the wise leadership of President Jimmy Carter."

If the president was aware that the signing could cost Rabin his life, despite the support of over 60 percent of Israelis, as it had once cost Egypt's president his, he did not show it. He was, observers noted, in his element—indeed for a moment it looked as if he might actually be finding his true métier, alongside former president Jimmy Carter. Rabin, twenty years his senior, confided over lunch that holding on to the West Bank, as Israel had done since the war of 1967, was pointless now, since it would no longer guarantee Israel's security; Palestinians would eventually outnumber Israelis in Palestine, so that the only way forward was to grant autonomy to the Muslims, and agree to a sort of partition such as had been put forward by the British in the 1930s, under their League of Nations Mandate, and again before their ignominious withdrawal in 1948.

As Rabin flew home on September 13 to sell the peace accord to the Knesset and his electorate, Bill Clinton was, meanwhile, almost levitating. The ceremony had brought to mind three previous landmark events of the age—the fall of the Berlin Wall, the dissolution of the Soviet Union, and Nelson Mandela's release from prison. Now, center stage in world history, Bill Clinton was empowered to do the good he craved: no longer being rolled, but on a roll. That very night he hosted a dinner for three former presidents and twenty-five couples, including Democratic and Republican leaders from the Hill—for the next day he had arranged to launch his next great initiative of the fall: NAFTA.

Launching NAFTA

Like his economic bill earlier in the year, the campaign to get Congress to ratify the North Atlantic Free Trade Agreement showed what could be achieved by the freshman president when served by a team that was experienced, focused, well-directed, and following a tight script. Clinton was certain that *patience*, not gung-ho moral absolutism, would win for America the post–Cold War challenge of the global capitalist economy. After all, had not patient containment won the Cold War, while the United States developed its free economy? To this end he was willing not only to place deficit reduction foremost among his programs, but to place it side by side with the embracing of economic expansion through free trade—pressing Congress to ratify the NAFTA agreement that President Bush had signed on December 17, 1992, shortly after the 1992 election.

Among traditional Democrats, both policies were seen as deeply flawed. In the summer, egged on by her advisers and even some of the president's, Hillary had done her best to dash the hopes of the NAFTA brigade on the president's staff—indeed she even managed to get Mickey Kantor, the new U.S. trade representative, to offer to sabotage the bill in Congress. Poll after poll, after all, showed less than a majority of the electorate in favor of the bill—and fewer than enough members of Congress to pass it. Its chances of successful passage appeared so poor, in fact, that the Mexican president, Carlos Salinas de Gortari (who would be up for re-election the following year), was reduced to backtracking. Mexicans, he acknowledged, "know the agreements and treaties will not by themselves solve our problems," and NAFTA might not, therefore, be the right step at this stage. "Until now," the *New York Times* reported, "Salinas has virtually ignored the possibility that the agreement might not go into effect."

It was at this point, when supporters of NAFTA were beginning to despair, that the president showed just how effective a warrior he could be, once he himself felt the cause to be right.

A Giant Sucking Sound

Even Republican Minority leader Bob Michel had worried that NAFTA support in Congress was losing ground—indeed, one lobbyist for the trade agreement declared that "NAFTA is dead. I've counted noses enough on Capitol Hill." A scholar at the Carnegie Endowment for International Peace declared, "It's looking worse all the time." The House Speaker, Tom Foley, agreed, saying, "The passions are flowing against it." True to his sound-bite style, Ross Perot warned of a "giant sucking sound" of jobs being lost to Mexico under NAFTA.

It was in this situation that all now looked to the White House. There, on September 14, the big Arkansan once again strode into the East Room for a second great photo opportunity in two days, flanked by three presidential predecessors: Republican former president Gerald Ford, Republican former president George Bush, and Democratic former president Jimmy Carter.

"Yesterday," the president began, after he'd extolled the time and effort they had invested in reaching the Oslo peace agreement, "we saw the sight of an old world dying, a new one being born in hope and a spirit of peace. Peoples who for a decade were caught in the cycle of war and frustration chose hope over fear and took a great risk to make the future better. Today we turn to face the challenge of our own hemisphere, our own country, our own economic fortunes." The fight for NAFTA in Congress would be tough, he acknowledged. "It will be a hard fight, and I expect to be there with all of you every step of the way. We will make our case as hard and as well as we can. And though the fight will be difficult, I deeply believe we will win. And I'd like to tell you why."

Once Bill Clinton was in campaign mode, it was difficult to resist his unique blend of political proselytizing. "As president, it is my duty to speak frankly to the American people about the world in which we now live," Clinton asserted. "Fifty years ago at the end of World War II, an unchallenged America was protected by the oceans and by our technological superiority and, very frankly, by the economic devastation of the people who could otherwise have been our competitors. We chose then to try to help rebuild our former enemies and to create a world of free trade supported by institutions which would facilitate it." The benefits, to America and to the free world, had been enormous. "As a result of that effort, global trade grew from $200 billion in 1950 to $800 billion in 1980. As a result, jobs were created and opportunity thrived all across the world. But make no mistake about it, our decision at the end of World War II to create a system of global, expanded, freer trade, and the supporting institutions, played a major role in creating the prosperity of the American middle class."

In that expanded global marketplace America had now to face up to the challenge of new technology, swifter communications, greater competition for investment, and wealthier competitors—which inevitably affected the American middle class. "Most Americans are working harder for less," he acknowledged. "They are vulnerable to the fear tactics and the averseness to change that is behind much of the opposition to NAFTA.

"But I want to say to my fellow Americans, when you live in a time of change the only way to recover your security and to broaden your horizons is to adapt to the change, to embrace it, to move forward. Nothing we do, nothing we do in this great capital can change the fact that factories or information can flash across the world, that people can move money around in the blink of an eye. Nothing can change the fact that technology can be adopted, once created, by people all across the world and then rapidly adapted in new and different ways by people who have a little different take on the way the technology works. For two decades, the winds of global competition have made these things clear to any American with eyes to see.

The only way we can recover the fortunes of the middle class in this country so that people who work harder and smarter can at least prosper more, the only way we can pass on the American dream of the last forty years to our children and their children for the next forty is to adapt to the changes which are occurring.

"In a fundamental sense, this debate about NAFTA is a debate about whether we will embrace these changes and create the jobs of tomorrow, or try to resist these changes, hoping we can preserve the economic structures of yesterday. I tell you, my fellow Americans, that if we learned anything from the collapse of the Berlin Wall and the fall of the governments in Eastern Europe, even a totally controlled society cannot resist the winds of change that economics and technology and information flow have imposed in this world of ours. That is not an option. Our only realistic option is to embrace these changes and create the jobs of tomorrow."

One by one, with his remarkable ability to choose the telling detail, the president relentlessly demolished the arguments of those who, he claimed, were looking backwards, not forwards. "Most Americans don't know this," he gave as an example, "but the average Mexican citizen, even though wages are much lower in Mexico, the average Mexican citizen is now spending $450 per year *per person* to buy American goods. That is more than the average Japanese, the average German, or the average Canadian buys; more than the average German, Swiss, and Italian citizens put together.

"So when people say that this trade agreement is just about how to move jobs to Mexico so nobody can make a living, how do they explain the fact that Mexicans keep buying more products made in America every year? Go out and tell the American people that. Mexican citizens with lower incomes spend more money—real dollars, not percentage of their income—more money on American products than Germans, Japanese, Canadians. That is a fact. And there will be more if they have more money to spend. That is what expanding trade is all about. . . ."

Republican senator Bob Dole was ecstatic. "President Clinton hit it out of the ballpark," he commented, while his colleague Senator John Danforth declared that no one "can now doubt the commitment of President Clinton."

All agreed it was a *tour de force*—by a veritable force of nature. "I thought that was a very eloquent statement by President Clinton," even President Bush acknowledged afterwards, "and now," he added with good grace (it was the first time he had seen his successor since the inauguration) "I understand why he's on the inside looking out and I'm outside looking in."

A Golden Month

With the president's polls surging from a low of 35 percent back to above 50, White House advisers from Gergen to Begala were jubilant. Comparing his economic team with his other White House crews, Alice Rivlin felt the fight for NAFTA was yet again a tribute to the directing mind of Bob Rubin, the cohesion of the economic squad, and the sheer *ability* of the president, once harnessed. "One other exception to the chaos [of the White House] was NAFTA," Dr. Rivlin recalled. "It was again a very good process and the right decision. And courage! I remember I was in the cabinet meeting that they had towards the end, because Leon [Panetta] was out of town. The president lined up those who were for it, and the people against it. And he had everybody speak. He was running it himself. Then at the end he said what he had decided. I think he'd already decided before the meeting—but it was a *good* way to handle it."

For the president, September 1993 seemed, then, to be his golden month: an Indian summer in which he was able to wave a magic wand and make everything he touched go right. Insisting he devote as much proselytizing effort into her health care reform bill as he did into NAFTA, Hillary brought the president out on the White House lawn yet again several days later, on September 18, as she urged dozens of American health care "victims" to recount their tragedies in person, broadcast on live breakfast television, in a bid to counter health care reform scare-stories similar to those that Ross Perot had been lobbing at NAFTA.

This time, however, as Dr. Rivlin pointed out, there was no Bob Rubin to manage the team. Instead of a *Meistermannschaft* of experienced economists and policymakers there was only a chaotic group similar to the convict-scientists in Solzhenitsyn's great novel *The First Circle,* led by an inexperienced first lady and her deputy, a mad, secretive management consultant who had been to Rhodes House with the president two decades before, that—working night and day against the clock—was currently completing the draft of a legislative plan almost fourteen hundred pages long!

CHAPTER TWENTY-ONE

ADDRESSING
HEALTH CARE REFORM

Something Inspirational

If Bill Clinton's launch of the NAFTA debate was a tribute to his energy, intelligence, and focus, his planned speech to a special joint session of Congress on Hillary's health care reform proposals on September 22, 1993, by contrast, threatened to be a disaster.

"When the president and, I guess, Mrs. Clinton read the [first draft of the] speech they didn't like it," David Dreyer recalled—in fact, the speech was so lame they "didn't even view it as a basis for starting over. It was an eleven-page document that described a thousand-page goal, you know. It would probably have been easier to do a thousand-page speech! It was just too complicated. In any event, David Gergen comes to me and says, 'The president doesn't like the text he's been given, and he likes the way Jeremy Rosner writes, and I put you forward because I like the way you handle yourself.'

"Gergen talks that way," Dreyer said, mocking the *basso profundo* of his former boss. "It seemed vaguely onanistic to me," he said, laughing—but with less than two days to go, there had been no time for schoolboy humor. "Something inspirational!" Gergen demanded—and after a couple of brief interviews with the president and first lady, Rosner and Dreyer produced a new first draft on September 21, the night before the event. The next morning it was returned to them with edits, and by the early evening the president

181

was able to practice it in the White House theater, in the basement, before leaving for the Hill.

"We would put it on the teleprompter," Dreyer recalled, "and he would read the speech as if he were delivering it. But he'd stop, sometimes every sentence, or in the middle of sentences, and say, 'No, this word should be A instead of B,' or 'No, let's move this to the end or the beginning. . . .'"

As with his inaugural speech, the presidential speechmaking process was excruciating—not merely because the president's last-minute attention to stylistic detail was exhausting, but because the focus on getting the rhetorical performance right masked the problem of the hugely ambitious plan itself, and the haste in which it had been prepared. In essence, the president was attempting to paper over an appallingly complicated, rushed, divisive, and unappealing proposal with fine words that sounded unconvincing, unfortunately, and were now, at the eleventh hour, even more rushed than the proposal itself.

Mounting the House podium, the president became aware that something else had gone wrong, too.

As welcoming applause for the president echoed through the House, Clinton whispered to Vice President Gore. Gore summoned George Stephanopoulos, who was standing nearby. "And George doesn't move!" Dreyer recalled. "George and Gore are [at this period] not on the best of terms—George somehow thinks that Gore is calling him up to get him into the picture, or embarrass him in some way, or has some agenda. Anyway, Gore finally persuades him that this is something that George really has to do. So George goes up there and talks to the vice president. And comes back. This is a man who has an olive-skinned complexion—and who now looks like every red blood cell has been sucked out of his body. And he says to me: 'The wrong speech is in the teleprompter, you have to fix it!'"

Dreyer left the chamber, sent a security officer to the majority leader's office to fetch his laptop, took this to the teleprompter control room, instructed the operator to hand over the offending diskette, wiped it clean, copied the new speech from his hard drive to the teleprompter diskette, reinserted it into the machine, reviewed it on screen, incorporated the final-final edits the president had made in the limousine on the way to the Hill, then scrolled through the text from the start to catch up to the point where the president, in the intervening seven minutes, had gotten without the aid of the teleprompter. . . .

No one in the House had even noticed. With pauses for applause and his unique ability to connect with an audience, the president didn't *need* a teleprompter. For sixty minutes he simply kept his congressional and national television audience transfixed as he went over, in outline, the parlous condition of health care in America, the benefits of Hillary's plan, and the moral righteousness of the mock plastic health card he held up, which all Americans would be entitled to carry—if Congress passed his bill.

Watching and listening to the charismatic president, even skeptical figures within Hillary's health care team began to feel, for a brief moment, that the plan had a chance. If "Bill and Hillary Clinton can bring it off," Rupert Cornwall had explained to British readers, "the prize is huge. Even if the first Democrat in the White House in 12 years achieved nothing else, his presidency would be a success. For his party, too, health care reform has the making of a copper-bottomed winner"—indeed, Cornwall posited that "success could usher in a post-Cold War generation of Democratic power focusing on America's domestic problems, matching the quarter-century of Republican dominance between 1968 and 1992."

With the stakes so high, then, why was the president, with his already legendary political antennae, so deaf to warning signals coming out of Congress and the states? Why, as he had in his launching of NAFTA, had he not tried to line up former Republican presidents to back a *bipartisan* approach to health care reform?

The Gathering Storm

As with the NAFTA bill, many Republicans were still willing to vote for a health care reform bill; two weeks before the president's address, Republicans had put forward two modest reform packages themselves, accepting many of the Clinton plan ideas, even coverage of the uninsured. Given Hillary's insistence on federal compulsion and new taxes, however, such Republicans had drawn the line.

This was a tragedy—as even the Republican counselor Clinton had employed to help sell his communitarian message acknowledged, in retrospect. As David Gergen later commented, the Clintons were still running "what amounted to a co-presidency in a variety of serious ways." Hillary wasn't "making all the decisions," he explained, "but she did have veto authority over some important issues. And that put her in a situation which I think is unprecedented in American history. You can perhaps go back to the late period of Woodrow Wilson when he had a stroke and his wife, Edith, was making many decisions. But there's no other, I think, comparable time when we've had, in effect, a co-presidency. And as much as I admire Mrs. Clinton's capacity because she truly is a very talented woman—she's passionate about the causes she believes in, and I think she's a well-centered person, but there is no room in the White House for a co-presidency. It just does not work. You cannot have two different camps running the White House. You can't have a war room that goes off and does a budget and another war room goes off and does NAFTA and then you have a war room who goes off and does health care. You need an integrated process. And frankly, I think the president would have been better off had he asserted himself, his own authority, in doing that." Not all the rhetoric in the world, with or without teleprompters, could thus have avoided the gathering storm.

A SHIP OF FOOLS

CHAPTER TWENTY-TWO

BLACK HAWK DOWN

Smoldering Troublespots

The third major speech President Clinton was scheduled to give in September 1993 was to the United Nations in New York, wearing his full robes as president of the world's last remaining superpower.

The Principals Committee of national security advisers to the president had met in the White House on September 17, in advance of the UN speech. The meeting had not gone well: there had been a sort of gunfight at the O.K. Corral. The ambassador to the UN, Madeleine Albright, argued for increased intervention abroad and nation-building, while General Powell cautioned against mission creep, as well as unwise intervention in intractable problems that did not directly affect U.S. security or interests. Secretary Christopher was unable to make up his mind what was best. Secretary Aspin found himself torn between his long-time support in the House for multilateral operations, on the one hand, and the uncomfortable sense that he was despised and beleaguered at the Pentagon.

In these circumstances, National Security Adviser Anthony Lake was concerned lest American attention to major international security issues—such as the future direction of Russia—become further skewed by unclear American goals in UN operations. He had strong-armed the European allies behind a NATO air-strike consensus—albeit under "dual-key" NATO-UN control—that had caused the Bosnian Serbs to pull back their forces temporarily, but was aware that the Balkans remained a brushfire that could at any moment become a forest fire. And then there were other smoldering trouble spots, such as Somalia.

The president, committed by his calendar to address the UN, had somehow to paper over the disagreement between his advisers. He would do so, he decided, by serving up a Clinton concoction: a one-hour smorgasbord of everything. In support of Madeleine Albright he would offer general backing for the UN, but no support for a UN rapid-response army, or even an American unit trained to carry out such a rapid-response mission in support of a UN mission. Indeed, in support of General Powell's view, he wanted a tougher new attitude towards the very notion of UN missions.

The president's UN speech leaked, and, according to the *Times* of London, was expected to "cast a pall over the world's expanding peacekeeping operations," especially at a time when the president was already facing formidable battles in getting Congress to pass his NAFTA and health care reform bills. His predecessor, President Bush, had sent in troops to Somalia with the best of humanitarian intentions, but now the deaths of eleven American soldiers there, including three in the downing of a Black Hawk helicopter on September 26, 1993, "prompted congressional calls for the withdrawal of the 4,700-strong force there, most of which is under UN command. The administration's official line is that policy towards Somalia and Bosnia will remain the same. The White House press secretary said that the weekend killings 'underscore the need to re-establish security in Mogadishu to prevent the international humanitarian efforts from being undermined' "—but how was this to be achieved, at a time when Congress was becoming less, not more, interventionist?

Edward Mortimer, writing in the *Financial Times*, lauded Mr. Clinton for his high intelligence and for "bringing with him into government a formidable array of intellectuals who have been honing their brains and refining their ideas in think-tanks and universities during the long years of opposition"—but wondered whether, in the brutal world of ethnic and tribal hatred, think-tankers would be effective. How could a group of intellectuals provide the sort of backbone that the world's last superpower was required to show—especially given the inherent powerlessness of the UN itself? "The weakness of the administration's 'think-tank' approach to policymaking is, precisely, that it does not facilitate quick or decisive reactions to unexpected events," Mortimer warned. "A problem like Bosnia, and perhaps still less Russia, cannot be relied on to sit still while six committees of brilliant political scientists hammer out a policy statement, writing incisive minutes in the margins of each other's drafts; or while the president conducts a thoughtful and well-informed debate with himself in the presence of his advisers, or sometimes of astonished journalists." All too soon Mortimer's fears would be realized.

Ship of Fools

As the diplomats and governments of the nations of the world took stock of the new "Clinton Doctrine" (that the president would first have to seek "a clear expression of support" from the Congress before countenancing the loss of a single American life abroad), the weakness of the new approach was vividly illustrated when American troops in Somalia, having been reduced in number from 35,000 to 4,700, were asked to undertake bold new tasks, with an insufficiency of arms.

Foreign diplomats and governments were not the only ones made anxious by President Clinton's mixed signals. Three days after Clinton's UN speech, General Colin Powell, the man Bill Clinton ought to have made his secretary of state, stepped down as chairman of the Joint Chiefs of Staff—the same day that the *Harlan County* set sail for Haiti. Relieved of his burden of traditional loyalty to his defense department superior, Powell now warned President Clinton that Les Aspin, the defense secretary, was a disaster, and should be fired immediately, before America was humbled.

An atypical reaction to medical shots before flying out to Somalia in the summer of 1993 had meant that, as defense secretary, Aspin had never even gotten to see the country where some two American divisions were deployed on active service. Nor had any other senior Clinton official, except Madeleine Albright—who was all for "nation-building," along with UN Secretary-General Boutros Boutros-Ghali. In this way, not only was the worsening situation in Somalia not properly investigated by, or on behalf of, the secretary of defense, but the rising level of anti-Americanism in the wholly Muslim country was simply ignored. Requests by the struggling U.S. peacekeepers for more armor were turned down by Secretary Aspin. "Amazingly," wrote David Halberstam, "there was no high-level national security meeting at which the potential for greater violence inflicted on American troops was fully addressed."

The president listened to Powell, but ignored his advice. Not only was Bill Clinton still almost constitutionally unable to dismiss anyone he had himself appointed, he was still unable to appoint a chief of staff who would carry out such necessary dismissals for him. Moreover, for the very reason he admired Colin Powell as the most distinguished living black American, Clinton also feared the general as a potential rival. *What if Powell decided to run for president in '96?* Clinton was thus loath to do anything that might further inflate Powell's reputation and popularity—refusing, for example, to grant Powell a fifth star in recognition of Desert Storm, such as had been awarded to General Eisenhower during the World War II campaign in Europe, and General Bradley during the Korean war. Indeed the president refused even to offer Powell a post-military assignment or honorary position commensurate with his talents, anxious lest Powell then accept it, as Eisenhower had done in becoming supreme commander of NATO forces in Europe in 1951, which became one of his stepping-stones to the Republican Party's nomination-by-acclamation.

Such a mean-minded attitude by an otherwise generous president was illustrative of Bill Clinton's flip side. His inability to function as a manager of men and women in a structured environment, as well as his underlying distrust of anyone close who might overshadow him as an equal (rather than a revered older man or woman, preferably foreign) was typified in his treatment of Colin Powell—and his rejection of Powell's urgent warning.

The Darkest Day

Three days after Powell's warning, disaster struck. A lightning attack by U.S. Rangers to capture two top lieutenants of Mohamed Aideed—the clan leader causing the worst of Somalia's civil strife—turned into a massacre. Some eighteen American soldiers were killed and ninety wounded. Recorded in print and dramatized on film as *Black Hawk Down*, "it was certainly one of the darkest days of the last eight years," Lake's deputy national security adviser, Sandy Berger, later recounted. "We got called in the middle of the night. I think Tony Lake called the president. It was Sunday morning, October 3, 1993. We came into the White House. The beginning of any of these episodes always has conflicting facts, and the facts change—how many people are killed, and is there still something going on? Initial facts are always false. That's the premise that I inculcate in my staff—don't jump to any conclusions based on the wire story. But, obviously, as we learned more about this, it was clear we had suffered a terrible loss. It was a very, very difficult day."

"Difficult" was an understatement, born of the difference between the instantaneousness of modern newsgathering via satellite, and the ponderous transmission of information via government agencies. "News organizations have better coverage than the CIA does in many areas," Tony Lake would later acknowledge. "When you're working information through the intelligence system—either through the Pentagon or through the CIA or the State Department—it has to go through layers because people are trying to turn the information into intelligence": in other words, not only "raw data, but also what it means."

The raw information from Mogadishu, however, was all too clear—graphically portrayed in indelible images beamed back to America by CNN. Pouring into Mogadishu's downtown area to attack the surrounded Rangers and Delta Force troops General Powell had dispatched *in extremis*, the Somali attackers met a veritable storm of fire, in which possibly as many as a thousand Somalis were killed. In many ways, the scene resembled a John Wayne or Sylvester Stallone movie—except that this was real, and that real American soldiers, too, were getting slaughtered. As Halberstam chronicled, "It was in all ways an American disaster, and by the end of the day video clips were being broadcast of a dead American soldier being dragged through the streets of Mogadishu to the cheers of local crowds."

President Clinton's "first reaction was, of course, horror at what happened and dismay at it," Lake recalled. He was "revolted and furious," Berger remembered, "both at the Aideed forces for having perpetrated this on the United States, and in trying to determine how this had happened and what had gone wrong." Not having taken any prior interest in the "seize Aideed" operation being undertaken by the Rangers, the president was at a loss to understand, or to know what to do. "It was absolutely the bottom of [my] four years on national security issues generally," Lake reflected later. Stunned and conflicted, the president didn't, Lake recalled, "have a first reaction, a first decision. He wanted to hear from his advisers and from congressional leaders on what we should do."

Tony Lake was aghast—not at the president's desire to involve the Hill in any decision he might make, but by Clinton's mien. "His first meeting with congressional leaders after Black Hawk Down was a disaster, in my view," Lake recalled candidly. "Because he went in there and simply asked them what they thought we should do. Which is like cutting your finger in a shark tank."

Senators Byrd and Dole called for withdrawal, while Lake and others pleaded to keep American troops there, at least until others could take their place. "I remember arguing in front of the president that if we got out too quickly, we'd put a bull's-eye on the backs of American soldiers around the world," Lake recounted. "The message would be: You kill Americans, America withdraws from that situation."

In the end, the president decided to withdraw the troops—slowly.

The Bay of Pigs

The damage, however, had already been done. As Halberstam put it, Mogadishu was a "major league CNN-era disaster." U.S. forces had originally been ordered in by President Bush to feed a starving civilian population on behalf of compassionate Americans recoiling at the sight, on CNN, of emaciated, dying children. Now, thanks to the same CNN, Americans were seen slaughtered and their bodies dragged in the dust. Understandably, American citizens at home were outraged.

The truth was, despite having been reduced to almost a tenth of the original number sent by President Bush, U.S. military forces had been asked to fulfill, under UN command, a new UN "nation-building" mission, at the behest of Secretary-General Boutros Boutros-Ghali and the encouragement of Ambassador Madeleine Albright—a mission for which the troops were not numerous enough, nor properly equipped, fighting traditionally fractious Somali Muslim warlords whose men were armed with free weaponry given to them by successive western and communist governments throughout the Cold War.

It was, both metaphorically and in terms of bin Laden involvement, a replay of the Soviet Union's vain attempt to bring order and modern infrastructure to backward, Muslim Afghanistan in the 1980s—a country long famous for its warring tribes and anti-Western outlook.

"Somalia wasn't quite his Bay of Pigs," David Gergen later commented of President Clinton's dilemma, "but it came close. It was a situation in which I think he in retrospect realized that as president he had allowed the mission to expand, what's called mission creep, and at the same time he had been withdrawing down the number of forces who could do it. And he left his forces in a situation where they were overexposed to danger. And he knew that. And in retrospect, I think he blamed himself to some extent and I think to some extent he blamed some of his advisors."

This was Gergenspeak. Smarting from the devastatingly bad publicity in America, the president had in truth screamed abuse at his aides, demanding to know who was responsible, and how such a catastrophe could possibly have happened on his watch without his knowing.

In Clinton's circle of courteous hand-picked courtiers, however, no one dared tell the president the bitter truth: that it had been an accident waiting to happen—because of his style of White House executive management.

CHAPTER TWENTY-THREE

THE *HARLAN COUNTY* FIASCO

Theater of the Absurd

As if the victory of a puny Somalian warlord over the great United States was not enough, a week later there was a second, internationally televised American military humiliation, as the USS *Harlan County*, carrying deposed president Jean-Bertrand Aristide, finally arrived at Port-au-Prince. To the chagrin of its crew and troops, it encountered no Haitian military rulers vacating the country as promised, or even a docking slip ready: only a crowd of taunting, armed Haitians shouting, "Somalia! Somalia!"

David Gergen, Stephanopoulos, and other communications advisers all counseled immediate flight. "People blame me for some of this," Gergen later acknowledged, "but my argument to the president was: 'You got one of two choices. You either got to go in with force and take care of that unruly mob, you can take them in five minutes. Or you got to get the ship the hell out of there.'"

The president got them out of there, opting for a trade embargo rather than force. This did not go down well with a vexed public in America, however. The taunts of Haitian thugs and the fleeing of the USS *Harlan County* constituted "one of the most embarrassing moments in recent American history," as Halberstam put it—a new low for the Clinton administration. "The theater of the absurd," the official American negotiator called it.

Even Sandy Berger, Tony Lake's deputy and a die-hard Clinton loyalist, later reflected how mistaken it was to have failed to use American military power to enforce the agreement. "Looking back on it, I would have done it differently," he conceded. "Three days after we pulled the *Harlan County* out, we took six warships and put them out around Haiti, and said, 'We're going to enforce this embargo a hundred percent.' And I've often thought if we'd put the six warships around Haiti on day one, the *Harlan County* could have left on day five, and no one would have paid any attention. There's a good example; symbols do matter. I think the way we handled it was a tactical mistake."

To those watching at the time—and historians assessing the fiasco later—the flight of the *Harlan County* was far more than a tactical mistake, however. General Gordon Sullivan, as U.S. Army chief of staff, was appalled. "I remember it vividly. I was at Fort Drum, New York, to pay a visit. I guess it was around Columbus Day, it was a holiday, and I flew down to Norfolk, navy Norfolk, to see Admiral Paul David Miller, who was commander of all American and NATO forces in the Atlantic, and we talked about the *Harlan County*. And that wasn't a great day. Because this warship—essentially a warship, a supply ship, it was a troop carrier really—pulled up to the pier in Port-au-Prince and a bunch of thugs, probably half-smoked up with whatever dope they were smoking or whatever they were drinking, drove 'em away! And the *Harlan County* weighed anchor—and left! And the gist of the conversation between the two of us was: 'Well, we've gotta figure this out, 'cause this is not . . . we can't live with this!'"

The *Harlan County* Fiasco, as it became known, seemed yet another manifestation of the president's erratic interest in foreign affairs, his still-distressing inability to choose effective subordinates, his ignorance of power-politics involving actual or potential military action, and his grave decision-making deficits.

As in 1980 when he lost the governorship of Arkansas, Bill Clinton would, however, shoulder no blame—though the problems were as clear as day to journalists. "A string of policy failures has led senators to publicly chide the president for spending too little time on foreign affairs, and for surrounding himself with weak advisers," the *Boston Globe*'s Mary Curtius reported. And she added the fact that "Rumors are rife that one of the president's advisers—either Lake, Secretary of State Warren Christopher or Secretary of Defense Les Aspin—may be forced out if embarrassing crises keep accumulating."

Basically Isolationists

Somalia, David Halberstam wrote, "confirmed the worst suspicions about the Clinton administration": that it was unable to back up its rhetoric. Anthony Lake agreed, in retrospect. "It does no good to be prepared to use force, or other instruments of power," he later wrote, "if others do not believe you have the political will to actually use it in a sufficiently coercive manner."

Somalia might have confirmed people's suspicions, but they did not do justice to Bill Clinton's ambivalence at this moment in history. His instincts were the same as any red-blooded American's. "We're not inflicting pain on those fuckers," he'd snarled at Stephanopoulos, as the catastrophe in Somalia unfolded. "When people kill us, they should be killed in greater numbers," he'd remarked (unaware that American troops were, indeed, doing exactly that). Stephanopoulos recalled how, pounding his thigh, his face going red with apoplexy, the president had turned on Tony Lake, his national security adviser, and declared: "I believe in killing people who try to hurt you"—adding, "I can't believe we're being pushed around by these two-bit pricks." When the fiasco in Haiti then followed on the heels of the tragedy in Somalia, the president had called Lake from his helicopter, *Marine One*, over North Carolina, screaming as the USS *Harlan County* steamed back to Puerto Rico in disgrace: "The Reagan people were much better at the politics of foreign policy than we are. Look at Lebanon"—where more than two hundred marines had been killed by a terrorist bomb in 1983. "They [American forces] went into Grenada two days later and fixed it." Stephanopoulos had been aghast when Lake recounted to him the tirade. "Grenada?" he'd queried in his mind. "I couldn't believe what I was hearing. *If you really feel that,*" he'd mused at the time, "*then why'd we turn the damn ship around?*"

The answer was, the president was still uncertain where the world was heading, and how he might prepare the American people for an uncertain future, in terms of national security. The men he'd appointed as secretary of state and secretary of defense had turned out to be incompetent—leaving the full weight of such security concerns on his inexpert shoulders. Uncertain, he had turned to the latest polls—which legitimized, he had felt, a gradual withdrawal of all American troops from Somalia and the avoidance of trouble in Haiti, as well as Bosnia. "Americans are basically isolationists," he'd told Stephanopoulos after church on the very day of the Mogadishu humiliation. "Right now the average American doesn't see our interest threatened to the point where we should sacrifice one American life."

Passing the Buck

The problem with Greenberg's polling was that it could tell the president what average Americans felt *in response* to questions about policy and priorities, but nothing *proactive* about leadership, or, indeed, ways of combating the fast-diminishing stature of the United States on the world scene. To his consternation, Stephanopoulos watched as leaks of Clinton's fury with his own foreign policy team appeared in the press, and American international standing declined even further. When the president was asked on NBC's *Meet the Press* whether Aspin and Secretary of State Warren Christopher might be fired, Clinton merely responded that "they have done well on 'many big things,' and that 'some of the attacks' on them were unfair."

Some? A senior administration official said Clinton was warned in advance that such an ambivalent answer, which he had rehearsed in a mock interview before the show, "would leave the impression of lukewarm support"—but it had not stopped the president from passing the buck. "Mr. President, you just have to . . ." Stephanopoulos began a weak attempt at reinforcement, a few days later. "I know it's hard now, but you really have to, around other people, you have to stand by your people. You have to communicate confidence down the ranks."

But Bill Clinton *had* no confidence down the ranks of men whom he himself had chosen, or mischosen! "No one told me about the downside," he wailed about the Mogadishu fiasco. Comparing Waco with the latest disaster, he said, "At least I knew what was happening [at WACO] and that it had the potential of going bad."

The shame of having to be lectured to by a thirty-two-year-old, however, was only the latest of Bill Clinton's consequent humiliations. By screwing up as commander-in-chief he had further infuriated a traditional right wing in America, which placed great store on national pride and American standing in the world. Of this, the president would eventually become aware. "I'm never going to wimp out," he would tell his aides later, on a visit overseas, "like I did in Haiti again." But by then it was too late.

America Is Weak

Somalia and the *Harlan County* episode, General Sullivan later reflected, had "a huge knock-on effect." In the "poisoned atmosphere" at home, where a divided nation expressed itself in intense political partisanship in Congress, American overseas involvement in peacekeeping and nation-building became "discredited terms": "a shock to the American system" that left ordinary Americans wondering what were the national interests of the United States of America that would cause the U.S. to become involved in a firefight in Mogadishu—or anywhere else, abroad. "Nation-building becomes a hot . . . it's like radioactive," General Sullivan recalled. "And all of that played itself out in our involvement in the Balkans."

It was in this context that, with President Clinton blaming the staff he'd appointed, and preoccupied with his next domestic agenda—the launching of Hillary's health care reform bill and the ratification of NAFTA—a cruel attack was readied: one that was not, originally, intended to topple the new president in the American White House so much as to force Bill Clinton—as the plotters had forced President Yeltsin in Russia—to show more muscularity in leading his country.

TROOPERGATE

CHAPTER TWENTY-FOUR

INSPECTOR JACKSON

"Not Some Holier-than-Thou Guy"

Looking back, years later, at the national scandal that erupted late in 1993, Little Rock attorney Cliff Jackson was at pains to assert that his own role had been honorable: that he was not part of a "vast, right-wing conspiracy," as Hillary subsequently claimed.

Jackson harbored no grudge against his old Oxford friend in terms of Vietnam service, he said. He himself had gotten a medical deferral. *"Millions* avoided the draft," Jackson pointed out. "And I *helped* him avoid the draft, for Pete's sake! So I'm not some holier-than-thou guy who's pro-war, or pro-American involvement in Vietnam.

"I always thought he would be president," Jackson later explained, "because he and I had had a lot of discussions about it. I knew that was his ambition, and I knew he was capable of meeting it." Asked why, Jackson was forthright.

"Okay," Jackson began, articulating each word in his distinctive, rolling southern drawl, "Bill Clinton is the very best politician this country, and you're probably gonna think I'm hyperbolizing—but he is the very best politician this country *has ever seen!* Now that's a statement, isn't it? That is *a mouthful!* But I believe it, because he has the techniques of campaigning and politicking in elections better than anybody I know in history—and I'm a history major! I mean, I *study* American politics! He *knows* how to do it: the nitty gritty, the nuts and bolts. He is great personally at networking. He has this charisma and ability to connect; the ability to dance on the head of a pin with twelve different positions, with twelve different people in a room, all on an issue that is critical to their vote for him. And he will look them each in the eye and he will smile and he will engage the eye contact, he will listen to what they have to say as if they are the only person in the room. He will then make some comment that conveys to each one of these twelve people that he really is on their side, despite what he may have said to the other eleven. And every one of them will leave that room thinking, 'Well, he did say some things in favor of the other eleven positions—but he's really for me!' And that's a tremendous gift, you know.

"So he has the innate ability to get elected. That's one aspect of it. The second aspect of it: he has this drive to power that exceeds, in my opinion, Richard Nixon's and Lyndon Johnson's—and I never thought I'd ever see anybody above Lyndon Johnson's, after reading Robert Caro's book— because Johnson would walk over his *mother* to get elected! I would tell re- porters in '92—they'd say, 'what's Bill Clinton like?' I'd say: 'Go read Robert Caro's *Path to Power*! I'll say no more—*just read the book*!'

"So he has this tremendous drive to power. And then the third aspect is this—which I perceive as a negative in terms of a human being in gover- nance, but in terms of being able to be elected, it's positive. His *malleabil- ity*. His lack of principle. His willingness to be anything to anyone, to adapt to any position, to say anything, in order to get elected. And to do it without being caught at it. To wiggle through the inconsistencies of political amorality. . . .

"And you combine those three elements, and I think you have an ex- tremely high likelihood that this man will be successful.

"I think you also have a potential for an extreme danger to the republic, if truth be known—because a person such as that, I think, could pose a dan- ger. Not that he *would*, but he could. Because that's an *awesome* combina- tion." Jackson shook his large head admiringly. "It's an awesome combination."

Two Different People

Bill Clinton's progress from the Arkansas attorney general's office to the Governor's Mansion in Little Rock had seemed to Jackson, even at the time, to be inexorable "steppingstones to the end goal" of the presidency. When Clinton gave his New Covenant speech in 1991, Jackson had been thrilled. "I thought it was wonderful! I mean it was superb! If I had been writing it, I could not have been more eloquent! I mean, he expressed ideas and thoughts that I have had—I mean if I had not known him, if I had believed he really believed that, I would have been enthralled by the man.

"But I *do* know the man," Jackson was quick to add, as if addressing a jury. "And what I know is *this*: that he made that speech, and it went over well. And the very next day he is capable of giving a speech that is a hundred and eighty degrees opposite of the sentiments, the ideas, the philosophy that he expressed at that particular moment. So the question is not whether Bill Clinton has good ideas. He does! The question is, does he *mean* it when he says it? Does he *believe* it when he says it? And there's a division of opinion on that. I know [Arkansas journalist] John Brummett thinks he does—but [that he] then changes it. I'm not so sure. I'm not so sure that he isn't just . . . *malleable*, you know—that there's no center there."

Had Bill Clinton always been so? "*Yes!*" Jackson responded emphatically. "*The essential Clinton has not changed.* Not at all! From the time I first met him at Oxford until today, I would say, the essential Bill Clinton has not changed.

"He and I are entirely two different people.

"I mean what I say. *I say what I mean.* I'm very direct. I'm very intense. I'm very personal. I will get inside people's heads. I will make people uncomfortable," the attorney admitted—recalling how his opposition had needled the Clinton campaign sufficiently that the governor had been compelled to go on talk radio in New Hampshire in 1992 to nix the ads of Jackson's Independent Action Committee. In doing so, Clinton had portrayed his old friend, Cliff Jackson, as "a long-time, bitter Republican who has for years tried to bring me down."

Given Jackson's twenty-year withdrawal from the political fray in Arkansas, Clinton's counterblast, Jackson felt, was completely untrue. Far from having for years tried to bring Clinton down, he maintained, Jackson had wanted so much to build Clinton *up*, from the time he'd put his own Republican career and credibility on the line to help Clinton get out of the draft—hoping against hope that his fellow Arkansan, with such veritable genius at politics, would mature with Hillary's help and grow a center, a core, that people in turn could grow to trust. "I'm no innocent," Jackson insisted. "I understand that politicians wiggle—that it's a necessity of a successful politician, the ability to wiggle, the ability to move out of situations, to be a little bit malleable. But at the core there needs to be some firm, guiding principles and commitment to something or someone, other than yourself."

Clinton's flip-flopping performance in the White House after his inauguration appalled Jackson, from the "gays in the military" fiasco through Travelgate: exposing the incompetence not only of the president but of the White House staff. "Wiggling" was producing a mockery of the office of president and, despite a Democratic-led Congress, worse gridlock on Capitol Hill than ever. It was 1978—Clinton's first term as governor of Arkansas—*all over again*! Clinton was indeed, as in the slogan of the Independent Action Committee in the '92 election, doing unto America what he had done to Arkansas.

Thus, when the telephone had rung and Lynn Davis, a fellow Little Rock attorney who had once been director of State Police under Republican governor Winthrop Rockefeller, had called to ask Jackson's help, the trial lawyer had listened very, very carefully.

A Feeling of Illegitimacy

A sense that President Bill Clinton was somehow a usurper had swiftly come to replace the excitement, indeed euphoria, that had characterized the inauguration of the nation's first baby-boomer president, Jackson maintained. As the new president failed to earn the support of a Democratic-controlled Congress, and as the White House stumbled from one mess-up to another, the hopes of millions of patriotic Americans had become frustrated, as Jackson saw it. "A large segment of the population looked at him, and the personal flaws, and said: 'How did he ever. . . ? I mean, it's surreal! I mean, this guy's *president*?' Again, not that he avoided the draft, but the *manner* in which he did it. 'And now he's commander-in-chief, asking our young men to go in harm's way!' And with the military, that's a big issue! I mean, with the story coming out about his 'loathing the military'—you can understand the feeling of illegitimacy."

A meeting with Lynn Davis and a group of Arkansas state troopers, held at Jackson's office in Little Rock, now added to this sense of illegitimacy a new concern: immorality.

Troopergate

There had originally been, Lynn Davis later explained, five state troopers. One had then backed out. The four remaining policemen seemed nervous, Jackson recalled—aware that in coming forward with their stories they were tempting fate, and their careers would be on the line. One after another, they unburdened themselves to Jackson. Their accounts were mind-boggling.

"We lied for him. We helped him cheat on his wife. And he treated us like dogs," the troopers told Jackson.

Cheating was, if anything, a euphemism. Jackson had known of Bill Clinton's susceptibility to the charms of young female campaign volunteers going back to his first congressional fight in 1974, but the troopers' stories of the governor's philandering in the Mansion in Little Rock, in the Mansion's grounds, in women's cars and trucks, and in their houses and apartments, was reminiscent of ancient Rome.

Power corrupts, and absolute power corrupts absolutely, Lord Acton had written. Bill Clinton had not held absolute power in Arkansas by any means, but he *had* wielded extraordinary power over some women, while expecting his detail of Arkansas state troopers, it appeared, not only to protect him but to procure, drive, ferry, conceal, and lie for him—especially with regard to his wife, Hillary.

No man, of course, can be a hero to his valet, whose discretion had for centuries been considered as sacred as a gentleman's word. Those times had changed, however. *The Remains of the Day*, from the novel by Kazuo Ishiguro, was about to hit the nation's screens in November 1993, with its excruciating portrayal by Anthony Hopkins of a loyal butler who recognizes that his absolute faithfulness to his master, Lord Darlington, has been misplaced. It is the master who is faithless. The film, set in the 1930s, would strike a deeply contemporary note. Fuelled by an insatiable public curiosity about the private lives of prominent people, there was a growing willingness among servants and subordinates across the world to reveal to tabloids what they knew of their masters and mistresses. From *People* magazine to celebrity programs on television, the media was responding to public voyeurism in the West, epitomized in the word "paparazzi." The troopers at the Governor's Mansion in Little Rock were trained policemen, acting as personal, armed bodyguards for the governor, to protect him from harm. What they now revealed to Jackson raised fresh and serious anxieties about the character, morality, behavior, and integrity of the five-time former governor.

Jackson was not a courtroom lawyer for nothing. He grilled each trooper in turn. "I am a trial lawyer, and I read people," Jackson later explained. "Yes, I was absolutely persuaded they were telling me the truth. These were straight-shooting guys."

Each individual, in the unfolding saga that would be called Troopergate, had his own motivation. At the heart of the matter, however, was the fact that they had all seen their boss, Captain Raymond "Buddy" Young, promoted from a poorly paid ($25,600 per year) Arkansas job to a well-paid federal position as director of a regional Federal Emergency Management Agency office in Texas, at a salary of $98,000 per year: a quadrupling of his income, and an ample reward for his years of loyal service to Governor Clinton. The troopers themselves had also been assured that the governor would "look after them," if and when he got to the White House.

In Bill Clinton's mind, however, the troopers symbolized not the many years of loyal service beyond the call of duty, but a trail of private shame to which they were uniquely privy, and which the president presumably would rather not think about. Instead of ensuring that the troopers were looked after, therefore, he had stupidly ignored them, hoping they would somehow go away.

But they hadn't—and their revelations would not only stigmatize the otherwise noble efforts of the freshman president, but inadvertently give rise to a lawsuit that would dog Bill Clinton to the day he left the Oval Office.

Clinton's Bad-boy Behavior

Amazingly, none of the Arkansas troopers guarding the Governor's Mansion in Little Rock had talked to the press during the 1992 presidential campaign. Governor Clinton, after all, was still their master, with two more elected years to run in Arkansas if he failed to unseat the incumbent president, George H. W. Bush. Yet even after his victory in November, he had, according to Trooper Roger Perry, expected his bodyguard to facilitate his adulterous trysts, such as get-togethers with his favorite mistress, Marilyn Jo Denton, who would even come, Monroe style, to the Governor's Mansion, wearing a trench coat and baseball cap, pretending to be a transition staffer. The state police officer "was instructed to stand at the top of the stairs leading from the basement to the main floor of the residence and to alert Clinton if Hillary woke up," he later revealed. The ruse, performed early in the morning only two floors below the marital bedroom, was pure JFK-Jackie behavior: the proximity of a sleeping wife providing a crucial element of sexual bravado, of tempting fate as well as marital-maternal wrath.

JFK had at least known what he was doing—namely, that the press would never dare expose his philandering. Thirty years later, in 1992, the press would gladly do so—the more so since there was widespread concern, in spite of the famous CBS *60 Minutes* broadcast, that the Clinton marriage might be a sham, and that Hillary had her own, feminist agenda. "More than most presidential marriages, the Clintons' will need to have a happy public face," reporters Michael Kelly and Maureen Dowd had warned prominently in the *New York Times*. "The image of the incoming president as an honest, decent man depends on the carefully cultivated idea that though he may have sinned, he has been redeemed. 'He can't play J.F.K.,' says a top Democrat. 'If he does, it would be a killer. All bets would be off.'"

Now that Bill Clinton *was* president in Washington, D.C., however, and no longer their paymaster, the troopers were no longer constrained in revealing what they knew of Bill's—and Hillary's—behavior, behind the scenes. Threatening to go public with their true stories of Governor Clinton's bad-boy lifestyle would force the young president to make good on his promises of better jobs, they reasoned. If he did not—indeed, even if he did—there was always the possibility they could make their stories into a book, as FBI agent Gary Aldrich was to do with his White House experiences, and both Hillary and Bill Clinton also, with *their* White House experiences, for historic sums of money. Finally, there was the matter of security in the Governor's Mansion, as in the White House. As a former police director, Lynn Davis was already aware, from the many stories that had passed around the homes and bars of Little Rock, that there existed a real "danger of compromise" in the case of William Jefferson Clinton: a reckless politician whose promiscuous private life not only made it difficult for his bodyguards to protect him physically, but held out the danger of potential blackmail by his enemies, even foreign powers.

In this respect Davis was impressed that, of the five troopers who originally came forward, none seemed to have a personal dislike or animosity towards the president. "It was not hate of Clinton," Davis was at pains to make clear, later. "I don't think anyone hated him in the group. All of them had good feelings about Clinton."

The troopers' good feelings did not blind them, however, to the governor's problem with women. "None of the troopers had any doubt about Bill's predilections of a sexual nature," Davis said, but he explained that none of the troopers held the president's lifelong promiscuity against him, either, since none felt themselves, as fellow males, to be necessarily any better, morally speaking. Unrewarded for their years of special, supra-professional loyalty—so far beyond the call of duty—the troopers felt justified in coming forward and, if necessary, "going public" with their testimonies, if the president continued to ignore them. It was, in essence, conspiracy and blackmail, but, they claimed, blackmail to avoid more serious potential blackmail, since they wanted "to address the danger of compromise," Davis recalled—that is, the danger of the presidency being compromised. Bill Clinton, after all, was no longer simply the governor of a small southern state. Of course, the governor of any state, large or small, "doesn't have a finger on the nuclear trigger," Davis added, "with the security of the western world in his hand." Behaving recklessly with women was to risk the safety of the world.

The Fox and the Lion

None of the troopers were, at this early stage, overtly Republican, right-wing, or ideological. Jackson's involvement would, Davis assured the troopers, ensure that they were represented by a tough trial lawyer, if he took on their cause, a man who kowtowed to no one—not even his old Oxford buddy, the president of the United States.

Some 480 years before, in 1513, a great Renaissance political analyst, Niccolò di Bernardi Machiavelli, had penned a treatise that explored the exigencies of political survival. In a chapter on the avoidance of "contempt and hatred," Machiavelli had warned against a princely ruler acting despotically by taking "the property and the women of his subjects. He must refrain from these." Equally, he should avoid gaining a reputation "for being fickle, frivolous, effeminate, cowardly, irresolute." A prince must avoid such a reputation "like the plague," he warned, lest he give rise to disappointment, resentment—and conspiracy.

A successful prince, Machiavelli made clear, was not necessarily a man who was a saint or even truthful—in fact, "contemporary experience shows that princes who have achieved great things have been those who have given their word lightly, who have known how to trick men with their cunning, and who, in the end, have overcome those abiding by honest principles." Thus, Machiavelli argued, to be successful a prince "must learn from the fox and the lion"—because "the lion is defenseless against traps and a fox is defenseless against wolves. Those who simply act like lions are stupid. So it follows that a prudent ruler cannot, and must not, honour his word when it places him at a disadvantage, and when the reasons for which he made his promise no longer exist." It was only necessary to know "how to colour one's actions," and to be what Machiavelli called "a great liar and deceiver. Men are so simple, and so much creatures of circumstance, that the deceiver will always find someone ready to be deceived. . . . A prince, therefore, need not necessarily have all the good qualities I mentioned above, but he should certainly *appear* to have them. . . ."

"There are two things a prince must fear," Machiavelli had especially noted, however: "internal subversion from his subjects; and external aggression by foreign powers." With regard to the first, "the prince's chief fear must be a secret conspiracy." In this, the prince was accorded, however, a distinct advantage over conspirators. Mounting any kind of attack against a prince who was "highly esteemed" was never, Machiavelli explained, an easy option—indeed, "open attack is difficult, provided he [the prince] is recognized as a great man, who is respected by his subjects."

Here, the difference between JFK and Bill Clinton was most pronounced—though it had not saved the Massachusetts hero from assassination. President Kennedy had been widely respected as a leader, in the White House, running a superlative cabinet and staff; President Clinton appeared to be constantly on the point of failure, despite his good intentions.

In short, had Bill Clinton performed effectively and resolutely in the White House *as a leader* in his first year, there is considerable doubt whether the "conspirators" in Arkansas would have found traction with their complaints. "To put it briefly," Machiavelli had written (after being tortured by the Medicis, and forced to retire from Florentine government), "I say that on the side of the conspirator there is nothing except fear, envy, and the terrifying prospect of punishment; on the side of the prince there is the majesty of government, there are laws, the resources of his friends and of the state to protect him. Add to these the goodwill of the people, and it is unthinkable that anyone should be so rash as to conspire."

Mixed Motives

Quite why the troopers had decided to seek Davis's help in making their grievances public at that moment in American history Jackson could not afterwards explain. "They were terrified at the step they were taking," he said—afraid for their safety, and afraid they would lose their jobs. "They didn't think, they *knew* that once they spoke, their jobs were ended": not only their jobs at the Mansion, as state troopers on bodyguard duty, but also the second jobs on which many policemen in Arkansas, drawing minimal state pay, relied.

Machiavelli had pointed out the difficulty of preserving unanimity of purpose and conspiratorial trust, since each new person drawn into the conspiracy is thereby able—and is often tempted—to inform on the others: the Judas syndrome. "Seeing the sure profit to be won by informing, and the highly dangerous and doubtful alternative, a man must either be a rare friend indeed or else an utterly relentless enemy of the prince," Machiavelli had observed, "to keep faith with" his co-conspirators.

Machiavelli was right. Certainly "Prince" William Jefferson Clinton learned through a Judas in the fall of 1993 that there was a "plot" brewing in Little Rock. Unlike President Kennedy, who had used his millionaire father and loyal "Boston-Irish mafia" to protect his throne, Clinton had no millionaire father, no barons to call upon to help him, and no tough chief of staff—since he had deliberately not appointed one.

Unwilling for the moment to bring back the enforcer—his old chief of staff from the time he was governor, Betsey Wright—the multi-tasking president decided that, in relation to the Arkansas troopers' conspiracy, he would try to manage everything *himself*, with the help only of Buddy Young, the former captain of his Arkansas police detail. On taking over the office of the presidency he'd ordered an immediate revamping of the old White House telephone switchboard, which until then was still employing a central operator who could listen in to calls. Under the new system he had become able to make, and receive, unmonitored calls. The president of the United States therefore called the conspirators himself!

By talking directly to the troopers the president hoped he could "divide and conquer." Certainly he divided the plotters. His telephone conversation with Buddy Young, appealing to Young to persuade the troopers to desist, either in return for the promise of federal positions or reprisals, was followed by several direct telephone negotiations with Trooper Danny Ferguson. Ferguson, in due course, caved in—but with the entry of Cliff Jackson into the arena, the president soon realized, the terms of the conspiracy had altered.

As fast as the president sweet-talked Ferguson to persuade him to withdraw from the conspiracy in the fall of 1993, Jackson worked to hold the plotters together. The president's successor as governor, Jim Guy Tucker, threatened to have the "squealing" troopers run off the Arkansas reservation if they "blabbed": well, then, he, Jackson, would find the men guarantees of alternative employment. With this in mind Jackson went to a prominent conservative financier, Peter Smith, to seek assurances, if possible, that the men would be offered jobs paying up to $100,000 per year for seven years. Speaking quietly into the receiver in the Oval Office, Clinton listened as Trooper Ferguson snitched on his colleagues. "All mad because I didn't give jobs," the president unwisely scribbled (his barely legible but duly transcribed notes subpoenaed and later used as a deposition exhibit in the investigation by Independent Counsel Kenneth Starr). "Troopers being talked to by lawyer—offered big $."

This news was bad enough. In a second call, however, conspirator Ferguson revealed more. The "lawyer" the men had gone to was none other than "Cliff Jackson," as the president noted, "—with another lawyer": Lynn Davis. Trooper Ferguson meanwhile assured the president that he himself had never intended to join the conspiracy, but "went to first meeting to see what they were doing, played along with [it]," Clinton scribbled, and he went on to take down the details of particular stories and allegations the men intended to make public, involving "Beth Coulson," "K[atie] Arnold," "Susie," and "GFlowers" (sic).

The president protested his innocence of any wrongdoing in his notes—but it was *pour l'histoire*. Better than anyone, Ferguson knew how enamored of extramarital recreation the former governor was, and how much he had relied on his trusty bodyguards to facilitate his trysts. Nor had Ferguson ever objected. Ferguson "says he knows [the truth] but wants to stay out of" it, Clinton scribbled. Ferguson was assured by the president: "If you tell me what stories Roger and Larry are telling, I can go in the back door and handle it and clean it up."

The fight was now becoming a battle between the Fulbright Fellow and the Rhodes Scholar; the courtroom lawyer against the former constitutional law professor; the moralist versus the pragmatist.

The Lack of an Inner Core

Listening to the intimate stories of the Arkansas conspirators and Bill Clinton's abuse of gubernatorial power, "Inspector" Jackson was more than ever disappointed in his Oxford friend. What especially concerned him was not simply that Valjean-Clinton had—so the troopers alleged—continued his promiscuous lifestyle even after the presidential election, but that President Clinton was failing to assert the kind of moral and executive leadership worthy of the presidency of the United States.

"I went to a little three-roomed country school where we pledged allegiance to the flag every day and we sang 'God Bless America' and 'The Star Spangled Banner,'" Jackson later explained. "I'm a patriotic-type person. And while I respect the governor of Arkansas, I revered the presidency. I mean, I placed the presidency . . ." The trial attorney's voice trailed away. "The presidency is a position of *moral leadership*," he went on. "A person in that position has the potential to effect great good—or great evil. And great evil can be effected by either omission or commission."

The troopers' stories had confirmed what Jackson had always suspected—that Bill Clinton had not changed since his days at Oxford. "For him, evil starts, I think, with an absence of commitment to principle. And that's what I saw. And that concerned me. It had nothing to do with the womanizing—the womanizing was a symptom. The disease was something bigger! The draft avoidance was, similarly, a symptom. The disease was *who he was*—that lack of an inner core."

Playing Horse

At Oxford, Jackson recalled, Bill Clinton had been not only fiercely competitive, but determined to win at all costs. Sometimes, Jackson remembered, the two of them would spend *hours* on the basketball court playing "Horse" until they dropped—the Rhodes Scholar loath ever to concede victory, willingly, to the Fulbright scholar. To do so now, twenty-five years later—and to a former Republican who had worked against him as an independent during the presidential primaries—not only would be to concede defeat, Clinton recognized, but would allow Jackson to hold a moral sword over his head, able at any time in the future to use it.

Was there a way in which they could reach a compromise, however, the president wondered? In his pursuit of NAFTA, after all, he was willing to dine with sworn enemies. In his quest to counter opposition to his health care reform bill, he had agreed to meet die-hard foes, such as the president of the National Federation of Independent Business, Jack Faris, not merely once, but a number of times—enduring, witnesses said, such wanton rudeness from the little Tennessee businessman, a Republican, that the White House staff was stunned.

Had the goal been successful passage of legislation, then, the president would not have thought twice. He would have called Jackson, as he had called Kerrey, earlier. But this was different. This concerned his *private* life, his marriage—or extra-marriage: his foraging relationships. . . .

Cliff Jackson, the president knew, was from the same background of rural Arkansas poverty as his own, with its accent on morality, evangelical certainty, suffering, and redemption. As president he himself was no absolute monarch, but Jackson was an absolute Christian. There was, Clinton understood, simply no way in which the trial lawyer, with his black-and-white approach to life, would accept a compromise, or an ignoble outcome. He would want the troopers rewarded for their past loyalty, but he would also want Clinton to fess up to having abused their status as state troopers, guarding the governor. And this, the president could not, would not do.

The very thought made Bill Clinton, undefeated in any election for the past ten years, anxious. Apologizing did not come easily to such an ambitious, relentlessly competitive person. He had collapsed in tears at his electoral defeat in 1980, yet only after profound wrestling with his soul and pride had he agreed to Dick Morris's recommendation in 1981 that he make a televised apology for raising ordinary people's car tag taxes in Arkansas, and promise never to do anything like that again. That apology had worked like a charm in a southern Baptist state where human redemption and forgiveness, on earth, was a key feature of southern culture. Yet for complex reasons relating to his psychological makeup, it was not something Bill Clinton would ever, willingly, repeat—as would become all too clear in the years ahead.

How could he, after all, when all his early life he'd had to shut out his stepfather's alcoholic abuse in order to survive—and to bury his shame, both at his stepfather's behavior and his own secret thoughts and desires? "Apparently a lot of people who grow up in difficult circumstances subconsciously blame themselves and feel unworthy of a better fate. . . . My internal life was full of uncertainty, anger, and a dread of ever-looming violence," he would later confess—but only after leaving the Oval Office.

Fiercely loving his mother, basking in her pride at his achievements yet uncertain of her feelings at a deeper level (especially when she remarried Roger Clinton after getting her son to testify on her behalf, as part of her application for a divorce from Clinton), Billy Blythe IV, named after Virginia's first husband, William Jefferson Blythe III, had become almost pathologically unwilling to admit fault and thereby surrender the initiative, and control over his life, to anyone else. He had become, as he later revealed, secretive, leading what he himself called "parallel lives," and only with great difficulty "letting anyone into the deepest recesses of my internal life. It was dark down there." In this respect his almost literally pathetic need to be liked concealed a deeper fear of the opposite: of being disrespected, even abused. The word "like" was thus, to an extent, inadequate, for it was not affection he needed, on a massive scale, but affirmation. "It appears that Clinton does not want to be liked so much as validated," wrote Stanley Renshon, a political science professor and psychoanalyst, in a perceptive study of Clinton's psychology that year. "He wants others to accept the view of himself that he holds, and when they don't, he disowns them and turns against them angrily."

Jackson's view of Clinton's character, Bill Clinton knew, was at marked variance with his own. Ergo, he would never be able to cut a deal with Jackson, short of promising to reform his lifestyle, his vacillations over issues, and his faulty White House command structure. Yet if he did not cut a deal with Jackson, what could he do to head off the looming scandalous revelations?

Big $

As at Oxford, the president did not give up, he merely played harder—working through Captain Young and Trooper Ferguson to bribe, threaten, or otherwise persuade the plotters to desist.

Ignoring Jackson did not, unfortunately, make the trial attorney go away. The more Clinton attempted to head off the disgruntled troopers, the more, the president realized, his nemesis would raise the stakes. His chief informant, Trooper Ferguson, confirmed this—tipping him off, during the latter's second telephone call, that there were "big $ in [it] maybe from T[e]x[as]" behind Jackson." The big bucks, the president knew, heralded political dirty tricks. Ferguson reported that the "GOP [Republican party] in on [it]—now talking about 100G/7 years—job and whatever get from book"—which alone might net the men millions (as Clinton's own memoirs would later net him).

Would a publisher dare print such defamatory stories about a serving U.S. president, though? In snitching on his colleagues, Trooper Ferguson revealed that Cliff Jackson had told the conspirators: "if [three] would say same thing, anyone would print." Therefore, two would not be enough.

Suddenly the math looked doable. Clearly Trooper Ferguson was not going to go with the conspiracy. The president had therefore only to pick off *one* more trooper, and he'd be safe—for the remaining two would never be believed by responsible publishers or newspaper editors. Even if the remaining two troopers *did* find a trash outlet for their stories, they could easily be hosed away by the White House's spin doctors—for the troopers, Clinton knew, were themselves no saints.

With Captain Young's help, a third conspirator was thus duly prised away—and the president breathed a sigh of relief. He would survive—and Hillary's feelings would be spared.

Rationalization

Bill Clinton owed his wife everything. On transplantation to Little Rock, Hillary had not only earned top dollar for years as the chief breadwinner of the family, but had borne him a daughter he adored, and had on his behalf acted as a political sparring partner such as had rarely, if ever, existed in the annals of American government. For that he had always been both grateful and proud—and was so, still. Nor did he blame Hillary, as others did, for being often cold, unlikable, or unexciting. In the intimacy of her own home, he knew, she could be warm and cuddly, even fun. Besides, no woman could be everything, and Hillary was already far more than most. She stood by him when he was attacked, kept him on his political toes, and above all, after seventeen years of marriage and political warfare, believed that he *did* have a core within him, a conscience, despite his enemies' accusations—if only because it was, to a large extent, *her* core: projected, transferred, strengthened by her faith.

Extramarital gratification was thus, in the president's own mind, a minor sin within such a devoted relationship, where genuine affection, loyalty, and mutual respect were the crucial factors, not sex. After all, had not their biblical forefathers had mistresses, harems, handmaidens? Did that mean they did not love their wives? "After all, it isn't like I *stole* anything!" he once protested to his former chief of staff, Betsey Wright. He did not seduce virgins, or married women, generally. Nor did he go to brothels, as so many of his southern male colleagues did—willfully subsidizing sex slavery. On the contrary, he *liked* women, indeed *loved* women: their aura, their femininity, their bodies, their clothes, their spirited personalities, their tantalizing accessories. On one occasion, addressing a married woman at a fundraising party in Little Rock, he had paid such embarrassing compliments on the brooch pinned to her ample bosom that she had taken it off and given it to him in disgust, furious that he had so shamelessly mentally undressed her. Unperturbed, Bill had pocketed it—only for the woman to see it, some months later, pinned to Hillary.

Besides, the president rationalized, the form of sexual gratification Bill Clinton preferred had been far less overt than that of President Kennedy or Lyndon Johnson. He had, in fact, challenged one of the current conspirators, Trooper Larry Patterson, to prove him wrong. He'd researched "the subject in the Bible," the governor had told the trooper—in words that would have haunting resonance in later years—"and oral sex isn't considered adultery." It was, he claimed, merely heavy petting.

Sex Appeal

The brooch story—the brazen but unwelcome pass, and the casual giving of the costume-jeweled item to his wife thereafter—somehow encapsulated Bill Clinton's wayward, undisciplined self, at once questing and happy-go-lucky. He was, as Betsey Wright put it, careless. "That's the way I would put it: careless. Given the moral strictures. *But he always was.* I used to beg him to stop—when we had our photo sessions in these public, proclamation sessions—to stop putting his arm around every female that got her picture made. . . . I mean, I was *constantly* fighting this womanizing thing."

Betsey was recalling her former boss's affliction as a needless impediment to his performance while governor of Arkansas. Worse still was the carelessness when he was president of the United States and leader of the free world. How, in an age of literal media magnifying glasses, or lenses, could he continue to be so unconcerned?

In his defense, however, it could be argued that big Bill Clinton understood, instinctively and better than any other politician of his generation, a factor that even Betsey Wright, his most professional political operative, did not—and that would indeed save him from impeachment in time, against all predictions. That factor was—as with President Kennedy—sex appeal.

According to congressional electoral research, almost the same (41) percent of married women had voted for Bill Clinton at the 1992 election as for President Bush (40 percent). Among *un*married women, however, there was a huge disparity. No less than 53 percent of unmarried women had voted, it was reckoned, for Clinton, against only 31 percent for Bush. This yawning difference would grow ever larger during Clinton's first term in the White House, despite all his travails—indeed, by the time of the subsequent presidential election almost *70 percent* of unmarried women, among those voting either Democrat or Republican, would vote for young President Clinton in preference to his septuagarian contender.

Few pundits took heed. Betsey Wright might quail at Bill Clinton's need to hug and impress women, but the simple fact was this: that the president's predilection for women was amazingly often reciprocated, overtly or even subliminally. Despite knowing that Bill Clinton was a married man, millions of American women were now susceptible to his charms. Indeed women, literally, *dreamed* of him, as a new survey, *Dreams of Bill*, had shown.

Made curious by their own vivid dreams of the new president, Julia Anderson-Miller and her husband, Bruce, had placed ads in newspapers across the country, soliciting examples of similar dreams. The response had been torrential. "Would you mind if I kissed you?" a nearly seventy-year-old retired advertising executive in Colorado recorded, for example, of a dream in which she'd been driving presidential candidate Clinton to his quarters for the night. "I was aware that this was terribly bold, but I was much taken with him. He threw back his head and laughed, saying, 'Not at all!' And he embraced me in a great bear-hug and kissed me on the mouth—a long, soul-melting kiss that was delightful," she recalled: "a kiss so satisfying and real that I remembered every detail and feel of it on awakening." Having introduced him to a crowd of people, she then retired to her room, "got into bed, and began reading with the lights on. Bill sort of wandered in wearing only his shorts and said there didn't seem to be any bed for him and could he share mine? I said half alarmed and half sexily, 'Well, why not?'"

A housewife in St. Louis, Missouri, though, dreamed she was inveigled into the president's limousine, wondering "what my husband would think." Bill had told her not to worry—and she hadn't. "Next thing I know, we're in bed together, and let me say it was great. He was the best lovemaker in the world. He kissed so *good*."

Clearly candidate Bill Clinton had touched the erotic nerve of many American women like no other presidential candidate before him. The Arkansas giant might lack the toughness, born of crippling Addison's disease, of war in the Pacific and of the deaths of his siblings, which had steeled the heart of his hero, JFK. Nonetheless he had the same bushy-thick wayward hair, the same blue eyes, tall stature, and broad forehead as JFK, the winning smile and bright intelligence—emotional as well as intellectual. He felt people's pain because he clearly had known domestic suffering himself, as a youngster. Moreover, he'd traveled, and had a real respect for different cultures, even where he disagreed with their ideologies. As he aged, his hair had gone prematurely gray and his nose had become more bulbous, while his big jaw had widened (as had JFK's, after steroid treatment for his Addison's disease), yet he remained vibrantly youthful-looking and energetic—a big, confidant man with a high-timbred voice but a commanding presence, able to hang out with the Kennedys, the Kerrys, and the Grahams on the Vineyard, the Sharon Stones and Barbra Streisands in Hollywood, yet able always to connect with ordinary people, without condescension or inverted snobbery: a man who had not forgotten his origins.

CHAPTER TWENTY-FIVE

HARRY AND LOUISE

Choking on Complexity

While the president struggled to blunt the growing conspiracy in Little Rock, the first lady was struggling to keep her health care reform bill afloat. Despite the president's miracle performance before Congress in September, and Hillary's stalwart, campaign-style proselytizing throughout the country thereafter, the gigantic legislative proposal was meeting with more and more opposition.

To present the outline plan the first lady had personally testified in a "marathon week" before five committees of Congress—her appeal to the members having a feminist ring: "I'm here as a mother, a wife, a daughter, a sister, a woman. I'm here as an American citizen concerned about the health of her family and the nation," she'd declared. "I know what it's like to be overrun with forms and regulations and confusing choices when a family member is dying." The system was choking on its own complexity—and failing. It had to be reshaped, and she was determined to see that done, on behalf of the American people. "She came, she saw, she wowed 'em," gushed CBS's Bob Schieffer. First reactions, thought Bob Franken of CNN, "bordered on ecstasy," while Tom Brokaw spoke of a "love-fest for the first lady."

Certainly no other first lady had ever held such a high-profile torch, involving such high-profile stakes, affecting one-seventh of the national economy. However, darker clouds were appearing, too. A poll showed only 52 percent of Americans thought the health care system was "fundamentally unsound." More ominously, only 21 percent thought it needed to be completely rebuilt. Moreover, on the same day Hillary testified, the American Medical Association sent out a letter to some seven hundred and ten *thousand* doctors and medical students, expressing "serious reservations"—and warning that Hillary Clinton's plan could "limit choices" and "undermine the quality of medical services and lead to federal control of medical education and the physician workforce."

A month later, the omens looked substantially worse. On Wednesday, October 27, 1993, the president and the first lady had handed over the final, complicated 1,342-page legislative proposal in the Capitol Building's National Statuary Hall. Universal coverage was the key to their reform of the American system, the plan declared. Such coverage would be paid for by employers (80 percent) and employees (capped at almost 4 percent of annual pay), augmented by a 75-cent tobacco tax. Before banks of television cameras and beneath the bronze and marble statues of the Founding Fathers, President Clinton banged the podium to emphasize the moral urgency of such legislation. "Let me just make clear to you the central element of this plan that is most important to me. It guarantees every American a comprehensive package of health benefits that are always there and that can never be taken away. That is the most important thing. That is the bill I want to sign. That is my bottom line. I will not support or sign a bill that does not meet that criteria."

Universal coverage? The president *sounded* emphatic. But was he *really* saying he would veto a less revolutionary proposal? Was it bluster? Despite the fact that the first lady's latest proposal postponed the introduction of full universal coverage for five years, the very notion of floating a $331 billion package during a continuing national recession seemed a tremendous pill for Congress to swallow. It required legislators and the public alike to believe that America's economic ills—which included the increase of health care costs from 7 percent of GDP to 14 percent over the past twenty-five years—could be solved in major part by Hillary's refashioning of the health care system. Waste there was—but was it right to create a potential government monster to eradicate it? people wondered. Even Democrats began to jump ship. "Once we get hold of it, we keep it for the rest of the game," warned one Democrat in the House. "That's what democracy is. The president makes a proposal, and the Congress disposes of it."

Among Republicans, opposition became even more hostile. Senate Minority Leader Bob Dole warned, for example, that "turning over one-seventh of our economy to the United States government is an idea that has many Americans—Republicans and Democrats—very concerned." Not only did the proposal still lack vital and credible statistics, but even Bob Michel, the mild and thoughtful House minority leader, announced that he had "substantive and profound policy differences" with the Clintons—"real differences that cannot be glossed over. The debate that begins now will be about nothing less than conflicting visions of what America means—not just about health care reform itself, but about the role of government in our society . . . whether our health system is essentially to retain its private sector character . . . or embark on an uncharted course of government-run medicine."

Michel's deputy, Congressman Newt Gingrich, simply refused to attend the Clinton ceremony in the Capitol, calling it a "circus." In words that chilled those who heard the die-hard Republican (and future presidential hopeful), Gingrich not only characterized the Clinton plan as "a power grab," but put the Clintons on notice that their plan would be rejected, because it was too expensive and too bureaucratic for an American government to undertake. "If you've seen public housing, you've seen public medicine," he snarled, "and it's not a pretty picture."

"Distracted by overseas crises, Mr. Clinton has dissipated much of the support generated by his stirring address to Congress," Martin Fletcher explained at the end of October to British readers—indeed, since September 22, "at least 200 senators and congressmen out of a total of 535 have lined up behind half a dozen alternative plans proposed during the hiatus."

Ominously, the image of Hillary Clinton, health care reform czarina, was also shifting; no longer was she the small but brave first lady, humbly bringing her homework for Congress to correct. She was now being tarred with the label "Big Sister"—and with that, the real shooting began.

Harry and Louise

All too quickly, as the health war heated up, it became clear that Hillary Clinton had been overambitious. Because she had tried to do too much, too soon, too secretively, at too high a potential cost and with too vague a notion of the real savings, the plan was in danger of failing.

The critical point came with a series of television commercials: the "Harry and Louise" ads. Designed earlier in the year after careful research, they were paid for by the Health Insurance Association of America, the president of which, former congressman Bill Gradison, Hillary had refused to meet when drawing up her reform proposals. Ignoring the slight, Gradison had at first objected to the fear-mongering ads. They would not, in all probability, have been aired if Hillary had pursued a less strident campaign on health care reform throughout the summer. As a result of Hillary's angry accusations, Gradison's objections to the ads had faded. "We're going to crack down on profiteers who make a killing off the current system," one of Hillary's White House attack memos to Democratic members in Congress had warned in August—incensing the HIAA. Two million dollars were allocated for fighting back through television advertising, focusing on a fictional American couple, "Harry and Louise."

The ads began only in Washington, New York, and Los Angeles, on CNN. Kathleen Hall Jamieson, dean of the Annenberg School for Communications at the University of Pennsylvania, observed that the "impact is not going to be on the citizenry at large. It's going to be on the people who make the decisions"—but, thanks to Hillary, she proved wrong. "Harry and Louise" were depicted as a typical middle-class couple in their kitchen, discussing the implications of Hillary's health care proposals. The couple always acknowledged the need for reform, but ended with the refrain: "There's got to be a better way."

Stung by the ads, and unwilling to countenance a better way, Hillary lost her composure. Though begged by her advisers not to retaliate, but rather to "be quiet and go out and sell the Pablum," she went before the American Academy of Pediatricians in Washington on November 1, 1993, and fired back, without notes or text.

Her speech was a public relations disaster of the first magnitude—indeed, the damage it did would, in the event, prove irreparable. "Rarely, if ever, has a first lady publicly attacked any American industry or industry group—and certainly never in such strong language and such a furious manner," wrote the chroniclers of the health care fiasco, Haynes Johnson and David Broder. The next day, both newspaper and television editors were rubbing their hands with glee—for a story without controversy was no story. Now they had one.

How Hillary could have made such a mistake was difficult, in retrospect, to imagine—for the first lady's visceral reaction brought the otherwise unspectacular ads to public prominence in a way that nothing else could have done. "In the most scathing administration assault to date on the health insurers, Mrs. Clinton said that the insurance companies 'like being able to exclude people from coverage because the more they can exclude, the more money they can make,'" said one typical news story—fanning flames that were soon out of control.

Unwilling to compromise, Hillary had decided to use the tactic she and Bill had used years before when the Arkansas teachers' union refused to embrace teacher testing: direct gunfire, with live ammunition, aimed at spotlit targets. "Mrs. Clinton blamed the insurers for bringing the health-care system to 'the brink of bankruptcy'" front-page reports ran. Others described Hillary's speech as the transition from gentlemanly boxing to bare-knuckle fisticuffs. "Taking the gloves off in the escalating fight over health care reform, Hillary Rodham Clinton lashed out yesterday at the nation's health insurance companies, accusing them of telling 'great lies' in television ads deriding the administration's proposal," the *Boston Globe* reported. "She acknowledged that the White House plan would make 40 percent of Americans pay more for health insurance," the newspaper pointed out, "but said 25 percent would gain much better coverage and the other 15 percent 'are the cherries that the insurance companies love to pick'—those who were no risk."

"Enough is enough," the first lady had told the pediatricians' convention. She blamed the big, bad health companies—"many of them headquartered in New England," as the *Globe* recorded. Hillary was quoted as saying: "It is time that we stood up and said we are tired of insurance companies running our health care system." Dipping polls greeted Hillary's attacks. As the *Globe* noted, a "*Wall Street Journal*/NBC News poll published last week indicated public support for the administration plan has eroded in recent weeks and that growing numbers have negative feelings about Mrs. Clinton, the plan's principal champion."

Such a report should have set off alarm bells in the White House, especially given the president's supersensitive ears. But with her own offices in the West Wing, and in the East Wing, and in the Old Executive Office Building—not to speak of the marital bedroom on the second floor of the president's private quarters—Hillary's Four-Power complex had become greater than that of the president of the United States himself over the health care issue. No one *dared* contradict her. Ira Magaziner was near to breakdown, but Hillary's feminist cohort continued to worship her: watching with compassion and admiration how, in the privacy of their company before giving a speech or addressing a panel, she would tremble with fear, or snap at them as if half out of her mind with anxiety, yet on the stage would present a picture of composure. Faced with such a challenge to the first lady's courage and determination, her courtiers therefore dared not tell her the bitter truth, lest they undermine her incredible act of will.

Later, Bill Clinton, who was nothing if not a microbiologist of politics, would claim that the opponents of health care reform had "more and more moved to a position of total opposition"—yet he simply refused to see this as a response to the very person he had appointed, despite legal injunctions and warnings, to head up his health care reform task force. Instead he blamed the people with whom Hillary negotiated, from HMOs to general practitioners: constituencies who agreed on the need for improvement and reform, but who never coalesced, and "were always thinking about how they could get a better deal," the president observed. "That was very frustrating."

At the time Hillary made her terrible health care *faux pas*, however, the president had had other problems on his plate—particularly NAFTA. "The fault here was that the president was not in it." Judy Feder, attempting to shepherd Hillary's guargantuan proposal through congressional committees at the time, later lamented. "This was not a team effort. The president was out—and the rest of the administration hated it like the plague. We took on an impossible task. But that does not mean the interest groups did not do a phenomenal job—they did. But we had no counter-campaign—we just didn't have our act together."

As more and more Congressional Democrats heard from worried constituents, they began to leap like proverbial rats from the sinking health care reform ship—without being replaced, as they were in NAFTA, by Republicans.

A Big, Fat, Ugly Bill

Whether Bill Clinton, as president of the United States, could have personally rescued Hillary's health care plan had he delayed its presentation until after the NAFTA bill is debatable. Senator Jay Rockefeller felt he might have succeeded, given the president's late-October speech in Statuary Hall, in which he demonstrated a power of oratory the country had not seen since Ronald Reagan. "I mean, he was absolutely on fire. He brought the place down. That's the Clinton I want out during the spring and summer fighting for reform."

Instead, Rockefeller had got Hillary: noble, feisty, smart—and tin-eared. Bob Boorstin, an assistant working for Hillary, admired her sincerity and relentless determination to solve the nation's health care mess in one fell swoop, but afterwards lamented their hubris. "We came up with such a big, fat, ugly bill that was such an easy target," Boorstin confessed candidly, once it was over. "We created a target the size of Philadelphia."

As Senator Bob Bennett later put it, Clinton's "incomprehensible health plan came to symbolize everything people hated about government": a plan so complicated that it cost forty-five dollars per copy to read, that was so long and convoluted the press had to be given it on computer disks! When trucking it to Congress Hillary had got the president to disclaim authorship and ask Congress to assume copyright—but, with Hillary and Ira Magaziner's wording, style, blind assumptions, and ignorance about Congress's arcane way of passing legislation, had found no congressional takers. It was doomed to defeat.

At the last moment Bob Boorstin attempted to remove the most flagrant examples of arrogance, bureaucracy-speak, or gifts to opponents—words like "capitating," or ominous sentences such as one about the assignment of patients to health plans, if some were oversubscribed, "on a random basis." It wasn't, frankly, "a working document," Boorstin felt—yet he and the rest of Hillary's 620-man team were expected to go out, fight, and if necessary die, professionally, for it. And with Hillary remaining at its helm, it became easy for lobbyists, Republicans, and anti-feminists to caricature the unpopular proposal, together with its author.

The surgeon general, Dr. Joycelyn Elders, had been permitted only minimal input—despite having been a member of Republican President Bush's committee on health care reform even before her appointment as S.G. Her view of the completed task force report was less than laudatory, but ignored. None of the report's architects—Hillary, Magaziner, Shalala, Feder—were medical doctors (Hillary had a law degree, Ira Magaziner an undergraduate degree from Brown, Dr. Shalala a Ph.D. in public policy, not medicine, and Dr. Feder likewise), whereas Dr. Elders, as a distinguished doctor with over a hundred and sixty papers in pediatric endocrinology and medicine to her name, had warned they *must* co-opt the doctors of America to their cause if they were to have any chance of legislative success. "I'm saying: Involve the doctors!" she had pleaded. "You can't have health care without the doctors!"

Dr. Elders, in retirement, never claimed that, had she been made secretary of Health and Human Services herself (she had been director of health services for the state of Arkansas), she could have gotten the Clinton health care reform bill passed, any more than Hillary had done—but she did feel she could have guarded against its overambitious, premature still-birth. One problem was that health care reform in 1993–94 was not only disputatious, it lacked a constituency of people who needed it to happen, since "most people who were working *had* insurance, and the poorest had Medicaid"—leaving only the working uninsured, rather than the majority of insured people, to back Hillary. "We introduced it too quick," Dr. Elders later recalled. "I think we were in a real big hurry to get it on, get it done, get it passed, and get it through. I think it should probably have cooked for a year or two."

Alice Rivlin, as deputy director of OMB, was especially disappointed, because she hadn't felt NAFTA and health care reform *could* be tackled simultaneously, either in terms of the research that was necessary, or the legislative difficulties. Ratification of NAFTA had to be completed, by the terms of the treaty President Bush had signed in 1992, by November of 1993. "Health care, meanwhile, was consuming an enormous amount of energy," Dr. Rivlin remembered. "There was this elaborate process that Magaziner had set up, and OMB was involved because we had to be: we were the keepers of the numbers. And so I had staff people who were heavily involved in this. And then there would be higher-level meetings—lots of them. What should we do about Indian health? What should we do about pharmaceuticals? All different aspects of this thing. Was it necessary? Well, I *never* understood the Ira Magaziner thing. He had this elaborate setup with all these 'working groups,' and things he called 'tollgates'—and it was laid out on charts. My husband teaches in the management department at the Wharton School in Pennsylvania. So I took this chart home one night and showed it to Sid, and he laughed! He said: 'This is never going to work. It's just overorganized, over-everything.' And he was absolutely right. I mean, the process was laughable! And yet we couldn't not participate in it, because it was happening and because it was important. It was quite distressing for Leon and me and the rest of the economic team who, after our big [economic bill] success, but with lots of other things to be done, saw this thing about to crash and burn. But there was nothing we could do about it."

Dr. Feder, Ira Magaziner's deputy, was equally disappointed by the strategic fiasco. "Inevitably it was going to be a very difficult congressional issue. Public opinion is either permissive, or not—it can go either way. I think on health care they *are* permissive—but you've got to keep them with you. And that is part and parcel of working with Congress. So what you didn't have: you didn't have a plan to get the damned votes. That's what you didn't have."

Without the votes, the plan looked shaky, and its opponents each day more confident. The Harry and Louise television ads, begun on a minimalist scale, now migrated to radio as the insurers' campaign coffers filled with new money. Soon funding was flooding in. The HIAA budget for advertising went from $2 million to $4.5, then $5.5, then $6.5, and finally reached $10 million. Soon there were T-shirts for sale at health care conventions reading: "Doctor Feelgood: Her Prescription Could Kill You."

CHAPTER TWENTY-SIX

NAFTA PASSES

Gingrich to the Rescue

As Hillary attempted to steer her listing health care reform ship into port, the president was working frantically on the North American Free Trade Agreement, lest that too fail to make land.

With the help of Vice President Al Gore, Clinton focused his prodigious marketing skills on the task, guiding his NAFTA vessel over the shoals of his own liberal colleagues such as Reich and Stephanopoulos, and even the blocking tactics of the Democratic majority leader, Congressman Dick Gephardt, and his chief whip, David Bonior. He played golf with fence-sitters, and wheeler-dealt with so many special interests to get their backing that comedians joked the White House should sport a sign that read "For Sale." Yet the president's tactics worked—as they had for President Lyndon Johnson once he badly wanted something passed in Congress. In a marathon nationally televised debate on November 9, 1993, Vice President Gore crushed their arch-NAFTA opponent, businessman Ross Perot—exposing Perot as "shallow, opinionated, poorly informed, egocentric and erratic."

With public support for approval of the NAFTA bill finally beginning to run his way, President Clinton was then able to make a deal with the minority whip in the House, Congressman Newt Gingrich. If the Democrats could muster 100 votes for NAFTA, Gingrich assured the president, his Republican colleagues would furnish the other 128 necessary to push it over the top.

Gingrich's help stunned the liberal press. "That 'giant sucking sound' you may have heard last Wednesday afternoon was not," Mary McGrory commented on November 21, "Ross Perot's dire prophecy about jobs going south coming true. No, it was made by scores of Republicans rushing to the pro-NAFTA side hours before the vote. The tour guide for this extraordinary late-forming expedition to rescue the Clinton presidency was none other than Newt Gingrich, Republican whip and scourge of Democrats.

"Gingrich, a master of the blow-torch rhetoric favored by Republicans who speak after hours on CNN, has a square, rosy face and a rough thatch of gray hair. With his darting eyes and alert air, he looks like a mastiff. He is eternally on the watch for slights and moral decay on the part of Democrats. He barks about 'institutional corruption and hypocrisy.' He bites, too. But that was the pre-NAFTA Gingrich. As a candidate for the post of GOP leader, a question hung over him: Can he work with Democrats? The answer came loud and clear Wednesday night: Can he ever! He delivered an astonishing 132 votes to Bill Clinton, a man who hitherto attracted only his corrosive contempt."

Clinton's NAFTA campaign was succeeding against all expectation. By endorsing side agreements with Mexico to protect Florida's winter output of citrus fruit, fresh vegetables, and sugar against cheap Mexican imports, for example, thirteen of Florida's twenty-three representatives were won over—an example of presidential bartering that traversed the country. "There was more to the victory, however, than vote-buying," Geoffrey Stevens, a veteran Canadian parliamentary correspondent, noted. "Recruiting Bill Daley, son of the late Chicago mayor Richard Daley, to direct the NAFTA campaign, the White House devised a strategy, stuck to it and implemented it flawlessly. A key element was Clinton's Sept. 13 appearance with former presidents Carter, Gerald Ford and George Bush to give NAFTA their joint blessing. That event reinforced NAFTA as a bipartisan initiative, stopped the hemorrhaging of congressional support from the agreement, and underscored Clinton's commitment to it." The NAFTA vote in Congress on November 20 had thereafter been an unexpected pushover: 234–200 in the House on November 17, and 61–38 in the Senate, three days later.

Columnist Anthony Lewis spoke for many when he drew the lesson of this phenomenal performance. "To be effective, a president must focus on objectives crucial to him and the country. And then he must be resolute in pursuit of those objectives. Clinton was slow to focus on NAFTA. . . . The opposition got so far ahead that many expected the president to back away from NAFTA. Instead he went all-out and won. Too often before now Clinton has backed away from declared positions. There was a widespread belief in Washington that if you made something difficult for him, he would cave. In politics that perception is disabling. Clinton will have dispelled it if he follows up his NAFTA performance with resolve on other issues."

Brimming with pride in his victory, the president now rushed to do just that: to help his wife with her health care reform bill. By then the Harry and Louise ads had taken their toll, however. Prematurely launched, the leaking vessel had begun to take on serious water. By December 1993 it was visibly and dangerously listing. Small firms, realizing the implications of mandatory employee health insurance, were beginning to organize grass-roots opposition to target senators and congressmen. As the lady captain was peppered with more and more enemy shot, the true irony of the situation became clear. The Fleet Admiral-president had appointed his own wife to command of the battleship—but he could not now cut her adrift, as his own beloved wife and partner.

CONSPIRACY

CHAPTER TWENTY-SEVEN

SHAMING THE PRESIDENT

Holiday Homily

As December unfolded, the first lady decided U.S-made decorations should be the theme of the Clintons' first Noël in the White House, and all-American crafts were solicited from "artisans around the country" to adorn the more than twenty Christmas trees in the building. "We hosted, on average, one reception or party every day for three solid weeks," the first lady later recalled in her memoirs, *Living History.* "I liked planning menus and activities and overseeing the dozens of volunteers who flock to the White House to help hang ornaments. That first Christmas season, some 150,000 visitors came through the public rooms to view the decorations and sample a cookie or two. Because we wanted to include people of all faiths in the holiday season, we lit the menorah I had commissioned for the White House that December to celebrate Chanukah. . . ." Later, she would even hold the first Eid-al-Fitr event in the White House to celebrate the end of Ramadan.

For the holiday the president had drafted a homey message to all Americans to be published in *Parade*, the syndicated color magazine distributed with Sunday newspapers throughout the nation. "A Holiday Message From Our Family to Yours" the article was to be headed in huge type. "Across our nation this holiday season," it would begin, "our family and other families are gathering to celebrate and take stock of another year passed. It is time to reconnect with relatives, a time to reflect on good deeds and failings, a time to reawaken ourselves to the spirit of giving."

There had certainly been joy and suffering in Bill Clinton's own family—with more to come. Thinking of the death of Hillary's father and of Vince Foster, the president could not but contemplate the waning days of his courageous mother, whose life was now drawing towards its painful, cancer-afflicted close. As the president's homily ran, "there were days when we reveled in the love we felt from relatives and friends; there were days when we ached with sadness over the passing of those dear to us. No matter what highs and lows any year brings," however, he went on, "the holiday season for us is always a time to celebrate family and faith. By coming together every December with our parents, brothers, sisters, aunts, uncles, nieces, nephews and friends, we reaffirm the common bonds that make us family."

From domestic family the president then moved to the larger American family, whom he so wished to help through the programs he'd promoted and in certain cases already achieved—such as Congress's Family and Medical Leave Act, the National Voter Registration Act, the National and Community Service Act, and (the day before Thanksgiving) the Brady Bill, which mandated a five-day wait and background check before a handgun license could be granted. "Today, as our nation struggles with new challenges, family and faith are more important than ever," the president emphasized. "That's why, during this holiday season, our family asks all Americans to join us in reaffirming America's spiritual richness and sense of community. . . . "

Behind such homilies, however, both the president and the first lady had cause to be anxious, knowing the postmodern media never slept, nor relented in their quest for news stories—the more contentious the better, since they garnered more viewers, more readers, more sales, more advertising. What Hillary called "the media fixation with Whitewater" had since October been gathering steam. Jim McDougal, who had once worked for Senator Fulbright and then Governor Clinton, had inveigled the Clintons into investing twenty thousand dollars in a resort complex in the picturesque Ozarks, by the White River, as part of McDougal's expanding entrepreneurial activities conducted with his wife, Susan. The Whitewater Development Corporation project had failed to attract homeowners, however, and instead of making a profit, the Clintons had not only lost their investment, but as sleeping minority partners in the corporation were nevertheless responsible for McDougal's losses also. From McDougal's tangled figures, they had declared a tax loss, initially, of sixty thousand dollars. When this was later determined to be more than the final loss (which was partly covered by the government), they repaid the two thousand dollar over-refund they had received from the IRS.

How this minuscule failed investment from 1978 would ultimately be inflated by the media into a Congress-backed investigation of supposed Clinton malfeasance must remain the ultimate example of the madness that took over so much of the American "infotainment" industry in the 1990s, from tabloids to television, and even the once-serious press. Indeed, it was a *New York Times* reporter, Jeff Gerth, who had begun the business during the Clinton election campaign in March 1992—confusing McDougal's later misfortunes as the director of a savings and loan bank, Madison Guaranty, which had nothing to do with the Clintons, with their earlier partnership in Whitewater, and never withdrawing or apologizing for his misrepresentation of the facts. Based on the crazed claims of Mc-Dougal—who was not only destitute but divorced, living in a trailer on Social Security, and suffering from mental illness—Gerth's front-page allegation then metastasized into a cancerous proliferation of unfounded accusations by Clinton-bashers, haters, and opponents, once Clinton won the Democratic nomination and defeated the incumbent president, George Bush. When the Resolution Trust Corporation finally submitted its official recommendation for criminal proceedings against Jim McDougal for his misuse of funds at the Madison Guaranty, despite his ill-health and bipolar disorder, the Clintons were notified they would be required to be witnesses in his trial, though they were not, initially, in any way implicated in the RTC criminal referral.

The media—now headed by the *Washington Post,* which had picked up on the story—wanted evidence that McDougal's former partners were untainted by the case. The newspaper therefore insisted that it be allowed to see the Clinton records. The first family balked, regarding this as an invasion of their rightful privacy in a matter that was not the subject of the RTC referral, until finally they had to make up their minds. It was, however, the wrong mind, in even the president's subsequent view.

Flipping a Switch in His Head

"If a genie offered me the chance to turn back in time and undo a single decision from my White House tenure, I'd head straight back to the Oval Office dining room on Saturday morning, December 11, 1993," Stephanopoulos would later write. That fateful morning he learned that the first lady, with her old boss, Bernie Nussbaum, and the Clinton family's new lawyer, David Kendall, had "persuaded the president to stonewall the [*Washington*] *Post*."

To Stephanopoulos this was crazy—the lawyers' attitude was "more appropriate for corporate litigation than presidential politics." Mack McLarty, as the president's chief of staff, should have taken charge of the matter, but it was left to Gergen and Stephanopoulos to make their case that "the country probably wouldn't care about the ins and outs of an old land deal, as long as it didn't look as if the Clintons had something to hide."

"I don't have a big problem with giving them [the *Washington Post* and *New York Times*] what we have," the president replied. "But Hillary. . . . "

Hillary was a problem—indeed Hillary, it turned out, was *the* problem. In a disembodied but loud voice—"as if he were a high school debater speeding through a series of memorized facts"—Clinton now told Stephanopoulos he was wrong. "The questions won't stop," he warned his political aide. Recalling his experience with Washington correspondents at a breakfast in 1991, Clinton said, "I answered more questions about my private life than any candidate ever, and what did that get me? They'll always want more. No president had ever been treated like I've been treated."

This was true—but missed the point, as Stephanopoulos would have pointed out had he been able to dam the flood. The correspondents' breakfast and the CBS *60 Minutes* broadcast, during which Clinton tacitly confessed to adultery as governor of Arkansas, had been the very things that had served to *inoculate* him against the worst that Republicans and pro-Republican journalists could throw at the candidate. The president, having clearly beaten all rivals for the post, could only *gain* from public disclosure. . . .

Clearly, there was another agenda that was stopping Bill Clinton, the president of the United States, from leveling with the press. But what was it? Hillary's concerns? Or concerns *for* Hillary, in view of something else that was about to implode?

Neither Gergen nor Stephanopoulos yet knew—but the reason was not long in coming.

The Plot Goes Pear-shaped

Seeking funding for the two remaining troopers, in case they lost their jobs, trial attorney Cliff Jackson was disappointed. He had approached Peter Hunt, a right-wing maverick millionaire, for financial guarantees or help in finding jobs for the troopers, but had come away empty-handed. Hunt, however, did something that would change presidential history. He recommended a man he considered the perfect co-author or ghostwriter for a book telling the troopers' stories: David Brock.

The story of how Brock deceived and betrayed everyone, from the editor of the *American Spectator* to the Arkansas troopers, would become one of the foulest in modern American presidential annals, as even Brock would afterwards acknowledge. At the time, however, the thirty-one-year-old author of *The Real Anita Hill* (a book that turned out, as its author later admitted, to be for the most part an assemblage of lies) was at a crossroads in his own sexual life as a practicing but closeted homosexual. Having paid Brock "on the side" for the poisonous work on Anita Hill, Hunt now paid for the writer to fly to Little Rock to meet Jackson and the Arkansas conspirators.

Ironically, as a closet homosexual Brock had been completely uninterested in President Bill Clinton's loose heterosexual morals, which paled beside his own gay-dance-club-cruising lifestyle. Listening to the troopers' accounts, Brock's deepest, meanest, and most personal ambition as a journalist was, however, ignited. As a "self-loathing" homosexual, as he himself later put it, he recognized immediately how he could turn the story to his own advantage, not that of the troopers.

Here, then, was the very last person Cliff Jackson, as a devout Pentecostalist, should have trusted to join the plot—indeed both he and Lynn Davis, the former police commissioner, had qualms about him. "I was negatively impressed by David Brock," Davis recalled. "Later, my impression was proved to be right."

Having got the troopers to tell their stories on tape (his own), as "background," the young best-selling author, once back in Washington, subsequently declared, to their chagrin, that he was not interested in writing a book *with* them. As he later candidly confessed, this was because he would then have had to share the very proceeds they needed to protect them financially, if and when they lost their jobs.

As a freelance contributor to the right-wing quasi-satirical monthly the *American Spectator*, and a gay Republican frightened of being "outed" at any moment, Brock had a very specific personal motive in abetting the conspiracy. If he played his journalistic cards right he would land himself a permanent job on the magazine before his sexual orientation could be exposed by jealous colleagues or homophobes. What he needed, then, was not a book contract favoring the troopers, but an immediate journalistic scoop favoring himself—an objective that placed him in direct competition with two reporters, Bill Rempel and Doug Frantz, who had been given an exclusive on the story for the *Los Angeles Times*.

Brock's new, competitive role in the Arkansas troopers' plot now transformed the conspiracy into something more like a French farce, redolent with misunderstandings, cross purposes, threats, and counter threats—all masking the homosexual secret that, at that time, none of the plotters or even the president knew.

The Prospect of Open Combat

Unaware of Brock's deeper sexual motive, Jackson meanwhile attempted to hew to his original script. The prospect of a tough battle with his old friend, the Yale Law School–educated presidential candidate, had caused Jackson's blood to run faster the previous year, but in the cold light of day a fight with the *president of the United States of America* seemed a tall order. How could one hope to win *that*? "Would I do it again?" Jackson later reflected, recalling how his telephone was bugged, the intimidating surveillance by a stalker, the unregistered car that followed him everywhere. . . . "Probably not," he admitted.

This was said, however, in retrospect. At the time, Jackson's wife begged him not to undertake the case, but Jackson was undaunted by the president's intimidators; in fact, the prospect of *open* combat with the president was preferable to a secret struggle, in which he would be at a disadvantage. The thing that made Jackson most anxious, ironically, was the danger that what he saw as his moral crusade to reform his old friend might be turned into a mindless sex-opera unless he could control the presentation of the troopers' stories. He therefore became infuriated by Rempel and Frantz's editor at the *Los Angeles Times*, who refused to publish the journalists' serious account, based on their painstaking research and interviews with the troopers and others—thus, as Jackson saw it, forcing him and the plotters back into the arms of Brock, whose motives were at best suspicious, and whose understanding of the moral scenario was tenuous in the extreme.

"This is a misuse-of-power issue," the trial lawyer lectured the still-closeted homosexual, "a misuse-of-taxpayer-money issue, a misuse of tax-paid employees issue." Brock, fifteen years younger and belonging to a different generation, simply returned Jackson's stare.

"It's an *exploitation of women* issue," Jackson tried again. "It has sex in it," he allowed, "but that's not the primary thing." For Brock, however, it was.

In vain, Jackson and the plotters demanded that Brock return the tapes he'd made, if he was not willing to work with them on a book. It was too late, however. Brock had made copies of the tapes, and had been told by his friend, federal judge Laurence Siberman, that if he published the story, "in conservative circles, I would be king." To Lynn Davis's demand Brock therefore retorted that he "hadn't spent three months working on it for nothing, and [would] publish it without their permission."

The situation now turned from farce to thriller—a cross between a Feydeau farce and *All the President's Men*. "Deep Throat" now took on a whole new meaning as Rempel and Frantz, on the one hand, drafted their series of articles drawing serious attention to President Clinton's lapses of ethical judgment as governor of Arkansas and predilection for oral gratification, while Brock, afraid of being beaten to the tape—in both senses— milked the troopers' transcribed revelations to manufacture a "salacious bombshell" some eleven thousand words long. "I threw in every last titillating morsel and dirty quote the troopers served up," the Republican hit man later admitted, ignoring the extent to which, in background conversation relating to an eventual book project, their scandalous anecdotes might have been exaggerated in joshing banter and barroom-style speculation. "With my gonzo spirit on overdrive," Brock recalled, "I tossed it all into the piece, details that had no conceivable news value," down to "devoured apple cores" and "feminine napkins."

Gone was any attempt at serious journalism—indeed, so nervous about the draft was Brock that, having shown it to Troopers Larry Patterson and Roger Perry, without whose permission he could, under copyright law, not quote their words, and having received an unannounced, menacing visit from an irate Lynn Davis in Little Rock, he left his rented car in the parking lot and took a cab straight to the airport and boarded the first flight back to Washington and its gay dance bars. "I actually thought Roger Perry might pull me off the road and kill me," he later recalled.

Trepidation and Anxiety

Had Perry done so, the story would only have become yet more nefarious. With no book contract, Jackson was unable to get financial guarantees for the two remaining troopers willing to go public—men who were now certain to (and did) lose their jobs over the deliberately salacious piece of "journalism" that Brock wrote.

"After we saw the draft version of David Brock's story," Jackson recalled, "we were mortified. It's one thing to sit around a room and listen to these anecdotes, these stories—you know, it was sort of like a college beer session, where you're sitting there and everybody's rolling on the floor listening to this. None of us could believe that Bill Clinton would do these things. I mean, they were sad in the sense that he would compromise himself to this point, but it was just hilarious, the way these guys would tell the anecdotes. But to see it in black and white, and see the way Brock packaged it, you know, really as a hatchet job, turned us all off. So, particularly after we saw that, we were adamant that we didn't want him to publish the story before the *Los Angeles Times* put it into, from my point of view, the right perspective."

Brock's boss, editor R. Emmett Tyrrell Jr., was, by contrast, screaming with delight at the prospect of skewering the democratically elected president of the United States—indeed, nervous about losing the scoop, he now offered to pay the troopers anything they asked. Brock refused to convey the offer, though, as he thought it would diminish his role in the exclusive—as well as forcing him to share the financial proceeds from it.

At the *Los Angeles Times*, Rempel and Frantz's more serious story meanwhile met a very different reception. Although the newspaper had published Rempel's frank reports during the 1992 primaries concerning Governor Clinton's draft avoidance, the question of Bill Clinton's moral character had been settled by the presidential election of November '92. William Jefferson Clinton was now the forty-second president of the United States, and it was bordering on treason to deliberately traduce his presidential stature in the public eye, as leader of the Western world, in a serious daily newspaper. So nervous did Shelby Coffey, the editor of the *Los Angeles Times,* become about a leak by his Washington bureau chief to the White House—and possible pressure from that quarter that might prejudice the newspaper's future access to the highest levels of the administration— that he authorized Rempel and Frantz to pretend, among their colleagues, they were researching another story: the McDougals' Whitewater real estate venture and their savings and loan bankruptcy in Arkansas.

Thus, as the end of the year approached, there had been trepidation and anxiety in every quarter, from the offices of the *American Spectator* and the *Los Angeles Times* to the offices of attorney Clifford Jackson—and of the president, William Jefferson Clinton.

Attacking the Presidency

Unlike David Brock, Bill Rempel and Douglas Frantz had done a highly professional investigative reporters' job. One by one, researching in Arkansas, they had attempted to check out each of the troopers' stories—in the course of which they discovered that the president had, since learning of the plot, become personally involved.

According to Captain Buddy Young, the former captain of the governor's security detail, the president had been in direct personal touch on numerous occasions about the issue. Captain Young even tacitly admitted to the journalists that he himself had brought pressure on the troopers not to speak out, on behalf of the president, telling Rempel and Frantz "he had called three of the four troopers after talking to Clinton," and thereafter "reported on the conversations to the president."

The president's personal involvement in the outcome of the troopers' blackmail now gave the plot a further dimension, as the conspiracy approached its climax. Hearing of the president's intercession, Jackson accused Shelby Coffey of being "spineless" in backing off. Here was a serving president of the United States known to be buying off or intimidating his former bodyguards—though the veteran trial lawyer later accepted that he was seeing the saga from his own perspective.

Clinton's successor as governor of Arkansas, Jim Guy Tucker, certainly saw it from another. He also knew of the *American Spectator*'s looming exposé by early December 1993, and the role of the troopers in it—the very men who were currently "protecting" him at the Governor's Mansion in Little Rock. "These people are not your friends," the governor cautioned Roger Perry one morning, as the trooper came off duty at the mansion. "You are not attacking the president, Bill Clinton," he argued. The matter was far, far more serious than that. "You are attacking the presidency."

This was a grave assertion, yet Governor Tucker made it in all seriousness. A former prosecuting attorney, he had served as a war correspondent in Vietnam, and been chairman of a cable and television empire as well as a congressman and corporate lawyer, with a special interest in helping the retarded and those suffering multiple sclerosis.

Unaware that he himself would one day be indicted, forced to resign, and sentenced to prison in consequence of the right-wing war on Bill Clinton, Governor Tucker begged the troopers to think again before going public with their stories. "Roger, you will not survive this," he warned. "Your reputation will be destroyed. You can never work in law enforcement again."

Perry, a policeman to his core, was not to be intimidated, however. It was too late, he countered. "Things have gone too far to turn back, even if I wanted to." In fact, the trooper said, tilting up his jaw, "The more I'm threatened, the more determined I become."

The next day Perry was ejected from the governor's security detail and transferred to a backwater narcotics investigation. The firing had, literally, begun; the phony war was at an end.

A Declaration of War

Aware through Captain Young and Trooper Ferguson of the impending *American Spectator* article, the president swallowed. Once the details of his extramarital escapades were in print, Clinton knew, he would be subjected to Hillary's notorious wrath. In this situation it was not only not possible to think of firing her from her role as chair of the president's health care reform task force, but impossible to press her to open up their records relating to Whitewater and her work at the Rose Law Firm.

The president could be forgiven for feeling that a dragnet was being cast over his associates and now the first couple. Vince Foster was dead, Roger Altman had been forced to resign from the Treasury (for alerting the Clintons to the Whitewater criminal investigation), Webb Hubbell—after spending prodigious time defending Hillary against a lawsuit claiming her appointment to head the health care task force was illegal and unconstitutional—was facing the prospect of becoming ensnared in the Whitewater imbroglio himself. Calls for a special Whitewater investigator were mounting each day—in fact, causing such panic at the Rose Law Firm in Little Rock that newspapers began to report "that the Rose firm was shredding records." Bill Kennedy, Hillary's second man in the legal office at the White House, denied it, but Hubbell "wasn't so sure. No law firm wants its skeletons held up for public inspection," he later noted. Certainly he "never found out what they were shredding," but whatever it was, it wasn't his own misdeeds. Going through their records, the partners came across serious company credit card irregularities among Hubbell's papers—and though he offered to pay the company back, the partners, aware of the Madison Guaranty criminal investigation gathering steam, decided he must become the company scapegoat, thereby deflecting attention from Hillary's and their own past actions.

Hillary's past was, unfortunately, peppered with dubious acts. The whole saga of her hundred-thousand-dollar profit on cattle trades, for a start, would become public knowledge if journalists were permitted to investigate. Then there were the numerous conflicts of interest that had arisen over the years, including the fact that Madison Guaranty, Jim and Susan McDougal's savings and loan bank, had retained Hillary and the Rose Law Firm as their legal representation—yet the Rose Law Firm had later *also* represented the FDIC in recovering customers' lost deposits and loans from the same S&L when it went bankrupt. Again and again when such conflicts of interest—especially legal work for the state of Arkansas while Bill Clinton was governor—had been raised during the 1992 campaign, Bill Clinton had deflected them as his modern, working wife's affairs. Now, however, if the press had their way, the record of those long-buried affairs would be exhumed and questioned—something Hillary was determined to avoid.

It was in this situation that the president concluded the White House meeting with his advisers Gergen and Stephanopoulos—telling them that, with regard to the urgent furnishing of his and the first lady's financial records to the press, he would "think about it some more."

If the president did think more about it, the answer remained the same. To David Gergen's consternation, the following day the first lady exercised her unelected, marital veto power.

Gergen had already called the editor of the *Washington Post* to ask for another week's grace before handing over the requested Whitewater documents. No sooner had he done so than McLarty called Gergen with the bad news. "I'm sorry, there will be no re-argument," McLarty told the hapless counselor and de facto head of White House communications. The decision was, apparently, "final"—and that evening Bruce Lindsey, the president's "slight, nervous and perpetually suspicious" (as the *Post*'s reporter, Michael Isikoff, described him) personal confidant, a man regarded as "the keeper of all secrets, Clinton's all-purpose Mr. Fix-It," wrote on behalf of the president to the *Post*'s editor, "We see no need to supplement the March, 1992 CPA report [by an independent accounting company on the loss-making Whitewater investment] or to provide further documentation."

It was, both sides were clear, a declaration of war: *Hillary* v. *the Press.* The editor's reaction was inevitable. "I just want to tell you," he said to the White House director of communications three days later, "that this is a serious mistake. We're not going to drop this. We will go full-bore on this investigation."

By then, however, the Clintons' world was imploding, ignited on all sides.

CHAPTER TWENTY-EIGHT

A NEW ERA OF VOYEURISM

Vile Stories

In the West Wing of 1600 Pennsylvania Avenue, Hillary was hosting a reception on Saturday, December 18, 1993, when she was summoned to take an urgent phone call from the new family attorney, David Kendall. "Hillary," Kendall said, "I've got to tell you something very, very ugly. . . . "

As Hillary sat down to hear the news, Kendall summarized to the pale, stunned first lady "the most vile stories I had ever heard, worse than the salacious garbage in supermarket tabloids," she later wrote. In Brock's account, her marriage to Bill was portrayed as a sham, her character traduced as demonically evil, her relationship with Vince Foster as an affair, and Bill's behavior caricatured as that of an amiable buffoon—unable to keep his pants zipped. Kendall told her, "You've got to be prepared."

Hillary's husband had been negotiating with the troopers for months; Brock had already talked directly to the president's *consiglieri*, Bruce Lindsey, and the president himself had already seen a proof of Brock's article, which the *American Spectator* had begun faxing to television and press newsrooms across the country! The president had already put Betsey Wright on the case; Betsey had already had a copy of Brock's article slipped under the Embassy Suites Hotel door of the *Los Angeles Times*'s reporters that morning (to further shame the newspaper into backing off such a tacky story) and was on her way to Little Rock to try to obtain an affidavit from Trooper Ferguson denying that the president had ever offered him a federal position in return for his silence. Was it conceivable, then, that Clinton had not told Hillary, his co-president, *anything* before the December 18 call from Kendall?

If true, it was typical, however, as Betsey Wright knew—as much a component of Clinton's Achilles heel as the need to consort with inappropriate women. Only Hillary, in any event, could know the truth of what transpired between herself and the president that evening in their private quarters. Understandably, she was not disposed to make it public, then or later. Instead she confined herself, in her memoirs, to describing Cliff Jackson as "another of Bill's most vehement enemies in Arkansas" and Brock's article, with "certain specifics" that could be "easily refuted," despite "a veneer of credibility" owing to their state trooper sources, as "vague tales."

Here, however, Hillary was clearly *not* telling the truth—or if she was, it revealed how little she and her husband were willing to confide the truth to each other, and the effect this would now have upon the nation, indeed the world—for as Betsey Wright had confided to David Gergen, the White House communications supremo, "as far as she could tell, the troopers were telling the truth." *Que faire*, though? A communications counteroffensive was urgently needed, if the troopers and their "vile" stories were to be trashed. Bruce Lindsey therefore convened "an ad hoc group to discuss the problem, which included Stephanopoulos, Gergen, Gearan, Nussbaum, and the first lady," as James B. Stewart later recorded in *Blood Sport*, his chronicle of the systematic hounding of the president. "It was especially awkward discussing the troopers' allegations in front of Hillary, but she didn't seem to flinch. Just about everybody in the group was indignant that troopers' allegations were even being raised."

With great matters of state to deal with—domestically and internationally—the situation was indeed ridiculous. Yet in its strangely surreal way it marked a new stage in the cultural history of the West: a marker of a new nineties era in which not even the serving president of the most powerful nation in the world would be immune to media investigation of his most private life—part pandering to the voyeurism inherent in an age of celebrity-itis; part product of an American tradition of democratic rules that did not spare any mortal, especially a monarch, from scrutiny; and part fascination, since Jackie Kennedy, with the life of the first lady as a projection of the destiny of all wives.

It was the last of these that now consumed the attention of the White House staff. In the cabal of advisers that Lindsey collected at the White House to plan the White House response to the troopers' stories, the protection of the first lady's honor and pride seemed now to dictate policy as much as defense of the president himself.

Over a Hundred Partners

Hillary's situation certainly mirrored that of millions of hard-working, faithful wives in the world. Their long partnership since cohabitation at Yale Law School had helped promote and stabilize Bill Clinton's political career, but had never, however, come to grips with Bill's "JFK complex": his need to philander. From the tales the troopers were telling it was clear that that need had become addictive—and that the therapy Hillary had insisted her husband undergo, after their near divorce in 1989, had not worked.

Trooper I. D. Brown, another of the bodyguard detail at the Governor's Mansion in the 1980s, later claimed to have solicited "over a hundred" sexual partners for the governor during his period of service at the mansion. This was hardly Hillary's fault—but it was certainly her own responsibility that, knowing something of this, she had pressed her husband to declare his presidential candidacy in 1991, in spite of Betsey Wright's warnings.

Hillary might rightly rail against the hypocritical, cynical, and malicious muckraking of modern tabloid journalists—but to do so was to ignore Betsey's warning: that the Clintons could not make the moral rules of the nation. To cover up the moral transgressions of her husband would necessarily involve spinning, deceit, evasions, and an orchestrated media counterinsurgency that would permit the Clintons to survive, but would leave a terrible trail of wounded, subpoenaed, blood-soaked bodies—those of their innocent staff and supporters. What of *them*?

Sadly, the concerns of the White House staff to protect the first couple were not reciprocated. Unwilling to turn the tables on their critics by an open display of honesty, the Clintons would doom their administration to years of moral, cultural, and political siege—with endless lying necessary, and untold numbers of innocent victims sucked into the mêlée.

Black Saturday thus became Bleak Sunday, December 19, 1993—in Bleak House. Hillary even accused David Gergen of being disloyal—a tactic that she had often used to put staffers and advisers into loyalist superdrive. It certainly worked on this occasion. The editor of the *Los Angeles Times* had been a college friend of David Gergen; skiing in Colorado, he was duly "leaned on" by Gergen to hold off his reporters for a few days.

This would, Hillary and her communications cohort felt, allow time for the White House to trash the *American Spectator* and sideline the more serious aspects of the allegations: claims that Bill Clinton had misused his prerogatives as governor of Arkansas.

In other words, there would be no confession of misbehavior, only a barrage of counter-artillery so dense that the public would not know what to think.

Early on the evening of December 19, 1993, the Battle of the Beltway thus began, with CNN television firing the first official salvo in what was instantly termed "Troopergate." As their *raison de reportage* CNN used the *American Spectator* article, scheduled for publication the next day: a story entitled "His Cheatin' Heart: David Brock in Little Rock."

Brock was over the moon—he danced for joy in his Washington apartment. His salacious article would make him famous. He could come out as gay, and would be put on the permanent staff of the right-wing journal. And the great LA *Times* would be scooped.

The first lady, meanwhile, was hosting yet another of her Christmas parties—this time for relatives and friends. As news came in that CNN was leading with the troopers' story, "the full effect" of the allegations finally hit her.

Going paler by the second, Hillary listened as her press secretary, Lisa Caputo, described the CNN segment on the troopers, with filmed interviews, as well as the news that the "*Los Angeles Times* was about to publish its own version of the troopers' allegations." As she herself recalled, "It was too much." She "sank into a small chair" in the center hall, under the twinkling mock candles of its Christmas trees and glittering all-American ornaments.

Bob Barnett—her personal attorney and literary agent, who would later sell Hillary's and Bill's autobiographies for $20 million in advance royalties—"knelt in front of me," Hillary recounted. The troopers were, after all, "shopping around for a book deal"—thereby "doing a reasonable job of discrediting themselves," as she later put it, "shamelessly boasting that they expected to cash in on their stories. With his oversize glasses and mild features," Barnett was "talking in a soothing voice, clearly trying to see whether after all that had happened this year, we had the strength for yet another struggle."

Did she? Did Bill?

"I am just so tired of this," Hillary said with a sigh.

CHAPTER TWENTY-NINE

LOW TIDE

Sticking It Out

The sight of the president's lawyer on his knees before the co-president, next to an illuminated Christmas tree, was moving and symbolic. Nothing like it had ever been known in the White House—at least not since Henry Kissinger was made to kneel and pray beside President Richard Nixon, during the Watergate scandal. "The president was elected, and you've got to stay with this for the country, for your family. However bad this seems," Barnett begged, "you've got to stick it out."

It was not, Hillary recalled, the first occasion that she had been "advised that my actions and words could either strengthen or undermine Bill's presidency." As she confessed, she wanted to point out that "Bill's been elected, not me!"—but she held her tongue, knowing that she had overstepped the boundaries of first lady since the transition, and that her health care reform crusade was a shambles, while Bill's deficit-reduction bill, NAFTA, and a dozen of his smaller legislative programs had proved to be triumphs. She felt "very much alone" at that moment. CNN was not only airing but with new interviews instancing the past sexual misbehavior of the nation's chief executive—such as the story of his arriving at the Little Rock airport in January 1993, prior to the inauguration, and one of his mistresses brought personally by Trooper Patterson to take her leave of him. Hillary, as impending first lady, had naturally been furious. "What the f– do you think you're doing?" Hillary had allegedly yelled at Trooper Patterson. "I know who that whore"—by then a state judge—"is. I know what she's doing here. Get her out of here."

Hillary wanted to "go upstairs with Bill for a few minutes to talk it over," but receiving the brunt of his wife's fury in private was the last thing Bill Clinton was prepared to do. Instead, the president "paced in the center hall"—painfully aware that, yet again, his extramarital addiction had put his political career in jeopardy. He felt it was all so unfair; after all, in France such behavior, even on the part of a president, would be considered *de rigeur*—President Mitterand's wife and mistress both attended his funeral several years later. At least, though, in prudish America President Clinton's election to the highest office had avoided the scourge of background FBI checks and a Senate hearing such as Judge Clarence Thomas had endured—and which was currently facing Clinton's latest nominee, Admiral Bobby Inman, to replace Secretary of Defense Les Aspin. (Inman was being "outed" in gay circles for being a bisexual—an unfounded rumor that, along with indications that he had not paid taxes on his children's nanny, would make his confirmation by the Senate a dubious proposition, despite his distinguished past.)

Again and again the president thought of his predecessor and hero, John F. Kennedy. JFK had gotten away with extramarital excesses even in the White House—but as Clinton had learned in reading the recent bestseller by Richard Reeves, the press was muzzled in that era by convention, by male camaraderie, and by fear of retaliatory banishment from the White House press corps if any journalist dared blow the whistle. Kennedy's assassination had then sealed the lips of revelators for a further decade. With the fall of Richard Nixon in 1974, however, the media's gloves had come off. By 1987, when Bill Clinton contemplated a first run for the presidential nomination, the moratorium was over, as Betsey Wright had lectured him: the fourth estate was licensed to investigate the private as well as the public lives of the candidates.

While Rempel and Frantz waited in the lobby of the West Wing beside a Razorbacks-decorated Christmas tree, hoping for a White House response to the more serious allegations (of misuse of public funds in Arkansas) that they had drafted for the next day's *Los Angeles Times,* the first lady summoned her courage and will. Calling for Bruce Lindsey, Bernie Nussbaum, Dee Dee Myers, and David Gergen to meet with her and go over the sworn affidavits the journalists had dutifully submitted as evidence for their story, Hillary was in no mood to give an inch. Nor did she have any qualms afterwards about her tough response. "I realized that attacks on our reputations could jeopardize the work Bill was doing to set the country on a different track," Hillary wrote. Lindsey, reading through the affidavits, spotted inaccuracies that could be used to counter-trash the troopers and other whistle-blowers. His team therefore cross-examined the reporters on their sources, telling them like errant schoolboys to then wait outside for their verdict.

From despondency Hillary now felt sudden triumph—a lawyer not only by training but by upbringing and character. The mistakes in detail, and the lack of substantiation by any of the women who had been mentioned, made it unnecessary for Bill to make a confession, or to apologize, she was sure. The president and first lady could simply deny everything as "ridiculous" and stonewall, as they had decided to do over calls for their Whitewater documents. She thus "went back downstairs to rejoin the party," she recalled: a new woman, a warrior in shining armor—while the president's disconsolate staff were sent into combat without bulletproof vests, expected to defend the president from "attacks" without knowing themselves if the allegations were true.

Bearing Out Dreams of Bill

Having waited in the White House lobby again for an hour, cooling their heels and wondering whether they could possibly now meet the deadline for Monday publication, Rempel and Frantz had hoped to meet with the president, but as James Stewart chronicled, Hillary's denial strategy was now "firmly in place." The president would be kept in purdah, while staffers protected him using their own words as their only weapons (and their pocketbooks when later subpoenaed). Finally, belatedly, the journalists were handed a written response. It was signed by Lindsey.

Their hearts sank. In what Elizabeth Drew described as misleading and fractured syntax, the first of a series of "nondenial denials" met their astonished gaze. "Similar allegations were made, investigated and responded to during the campaign," Lindsey pointed out, "and there is nothing here that would dignify a further response." Brazenly Lindsey denied the president had made any job offers to Trooper Ferguson and called the journalists "irresponsible," hurrying them to the exit. "I think," said Rempel to Frantz, "we've just been thrown out of the White House."

They had—while outside the White House, a call to arms was sounded for staffers to come in and save the president. Mark Gearan, the deputy director of White House Communications, was, for example, giving a party at his house in Alexandria, Virginia, for two prominent White House staffers who had decided they could not go on serving the president. One by one Gearan's guests—Mack McLarty, Bernie Nussbaum, and others—returned to duty. Finally, at 8:30 P.M. Gearan, too, joined them—the staff instructed to get in touch with the most powerful players in the press corps and enlist their help.

Begged by phone, journalists such as Anthony Lewis, R. W. Apple, Paul Duke, and even Gary Wills condemned the *American Spectator* for publishing such garbage. Thanks to Gergen's influence with its editor, the LA *Times* still sat on the troopers' story, too. Others could not be so easily influenced. France, Germany, Britain, and other major European powers might condone extracurricular activity, in terms of public morality, but they also operated strict libel laws. The reverse was the case in the United States: strict moral expectations but the laxest libel laws in the universe. Once broken, the troopers' stories could not fail to ignite the curiosity and speculative interest of the nation. With the *American Spectator* now officially on newsstands, and almost all major American television networks ignoring the White House attempts to silence them, "Troopergate" took on a life of its own, bearing out the "Dreams of Bill" that the Millers had been collecting for their book.

On Tuesday, December 21, 1993, four days before Christmas, the *Los Angeles Times* finally printed Rempel and Frantz's account. Beaten by other journals, however, Shelby Coffey gave it the lower-right-hand-corner treatment. It was too late, anyway. Rempel and Frantz's serious, painstaking investigation had been made redundant by the tantalizing, salacious details Brock had touted—details that were already feeding a vast public appetite for Jerry Springer-like Christmas fare and rumor.

As even the august *New York Times* began to lead with the story, Christmas week for the Clintons—a presidential couple with a "deep commitment to lead ethical lives," and parents of a beloved thirteen-year-old daughter—became a nightmare, capping an *annus horribilis*.

A Plea to the President

"They did a masterful job blunting the thrust of the troopers' story," Lynn Davis later said of the president, the first lady, and the White House's spin machine. Davis himself knew "more than I could ever say, for there *were* inducements," he insisted—offers made to the troopers both directly, and on behalf of, the president. But what, in retrospect, did such inducements matter when the whole story had become but a pawn in other people's agendas—right against left, journalist against journalist, television network against network, television network against cable, public broadcasting against rabid AM talk shows, gender against gender, in the continuing culture wars of the nineties?

In vain Cliff Jackson tried, he maintained, to hew his way back to high ground, away from the smut, writing to the president after Christmas to apologize and to assure his old friend that he had meant well in challenging him to be more of a *leader*: a real leader, aware of his new and immense responsibility in assuming the presidency. "As the president, you are the moral repository of American values," Jackson wrote. "You, and only you, can shape America—for good or evil—by the force of your moral suasion—or lack of it. As you go, so goes America." He begged his old Oxford friend to embrace change—personal change. "I know that you are capable of change. We all are. If you change and assert moral leadership, America will follow you, and I believe that you will then have the potential to be one of the most effective presidents this country has known."

By reform, Jackson was at pains to point out in his letter to the president, he did not mean just the president's "sexual peccadilloes. They are the symptoms, not the disease," he emphasized. "I am not judging you; I am not condemning you, I am not casting stones. It is much more fundamental than mere sex. I am talking about your fundamental nature—seemingly inbred and long-polished—and your casual willingness to deceive, to exploit and to manipulate in order to attain personal and political power. I am talking about your willingness to compromise principle until there is no longer any principle left to compromise. I am talking about your expectation," he chided, "that others around you practice the same traits to cover up for you."

This was no less than the truth. Dee Dee Myers, the White House press secretary, had simply refused to give any press briefings for two days after publication of the troopers' story, until she could compose herself, and force her feet back onto the treadmill of the president's spin-machine. George Stephanopoulos was reminded of the year before, when, in Dee Dee Meyers's pumps, he too had defended his boss against Gennifer Flowers's allegations.

Was it right for a president to expose his own troops to such withering enemy fire, knowing he hadn't told them the truth? "So none of this ever happened?" a journalist at a White House press conference asked the president. Clinton had "stammered and hesitated as he didn't on any other subject," Elizabeth Drew chronicled. "We, we did, if, the, I, I, I, the stories are just as they have been said," the president had declared in gobbledygook—ending: "They're outrageous and they're not so."

When the tape of the troopers being interviewed was played on one of the network news broadcasts, Drew commented, "the effect was very damaging"—since each "trivialization of the presidency undermined both the presidency and Clinton's moral authority, which could have real consequences."

This was certainly what worried not only White House staffers but Cliff Jackson, who was beginning to sicken at the morass to which his own miscalculations had contributed. "Without trust and integrity, there can be no new covenant," Jackson warned his old friend, referring to Clinton's 1991 speech he had so admired, "between the government and the governed. There can only be a perpetuation of the current pandemic distrust and cynicism which now eat like a cancer at the very fabric of our society." Thus the former Fulbright scholar pleaded with the Rhodie president for a return to traditional values—most especially, truthfulness. "I believe in these values," he wrote, "not because they are old, but because they are timeless; not because they are traditional, but because they are true; not because they are American, but because they are universal. Moreover, these values are not the exclusive domain of either the Republican or Democratic parties, nor of either the political left or political right. Universal values are ideologically neutral."

Jackson was sure that Bill Clinton, in his heart of hearts, understood. "Without responsibility and accountability on your part, however, and without a change in your fundamental approach to people and in your basic method of operation," he warned, "I fear for you, your presidency and America"—and he added: "Forgive my role as an attorney for the troopers . . . in inflicting such public pain upon you and yours." He closed by hoping and praying that "good and truth will ultimately triumph along this future timeline, that you will lead this country into a bright new era of change, and that a renaissance of the spirit, beginning with and led by you, will sweep across our people and propel a reinvigorated America into the 21st century." He signed himself "Your friend (still), Cliff," and in a postscript added that Lynn Davis and the troopers themselves joined in the "thoughts and sentiments expressed in this letter."

Low Tide

In the Oval Office President Clinton read the Little Rock missive. He did not answer it. Aides described him, in the wake of Troopergate, not only as distraught but "distracted," and both Clintons as volcanic, with tensions in the family quarters "said to be high. Clinton called a friend and said it was terrible to go through this with both his mother and his wife's mother in the house."

Hillary, defying the agreed line that the president and first lady would refuse to speak on the issue themselves, lashed out in an interview with the wire services against the "outrageous, terrible" stories being published about her husband, claiming they were part of a Republican plot to smear the president, just as "he is on the verge of fulfilling his commitment to the American people." Meanwhile the president did seem chastened. In response to a request by Arkansas reporters to define his personal character, he had responded: "I think character is something that you have to demonstrate rather than try to define." His response, they felt, "fell short of an outright denial of extramarital affairs."

Mixed with media and congressional calls for further investigation of Whitewater, thanks to Hillary's refusal to permit sight of her past records, the Clintons had become embattled. Hillary began wearing dark glasses, despite the winter. Mark Gearan, asked about the latest Inman story, blurted out: "I can only deal with one nightmare at a time." Hillary's press secretary told reporters they could only interview the first lady about Christmas celebrations at the White House—celebrations that had fizzled out like wet fireworks. The atmosphere turned eerie, indeed resembled a morgue more than the first residence of the nation—the first couple spending only five minutes with the White House staff at the traditional Christmas party, and looking understandably strained.

THE BLACK PEN

CHAPTER THIRTY

THE SWING TO THE RIGHT

Polls Remain High

Mindful of the lessons of the trooper scandal, the president did try to put the past behind him and demonstrate better moral leadership as the New Year unfolded. He flew to Europe and, in two weeks of brilliant personal diplomacy, got the liberated countries of central and Eastern Europe to join NATO as part of a slow-but-steady program called "Partnership for Peace"—while in Moscow he persuaded the Russian president, Boris Yeltsin, to consider joining NATO, too, and not feel threatened by the defection of their once-vassal states. By offering American aid he then got the Ukrainian parliament to agree to hand over to the Russians their huge arsenal of atomic weapons. And when he returned, as a sort of conquering hero—certainly the most popular U.S. president in Europe since JFK—to Washington, he felt he was on a new roll. Beyond the platform of the Democratic Leadership Council he had no real constituency, such as trade unions or the old-established organs—local, regional, and national—of the Democratic Party. In Congress, it was true, he had lost much support among members of the House thanks to his poor leadership skills in the White House. Nevertheless, he was not completely without friends, for in the minds and hearts of the general public he was still an extraordinarily young and charismatic president, attempting to do his best. And in this respect, his generous, southern personality had proven a tremendous advantage, notwithstanding the scandals punctuating his first year in office. Pollsters thus noted with amazement how, in the wake of Troopergate, the president's rating remained consistent from December 1993 into January

1994—in fact, his favorability rating actually improved from 55 percent in November to 62 percent in January.

What, then, went wrong, that in his second year as president, despite the noblest of intentions and every effort to rise to his former Oxford friend's prescription of leadership, the president should have failed so spectacularly that by year's end the Republicans had been able to morph his image onto Democratic candidates and win both houses of Congress for the first time in forty years?

It was a question that would vex a thousand political pundits at the time, and scores of historians and political observers in the years afterwards—for the loss of Congress would doom Democratic legislation for an entire decade, as the Republican machine sought to control the American national agenda.

Was it Bill Clinton's fault? Could the big Arkansan with the silver tongue have changed this? What, we ask again, went so *wrong* in year two of the Clinton administration?

Yesterday's Wine

Some observers, assessing the swing to conservatism in America in the 1990s, considered it inevitable, and irreversible. "The tide was indeed turning and there was nothing Clinton could do about it," the *Washington Post* writer Tom Lippman, for example, later reflected. "Clinton came along at a time when a lot of the ideas that had people like Noam Chomsky and Herbert Marcuse lionized on American campuses were [now] yesterday's wine in yesterday's bottles. The country had outgrown that. And with the approach of the 1994 election, in my opinion, what happened was that the Marxist pig finally passed through the python of American politics. The country had gone as far as it was going to go in the direction of political and social liberalism and was now going to go back the other way."

Many political and presidential historians, in after years, agreed, picturing the Clinton presidency as not only irrelevant but doomed from the start, just as Jimmy Carter's had been: in a period of broadly Republican retrenchment regarding public expenditure and entitlements outside of defense, and rising moral certitude over issues such as abortion, they asserted, the president's room for maneuver had been so limited that even had he been a better executive leader, he could not have altered the outcome of American political history in 1994, with the long, faltering Democratic majority in Congress already leaching away, as Senate and congressional seats as well as state governorships began to fall inexorably to the Republican right. Democratic senator Wyche Fowler lost to Republican Paul Coverdale in Georgia; Lloyd Bentsen's vacated Senate seat in Texas went to Republican Kay Bailey Hutchison in a landslide. The Governor's Mansion in Virginia went to a very conservative Republican, while in New Jersey Governor James J. Florio fell to Republican anti-tax challenger Christine Todd Whitman. Two of the largest U.S. city mayoralties switched to Republicans.

Why, then, did the most seismically sensitive president in modern times not see what was coming in November? Above all, why did he try to bulldoze through Congress a massive, increasingly unpopular health care reform bill with no concession to looming reality? Instead, on his return from Europe, the president went before Congress for a second major, televised address and, holding up an ominous black pen, threatened members of his own party that he would veto any bill that offered less than Hillary's insistence on universal health coverage!

The Black Pen

"For twenty years this country has tried to reform health care," the president began his Periclean speech, after mounting the podium of the House of Representatives on January 25, 1994. "President Roosevelt tried, President Truman tried, President Nixon tried, President Carter tried. Every time the special interests were powerful enough to defeat them. . . . But not this time!"

Courage was certainly not lacking as the president acknowledged the arguments of his opponents. "I know there are people here who say there's no health care crisis. Tell it to Richard and Judy Anderson," he challenged, evoking the names of two Reno residents who had written to the first lady after they lost their jobs and insurance. "Tell it to the 58 million Americans who have no coverage at all. . . . You tell it to those people, because I can't. This is another issue," he lectured the packed chamber, "where people are way ahead of the politicians. That may not be popular with either party, but it happens to be the truth." And with that he made the single worst political error of his presidency thus far. Raising a black pen above the lectern like a nasty teacher in science class, he warned: "If you send me legislation that does not guarantee every American private health insurance that can never be taken away, you will force me to take this pen, veto the legislation, and we'll come right back here and start all over again."

An hour later the president finally left the famous debating chamber—little imagining what Republicans had in store for him, once the minority leader of the Senate exerted his right to respond.

Senator Robert Dole was not known as a great speechmaker—though he was admired for his courage as a young infantry officer in World War II in Italy, when his right arm was shattered during a rescue attempt. Dole had had surgery for prostate cancer in 1991 (covered in full by his Senate health insurance), and had previously supported legislation aimed at improving the convoluted administration of health care in America. In speaking on behalf of Republicans in Congress Senator Dole therefore welcomed, first, the president's belated attention to Republican welfare concerns (which the president had outlined in preliminary proposals for welfare reform that he intended to put before Congress) and his concern with health care reform—in support of which the first lady had submitted her 1,340-page legislative application to Congress. Then Dole proceeded to ridicule the president's health care proposal.

Before the cameras the Senate minority leader produced his own tele-gimmick—one that proved far more effective than the president's black pen, as, pointing to a huge wall chart, Dole poured scorn upon the White House's *über*complex proposals. "Our country has health care problems," the senator acknowledged, "but no health care crisis. But we *will* have a crisis if we take the president's medicine—a massive dose of government control. More cost. Less choice. More taxes. Less quality. More government control," he repeated. "Less control for you and your family. That's what the president's government-run plan is likely to give you.

"We can fix our most pressing problems," Senator Dole assured viewers, and Congress could do so, moreover, "without performing a triple bypass operation on our health care system." He finished by pointing to the bottom of a "dizzyingly detailed flow chart of Bill Clinton's health care legislation—a prop so full of twists and turns that on television it looked downright intestinal," as the *Washington Post*'s reporter wrote. "'You and I are way down here, somewhere,' Dole said, grinning into the camera, with his best 'Mister Rogers-meets-Freddy Krueger' smile.'"

Given Bob Dole's own top-class guaranteed Senate health insurance for life, the senator's self-identification with poor people at the bottom of the chart was a trifle disingenuous—but his appeal to viewers rather than members of Congress was devastatingly effective. "The chart, even more than Dole, was the star of Tuesday night's official Republican response to the president's State of the Union address," the *Post* chronicled—"200-odd reddish organizational boxes linked by a dense web of angry lines, and Dole continued to brandish it yesterday as he lampooned Clinton's proposal on all the morning talk shows."

"If a picture is worth a thousand words, a chart is worth more than a hundred agencies," boasted Republican senator Arlen Specter, who had provided Dole with his weaponry. Specter claimed to have received more than two thousand phone calls from people asking for a copy of the chart—boasting that "My wife couldn't even get through."

To the surprise of Republicans who had assumed that, with a Democratic administration and a Democratic Congress, some sort of health care reform was inevitable, the president's universal-care plan was now, Dole pronounced, "in trouble"—deep trouble, with the first congressional votes on the bill due to take place in about four months. The president, Dole warned, is "going to have to drop a lot of these price controls, mandates, the mandatory health care alliances, before we make any real inroads," for Clinton was asking the American people to "trust the government more than you trust your doctor."

One of Hillary's Biggest Admirers

White House staffers and Democratic Party officials were mortified. "At that particular moment, the people in this country learned more about the Clinton health care plan than from all the rhetoric and talking heads that came before, and it had a bigger audience," a Republican political analyst said—indeed the GOP response got a combined rating of 26.2 on the three major networks, or 24.7 million American homes.

Jeff Eller, communications aide and computer manager in charge of the Clinton health care team, attempted counter-battery fire from his emplacement in Hillary's boiler room operation in the Old Executive Office Building, dubbed "The Delivery Room." "We think that chart is very misleading and very inaccurate," Eller complained, while White House policy analyst Christine Heenan attempted to inject a little balance into the debate. "What you don't see on this chart," she said, "is the amazing morass of truly bureaucratic boxes and lines and arrows that represent today's health insurance system that basically result in administrative costs and no consumer control."

Why substitute one morass for another, though, was the question that went through most voters' minds. The person who had actually drawn up

Dole's devastating chart, Sharon Helfant, was even a Democrat! The chart itself was not really a surprise—it had, newspapers reported, been in circulation since the previous October, when Helfant had "sat down at her dining room table with a straight-edge, a pen, Wite-Out and 10 pieces of paper taped together. Oh yes, and the thousand-plus pages of Clinton's health care legislation. 'In my view it's very conservative,' Helfant said of her handiwork"—which pictured some 207 boxes, but could have included more. "'There's only one state government box, for instance, and not 50. And I don't think it really conveys to people the power and authority of all these new entities like national health boards which can negotiate premiums for people, which is very significant.'" The long-time Democrat insisted that the last thing she wanted to do was "distort Clinton's plan for crass partisan political purposes. Not at all. 'I'm a Democrat and I voted for Bill Clinton,' she said. 'I'm one of Hillary Clinton's biggest admirers.'"

With admirers such as these, however, the Clintons had no need of enemies.

Tracer Rounds over Baghdad

Just days before the president's speech to Congress, a devastating earthquake struck the Los Angeles area, killing dozens and leaving thousands homeless. Most Republicans conceded that Clinton responded magnificently, flying to the scene to make sure that effective federal help was forthcoming.

So exhausted was the president by his trip to Los Angeles and then his address to the Joint Session, that the next day he was ordered by his doctors to cancel all speaking engagements, to alleviate his laryngitis. The battle of health care reform was now joined, however. "In the president's absence," reporters for the Cleveland *Plain Dealer* noted, "his supporters, from Vice President Al Gore down, and his opponents, led by Senate Republican Leader Bob Dole, R-Kan., filled the airwaves with sound bites like tracer rounds over Baghdad during the Persian Gulf war."

The president's confrontational challenge, however, did no good. "Health care was once Bill Clinton's poster child. It is now becoming his tar baby," William Kristol, former chief of staff to Vice President Dan Quayle, soon commented, insisting that the president's threat of veto showed "that he fears support for his plan is eroding."

"White House aide George Stephanopoulos said today that Clinton would not budge from his demand for coverage for every American," the *Buffalo News* reported. " 'On that fundamental point, we can't move. Because if we don't have universal coverage, you'll never get the costs under control.' "

This was a strange argument for what had become, as universal coverage, a *moral* imperative more than cost-control—costs that even the bill's supporters accepted *could not* easily be controlled.

As the contribution of health care reform to deficit reduction had wilted before OMB's numbers and Treasury warnings, the president's commitment had become more and more *ethical*: that covering the uninsured was the *right* thing to do—*now*. In this way, Bill Clinton had hoped he could mollify most of those Democratic constituencies most opposed to the NAFTA bill he'd got through Congress—without recognizing that, as the economy picked up, not only did the number of voters worried about their own health care coverage lessen but their humanitarian concern for the uninsured dipped at the thought of their own premiums rising. "If there's not a recession," Judy Feder pointed out, "then people are not worried about it."

In an improving economy, health care accompanied new jobs anyway. Even had this electoral consideration been properly understood by the president, however, the room for maneuver without spending new money was limited. As Dr. Feder pointed out, a transitional, step-by-step approach was hard to devise, because it was "hard to get any money from cost-containment *unless* you did something massive. Now you could, of course—if you'd taken the $60 billions you took out of Medicare and that were used for deficit reduction, you could have done universal coverage, or something like it. . . . It's doable, but not without money." And thanks to the profligacy of previous Republican administrations, there *was* no money, until the economy picked up some more. Meanwhile, despite a marked turnaround that was beginning to take place in the economy, it did not look as if there would be the electoral support for radical legislation that would actually raise, not lower, the premiums of those already insured—who constituted 85 percent of the population.

Fighting the rising Republican tide of negative advertising would be an uphill struggle for individual members of Congress in their home districts—yet it was a battle Bill Clinton, having begun the hostilities, insisted he could not close down, given that his own wife had traveled the country to promote it, and had become so identified with its success or failure. It was Hillary's baby—and Hillary, as he'd announced proudly the year before, was not a quitter.

By contrast, Bill Clinton was a realist and a quitter—but could not afford to quit Hillary.

Alarm Bells

The president and first lady thus felt compelled to continue their health care reform offensive, without the troops to guarantee victory.

By demanding unconditional surrender—that as president he would sign no bill that did not include universal coverage—the president might *sound* firm, but he was standing on marshy ground, as all who looked carefully could see.

"The consensus on Capitol Hill is that some reforms will be enacted but change will be incremental—not the sweeping policy and economic shift Clinton wants," *USA Today* predicted—quoting Republican Senator David Durenberger of Minnesota, who advised a more cautious, step-by-step approach. "The important thing is to get started," Durenberger emphasized. "You can't change the way 257 million Americans buy their medical care or the way 500,000 doctors and 7,000 hospitals deliver it overnight."

In the House, Republican congressman Richard Armey of Texas had remarked that the Clinton bill "is still a bureaucratic nightmare that will kill jobs, and it can't pass Congress in its present form." Alarm bells should have sounded in the West Wing and in "Hillaryland." But the truth was, there were louder bells tolling—bells that pealed other problems: Whitewater, and "Paula."

One-minus-One

Whitewater was emblematic of a post-Watergate conspiracy-victim culture that had overtaken much of America after the Vietnam War in the 1970s. How to deal with it was a conundrum. Hillary had been part of the Nixon impeachment process. She thus knew how unlikely it was that she and Bill could stonewall forever, yet her character was that of a Republican: averse to compromise. It was her strength, and—in a world of New Democrats— her weakness. By contrast, Bill's political genius was one of riding the waves of public concern, anxiety, and hope—as an expert surfer, able to tumble and get up again on his board.

Hillary was loath to tumble in public—as both Stephanopoulos and Gergen had found. Instead of riding the investigative wave, therefore, with the possibility that she might be censured at some later point, Hillary had insisted, with the backing of her loyal cabal of female advisers, that she'd never done anything wrong, despite her partnership with, and then legal representation of, Jim McDougal, and that she had no obligation to help put the decade-old matter to judicial rest. The president had snapped at a reporter when asked about the call for a congressional inquiry: "I have nothing to say about that. I've said we would turn the records over. There is nothing else for me to say about that." But he hadn't handed over the records—at least, not all his records—and his snappy response didn't make the matter go away. The law empowering Congress to appoint an independent counsel was expiring in January. Should he have let it die, and vetoed any attempt at congressional resurrection? Or would he have been overridden by a two-thirds majority in Congress? Was it not best to encourage the attorney general to appoint her own special counsel to investigate Whitewater? Eventually—and reluctantly—Hillary had given in.

To be sure, Bernie Nussbaum's prediction that the more the attorney general's investigator might find, the more Republicans would press for further investigation, was to prove eerily accurate. What President Clinton didn't admit at the time, but later addressed when he came to compose his memoirs, was, of course, his own wife's absolute determination, from the start, not to release their Whitewater files to the *Washington Post*—thus fanning a suspicion in the serious press that the Clintons had serious things to hide. "What I should have done," Clinton admitted in retirement, "is release the records, resist the prosecutor, give an extensive briefing to all the Democrats who wanted it, and ask for their support." But that had been something Hillary, for a mix of reasons, had refused to countenance (and Bill refused, in retrospect, to chide her for) until it was too late.

The "two-for-one" advantage of the forty-second president began to look uncomfortably like one-*minus*-one as the president continued to pursue his doomed health care reform plan in early 1994, while hoping that the newly appointed Department of Justice investigator—an impartial Republican former prosecutor from New York—would wrap up a quick examination.

CHAPTER THIRTY-ONE

PANDORA'S BOX

Alone in a Whirlwind

In an exquisite colored line-drawing cover illustration for the *American Spectator,* Bill Clinton tiptoes stealthily down a back alley, past a garbage can, shoes in hand, beneath an arching cat and crescent moon. In another illustration, Clinton has his hand on the thigh of a transfixed, short-skirted secretary. In a third, a ruddy-faced Bill poses with a bright, complacent smirk—his arm around a shorter, almost shrunken colleague, who looks up at him with a worried frown. It is JFK.

However amusing the illustrations for "His Cheatin' Heart: David Brock in Little Rock," and however far the ripples of the scandalous allegations had spread, the actual text had but a tiny circulation—which, in Arkansas, did not extend much beyond the main library. By contrast, Little Rock's daily newspaper, the *Arkansas Democrat-Gazette,* had a huge circulation in the state, and had been doing its own reporting on the trooper story. On December 23, 1994, the *Democrat-Gazette* had run a banner headline across its front page: "Clinton confronts troopers' charges—Tells media allegations are 'not so.'" Beneath a photograph of what appeared to be a group of condemned men another headline read: "Troopers scared, alone in whirlwind."

As the Christmas from Hell had given way to the New Year at Hilton Head, a little girl had stood up at one of the Renaissance weekend events and urged the president "not to let the tension of being president hurt his family and not to get divorced because it is hard on children." As the president's polls had gone up, it had not looked, in other words, as if President "Machiavelli" Clinton would be more than temporarily embarrassed.

All too soon, however, there was a glitch. A young clerk, mentioned only by her first, given name in Brock's nefarious piece, took umbrage—and sued not Brock or the *American Spectator*, but the president.

"Paula"

"The names of the mistresses with whom [Trooper] Patterson was familiar, some of whom are married and have children, are known to me," Brock had claimed, "but will not be revealed here, so as not to exploit them more than Clinton already has, or to punish innocent family members."

Why, then, had Brock left the given name of the clerk-receptionist in the Excelsior Hotel, who had allegedly been invited up to service the Arkansas governor during Clinton's final term in office in Little Rock?

Brock never explained. After her encounter with Clinton, "which lasted no more than an hour as the trooper stood by in the hall," according to Brock, "Paula" told the trooper she was "available to be Clinton's regular girlfriend if he so desired." The obvious implication was that "Paula" had not only serviced the governor but was willing to do so again on a regular basis.

Since the 1991 incident—which the receptionist had never reported, at the time—she had married her fiancé, Steve Jones. As Mrs. Jones she had moved to California, where she'd had a baby. On a visit home at the end of 1993, however, she'd heard about the trooper scandal that had been emblazoned on the front page of the local daily newspaper, but had no idea she had actually been named as "Paula" in the *Spectator* article.

However, a friend, Debra Ballentine, who had originally gotten Paula the temporary job as a clerk-receptionist, *had* read Brock's text. Knowing the account was untrue, Ballentine had called Paula's mother's house, and read out to Paula the offending passage—from a journal the very existence of which Paula had at that time no idea. It was in this upside-down way that one of the most extraordinary legal challenges to the presidency in American history had begun—a challenge that would haunt the president for the rest of his time in the Oval Office.

David Brock's claim that "Paula" had had consensual sex with Governor Clinton infuriated Mrs. Jones—especially when, meeting Ballentine at the Golden Corral steakhouse in North Little Rock with their two babies shortly afterwards, she happened to see Trooper Ferguson: the trooper who had ushered her into Governor Clinton's hotel room. "Now, Paula, I got dragged into that deal and I never gave out your last name, so nobody knows who you are," Ferguson said, adding—when Paula protested she had rejected the governor's advances—"Clinton told me you didn't do anything anyway."

Anxious lest Paula go after him for slander, Ferguson had then sought to deflect her anger by pointing to a potential pot of gold, should she wish to pursue it. He suggested that the *National Enquirer* tabloid magazine would probably pay her a million dollars for her story, if she chose to tell it. After all, the trooper reasoned, the story of Clinton's sexual proposition (as opposed to consummation) was true, yet "he always gets away with it."

Without a job in California, Paula had indeed been intrigued by the prospect of "big money"—whether suing Trooper Ferguson and the *American Spectator* for defamation of her character or seeking bigger bucks still for telling her tacky story in public she was as yet unsure, according to her sister, Charlotte, who begged her not to pursue such a course, which would, she feared, "kill their mother."

A century before, in France's *Belle Epoque*, virtually the entire Gallic nation, and much of Europe, had become polarized over the issue of whether a terrible injustice had been done to a Jewish artillery officer, Alfred Dreyfus, who was wrongfully accused of treason, then tried, convicted, and sent to prison for life in 1894, on Devil's Island. That case, filled with its racist undertones, had pitted French conservatives against liberals, but it had at least revolved around national security and the betrayal of state secrets to the Germans. The Dreyfus and Jones cases are, of course, enormously different, but each became the iconic cultural clash of its time—the one in traditional terms, the other in full postmodern, wacky regalia. The case of Paula Corbin Jones was all-American: a diminutive, buxom female employee, with fantasies of a career in Hollywood, wrongfully trashed in a national conservative-Republican satirical magazine, who now sought redress not from the magazine that had printed the untrue story, but from the president of the United States.

Wanting an Apology

Since Paula knew no lawyer to consult, her friend Debra Ballentine called Danny Traylor, a Little Rock attorney, whose main work was divorce, real estate, and wills. Traylor had little confidence Paula would make any money out of the case, even though he believed her story—indeed, Traylor warned her that far from making a fortune "there may be no money and even so, it's not worth the grief." Because she pursued the matter, however, everyone in America, indeed everyone in the world, would soon be party to the grief.

Traylor, mistakenly thinking that Cliff Jackson was Danny Ferguson's attorney, called him in Little Rock. With his colleague Lynn Davis, Jackson had then met Paula Jones in Little Rock, subjecting her to his characteristic interrogational style of pre-trial cross-examination. "Again, I did what I did with the troopers," Jackson recalled. "I listened. I looked her in the eye. I watched her body language. I read her. This was a woman in distress. She cried—not a lot—teared up when she described the incident. So my take was: She was either telling the truth or was a *very* effective actress.

"Her version was that he was the governor, and she was intrigued when 'he told me that I'd made his heart flutter or something, and he'd wanted to meet me. And here am I, a lowly state employee, this is the governor. . . . And it's a state trooper who's taking me up, after all, and I no sooner got into the room, than'—and she went into her story."

The story of a governor unable to curb his lust was disgusting—but sadly in character. In the end, the courtroom lawyer became convinced that Ferguson was mistaken in what he'd inferred to Brock. Paula Corbin Jones was, he felt, telling the truth, for her account of what had happened seemed too genuine to be invented. "I told Danny Traylor, afterwards, 'I believe Danny Ferguson has not told the truth [to David Brock].'"

"Their objective was very simple," Jackson explained the Jones-Traylor agenda at that point, in January 1994, almost three years after the alleged incident. "It was: 'We want an apology. We want [the president] and Danny Ferguson to admit that this was not true.' Because she said it was hurting her with her husband, and she was embarrassed by it."

Blood in the Water

Mulling it over, Traylor—whose father had been a Democratic alderman—decided to first be a gentleman and approach the president privately. Via a friend of his, Traylor found an Arkansas intermediary: an F.O.B. who agreed to approach President Clinton directly, with a view to getting not only an apology but a job in California for Paula—preferably in acting, possibly through the Hollywood couple, the Thomasons, who had made *The Man from Hope.*

A "man in Little Rock" got in touch "with my office," Clinton himself recalled, ten years later, "telling us that the lawyer [Danny Traylor] had said that her case was weak and that if I would pay her $50,000 and help her and her husband, Steve" to obtain jobs in Hollywood, "she wouldn't sue me." As in the story of the Sibylline Books, this sum, if true, would come to seem a bargain in later years. In February 1994, however, the president was in denial, both over Whitewater and over Troopergate. To admit publicly to having solicited a state employee, while confessing that the employee had turned him down, was beyond the president, and would have been beyond any official or employer in such circumstances.

Though the chosen intermediary, George Cook—a long-time supporter of Bill Clinton—did his best to negotiate, it was no use. In the context of the president's latest polls, as he reported back to Traylor, there was no reason for the president of the United States to cut a deal. "We had been through that before," Stephanopoulos later said of the thinking in the White House. "And basically, I thought we had learned that these sex stories just weren't going to make that much difference." The news for Mr. Cook was thus negative. "We can't do anything for you. We can't do anything with you" was the White House verdict. "People don't care about Clinton's extramarital affairs."

The White House's response spelled a six-letter word: hubris. Traylor—who had said he would act on contingency—had been hoping for a mere $1,000 fee and an apology for Paula. Getting neither could not but inflame Paula's ember—pushing her into the arms of right-wing conspirators only too pleased to stumble on ammunition with which to shoot at the usurper who had unseated their sitting Republican president, the patrician George H. W. Bush.

Sound Advice

"Ladies and gentlemen! Out of deference to the first family [and] the presidency," Traylor said in a press conference held in the Diplomat Room of the Shoreham Hotel in Washington, D.C., on February 11, 1994, "I do not want to appeal to the prurient interests of us all. But let me assure you what transpired in that room [in the Excelsior Hotel, Little Rock, in 1991] is the legal equivalent of on-the-job sexual harassment."

The press, still exercised over the business of Whitewater, were nonplussed. Was this quiet Arkansas lawyer, with his southern drawl and a practice devoted to divorce and real estate, intending to sue the president of the United States for pre-presidential *harassment*?

Traylor had, he explained to the journalists, spent many a sleepless night over the best way to resolve the matter. He had finally decided to send a letter to the president, as well as one to Trooper Ferguson. "All Clinton had to do was acknowledge his misbehavior, apologize to his client, and set the record straight that there had been no sexual relations between them," the *Washington Post*'s reporter, Michael Isikoff, later recalled. "Then he and Jones would go away." Traylor was so apologetic, in fact, he had even pointed out the relative triviality of the matter. "We've got Bosnia. We've got a health care crisis. We've got eighteen children living in a room without a father. Mr. President, this is something that shouldn't occupy your energy and your attention. I would encourage you to come forward and . . . tell the American people what the truth of this matter is. If you made a mistake, the American people will forgive you."

As with attorney Cliff Jackson's New Year's letter, Traylor's appeal fell on stony ground, however—not only at 1600 Pennsylvania Avenue, but at the Omni Hotel. "There were a bunch of questions," Jackson recalled, as reporters demanded specifics, "and Danny wouldn't let [Paula] say anything—just in vague, general terms," which gave the impression of a hoax. "And finally Reed Irvine, representing Accuracy in Media, asked something to the effect of: 'Was whatever he did something that can be done with your clothes on?' And everyone hooted and howled."

Too shy to retell in public her intimate story of sexual humiliation, the diminutive, inarticulate Mrs. Jones was now humiliated a second time: more or less booed off the Washington stage. It was a poor omen for her future in Hollywood movies, and even less encouraging for her appeal for her given name to be cleared. As Jackson recalled, "It was a disaster! The media just—I mean, there weren't any [news] stories. There was no coverage of it. And I can understand why.

"I went again to their room the next day, after there wasn't anything on the networks, or TV. They were totally depressed—abjectly depressed. Theirs was a wasted journey."

It certainly seemed so—Clinton's staff having little difficulty, thereafter, in trashing the Arkansas whistleblower and her request for an apology. "Basically we just pointed to the messenger and said as little as possible," Stephanopoulos later recounted. "And basically it worked. There wasn't a lot of evidence behind it. The charges were flimsy at first, and she was being promoted by these Clinton haters. Let the picture speak for itself."

Jackson's advice to Traylor was, rather, to find a sympathetic journalist, and rely on him or her to research and authenticate the real story. "Danny was way over his head, didn't know what to do. He would call me about it. And I would say: 'Danny, I told you repeatedly: Stay away from Republicans, stay away from conservatives, stay away from them!' And to his credit, he tried. He called the National Organization for Women, he called the liberal interest groups—trying to involve them, trying to get their assistance. And nobody would help him. And so, ultimately, how they got to know Gilbert K. Davis I'm not sure. But I think, only because they didn't have any alternatives." Again and again, Jackson urged Traylor "to have some mainstream lawyers, if not liberal lawyers. Because this is an issue about women's rights. . . ."

Jackson was talking to the wind. By the time feminists and civil rights organizations did finally wake up, in the summer of 1994, to the women's rights issue involved, it would be too late; ambitious lawyers and right-wing political extremists had already hijacked the story.

Petite, long-nosed, and big-breasted, the former Arkansas receptionist would become Bill Clinton's nemesis by default, since Clinton refused to admit to wrongdoing—indeed, initially, to ever having met her. This was fatal. His staff, meanwhile, compounded his error. As Paula's lawyers would put it, "On several occasions on and after February 11, 1994, Clinton, and his agents and employees acting pursuant to his direction, maliciously and wilfully, defamed Jones by making statements which Clinton knew to be false. These statements were made with the intent and certain knowledge that they would be reprinted in the print and other media. Such statements by Clinton, his agents and employees, characterized Jones as a liar and as being 'pathetic,' and damaged her good name, character, and reputation."

Blessed with outsize lips and a contrary character, Paula was, even to her lawyers, a loose cannon—as prepared to risk her marriage and her well-being to get the president to confess his original sin as she was intent on making big money and getting her fifteen minutes of fame. "I was a small little entity in this big vast whatever-you-want-to-call-it that got erected," she would later confess once Bill Clinton, in retirement, gave his version of the long, sorry road to his impeachment. "It started with me—and they [right-wing Republicans] did use me for their own agendas."

Paula Jones Uncovered

Count III of the $700,000 lawsuit that Paula Jones's new lawyers developed against the president of the United States in the spring of 1994 went under the title "Intentional Infliction of Emotional Distress." A penalty payment of $175,000, plus legal fees, would be demanded for this, on the grounds that the "conduct of Clinton herein set forth was odious, perverse and outrageous. Not only were the acts of sexual perversity unwelcome by Jones, but they were wilful, wanton, reckless, intentional, persistent and continuous in the hotel room."

By giving in to what Bill Clinton would himself later term his "old demons," his "dark alley," the president—though he had mercifully *not* forced the young Arkansas employee into having oral sex with him—had nevertheless put himself at the mercy of the whims of a now twenty-four-year-old from Little Rock. Under state law in Arkansas (by 1994 overturned, but still operative retroactively in terms of the alleged 1991 incident), Paula Corbin Jones had been entitled to three full years in which to file a complaint. Her opportunity for legal redress was due to run out on May 9, 1994—and had already run out under federal harassment law. The president thus had three urgent choices: a full confession of his bad behavior, together with the apology Paula demanded; a partial admission, such as that he had made a mere pass at Paula but that it had been rejected, along with a formal, total repudiation of the *American Spectator*'s libelous assertion that Paula had had sex with him; or, finally, a denial of the entire episode and the hope that presidential immunity, under constitutional law, would keep the matter from going to court during his term of office.

Having already set Stephanopoulos and his dogs on Paula, however, the president found himself unable, or unwilling, to call them off. He therefore chose the last alternative.

Had President Clinton told the truth, or even half the truth; had he, at the very least, immediately and categorically signed an affidavit denying Brock's assertion that he had had sex with Paula, he would have removed the worst of Paula's blood from the Washington water—just as, had he handed over all his and Hillary's Whitewater documents at the very first suggestion of possible impropriety, he could have avoided a formal Justice Department special inquiry, and certainly a congressionally ordered investigation by a prosecutor.

Such hindsight, however, is to overlook the situation in which the president found himself in the early spring of 1994. Following the Los Angeles earthquake, a series of winter storms produced devastating floods and property damage in states as far south as Florida and as far north as Michigan—often twice that spring. As president, Clinton crisscrossed the nation, speaking with governors and invoking federal disaster relief. At the same time he met with the prime ministers of Ireland and Great Britain to further the Northern Ireland peace process; conferred with ANC president Nelson Mandela on the transition of South Africa to post-apartheid democracy; pressed President Hosni Mubarak of Egypt, President Hafiz al-Assad of Syria, and Prime Minister Yitzhak Rabin of Israel toward rapprochement; met with President Zhou of China; and negotiated with the prime minister of Japan on liberalizing Japan's restrictive import culture. Simultaneously he continued to pressure congressional leaders to pass his major health care reform bill, his assault weapons ban, his crime bill, his forthcoming welfare bill. . . .

In view of such grave responsibilities, it seemed inconceivable that a private citizen could disrupt the business of government of the world's sole remaining superpower—especially over an allegation about a non-criminal event that had taken place before Clinton became president. And yet the inconceivable was now fact: a fact that would lead, inexorably, to the possibility of impeachment.

CHAPTER THIRTY-TWO

PROXIMITY TO DISGRACE

Presidential Immunity

For several years in the early 1970s Clinton had taught criminal law at the University of New Haven while still a student at Yale Law School, and after that antitrust law as a professor at the University of Arkansas Law School in Fayetteville, before becoming attorney general of Arkansas. Article 2, Section 1, Clause 1 of the United States Constitution clearly stated, "The executive Power shall be vested in a President of the United States of America," and for over two hundred years this statement had been taken to mean that, save for impeachment, the president of the United States was immune to civil lawsuits during his term of office, lest he be distracted from his great responsibilities. Impeachment could only be sought by the House of Representatives, and then only for "Treason, Bribery, or other high Crimes and Misdemeanors" (Article 2, Section 4)—lest Congress, too, distract the president from his executive duties.

Allegedly exposing his private parts, in private, to an employee before becoming president of the United States hardly constituted treason, bribery, or a high crime or misdemeanor. Ergo, it did not, on the face of it, seem possible to the president or his legal counsel that Ms. Jones's new lawyers, however rabid, could pursue her ramped-up claim. Or that, if they did, the president would be liable to respond before the end of his presidential term in 1997 or 2001.

Certainly no one had ever successfully brought a civil suit against a serving president since the beginning of the Republic. But did that mean there could not be a first time? After all, a disgruntled federal employee *had* once brought suit, Clinton knew, against President Nixon, *while Nixon was in office*. Though the suit had not prevailed, the Supreme Court had reviewed presidential immunity from prosecution—and had perversely ruled that Nixon was indeed immune from prosecution for his *official* acts, but could be sued for his private acts.

What if Paula Jones's lawyers decided, as a result of his denial, to challenge the doctrine of presidential immunity from private litigation over private acts? If Hillary sued him for divorce, for example, over his sexual misbehavior towards women such as Paula Jones, would he be allowed by the courts to defer the suit for another potential seven years? His mind whirring, the president rehearsed potential outcomes.

In a new world in which every member of his staff and administration, thanks to Whitewater, was potentially liable to subpoena and interrogation by virtue of ever-expanding American laws of "discovery," the president's friends and colleagues were being toppled—indeed, the resignations of administration staff were already becoming a veritable exodus. The latest was Clinton's old golfing partner Webb Hubbell, number three at the Justice Department, who resigned in March 1994. With Hubbell going down—he would be sentenced the following year to twenty-one months in federal prison, despite having offered, from the start, to repay the money he had overcharged on his company's credit card—there was no one in Washington with whom the president could share his anxieties, let alone his "dark alley" secrets.

Apart from Trooper Ferguson, the lonely president reflected, there was no credible witness to corroborate Paula Jones's story. Thus he continued to deny having ever *met* Paula Corbin Jones. As reports reached him that Paula had witnesses to whom she had confided the episode, *on the very day on which it had happened in May 1991*, the president began to rethink his strategy, however, and by the first week in May 1994, he started to back down. "In a desperate attempt to avoid a sexual harassment lawsuit, President Bill Clinton has offered to apologise to his accuser, although he denies ever having met her," the Washington correspondent of the London *Sunday Times* reported. "Clinton was prepared to say that if he had met her, and something had happened to upset her, he was sorry." Such an apology, however, was too little, too late—for Paula's lawyers were now out for blood.

This state of affairs didn't make sense, was surely not in the best interests of the country, and certainly did not seem in tune with the intentions of the Founding Fathers. "Welcome to the 1990s" was all Bill Clinton's capacious mind could register. But his more vulnerable inner self was wracked by the business—indeed, he could only thank his maker that his mother, Virginia, who had passed away in January, was not alive to witness it.

Epitomized in David Mamet's controversial 1992 play *Oleana*, sexual harassment had certainly become a complicating factor in the cultural wars—often pitting liberal males against liberal females, and raising the question of deeper agendas. In the wake of Paula Jones's allegations, the National Organization for Women (NOW) had at first issued a bold statement that "sexual harassers are everywhere—in high public positions, in executive suites and even in pulpits," powerful men who "treat harassment as a fringe benefit, a privilege of power." As NOW initially stated, "Every Paula Jones deserves to be heard, no matter how old she is and how long ago the incident occurred, no matter what kind of accent she has or how much money she makes, and no matter whom she associates with."

The people Jones associated with did matter, however, in this case— and gave the executives of NOW, the largest women's group in the country, growing cause for anxiety, as did Jones's obvious indifference to the feminist aspect of the suit. "When the case was first filed, [Patricia] Ireland [president of NOW] agreed to a conference call with Paula Jones, and even offered to fly out to California at NOW's expense to meet with her," the feminist organization later recorded. "At the last minute, her lawyer told Ireland that Jones was shopping for a dress for a court appearance and couldn't be on the call." Nor did Paula's lawyer take up the offer of NOW support. "NOW leaders talked with Jones' attorneys in 1994, but they never asked for NOW's assistance. We wouldn't force ourselves on an unwilling plaintiff anymore than a man should force himself on an unwilling woman," NOW commented, ruefully—regretting that Paula Jones had chosen to align herself "with Pat Robertson, right wing publicist Floyd Brown and 'Operation Rescue' [anti-abortion activist] founder Randall Terry."

Even die-hard feminists became wary of championing the lowly Arkansas receptionist, with her fantasies of Hollywood stardom and her strange choice of funding allies. "We were not born yesterday," a spokeswoman for NOW was soon quoted. "We know that [Clinton enemies] Cliff Jackson and Floyd Brown are behind this and that they do not have the best interests of this woman in mind. Their agenda is not to fight sexual harassment but to bring down Clinton. We're not going to be a part of that."

NOW wouldn't—but thousands would. Hyping scandal via allegations of private sexual behavior (or misbehavior) while Rome burned would become a media obsession of the 1990s—an obsession that would preoccupy the world's wealthiest and most powerful nation while a continent away almost a million black African Tutsis were murdered, that spring, without the U.S. or the UN lifting a finger.

CHAPTER THIRTY-THREE

AN AMERICAN PLATONOV

Hunter or Prey?

In certain ways Bill Clinton resembled Chekhov's famous character Platonov: a brilliant educator, a married man, proud father of a child, but also a male who magnetizes the womenfolk of his community because, surrounded by greedy, vain, and pompous individuals, he is so much more dynamic and intelligent than his contemporaries. Irresistible to the opposite sex, and admired—as well as envied—by his fellow males, Chekhov's Platonov had reversed the Don Juan tradition by being the *prey* as much as the hunter. It was a scenario that the case of Dolly Kyle Browning, in the summer of 1994, exemplified in real life.

Dolly was a Hot Springs High School classmate of Clinton's who'd become a public defender, and a self-confessed sex addict. As she later chronicled of her connection with Bill Clinton in a sworn affidavit, under penalty of perjury: "During the period from the mid-1970s until January 1992, we had a relationship that included sexual relations. The frequency of our contact with each other, and the frequency of our sexual encounters, varied over that time period, but we did have sexual relations many times. . . ."

What happened, however, in such modern "sexual relations" when Clinton either wished to become monogamous, or for reasons of his career had to decline further contact? American voters might later rue the president's inability, over Monica Lewinsky, to change his behavior, but Dolly Kyle Browning's case provided a vivid example of how difficult that was. As she explained, "Our relationship ended abruptly in January of 1992 when

Billy would not return my telephone call. I told his secretary, Linda, that a tabloid had the story about me and Billy. I asked her to have him call me and he refused. Instead he had my brother, who was, at that time, working in the 1992 Clinton presidential campaign, call me from Billy's New Hampshire apartment or office. My brother said that Billy was afraid to talk to me because everyone thought that I might record the conversation as Gennifer Flowers had done. He said 'we' think you should deny the story." When she had balked at doing this, her brother had been reduced to threatening her. "He finally said: 'if you cooperate with the media we will destroy you.'"

Although Dolly understood the dire context in which candidate Bill Clinton had, at that moment, been fighting for his political life, she had been hurt by the rejection, and the cold, intimidating manner of it. Thereafter she had kept silent and kept away—as had he. But at the thirtieth reunion of the Hot Springs High School class of 1964 in Hot Springs on July 23, 1994, it became inevitable they would meet, and have words.

Throughout the reunion, Dolly also recalled on oath, she had sedulously "avoided contact with Billy." But Billy Blythe would not have been Bill Clinton had his curiosity—and conscience—not piqued him to find out where they now stood. "He approached me sometime around midnight. He greeted me, saying 'How are you?' I responded: 'You are such an asshole, I can't believe you'd even bother to ask!'"

Deflecting the reactions of the Secret Service officers to such *lèse majesté*, the president listened to his friend for almost three-quarters of an hour, hoping to assuage her anger and make it up to her. "During this conversation, we sat in two chairs in front of a large column in the ballroom where our reunion dance was being held," Dolly recalled. "There were several hundred other people in the ballroom. Dance music was playing almost continuously during our conversation." Their faces were "close together. We were speaking in a volume that was only just loud enough to hear each other over the background noise. The only people within at least six feet of us during our conversation were two male Secret Service agents.

"Our conversation began," Dolly recalled, "with my confronting him for not returning my call in early 1992. This lead to a discussion of many things, including his affair with Gennifer Flowers." Dolly was completely forthright. "I reminded him that he had threatened to destroy me and he said he was sorry. We discussed many other things."

One of these "other things" was Dolly's latest proposal. She was minded, she told him, to write a book, concerning an attractive southern blonde and the blonde's childhood sweetheart, who becomes a governor and then the president of the United States. It would, of course, be a fiction—but then. . . .

The scene was both extraordinary and comic as, against the background of deafening dance music, the president of the United States nervously strained his ears to hear *more* personal trouble in the making—thanks to his adulterous past.

This time the president sought to defuse the situation not by secondhand threats of personal destruction, or by public denial of the relationship, but by negotiation and soft-talking—as well as job offers. "The Secret Service agents were standing one on each side of us so that we, Billy, the agents and I, were effectively in a row with an agent at either end. There was one agent approximately one foot from me and a second agent approximately one foot from Billy," Dolly remembered. "At one point a Caucasian woman [Marsha Scott] whom I do not know interrupted us and told Billy that the party was over, they were closing the bar and that he needed to say goodbye to some people. Billy said to tell them to keep the bar open. She asked: 'Who is going to pay for that?' He replied: 'We will.' "

In his own notes on the episode the president afterwards jotted down that Dolly was writing her putative book because "she didn't have much money to live on"; she had loved him since schooldays, he noted, but occasional companionship wasn't enough—he had "never really been there for her because it wasn't my friendship she wanted," he concluded, but either long-term sexual availability or his hand in marriage. Both were clearly now impossible, given his status as president. Dolly had been, he added, quite candid about her mercenary motives in writing her book: "she needed the money and she didn't care if it hurt me or the presidency"—after all, "others had made money and she felt abandoned."

Was Dolly Kyle Browning seeking to blackmail the president, as the Arkansas troopers had done, by threatening to write an account of the affair she'd had with him over so many years? And if so, what payment did she want—money, or in-kind remuneration?

The president seemed to know. "At the end of the conversation he asked me to come to Washington. He said, 'You can live on the hill. I can help you find a job.'"

The implication was obvious. Bill Clinton, as always, had sought to as-suage the anger of a woman as best he could—by offering himself.

The complexity not only of Platonov's character, but of the intersection between his character and late nineteenth-century economic and social con-ditions in Russia, had in Bill Clinton's case been matched and expanded, *en plus*, by the infotainment conditions of America a century later: a media-fanned voyeurism had become by the 1990s a sort of throwback to Roman times and the entertainment of the masses in the Coliseum—a license for-merly given to tabloids on the tacit understanding that no one took seri-ously the trash they printed, whether or not it might be true, was now accorded to members even of the serious press.

In this new era of "Gotcha" journalism, the once higher ethics of media communications had been jettisoned in an evolutionary rat race for sales, advertising, and survival, epitomized in the rise of Rupert Murdoch's News Corporation/Fox News empire. All that came to count was the cutting of costs and selling more copies, or broadcasting into more homes, than one's competitors, in order to attract more advertising. Since voyeurism was the common denominator of infotainment, and the epochal *New York Times Co. v. Sullivan* case had virtually ended libel protection for "public figures" in America in 1964, even serious newspapers, television, and radio programs were now compelled to poke intrusively into the private lives of public fig-ures—figures who could no longer sue, however mean the agenda or primi-tive the reporters' understanding of complex human beings.

Such growing cultural anarchy was not, moreover, confined to the United States, thanks to the global reach of American entertainment media. It was, rather, a pandemic threatening in the 1990s to infect the entire West-ern world—a trend held at bay abroad only by remaining legal protections of rights of public figures to privacy and protection against libel and slan-der. (Soon, this protection, too, would prove vulnerable to the expansion of the Internet.) Even in those countries where libel law successfully kept me-dia snoopers at bay, journalists responded by turning their paparazzi lenses onto public figures who were known not to sue—such as, in Britain, the various members of the British royal family.

In short, with a president in lieu of a king, and lacking libel protection for public figures, America's infotainment coliseum raised the spectacle—and specter—of a revised version of Orwell's *1984*: a new world in which individuals would become victims not of political and industrial bosses, but of *media* bosses. Such a new Orwellian *1994* held out the nightmare prospect of a *fin de siècle* madness, an explosion of unregulated, secular, market-driven, democratic madness in which members of the proletariat and petite bourgeoisie would be encouraged, even paid, by unscrupulous sections of the media not only to perform on reality television to amuse a bored public, but even to accuse their own chief executive and head of state: the forty-second president.

CHAPTER THIRTY-FOUR

THE PRESIDENT
NEVER ADJOURNS

Constitutional Indispensability

Six years later the Republican-dominated Supreme Court would decide the outcome of the post-Clinton 2000 presidential election on the basis of the national interest—the need for stable transition and executive authority in running the world's most powerful country. Under a Democratic president the Paula Jones case had elicited, however, no such concerns on the part of the distinguished justices.

Disagreeing with his colleagues' misjudgment, or lack of good judgment, Supreme Court justice Stephen Breyer protested in words that became a landmark caution to his countrymen. "The Founders," he declared, had deliberately decided to "vest Executive authority in one person rather than several. They did so in order to focus, rather than to spread, Executive responsibility, thereby facilitating accountability. They also sought to encourage energetic, vigorous, decisive, and speedy execution of the laws by placing in the hands of a single, constitutionally indispensable individual the ultimate authority that, in respect to the other branches, the Constitution divides among many." As Breyer added, movingly: "For present purposes, this constitutional structure means that the President is not like Congress, for Congress can function as if it were whole, even when up to half of its members are absent. It means that the President is not like the Judiciary, for judges often can designate other judges, *e.g.,* from other judicial circuits, to sit even should an entire court be detained by personal litigation. It means that, unlike Congress, which is regularly out of session, the President never adjourns."

Certainly Bill Clinton never adjourned. Day after day he sought to do his best as president in the spring and summer of 1994—ordering emergency flood disaster relief funding in the Midwest, highlighting health care issues around the nation, discussing an assault weapons ban with congressional leaders, preparing to fly to Europe for the fiftieth anniversary of D-Day, and conferring with world leaders from African National Congress president Nelson Mandela to Prime Ministers Hosokawa and Hata of Japan, Prime Minister John Major of the United Kingdom, President Francois Mitterrand of France, and UN Secretary-General Boutros Boutros-Ghali. Had Bill Clinton proved a better executive leader from the day he was elected, it is doubtful if either the press or conspiratorial opponents could have gained real traction with their *ad hominem* attacks. Instead he seemed as president always to be running, in Alice in Wonderland fashion, just to stay in the same place. Thus, in the sixteen weeks between Paula Jones's failed press conference on February 11 and his D-Day anniversary trip to Europe in June 1994, the president made more than twenty journeys to eighteen states, speechifying before audiences high and low, as if on a perpetual presidential campaign to open America's eyes to its opportunities, challenges, and responsibilities. He pleaded for reform in health care, in welfare, in tackling crime, and in reconciliation between warring parties, institutions, communities, religions, nations—one of the most indefatigable, loquacious, energetic, and ardent speechgivers in American presidential history.

Nor did the president lack courage in addressing chosen issues. He risked the ire of British officials by granting, for the first time, a U.S. visitor's visa to Sinn Fein's leader, Gerry Adams, in the hope that it would help advance the Northern Ireland peace process—something it undoubtedly did. He attended the funeral of the very man whose impeachment his own wife had worked to engineer: former President Richard Nixon, whom he had invited to send him a personal memorandum on Russia's future before his January visit to Moscow, and with whom he had spoken repeatedly on the phone. On the economic front, his courageous insistence on deficit reduction had upset traditional Democrats appalled by the social ravages of recession, but it had already paid off in lower short- and long-term interest rates that increased bank lending and led to higher business confidence, lower mortgages, and rising employment figures: a total of 3.5 million new jobs were created in the first year and a half of his administration alone.

A Tough Decision

In the gathering high political drama of the 1990s in America, Clinton's personal brilliance was simply not enough. The majority of Americans wanted a strong leader, not simply a bag of hot air; they wanted a chief executive who could demonstrate in the running of the White House the sort of executive command that helped citizens sleep better. The missteps, leaks, scandals, investigations, and lawsuits that had beset his presidency, even where allowance was made for inexperience in the White House, had left many voters with the impression of a weak leader—the very moniker that had felled Jimmy Carter, for all the noble causes and peace initiatives he had advanced as president (and former president). Above all, President Clinton had failed to rein in his co-president.

As Hillary's health care reform bill headed towards defeat in the late spring of 1994, the president finally opened his eyes and recognized his mistake. Failing to appoint a tough chief of staff, lest he thereby have to delegate real power, he had merely empowered Hillary in McLarty's place. Therefore, Mack McLarty must be replaced by a tough chief of staff, and the first lady sidelined—or the Clinton presidency, despite its noble ideals, would fail.

THE FURY OF AN
AROUSED DEMOCRACY

CHAPTER THIRTY-FIVE

DRAWING THE LINE

No Adult Supervision

Years before, Tom Lippman had watched the spectacle of Jimmy Carter's difficulties in Washington—yet they were as nothing compared with the current ineffectiveness of the forty-second president. "Jimmy Carter was an officer in the nuclear navy. He was as structured as Clinton was ramshackle," Lippman recalled. "Clinton was a ramshackle personality anyway—from way back. He was a back-slapper and a tobacco-chewer and a barbecue-eater *by nature*, in a way. One wonders how he ever got through Yale Law School—except through sheer brilliance. Sheer brilliance."

Brilliance was not, however, enough to run a country. "The sheer topsy-turvy craziness of the first year or so prevented any really valuable thing from getting done," Lippman recalled. "You have all this stuff about Zoë Baird, and the nannies . . . and gays in the military, Travelgate, Troopergate, and the health care plan. You just had one *non-thing* after another—while at the same time the country was changing politically. And they were getting beaten up about Bosnia. . . . There was a *lot of stuff* going on—and there was *no adult supervision*. Except the Treasury Department. At the *Washington Post* we would go to work every morning with no idea what we would be talking about by lunchtime. You know: because something bizarre was going to happen. . . . Something completely unpredictable. Or something that was not part of any known agenda. Because there *was* no known agenda."

It was in this situation that, on the plane to Europe for the fiftieth anniversary of D-Day, traveling with the director of OMB, Leon Panetta, that

President Clinton had a heart to heart with the man who would transform his presidency.

The Unvarnished Truth

The president's father, William Jefferson Blythe III, had served as a tank maintenance mechanic in Italy, after bigamously marrying the president's mother in 1943. Prior to leaving, the president had summoned the finest American World War II military historians to fill him in on what had gone wrong in the near-disastrous American landings at Salerno, in September 1943, and at Anzio, in January 1944. He had also asked what had gone right in the greatest and most successful amphibious invasion ever mounted: D-Day, June 6, 1944, on the shores of France. Clearly, the president had good reason to be interested in the difference between success and failure.

Leon Panetta, appalled by the president's process, or lack of process, had watched aghast at the way the White House operated—especially at the way the president kept asking the Democratically controlled Congress "to walk the line on the economic bill, then to walk the line on NAFTA, and to walk the line on the crime bill." And with health care reform, "this was just one too many lines!" Panetta exclaimed.

It was Italy in 1943 and 1944, all over again—too many bold operations mounted with insufficient planning, and disastrously poor executive leadership. It was imperative, in these circumstances, to run a tougher White House operation that offered Republicans the very smallest of targets. Yet for all his smartness, the president had failed to do that.

"In May, the president asked if my wife and I would go with him on the trip to Normandy, for the fiftieth anniversary. On the trip over, I was on Air Force One. He called me over and said—it was just a one-on-one conversation, we were sitting on one of the couches in the plane—'What would you do to try to tighten up the operation in the White House?'"

Panetta's great gift was to be able to tell the unvarnished truth, in the friendliest and most straightforward manner. "So I gave him my sense of it: 'I don't think there's enough discipline. I think there aren't clear lines of supervision. You've got too many free-floating people who are general counsels'—I just gave him a sense of what I thought needed to be done."

No discipline—this was an understatement, as Bob Woodward's latest book on the presidency, *The Agenda*, made scandalously clear when published that June.

Lessons of D-Day

Thinking no further on the matter, Panetta, after attending the ceremonies in Italy, returned to the U.S. while the president flew on to England and Normandy. There, reflecting on the greatest military undertaking of the twentieth century—the amphibious invasion of France by two million Allied troops, backed by vast navies and air forces—the president at last recognized the need not simply to lead by rhetoric, intelligence, and encouragement, but by command: making effective appointments and decisions. And selecting a chief of staff, *not his own wife*, to see that the decisions were carried out.

Asked by reporters aboard the U.S. Navy's latest and largest nuclear-powered aircraft carrier, the USS *George Washington*, what were the lessons of D-Day, the president made clear how the anniversary had made him rethink the history and nature of American liberty—especially the time it took, inevitably, for the nation, its leaders, and its people to fully understand and ultimately commit themselves to action on the world stage. The United States had entered World War II in December 1941, but it had taken two-and-a-half years before it was able to demonstrate the full force of what General Eisenhower called "the fury of an aroused democracy." As the president reflected, "Yes, maybe we were a little slow, you can argue in hindsight, to respond to Hitler's aggression, but the fact that we were a free people, full of young, gifted men and women, like these young men sitting behind you today, who figured out how to win this war and would not be denied," he maintained, "is still the best [lesson]." American democracy was by its nature "disorganized to some extent or messy but at least it allows us to govern ourselves from the inside, from our genuine emotions." The triumph of D-Day had led, inexorably, to the ending of World War II, but even so, it had not thereby solved the problems of the world, or even shown America where to draw the postwar line. "It took some time to figure out, you know, what was NATO going to do, what was the Marshall Plan all about, what was our position in Asia going to be. And"—thinking of the current standoff over North Korea's threat to develop nuclear weapons—"that's the period we're in now. We're working at the line-drawing."

Containment had proven the wisest postwar course, not precipitate action. In a remark that would become profoundly apposite ten years later, the president added, a propos Vietnam: "One of the things that I think we learned from that war is that even when we are extremely well-motivated, heroic, and willing to die in large numbers, we cannot win a fight for someone else. We can support other people on their own land fighting for their own destiny, but we can't win a fight for someone else. There are limits to what we can do. . . . And what I'm determined to do is learn as much as I can from history but not be imprisoned by it and certainly not be bogged down by it. I have a job to do now. And nobody else in the world has it but me. And one thing I owe these people who are in the armed services is to get up every day and do it the very best I can, unencumbered by anything anybody else says about it but always listening to other people."

Clinton had been touched in Italy, he said, by "the World War II veterans who in such large numbers said they were supporting me." In England and France the same held true. "He was cheered wildly by the *George Washington* crew," the *Houston Chronicle* recorded, and "many sailors said they were impressed with Clinton's remarks and how he 'handled' himself. 'I think he feels the stigma [of not having served] more than we in the military do,' said one crew member." Back in Somerville, Massachusetts, where veterans and the relatives of veterans watched the ceremonies on television, the *Boston Globe* reported how "Virtually all residents interviewed said they felt the media was unfair to Clinton, digging up dirt on sex scandals and confused financial dealings that mean little or nothing to them. They said they believe he is not getting a fair chance to get things done."

A forty-seven-year-old fireman had voted for Clinton because "he was the best guy to fix the economy," and since his wife had been laid off, it remained his primary concern. "I think we watch how he is doing the economy a lot more than what he is doing in Bosnia. It hits us right at home. But I think he knows that, I think he's trying to do the best he can." At the Coin-op laundry a young architect agreed. "I truly believe if people—the media, the politicians, everyone—would lay off the dirt, I think the president and all of us could get a lot more done in this country."

Clearly the president was mindful of his great responsibility in figuring out where the world was heading, and how best to manage America's role on that journey. And the more he thought about it, the more he realized that the most important thing he must get done, in the aftermath of the D-Day anniversary, was the tightening up of his White House operation—by firing Mack McLarty.

CHAPTER THIRTY-SIX

MCLARTY IS REPLACED

A Bombshell for Panetta

Before the president could deal with his chief of staff problem, however, he had to deal with an international military crisis. For years the true extent of the saga—a smaller version of the Cuban Missile Crisis—would be kept quiet. "The American people will never know how close we were to war," a diplomatic source in the Clinton administration later admitted. "It went down to the wire."

The United States had withdrawn its nuclear weapons from South Korea in 1991, in pursuit of a nuclear-free Korean peninsula. North Korea, however, was suspected of doing the opposite: secretly extracting plutonium from its reactor at its Yongbyon nuclear power plant in order to make and house atomic weapons on the peninsula. It had announced its withdrawal from the Nuclear Non-Proliferation Treaty in March 1993, following provocative U.S.-South Korean military maneuvers; by the summer of 1994 the situation had reached crisis point. The International Atomic Energy Agency, under Hans Blix, had been denied access by the North Koreans to the spent nuclear fuel rods that would allow the UN team to determine whether fuel had been reprocessed for atomic bomb-making; North Korea probably possessed, the CIA estimated, enough plutonium for two nuclear bombs. The UN was preparing economic sanctions against North Korea, but, in a Catch-22 situation, such economic sanctions would be considered by North Korea to be a declaration of war, since they would abrogate the 1953 Armistice. Republican senators Bob Dole and John McCain advocated a preemptive U.S. strike on Yongbyon to destroy the North Korean nuclear facility. By contrast, William Perry, the former deputy secretary of defense, whom Clinton had reluctantly promoted to take Les Aspin's place, warned that a surgical strike would inevitably "result in all-out war." On June 15, 1994, therefore, President Clinton assembled his top security and military advisers, and had to decide whether, indeed, to launch a preemptive attack. Perry's plans for a strike by cruise missile and F–117 stealth fighters to demolish the Yongbyon installation might or might not lead to atomic irradiation of the region, but the conventional war that would follow would result in an even more terrible outcome—indeed, it was openly reckoned at the Pentagon that up to a million lives would be lost.

General Gordon Sullivan later recalled the seriousness of the situation. "Korea. It never became public. The chiefs knew, most of the troops did not. We allocated forces from Fort Hood and Fort Campbell, we earmarked forces to go to Korea, but that was all done at a very high level." General John Shalikashvili, chairman of the Joint Chiefs, and Secretary Perry were briefing President Clinton and other top officials on June 15, with preparations to evacuate all American civilians in South Korea prior to planned combat, when "the door of the room opened and we were told that there was a telephone call from former president Carter in Pyongyang and that he wished to speak to me," Bob Gallucci, the assistant secretary of state for political-military affairs, later remembered.

With President Clinton's wary imprimatur, Jimmy Carter had nobly traveled to South Korea—and had crossed the famous forty-ninth parallel to speak in person with Kim Il Sung. Carter was now reporting a breakthrough—that, in return for two new, smaller nuclear reactors that would not produce weapons-grade plutonium, along with oil to help meet North Korea's energy needs, Kim Il Sung was agreeing to freeze North Korea's nuclear program and to allow full inspections.

It was a merciful resolution—one that would guarantee peace on the peninsula for a further decade. But the former president's triumph of personal diplomacy did not lessen the need for the current president to put his White House in order—especially once Woodward's latest exposé of presidential ineptitude hit the bookstores and newspapers. "The president has returned from Omaha Beach to find he is under fire at home," Godfrey Sperling commented, for example, in the *Christian Science Monitor*. "Actually, the cannon sending shells into the White House is only a book—but what a book! It's by investigative reporter Bob Woodward who, along with Carl Bernstein, did so much to bring down President Nixon. . . . The book . . . depicts a White House in chaos and a president who is indecisive and reluctant to delegate."

Other newspapers were even less charitable. As a consequence, immediately following resolution of the North Korean crisis, the director of OMB was approached by Vice President Gore, who delivered a bombshell to Panetta: "Leon, the president is seriously thinking about asking you to be chief of staff."

Panetta recalls replying, " 'You know, I really don't think that's the right step. And I have to say, I've got this great job as director of OMB. We've passed the economic plan. I know what I'm doing. I've got a good team of people working for me. . . . I think I can serve you better as director of OMB.' And he warned me, 'Well, he's serious about it.' "

Clinton was. Several days later Leon Panetta found himself in a Marine helicopter, being whisked by the vice president to Camp David. There he was ushered in to see the president.

"It was Hillary, the president, Al Gore, and Tipper, his wife—and me," Panetta recalled. The president's chief of staff was conspicuous by his absence. "The president said, 'We really want you to become chief of staff.' "

The "we" was both stunning and indicative of all that was wrong about the president's command setup. "I said—I told them the same thing that I told the vice president. I said, 'I really think I'm much more valuable to you as director of OMB. . . . I know the appropriations process, I know the people on the Hill. I think I'm doing a good job for you on that basis.' And the president said something I'll never forget. He basically said: 'Leon, you know, you can be the greatest OMB director in history. But if the White House is falling apart, nobody's going to remember you.' "

"Before I knew it we had flown back to Washington and they decided to make the announcement, I think it was almost the next day, which was my birthday, the twenty-eighth," Panetta recalled, having given in to the president's entreaty. As Washington's hostesses duly sharpened their tongues— and journalists their quills—however, there was an amazing revelation within the building. It was one that, to Panetta, explained everything about the White House's operations over the past year and a half. "We made the announcement," he recalled, "then I remember going to [McLarty] and asking, 'Do you have an organization chart for the White House?' And Mack said, 'I don't think I do.'

"And I thought: 'Oh, man! We *are* in trouble!' "

Was it really possible that the richest and most powerful nation in the world could have been ruled since January 1993 from an operations center that did not even have an organization chart? A White House that incurred hundreds of millions of dollars per year in costs and employed a *thousand* people in myriad departments, from national security to advance scheduling?

It was small wonder McLarty had failed to cut the mustard as chief of staff. Yet even the most savage criticism of McLarty in the press was tempered by knowledge that the president had only himself to blame.

Panetta had asked the president to give his solemn assurance that he would be given "full authority" to manage policy and personnel in the White House, making whatever changes were necessary to streamline the White House operation. Above all, it was agreed, he was to be empowered to fire whoever was redundant or ineffective. Yet by 11:30 P.M. on the very night of Panetta's appointment the president was telephoning his chief of staff to tell him *not* to fire Dee Dee Myers, the president's press secretary.

Nor was David Gergen (whose effectiveness had been undercut by Hillary and by the left-leaning coterie around the president) discarded—he was asked to stay on as presidential adviser but work as communications guru to Secretary of State Warren Christopher until the end of the year. With Mack McLarty taking Gergen's title of counselor to the president, the appointment of the new chief of staff seemed more musical chairs than radical surgery. "Unless you hijack a helicopter in order to play golf," mocked columnist Roger Simon (in a reference to the resignation of David Watkins), "you never get fired, you just get shuffled."

As director of OMB, Leon Panetta had been "a pillar of strength for our administration," the president said of his new chief of staff—a man who would "go down in history as the budget director who began to slay the deficit dragon." But could the dragon-slayer handle what Stephen Hess called the Clinton octopus: the president's illusion that he had eight legs?

It was imperative that the president begin to shape up, to start to project, with a new and tough chief of staff at his side, new strength and new clarity of purpose, before the midterm elections.

"In an organizational sense President Clinton is the unmade bed of American politics," a *Boston Globe* editorial lamented. But could Leon Panetta make the bed tidy—and would that even be enough? "Clinton has to take ultimate responsibility for the administration's wobbling world view, but he is ill-served by the wrong secretary of state. Warren Christopher may have worked out under a different president, but he is respected neither at home nor abroad. Both he and Gergen should be encouraged to retire early."

Democratic observers could only hope against hope that the arrival of Leon Panetta next to the Oval Office would mitigate the president's executive weakness: that with the mix of humor, experience, and straightforwardness that had made him a legend on the Hill, the former California congressman might turn things around before the nation cast its November judgment.

Not even Leon Panetta, however, could save the health care reform bill, now—or its charioteer, First Lady Hillary Rodham Clinton.

CHAPTER THIRTY-SEVEN

EXIT HEALTH CARE REFORM

Whitewater Eclipses Health Care

If, in the wake of Troopergate and the Paula Jones scandal, matters of a personal nature were daunting for the president, they were even more so for the first lady. Hillary had, after all, led an untarnished personal life. Whitewater allegations concerning her professional life, however, were now being raised continually, drawing reporters to look deeper and deeper into Hillary Clinton's financial transactions in the past.

In April in the State Dining Room of the White House, in what was called her "pretty in pink" special press conference—the first she had ever given—the first lady had faced down journalists anxious to know more about Whitewater, and about the three hundred thousand dollars she'd made on a thousand-dollar investment in cattle futures many years before. Reporters had been respectful of the first lady, and the conference was broadcast live on CNN, and even the major news networks had cut in on it, ignoring U.S. threats of NATO intercession in Bosnia. Intended to defuse press suspiciousness—Hillary joked that she had mistakenly clung to an old-fashioned "zone of privacy" but guessed she'd been rezoned in the new world—the conference did little to alter the growing public perception of a woman who could admit to no wrong, had a shady financial past, and as a result was not to be trusted over reform of the nation's health care system. Who was she, viewers wondered, to accuse the drug and insurance companies of profiteering? Her poll numbers plummeted even more than those of the president. Worse, a seventeen-point majority in public support *for* her health care reform bill in December 1993 had dropped, by the spring of 1994, into a majority *opposing* it—and every day things got worse.

"More Whitewater stories," Haynes Johnson and David Broder lamented in their chronicle of the demise of health care reform, "were published in major papers than on the combined total of health care, welfare, and crime legislation"—with Whitewater congressional hearings taking place in mid-June, 1994, just at the time it had been hoped health care reform bills would pass out of committee onto the floor of the Senate and the House of Representatives.

The Hill Becomes a Mountain

For the Republicans, Whitewater was akin to Watergate. Twenty years before, Hillary had been on the Senate investigating staff, while her professor-boyfriend had unabashedly used the issue to try to unseat Congressman John Paul Hammerschmidt. Now the situation was reversed, as the Clintons found themselves under continuous enemy fire. The first lady vainly attempted to keep the nation's attention focused on the need for health care reform, while her husband attempted to run the country as its chief executive, both of them simultaneously having to deal with Whitewater issues.

"We talked about it all the time. We thought it was just crazy. Here we are trying to do something that needs to be done," the president afterwards told Johnson and Broder. "It's the opportunity of a generation, and every day there's three times as much coverage on this deal where we lost forty-eight thousand dollars that neither of us had anything to do with until that whole thing came a cropper. . . . It was maddening to me, frankly. . . . I didn't know what had happened to my country. I just thought it was bizarre. I had to fight hard to keep my mind and my spirit in the right frame so that I could focus on what I was trying to do for the people. In that period, I was more bewildered than anything else"—for it seemed impossible "we would squander this historic opportunity to solve a major problem on something that didn't amount to a hill of beans."

Friends and colleagues would testify to the president's torment—"the most gushing outpouring of rage, humiliation, frustration, I've ever heard," one senator described the call he got from the White House. Another, a cabinet officer, worried that the president and first lady had become, understandably, "paranoid. They think people are out to get them—this right-wing conspiracy. They feel sorry for themselves. They talk about it all the time."

The hill of beans, however, was becoming a mountain, while Capitol Hill, that summer, came to resemble a Tolstoyan battlefield, covered in smoke, with a hundred firefights, hand-to-hand struggles, and skirmishes taking place, but no general able to control the combat area, or the troops.

With the prospect of last-minute victory on the crime bill, the president and Democratic congressional leaders George Mitchell and Dick Gephardt hoped against hope for a "one-two punch-and-we're through" ultimate victory on health care also, even if the first lady's bill had to be modified to win Republican support—in fact, Senator Mitchell, who had secretly agreed on his own compromise bill with the president, warned his colleagues that no one was going on summer vacation in August until both bills were passed.

The Republicans, however, refused to lay down their arms. To herald the final push for health care reform, Hillary's office had organized a "Health Security Express"—a publicity gimmick in which a series of buses would carry doctors, nurses, and seriously ill people not only to the capital but to the steps of the U.S. Capitol, in a final effort to goad Congress into voting for her reform plan before the summer recess. In 1992, the Clinton-Gore road trip, after all, had stirred the nation with its grassroots appeal by young, fresh, and innocent-looking candidates traveling by bus and calling for change. Now, two years later, the cavalcade, filled with "Reform Riders," ran into reality—symbolized by the first lady's experience in Portland, Oregon.

As celebratory balloons lifted into the sky to wish Hillary's Express good luck, spectators saw a plane appear above them, dragging a banner with the words "Beware the Phony Express." Moreover, when the caravan reached the first highway, there was a broken-down bus swathed in red tape and bearing a forbidding notice: "This is Clinton Health Care."

Hillary was stunned by the numbers of protesters, and by their anger. "They were men in their twenties, thirties, forties. I had not seen faces like that since the segregation battles of the sixties," she recalled—faces full of hate. "Those faces, that's what scared me, that's what really bothered me."

August 1994: a Nightmare Month

Where did such hate come from? Who had inspired it—and how? August 1994 became a nightmare month for the Clinton administration and the Democratic leadership in Congress. Rural Democrat congressmen began defecting from the crime bill, in fear of the National Rifle Association, as did some senators; by means of a filibuster, the Republicans were able to hold up (though not passage of) the bill for a full week. In the end the Senate accepted a compromise, which outlawed assault weapons without special license, but the chance of a "one-two-and-we're-through" passage of both the crime *and* health care reform bills was defeated. The Clinton administration looked set for a major defeat of the most ambitious legislative proposal since Social Security in 1935. More Harry and Louise ads were being aired on television. The response of voters to Hillary's health care reform bill had turned not only negative but downright hostile, even hateful. With midterm elections approaching, the Democratic Party in Congress suddenly looked as chaotic and contradictory as had been the Clinton White House since the inauguration.

"Don't let the fear-mongers, don't let the dividers, don't let the people who disseminate false information frighten the United States Congress into walking away from the opportunity of a lifetime," the president had begged his audience in Liberty State Park, New Jersey, on August 1.

It was no good. On August 11, 1994, the Democratic leadership was unable to find the procedural votes to bring even the crime bill to the floor of the House. In the Senate, Mitchell's health care compromise bill produced forty *hours* of Republican opposition speeches over six days.

The unity of the Democratic Party in Congress was breaking up, and the president, at his headquarters on Pennsylvania Avenue, not far away, could only watch with disbelief as his army self-destructed.

A week later, on August 19, the Mainstream Coalition, a bipartisan group of senators, in a desperate attempt to produce a compromise health care bill that would break the congressional deadlock, produced its own alternative proposal, in the hope of some sort of "negotiated settlement," as Senator Jay Rockefeller put it.

President Clinton was not optimistic—indeed, in a call to Senator Durenberger he said the last few weeks of warfare on the congressional battlefield had been like "acid in the stomach" to him, as he surveyed the scene. For his part, Ira Magaziner subsequently saw it as the day the battle was lost—"the day when I knew this thing was going down."

But what had the Republicans to gain by compromising late over a proposal they had now successfully trashed in the public mind? Polls everywhere were showing that in the November election the Democrats could well lose their majority in the Senate, and Republicans come close to parity in the House.

On August 24, Hillary summoned the former surgeon general, Dr. C. Everett Koop, to the Map Room in the White House to see if an armistice could be offered, in the way of a bipartisan commission being appointed.

It was too late, aides recognized—Hillary should have made her task force a bipartisan affair right from the start if she had wanted Republican help. Now the battle was over. Despite a Democratic majority of 257 to 176 seats in the House, and 56 to 44 in the Senate, the Clinton administration had failed to win health care reform—*in any form*. After talking with the White House and other Democratic leaders, Senator Mitchell—flanked by the president's new chief of staff, Leon Panetta—made the tragic announcement on August 26. Comprehensive health care reform in America was dead.

"We've lost our compass a bit," one top adviser to the president said as the Clintons flew off to Martha's Vineyard that evening—aware that, with the appointment of a new Republican prosecutor, named Kenneth Starr, to head up an independent counsel investigation of Whitewater in place of Robert Fiske, more monsters could yet emerge from the deep.

WAR IN HAITI

CHAPTER THIRTY-EIGHT

EXPRESSIONS OF PERSONAL HATRED

Wafflin' Willie

The Washington air in the summer of 1994 seemed thick with artillery, mortar, machinegun fire, and sniper fire. The NRA's arch-patron, Charlton Heston, best known for his portrayal of Moses in the epic film *The Ten Commandments*, had been incensed by the recent assault on assault weapons in the president's crime bill. "Moses brought down, through God, seven plagues to force the pharaoh to let his people go," Heston said. "I think God brought the Clinton administration to show us how bad it can get in this country." He added that people joked about Clinton programs "because if we didn't laugh, we would cry." There was even a new board game, "Wafflin' Willy"—inspired by the relentless ribbing of talk-radio host Rush Limbaugh, and marketed to appeal to Limbaugh's twenty-two million-strong audience. The game was for "two to four players, each of whom has a different Bill Clinton figure (in red, blue, green or purple shorts), starting in the middle of the board and, appropriately, trying to move left to amass votes. Along the way, players face such hot-button issues as gays in the military, Somalia and controversial appointments. You can deal with each issue (lose votes), waffle (keep your votes) or go to Congress (take your chances). But, as art imitates the presidential life, 'The Past' is slowly trailing you—and if it reaches you, you're out of the game."

Such board games were, however, the least of it. "The Clinton presidency has inspired a veritable cavalcade of tacky gag gifts poking fun at the 'man from Hope.'" *Human Events* also reported. "For instance, there's the eight-inch 'I Feel Your Pain' Clinton doll/pincushion, the 'Slick Willie' doormat, a glass ashtray 'to put your butt in Bill's face' and the various T-shirts, bumper stickers and coffee mugs with any number of anti-Clinton slogans such as 'Slick Willie is spending my kids' inheritance' and 'I don't like President Clinton . . . or her husband either.'"

Merchandise pages in the *American Spectator* were even more poisonous, featuring advertisements for "Cowardly Clinton," "Commie Clinton," and "Impeach Billary" T-shirts, while there were bumper stickers to be had with slogans like "It's Hillary Rottweiler Clinton," "Doin' Time in San Clinton," "From A Chicken in Every Pot to a Chicken Smokin' Pot," and "Clinton 'Loathes the Military'. . . It's Mutual."

The *Atlanta Journal and Constitution* commented in a thoughtful editorial that although presidents had always been the focus of national media attention, "the Clinton case is something special. To a remarkable degree, Bill Clinton has become the subtext to every political debate that occurs in Washington, the distorting prism through which every issue is viewed. As a result, our elected representatives no longer vote simply on health care, gun control or other issues. They vote for or against the president. Even on something as visceral as the crime bill, a lot of votes were cast not on the basis of the policies involved, but on how closely a particular politician was willing to be identified with Clinton."

The Republican intifada against the co-president was, the newspaper noted, as virulent as Republican antipathy towards the president. "At a pro-tobacco rally in Kentucky over the weekend, an effigy of Hillary Clinton was doused in gasoline and set ablaze, with a rally organizer gleefully chanting, 'Burn, baby, burn.'" This was not even amusing. "Mrs. Clinton's health-care reform plan calls for higher taxes on tobacco products, and that has caused some understandably hard feelings in tobacco country. But burning people in effigy is not a political statement; it is an open expression of personal hatred seldom seen in the political mainstream."

Viewed in retrospect, the worst part of the Limbaugh-style trashing of the Clintons was that it caricatured a complex, talented, genuinely idealistic, and not uncourageous president and first lady. It was easy enough to mock a president who "feels your pain," but how many presidents had ever used that pain to bring a major health care bill, however convoluted, to the very floor of the House and Senate? How many presidents had ever dared use Martin Luther King Jr.'s words to challenge black communities over their own responsibility for the guns, violence, drugs, teenage pregnancy, and intimidation that still scourged them—and how many presidents had gotten a gun-reducing crime bill, banning assault weapons from the streets of America, passed within eighteen months? Were those efforts alone not the mark of political and social beliefs? And what of AmeriCorps, the national program of voluntary work among the economically and socially disadvantaged? What of the Family and Medical Leave Act, and the Brady Bill? What of President Clinton's courage in tackling the "economy, stupid"—bravely addressing the national deficit rather than loading it upon the next generation—and passing the North American Free Trade Agreement, even though it meant delaying stimulus and investment programs favored by the Democratic Party? And why was the president's belief in diversity—economic, social, racial, cultural—so despised by the warriors of the right?

As a voracious reader, with a near-photographic memory, President Clinton devoured political biographies, mystery stories, high literature, and thrillers. Gabriel Garcia Márquez and Carlos Fuentes, on Martha's Vineyard, were "bowled over" by the president's ability to quote from his favorite Faulkner novels, as well as his knowledge of Mexican literature, William Styron told reporters. Styron himself thought it "of profound importance to the entire world to have a president who knows and enjoys literature," in contrast to certain predecessors who hadn't "cracked a book to anyone's knowledge"—but then, literary literacy was not synonymous with efficacy, it had to be admitted. Indeed, voters, witnessing the train of ineptitude and chaos of the Clinton White House, were entitled to ask whether *über*literacy led, in fact, to *in*efficacy in the tough, practical outside world.

Whatever the truth, the fact was that the president, by virtue of his undisciplined, chaotic approach to management, had given an unfortunate impression of dithering, indecisive, faltering leadership at the top, both at home and abroad. With a tough new chief of staff—if the president would only empower him to *be* chief of staff—could that impression be reversed? And if so, would it be enough to save the Democratic Party in November that year? Certainly the president was willing to try—having decided to mount his own D-Day invasion, in the Caribbean.

CHAPTER THIRTY-NINE

CLINTON'S WAR

Fed Up

At the end of summer Chelsea was sent back to Washington, after Labor Day, to start school. The president remained on the Vineyard, however, only returning to the capital on September 7, 1994—for he was determined there be no leaks this time.

Stan Greenberg, the president's chief pollster, had produced new figures showing the president's overall approval rating "the lowest it had ever been"—down to between 36 and 38 percent. His health care reform, which would have given both the Democratic Party and his presidency the blood transfusion they needed, was now toast. Bill Clinton felt he must do something spectacular, before it was too late. How long the president had been mulling his *coup de surprise,* in his own mind, he would not say in his memoirs. Nevertheless, he was aware of Field Marshal Foch's famous signal during the Battle of the Marne in 1914: "My centre is giving way, my right is retreating, situation excellent. I am attacking." As Clinton later wrote of Haiti, "I was fed up. General Cedras and his thugs had intensified their reign of terror. It was time to throw him out." Preparing his own D-Day, the president had in mind an assault on the Caribbean island with twenty-thousand (later increased to twenty-five thousand) American para-troopers and Marines.

Such a massive and expensive military invasion of Haiti seemed strate-gically daft, given that the island posed no security threat to America—and it was certainly opposed by Congress, as Clinton knew. "Republicans were solidly opposed, and most Democrats, including George Mitchell, thought I was just taking them out onto another precipice," Clinton himself later admitted, "without public support or congressional authorization." At the time, however, the president was determined to win his belated spurs—in fact, when a flurry of plaintive phone calls came from members of Congress concerned about the electoral implications of such a militarily unnecessary act, the president turned to Stephanopoulos and his new chief of staff, Leon Panetta, with the fighting words: "After those fucking phone calls, I guess we'll have something to show those people who say I never do anything unpopular."

With congressional support unlikely to be given formally for an invasion, however, there arose the question of legality. Could the president go to war without a congressional vote? Would he be impeached if he did? Histories were quickly consulted, including Doris Kearns Goodwin's charming new biography of Eleanor and Franklin Roosevelt, *No Ordinary Time*. The State Department was directed to produce a "white paper" that would make the case for unilateral action by presidential executive order. Since the State Department, under the vacillating Warren Christopher, was against a military invasion, this was, however, somewhat meretricious. No one, Stephanopoulos later admitted, was "clamoring" for an invasion of Haiti—in fact, it was "our most unpopular act since gays in the military." Yet for the president, he allowed, "it could be a political plus. Clinton was constantly being called 'spineless' and 'wishy-washy.' " Resolute action might alter the public perception—"the best way for Clinton to demonstrate presidential character."

This was easier said than done, however, with American soldiers' lives at stake. The man Clinton had deliberately chosen over all others to be his secretary of state was a cipher in regard to Haiti—an island and an invasion that, like Rwanda, would be completely omitted from Warren Christopher's memoirs, *Chances of a Lifetime*. For Christopher the chances of successful action there were remote. Urbane and uptight, Christopher was not impressed by President-in-exile Jean-Bertrand Aristide, who had sent conflicting messages about whether he actually wished to be restored to power by the American military in Haiti. The United States had, after all, invaded the country in 1915 and had subsequently controlled it for twenty years, with no solid democratic institutions to show, only racism and worse poverty than ever.

Christopher was not alone among cabinet colleagues in opposing invasion. There were many others, too, who questioned whether it was worth returning the Reverend Aristide, a Marxist priest with no successful governing experience—an elected president who had been expelled by the Haitian military for his perceived incompetence.

Senator Sam Nunn, the Democratic chairman of the Senate Armed Services Committee, not only staunchly disapproved of military invasion, but opposed Aristide's restitution. The undersecretary of defense for planning, in particular, was overheard to say he had no intention of risking American lives "to put that psychopath back into power." Clinton's new secretary of defense, Dr. William Perry, who had shown his mettle over North Korea, in the way he prepared for a huge movement of American forces into the region, was dubious about the consequences, even if an American invasion did prove painless. His deputy secretary, John Deutch, felt the same; the "first few days may be easy, but I'm afraid we might get three or four boys hacked up in a few months," during the inevitable and expensive American occupation. True, the processing and housing of an ever-growing flood of Haitian refugees and boat people sailing to America in rickety vessels was (as the earlier Cuban exodus had been) costly—$200 million, Clinton claimed; yet the disastrous Bay of Pigs invasion of Cuba in President Kennedy's first year in office had taught that it was still cheaper to take in refugees and wait out the withering of dictators, even if this took decades, than to take unilateral action that risked expensive failure in lives and dollars, and moreover—given the endlessly feuding Haitian factions and the lack of democratic traditions or institutions in the country—might tie down American occupation troops and officials for years in the aftermath.

Against these considerations, there were the reports from UN aid workers and others who described alarming abuses of human rights and worse—assassination, rape, and torture—amounting to a moral imperative on America's doorstep such as the U.S. had completely balked in far-away Rwanda that spring. The Cedras junta, comprising the army commander, General Raoul Cedras, his chief of staff, and the chief of police, had expelled UN human rights observers after the U.S. threatened military action, but copious photographic evidence had emerged of what Clinton later called a "reign of terror, executing orphaned children, raping young girls, killing priests, mutilating people and leaving body parts in the open to terrify others, and slashing the faces of mothers with machetes while their children watched."

Still, the fact was that such photos were hardly the same as the haunting pictures of Russian nuclear-tipped ballistic missiles in Cuban silos, pointing at America, as in 1962 when President Kennedy prepared direct U.S.

military action; $200 million a year was sustainable in a swiftly improving American economy, whereas the $1 billion cost of sending in and stationing American troops on the island would far offset the saving.

Which left the larger, international strategic goal: re-asserting American leadership in an increasingly fractious world.

Constant Flip-flops

In May, in a CNN town hall special, the president had spoken with moving seriousness of the post-Cold War world and America's new interests and responsibilities. America could not, he emphasized, seek to "solve every problem, nor should we try." Nevertheless, in an "era of change and opportunity and peril, America must be willing to assume the obligations and risks of leadership. And I am determined to see that we do that." Pressed by the program host to say whether the U.S. was intending to use military force in Haiti, and what the American goal in doing so would be, the president had assured viewers that the mission was "to restore democracy, to start a multinational effort to help Haiti function and to grow again"; however, "we have not decided to use force; all I've said is we can't rule it out."

CNN's Christiane Amanpour, standing in Serb-shelled, UN-protected Sarajevo, was skeptical. She had asked the president why it was taking him so long to come up with a consistent American policy there. Didn't he think "that the constant flip-flops of your administration on the issue of Bosnia set a very dangerous precedent?"

It had been a stunningly direct question (later paraphrased in the official government publication of the exchange). "He was obviously angry," wrote David Halberstam, who described the president's face growing "hard and his voice icy" as he retorted that there had been "no constant flip-flops, madam. I ran for president saying that I would do my best to limit ethnic cleansing and to see the United States play a more active role in resolving the problem in Bosnia. And we have been much more active than my predecessor was in every way from the beginning. . . ."

If so, no one in the worsening conditions of the "living hell" of Sarajevo or in other Serb-assaulted Muslim enclaves was aware of it.

The fact was, Bill Clinton had not focused consistently on foreign policy, either while running for president or after his election. Instead, he had deliberately appointed a low-key, older man—a corporate attorney—to keep his desk at the White House clear of such foreign problems. Warren

Christopher had done his dutiful best, but his very facelessness and his anxiety never to be caught holding the ball meant that the responsibility for foreign policy "flip-flops" was laid at Clinton's door.

Since he was against the use of force in Haiti, Secretary Christopher was now keeping a low profile. Nevertheless, with a protracted Orthodox Christian/Catholic Christian/Muslim civil war involving acts of mounting genocide in Bosnia that defied international solution, with black-on-black genocide in Africa that the West was deliberately ignoring, as well as a Middle East in which the memory of the massacre of 216 marines in Beirut would never go away, the fact was, Haiti was the only place on earth where President Clinton could make a distinctive military impact—an island less than two hundred miles off the shores of the United States, with a UN-approved mandate to restore an elected leader, and without the prospect of heavy casualties. "Haiti had no military capability," Clinton would himself acknowledge, later; "it would be like shooting fish in a barrel."

President Reagan had ordered an invasion of Grenada, after all, and President Bush the invasion of Panama, on the flimsiest of pretexts. Such flexing of American military muscle had enhanced their images as tough commanders-in-chief of the nation—and the world. Why shouldn't Bill Clinton do so too?

Thus, before leaving for Martha's Vineyard, the forty-second president of the United States had already ordered a reluctant Pentagon to go ahead with the planning. Now, after a confident presentation of the plan on September 7 before the national security team by General John Shalikashvili, the president, "without hedging or hesitation," Stephanopoulos recalled with admiration, gave the command: "It's a good plan; let's go." The invasion was to take place a week later, in mid-September, seven weeks before the midterm elections.

It would be Clinton's first official war.

CHAPTER FORTY

THE JUNTA'S TIME IS UP

What If Things Go Wrong?

"I think all of us in the military felt it was important to do it," recalled General Gordon Sullivan, who had felt deeply the humiliation of the *Harlan County* the year before—and had vowed with Admiral Paul David Miller, commander of American and NATO forces in the Atlantic, that such an event would never be allowed to happen again. "It was a two-pronged approach. One would kick down the door and really go in and *fight*. We had the 82nd Airborne Division, of the 18th Airborne Corps, but the 82nd mainly, to do that. And then, once again, the 10th Mountain Division, which had been in Somalia, was the other force that would go in and land in the helicopters."

Vengeance would be sweet. As the date of Operation Uphold Democracy approached, however, the president himself "was not always pretty to watch," Stephanopoulos allowed, while the performance of his communications team, under the hapless Dee Dee Myers, whom the president had failed to fire, was even more wretched.

Visiting the Allied battlefield at Anzio in June, the president had been reminded not only of the casualties of war, but of botched invasions. In a sort of World War II Gallipoli, an entire Anglo-American army had, in 1944, been pinned down on a small Italian Mediterranean beachhead for almost five months, at the cost of almost ninety thousand American and British battle and medical casualties—for no tactical gain whatever.

The president had also visited the Pointe du Hoc cliffs, overlooking Omaha beach, in Normandy, where the left wing of American landings had been held up for most of D-Day by fierce German opposition. The anticipated heavy German guns had, mercifully, still not been installed by June 6, 1944, brave American Rangers had found when they scaled the steep cliffs; nevertheless, overall Allied casualties in the air and seaborne landings had amounted to ten thousand in a single, longest day.

Bloodless victory in war was seldom, if ever, a reality. *What if things went wrong?*

At the daily White House press conference a train of reporters harassed the president's press secretary:

QUESTION: Dee Dee, on the question of a congressional vote or approval of some kind, when the missions to Grenada and Panama were undertaken, it was at least argued that time was of the absolute essence because the safety of Americans was at stake and that it was an emergency action, and the time did not permit a congressional debate on the matter. That appears not to be the case here. Could you explain further what the administration's thinking is on why congressional—not consultation, but advice and consent—is not required? I take it that's not part—the safety of Americans, time of the essence, is not part of the argument.

Myers admitted that time was not, though there was concern for some three thousand Americans living in Haiti.

Q: You're not [claiming they are in more] danger today than they were a week ago or six months ago, are you?

MYERS: No. What we've said is that, first of all, we believe that the president has authority under the United States Constitution to introduce forces if he sees—believes it's in the United States' national interest to do so, and that's one of the things that he'll be talking about tomorrow night, exactly what our interests are. . . .

Q: You're not making the argument . . . that there is any immediate time pressure involved in the president having to make a decision to send in the troops. Between two-thirds and three-quarters of the American people in the two latest polls oppose this. Senator Glenn, among others, said today that if a vote in Congress were taken, you would lose. Some say you would lose overwhelmingly. The American

Legion wrote a letter to the president today saying, do not invade, there's no reason to. Why are you then saying that there is—this is not a time for debate—everybody should close ranks behind the president. It seems like the president perhaps might want to listen to the American people.

Ultimately Dee Dee Myers was reduced to pleading: begging journalists to understand that "the president believes the United States interests are at stake here. We have consistently pursued a policy aimed at getting the dictators to leave peacefully. We worked through negotiations. We worked through sanctions. We've made it clear to them for weeks and weeks and weeks that if they did not leave voluntarily, they would be forced to leave involuntarily. They must know that we're serious about this and that time is running out."

Must? At what point in the Clinton administration's twenty-month history had any nation, save perhaps North Korea, been made to feel the U.S. government was serious and time was running out? White House correspondents, operating in the great democratic tradition of the United States, were, at any event, not impressed.

Pressed to explain more fully exactly what were the national security interests that demanded immediate action, a year after the U.S. had been content to recall the USS *Harlan County*, Myers reiterated:

We have an interest in democracy, particularly in our back yard. Democratically ruled countries make better trading partners. The habits of democracy are the habits of peace. There's certainly, when governments are democratic, a lot less likelihood that there will be internal abuse of power or that there will be external conflicts between countries. Certainly, we have an interest in seeing human rights abuses stopped. We have an interest in seeing stability in the region because of, among other things, migration questions. I think we certainly have a security interest in not seeing a massive outflow of refugees from a country that is a hundred miles or so or a hundred and fifty miles off of our shore.

So there's a number of national security interests at stake, and that's something that we've talked about consistently and the president will address tomorrow.

Q: Dee Dee, most of the conditions you've just talked about also apply to Cuba. And is the difference here that Cuba—an invasion of Cuba would obviously be a very bloody, protracted event? Does the United States see that it has like a higher moral demand to do this invasion of Haiti because it can be done easily and relatively cost-free?

Wearily, Myers could only speak in platitudes. In the final resort, she concluded, "it's something the president feels is important."

The Die Is Cast

Watching Myers field the hostile questions on his television monitor, the president saw his dream scenario vaporizing. His plan to take tough military action that would end the flip-flopping and assert new presidential character was turning into a morass of conflicting, cacophonous views on the legality, advisability, human cost, and long-term consequences of the planned invasion—with the press secretary whom he'd retained, in direct counter to the empowerment that he'd promised his new chief of staff, unable to make a clear and plausible case for invasion.

At one point, Stephanopoulos recalled, the president broke down. "I can't believe they got me into this," he raged in private. "How did this happen? We should have waited until after the elections."

It was too late, however. The die was cast. He would have to step up to the plate and convince a skeptical nation.

Scoop

Evelyn Waugh would have had a field day. In *Scoop*, the comic masterpiece Waugh wrote in the aftermath of the Italian invasion of Abyssinia almost sixty years before, the scabrously unsentimental novelist had parodied the medium of journalism. Newspaper correspondents were paid by cynical moguls, whose journals were staffed, he mocked, by a frivolous, sensational, and dishonest assortment of utterly self-serving individuals, in spite of their being charged with reporting on the serious matter of war.

Now, in 1994, it was the serious journalists who were seriously questioning the frivolous escapade of the president, before it even began. Over twenty thousand troops were donning war paint. Meanwhile an American warship, scouting the shoreline ahead of the invasion, ran aground—to the mockery of watching Haitians. Congress was bewailing the president's rush to war, and contesting the legality of his doing so—indeed, as the *Congressional Quarterly*'s weekly report noted, the strangest of reversals was evident. Democrats had traditionally insisted upon the president's need to seek Congress's approval before going to war; Republicans had not. Now, Republicans "who previously defended the broad authority asserted by GOP presidents to dispatch troops abroad," the *CQ* pointed out, "have become born-again defenders of congressional prerogatives."

There was also the question of whether President Clinton was *capable* of conducting a successful war. It had been arranged that the president would address the nation—and the world—on television at 9 P.M. on Thursday, September 15, 1994. At the White House press conference that morning, Dee Dee Myers openly joked that the president, currently at work in his office on his script, would be unlikely to have advance copies of his address ready for reporters by noon, as they'd requested. Later that evening, perhaps at 8:45 P.M., might be a better guess, she felt—and even then it was uncertain. "I'm a merchant of hope," she remarked breezily, to which a reporter responded: "We're a merchant of doubt." Another quipped: "Yes, but we're not buying."

"Yes. That's always the problem in this relationship," Myers had commented sadly, as the next volley of tough questions streaked at her, like SCUD missiles. "Dee Dee," another correspondent asked, "if it is the most brutal regime in the hemisphere, how does the president then justify a willingness to allow them [the junta] to walk away from whatever crimes and brutality and violence they've inflicted and get away scot-free, were they to leave in advance of an invasion?"

Embarrassed, Myers quoted the Governor's Island agreement of the year before. This had laid down the carrot-like terms by which "the military dictators would be able to leave without retribution." Another then called attention to the ship, the USS *Monsoon,* "that ran aground." Did she have further information? "Only that it did, in fact, run aground," she admitted. "Obviously, we've seen pictures of it, and that they expect it will be freed up soon"—which raised a journalist's mocking question of whether the Haitians were using voodoo.

It was at this point that the most dreaded missile came, asking Myers to respond to charges being made by conservatives "that the president's action"—which was to say, "an invasion of Haiti"—"is meant to enhance his credibility and his political standings."

For Dee Dee Myers this was the most lethal charge—the same charge Democrats had thrown at Presidents Reagan over Granada and Bush over Panama. *Was* the president deliberately wading into Republican waters to bring out the patriotic vote, before the midterm elections? Why had he chosen this moment to launch an invasion, using almost as many airborne troops as had dropped on D-Day in World War II—or, more worryingly, at Arnhem, in September 1944: the "Bridge Too Far"?

Myers, stammering, sought to meet the missile in mid-air:

MYERS: Well, I think we've—the president has said and others have said that the credibility of the international community and the credibility of the United States' commitment to democracy, particularly in this hemisphere, are at stake. There's no question about that. But to suggest that there are political motives, it's really—it's sad.

Was it, though? If it was untrue, why was the invasion secretly set for Sunday, September 18—the day before Congress returned from its summer break to debate the issue? Would the president consider going forward with an invasion before the House had a chance to vote on it on Monday, September 19, one reporter had asked? "Our timing is—our timing is in no way connected to what happens in Congress," Myers had retorted. "So the invasion's on Monday?" Myers: "No, I think Congress is in session on Monday."

When Is War War?

For two hundred years the president and Congress had feuded over the wording of the U.S. Constitution, Article I, Section 8, which reserved to Congress rather than the president the power "to declare War." But when was war "war"? Was President Clinton, in warning the Haitian junta to leave—and preparing to send in tens of thousands of U.S. troops whether or not they did—threatening to declare war, as Prime Minister Chamberlain had done when responding to Hitler's invasion of Poland in September 1939?

Article II, Section 2, of the U.S. Constitution specified that "The President shall be Commander in Chief of the Army and Navy of the United States." Did that role allow him to embark on potential hostilities, or not? Congress's War Powers Resolution of 1973 had required the president to consult with Congress "in every possible instance" before committing U.S.

forces abroad, and had necessitated the termination of any American troop commitment within sixty days unless Congress specifically authorized continuation of the operation. But the resolution had not actually amended the Constitution—allowing President Nixon and his successors to treat the congressional resolution itself as unconstitutional.

For the first time in recent American military history a *Democratic* president would be attempting to bypass Congress—knowing that, if it came to the floor of the Democrat-controlled House or the Senate, he would probably lose the vote of his own party!

"It's a mistake," warned Republican Senate minority leader Bob Dole, who spoke to reporters in Lincoln, Nebraska, before Clinton's address—despite having finally been given special advance draft excerpts from the speech. "There's not a single American life threatened in Haiti"—and the Senator claimed to reporters that telephone calls to his office that Thursday were running 147–2 against an invasion. The day before, they had been 967–0 against—more, it was pointed out, than had protested against gays in the military.

Finally at 9 P.M. on Thursday, September 15, the president addressed the nation from the Oval Office.

An Impossible Task

The *Times* of London considered it an almost impossible task for the American president to convince his fellow Americans in a single, brief Oval Office address that their "overwhelming aversion to invading Haiti" was misguided. Clinton's speech would thus be, possibly, "the single most important appeal of his presidency."

In the many months prior to Operation Desert Storm President Bush had deliberately "softened up" the American people for an invasion of Iraq, in a veritable campaign of addresses, as well as White House-encouraged congressional debate—thereby transforming a meager 11 percent public support for war into 70 percent approval. By contrast, prior to his television address on September 15, as the *Times* afterward noted, "Mr. Clinton had done almost nothing to prepare the American people for military action. His address was thus a critical test of the celebrated eloquence, some say glibness, that has served him well in the past. The odds against him winning the public round in just ten minutes were, however, extremely long." Not only was General Cedras nowhere near as fiendish an enemy as Saddam Hussein or earlier Haitian dictators such as Papa Doc and Baby Doc Duvalier, the *Times* correspondent pointed out, but the man President Clinton was seeking to reinstall was considered mentally unstable by the CIA and, though a priest, was known to condone violence—such as "necklacing," or using burning tires to kill a victim—on a par with the junta.

"Mr. Clinton's other big handicap," Martin Fletcher wrote, "is himself." The president's record "renders him singularly inappropriate to be arguing for military intervention. He spent his young manhood resisting the unpopular Vietnam War. He avoided military service while Robert Dole, John McCain and other leading opponents of the invasion in Congress have extremely distinguished war records." It was hardly surprising, then, that "many Americans suspect his motives."

Aware of the magnitude of the challenge, President Clinton faced the cameras, and in strong, measured language explained the situation to the nation. Gone, viewers noted with relief, was the embarrassed, awkward defensiveness of his press secretary and the White House communications staff over the past days. Gone was the secretary of state's hesitancy, the confused rhetoric of the State Department and officials at the Pentagon. The president's articulate declaration suddenly elevated the invasion into a realm of nobility that tapped into America's native idealism—the same idealism that had inspired President Kennedy's peace corps, and was motivating the current AmeriCorps.

"Mr. Clinton is one of the most skillful of modern presidents in stating his case," the *New York Times* reported, "and he did so effectively tonight. Blending elements of the Monroe Doctrine and the Truman Doctrine, Mr. Clinton argued that if General Raoul Cedras refuses to yield power, the United States would have no choice but to invade to protect its interests, 'to stop the brutal atrocities that threaten tens of thousands of Haitians, to secure our borders, and to preserve stability and promote democracy in our hemisphere, and to uphold the reliability of the commitments we make and the commitments others make to us.'" As the USS *Eisenhower* and USS *America* made course for Haiti, the president warned: "The message of the United States to the Haitian dictators is clear: Your time is up. Leave now, or we will force you from power."

With that threat, the once-vacillating, indecisive, and timid president had finally shown his mettle—wielding President Teddy Roosevelt's big stick. The next question that arose was: would the stick work?

An American Fleet Steams Toward Battle

A huge American fleet was now steaming towards Port-au-Prince, with stripped-down U.S. aircraft carriers being used for the first time as staging platforms for thousands of infantry and specialist troops. Paratroopers were assembling; high-speed civil and military policing response preparations were being tested by the Pentagon in real-time, not merely high-tech, death and destruction.

"Defiant even as U.S. warships steam toward his besieged Caribbean nation, Haiti's principal military ruler, Lt. Gen. Raoul Cedras, said he would rather die than step aside," the *Washington Post*'s Douglas Farah meanwhile reported from Port-au-Prince, "and he warned that a U.S. invasion would bring civil war and widespread bloodshed here." The outcome remained to be seen, clearly, but in terms of American popular opinion, the predictions of hostile Republicans suddenly began to look silly. The public's approval rating for invasion rocketed from barely 41 percent to 56 percent overnight—the biggest single leap of Clinton's presidency.

Though pacifists, left-wing radicals, and die-hard conservatives deplored a Democrat rather than a Republican making a show of American force, the majority of Americans applauded the president's decision as a mark of true leadership, however belated. Said Sean W. Foster-Nolan, of Issaquah, Washington: "If you have a next-door neighbor who's beating his wife and kids on a regular basis, don't you have a moral obligation to do something about it?" Dan Lindsay of Bellevue was equally won over: "I support the president on the Haiti decision completely. I think his reasons are far better than any of the decisions in Grenada, in Panama, or in the Persian Gulf. We have a situation that's close at hand, we have something that needs to be done, and we have given every opportunity for every other method to work and it hasn't. I think he's absolutely right."

Heather Lorimer of Seattle was unsparing in her analysis of the alternative. "I'm generally not an advocate for physical force of any kind; there always should be some other solutions. But the arguments against intervention in Haiti are very disturbing to me. I worry that we've become amoral, greedy, and self-centered. Haiti may not be able to provide us with a lot of oil wealth, or make us fear for our lives, but what about truth, democracy, and stability? When your neighbor needs help, do you first ask what's in it for yourself? Why is it that so many Americans think that one

American life is worth more than hundreds of non-American lives? Have we lost our moral fiber? Did we ever have moral fiber?"

All now depended on how the invasion progressed—as well as on former President Carter's new, secret mission.

The Time for Negotiations Is Long Past

What might have happened had former President Jimmy Carter not interceded? historians pondered later.

With the Cedras junta no more willing to surrender power than it had been the previous year when the *Harlan County* was turned away, steel nerves were required. In an interview with wire service reporters the day before his television broadcast, the president had shot down the notion of former President Carter, or Secretary Christopher, or anyone else, flying to Port-au-Prince—"There is nothing to meet about, unless they [the junta] are leaving," he had insisted.

It was in the immediate aftermath of President Clinton's tough television broadcast on September 15, ironically, that former president Carter, who had vainly offered his services as an intermediary over the past week, yet again urged President Clinton to let him travel to the lion's den and deal directly with General Cedras, as he had done with Kim Il Sung. State Department and White House advisers had hitherto painted Carter as a "loose cannon" who might weaken the tough threat of American military force in getting the Cedras junta to leave, but at this moment Clinton demonstrated the very *leger de main* that had escaped him over his wife's health care reform struggle. Admitting the danger of sending mixed signals to the junta, Carter had suggested he go to Port-au-Prince not alone, but with two other senior emissaries: Senator Nunn, the anti-invasion chairman of the Armed Services Committee (thus involving Congress directly in the negotiations) and, as a mark of military backbone, the former chairman of the Joint Chiefs of Staff of the U.S. armed forces, General Colin Powell. Born in Harlem of Jamaican parents, General Powell was a hero throughout the Caribbean. Carter had already contacted the two men, he explained to President Clinton, and they were both willing to go. The president, trusting his instinct, decided to back Carter's plan—and thereby ensure, he hoped, a bloodless victory.

Eyeball to Eyeball

General Powell certainly thought the diplomatic mission was going to fail, once he met General Cedras. Cedras—"a lean, sallow man with a long, pointed chin and nose," as Powell later described him—proved immune to reason, to bribery, or the prospect of death. Moreover, if Cedras was lean, the parliamentarians and business leaders whom the American plenipotentiaries met appeared surprisingly "well-fed and well-dressed," given "almost three years of economic embargo [that] had impoverished their countrymen. So much," Powell later wrote, "for [UN] sanctions."

Cedras remained implacable. A noble demise, defending his beloved island, whose independence went back to Napoleonic times and the overthrow of white French slave-owning imperialists, seemed to Cedras preferable to kow-towing to white militarism and a mad black priest, steeped in voodoo. Nothing that the American plenipotentiaries offered was sufficient to convince him, save force.

Unknown to the press, yet obvious to most, the invasion had been set for midnight, Sunday, September 18. Former president Carter offered amnesty, pensions, and free passage into safe exile. General Powell appealed to military honor and realism. Senator Nunn claimed, less convincingly, that Congress would back the U.S. president's decision to go to war. Nothing worked.

By midnight on Saturday, September 17, there had been no breakthrough. At 2 A.M. the next morning the follow-up meeting with the junta ended, in fact, with yet another Evelyn Waugh touch. Shaking hands with former president Carter, the chief of personnel in the Haitian military, Colonel Carl Dorelien, suddenly withdrew his arm, alarmed. He asked Carter if he had shaken hands with Jean-Bertrand Aristide lately. When President Carter said no, but asked why, Colonel Dorelien replied: "His spirit would still be on you, and I would not like to be touched by it."

That night, according to General Cedras's strikingly beautiful wife, Yannick Prosper Cedras, the children joined their parents in their marital bed, in their Mediterranean style villa set in green tropical gardens. They had been told it would be their last night on this earth, for it was better to "die with American bullets in our chests, than as traitors with Haitian bullets in our backs."

Time was running out. Vainly Carter, Nunn, and Powell attempted to convince both Yannick and Raoul that President Clinton meant business—that the invasion would take place in a few hours, and it was no dishonor to cede to overwhelming American military force. All Sunday the Carter team attempted to negotiate. On the wall of his office General Cedras had the framed photographs of six of his military predecessors: the U.S. officers who had been dictators of Haiti between 1915 and 1934, when President Roosevelt pulled out American occupying forces. Told of the magnitude of American military might, poised to descend upon the island sixty years after their last appearance, Cedras commented, "We used to be the weakest nation in the hemisphere. After this we'll be the strongest"—but he and his colleagues refused to be forced into exile, or to cede power and be given an amnesty within a month, as President Clinton demanded. That, Cedras made clear, was up to the Haitian parliament to determine, not the U.S. president.

With the supposed Haitian dictator suddenly behaving like a model parliamentarian and the hours before the invasion ticking ominously away, a metaphorical explosion did finally take place, around 5 P.M. Former president Carter had gone into another office to talk to President Clinton and beg for more time. "This is uncomfortable for me," Clinton told Carter. "We've been friends a long time. I'm going to have to order you out of there in thirty more minutes. You have got to get out." As they spoke, there was a commotion next door. Cedras's chief of staff, Brigadier General Philippe Biamby, burst into the room and announced that the American invasion had begun. "He just kind of exploded," Nunn later recounted. Addressing General Powell, his retired American counterpart, Biamby accused the former chairman of the Joint Chiefs of Staff of being "part of a trap."

Powell was genuinely at a loss. Since the Americans had been told H-hour was another six *hours* away, he asked how Biamby knew for sure the invasion had begun. It was then that Biamby confessed he'd heard it on his new cell phone from a spy he had at Fort Bragg. The 82nd Airborne division was emplaning at Pope Air Force Base, and planes were already taking off. "Not bad intelligence, I thought, for a poor country," Powell remembered thinking.

"We must immediately break off these talks," General Biamby concluded, urging his chief, General Cedras, to move to a command post and begin the defense of the island. "They were going to take off their uniforms, get their guns, and go into hiding," General Powell later explained the Haitian guerrilla-warfare plan. "There wasn't going to be an opposition army in uniform sitting there in formation on tanks on the docks. They were going to be civilians with guns."

The Invasion Stays On

War in the Caribbean was commencing: guerilla war. In the White House President Clinton was uncertain whether his envoys were now captives or in danger of being killed: the very scenario he had wished to avoid. Should he delay or postpone the invasion? His national security adviser, Tony Lake, had developed such a bad toothache that he had to leave the president's side and see a dentist. Having spent the entire day, after going to church, in the Oval Office waiting for the phone to ring and watching CNN vainly for signs of a breakthrough, Clinton thus ordered a hostage rescue team to assemble to try, if necessary, to save his envoys; but, as Biamby had learned, he'd also ordered the 82nd Airborne paratroopers into the air with two words: "Pack 'em"—and he refused to call them back. The invasion was on—and was staying on.

General Biamby remained convinced that he and his fellow Haitian leaders had been tricked by Clinton. The Carter team was only a diversion to keep the Haitians talking, in his view, while U.S. troops pounced from the night sky. The Georgia senator figured they had a "fifty-fifty chance, maybe better" of being held as prisoners of war, or as hostages—or killed.

News of the approaching U.S. warplanes "caused almost a complete breakdown," the other Georgian, Jimmy Carter, later considered. However, "we didn't have time to discuss it," said Senator Nunn, for it was now that former President Carter, recovering his wits, launched into an emotional plea for sanity. On the one hand, Carter declared, he empathized with the Haitian rulers and the suffering that a UN embargo had forced on the island nation's poor. "I said I was ashamed of my own country's policy," Carter later candidly admitted. But, he added, Haiti's leaders were showing just as little concern for their own people. "I began accusing the generals of just wanting to stay in office and being willing to sacrifice the people's safety," especially the safety of the country's children. "I didn't have to come down to Haiti," he reminded them of his own personal sacrifice in attempting to broker an agreement. "They were," he claimed, "taken aback."

Thousands of American paratroopers were meantime already airborne, and would be overhead in the next few hours. Someone suggested they put the matter to pro-tempore president Emile Jonassaint, in a final effort to halt the invasion. Racing from Cedras's military headquarters in a phalanx of cars to the presidential palace, General Powell sat with General Cedras. "Hand grenades rolled around on the floor," Powell recalled, later. "And in the back was a Haitian soldier clutching an assault rifle."

For Powell, architect of America's crushing victory over Iraq in Desert Storm, it would have been an inglorious end to a brilliant career had the Carter mission now ended in Haitian fiasco and bloodshed. President Jonassaint, however, was waiting at the palace, together with his ministers of information, foreign affairs, and defense—all considered illegitimate officials by the U.S. State Department. Dialing the White House number from a telephone in one of the palace offices, General Powell got straight through to the Oval Office. It seemed surreal—almost like a scene from *Dr. Strangelove.* "Mr. President, I think we've got some movement here," Powell explained. "We just need more time."

President Clinton countered that he was not going to halt the invasion; the airborne troops would continue on their flightpath, but the plenipotentiaries—whom he had originally ordered to be clear of Haitian soldiery or the palace by noon—could nevertheless keep talking, in a last-ditch effort to obtain voluntary surrender terms from Cedras.

The entire world seemed to be watching CNN, which had cameras in Port-au-Prince, picturing the movements, but not the negotiations, of the U.S. delegates. On board one of the aircraft carriers—each packed with helicopters and two thousand assault infantrymen—the invasion commander, General Hugh Shelton, six-foot-five inches tall and a much-decorated former commander of the 101st and 82nd Airborne divisions, was raging at his television set whenever Carter, Nunn, and Powell were shown, screaming: "Get out of there!"

In the Pentagon the head of press communications was still begging CNN's chief, Tom Johnson, not to broadcast his information that no less than sixty-one planes carrying paratroopers of the 82nd Airborne had already taken off, since this would enable the Haitian military to work out their drop time—allowing them to shoot American soldiers as they parachuted. (Johnson agreed not to broadcast the information.)

In the presidential palace in Port-au-Prince, meanwhile, the crisis reached the point of no return, as the Haitian minister of defense declared he would resign rather than accept President Clinton's "outrageous" terms.

The eighty-one-year-old Haitian president stared at the minister in absolute calm, despite the tension.

"Then resign," he challenged him.

The Haitian minister of information then piped up. He, too, threatened to resign over the "disgraceful" terms.

"We have too many ministers already," Jonassaint replied—to President Carter's amazement. "I thought that was funny."

Then came the longed-for words: "I am going to sign the proposal," President Jonaissant now declared. "I will not let my people suffer further tragedy. I choose peace."

All eyes then turned to General Cedras—who swallowed deeply, and agreed to obey his president. Former president Carter almost leaped for joy. Still skeptical, General Powell was concerned about the lives of his former soldiers; he demanded a personal assurance from General Cedras that, if the paratroopers were recalled in midair, no member of the Haitian army would resist when American infantry forces came ashore to police the agreement the next day, rather than dropping by air. Cedras gave his assurance.

It was over. By nightfall on Sunday, September 18, 1994, as plenipotentiaries Carter, Nunn, and Powell flew back to Washington, President Clinton had won his first war—without a shot being fired.

In the Glow of Heroes

As U.S. soldiers were televised landing peacefully in Haiti on Monday, September 19, 1994, and took up their stations to control the nation in anticipation of President Aristide's return, most observers considered that President Clinton, together with former President Carter, had played a masterly hand. Republican opponents in Congress were, for one brief interval, confounded. Congressman Robert Livingstone, the Republican spokesperson on the issue, had predicted a guerilla nightmare. To his chagrin the House of Representatives overwhelmingly passed a resolution, 353–45, expressing its support for the troops and the emissaries who had negotiated their peaceful arrival, as well as applauding President Clinton's handling of the crisis.

The president's polls, already rocketing after his "Your time is up!" address to the nation, rose 22 percent, with 77 percent of respondents to a *New York Times*/CBS poll favoring the agreement under which the Haitian military would leave power by October 15, 1994, and 71 percent crediting the United States delegation led by former president Jimmy Carter with helping to resolve the situation.

Even members of the press were forced to eat their hats, and their words. *U.S. News & World Report* had headed its previous week's edition "Clinton's Quagmire," a somewhat "premature condemnation of a mission that has been a remarkable success," as Carl Rowan noted in the *Chicago Sun-Times,* "with American forces in anything but a quagmire—basking, really, in the glow of heroes."

Jack Payton, reporting direct from Haiti for the *St. Petersburg Times,* spoke for the vast majority of relieved Americans when writing that "Clinton and Carter have chalked up a real win for themselves. And in the process, they've also discovered something that many past presidents have known well—that diplomacy backed up by a credible threat of force can move mountains, even recalcitrant dictators.

"This credible threat of force is exactly what was lacking in previous U.S. policy toward Haiti as well as Washington's approach toward Bosnia," Payton pointed out, "and why the situation in the Balkans is still unresolved to this day. Nobody—not the United States, not the United Nations or NATO—had persuaded the Bosnian Serbs that they would have to pay dearly if the fighting in the Balkans dragged on."

General Sullivan agreed. "By this time, the Europeans were unhappy with Mr. Clinton," he later recalled. "*I* think Haiti *did* help. It helped our message abroad, certainly: 'Look, these guys are willing to apply power, and they know how to do it—and they're willing to do it.'"

On the international podium, the president's stature as leader and as peacemaker was immeasurably increased—indeed, with the triumph of Haiti under his belt the president met with the foreign minister of Japan, with the UN secretary-general, with the president of Bosnia, with the presidents of Croatia, Azerbaijan, and Mexico. He invited the crown prince of Jordan and the foreign minister of Israel to tripartite talks at the White House. He was slated to meet with the president of Russia at the new Russian embassy in Washington, with the prime minister of Ireland, the vice president of China, and Nelson Mandela, president of South Africa.

Simultaneously, the president's belated decision to appoint a strong, military-style chief of staff was having the desired effect.

THE CONTRACT WITH AMERICA

CHAPTER FORTY-ONE

NEWT GINGRICH

Newton Leroy McPherson

Looking back, Bill Clinton would kick himself for not seeing the enemy's attack coming.

Born three years apart and on collision course were Newton Leroy McPherson and William Jefferson Blythe—now performing as political stars of their respective parties: Congressman Newt Gingrich and President Bill Clinton.

MacPherson had been brought up—like Billy Blythe—initially by a maternal grandparent (a teacher, Ethel Daugherty) and an extended family in Pennsylvania, who had taught him to read and love books. His father, Newton McPherson, was a quintessential redneck, a farm boy from Fiddler's Elbow. Known as Big Newt—he was six feet three—the elder MacPherson was not a reader. From the age of "sixteen to thirty-five he was in bar fights," his son later recalled. "My mother was very frightened of him." When she became pregnant and Newt continued to slam her, his own father threw him out of the MacPherson family home, where they were living. Divorced by his wife, Newt joined the Merchant Marine. When Little Newt—or Newtie—was three, his mother, Kit, had remarried, choosing this time a man who worked on the Reading Railroad, Bob Gingrich. In return for being exempted from providing child support for Little Newt, Big Newt ceded to Bob Gingrich the right to adopt Kit's son, who asked (like Billy Blythe) to change his family name and became, once Bob Gingrich went to Korea as an infantry officer, an "army brat," living with his mother and adoptive father wherever they were stationed, around the world.

Like Billy Blythe, Little Newt possessed in childhood an abnormally high intelligence but suffered from obesity, with inevitable consequences among his peers. He loved animals, but had such poor eyesight that, until his disability was identified at age twelve, he "literally couldn't see people." It would be, even his staff agreed, a lifelong affliction.

Like Bill Clinton, née Blythe, Newt Gingrich would become the butt of his stepfather's anger—but also of his stern, unrelenting, and unmet military expectations.

"No, I don't think I ever impressed him," Newt later reflected on his stepfather, Bob Gingrich. "He and I fought from the time he adopted me until I was nineteen. It wasn't tough. It was just a fact." Bob did not disagree—though he hated sentimentality. "Some people thought I was too tough with Newt. I just wanted to get him out of the house and earn a living," he said. He certainly never hugged Newt. "You don't do that with boys. I didn't even do it with my girls"—Newt's two half-sisters. Disobedience had brought swift, unsparing punishment. When Newt stayed out till the early hours of morning as a young teenager in Orleans, France, and had to be brought home by the military police, his adoptive father—wakened by the MPs—felt shamed by such an unmilitary stepson. In a reverse scenario of the scene in Bill Clinton's childhood when Bill confronted his abusive stepfather, who was about to beat and rape his mother in Hot Springs, it was the stepfather who, in Gingrich's case, confronted his errant son. "I took him inside, grabbed him by the lapels, and I smashed him against the wall," Bob admitted. "We were face-to-face."

Gingrich—who was promoted to colonel—did not need to further intimidate the terrified thirteen-year-old. ("It is hard to be belligerent when your feet aren't touching the ground," Colonel Gingrich later said.) The message was unmistakable. "There was no need to shout. He didn't do it again."

A Man-boy

If Little Newt didn't impress his adoptive father, he became determined to impress other folks—especially older people.

It was as a self-confessed man-boy ("I was a fifty-year-old at nine," Gingrich later reflected) in his junior year at Baker High School, back in Columbus, Georgia, that Newt Gingrich fell in love with his math teacher,

Jackie Battley, who also ran the school's drama club. She was seven years older than her pupil.

"Persistent and persuasive," Gingrich got the math teacher to agree to date him, secretly—even persuading her to convert to the Lutheran church from her Baptist faith. When Colonel Gingrich tried to separate the pair by insisting Newt go away to college at Emory University, Jackie moved, too—obtaining a teaching position in Atlanta. Two days after his nineteenth birthday, the freshman student with the huge head and fountain of dark hair, Newton Leroy Gingrich, née McPherson, married Ms. Battley, the buxom math blonde, who was twenty-six. "He was her little boy," his mother, Kit—who, on the orders of her husband, the colonel, did not attend the wedding—recalled.

Hired by Jack Prince as Republican congressional campaign manager while still an Emory student, Newt Gingrich then became as committed to, and involved in, Republican politics in Georgia as Bill Clinton, an undergraduate at Georgetown, was in working for Democratic senator J. William Fulbright. Both boys possessed prodigious memories, gave relentless attention to detail, and had a love of strategy—Gingrich's fuelled by his upbringing in Europe in military garrisons during the Cold War, his visits to the First and Second World War battlefields, and his addiction to heroic Hollywood movies, especially those of "The Duke," John Wayne.

From Emory State, financed by Jackie's teaching, Gingrich went to Tulane University, in New Orleans, where he took his master's degree, then wrote his Ph.D. dissertation on the Belgian colonial education administration in the Congo, passing his doctoral orals with distinction. Teaching at West Georgia College from the fall of 1970, Dr. Gingrich applied the next year to become president of the college! Having failed in that endeavor, he applied the following year (also unsuccessfully) to become head of the history department.

Here, clearly, was a young academic in a hurry. His interest in environmental affairs led to him to transfer to the interdisciplinary geography department; he was "the most charismatic teacher on campus," in the opinion of the department chair, a "fantastic teacher," a "populist" able to think outside the box and challenge received ideas with wit, a wide range of learning, and a sometimes reckless disregard of consequences. Like Bill Clinton as a student, Gingrich had dreamed of writing a "great novel," but settled for reality. Eschewing state office, he launched his first bid for Congress, like Clinton, as a college professor and in the same year, 1973.

Gingrich and Clinton duly won their party primaries, and the two professors demonstrated skills that went far beyond academia: Clinton challenging
his opponent through charismatic, indefatigable retail politics—gladhanding
with a smile from morning till night, and exhibiting a shameless willingness
to ask for money—while Gingrich coached his team of volunteers like a star
football team, identifying his opponent's tactical weaknesses, and penning
endless lists of priorities to maintain focus. His "six basic rules for the campaign" had, in 1974, an almost military ring, reminiscent of Field Marshal
Bernard Montgomery's famous orders of the day:

1. Honesty in everything about the campaign

2. Co-sharing in power, information, etc.

3. We go slow now in order to go rapidly later

4. Keep everything simple, stick to fundamentals

5. Keep trying, openly admit mistakes, learn from each other

6. Have some fun along the way

Like Clinton an ardent admirer of Martin Luther King Jr., Gingrich de-
cried his Dixiecrat opponent's abysmally poor record on civil rights, and
spoke in numerous African-American churches throughout the sixth district as a fearless standard-bearer of the party of Abe Lincoln.

Both Gingrich and Clinton came three thousand votes shy of winning
their respective elections that fateful year, when President Richard Nixon
resigned in the face of certain impeachment proceedings. While Bill Clinton never did make it to Congress, however, Newt Gingrich proved successful in reaching the House of Representatives on his third attempt, in 1978,
when the incumbent retired and an anti-tax, fundamentalist New Right
wave swept the nation, giving Republicans new momentum in hitherto
staunch Dixiecrat districts. It was in this manner that Newt Gingrich became a young Republican congressman from Georgia, in the same year that
Bill Clinton became his state's youngest elected governor.

An Ambitious Bastard

Ironically, just as Clinton had taken on a Republican media consultant,
Dick Morris, to destroy his rival Jim Guy Tucker by using negative adver-

tising, so Newt Gingrich had used a Democratic media consultant and film-maker, Deno Seder, to destroy *his* rival, Virginia Shapard, a Democratic state senator.

There were other parallels, too. Like Bill Clinton, Newton Leroy Gingrich was not immune to the attractions of the opposite sex, despite being married. Anne Manning, an English campaign volunteer married to one of Gingrich's faculty colleagues at West Georgia College, was just one of his adulterous conquests—an attractive woman who found her candidate preferring the same sort of sex as Bill Clinton. In her hotel room in Washington, where she was attending a conference in 1977, Gingrich insisted upon oral rather than penetrative sex. "He prefers that *modus operandi*," Anne later asserted, "because that way he can say, 'I never slept with her.'" Before Gingrich left the room he'd warned her: "If you ever tell anybody about this, I'll say you're lying."

The parallel between Clinton and Gingrich, the two college professors, was certainly remarkable: both men proponents of the opportunity society; pro-business; well-funded; intellectually astute; interested in future trends; personally unavaricious but relentlessly ambitious in terms of their careers; tireless campaigners; and narcissistic—happiest when the center of admiring attention.

For all the genuine idealism that propelled them into politics, moreover, both men had quickly gained a record for hypocrisy, questionable loyalty, and amorality in the murky quest to win and retain power. Lee Howell, an early press secretary and friend, was quite candid. Gingrich's path to power, inevitably, was strewn with metaphorical bodies. "Newt Gingrich has a tendency to chew people up and spit them out. He uses you for all it's worth, and when he doesn't need you anymore he throws you away. Very candidly, I don't think that Newt Gingrich has many principles," Howell commented, "except for what's best for him, guiding him." Chip Kahn, who managed two of Gingrich's congressional campaigns, puzzled over which came first in Gingrich's life: his dreams of personal success, or success in steering his chosen party towards a new kind of Republicanism. "I don't know whether the ambitious bastard came before the visionary, or whether because he's a visionary, he realizes you have to be tough to get where you need to be," Kahn confessed. The result, however, for those working for and with Gingrich, was often cruel. As Kahn's wife remarked in 1984, "Newt uses people and then discards them as useless. He's like a leech. He really is a man with no conscience. He just doesn't seem to care who he hurts or why."

Nowhere was this hurtfulness more evident than in Gingrich's private life. He had eviscerated his Democratic opponent, Virginia Shapard, with negative ads in 1978 for opposing a cut in state taxes; for handing out money indiscriminately to welfare recipients; and, worst of all, for intending to go to Washington without her spouse. As one of Gingrich's team recalled of their full-page ads, under photographs of the two candidates, the caption for Mrs. Shapard—wife of a wealthy Georgian businessman—proclaimed: "If elected, Virginia will move to Washington, but her children and husband will remain in Griffin." Under the Gingrich photo the Republican caption boasted: "When elected, Newt will keep his family together."

Far from keeping his family together once elected, Gingrich had quickly dissolved his family, divorcing the teacher-wife who had changed her religious affiliation for him, financed his college and postgraduate studies, ceaselessly campaigned for him, and pictured him in public as a model church deacon and Sunday school teacher, while ignoring his philandering. Worse still, to the consternation of his friends and supporters, Gingrich had gone to the hospital where Jackie Gingrich was recovering from uterine cancer surgery, and with a yellow legal pad in hand had urged her to agree such disadvantageous divorce papers that her church would have to organize a collection on her behalf during the proceedings. "Newt can handle political problems," Gingrich's former press secretary attempted to explain, "but when it comes to personal problems, he's a disaster. He handled the divorce like he did any other political decision: You've got to be tough in this business, you've got to be hard. Once you make the decision you've got to act on it. Cut your losses and move on."

Aged thirty-six, the freshman congressman had considered his wife to be aging baggage he should discard as soon as possible. "She isn't young enough or pretty enough to be the president's wife," one aide recalled him saying. Another commented on the explicit hypocrisy. "Newt thought, well, it doesn't look good for an articulate, young, aggressive, attractive congressman to have a frumpy old wife"—despite the election platform Gingrich had put forward as "Mr. Family Values." As a result, his staff split over the issue, and Gingrich had been lucky to win re-election in 1980—after which, however, the narrowly re-elected Congressman felt safe to marry his girlfriend, Marianne Ginther, who had worked for him and was then employed as a clerk by the Secret Service.

The Last Three Options

Sadly, the same marital and extramarital saga would be repeated, with yet another aide. By 1989, as Gingrich was pushing his activist, partisan, and confrontational style in Congress in pursuit of a GOP majority and inventing the Conservative Opportunity Society platform with men like Dick Cheney and Trent Lott, he found himself bored at home and interested in new extramarital opportunities. He and Marianne separated frequently.

"Frankly," Marianne later told the *Washington Post*, "it's been on and off for some time." By 1993, Gingrich was enjoying a close relationship with Callista Bisek, a congressional aide more than twenty years his junior. "Newt is apparently trying to create a new hybrid form, Christian adultery," one hostile organization later maintained. "According to MSNBC, Bisek sings in the [Roman Catholic] National Shrine Choir, and Newt would often wait for her at the Shrine of the Immaculate Conception, listening to her sing while he read the Bible."

Interviewing Gingrich in 1984, author David Osborne had already challenged the congressman to explain his apparent hypocrisy—and had received a remarkably candid reply. "Looking back, do you feel your private life and what you'd been saying in public were consistent?" Osborne had asked—to which Gingrich had responded: "No. In fact I think they were sufficiently inconsistent that at one point in 1979 and 1980, I began to quit saying them in public. One of the reasons I ended up getting a divorce was that if I was disintegrating enough as a person that I could not say those things, then I needed to get my life straight, not quit saying them. And I think that literally was the crisis I came to. I guess I look back on it a little bit like somebody who's in Alcoholics Anonymous—it was a very, very bad period of my life, and it had been getting steadily worse. . . . I ultimately wound up at a point where probably suicide or going insane or divorce were the last three options."

Gingrich had *not* got his private life straight in the subsequent ten years, however. While continuing to trumpet Republican "family values," he had used his political ambitions to drown his inner fears and anxieties, and cover his philandering. As he himself would admit to an interviewer in 1995, "I think you can write a psychological profile of me that says I found a way to immerse my insecurities in a cause large enough to justify whatever I wanted it to."

In 1994, meanwhile, that cause became a *cause célèbre*: the overthrow of American big government, and its replacement by a new, activist Republican crusade combining "traditional American values" and "a conservative opportunity society" hungry for the benefits of "advanced technology."

CHAPTER FORTY-TWO

BLUEPRINT FOR THE NEO-REAGANITE FUTURE

Getting Attention

Why did Bill Clinton, possessed with such supersensitive antennae to political danger, not appreciate the missile that Newt Gingrich was preparing throughout the summer of 1994?

The situation was ominously similar to that of 1980, when as first-term governor of Arkansas Bill Clinton underestimated the growing support for his Republican opponent, Frank White—and responded too late to defuse the threat.

Newt Gingrich was, in the summer of 1994, simply a firebrand in Clinton's eyes: a controversial, attention-seeking, "confrontational activist" congressman; a clever man who understood the sea change that had taken place in media coverage of politics since Watergate, and with the help of moguls such as Rupert Murdoch had made his Faustian bargain with it. "You have to give them confrontations," Gingrich told a group of conservative activists. "When you give them confrontations, you get attention; when you get attention, you can educate." It was a feisty approach to self-promotion, but hardly the stirrings, in the president's eyes, of a real threat to the Democratic Party's hold on the House of Representatives.

How wrong he was he would now discover.

An Ethics Violator

Confrontation was certainly the key to Gingrich's strangely aggressive behavior. For years he'd made a name for himself as a lecturer and speaker, without ever getting significant press coverage. Then, one day, he'd deliberately crossed swords with the Speaker of the House of Representatives, Congressman "Tip" O'Neill, and had won the national attention he craved. "In the minute Tip O'Neill attacked me," Gingrich later boasted, "he and I got ninety seconds at the close of all three network news shows."

From there, Gingrich had gone on to achieve further television-grabbing notoriety on the Hill by charging O'Neill's successor, distinguished World War II veteran and Speaker of the House of Representatives Jim Wright, with ethics violations in 1988 over a vanity book he'd published. This soon rebounded, however, onto "bomb-thrower" Gingrich—indeed reduced him to a sobbing wreck when Democrats attacked him the following year as a neo-McCarthyite, and countercharged him with no less than eighty-four ethics violations of his own. A special prosecutor was appointed to investigate the charges—a process that would eventually cost American taxpayers $1 million.

Such had been the opening salvos in a series of bitter new, internecine, profoundly partisan, uncivil civil warfare in Congress that could only bring dishonor to the House.

Gingrich had only himself to blame. Drying his eyes, the Georgian Republican congressman had merely continued his antics. If that was the only way he could get his ideas written about, mentioned on television and radio, and debated in modern, tabloid America, then so be it, he reasoned—content to be considered, in his own words, "just about the most disliked member of Congress."

This was the very opposite of Bill Clinton—who wanted everybody to like him, and would go to almost any length to elicit approval. What President Clinton failed to acknowledge, however, was Gingrich's relentless if subversive generalship, compared with his own. Newt Gingrich's private life might be a mess, and his insensitivity to real people—especially ailing people—heartless, but his political drive and dogged organizing capacity were extraordinary. Where Bill Clinton threw himself into third-way consensus through an ever-compromising synthesis of different and often differing views of others, Newt Gingrich had for years sought to synthesize his own life's interest in different subjects from paleontology to filmography, manipulating them into a peppery political philosophy that in spirit if not in detail resonated with the beliefs, experiences, and aspirations of average voters in his state. By 1993, despite being the minority whip in Congress, he had begun giving a college course called "Renewing American Civilization" as an adjunct professor of Kennesaw State College, in Kennesaw, Georgia, through its School of Business Administration. Though he would in time be fined three hundred thousand dollars for ethics violations in relation to the non-profit funding and dissemination of his course for partisan political purposes, it was nevertheless a remarkable testament to Gingrich's sheer intellectual determination to define himself and his view of modern America. One by one he had highlighted what he saw as the core principles of the American way of life in the past, the present, and the future—the basis for a new Republicanism, or New Age Reaganism, as he called it.

"Renewing American Civilization" offered Kennesaw students (as well as satellite-connected off-campus students) ten two-hour lectures on "identifying and fostering the underlying values and attitudes that enable free markets, private enterprise, and democratic systems to prosper. The basic premise of the course," its outline explained, "is that there is a distinct American Civilization that has flourished for over 200 years. While the course examines the Foundations of American Civilization, its main purpose is to present a workable, practical, and positive blueprint for Renewing American Civilization." In notes prepared for his congressional staff—later subpoenaed by the special prosecutor, James M. Cole, as potential evidence of wrongdoing—Gingrich wrote that the course "is only one in a series of strategies designed to implement a strategy of renewing American civilization. Another strategy will be a series of legislative initiatives designed to transform the system from a welfare state to an opportunity society"—his most fundamental concern.

To this end Gingrich had proposed to his staff five immediate tasks, targeting specified groups:

1. Knitting together trade associations and activist groups that agree they want to replace the welfare state into an active movement.

2. Developing a national news media strategy that explains the concept of renewing American civilization so reporters, editors, and citizens can understand it.

3. Getting Republican activists committed to renewing American civilization, to setting up workshops built around the course, and to opening the party up to every citizen who wants to renew American civilization.

4. Identifying, publicizing, and knitting together Republican elected officials at the city, county, and state levels who are already developing specific building blocks to transform or replace the welfare state.

5. Identify, recruit, encourage, publicize, and knit together the activists in business, community service, and government who are already instinctively applying the principles of renewing American civilization.

These Ideas Don't Work

Clearly there was a messianic quality to the teachings of radical-conservative Congressman Newt Gingrich—something skeptics dismissed as psychologically inspired by his rootless background as the son of a manic-depressive mother and tyrant military stepfather: an attempt to create order out of disorder.

Whatever its source, and however politically biased its revivalist message, there was no denying Gingrich's intellectual fervor. "He takes complete possession of the room," journalist Peter J. Boyer noted of Gingrich's speaking ability, "even when he's speaking what one critic calls 'GobbledyNewt'—his philosophical mix of futurism, high technology, free enterprise, and space. A former college professor, he has the instructor's command, rather than the lawyer's equivocation, a compelling directness in a world of frayed smiles and glazed expressions. But most of all Gingrich has something that is of great practical value to the Republicans just now—the zealot's single-minded drive."

Gingrich did—a drive that was at once political and educational. His "Renewing American Civilization" was no dry recitation of traditional Republican ideas—especially libertarian ideas. It was, rather, a call to action, based on his life's study of what was unique to America—"American exceptionalism," in a phrase he borrowed from Everett C. Ladd. Gingrich had lived abroad as a child, in France and Germany, and had developed a deep personal sense of what it was to be an American, as opposed to a European. His claim was that an American did not inherit a nationality but that "you *learn* to be an American"—a surprisingly un-elitist, un-racist view, based on the freedom to own property, access to good public education, and participation in an opportunity society, within the great melting pot of races. "What I'm suggesting to you," he lectured, "is: we are multi-ethnic. We are the first world civilization in that sense," he proudly claimed, "a great country with good people"—a place where "there's an enormous level of trust in each other. . . . "

Trust was not a quality that Gingrich's behavior inspired in Congress, but there was certainly sincerity in his belief in a revitalization of the American economy and society by promoting a Reagan/Thatcher-like cultural shift from dependence on welfare to freedom of economic opportunity.

Since the American War of Independence, Gingrich claimed, "you have certain long sweeps that are more and more positive. We go from slavery to segregation to integration. We go from empowering wealthy white males to giving women the vote, to eliminating the poll tax and then . . . making sure everybody can vote." It was, however, a historico-cultural journey that had come to an end under Lyndon Johnson. "What's been happening, we [radical Republicans] would argue, is that from 1965 to 1994, that America went off on the wrong track—if you look at the first 300 years of American history, we're going in one direction, and then all of a sudden around 1965, with the rise of the great society, the counterculture, et cetera, you suddenly have a tremendous burst in a direction which is different from every other period of American history."

His critique, Gingrich emphasized, was "not ideological. It's not, 'I'm a conservative, they're a liberal,'" he claimed. "The critique is: *these ideas don't work.*" One by one he pointed to the ills of American society—and blamed Democrats for the well-meaning but patronizing notions that had failed to cure those ills. "The elite ideas of the last generation have failed, and in failing, have left America with more poverty, more violence, more red tape, more bureaucrats, more litigation, more power in Washington. And ironically, after all those 'mores,' with less ability to actually get problems solved and less ability to get opportunities developed."

In Gingrich's view, America's great civilization wasn't working.

Bookworm, lecturer, and proseletyzer: Newt Gingrich was, in the context of his "Renewing American Civilization" fantasy, determined now to go one step further in his long campaign to convert younger people to Republican opportunity-led values and wrest the House of Representatives from Democratic control. He was already the party's whip in Congress. Bob Michel, the gentlemanly minority leader, was intending to stand down at the end of the 103rd Congress—offering an opportunity for Gingrich not only to succeed him as minority leader of the House but, if the Republicans could win enough seats in the forthcoming 1994 midterm elections, or in 1996, for Gingrich to become Speaker of the House.

For Republicans to win back control of the House after some forty-one years, however, they would need a document, a solemn declaration, a manifesto, Gingrich reasoned: a clearly defined agenda of political goals that would distinguish them from their opponents.

Traditionally, midterm elections were fought locally, not nationally. In a step that would put Newton LeRoy Gingrich into the political history books, he decided to reverse that approach. In the 1994 gubernatorial, senate, and congressional election campaigns the GOP would wage war as a *national* revolutionary army, controlled from a central headquarters, not as guerrilla warriors fighting in penny packets.

As a student of military history, the stepson of a colonel, an "army brat" who'd visited the battlefields of Normandy, the Somme, and Verdun, and who'd probed the battles of the Revolution and the Civil War for their lessons at home, Gingrich thus presented himself as a new kind of Republican general. A man of ideas. And an inspiring, if insensitive, trainer of troops.

Catching the President Unawares

Bill Clinton, though *ex officio* commander-in-chief of the United States of America's military, had perilously few forces to face insurrection at home. Indeed the problem for General Clinton in America was his party. As Republicans constantly reminded him, he had not won a majority of votes in the 1992 presidential election, only a plurality in a three-way fight. His brand of Democratic centrism, as a New Democrat, had appealed to many voters tired of liberal-versus-conservative ideology and gridlock, and responsive to the promise of a new, middle-of-the-way forward. But his subsequent administration hadn't cured gridlock, despite a three-way lock on the White House and the Capitol.

Instead the president had stumbled through his first year and three-quarters in office, with a number of significant accomplishments to his administration's name. Except for deficit reduction, however, these were bi-partisan achievements. In the one great Democratic initiative that would have placed him in the FDR-Truman-Kennedy-LBJ pantheon as a Democrat—namely, health care reform—he had singularly failed, leaving the Democratic Party without a coherent leader or an ideological philosophy with which to combat the approaching Newtonian cohort, a revolutionary army making for the capital, and with an agenda aimed straight at Clinton's centrist heart.

Contract With America

Monday, September 26, 1994 became in its way the blackest day of the whole Clinton administration—for on that day Senate Majority Leader George Mitchell, who had turned down the possibility of a seat on the Supreme Court, announced the final death of health care reform, saying he could not muster the sixty votes needed to stop a Republican filibuster not only of Hillary Clinton's proposal but of any Democratic compromise plan, including the one he had been pushing since August 9, his own.

"This journey is far, far from over," the president warned in a statement—unable yet to grasp the magnitude of his mistake in putting his wife in charge of the project and then waving his black pen at lawmakers. Hillary, too, seemed not to understand—having held a meeting with her health advisory team at which she assumed she would simply revive her plan in the 104th Congress. "This wasn't a person who acted like she's given up," a doctor present at the meeting reported. "This is not a dead issue."

Whatever the Clintons believed, however, her plan *was* dead.

Amid the national lamentations there were, inevitably, doomsday prognostications about its likely effect on the Democratic Party's performance in the November elections. But before Dee Dee Myers could try to pin the defeat of health care reform on Republican obstructionism, the Democrats in Congress and the White House found themselves completely outflanked. On Tuesday, September 27, 1994—one day after the final, official announcement of the death of health care reform in the 103rd Congress—Newt Gingrich launched his SCUD missile. Standing on the steps of the Capitol's West Front beneath a vast banner rippling in the late summer breeze, and accompanied by a brass band, Congressman Gingrich stepped forward to face the banks of assembled cameras. He was there, he declared, to make a solemn promise to the nation, along with no fewer than 375 other congressional and would-be congressional signatories. The American welfare state was over; the era of opportunity was about to unfold. And to kick it off, the signatories were putting their names to a sort of Bill of Rights for Conservatives—a "Contract With America"—based on ten bills that Republicans would present in the House of Representatives, if they defeated the Democrats in November 1994:

1. Balanced budget, including line-item veto.

2. Anti-crime package, including effective death penalty.

3. Banning welfare to teenage mothers, and instituting "two-years-and-out" welfare provision, with work requirement.

4. Family reinforcement, including stronger child pornography laws.

5. $500-per-child family tax credit, and repeal of marriage-tax penalty.

6. Increase in defense funding, no U.S. troops to serve under UN command.

7. Raise in Social Security earning limit for older people.

8. Job creation incentives and capital gains tax cuts to help small businesses.

9. Legal reform, placing limit on unreasonable damages, curtailment of "endless tide of litigation," and enacting "loser pays" legislation.

10. Term limits to replace career politicians with citizen legislators.

The legislative program was, as Gingrich later admitted, poorly received by the press, and soon trashed by the White House. But—as the House Republican Party whip knew from a prior, four-day flight around the country—it was exactly, emphatically what Republican candidates and voters had longed for: a blueprint for the neo-Reaganite future: a renewed "morning in America."

CHAPTER FORTY-THREE

MIDTERM MELTDOWN

The President Doesn't Stand for Anything

Without a new manifesto of their own, or a centralized, national-agenda approach to the midterm elections, the Democrats now found themselves helpless to defend their party against Gingrich's onslaught. Panicking, they fired a series of Patriot-style missiles to intercept, and if possible shoot down, Gingrich's ten SCUDs. The president's closest tactical advisers—Stephanopoulos, James Carville, and Panetta's policy deputy, Harold Ickes—quickly coined the term "Contract *on* America," but the moniker didn't stick. Nor did the battery of statements they issued, ridiculing Gingrich's faulty math and pie-in-the-sky promises. As Clinton traveled around the country following the death of health care, he realized the Patriots weren't working. Gingrich had done his homework, and the SCUDs were reaching their targets, unscathed.

Anxiously, Hillary called their old pollster, Republican Dick Morris, asking him to speak to the president and conduct a secret poll on their behalf. "I'm not satisfied that I know how to handle what the Republicans are doing to me," the president explained to Morris. "I'm not getting the advice I need."

Morris, who was at that moment working to elect two Republican governors and re-elect two other Republicans in the race to reclaim Congress, was a politician's dream consultant: a hired gun with a near genius for conducting and reading polls, who would fire in whatever direction he was ordered. He agreed to help—immediately contacting some eight hundred voters across the nation, and asking them to respond to questions that the president personally reviewed in a two-hour session—a session that surprised Morris, who'd assumed the president would be too preoccupied with affairs of state to micromanage his own poll.

Morris was wrong (as he had been in advising Clinton not to invade Haiti). To the arch-pollster's astonishment the president "lovingly detailed each of his achievements" he wanted Morris to insert in his survey questions, "citing to the nearest thousand the number of jobs that had been created while he served as president, the amount by which the deficit had been reduced, the number of trade agreements that had been signed, the amount by which the default rate on student loans had dropped and the collection rate on child support judgments had risen." Even Morris was shocked, however, when he tabulated the results.

"Voters believed that the president had not accomplished much," Morris reported, "and didn't stand for anything." This was alarming. In such circumstances, did it make sense for Clinton's aides to go on shooting at Gingrich's SCUD missiles? Should they not swiftly draw up a positive, counter-manifesto?

If the public, according to Morris, was ignorant of the achievements of the Clinton administration, could those achievements not become the core of a Democratic manifesto? Clinton himself was all for a massive new campaign to persuade the public of the wonderful things he had achieved in his administration—especially raising employment levels, tackling the deficit, improving trade.

Morris shook his head. It was, he argued, too late. Clinton was caught in the same nexus as his predecessor, George Bush, who had counseled patience as the recession bottomed out, maintaining that good things were on the way—while all the time the Democratic presidential nominee, Governor Bill Clinton, had lacerated Bush's record.

Now, in the selfsame position as President Bush had been, Bill Clinton wanted to boast of his macro-economic success—rising exports, more jobs, declining deficit, lower interest rates—while ignoring the fact that most ordinary voters hadn't had time to feel the effects of such success in their own lives.

The president was "in deep, deep trouble"—yet the deepest trouble was that he refused to believe Morris's poll. What, the president asked Morris, did respondents say "when we tell them we've created millions of jobs and cut the deficit for two years in a row? They can't deny that. It's a fact."

Morris could only laugh. The situation was similar to the one in which he'd been asked by Clinton to poll a representative sample of Arkansas voters to see if they would vote for Hillary as governor, if he divorced her in 1990 and did not run again; Clinton refused to believe the results of Morris's survey, and insisted upon rewriting the questions—with even *worse* results! Morris thus told him it was fatuous. There was no hope of changing people's perceptions about macroeconomics at this late stage: "This is about the economy that's right in front of them. If they don't agree that you've created jobs or they believe you shouldn't get the credit, you'll never convince them otherwise. Never. It's a total waste of money to try." The president should, instead, stress his small but visible achievements, and be as calm as possible: patient, positive, presidential. Above all, with a strange, almost vengeful mood towards traditional Democratic incumbents across the country, the president should stay away from the campaign trail, in an election that wasn't his to win, only to lose.

Carter II

As Morris noted, Bill Clinton was incapable of sitting still, however. He was, and had always been, a multi-tasker. Even when speaking to him on the telephone, Morris would know that the president was simultaneously speed-reading the newspaper or doing the *New York Times* crossword puzzle. To ask him to confine himself to presidential activity and contentment, while only reminding people of the small but worthwhile achievements of the past two years, was not in Clinton's nature. Nor was it acceptable to the liberal members of his White House cohort, who urged him to put on his armor and do battle against the barbarians, now assembling at the gates of Rome.

True to form, however, Bill Clinton tried to please both those who wanted him to be presidential and those who wanted him to be a political warrior—spending about half the remaining six weeks pursuing international initiatives as president of the United States, and the rest rooting passionately for individual Democratic candidates in the upcoming election. Thus when Saddam Hussein massed his armies on the border of Kuwait, once again, President Clinton ordered the immediate deployment of thirty-six thousand U.S. troops to Kuwait, backed by an aircraft carrier battle group and fighter planes, with Tomahawk missiles targeted on Iraq—forcing Saddam Hussein to withdraw within days, and the Iraqi parliament to formally recognize Kuwait's sovereignty and borders. Thereupon President Clinton immediately flew off to offer campaign help in Florida, where Hillary's carpetbagging brother Hugh Rodham was standing for the U.S. Senate. After that the Clintons flew back to Washington, proceeding the next morning on the campaign trail to New Mexico. It was aboard Air Force One, campaigning early on October 17, 1994, in fact, that President Clinton heard by phone directly from King Hussein of Jordan and Prime Minister Yitzhak Rabin of Israel. After a year of intense, largely secret negotiations, their two countries had agreed on a historic peace accord, the ceremonial signing of which would take place the following week, on October 26, 1994, at the remote Araba Crossing on the border of the two nations—a ceremony they hoped the president would attend.

Even if this was Carter II, Bill Clinton felt it was worth it, in terms of world peace. He agreed to go. In the meantime, however, he continued to crisscross the nation, fundraising and speechmaking on behalf of Democratic candidates and his administration's wonderful record—in New York and then Boston on October 19, back to Washington for another breakfast fundraiser for Hillary's brother Hugh, then off to San Francisco, then to Seattle, and from there to Cleveland, before returning to D.C. to pack for the flight to Egypt, on October 25.

Enemies on the Warpath

From Cairo, where the president met with President Mubarak and the chairman of the Palestine Liberation Organization, Yasser Arafat, on October 26, the president and first lady flew to Jordan for the Israel-Jordan Treaty of Peace signing, then to Damascus to see President Assad, and from there to Tel Aviv, where he saw Prime Minister Rabin at the King David Hotel—ironically, the very hotel that Rabin's colleague, Menachem Begin, had in 1946 blown up while masquerading as an Arab and using explosives concealed in milk churns, murdering ninety-one people.

Palestine was a melting pot not only of religions, but of ironies. War upon war since 1948 had established, challenged, and then extended the borders of Israel, transforming the Muslim inhabitants of the region into refugees, while hundreds of thousands of Jewish refugees and immigrants drawn from across the world occupied their erstwhile land, houses, and orchards. It had become an intractable, impossible situation: a tinderbox in the heartlands of the three largest monotheistic religions of the world, and one that could re-ignite again at any moment. Not even President Reagan, despite his tough stance towards the Soviet Union, had been able to make a difference in the region. Using American carrot and more carrot, President Clinton was nevertheless determined to extend the Oslo Accords of 1993 into further normalization of relations between Israel and its Arab neighbors—assuring security in the Middle East. "Here at the first of many crossing points to be open," he remarked in his speech at Araba, the future of the region would be rehearsed. "There are resources to be found in the desert, minerals to be drawn from the sea, water to be separated from salt and used to fertilize the fields. Here where slaves in ancient times were forced to take their chisels to the stone, the Earth, as the Koran says, will stir and swell and bring forth life. The desert, as Isaiah prophesied, shall rejoice and blossom. Here your people will drink water from the same well and savor together the fruit of the vine. As you seize this moment, be assured that you will redeem every life sacrificed along the long road that brought us to this day. You will take the hatred out of hearts, and you will pass to your children a peace for generations."

Moved by the president's sympathy for both sides in the Middle Eastern imbroglio, many wept. Indeed, in the chilly capital of Sweden, Prime Minister Rabin, his foreign minister, Shimon Peres, and the Palestinian leader, Yasser Arafat, would all share the Nobel Peace Prize that winter. But for Bill Clinton, president of the United States, there would be no prize for peacemaking, nor for his moving rhetoric of reconciliation. Flying back to Washington from Kuwait and Saudi Arabia at the end of October 1994, the president realized he had fostered growing peace in the Middle East, but had failed to achieve it at home. His enemies were on the warpath—and were taking no prisoners, least of all the Man from Hope.

Drinking from the Cup

A hundred members of Congress appealed to the president to campaign in their states and districts in the days running up to the election. But should he agree—and would it even help? Yet again Morris warned Clinton, if he did so, not to claim premature credit for ending the recession, because too few had seen the benefits in their personal lives and communities. Better, in Morris's view, that Clinton should point away from the big domestic issues, given that there were big failures such as health care reform, and highlight his smaller but real achievements. Apart from that, he should now stand aside and act presidential, using his increasing popularity and approval rating after Haiti, Iraq, and the Jordan-Israel peace agreement to take a more Olympian stance in the White House. "Your ratings are up because they don't see you as a politician," Morris pointed out, in perhaps the most profound advice he ever gave Bill Clinton; "the voters see you as president. Now if you start campaigning again, you'll become a politician again."

But the president wouldn't listen. He was still feeling "battered" by his defeat on health care reform, and was determined to drink from the cup of public attention. Day by day Morris would watch with fascination and a sinking heart as the rise in the president's approval rating, following his trip to Jordan, began to falter and lose momentum. It was like gazing at a July 4 rocket reaching its zenith and exploding—and its fading starburst starting to fall. "This babykissing, handshaking, hamburger-eating politician was not the president who had led the Middle East to peace the week before," Morris noted. "As the president dipped," moreover, "so did his candidates."

Tax Cut Fever

Polls now pointed to catastrophic Democratic meltdown in November, as Republican voters got with Gingrich's program but Democrats offered no competing program to get with. Increasingly, Democratic voters decided to stay at home, even to vote against their Democratic governors, senators, and congressmen as a mark of their displeasure over gridlock.

"Tax cut fever is sweeping state capitals across the country," the *Washington Post* reported—even if the Republicans were vague about how to pay for such largesse while balancing the budget, as they claimed to be anxious to do, and increasing military spending.

Clinton's advisers remained in wolfpack mode—Laura Tyson, chair of the president's Council of Economic Advisers, having quickly denounced Gingrich's Contract as "Voodoo Two." The chair of the House Budget Committee, Congressman Martin Sabo, mocked it as "a riverboat gamble," while others painted Gingrich's 376 signatories as the "Stepford candidates"—robots in the service of the man with the "melon head and the Cheshire cat smile."

To ridicule Gingrich and his revolutionaries, however, proved a fatal misjudgment. While journalists and commentators sneered at Gingrich's statistics as "warmed-over Reaganomics," they could not overlook polls that showed a massive shift taking place across the nation: a shift that Gingrich seemed to be tapping into but that Clinton's party was not. Gingrich had, moreover, dropped school prayer and anti-abortion from his Contract, so the final document avoided two of his party's most contentious moral issues and allowed the popular Christian conservatism of the South to line up, silently, alongside the patrician, socially liberal Republicanism of the Northeast for the first time since Reagan. "Clinton is in such trouble with the American people that our job is to go out and offer a clear, positive alternative," Gingrich declared—pounding his familiar drum as in a Pueblo Indian turtle dance: that it was "impossible to maintain American civilization with twelve-year-olds having babies, fifteen-year-olds killing each other, seventeen-year-olds dying of AIDS and eighteen-year-olds getting diplomas they can't even read."

The lament of the chair of the House Rules Committee, Joseph Moakley, that Gingrich's Contract would cut important programs and jobs, sounded all too lame after forty years of Democratic control of the House, as did his assertion that "government has a very strong function—to take care of the people, particularly those least able to take care of themselves." The government *did* have such a duty—but such statements didn't excite voters in the fall of 1994. "Every item in our contract is supported by 60 percent of the American people," Gingrich boasted—and polls confirmed his claim. As Dick Williams, a television news director, noted in the *Atlanta Journal and Constitution*, "They laugh, they scoff, they offer a Bronx cheer, but the national Democrats know Rep. Newt Gingrich and the Republicans are on to something." The Democratic Party "could not produce such a document today, or at least one so detailed. Its disparate wings would collapse into each other, just as they did with health-care reform." Moreover, Williams pointed out that "some 60 million families would benefit. Almost 5 million would be lifted from all federal taxes. A middle-class family earning $40,000 would see its tax bill cut by 10 percent." The Contract was, in Williams's view, "a powerful medicine for so many ailments. The GOP deserves credit for putting it on the table. The scoffers do so at their own peril."

Gingrich's Hour Comes

The scoffing would continue to the bitter end. Meanwhile, pollsters looked with awe as the indicators swung more and more decisively towards the Republicans. Gingrich had counted on winning an extra twenty to thirty seats in the House, which would place the Republicans in a position to win control in 1996. Despite widespread ridicule by the "Praetorian Guard" (as Gingrich termed them) of the Washington press—fed and victualled by the White House—the omens suggested that he might *already* be on the way to becoming Speaker: empowered to preside over a "Gingrich Era."

Esquire magazine might jeer at "General Gingrich," and *The New Yorker* dump on the "representative from Madderthanhell," but it was the voters who would decide, Gingrich knew. "The chances are two in five" of winning the House, Gingrich had commented on October 18. "If we get thirty seats, we'll be close enough to a majority to get a few Democrats to switch" when tackling congressional business, in the following Congress. As the last days before the election went by, however, such predictions seemed altogether too modest. Gingrich's hour, it was apparent, had come. His own boss, Bob Michel, was openly skeptical about the viability of the Contract, but Michel was retiring from politics and out of the loop; the Contract was nothing short of a stroke of political genius at such a moment: a rallying call for Republicans that had left the Democrats spluttering and moaning, and with no counter-document. By the first week in November, Newton Leroy Gingrich was on the cover of *Time*.

Four days before the election, Dick Morris warned the president he was going to lose the Senate and the House.

"Not the House, no way," Clinton responded.

"*And* the House," Morris emphasized. "And by significant margins."

THE FUNK

CHAPTER FORTY-FOUR

AT THE CROSSROADS

A Republican Avalanche

"No way, no way, not the House. Not the House. You're wrong. You really think so? You're wrong," the president had said of his Republican pollster's prediction. The sheer magnitude of the Republican victory in 1994 stunned him and the White House—"a full-blown disaster," as the first lady described it. Clinton himself later lamented, "On November 8, we got the living day-lights beat out of us, losing eight senate seats and fifty-four House seats, the largest defeat since 1946; Gingrich had proved a better politician than I was."

At state level, too, the conservative sweep was a veritable tsunami: Re-publicans won thirty of the nation's fifty governorships (up from nineteen), their first gubernatorial plurality in the United States for almost a quarter of a century. Even within state legislatures, Republicans would now boast a plurality of controlling majorities in America: forty-eight legislative houses under Republican control across the nation, against the Democrats' forty-seven.

Many famous politicians were felled. Mario Cuomo, once considered the Democratic Party's brightest star, was voted out after long and distin-guished service as Democratic governor of New York; Tom Foley, the Dem-ocratic House Speaker, lost his seat, as did the indicted Dan Rostenkowski of Chicago, chair of the Ways and Means Committee. Popular Democratic governor Ann Richards of Texas lost to the former president's son, George W. Bush. Moreover, not a single Republican incumbent governor, senator, or congressman lost his or her seat. With Senator Richard Shelby of Al-abama switching to the Republican side (or tide), the Republicans would hold 53 Senate seats. In the House of Representatives they would hold 227—clear and decisive majorities.

What to Do?

Who was to blame? The Democratic Party? Low turnout? The president? The first lady?

Most observers blamed the president. David Gergen, who had asked to leave the administration prior to the midterm elections, put the matter harshly: "a negative referendum on the Clinton presidency."

Even Democratic pundits assumed that the forty-second president was now washed up—a "lame duck" who would be swept out of the White House at or before the end of his first term, like his Democratic predecessor, Jimmy Carter.

The atmosphere in the White House was, as Hillary later described, "funereal." She wondered how much she herself was responsible "for the debacle: whether we had lost the election over health care; whether I had gambled on the country's acceptance of my active role and lost." She also puzzled, in retrospect, over why she seemed to have become such a "lightning rod for people's anger"—indeed, in a specially convened meeting of her ten top female colleagues, nicknamed "The Chix," who had been summoned to the refurbished Map Room on the first floor of the Presidential Residence, she broke down. "Fighting back tears, my voice cracking, I poured out apologies," she later recalled.

Dick Morris, speaking to Hillary on the phone, found her for the first time in his experience depressed, rudderless, and confused. "I don't know how to handle this," she confided to him. "Everything I do seems not to work. Nothing goes right, I just don't know what to do."

The President Explodes

Writing his memoirs ten years after the event, Bill Clinton saw himself as a superactivist, a political leader who had run ahead of his country, just as he'd run ahead of his state in 1980. "I had forgotten the searing lesson of my 1980 loss: you can have good policy without good politics, but you can't give the people good government without both." By poor politics, however, he understood poor political communication: that he'd failed to ensure that "the people" knew of all his good deeds. "I felt much as I did when I was defeated for reelection as governor in 1980: I had done a lot of good, but no one knew it."

This was a true representation of his defeat neither in 1980 nor in 1994. Moreover, it gave no indication of his angry response, in the White House.

"I was present with him at the first meeting to evaluate what happened," remembered Henry Cisneros, the housing secretary. "And he was the maddest I have ever seen him. And somebody—I think it was Panetta—dared to suggest that it was at least partially his fault. And he said, 'God damn it, I've worked my ass off! You treat me like a damn dog! Like a mule! You trot me out every day, and all I'm doing is what you're *telling* me to do! And if you're telling me it's my fault, then it's *your* fault, because you're the ones who're putting me out there, exhausting me, spending all my time. . . . I never have time to think, I never have time to reflect, I never have time to strategize—you just treat me like a pack mule!' I mean, he *exploded*!"

George Stephanopoulos bit his tongue, knowing how the White House staff had been unable to *stop* Clinton from campaigning, instead of being presidential. "He crisscrossed the country to raise money for the party, and appeared at rallies and fund-raisers for any Senate candidate who would have him," Stephanopoulos recalled.

Oblivious of the real reasons for the Democratic catastrophe, Bill Clinton was determined that more heads would have to roll on his communications team: his "spin machine." He had always found the business of dismissal too hateful to undertake himself, however—which put him in an even angrier state.

David Gergen, by letter of resignation, had already gone. Dee Dee Myers was slated to go at the end of the year, after Panetta had cut her a face-saving deal. Possibly Stephanopoulos, also, would have to be ditched. "I never should have brought anyone under forty into the White House," the president was overheard complaining in the corridors of the White House—yet for the moment he held off firing the young aide who had, after all, helped him catch the public mood and triumph in 1992.

But was it really a matter of communication? On his own insistent volition Clinton had "communicated" his message and his achievements until he was hoarse—on the stump, before cameras, into microphones, in interviews, one-on-one. Articulately and almost *ad nauseam* he had pointed out his administration's accomplishments to all who would listen—and many who wouldn't. His presidential papers, when bound and published, would encompass more "communication" speeches in the course of his first two years than the "Great Communicator" himself, President Reagan. His State of the Union addresses were probably the best ever given by a president in the twentieth century. His town hall-style question-and-answer sessions would become as classic as JFK's press conferences in the history of the presidency. His interviews with television and print reporters numbered in the hundreds. No man, it had to be said, was a better "communicator" than Bill Clinton.

To the extent that the midterm election was a referendum on Clinton's presidency, then, the result was not, arguably, a critique of Clinton's communication skills. Rather, it was a criticism of the president's perceived incompetence behind such high rhetoric. As the *Boston Globe* had reported in late October, "In many races, Republicans are having the most success in tying their Democratic opponents to Clinton, with the most popular device being a commercial in which a Democrat, via computer imagery, 'morphs,' or is transformed, into the president."

The morphing advertisements naturally took their "toll on Clinton's psyche," Stephanopoulos later recounted. Not unnaturally the president was appalled at being caricatured as "a cardboard cutout of myself." Yet he stalwartly resisted the clear reasons for the cardboard: that he was still perceived by most people as well-meaning but weak, ineffective, and verbose —dogged by scandal, as well as incapable of prioritizing legislation he wished to see passed by Congress, and driving it through.

Unacknowledged by Bill Clinton was a very real problem, then: namely the extent to which, after arousing public expectations by charismatic prepresidential performances on the campaign trail, he had failed to show himself a strong president, or to deliver on his much-vaunted health care reform, once he'd prematurely announced it. By deliberately surrounding himself with mediocrity, especially in the chief of staff's position, lest his own role be overshadowed, had he not, with the best of intentions and the best command of rhetoric, proven the least effective commander in the White House since World War II, and compounded his own executive failure? Moreover, what specific vision of the future had he offered voters, after the defeat of his health care reform proposal?

Almost every member of Congress associated with Bill Clinton and his chaotic presidency had been wounded or felled in the midterm election, even the Speaker of the House of Representatives—the first time such a thing had happened since the Civil War. It was small wonder that Congressman Newt

Gingrich, basking in the glow of his imminent role as Speaker of the 104th Congress, third in line to the presidency, gloried at his good fortune.

The morning after the election, on November 9, the president therefore called his Republican strategist—early. "You were right," Clinton admitted to Morris. "You saw I gave your statement," he added, referring to the announcement Morris had faxed him, three days before the "avalanche" that Morris had predicted.

It was the closest Bill Clinton could come to an apology for ridiculing his pollster's warning. It was followed by something close to a sigh. "What should I do?"

Wishy-washy

For a start, Morris instantly made clear, Hillary would have to be dumped as co-president. Unfortunately this was the toughest of all realities for the president to face up to. In Bill Clinton's eyes Hillary could do no wrong. "President Clinton never, ever criticizes Hillary in public or in private," Morris later noted. "He criticizes himself all the time and goes after everyone else when he's angry. But he never says a negative thing about his wife. This is a strength and a blind spot, but it's how he is."

To some, such deference was a rather endearing trait—the loyalty of a supersmart son and surprisingly feminine husband to the strong women in his life. James Morgan, who had ghosted Virginia Kelly's autobiography, *Leading With My Heart*, before her death, had often reflected on how *masculine* Virginia was: decisive, risk-taking, swaggering. She'd earned her own livelihood all her adult life as a nurse anesthetist, had been bigamously deceived by one husband, physically abused by another; had seen one of her sons taken away to prison, the other become the president of the United States. She adored nightclubs, makeup, dancing, glitz—and had remained fond of the thrill of horseracing and betting, despite all the money she'd squandered over the years at Oaklawn, in Hot Springs, to the very end. "A race track," she'd stitched on one of her needlepoints, "is a place where windows clean people." In her own, completely different, somewhat standoffish way, Hillary, too, was a fighter: resolute, also an only daughter, also trying to break the glass ceiling men had erected to contain her gender.

As Morris explained to the president, however, the polls he'd taken demonstrated that, far from providing great value as a "two-for-one" presidency for American voters, the president's homage to his supersmart wife had proved an electoral disaster in office. The president and first lady were "locked in a sort of zero-sum game," Morris recounted his conversation later. "The more powerful she seemed, the weaker he seemed. The voters who protested Hillary's power, telling our pollsters, 'Who elected her?' were the same ones who five minutes later described the president as 'weak, wishy-washy, ineffective.'"

A struggle over Hillary's role in her husband's presidency now began, and continued for many weeks. To her intimate "Chix" Hillary initially declared she wanted no further political position in the Clinton administration—but this did not translate into surrendering her co-presidential role within the White House, whatever Morris might argue. News of a "bitter row between President Clinton and his wife, Hillary," spilling over at a top-level White House staff meeting soon leaked. "Reports said the first lady 'blew her top' in a row that has been raging in private since the poll. Mr. Clinton, now seen as a lame-duck president, has indicated he may well lean to the right in backstage compromise deals with the Republicans, who now control both the Senate and Congress. But Mrs. Clinton, a diehard liberal, virtually called her husband a 'traitor to his principles' in an open political split which shocked some senior staff."

The spat mirrored, in its way, the argument raging within the Democratic Party, in the wake of electoral defeat. "Leading Democrats are openly declaring that Mr. Clinton must be dumped if the party has any chance of keeping control of the White House at the next presidential election in two years' time," newspapers announced. If that was the case, the president pondered, was it better to go down fighting—or float with the incoming Republican tide?

Though Bill Clinton would never admit it, it was the very fact that he had lost his first great fight with Gingrich, the political pirate, the mutinous Fletcher Christian of America's *Bounty*, that most rankled in Bill Clinton's competitive heart. For in truth his own destination, in terms of national prosperity and policy reform, was in many respects the same as Newt's—it was command of the vessel that had proved wanting! How, then, was he to wrest control of the ship of state from the eager hands of the new mate? Or should he actually bother—trusting that Newt, who would inevitably struggle to maintain order among the disparate elements of his own new mutinous crew, would end up on the shoals?

Panetta had counseled the president to take a passive-defensive approach, assuring him that Gingrich and the Republicans were likely to overreach. What if the ship *didn't* founder, however? What if Newt proved himself a competent mate, while Captain Clinton locked himself in his cabin? What if Newt's new, direct course proved successful, moreover, and the Northwest Passage navigable—allowing Republicans to claim ownership of that centrist territory? Would Clinton then be removed by the electorate in November 1996, perhaps even by his own party in the presidential primaries?

It was small wonder the president slept badly, and that Hillary worried for him. Others did, too—especially when the incoming new chairman of the Senate Foreign Relations Committee, Republican senator Jesse Helms, labeled the president not only a political failure but "unfit" to command the armed services of the United States as commander-in-chief!

A Portent of Things to Come

Senator Helms, an arch-protectionist, boasted a long record of bashing communist, ex-communist, Third World, and other governments. In a recent letter to the president, Helms had asked President Clinton to delay a vote on the General Agreement on Tariffs and Trade (GATT) pact until the next year—when he planned to eviscerate it.

The president was aghast. An agreement between 123 countries, GATT had taken twelve years to negotiate, and any changes would kill it—as Helms knew. "If you will agree to this," Helms nevertheless assured the president, "I can assure you that it will have an exceedingly positive effect on my making certain that the administration's position on all foreign policy matters during the 104th Congress will be considered fairly and fully."

The president had resolutely ignored such political blackmail, and had flown to the Philippines and Indonesia for a long-planned meeting of the leaders of APEC, the eighteen-member group of Asia-Pacific Economic Cooperation nations—thereby enraging Helms, the son of a police chief, to the point of open spite. In an interview on CNN's *Evans and Novak* program, the North Carolina senator, infamous for his angry-white-male Christian fundamentalist racism, now derided the president's foreign policy in Haiti, Russia, the Middle East, and elsewhere. Asked if he thought Clinton had demonstrated an ability to command the U.S. military during the two years he had held the presidency, the arch-conservative responded, on camera: "You ask an honest question, I'll give you an honest answer. No, I do not. And neither do the people in the armed forces."

Evans and Novak blinked—then pressed the senator to name someone in the armed forces who claimed Clinton was not competent to be their commander in chief. Helms sneered. "Well, for openers," he began, "just about every military man who writes to me." He added that those who agreed with him included active-duty officers—including some of *general*'s rank. Did any of those generals include members of the Joint Chiefs of Staff? Helms pursed his lips. "No comment," he said, smirking.

No comment? As news of Helms's challenge to the absent president spread, alarms sounded across the capital. Even some of Helms's colleagues in the Senate were concerned. Was this treason? Senator Chris Dodd, in whose state, Connecticut, nuclear submarines were constructed and immense amounts of war material were produced, was quoted saying that Mr. Helms's "very, very reckless" comments amounted to "aiding and abetting insubordination" in the military.

General William J. Taylor, a former army commander and senior vice president at the Center for Strategic and International Studies, pointed out that "Bill Clinton is still our president. He is still our commander in chief. If you want to go after the policies or the planning, fine. But to go public and to say our president is not fit to be the commander in chief, I take great exception to that. This man is our president. This nation must have a national security policy and strategy, and we should not try to undercut it for domestic political reasons."

Patrick Glynn, former diplomat in the Reagan administration and a scholar at the American Enterprise Institute, was almost disbelieving that a soon-to-be chairman of the Senate Foreign Relations Committee could be so outspoken. "That's a mistake. You may dislike Clinton, you may hate Clinton. But he is the commander in chief, and there is a real limit as to how far you want to go to weaken a president. He still has to conduct foreign policy. He still may have to order troops into battle."

A shudder of revulsion seemed to go through Washington. General John Shalikashvili, the chairman of the Joint Chiefs of Staff, decided to wade into battle for his commander in chief—who was still abroad. Shalikashvili personally telephoned senior newspaper journalists from the Pentagon to assert his confidence in the president, emphatically denying any impression people might get that the military leadership of the United States was endorsing Senator Helms's assertion. "I was taken aback by the implication that [Helms] left that somehow the Joint Chiefs of Staff and I shared his view on President Clinton," declared the four-star general, who had headed the Joint Chiefs for thirteen months. "Nothing could be further from the truth." To another journalist he slammed Helms's diatribe in greater detail. "I do not share that view. I have been with the president in difficult deliberations and have always found him able to understand the issues, ask the tough questions, and make the hard decisions. He always has given me the opportunity to air my views. I feel very satisfied with my relationship with the president." The general also issued a written statement on behalf of his colleagues, carried by all national and international news agencies, saying, "President Clinton is our commander in chief. He has and will continue to have the loyalty and full support of the Joint Chiefs of Staff."

Even Senator Bob Dole, the Senate majority leader-elect, was moved to turn against Helms, his fellow Republican, in favor of his Democratic commander-in-chief. "I had some reservations early on," Senator Dole said on ABC's *This Week With David Brinkley*, "but I think he's up to the job now."

As his travel clothes were unpacked and put away for him at the White House, on his accelerated return from the Far East, the president not only breathed a sigh of relief, but saw that Panetta was right to be optimistic. The Republicans had overreached, *already*. God might yet be on his side. As Bill Clinton he might be hated by some, and disrespected by the majority of his countrymen (according to the latest poll data), but he was, in the end, the president of the United States of America. He'd reached rock bottom—and could only rise, now, in public estimation, if he played his cards right.

CHAPTER FORTY-FIVE

WOOING THE DLC

The Essence of the Modern Presidency

By raising the matter of President Clinton's fitness to command America's military forces in a post-Soviet world, Senator Helms had drawn public attention to the president's foreign policy record—a record that, after a shaky start, had, as Senator Dole conceded, improved beyond all recognition. The latest Asian trade agreement in Indonesia, following Clinton's decision to go into Haiti, and a U.S. decision to authorize NATO air attacks on Serbian forces attacking UN-protected Muslim enclaves, gave hope that the president was at last finding his presidential feet, not simply as commander-in-chief but as a world leader.

If the president was, by contrast, unable to control Congress over domestic legislation, was that necessarily a bad thing? some pundits asked. Presidential scholars had argued from the founding of the United States that the separation of powers between the White House and the Capitol was a central feature of American democracy, in contrast to monarchical tyranny. Had not Harry Truman, a Democrat, proved an unexpectedly great president after control of Congress passed to the Republicans in 1944? Were not European presidents from France to Finland charged primarily with foreign affairs, while a prime minister dealt with domestic policy?

"I'm wondering in the light of this meeting," a reporter had asked at the APEC meeting in Indonesia, "and the other meetings you've had previously to this, if it's not perhaps beginning to seem to you that perhaps foreign affairs and foreign trade is really the essence of the modern presidency, more so than domestic . . . ?"

The president winced. No American president could be elected, or re-elected, solely on his record for foreign trade and foreign affairs: indeed, in an expanding global economy in which the United States was still the world's linchpin, the irony was that the majority of American voters had less and less interest in foreign affairs—including the president's affairs. President Bush had lasted but a single term because of his relative neglect of domestic issues.

To be re-elected, President Clinton knew, he *must* cater to that domestic, inward-looking constituency, however much he was hated by gun-toting segments of it. He had raised taxes on the wealthy, he had been damned by Republican candidates and spinmeisters in the midterm campaign, and he had lost control of Congress, to be sure. After forty years in the wilderness, Republicans had now been called to show their ability to manage congressional power, rather than caviling from the sidelines—but already, even before the January handover in Congress, they'd shown that they could be as hard to unite as Democrats had been. Why, Helms's boil had been easily lanced, without Clinton's needing to be in town! Even the threatened Republican opposition to GATT faded away, after the snuffing of Helms's treason. Attempting to trivialize GATT as something of which only 2 percent of Americans were aware merely made the seventy-three-year-old senator look silly, as Republican economists and business leaders across the nation asserted how crucial was GATT for America's finally re-burgeoning economy. Newt Gingrich, as a former interdisciplinary geography professor, expressed himself 100 percent in favor of GATT; Bob Dole, who had sat on the fence for some time over the issue, now came down on the side of the president, and of bipartisanship.

On the night of December 1, 1994, GATT was formally ratified by the Senate, in one of the last votes of the outgoing 103rd Congress. President Clinton had won out—proving himself, after Haiti, not only the nation's commander-in-chief but its trade promoter-in-chief.

A Secret Meeting

In a secret meeting in the White House's Treaty Room, Dick Morris now urged the president to embrace Gingrich's Republican agenda—even instancing the way President Mitterand, a committed socialist, had considered it to be the will of the people when Jacques Chirac won the parliamentary elections in France and became prime minister. Mitterand had responded by pushing Chirac's privatization agenda even faster than Chirac had himself intended. With that, Morris gave Clinton a five-point memorandum on how to be president of the United States.

Clinton read through the points, and disagreed with none. But all five were *tactical* methods. They didn't actually address the problem of definition: who is Bill Clinton—and what does he really stand for?

Here, Morris's advice was deficient. For all his strategic and tactical brilliance, Morris saw the challenge ahead simply as one of personality—the notion that William Jefferson Clinton was capable of becoming "a great president" if only he could learn to exploit and maximize the skills in which he was "uniquely qualified," ruthlessly shedding his liberal image in order, quite literally, to "redefine the job of president" and then show his presiding genius for "compromise, reconciliation, values and healing."

Nowhere in Morris' prescription was there mention of a Democratic team or teamwork. Indeed, there was no mention of the Democratic Party, period. Did Morris really expect the president to abandon the party that had nominated him in New York in July 1992—and would have to renominate him if he was to run for re-election in 1996? What if his party then turned against him? What if it labeled him a renegade, and put up its own alternative candidate or candidates in the '96 primaries? What if Al Gore, who was gifted with a fine mind and great executive skills, chose to run against him on behalf of the Democratic Party? Gore's Harvard mentor had once assured Governor Clinton, when he was selecting a vice presidential candidate in 1992, that Senator Gore was incapable of disloyalty. But would a Gore defection not be seen as *higher* loyalty to his party, if Clinton abandoned it?

In the end Clinton dismissed the fear of a Gore defection, as well as the threat from other possible Democratic rivals, since, ironically, the midterm rout he'd caused had removed most of his potential rivals for the 1996 Democratic crown. Dead and severely wounded Democratic bodies littered the political battlefield. In particular, Cuomo's defeat in New York had vaporized the one Democratic politician whose possible candidacy Clinton had desperately feared in 1992.

What, then, of the New Democrats? Could *they* form up and field a challenger against the incumbent president, if Bill Clinton "went native" and became, to all intents and purposes, an independent? Eyeing the tenth anniversary of the founding of the Democratic Leadership Council, Bill Clinton looked into his own soul, wondering if he could provide an answer. For if he could swing the DLC behind him, he instinctively felt, he would have a chance of reenergizing the entire Democratic vote in America, just as he had done in 1992.

The Heart of an Old Democrat

The omens for DLC support at first looked poor. Congressman Dave Mc-Curdy, chairman of the Democratic Leadership Council, had recently been quoted saying Bill Clinton was but "a transitional figure"—a politician who had cost Democratic moderates all credibility, after they'd worked so hard and for an entire decade to release the party from its liberal moorings. "While Bill Clinton has the mind of a new Democrat," McCurdy declared in public, "he retains the heart of an old Democrat. The result is an administration that has pursued elements of a moderate and liberal agenda at the same time, to the great confusion of the American people."

Other DLC members felt likewise. Of the nearly $40 million the Democratic party had raised, Senator Dianne Feinstein of California reminded her DLC colleagues, most had been "spent to promote the health care plan and to hire consultants." Failure of Hillary's overcomplicated, overambitious health care plan had meant, however, that all the consultant spinners in the world could not have rescued the Democratic Party at the midterm election, despite a raft of positive legislation that had passed. Feinstein herself had narrowly beaten the Republican millionaire Michael Huffington in California in one of the year's most volatile races, but the senator was now devastatingly frank about the mess. Democracy vested political power in the hands of the people's representatives via the ballot box—and woe betide those politicians who then ignored their ballots. "We Democrats listened to the 15 percent of the people who had no coverage," Feinstein remarked bluntly. "Republicans listened to the 85 percent of the people who had coverage." The Democrats must move further to the center, she felt—or have their center stolen by Gingrich's Republicans.

The president a "transitional figure"? The president even *expendable*? Such criticisms sounded harsh, only two years into President Clinton's first term. Along with Senator Feinstein's condemnation of Hillary's approach to health care reform, the criticisms were painful—yet in truth also music to Clinton's ear. He had himself been a founding father of the DLC, and the *center*, not the left wing, was where he *wanted* to be. Straightaway the president telephoned to invite half a dozen of the most senior DLC leaders to meet him personally in the White House to gauge their temper—and at the DLC anniversary gala held in the Sheraton Washington ballroom on December 6, 1994, he gave his first spirited speech in public, one month after the midterm disaster.

A Slip and Not a Fall

"You know, I was trying to think of what I ought to say here tonight," the president began. "They gave me some remarks at the office. I didn't like them, so I wrote some down," he explained—and thereupon the president launched into what attendees felt was the best, most classic extemporaneous Clinton speech he had ever given.

It was time, Clinton knew, to "get over it," and "get it on." Starting his analysis of the midterm Democratic defeat, he told two symbolic stories. The first was of a self-made millionaire from New York who is struck by lightning when he retires, and complains to God at the unfairness. "How could you do this to me?" the millionaire asks God. "Oh, Jake, I'm sorry," God apologizes, "I didn't recognize you."

The ballroom erupted in laughter. "So maybe, you know, there was a little bit of that in this election," the president commented—voters not actually recognizing how much had been done by the Democratic-controlled Congress and new administration on their behalf. The second story was more bittersweet. It concerned an old couple, married for over fifty years, rocking one night on the porch. The husband lists the way his wife has loyally stood by him throughout the many travails that have befallen him during their married life. Concurring, she accepts his gratitude. Finally he adds: "Well, before it's too late, I want to say one thing to you." The president paused. "Sarah, you're bad luck."

Again, the audience erupted—thinking not only of the public's rejection of congressional Democrats, but of Hillary.

Before he addressed the problems facing the nation the president was anxious to warn his audience not to be of faint heart, or to give up. When President Lincoln sustained a defeat, he pointed out, "he said that it hurt too much to laugh and he was too old to cry, but it was a slip and not a fall."

With this caveat the president wanted, he explained, to begin by talking about "what's really going on in this country. Not about the Democrats and the Republicans and who loses and who wins, but who loses and who wins out in America." He had run for president in 1992 "because my experience as a governor made me believe that you really could roll up your sleeves and reach across party lines and other lines and solve real problems that real people have. I ran because the DLC made me believe that ideas could matter in national politics just like they do in other forms of national endeavor. And when I started this campaign," he added, "nobody but my mother gave me much chance to win.

"I knew that there were many dangers. One is, just taking on tough issues. If they were easy issues, somebody else would have done them because a poll would say it was popular to do so. The second is, if you try to do a lot of things in a short time, you're going to make some mistakes. And I've made my fair share, and I accept that. The third is, that it is easy to be misunderstood in a difficult time when you're a long way from where people live," since your opponents were free to trash and burn you in effigy, without recourse. "Ask Mr. McCurdy and Senator Robb," he said, knowing what defamatory blizzards they had been through. It was all too easy to be "demonized when you're a long way from where people live so that the very people you try hardest to help are those who turn away.

"That's the thing I regret about this election more than anything else," the president lamented. "All the people who are trying to follow the rules and are sick and tired of people benefiting who don't, who take advantage of the system whether they're rich or poor or somewhere in between—those are the folks that the Democratic Party ought to be championing and the ones who ultimately will benefit if we stay on the right course.

"Well, we did a lot of things that they didn't like very much, especially after 'it got explained to them,' as we say at home." And with that, he gave his own explanation of the Democrats' defeat.

"I think I was right when I opposed discrimination and intolerance," Clinton maintained of his gays in the military fiasco, "but a lot of folks thought I was just more concerned about minorities than the problems for the majority.

"I believe we were right when we stood up to the NRA and said we ought to take these military assault weapons off the street. But a long way from the battlegrounds of the inner cities, a lot of folks out in the country said, 'My Lord, I'm paying too much in taxes, I can't hold my job, and now they're coming after my gun. Why won't they let me alone?'

"I believe we were right when we fought to bring this terrible deficit down," the president went on. "Next time you make out your federal income tax check, 28 percent of it is going to pay interest on the debt accumulated in the last twelve years before we took over. So I think we were right to do that.

"And yes, I think we were right to try to find a way to stop health care costs from going up at three times the rate of inflation, to stop people from losing their health care or having it explode if they have a sick kid or if they change jobs; to try to find an affordable way for small business people and self-employed people to buy private health insurance. But by the time it got to the American people, in both cases, it was characterized as 'the Democrats are the party of government and taxes.' And they don't have a lot of faith in government because they're working harder for less, less money. Males in this country without a college degree are making 12 percent less than they were making ten years ago [and] working a longer work week. We are the only country in the world with an advanced economy where the percentage of people with health insurance under sixty-five is lower today than it was ten years ago."

A few days previously, Newt Gingrich had caused headlines by repeating, on NBC's *Meet the Press*, his claim that the Clintons were "counterculture McGovernites," and that "up to a quarter of the White House staff, when they first came in, had used drugs in the last four or five years." Like Senator McCarthy's infamous 205 Communists who were "still working and shaping the policy of the State Department" in 1950, the unverified smear was enough to tip unhappy or suffering people into believing them—the infamous tactic of Goebbels's "Big Lie," or deliberate demonization. "That's why those numbers [of uninsured Americans] don't mean a lot," the president explained. Thanks to the relentless, negative smears of Republican radicals, voters shied away from positive programs—accepting Gingrich's tabloid portrait of current America: " 'My kid could get shot on the way to school. And all my money is going to people who misbehave.' "

No more insightful perception would ever be offered by President Clinton into the praxis of Republican politics at its dirtiest. "Communist," as the catch-all defamatory label of the right, had ultimately been removed from the Republican *ad hominem* arsenal—to be replaced, two generations later, by the label "misbehavior."

"Sometimes," the president reflected, "people make decisions when they are very, very angry, and sometimes those decisions are good. Sometimes they're not so good." It was important not to lose one's head. "One of the first lessons I was ever given at my mama's knee was, 'Count to ten, Bill, before you say something.' I still don't do it all the time, and every time I don't, I'm sorry.

"There is no prescription for a perfect world in a difficult time of change where every election works out and everybody is happy. But we've got to let these folks know that we heard them, because they're the very people that I ran as president to help."

The need to listen and heed the people's message had been the president's concern since the awful magnitude of the Democratic defeat had become clear. "I do think they sent us a message, and I tried to hear it," he'd quickly acknowledged to reporters. "They don't want the presumption to be that people in Washington know what's best," he'd acknowledged. Nevertheless voters did want "the government to protect their interest, promote their values, I think, and to empower them. And then they want people held accountable. So I'm saying that, to that extent, that message—I got it. I accept responsibility for not delivering. To whatever extent it's my fault that we haven't delivered back to the American people what they want on that, I have to accept my responsibility."

The fact was, Republicans had had a field day trashing the health care reform bill and other legislative measures involving higher taxation. By their slogans, negative advertising, and cynical travesties of complex reality they had whipped American voters into a punitive mood—as the president recognized. "Now, all my life, ever since I was a little boy, I have seen people like that mistreated, disadvantaged, and then I have seen them inflamed with anger and enraged and taken advantage of," he confided to his DLC audience. It was, he knew, one of the few advantages of coming from a humble home in a poor state, peopled with simple souls—white people who for centuries had vented in racism and bigotry their frustration at their poverty, both financially and in terms of knowledge and education. "So I'm telling you," the president warned his audience, "forget about us. We owe it to them to let them know we heard and we're fighting for them and we're going to deliver." As centrist Democrats they had now to do three things: restate their convictions clearly; restate the positive things they had already done, from deficit reduction to gun control; and thereafter be prepared to "engage with the Republicans in a spirit of genuine partnership and say, 'You have some new ideas. We do, too. Let's have a contest of ideas. But stop all this demonization and get on with the business of helping America to build this country.'"

And to remind his audience of the convictions of New Democrats, he quoted from the New Orleans Declaration of the DLC at its fourth annual conference in 1990, beginning:

> We believe the promise of America is equal opportunity, not equal outcomes.
>
> We believe the Democratic Party's fundamental mission is to expand opportunity, not government.
>
> We believe in the politics of inclusion. Our party has historically been the means by which aspiring Americans from every background have achieved equal rights and full citizenship.
>
> We believe that America must remain energetically engaged in the worldwide struggle for individual liberty, human rights, and prosperity, not retreat from the world.
>
> We believe that the U.S. must maintain a strong and capable defense, which reflects dramatic changes in the world, but which recognizes that the collapse of communism does not mean the end of danger.
>
> We believe that economic growth is the prerequisite to expanding opportunity for everyone. The free market, regulated in the public interest, is the best engine of general prosperity. . . .

Item by item he listed what should have been his "Contract With America," ending:

> We believe in the moral and cultural values that most Americans share: liberty of conscience, individual responsibility, tolerance of difference, the imperative of work, the need for faith, and the importance of family.
>
> Finally we believe that American citizenship entails responsibility as well as rights, and we mean to ask our citizens to give something back to their communities and their country.

Four years after that declaration, Clinton saw no reason to change a word—for the words had been largely his own. "It's just as good as it gets," the president commented. Issue by issue, the president then ran through the New Democratic agenda for the next two years: positive steps in a positive nation. And to cap this recitation, Clinton then issued a challenge to the members of the DLC. "We always talk about what other people's responsibilities are. What's *your* responsibility?" he asked. "It's to join me in the arena," he admonished, in a phrase that made headlines, "not in the peanut gallery." The midterm disaster and the tough debate with New Republicans had been, the president noted, a "great period of change. But let me tell you something, folks, this is a very great country. We can stand this conflict. This can be good for us. It can be good for our party, but more importantly it can be good for the American people. Never forget that it is no accident that it was the United States that was asked to be involved in putting an end to all this conflict that's gone on for centuries in Northern Ireland, the United States was asked to stand up to aggression in the Gulf or work on peace in the Middle East or restore democracy to Haiti. We are committed to the rest of the world," he pointed out, "but we should see ourselves sometimes a little more the way they see us. This is a very great country.

"The responsibility we have is not to win elections, it is to fight for the people about whom elections are fought. If we fight for them and their children, then the elections will take care of themselves. And if they don't, we'll still be doing what's right. That's my commitment, and it ought to be yours."

As the president sat down to thunderous applause, the DLC chairman was heard to exclaim: "That's the Bill Clinton we've been waiting for!"

Dump Bill

President Clinton mounted the steps of the White House walking on air. Outgoing senator David Boren had been reported saying the president should give "serious consideration" to not seeking re-election. Surviving Democratic members of Congress were complaining that their own political survival in 1996 might be jeopardized by having Clinton on the ticket. A "Dump Bill" campaign had been launched in the *New York Post*. And as if this was not enough, there was a new Times-Mirror poll writing the president off as a political cripple, with more than two-thirds of Democrats in the survey wishing to see other candidates challenge him for the Democratic nomination. The applause Bill Clinton won on the night of December 6, 1994, before the members of the DLC, was more significant, however, than any poll.

With barbarians at the gates of the Capitol—and more Gingrichites swarming towards it—the DLC members had had little alternative but to cheer their own president, Clinton judged, for, after "an awful lot of meetings and thinking" over the past month, as Leon Panetta put it, the president had "ended up, not surprisingly, where he started his presidency": reclaiming the center, where the DLC wanted him to be. Ergo, they must support him—not as a transitional figure, but as the *only* figure who could keep the White House in Democratic hands: his own.

That the president had proved less than an able chief executive was unfortunate. That he had failed to create and manage a team that gave the public confidence in the Democratic administration was sad. But he was, in the end, the party's star performer, and they would have to forgive him his failings, in deference to his larger strengths: his impressive grasp of global economics, his brilliant rhetorical skills, his sheer optimism about America and its future. With the DLC's backing in the bag the president was confident he could lead the Democratic Party out of its slough of despond. However, the biggest challenge of all, he knew, would be dealing with the "madderthanhell" Speaker, Newton Leroy Gingrich.

CHAPTER FORTY-SIX

IN THE TIGER'S DEN

Gingrich: A Psychodrama in Progress

If psychologists saw President Clinton as a complex specimen of abused, half-orphan, fatherless split personality, his new nemesis, the Speaker-to-be, was a veritable psychodrama in progress.

On Friday, December 2, 1994, Clinton had invited the majority leader-to-be of the Senate, Bob Dole, and the Speaker-to-be of the House, Congressman Newt Gingrich, to the Oval Office. Yet two days later, on NBC's *Meet the Press*, Gingrich had made his accusations that a quarter of the White House personnel took drugs!

The president's chief of staff, Leon Panetta, who'd attended the Clinton-Dole-Gingrich meeting on December 2, was outraged. "He's Speaker of the House of Representatives. Words matter," Panetta declared. As Speaker-to-be, Gingrich was not "just the minority whip in the House of Representatives, he's not the editor of a cheap tabloid, he's not just an out-of-control radio talk show host. He is one of the most powerful politicians in the country, and it's time he started behaving accordingly. As House Speaker, he is second in the line of presidential succession, behind Vice President Al Gore Jr." Gingrich's outrageous assertions about drugs in the White House, without names or evidence, smacked of McCarthyism. "It started with Jesse Helms," Panetta complained, "and now it's Newt Gingrich, in which basically there are reckless charges made, reckless accusations that impugn people's integrity. No evidence, no facts, no foundation, just basically smear and innuendo—the kind of thing that we rejected in this country a long time ago."

Certainly, when he appeared before reporters on December 8, Gingrich had turned himself back into an amiable bullfrog, a model of excited hope and conciliation. "Either I have to close down that part of my personality or I've got to learn to be more careful, more specific, about what I say," he reflected. "I do not think we should ever pick a fight with the president of the United States if it's avoidable." But he added: "I do not think we should shrink from a fight if it's necessary. Had I followed that advice last Sunday, we would've lost three days of news stories and the country might have been better off without it." He was, he confessed, "still too much the assistant professor being analytical and not enough the next Speaker being more careful and more cautious. Yeah, if I had it to say over again, I probably wouldn't say it." Even his own wife, Marianne, had advised him to "be responsible and go slow." With that in mind, he announced, "The president's got to reassemble his team, and I think he's going to work very hard at doing that." And the former assistant professor complimented the former law professor: "He's a terribly smart man." Together, they might achieve great things for the nation. "I think there's a big zone here," he remarked, "where you can have a New Democrat-D.L.C.-Republican coalition passing a lot of very, very interesting and positive things."

Could such a man ever be trusted, though? Given Bill Clinton's nickname "Slick Willie," it was interesting that the public expressed even *less* trust in "Slick Newtie." A *USA TODAY*/CNN/Gallup poll found fewer than one in five viewed Gingrich favorably, while three-quarters of those polled viewed him distinctly unfavorably after his motormouth remarks.

Yet Gingrich's sparring with the president paled beside his spat with the first lady.

Orphanages

Hillary Clinton loathed Gingrich—and as the Republicans gabbed about all they proposed to do in their first hundred days in power in Congress, she had found it impossible to resist belittling him. Talking to the New York Women's Agenda, a non-profit coalition, at the end of November, she had declared Gingrich's intention of building orphanages to reduce welfare rolls ridiculous. Any reform of welfare, she said, would have to address training, child care, and health needs, which "have to be met unless we want to see literally thousands . . . of people on our streets and face the unbelievable and absurd idea of putting children into orphanages."

"Unbelievable" and "absurd" were soon headlines across the country. Gingrich, on *Meet the Press*, lashed back. There were over half a million American children already living in foster homes, with a further eighty thousand already in emergency or long-term institutional facilities. "I'd ask her to go to Blockbuster and rent the Mickey Rooney movie about Boys Town," he remarked. "I don't understand liberals who live in enclaves of safety who say, 'Oh, this would be a terrible thing. Look at the Norman Rockwell family that would break up.' The fact is we are allowing a brutalization and a degradation of children in this country. We say to a thirteen-year-old drug addict who is pregnant, you know, 'Put your baby in a dumpster, that's OK, but we're not going to give you a boarding school.'" And as actual examples Gingrich mentioned specific Chicago boys who, he said, would have been better off in a home like the one in the movie. Eric Morse, a five-year-old, had recently been dropped to his death from a fourteenth-floor window of a public housing project by two older children— who were angry at him for refusing to steal candy for them. The other, Robert Sandifer, an eleven-year-old murder suspect, had been shot in the head, allegedly in an execution by two fellow adolescent gang members.

Deliberately using such stories to peddle simplistic, ignorant social solutions was sickening, but, as commentators pointed out, the sight of the plucky but self-righteous first lady baiting the off-the-wall "bomb-thrower" of Congress was an unedifying spectacle, too, as Gingrich prepared to don the robes of Speaker of the House of Representatives—the very place in which any lingering hope of resurrecting a less ambitious health care reform bill was vested.

Why did Hillary do it? Frustration? Disappointment? The White House, nervous about the implications for the relationship between the president and Congress, quickly pointed out that the first lady had spoken as a private citizen—no longer the president's spokesperson on health care reform, indeed any reform.

Hillary—who'd heard, to her fury, that Gingrich "regularly referred to me as a 'bitch'"—was even pressed to kiss and make up. Dutifully she sent the Speaker a handwritten note inviting Dr. Gingrich and his family for a tour of the White House and then tea. Along with his wife, Marianne, his sister, Susan, and his mother, Kit, Congressman Gingrich came. While they sipped from porcelain cups in the Red Room, according to Hillary, Gingrich looked at the period furniture and "began pontificating about American history. His wife soon interrupted him," Hillary recalled. "'You know, he will go on and on, whether he knows what he's talking about or not,'" Marianne said. Gingrich's mother, however, refused to kow-tow to the first lady. "'Newty is a historian,'" Kit Gingrich said. "'Newty *always* knows what he's talking about.'"

Even a decade later the memory still rankled Hillary Clinton. As a feminist and as a Democrat Hillary found Newt Gingrich irritating. And as an enemy of her own Ideal Husband, he was even more irritating. Hillary's idealization of her husband's genius—and derision for any other woman's idealization of a husband or son—was at once touchingly loyal and comic, in view of the risks the president took in his own behavior. "Shaking hands with Bill Clinton is, in and of itself, a full-body sexual experience, I promise you," the shocked novelist Judith Krantz remarked, in a phrase that was soon syndicated nationally. "He has the sexiest handshake of any man that I have ever experienced in my life." For Hillary this was par for the course—but woe betide any man or woman who challenged, let alone belittled, her husband on political matters!

Touched by his wife's forgiveness of his flirtatious signals, and by her combativeness towards his enemies, the president found himself more and more re-energized. Hillary had contented herself with taking tea with the Speaker-elect, but Bill Clinton had an even bolder strategy in mind, indelicately termed by his secret political consultant as "getting into bed with the Republicans."

CHAPTER FORTY-SEVEN

VEERING RIGHT

The Task of Dismissal

As the president drew up his confidential strategy for co-option and co-operation with the new Republican majority in Congress, there would have to be casualties, Dick Morris pointed out. For one thing, the president would have to discard those who disagreed with, or attempted to block, the new course. Yet firing people had, since the time he became governor of Arkansas, been Bill Clinton's worst nightmare. The task of dismissal had therefore always been assigned either to Hillary, to Betsey Wright, or to someone else.

Aware of this, Morris pointed out that the casualty list of the Clinton administration had already become, since the inauguration, an almost unending hemorrhage. It comprised, indeed, a veritable ABC of former F.O.B.s—Altman, Aspin, Espy, Foster, Gergen, Hubbell, Kennedy, Myers, Paster, Watkins—and there were more resignations in the pipeline, including that of the treasury secretary, Lloyd Bentsen. The secretary of state, Warren Christopher, had already tendered his formal resignation on Clinton's return from Indonesia, while the director of the CIA, James Woolsey, was also teetering on the brink of departure. (He would resign before the end of the year and vote for Clinton's opponent in the 1996 election.) Yet still Clinton seemed incapable of actually *firing* an employee.

Morris's advice did, however, sink in. As Clinton prepared himself for his new bipartisan partnership, he also readied himself, at Morris's urging, to show more symbolic backbone, in order to placate barbarian Republicans and traditional Democrats. Haiti had proved—to Morris's own surprise—

an impressive and popular example of Clinton's potential for leadership as commander-in-chief. It was time, Morris felt, that Bill Clinton also showed himself to be a real chief executive, capable of running the vast White House and administration staff with a firmer hand—to start firing people, not just having them resign under his faltering command.

It was not long before the first opportunity for such a symbolic dismissal came: the surgeon general of the United States.

A Sop to the Republican Wolves

Dr. Joycelyn Elders, though grudgingly approved by the Senate as surgeon general of the United States in the fall of 1993, had always been controversial among members of the Christian Coalition, who had deluged the Senate with objections to her confirmation. Such protesters had deplored the prominent Arkansas pediatrician's views on sex education, prophylactics—and, above all, on abortion.

In the struggle to prevent teenage pregnancy and sexually transmitted diseases, Dr. Elders had often found herself infuriated by the obstructionism of abortion rights opponents who, she once said sarcastically, "love little babies as long as they are in someone else's uterus." Such fundamentalists needed to face the reality of poverty, sexuality, crime, and the sheer numbers of unwanted pregnancies among young people in America, she felt—particularly in poor black and Hispanic communities. Rather than gratifying themselves in a "love affair with the fetus" they should actually involve themselves in helping the poor through education and work with teenagers. Tirelessly she pointed out that she was not in favor of abortion. "My ideas have been about *preventing* pregnancy," she emphasized—especially via the use of prophylactics. "The best way to prevent abortion is to prevent unwanted pregnancy," she insisted—but was then accused by Catholics of being the "Condom Queen," encouraging degeneracy. In near despair about concealment of sexual abuse by Catholic clergymen at the same time as the Roman Catholic church set its face against prophylactics, Dr. Elders had scorned the church publicly as "a celibate male hierarchy." A devout Baptist churchgoer, she'd counter-accused religious conservatives, referring to them as "the un-Christian religious right," and had accused them of "selling our children out in the name of religion."

Having an intimate knowledge of poverty in the South, as well as the bigotry of the Bible Belt, President Clinton had great empathy with Dr. Elders.

His own maternal grandparents, after all, had come from rural poverty; his grandmother Edie had been an auxiliary in-home nurse, and his mother had been a hospital nurse anesthetist all her working life. His relationship with Dr. Elders as his director of health services in Arkansas had sometimes been stormy—"Now I know how Abraham Lincoln felt when he met Harriet Beecher Stowe," the president had once remarked when introducing her, quoting Lincoln's legendary words "This is the little lady who started the great war"—but he genuinely admired the sharecropper's daughter from the hamlet of Schaal for her pioneering work on health clinics and education in schools. Her pilot scheme at Lakeview High School, in the heart of the Mississippi delta, for example, had reduced teenage pregnancy there to zero. She had even been asked to become a member of President Bush's committee on health care reform. But with Republicans baying for Democratic blood, her days were now numbered.

On December 9, 1994, the surgeon general was summoned to the office of Donna Shalala, secretary of Health and Human Services.

"Did you say masturbation ought to be taught in schools?" Secretary Shalala demanded.

Dr. Elders could hardly believe her ears. At a UN conference on AIDS more than a week before, Dr. Rob Clark, a psychologist, had asked Dr. Elders, in a panel discussion, whether, as part of the process of breaking down taboos on the discussion of sex so that the epidemic in Africa— where 50 percent of AIDS transmission was via heterosexuals—could be stemmed, there ought to be more discussion of masturbation as an aid to abstinence. Dr Elders had merely concurred. "I think that is something that is a part of human sexuality, and it's a part of something that perhaps should be taught. But we've not even taught our children the very basics," she said, "and I feel that we have tried ignorance for a very long time, and it's time we try education."

Dr. Elders's general but qualified concurrence had gone unremarked by the media present, but Donna Shalala had had an assistant there, reporting back to her. Whether the subsequent professional elimination was rigged or not, *U.S. News & World Report* was given the story—and nine days later Secretary Shalala had the pleasure of cutting adrift her surgeon general (and assistant deputy secretary), who had criticized the administration's health care reform plan. By the time Dr. Elders got back to her own office, the president's chief of staff was calling her. "Dr. Elders, I don't believe we can stand any more of these remarks," Leon Panetta declared. "They're just not acceptable. I want to have your resignation on my desk by two-thirty."

Dr. Elders refused to resign, however, unless the president personally ordered her to do so. She was thus trebly shocked when the phone rang again. Friends had begun to tell her they had heard of her resignation on the radio—the now accepted method of Clinton administration corpsing.

"Joycelyn, I'm sorry this is all happening," the president told her on the phone from Florida. "But I hear there are all these remarks going on, and we can't have them. I want you to get your resignation into Panetta's office this afternoon."

"Mr. President. Do you know what I said?" Dr. Elders asked, disbelieving.

The president *had* heard—at least the version given by Secretary Shalala's office. But as part of his McCarthyite barb on NBC's *Meet the Press* on December 4, the Speaker-elect had specifically targeted Dr. Elders, by name, as an example of administration officials whose views were out of step with those of mainstream America. The surgeon general, Gingrich explained, "has basically taken positions that are not just anti-Catholic but, in effect, represent an attitude toward permissive sexuality that by any reasonable standards in a middle-class sense is destructive. . . . [You] ask yourself, why does the president keep her? I assume he shares her values. I assume he thinks it's okay."

Tarred with the bombthrower's tabloid brush, Dr. Elders had been put on notice, and the president on the defensive. Five days after Gingrich's assertion, moreover, the masturbation remark looked a cut-and-dried case. "Yes, they told me," the president responded to Dr. Elder's question. "I'm sorry, we've just got so many things, and I'm sorry."

And that was the end of Surgeon General Elders—discarded from the United States Government to atone for the health care reform failures of her colleagues; to placate the anti-prophylactic, anti-abortion, un-Christian Coalition lions crying for her blood; to silence the loose-tongued, vitriolic propagandist preparing to take the Speaker's chair in Congress; and to stave off the demise of the president of the United States of America.

A dozen years later, the secretary-general of the UN would be appealing for *$22 billion* to counter the ever-proliferating spread of AIDS in Africa—the illness having "spread further, faster and with more catastrophic long-term effects than any other disease," thanks to the fact it had taken "the world far too long to wake up" to the pandemic.

Dr. Elders *had* warned—but far from being lauded for her medical foresight, the first black American surgeon general would go down in modern American history not for her prophetic concern over AIDS, but for having supposedly advocated "the teaching of masturbation in schools." With a heavy heart Dr. Elders had returned, that cruel December, to the University of Arkansas Medical School in Little Rock as a professor of pediatric endocrinology. Looking out across her modest tree-shaded lawn in later years, she would think back upon her saga, however: recognizing the larger context in which she had become the sacrificial lamb of a struggling administration, following its disastrous midterm election results. "I never got the impression that the president was too interested necessarily in medicine," she explained, candidly. "I think, though, he really wanted to get universal health care *for the country*. Well, that would be almost like getting a civil rights bill passed, or getting Social Security passed, or workmen's comp! You know, it would be a big thing that would be there forever."

Despite the failure of health care reform and the machinations of Donna Shalala as health secretary, "I really felt that the president supported me. And I still feel that he did. But I feel that things had gotten so he felt that I was causing. . . . "

Dr Elders paused. "His whole administration was shaking. I was kind of their hatchet-boy, the bull's-eye target [of the un-Christian right], so it was easier to let me go."

Giving Ignorance One More Chance

Conservative groups expressed elation at the news of their victory over the surgeon general. "This is the wisest decision President Clinton has made in two years," declared Beverly LaHaye, president of Concerned Women for America, a Washington-based conservative women's organization. Senator Don Nickles of Oklahoma, who had spearheaded Republican opposition to Elders's nomination in the Senate, announced in a statement that he, too, was "pleased" to learn of Dr. Elders's resignation, and called for the next surgeon general nominee to be "someone who reflects mainstream American values."

Liberals across America, however, saw in Dr. Elders's departure the writing on the political wall—and got the sad message. "This outspoken woman is out," Ellen Goodman wrote elegiacally, "guilty of the one unforgivable political act. Joycelyn Elders practiced unsafe speech."

Other Democrats, however, warned that the president's new appeasement policy would not satisfy the Republicans. "Bill Clinton could have flogged Joycelyn Elders with a rattan cane in prime time before demanding her resignation as surgeon general last week," Eric Zorn wrote in a syndicated column, "and even then—even then—not won over any Republicans. These people mistrust, dislike, and in many cases actively hate the president. I doubt even Nixon inspired the sort of dismissive contempt that dogs Clinton, and his stand against the very mention of masturbation in the context of public health and education isn't going to diminish it, by even one of whatever the units are by which we measure contempt (Borks?)." James Lileks, another columnist, was even more damning. "There's only one thing Bill Clinton has left to do—switch parties and become a Republican." Not only defect but "publicly admit that the only reason he's a Democrat is because it's the only way you get dates in college."

Humor was, for such disappointed spectators of Bill Clinton's about-face, almost the only recourse. Climbing on the anti-sexual-permissiveness bandwagon was, given President Clinton's own rich sexual history— "a man whose libidometer long ago zoomed into the red zone," as the journalist Patricia Smith put it—the height of hypocrisy. "Obviously," Smith wrote, "the Prez believes we should give ignorance one more chance."

Reading such fulminations by hitherto stalwart Democratic supporters, Bill Clinton could not but be hurt. He and his chief of staff claimed that the dismissal of the surgeon general was not "politically motivated," but Clinton knew that wasn't true. As Leon Panetta was heard to say, had Dr. Elders not resigned, "she would have been terminated."

The fact was, as foreign correspondents could see perhaps more clearly than their American colleagues, the Christian mullahs were massing in the South and Midwest. Secular East and West Coast liberals were left with an unappetizing choice: to go down fighting honorably, or to find a way to disarm the fundamentalists.

The president's conundrum was therefore emblematic of his time. Once before he had found himself in such a situation, when Ronald Reagan won the presidential election and immersed the country in Republican anti-tax, anti-government, anti-regulation rhetoric, making the communitarian tasks of a small-state governor like Bill Clinton immeasurably more difficult— especially when the rhetoric came wrapped patriotically in an American flag. Ominously, Newt Gingrich was a self-confessed neo-Reaganite—and would shortly rule the House of Representatives, with a more conservative agenda than even Reagan had promoted.

The Best Hope for America

Whether principled or unprincipled, Bill Clinton had the most sensitive antenna to political change in the whole of the United States. Had he sensed that the country was moving in an overall more liberal direction—as polls indicated Great Britain was doing, after almost two decades of Conservative government—Bill Clinton would happily have shifted to the left, a direction that embodied his "Boy Scout," communitarian idealism, as Dick Morris observed: the desire to do good, and be applauded for doing good. But the country, Clinton knew, was still moving to the right. Who knew what madmen lurked in the wings, behind Newt Gingrich's tabloid banner, or what damage they might do to American democracy if they were not cauterized? By bestriding the middle ground and embracing his own and Newt Gingrich's centrist vision of incentives, opportunity, strength, and firmness, he would, he hoped, slow or even halt the national slide towards Republicanism—at least in its more extreme forms.

Two years in the White House had taught the president many lessons, from the danger of making his wife his co-president to the need for a tough chief of staff, better liaison with Congress, and more attention to foreign affairs in his role as a world leader. He could take comfort, however, in having proved himself a successful steward of the American economy—which looked set for another boom. He had successfully guarded against Russian backlash over the potential expansion of democracy and NATO in eastern Europe; he had courageously revitalized the Northern Ireland peace process; had pressed hard for an Israeli-Palestinian settlement; had re-applied the UN-mandated tourniquet on Saddam Hussein in Iraq; had got the Serb siege of Sarajevo lifted and, introducing the U.S. directly into European negotiations for an ultimate Bosnian peace accord, had obtained a current cease-fire by threatening to abandon the Bosnian arms embargo and to enlist European consent for a more muscular NATO air approach to Serb military cleansing in Bosnia. He had promoted an extraordinary acceleration of global free trade expansion, from NAFTA to APEC, GATT, and the Summit of the Americas. And all the while cutting America's national deficit by an amazing $300 billion already. Could any Republican president do better for his country—let alone an alternative Democrat?

As 1994 came to an end, then, however much invective was aimed at him by disappointed liberal pundits, Bill Clinton had reason to feel bruised but not bowed.

The Republican tide could, the president felt sure, be ridden out. He had been forced to cut his surgeon general adrift, thanks to Donna Shalala, the right-wing trash machine, and the advance of the white, reincarnated-KKK fundamentalists—but that was, in the larger clash of cultures in America, a small sacrifice to make in saving the country from religious, right-wing ideologuery, such as was being practiced in Iran.

For himself, as president, he would be like a surfer, riding his board beneath the surging crest of the Big One. Right-wing Republicans might yearn to topple him, as the emblem of sixties "McGovernick" counterculture, but they would not catch him. He was smarter than they were, more politically adept, and more able to inhabit this centrist identity. Moreover, Bill Clinton had wit and the words to go with it: words with which to ensure that the debate over America's future was not framed in over-simplistic Republican gobbledynewt.

In short, for all his failings as the chief executive, President Bill Clinton was, in his own view, the best hope for America—backed by the best possible vice president, a tough new chief of staff, and two years still to run before his own job would be on the line.

BOOK TWO

PARADISE REGAINED

A COMEBACK FELLOW

CHAPTER FORTY-EIGHT

A PRESIDENT'S EPIPHANY

Soul Struggle

In a New Year's press interview with the president, reporters had begun by quoting a recent comment about there being a "struggle for the soul of Bill Clinton." At this the president jabbed the air with his long index finger. "This idea that there's some battle for my soul is the biggest bunch of hooey I ever saw," he retorted. "I know who I am; I know what I believe."

Gone, suddenly, was any sign of malaise or the self-pity that had marked the president's mood since November 1994. Yes, he had conducted, as they knew, marathon sessions to determine why the Democrats had lost Congress; had called hundreds of friends, advisers, and even adversaries: listening, apologizing, blaming, ruing. But now, it seemed, his mind was made up. He was amazed, he said, that people questioned whether he had core beliefs, or claimed that he had not fought for them. Had he not confronted—and beaten—the NRA over the Brady Bill, and brought about an assault weapons ban for the next *ten years*? Had he not tackled the national deficit *head on*? Pushed successfully (against all prognostications) for NAFTA, and imposed a major new *tax on the rich*? Tried with might and main to get *universal health care* coverage? Were these not signs of courage and conviction?

They were—but that was not, Bill Clinton knew, the real question in journalists' minds. No one claimed he was not an activist president. What they questioned was where the activist would go, now that his party had been hammered at the polls and in light of the fact that the new Speaker-to-be of the House was *also* an activist. Would the president roll over, would he fight

Gingrich—or would he "move to the center," as "unidentified sources" in the administration were suggesting?

"Well, let's stop right there," Clinton countered. "I think the American people are confused by all these anonymous quotes. I think everybody ought to have to be quoted by name."

Caught out, the journalists could name no one, and admitted that without anonymous sources there would be no stories. "But more of what you wrote would be *true*," the president admonished them. "What are you talking about—more to the center?" he demanded, and, without waiting for an answer, told them his intention. "What I'm trying to do is move forward and cooperate with the Republicans where I can. My strategy will be to stop this debate between left, right, and center, and to talk about synthesizing the debate. I'm kind of looking forward to it," he claimed.

The president spoke with absolute sincerity—looking as if he'd had a blood transfusion.

In a Very Good Humor

Morris might be right, Bill Clinton mused afterwards. Perhaps it was possible that he could become a great president. He had the charisma. He had the positive energy. He had the high intelligence. He had the sheer love of the political process. Moreover, he had experienced what increasingly seemed like an epiphany.

The United States was *not* Great Britain, where the prime minister is *ipso facto* the premier of Parliament, the master of the House of Commons, the star of the government. This was the United States, a nation where Congress had been constitutionally created to fulfill one function, the president another. As the president made clear to emissaries from the fourth estate, his period of grief and mourning was now officially over. He was not moving to the center so much as deciding what was important to him and to the people—the people who looked to him for presidential leadership, not legislative ability. He wasn't angry with the journalists for asking rude questions about his core beliefs. The pain was past. "I'm actually in a very good humor about this now," he explained to two interviewers from *Newsweek*. "It bothered me like crazy for a while, and then I realized the more it worries me, it's a waste of energy. Maybe it's because my so-called New Democrat philosophy has some liberal elements. Most thinking people, particularly the older they get, have liberal convictions *and* conservative convictions."

It was a simple insight, yet an important one. Bill Clinton's center was not a geopolitical position, cynically located by survey polls in order to appeal to the most voters. It was, rather, a place where Bill Clinton, born in humble circumstances in Hope, Arkansas, but exposed to the realities of a larger world, felt most comfortable as a citizen, a father, a husband, a brother, an educated man within a democratic society: a place in which progressive and conservative ideas mixed; a place in which optimism, energy, responsibility, compassion, and curiosity coexisted. "The Democrats," the president philosophized, "need to focus on rebuilding the middle class and restoring the sense of community, that we're not divided up—"

He paused, thinking of how, despite their triumph in the midterm elections, Republicans were undoubtedly masking a schism in their own church: one that might doom them in the next presidential election. To beat Republicans, Democrats needed to avoid the split between "angry white men, for example," and the various gender, ethnic, and other minority interests—a schism promoted by men like Rush Limbaugh and a hundred other loudmouth radio hosts polluting the American airwaves, decrying the iniquity of affirmative action, while in self-satisfied, evangelical white flight they hypocritically separated themselves socially, politically, economically, and geographically "from ethnics."

Bill Clinton would have cause to add "angry white women" such as Ann Coulter (one of the egregious Richard Scaife's "elves," soon chosen to spread venom about Clinton in the media). For the moment, however, the president found himself surprisingly at peace as he flew with Hillary to join their daughter at Hilton Head for the annual Renaissance Weekend—after which he was to be spirited away to Arkansas to spend time with Hillary's mother and southern friends he'd acquired over a lifetime.

The trip away from Washington did the president good. At home he went duck hunting, visited his dying patron, former senator Fulbright, and opened a new school named William Jefferson Clinton Elementary—complete with library named in honor of Hillary, plus a visitors' room named after his mother, Virginia. Even so, he found it hard to relax. Restored to confidence in himself, he was raring now to go, to get back in the race: the presidential race.

Despite his prominent newspaper interviews, neither the press nor the majority of political observers in Washington seemed aware of what was taking place: that, far from losing more sleep over the problem of governing

America without a Democratic majority in either the Senate or the House of Representatives, Bill Clinton was already preparing for the next election: *his* election.

Excellent News

Two days after Christmas, on December 27, 1994, Clinton had quietly met for breakfast with Terry McAuliffe, the fundraising head of the Democratic National Committee. He had been assured McAuliffe could raise some $25 million for the 1996 presidential campaign in no time and without difficulty—for the ominous victory of the Republicans in the midterm election would now make Democratic donors only more anxious to support their embattled prince, McAuliffe predicted. This was excellent news.

Three days later, behind closed doors, Clinton had met, in even greater secrecy, with his version of Nancy Reagan's astrologers: four self-help gurus with national reputations—Anthony Robbins, Marianne Williamson, Stephen Covey, and Jean Houston. Had they known, the press would have scoffed—unaware that the president, with the full support of the first lady, was girding his loins for battle, and wanted to be fit physically, mentally— and spiritually. Newt Gingrich was busy preparing his army for the 104th session of Congress, with a goal of driving his Contract through in a hundred days. Included was a provision not only to continue to reduce the deficit they had so recently sought to ignore if it required new taxes, but to bring the federal budget into positive balance: an impossibility without either raising huge taxes or making massive cuts in federal programs. Given the Republican mantra of no new taxes, it would inevitably be the latter: Republican "balancing" done at the cost of the poor.

Such an agenda made the president's blood boil. "In the beginning," he himself would chronicle, the fight seemed likely to "doom my presidency," but that was exactly how he liked it. Nothing raised his adrenalin level like the prospect of political combat in which he could engage his political and campaign skills. Members of the fourth estate were talking Gingrich up as a great general, a Genghis Khan, a Napoleon—but by visualizing Gingrich not as the Speaker of the House but as a potential presidential opponent, Clinton could see what others failed to see: that Newt Gingrich was more akin to Robespierre than Napoleon—at once imaginative and malicious, a revolutionary who would likely overreach himself and eventually be guillotined by his own party.

More likeable and less malicious was the new Senate majority leader, Bob Dole: a past and likely future presidential contender whom Clinton knew in his bones he could beat, despite what current polls predicted (Dole 47 percent, Clinton 37). Dole was as old as former president George Bush, and though an acknowledged master of Senate tactics, no master of the national stump, let alone of modern communications.

The fact was, as Clinton and McAuliffe had concluded at their breakfast, there was neither a Democratic nor a Republican campaign contender in the same electoral ballpark. The only possible challenger who could beat the president was a non-politician: General Colin Powell, who, in a meeting with the president on December 18, had declined to become secretary of state, and whose autobiography was in preparation. Bill Clinton had denied Powell his rightful fifth star; would that make him more likely to run—or less?

There was now less than two years to go, but from this point on, Bill Clinton was determined to make as few mistakes as possible, while backing the initiatives he felt were right for him and right for America, rather than standing for those that were right for his liberal advisers. With the spiritual backing of his self-help gurus, he was determined to get ahead of the game, and stay ahead—especially now that he had his secret weapon, Republican strategist Dick Morris.

In the meantime, Bill Clinton was aware that he needed a major new test that would, like Haiti, help define his presidential character and courage to himself.

CHAPTER FORTY-NINE

MEXICO: THE FIRST CRISIS OF THE TWENTY-FIRST CENTURY

Contagion

On the night of January 10, 1995, Bob Rubin brought his deputy Larry Summers from the Treasury building to the Oval Office. Ostensibly they were there for Rubin's swearing-in as the new Treasury secretary, succeeding Lloyd Bentsen. There was, however, another reason: namely to lay before the president the "first crisis of the twenty-first century," as it came to be called: the impending collapse of Mexico's financial system.

Ironically, it was Newt Gingrich who gave the crisis its name—and he was right. Before the decade was out there would be a whole series of potential (and actual) fiscal meltdowns, as countries with massive short-term debt in a global competition for investor funds found themselves unable to repay loans on time. When Summers finished his ten-minute presentation, the president turned to the new Treasury secretary. Rubin said there were risks in essentially bailing out wealthy American and European investors by shoring up the Mexican peso, but that it had to be done to avoid the collapse not only of the United States' new NAFTA partner, but of a model developing-nation economy. Meltdown not only would put back Mexico's economic miracle by five years, but could increase illegal immigration to the U.S. by as much as 30 percent and reduce the growth of the U.S. economy by as much as 1 percent.

George Stephanopoulos queried the amount required from the U.S. government: $25 billion in loans. Surely he meant $25 million?

Without blinking, Summers retorted, "Billion with a B."

The president eased his collar. The talk of consequences—"contagion"—meant what, in non-banking language? Panic selling? A Great Depression in Mexico? The loss of America's third-largest trading partner? And what were the chances of lending the $25 billion and losing it? Would his presidency be on the line if the bailout failed?

Whitewater, with its investment of a few thousand dollars in real estate in western Arkansas almost two decades before, seemed suddenly impossibly trite. Arguing on the sofas and chairs of the Oval Office the fate of millions of Mexican and 700,000 American workers, the crisis had a surreal, almost wartime air.

It was now that the president showed his new spurs. "Is not a patron, my Lord, one who looks with unconcern on a man struggling for life in the water," Dr. Johnson had famously quipped to Lord Chesterfield, who had failed to support the famous literary doctor in his quest to compile the first English dictionary, "and, when he has reached ground, encumbers him with help?" At least President Clinton would not be guilty of *that* kind of patronage. "This is what the American people sent us here to do," he declared—adding that he would not be able to sleep at night if he let Mexico founder.

Rubin, who had witnessed the president's dejection after the midterm election results ("He seemed off stride in a way that I hadn't seen before. . . . He seemed down and a little disorientated") was both surprised and relieved. Here was the commander-in-chief of the U.S. economy, alert to the implications of a Mexican default in a way that not even the bankers of Britain, Japan, and Europe were.

The president walked to his desk, picked up the phone, and asked to speak to Bob Dole, Tom Daschle, Newt Gingrich, and Dick Gephardt. He was now as incisive as LBJ at the height of his powers—and, as a result, all of them assured the president they would support him in getting the loan guarantee—raised to $40 billion to ensure that it worked—through Congress.

"Often, when I've heard criticism of Bill Clinton as indecisive or driven by politics rather than policy," Rubin later wrote, "I've remembered and cited that night as a response." The president had been at his best: utterly and determinedly presidential.

Uncivil War

The Mexican war was not won overnight, in the event—for even under its revolutionary House leader the new, Republican-controlled Congress declined to be taken for granted, as individual senators and congressmen assessed the consequences for their own local careers if they supported the president or challenged him.

The chairman of the Senate Banking Committee, Alfonse D'Amato, for example, had expressed initial approval for the Mexico bail-out, but soon backed off. As the chances of congressional support sank, Rubin's Mexico task force—involving even the deputy national security adviser, Sandy Berger—was driven to make history by recommending to the president that they raid the Treasury's ESF: its Exchange Stabilization Fund, reserved for currency intervention, not loans. The president concurred. History would thus be made by executive action, not—to Gingrich's disappointment—by Congress.

For Bill Clinton the Mexican crisis thus became a significant step in his "new" presidency: doing what was right for the nation and in the best interests of peaceful international prosperity. In the Map Room in the basement of the White House he had, only three days before, lamented the demise of civility in a strategy meeting with some of his closest advisers. "This is a cynical age," he'd remarked. "Doing good and right aren't sufficient anymore. Being mean isn't a disqualification anymore."

The Soul of America

The president had been right to contest the notion of there being a battle for the soul of Bill Clinton, for it was becoming as much as anything a battle for the soul of America. In this cultural war the lines were not conventionally drawn, as Reich had long supposed, between the haves and the have-nots, or between the mercenaries of conscience or self-interest. There was, rather, a civil war in progress over what constituted America and American values.

The very freedom of individualism—"making the world free for diversity"—which liberals had propounded and promoted since the 1960s—seemed to have produced an equal and opposite reaction, as in the fourth law of thermodynamics. Once the party of anti-slavery and federal authority, Republicans had, in the wrathful wake of flower-power, stolen the

South—appealing to white Dixiecrat conservatives worshipping in white, not mixed, congregations. Faith, for such adherents, was not a matter of rational opinions, but of blind loyalty and non-negotiable religious conviction—a Christian-American version of Islam. Remarkable in such growing, television-spread evangelical Christian belief was a marginalization of the very tenets of faith that Jesus of Nazareth had brought to modern monotheistic religion: tolerance and compassion. Reich, as a northeastern Jew educated at Dartmouth, Yale, Oxford, and Harvard, had no notion of the increasing power of the Christian Coalition; nor did Robert Rubin, who was also Jewish—as were Larry Summers, Sandy Berger, Roger Altman, and others in the administration. Even Christian political operatives like Stephanopoulos, whose father was a Greek Orthodox priest, were mystified by the punitive madness that had infected much of the nation and had swept the Democrats from power in Congress. "You all have to *help* me," the president had pleaded in the Map Room. "I don't want to use their tactics. I don't want to be *mean*."

But the team had been unable to come up with a strategy for turning that tide—at least, not without co-opting the pulpits of the South. One day, not far into his presidency, Bill Clinton had ruefully told Rubin that his gays-in-the-military disaster was "really going to hurt Democrats in the South for many years to come." Rubin had protested that it was a storm in a teacup and would soon be forgotten. But the boy from Hope knew better. "No, this is going to affect how people look at us for a long, long time," he prophesied. And he was right.

Newt Goes Ballistic

To bail out the Mexican government, avert its looming international loans default, and defend its rapidly depreciating peso through the early months of 1995 until stability was achieved and morbid speculators had been beaten off: this was a noble, courageous, and tenacious presidential decision—one that, in the most curious way, mirrored the president's stoic defense of his wife's honor in the Whitewater investigation, and his determination not to be crushed by the speculators in that protracted affair.

Chief among the speculators was former judge Kenneth Starr, the new Republican independent counsel, who had summarily discarded the preliminary report of his predecessor, Robert Fiske—a report that had discounted serious impropriety on the part of the president or the first lady. Starr had begun all over again—even re-examining the death of Vince Foster, which Fiske had rightly ruled was certain suicide, as a result of depression.

The appointment of Ken Starr had made a mockery of the term "independent counsel," for Starr had actually offered to write an amicus brief supporting Paula Jones's lawsuit against the president, before his own appointment as independent counsel. His indictment of Webb Hubbell, in December 1994, had therefore struck a note of grave alarm in the legal office of the White House, since it was feared Hubbell might, in return for a lesser sentence (for embezzlement unrelated to Whitewater), implicate the first lady in the somewhat contorted legal representation of Jim McDougal's failed savings and loan operation, Madison Guaranty. Hubbell didn't, however—and would pay for it by imprisonment and ruin.

In the wake of the summer '94 hearings in Congress that had caused the resignation of Roger Altman and others for illegally warning the White House what was coming, it was clear that a new variant of McCarthyism was beginning to sweep the land—a McCarthyism that might well accelerate, in the wake of the midterm elections. In lieu of Republican senator Joe McCarthy, the Senate now had Alfonse D'Amato—himself a former mob-related lawyer and associate of the notorious Roy Cohn—ordering his *own* renewed investigation of Foster's death on behalf of the Senate Banking Committee that he henceforth chaired, as well as continuing the investigation of Whitewater. Paula Jones's lawyers were also knocking on the gate—though to the president's immense relief, it was only an appeal, since federal judge Susan Webber Wright had ruled on December 28, 1994, that no *Jones* v. *Clinton* trial could take place until the president left office.

Paula Courts Infamy

In moments of self-doubt Clinton would see himself as presiding in the wrong period of history—"I would have preferred being president during World War II," he lamented one night. "I'm a person out of my time." But such lamentations were ahistorical—imagining an America solidly behind its chief executive, and ignoring Roosevelt's lifelong preparation for such wartime office: his role as undersecretary of the navy in World War I, his struggle with polio, and the Republican hatred inspired by his government actions in addressing the Great Depression.

The truth was, American politics was, and had always been, a cruel sport, whether in office or out, in war or in peace—and wishing it could be more gentlemanly was understandable, but unrealistic. In tyrannies such as North Korea or Saddam Hussein's Iraq, to contest the tyrant's authority was to risk incarceration, torture, and death; in America's democracy, by contrast, to contest the president's authority was to win media attention, big book advances, posses of fellow-travelers—and lawyers such as Ken Starr crowding for business and prominence.

Ross Perot had balked at such a reality, when running for president in 1992, and even President Bush had been relieved to leave it behind with the seals of office once defeated. However, what was important to remember was that, with an unfettered press and no recourse to libel for public figures, the playing field was level. The opponent, however rabid he or she might seem when on the attack, was vulnerable, too.

Paula Jones might be translating her fifteen minutes of fame into many, many hours. She was, however, courting infamy too—and not always in her opponents' camp. Readers of the January 1995 edition of *Penthouse* were thus treated to a Paula Jones very different from the sexually harrassed, diminutive state employee her right-wing lawyers presented. A former lover of hers, a bond trader boyfriend twelve years her senior, had decided he too could climb on Paula's bandwagon—by publishing his record of the affair he'd enjoyed with Paula in the late 1980s, including raunchy nude photographs of Paula at nineteen, together with open postcards from her that he'd kept. "I miss every inch of you," one particular message to him from Paula ran. "But I miss some inches more than others." Paula's own brother-in-law estimated she'd slept with fifteen different men before she was seventeen! Her lawyers' claim of extreme emotional distress and damage to her "reputation," ignominiously suffered as a result of Governor Clinton's unwarranted sexual proposition, was thus rendered deeply questionable, even without the president's redoubtable legal, paralegal, and illegal retaliation squads going into further action.

Paula's challenge was one thing, however. The more serious threat to the president was in Washington, farther up Pennsylvania Avenue, where the unpredictable congressman was raising his Speaker's gavel to begin the 104th Congress of the United States.

CHAPTER FIFTY

DYING BY THE SWORD

The Grinch

For a decade the Speaker's power in the House had steadily been growing, as his fiefdom encompassed not only the bills to be heard, via the Rules Committee, but the naming of chairmen to all House committees, and majority members of those committees. In a recent effort to reinforce this quasi-feudal power, Gingrich had even demanded GOP members sign his Contract before being considered for such posts. Gingrich now not only ended the traditional seniority basis for such appointments but limited each chairman's term to six years, and canceled the use of "proxy" votes of absent committee members. He decided which committees would hear legislation and created his own congressional task forces to report on his chosen Speaker's agendas, such as welfare and balancing the budget. He even claimed the right to control non-elected administrative officials of the House. "Today the House of Representatives will inaugurate a Speaker like none other, with clout unparalleled in recent history and an ego to match," it was reported on January 4, 1995. "Newt Gingrich—the rumpled history professor, futuristic lecturer and power-hungry revolutionary—formally takes office today with a promise to light the fuse on an explosion of Republican change across the country. He wants to do nothing less than dismantle the 'welfare state.'" And as an aside, the reporter noted: "The talk around Washington is he's positioning himself for higher office: the presidency."

Before the sitting president could become too alarmed, however, the missile launcher stepped in front of his own launch—taking him, effectively, out of the race.

Funding for Gingrich's *Renewing American Civilization* lectures had already drawn the attention of the House Ethics Committee. The news, on December 21, 1994, that the Speaker-to-be had then agreed a $4 million— soon revealed to be $4.5 million—book deal with Rupert Murdoch's publishing house, HarperCollins, added new fuel, however, to allegations of corruption. Gingrich's dire predictions of what he and fellow Republicans were planning to do to welfare recipients in the 104th Congress had led to his soubriquet as the "Grinch Who Stole Christmas." That the Speaker should deny the poor their meager handouts was one thing; that Gingrich should enrich himself as Speaker in a sweetheart deal to the tune of millions of dollars was another.

Not surprisingly, Gingrich's book deal became a scandal. Gingrich's ethical naiveté and dissimulation, in a Speaker-to-be, seemed, moreover, breathtaking. Though Gingrich attempted to brush off criticism—"Conservative books sell," he sneered. "I can't help it if liberal books don't sell"— and although his office issued a host of misleading stories and explanations, the Speaker was inexorably forced to fess up. Far from never having met Rupert Murdoch in his life, as he claimed, Gingrich had to admit he'd met Murdoch, in person, only a month before the deal—and in Congress, along with Murdoch's Washington lobbyist. They had had a full twenty minutes of private, unrecorded discussion. Even the assertion that they merely "passed the time of day" and had not talked about anything of substance was found to be a deliberate falsehood, since Murdoch's office admitted they had discussed Murdoch's current difficulties with the Federal Communications Commission. Moreover, the parallel with Murdoch's courting of Margaret Thatcher, and what looked like her multi-million-dollar pay-off for approving his satellite television merger, was uncomfortably close.

The Gingrich Era was getting off to a start more scandalous than Bill Clinton's in 1992—without the president having to lift a finger, let alone the phone. Clinton had nothing to do, indeed, but watch as, day after day, the Speaker was attacked in the House and in the press—and any presidential aspirations he might have had went up in smoke. By the third week in

January 1995 Gingrich was complaining at what appeared to be a concerted Democratic campaign designed to wreck his Contract With America agenda by spotlighting his book deal. "I think a strategy based on the personal destruction of somebody is pretty amazing," Gingrich declared at a press conference, looking battered.

What was more amazing was Gingrich's surprise that his own missiles were backfiring. In the lee of their notorious advertising hit man, Lee Atwater, Republicans had been waging a political war of personal destructions for years. Now they were getting a taste of their own medicine, and didn't appear to like it. "Damn it, every day I'm out there under attack and no one is defending me," Gingrich was heard to whine, in words identical to those of the president the year before. When the Speaker attempted to steamroller a gag order on the subject of his book deal, there was further uproar. Congressman John Dingell rose to his feet and shouted, "This is not the Duma, this is not the Reichstag. This is the house of the people."

As if this were not enough, two days later, at a Republican National Committee luncheon, the Speaker himself lost his head. His de facto chief of staff, Joe Gaylord, and his senior staff had warned him to stick to the political rather than the book contract, but the Robespierre of Congress was simply unable to contain himself. Calling Washington a "sick" place where Democrats and the news media conspired to halt the will of the Republican Party, and with his eyes "narrow in hate, his face moist with sweat from the glare of TV lights," Gingrich denounced the recent "grotesque and disgusting" attacks on his honor. "They will do anything to stop us. They will use any tool. There is no grotesquery, no distortion, no dishonesty too great for them to come after us. . . . I am a genuine revolutionary," he declared. "They are the genuine reactionaries. We are going to change their world," he warned—and, breaking the truce made after Hillary had invited him and his mother to the White House, he said sarcastically that he knew, of course, a number of important Democrats who would, for their part, have turned down advance royalties of $4.5 million without flinching. "They'd have said, 'I can make too much money in cattle futures.'"

Gingrich's invective brought the entire room to its feet in applause—but as the Speaker ranted on, it began to leave a sour taste, sending leakers to the telephones.

Such ranting did the Speaker no good. In the end he was compelled to turn down the entire book advance and accept a mere dollar until the two books were actually written—and sold. "This," James Carville observed, "is the first guy who tried to cash in before he was sworn in."

If You Live by the Sword

For Bill Clinton, so long excoriated, derided, and denounced by Republicans, the media's exposure of the Speaker's financial greed, as well as of his cynical lying, his snarling vituperativeness, and his ultimate climbdown was a welcome relief. As a child Billy Blythe had nightly watched on television the hateful white crowds chanting before Little Rock Central High, threatening injury and even death to the first black students attempting to go to the school. Gingrich was not a racist, but he possessed something Bill Clinton recognized better than anyone in Washington: the same Jekyll and Hyde split personality of so many cultural warriors of the South, alternately gracious and venomous. It was this insight that, while his staff urged him to pound away at the embattled Speaker, allowed the president to hold off and let Gingrich self-destruct. The Speaker might possibly win reelection in his predominantly white congressional district of Georgia, but there was little chance, Clinton concluded, he would ever make senator, let alone president.

"If you live by the sword," even the aging Republican majority leader, Senator Bob Dole, was heard to comment as Gingrich's poll-rating dropped precipitously, "you die by the sword."

As Dole filed as a candidate for Republican nomination for president, and Democrats gloated, Bill Clinton looked ahead. The Speaker had overreached, just as Panetta had predicted, and had destroyed himself as a potential Republican presidential opponent—a process that would be completed when Gail Sheehy, the veteran journalist, completed an article she was currently writing for *Vanity Fair*, detailing the Speaker's troubled childhood, marriages, and relationships. Who else, though, besides the senate majority leader, might come out of the woodwork to challenge the president?

CHAPTER FIFTY-ONE

THE GENERAL'S DOORBELL

The Joker in the Pack

Ever since the resignation of Richard Nixon, the nation had demanded—and got—likeable presidents: men able to take the heat, and with whom electors could "feel comfortable."

Senator Dole was certainly a comforting political figure—indeed, at seventy-one he was the nation's owlish grandfather. Not only had he twenty long years of experience in the Senate, but he'd already run three times for the Republican presidential nomination—losing on each occasion. In many ways he was even more lackluster than President Bush had been. If he won the Republican nomination, Bill Clinton would, if all went well with the economy and in foreign affairs, have no problem in defeating him in the election, providing the president waged a good campaign. The only figure who threatened that scenario was, once again, the Joker in the political pack, the non-politician and *real* general: General Colin Powell, who had declined to serve as his secretary of state.

Senator Dole was also worried about Powell—indeed, several days after Gingrich's self-destruction before the Republican National Committee the senator went to see the general at his residence in McLean, Virginia, to sound out his political intentions. Would the general run—and if so, for which party?

Powell's doorbell wasn't working, so while the distinguished general waited in the hall, the distinguished senator fumbled outside with a button that didn't operate—both men dreading the confrontation.

In truth General Powell was not ready to make a decision, and Senator Dole was reluctant to smoke him out—lest he tip Powell *into* running. Only after going back and calling Powell from his car phone was Dole able to gain admittance. After showing the senator around the six-bedroom residence, the general extolled the neighborhood, and mentioned some vacant houses.

"I'm looking for another house right now," was Dole's humorous response—and both men laughed.

Left unspoken in the discussion between the two men was whether Powell would run as a Republican, or be interested in running with Dole. That the general currently had the highest poll ratings in terms of public enthusiasm for a presidential bid, Dole had proof—in fact, he pulled from his pocket the evidence, showing Powell outstripping the current president of the United States.

It was a fateful moment in modern American history. Across the river, in the even larger house, to which Dole aspired, President Clinton was just as nervously aware of Powell's popularity.

The president was an inveterate reader of history and biography. He was reminded of a passage in David McCullough's 1992 biography of President Truman: the story of how Truman offered to step down and serve as vice president if General Eisenhower would return from his Supreme Commander's post at NATO and run as a Democrat in the 1952 election.

Bill Clinton could not see himself quite doing *that*. He had, after all, never run as anyone's lieutenant, and he did not propose doing so now. But would Dole, who had run for the vice presidency under President Ford in 1976? What if the senator now offered to serve *under* General Powell? Dole would bring decades of Senate experience to the Republican ticket as a vice president, with an entire Congress under Republican control for the first time in four decades. Powell, in those terms, could not lose. Backed by a distinguished parliamentarian, the general would present himself as the first African-American president in the nation's history—thus trumping Bill Clinton's own diversity agenda, triggered so many years before by racism in Arkansas.

Would Dole make such an offer, though?

Unknown to President Clinton, the former, brutally wounded second lieutenant, Tenth Mountain Division, did *not* offer to serve under the former chairman of the Joint Chiefs of Staff of the United States armed forces.

The visit to McLean after church, on Sunday, January 21, 1995, ended where it had started, with a silent bell—and in that missed opportunity, the fate of the two men, and of the American presidency, was sealed.

The Speechwriters Are Concerned

While Bill Clinton had no way of knowing the outcome of Dole's mission, his own genius for politics—both in understanding policy and in the myriad possible chess moves involved in a political campaign—told him what his staff could not. Thus while gung-ho subordinates counseled him to counterattack Senator Dole, Speaker Gingrich, and those Republicans leading the revolutionary charge in Congress, Clinton listened—but held his fire. Far from shooting at Gingrich or Dole, he had them both over to the White House on the day they became chiefs of their respective houses in Congress, and treated them almost as honorary members of his cabinet in dealing with the Mexican financial crisis. And when his speechwriters looked at the president's revisions to the proposed State of the Union address to the joint assembly of Congress, set for January 24, 1995, they were stunned. Far from being a call to Democratic arms, it looked to them like nothing so much as a surrender document.

CHAPTER FIFTY-TWO

A NEW STRATEGY

A Covert Operation Against the White House

As always, the president toyed with his text even in the limousine taking him to the Capitol. But for his staff that was not the real problem, as Dick Morris later revealed. Using the codename "Charlie" (taken from Charlie Black, a Republican consultant friend), Morris was maintaining an anonymous channel of communication that remained stunningly secret in a White House notorious for its leaks; not even Leon Panetta knew the source of the mysterious new passages that had crept into the State of the Union draft after Morris met privately with Clinton, in the president's family quarters, on January 19, 1995, for *five hours*.

George Stephanopoulos, like other loyalists, was outraged when he later learned that the president had consorted with the enemy—for Morris, in Stephanopoulos's book, was a sewer rat: an unprincipled, self-seeking, two-timing double agent, working for both Senator Trent Lott, the new Republican deputy leader of the Senate, and for President Clinton, *at the same time*. Given his Greek background, Stephanopoulos was minded to see the Clinton-Morris pact as treason, with the president engaging Morris "to run a covert operation against his own White House—a commander's coup against the colonels," as Stephanopoulos put it. "The two of them plotted in secret—at night, on the phone, by fax. From December 1994 through August 1996, Leon Panetta managed the official White House staff, the Joint Chiefs commanded the military, the cabinet administered the government, but no single person more influenced the president of the United States than Dick Morris."

This was a bold claim, but oversimple. Once his fury had subsided, after the midterm meltdown, the president had decided to keep Stephanopoulos as an adviser rather than firing him for his failure as White House communications director in 1993. Stephanopoulos was a tactical supernova, possessed with a brilliant ability to see the pluses and minuses of any proposal in Congress and in the traditional Democratic Party.

The midterm meltdown had, however, exposed the weakness of Stephanopoulos's grasp of voting patterns, and if the president defied Stephanopoulos's own expectations of dismissal, it was largely *because* the president was availing himself of the sewer rat. In other words, Stephanopoulos was allowed to keep his head—though not yet permitted to know of, let alone meet, Morris—in order to counterbalance the influence and ideas of the New Jersey Republican consultant. The idea was thereby to "triangulate," in Morris's later famous term, two opposing political advisers—listening to the ideas advanced by the former Greek Orthodox altar boy *and* those by the wholly unprincipled Jewish Republican maverick. Between them, the president reckoned, he would have at hand the best political antennae in the nation, left and right.

Reliance on opposing political proponents had, after all, been used to great effect by Franklin Roosevelt, who had replicated the system throughout his cabinet and administration. Besides, there was precedent for such triangulation already in the Clinton administration. Was Treasury Secretary Robert Rubin not encouraged to work "the markets" with Alan Greenspan to ensure that they were kept happy with the president's actions and speeches, while the labor secretary, Robert Reich, was encouraged to help keep labor happy with the president? Between deficit reduction and the raising of the minimum wage, the president sought, for example, to do the right thing for middle class America—*overall*. Listening to Rubin's recommendations regarding budget cuts and to Reich talk about the effects of the earned-income tax credit on whether poor people could be helped out of poverty, the president was enabled to assess the fairness both of policy and of policy consequences, in a manner that very few American presidents had ever evinced. It might be wonkery—but it was underscored with human compassion that went beyond that of most academics. "You can stop lobbying, Bob," the president thus assured Reich over the raising of the minimum wage. "I'll propose it in the State of the Union," he promised.

"Mission accomplished," Reich congratulated himself, thinking of the look on Panetta and Rubin's faces once they learned of the president's decision. *"Leon and Bob, eat your hearts out."*

A Secret Survey

In actuality, unknown to Reich or Stephanopoulos, a vast amount of triangulation had gone into the crafting of the president's State of the Union address. Sidelining Stan Greenberg, his Democratic pollster, the president had instructed Morris to carry out a new, secret survey of the electorate with no less than 259 questions, prior to the speech. The answers, moreover, had been deeply instructive. The mysterious left-handed ticks that Robert Reich saw the president apply to the mysterious memo he was reading as they sat in the armor-plated presidential limousine on the way to the Capitol were those of a new leader, repositioning himself in American politics.

No longer would he be, the president decided, the agent of change; he would be the *guider* of it. Newt Gingrich was calling himself a Republican revolutionary, aiming to defeat the government—indeed, to defeat government, period. Very well, then, the president would reorganize and pull back his outlying defenses. He was as much a policy nerd as Newt Gingrich, perhaps more so. He would not allow Gingrich to define the Democrats as left-wing reactionaries, but would encourage Gingrich to approach, indeed to feast, if he could, on the leaner carcass of government—the Clinton administration having already cut the federal workforce, under the aegis of Vice President Gore's Reinventing Government task force, by a quarter of a million jobs, and the deficit by 60 percent.

The president, in his new, hospitable mood, would welcome the Republicans to choose tasty looking federal morsels among the remaining dishes, and in doing so, to overreach—picking those delicacies that thanks to Morris's secret poll, the president knew the general electorate would *never* permit revolutionaries to consume, however brash their rhetoric: Medicare benefits and Medicaid guarantees. "Medicare cuts," Morris had noted in his memo, "are your single biggest weapon against the Republicans. They are hated by the public, old and young."

Putting down the anonymous memo, the president had looked up, over his half-moon reading glasses, at his diminutive Rhodie classmate, Robert Reich. "You're right," he acknowledged.

Reich, unaware of the origin of the memo, had imagined the president was talking about the minimum wage raise. But he wasn't—he was thinking of a much larger strategy.

"About the fights," the president had explained, "we'll be defined by the fights we have."

Gingrich would launch attack after attack, as would Senator Dole, now that he had filed for the Republican presidential nomination. Some, the administration would not contest. Others, however, it would fight to the death, thus redefining modern Democratic politics by the issues on which it most differed from Republicans. "We've got to pick them carefully. . . . They'll serve them up to us. We just have to recognize them when they come our way."

It was the start of a new approach—one that would require boundless patience and steel nerves over the coming months.

CHAPTER FIFTY-THREE

STATE OF THE UNION 1995

What a Debacle

As if to befog the invading barbarians, President Clinton's State of the Union address, delivered on January 24, 1995, was deliberately long and opaque. "Panetta was sick and disgusted," Bob Woodward chronicled, for the speech lasted almost as long as Fidel Castro's famous perorations: an hour and twenty-two minutes—much of it extemporaneous. "What a debacle, Panetta thought, and how embarrassing," Bob Woodward wrote of the White House chief of staff's disappointment. "The utter craziness of putting together a major speech in this way."

Panetta was certainly dumbfounded ("order and process had collapsed," he said of the way the speech had been prepared), but so was Morris— "horrified" that, after a clear preliminary outline of the new "opportunity-responsibility" centrist agenda, the president had seemed to go to pieces, finishing with a "thirty-minute self-indulgent, rambling monologue" that reminded Morris of a rabbi who, having longed for an audience all week in his empty synagogue, could not let go of the microphone, once called to speak.

As the days went by, however, Morris's polls revealed a different story. For two years Republicans and Democrats had waited for the president to get his act together and provide the kind of leadership associated with presidential authority and purpose. He hadn't, and his troops had been punished. Gingrich's army had now seized the high ground, and recast the nation's political agenda. Democratic politicians looked to their commander-in-chief for a strategy that would halt the Napoleonic army as it smashed through their homeland; the president, like Marshal Kutuzov in Tolstoy's *War and Peace*, had such a strategy, but he wasn't ready to reveal it clearly, lest Speaker Gingrich work out a revised military plan to counter it.

At the time not even Morris understood his master in this, though years later he accepted that he had misjudged the speech. "In those final thirty minutes, the public saw Clinton at his best," Morris wrote, "without artifice or pretense, genuinely enjoying his talk with them. . . . The informal style, his obvious enjoyment at having a chance to speak with them was deeply comforting to the American people, no matter how tedious it seemed to me."

Gingrich, fighting off accusations of unethical behavior over his book contract and lecture funding, while working eighteen hours a day to push ahead with his Contract With America, and Dole, concerned with emerging competitors in his own party for the Republican nomination, found the speech equally tedious. Both of them failed also to see what the president was up to: separating himself from the traditional thrust and tenets of the Democratic Party and repositioning himself as a man of common sense, of heart and conscience, without an axe to grind. In his elected post as president of the people, he was saying, he would be a moderator, a guide, an arbitrator between extremes that lobbied for power.

It was in this way that the president's warning about the fights he would choose over Medicare, Medicaid, and gun control—the three issues by which he would define and ultimately crush his Republican opponents—were swathed in the coddling clothes of Clintonese: an unrelenting torrent of facts, homilies, assertions, truisms, aphorisms, apologies, and appeals worthy of the Great Communicator himself. He allowed how he'd made mistakes, he admitted he had bitten off more than he could chew on health care reform, he claimed he was a committed, activist proponent of welfare reform going back to his days as governor of Arkansas, he said that balancing the budget was as much his aim as that of Republicans, he made clear he wanted Congress to help save the Mexican economy because it was in America's, not only Mexico's, interest. . . . And then, having woven his bipartisan, conciliatory magic, he'd addressed the issues he'd been exploring in his mind and meetings ever since the awful finality of the midterm meltdown: the role of *values* in American voting.

An Appeal for More Responsibility

Dick Morris and others were embarrassed by the president's folksy, southern touch—but a decade later, as Democrats yet again failed to secure the presidency or retrieve control of either chamber of Congress, Bill Clinton's antennae would be seen to have been remarkably sensitive—and prescient.

From anti-lobbying laws to SALT II nuclear disarmament and anti-terrorism measures, the president first demonstrated his mastery of rhetoric in raising and explaining complex issues to a vast national television audience for the State of the Union address—then used that achievement as a warrant for appending his personal, moralizing thirty-minute finale. With the sincerity of a parent and a concerned citizen he addressed head-on the moral challenges facing the nation: "the values and voices that speak to our hearts as well as our heads; voices that tell us we have to do more to accept responsibility for ourselves and our families, for our communities, and yes, for our fellow citizens. We see our families and our communities all over this country coming apart, and we feel the common ground shifting from under us," he acknowledged. Teenage pregnancy and the level of violence in Hollywood films were but symptoms of a social fabric that was unraveling, not binding. This in turn led the president to direct "a special word" to America's religious leaders.

"You know, I'm proud of the fact the United States has more houses of worship than any country in the world," he stated. "These people who lead our houses of worship can ignite their congregations to carry their faith into action, can reach out to all of our children, to all of the people in distress, to those who have been savaged by the breakdown of all we hold dear. Because so much of what must be done must come from the inside out and our religious leaders and their congregations can make all the difference, they have a role in the New Covenant as well"—reprising his 1992 slogan.

"There must be more responsibility for all our citizens," he implored, citing the need for adults who could ensure that kids in trouble stay off the streets, for adequate housing, for enough staff and volunteers to keep the nation's civic organizations running. "It takes every parent to teach the children the difference between right and wrong and to encourage them to learn and grow and say no to the wrong things but also to believe that they can be whatever they want to be."

In this difficult equation for American modernity, he confessed, politicians were doing as badly as the purveyors of violence in Hollywood. "Most of us in politics haven't helped very much. For years, we've mostly treated citizens like they were consumers or spectators, sort of political couch potatoes who were supposed to watch the TV ads," he admitted with stunning candor—politicians pouring money into cynically conducted campaigns that "play on their fears and frustrations. And more and more of our citizens now get most of their information in very negative and aggressive ways that are hardly conducive to honest and open conversations. But the truth is, we have got to stop seeing each other as enemies just because we have different views."

Such proselytizing, in the context of the current daily Democratic assault on the Speaker for his book deal, was unlikely to soften the hearts of Republican attack-ad makers, but in the context of a wide-ranging survey of domestic and international policy by the president of the United States, the plea for peace and goodwill between men of all political persuasions was uncannily effective with the wider public.

"If you go back to the beginning of this country," the president reflected, "the great strength of America, as de Tocqueville pointed out when he came here a long time ago, has always been our ability to associate with people who were different from ourselves and to work together to find common ground. And in this day, everybody has a responsibility to do more of that. We simply cannot wait for a tornado, a fire, or a flood to behave like Americans ought to behave in dealing with one another." And with that admonition the president then pointed to the gallery where, beside the first lady, there sat an AmeriCorps worker from Tennessee, a mother of four, whom the president asked to stand up and be recognized; a police chief from Kansas who had used community policing to great effect; a Haitian-American corporal who had returned to his native country as part of the U.S. contingent in Haiti; and two ministers of the A.M.E. Zion Church in Temple Hills, Maryland, who had started their congregation in their living room, and now had a church with seventeen thousand members, growing at two hundred a month—specializing in keeping couples together. Finally, there was a veteran of the great battle on Iwo Jima, who had thrown himself on an exploding grenade to save his compatriots, and thereby earned the Congressional Medal of Honor at age seventeen—attending the State of the Union address together with his son and grandson. All were "citizens," the president emphasized. "I have no idea what their party affiliation is or who they voted for at the last election. But they represent what we ought to be doing."

It was theater, televised for the nation, performed live on the stage of the House chamber by a president who only a few weeks before had been written off as a lame duck. As the audience stood up, applauding, after almost an hour and a half of Bill Clinton's new ministry, it was all too plain that the outgoing Treasury secretary was right when he'd warned journalists that Bill Clinton could be knocked to the canvas, but could never be knocked out. As right-wing Republicans still chattered excitedly on Fox TV about their midterm victory and the prospect of reclaiming the White House in 1996, Mr. Bentsen had warned them about underestimating the president. "Let me tell you about this president," he'd remarked in a tone reminiscent of his great debate with vice presidential nominee Dan Quayle in 1988. Clinton might be on the proverbial canvas, but it was a mistake to imagine he was beaten. "He's a comeback fellow," he'd cautioned.

A Bogus Charge

Reenergized by the challenge of the next two years, the president was almost visibly coming back to life, as he had done during his third, 1982 gubernatorial campaign in Arkansas. Interviewing President Clinton for NBC's *Nightly News* two days after the State of the Union address, Tom Brokaw found a president who was clearly back up on his feet and, like Mohammed Ali in his greatest days, bristling with self-confidence. "I always get the impression," Brokaw began after congratulating the president, "that once you get up there and get into a roll, so to speak, it's pretty hard for you to sit down, you love the art of political oratory so much"—to which the president happily agreed, ignoring the subtext of sarcasm. "It was a little longer than I wanted it to be," Clinton conceded, "partly because I was frankly not anticipating that the Congress and especially the Republicans would respond as positively as they did to some of the things that I said." He had been interrupted no less than ninety-six times by applause—from both sides of the aisle. Moreover, the speech had allowed him to "get back to the basic values and the basic ideas that got me into the race for president in the first place, really that drove my whole public service career before I became president."

Whatever the length of the speech, Brokaw had to admit that it had been well received in the majority of American homes. A new NBC poll showed that 60 percent of those polled supported the president's stated goals in the speech, with less than 10 percent in disagreement. Moreover, the president's performance rating had risen above the 50 percent approval bar. Other polls gave an even higher performance rating. The president, it seemed, was back in tune with the country.

One by one, under the klieg lights in the White House Roosevelt Room, whatever issue Brokaw threw at the president, Clinton seemed able to hit effortlessly into the bleachers—where the people, not the pundits, cheered. Asked if the president was a man of strong convictions, only 31 percent of NBC poll respondents thought so, Brokaw pointed out, accusingly, while 61 percent thought he "swayed."

"Part of the case against Bill Clinton that will be made even by your friends from time to time," Brokaw said, "is that you talk the talk but don't walk the walk." The president took the punch—but before Brokaw could take a breath, he went down with a left hook. "First of all," the president hit back, "who reversed twelve years of flagrant deficit spending? We did, by one-vote fights in both Houses in the most brutal fight anybody can remember. We did that. We walked the walk and took a lot of grief for it." He followed this with a blow to the Republican solar plexus. "And one of the reasons the Democrats lost this last session in this last election is because Republicans convinced the voters that we raised everyone's taxes when what we did was raise taxes on the top 1.2 percent, and a lot of those folks funded those campaigns. We took on the NAFTA fight. It was deader than a doornail when I became president, and we brought it back to life. We took on the NRA on the Brady Bill and the assault weapons ban. You may agree or disagree; no other sitting president has done it," he pointed out. "So this 'walk the walk' business is a bogus charge. . . ."

Clearly the president was in top form—which should have warned Gingrich and Dole that their revolution might be in trouble. But, each consumed with his own local problems, neither the military buff nor the former infantry officer could divine the president's plan behind the fancy footwork. They thus remained convinced they were on the path to a royal Republican flush—winning both houses of Congress, the majority of gubernatorial mansions, and the majority of state legislatures, as well as the White House in 1996—without realizing what they were up against.

A Road Map

One reason for such complacency in the Republican camp was the knowledge that they had a double agent working for them: Dick Morris, who reported back to Senator Trent Lott, the Republican deputy leader of the Senate, all that he was doing for the president in the White House—indeed, Morris was heard to predict, based on his private knowledge of Hillary's activities at the Rose Law Firm, that the Clintons would soon be indicted over Whitewater!

Years later, his standing ruined by his own scandalous relationship and loose talk with a prostitute, Morris would rail at Clinton for having bested him in this war of deceit and counter-deceit. By then, however, it was too late, Clinton having not only manipulated him into luring the Republicans to their doom, but having happily exploited Morris's best ideas for his presidential campaign and discarded most of the worst.

Chief among the former, to his credit, was Morris's notion that the president should launch his re-election campaign that very summer, a full eighteen months before the 1996 election, instead of waiting until challenged, and fighting only in the final year, like most sitting presidents.

In this respect, Morris had every right to crow, for the president's meeting with Terry McAuliffe to prepare for a fundraising campaign, and then his decision to follow Morris's idea of early television advertising—against the advice of the president's Democratic advisers—would prove a stroke of near genius. The advertising campaign, to be broadcast outside Washington and the main American cities, would radiate beneath the Republican national radar, month after month, without Republican leaders being aware of what was going on, let alone countering it.

Frightened that by giving Clinton his best ideas he was digging his own professional grave as a Republican consultant, Morris became almost hysterical in his dogmatic insistence that the president follow his prescriptions for success—and keep Morris in a position to remain employed if he lost his Republican clients. Meanwhile, liberal critics, along with the president's advisers, expressed concern that their president was giving away the candy store. "IT WAS CLINTON'S BIG CHANCE, AND HE BLEW IT" was David Broder's headline in the *Washington Post*, lambasting the president's failure in his State of the Union address "to define, for the doubt-wracked Democrats, the ground he would defend against Republican assault." "The hope that trailing behind a Republican Congress can bring him lasting lustre is simply absurd," the left-wing London *Guardian* newspaper also declared.

Had Clinton blown his chance, though? Hamish McRae, in the London *Independent*—the *Guardian*'s centrist rival—considered the president's decision to embrace good change and reject the bad to be "the best possible response of a decent and talented politician of the centre-left to the whirlwind electoral victory of the right." To govern again, liberals worldwide would have to accept that the old world of union solidarity and entitlements, in a global economy, was past its sell-by date, and that new liberalism could rise from its ashes only if it sought a new compact between politicians and the people. "It is a response that should be studied carefully by all politicians in Europe. For it signposts a way down the path they are likely to have to travel themselves. See this State of the Union not just as the squirming of a wrong-footed American politician; but as a road map which will be useful for us all," McRae urged—two years before Tony Blair's landslide victory over the Conservative Party in the British general election.

For the moment, then, Bill Clinton had to exercise every particle of patience. In speech after speech, meeting after meeting, broadcast after broadcast, he proselytized, clarifying and correcting the public on the real achievements of his first two years in office and calling for a new era of responsibility and compassion, while holding back on his actual battle plan— thus tempting Gingrich and his fellow revolutionaries to ride on into the valley of political death.

The Clinton administration's travails from gays in the military to the health care reform debacle had been cast by Gingrich as The Charge of the Liberal Light Brigade; now the president had a chance to turn the tables, luring the Republican cavalry onto *his* guns—"to let Gingrich, the Contract, and the revolution sort of crest and wash up on the shore," as Leon Panetta saw Gingrich's hundred-day timetable, before blitzing them with White House artillery where it would be decisive.

Newt Gingrich, tied up in Congress with his hundred-day march, was blind to the possibility. "February and March," Morris later chronicled, "were truly the Gingrich administration," rather than the Clinton administration. "Even Dole was an afterthought in the Republican revolution," Morris recalled, "who couldn't keep pace with his House colleague," so busy was he with his own presidential campaign preparations. "Clinton was invisible. The nation watched the Republican Congress grind on with its agenda. It was a withering sight."

No Colder Feeling on the Planet

Measure after conservative Republican measure, drawn from the Contract With America, was introduced and passed in the House of Representatives—requiring the patience of Job for the president and his chief of staff to watch Congress, yet hold their fire.

Hillary, shorn of her health care wings and the right even to attend strategy meetings, was especially frustrated. Unsure what, for her part, she should do, now that the health care task force had been abandoned and the midterm elections had produced such a negative referendum on the co-presidential experiment, she consulted the history books and their authors. Inviting Doris Kearns Goodwin, author of the recently published (and later Pulitzer prize-winning) biography of Eleanor and Franklin Roosevelt, *No Ordinary Time*, to stay over at the White House in the Queen's Bedroom, Hillary searched for a beacon of hope. "'She ought to stay at home, where a wife belongs; she is always getting her nose into the government's business; why, the way she acts, you'd think the people elected her president; she interferes in things that are not her affair,'" Goodwin had written, quoting public reaction to the first lady—Eleanor.

Interviewed after her night at the White House by Diane Rehm on National Public Radio, Goodwin pointed out that Eleanor, like Hillary, "kept yearning to have a job" in Franklin D. Roosevelt's White House. FDR had finally given in, and had appointed her to a Civil Defense post in late 1941. "It was a disaster," Goodwin commented. Eleanor had had to resign the following year under attack from critics and had vowed never to take another official government job. Ms. Goodwin had thus been sympathetic to Hillary's plight as a feminist, but fatalistic as an historian. As Goodwin explained, Eleanor had refashioned herself after her 1941 debacle, and had returned to being the "voice of outsiders. She would talk for blacks, for poor people, for migrant workers who didn't have access to power." Outside of government, Eleanor Roosevelt had been able to stand for causes and to take criticism—without the Roosevelt administration being held to account, or crippled. "In contrast, Hillary has chosen so far an insider's role—

that's just more fraught with conflict," Goodwin commented candidly. "It may well be that the experience of having been an inside, officially named player will not necessarily be repeated, and that may be a good thing."

This was excellent advice, from a first-class historian—though it overlooked the sheer hurt Hillary felt whenever her privacy was invaded. When in late January a new biography of the president came out—*First in His Class,* written by David Maraniss, a distinguished *Washington Post* journalist who had interviewed almost every living witness to the rise of the Man from Hope—Hillary went into one of her quasi-catatonic states, convinced that everyone was against her. Dick Morris had, like others, told David Maraniss of Hillary's "tin ear," illustrating its defective tympanic membrane by the story of Hillary's determination to build a swimming pool at the Governor's Mansion in Little Rock, at taxpayer's expense. Even more embarrassingly, Morris had revealed to Maraniss that both Clintons had told him of their plans to divorce in 1989.

Tens of thousands were fascinated by Maraniss's largely sympathetic account, which soon became a national bestseller. Hillary, however, was mortified. Supersensitive to criticism, the first lady was deeply offended to see such private information about herself and her husband, the president of the United States, in print—and Morris, along with scores of other "leakers," was summarily removed from Hillary's contact list. As Morris recalled, "When Hillary is stung, she reacts viscerally and closes up. After the Maraniss incident, she ostracized me. There is no colder feeling on the planet," he described. "She is intensely human and sensitive and feels every slap and aches with every blow. Her stoic exterior masks enormous pain."

It was not only pain on Hillary's own account, however. What Morris left unsaid was what the consultant confided to Maraniss, later—that "the few portions" of *First in His Class* that examined the president's sex life "upset the first lady so much that she had turned 'frosty' on the president for several weeks and had refused to talk to him or sleep in the same bedroom with him in the White House residence."

Maraniss—who titled his next Clinton book *The Clinton Enigma*—was perplexed. After Troopergate and the Paula Jones allegations, what possible revelation in his paean could have been news to the first lady, let alone cause her to go into Lysistrata mode? Not only Morris but Maraniss, too, had felt the effects of the Hillary chill—even the president refusing to give him, the *Washington Post*'s senior White House correspondent, a personal interview during his entire 1996 re-election campaign.

A Man of Foresight

While the Republicans were occupied with the excitement of their Contract, Bill Clinton, a decade ahead of most American politicians, was peering into the future, and seeing not the clash of issues qua issues, but a complex landscape of political power struggles in which *values*—religious, social, cultural—would be used as the new weapons of mass invocation and political destruction, in the U.S. and around the world.

The popular response to his State of the Union speech, expressed in rising polls, testified to the president's amazingly sensitive political antennae: his sensory receptors warning him of danger, and of opportunity. Fundamentalism was on the rise, not only in America but worldwide, and could be seen in many ways as a global response to the global economy—a reemphasis on ethical structure as social anchor in the tearaway expansion of world trade and swirling postmodern cultural relativism. In that context, the president's ability to connect and to articulate his understanding of people's religious concerns, at home and abroad, in reacting to the need to modernize the American economy in a post-industrial age, was admirable. It was, moreover, utterly sincere as an ambition, since he was, himself, such a genuine and ardent advocate of globalization. But as Jim and Tammy Faye Bakker as well as the Reverend Jimmy Swaggart had found in the late 1980s, whether teaching the prosperity-gospel or white fire-and-brimstone Christianity, the rule was the same: beware the moral expectations one raises as a moral preacher!

Who, skeptics asked, was Bill Clinton to preach a return to "moral values," given the revelations about his extramarital proclivities? In an interview with religious affairs journalists in the Oval Office on February 2, 1995, this was the first question that came up. "An awkward question, sir," the questioner said, apologizing for his candor in advance. "The moral crusade elements of the State of the Union Address—teenage pregnancy, as an example—sits well, except that there are investigations into your own conduct which some people say leaves an impression. Is this interfering with your ability to lead that type of crusade?"

Mouths dropped, but the president seemed completely unperturbed. "Not in my own mind," he responded. In a democracy, people were free to make up their own minds, and think their own thoughts. Refuting the notion that he was ill-suited for such an ethical campaign, he declared, "We live in an age where anybody can say anything and, unlike in previous times, it gets into print." And, without mentioning his former surgeon general, he truthfully pointed out that he had been involved in steps to reduce teenage pregnancy for many years; that he recognized that the temptations in the modern, youth-empowered world were greater than in his own earlier days; and that the statistics of increasing teenage pregnancy were skewed, in that they only appeared to be rising because legitimate, adult pregnancy rates were falling. . . . "But anyway," he said, dismissing the matter of his own ethical lapses, "you know, if folks want to use that as another excuse to attack me, that's their problem, not mine."

This was, indeed, the new mantra the Clintons had chosen to adopt—that it was someone else's problem, not his or Hillary's. "There have been an awful lot of attempts," he began to say, in response to a question about a Baptist minister, Jerry Falwell, who was selling a venomous video called *The Clinton Chronicles* on his television program.

In mid-sentence, though, the president thought better of dignifying such garbage. "I think there have been a lot of press stories refuting some of the specific allegations. But I would just say again, in the world we're living in—I'll say what I said at the prayer breakfast today—there is an inordinate premium put on the use of words used to destroy or to distract people. And it takes away from my ability to be president, to do the job with a clear head and a clear heart and to focus on the American people, if I have to spend all my time trying to answer charges about what people say that I did years ago. And I just can't do it; I just can't do it."

The president paused. "I do the best I can. Sometimes you can actually disprove something someone says about you. A lot of times, some people could lie about you in ways that you can't disprove. You can't always disprove every assertion. So insofar as whatever happened, I can't change yesterday, I can only change today and tomorrow."

Did this mean the president was promising to exercise more self-discipline in his private behavior, now, or simply that he was determined not to be swayed from his political work? It was unclear, as much to the religious affairs reporters as perhaps to the president.

But the president wasn't nearly finished. "There is a difference between reputation and character, and I have increasingly less control over my reputation but still full control over my character," he asserted. "That's between me and God, and I've just got to be purified by this." He would be, he appeared to be saying, a sort of martyr to the Supreme Court's 1964 decision to abandon libel law in America for public figures.

The reporters took deep breaths. *St. Sebastian*? Purification; the use of language to destroy rather than to build up; reputation and character; quoting Winston Churchill. . . . The president seemed to be conversing with himself as much as with them.

To the next question, a simple one about the president's favorite piece of scripture, Clinton actually instanced "a lot of the Psalms where David is sort of praying for strength to be sort of purified in the face of adversity and in the face of his own failures." The important thing, the president said, was "that I have to keep focusing on is what am I going to do today, what am I going to do tomorrow, how can I be free to call on the power of God to make the most of this job that I have for a little bit of time in the grand sweep of things. And that's just what I keep focusing on every day."

CHAPTER FIFTY-FOUR

THE TURNING POINT

An Olive Branch

It was April 7, 1995, and the White House staff had been led to expect a quiet, uncontroversial speech by the president on education.

The chief of staff was anxious, however. A recent spate of communications from "Charlie" had tormented Panetta, for the pseudonymous faxes had not only found their way into the president's draft speech, but in doing so, anonymously, they threatened to bring division, leaks, and disorder back to the White House. "I'm not going to take this shit," Panetta had eventually declared in a private strategy meeting with the president, vice president, and Morris, once "Charlie's" identity had been revealed. "I'm an adult human being and I've been around a long time, and I'm not going to take this squirt running around, gumming up the works."

The president, blushing, had attempted to pour oil on the bubbling waters. Morris's draft speech for Dallas, before a national gathering of newspaper editors, offered an olive branch to Gingrich and his Republican revolutionaries, but it was not a sellout, the president maintained. Instead it was a way to seize the high ground from under Gingrich's feet. "Leon, I want to do it Dick's way for now," he apologized. "I understand where you are coming from, but we've tried that way for two months now without much to show for it. I've got to get back in the game, and I think Dick's speech is the way to do it."

Supported by the vice president, it was "the turning point in the president's move to the center," as Morris later called it.

Deciding What Is Best for America

Assembling in the city where President Kennedy had been murdered, newspaper editors had been following the great march of Speaker Gingrich's first hundred days in the capital—and were stunned to hear the confidence with which the president described the political situation.

"We have entered a new era," the president declared, describing the disconnect between ordinary Americans and the revolutionaries currently dominating the airwaves of Washington. "For years, out here in the country, the old political categories have basically been defunct, and a new political discussion has been begging to be born. It must be now so in Washington, as well," he asserted. "The old labels of liberal and conservative, spender and cutter, even Democrat and Republican, are not what matter most anymore. What matters most is finding practical, pragmatic solutions based on what we know works in our lives and our shared experiences so that we can go forward together as a nation. Ideological purity is for partisan extremists. Practical solution, based on real experience, hard evidence, and common sense, that's what this country needs.

"We've been saddled too long with a political debate that doesn't tell us what we ought to do, just who we ought to blame. And we have to stop pointing fingers at each other so that we can join hands.

"You know, our country has often moved forward spurred on by purists, reformists, populist agendas which articulated grievances and proposed radical departures. But if you think about our most successful periods of reform, these initiatives have been shaped by presidents who incorporated what was good, smoothed out what was rough, and discarded what would hurt. That was the role of Theodore Roosevelt and Woodrow Wilson in the aftermath of the populist era. That was the role of Franklin Roosevelt in the aftermath of the La Follette progressive movement. And that is my job in the next hundred days and for all the days I serve as president."

It was apparent to the editors in Dallas that a new Clinton was talking—no longer the proposer, but the disposer, on behalf of the nation. And in that new role the southern dynamo might at last have found his historic role. It would not necessarily be, the president made emphatically clear, a negative one. "I was not elected to pile up a stack of vetoes," he declared, pursuing a line that Morris had written. "I was elected to change the direction of America. That's what I have spent the last two years doing and that's what I want to spend the next hundred days and beyond doing. Whether we can do that depends on what all of us in Washington do from here on out.

"So I appeal today to Republicans and to Democrats alike to get together, to keep the momentum for change going, not to allow the energy and longing for change now to be dissipated amid a partisan clutter of accusations. After all," the president added, "we share much common ground."

From that general overview the president had switched to the particular. One by one he pointed to the equivalence between his own 1992 New Covenant and the Republican Contract: on welfare reform; on cutting the federal deficit ("My administration is the only one in thirty years to run an operating surplus"); on shrinking the size of the federal government (which had already led to the cutting of a hundred thousand bureaucratic positions and was nearing the point where Clinton could claim to be running the smallest government since "President Kennedy occupied this office"); on "the toughest possible fight against crime" (involving a hundred thousand more police officers, limits on handguns, and a ban on assault weapons); on the line-item veto to remove "pork" spending. . . . "We are near many breakthroughs," the president asserted. "The real issue is whether we will have the wisdom and the courage to see our common ground and walk on it. To do that, we must abandon extreme positions and work together. This is no time for ideological extremism. Good-faith compromising, negotiating our differences, actually listening to one another for a change, these are the currency of a healthy democracy."

For another hour, the president of the United States had gone through in detail the tax cuts he'd like to see, and *not* see; the need for improved education in a competitive, global economy; the changing of tax regulations to allow parents to withdraw money tax-free from their IRA pension accounts for college education and health care and elderly-parent care; the need for welfare reform that compelled people to "take more responsibility for their own lives and for the children they bring into this world" but didn't at the same time punish young children for the sins of their parents. "Rich or poor, black, white, or brown, in or out of wedlock, a baby is a baby, a child is a child," he maintained. "It's part of our future, and we have an obligation to those children not to punish them for something over which they had absolutely no control. . . ."

One by one, the president had then finally warned, in public, what specific Republican House bills he *would* veto. It would not be a stack of vetoes, he re-emphasized, but he would use his constitutional right to kill legislation he felt inappropriate for the American people—including the recent House-passed temporary freeze on most new federal regulations, imminent legislation repealing his assault weapons ban and financing for a hundred thousand police officers, any reduction in environmental protection, and Gingrich's massive GOP tax cut proposal, which he labeled "a fantasy. It's too much. It's not going to happen. We can't afford it."

In Washington, D.C., Speaker Newt Gingrich ought to have been listening carefully. But to his own detriment, the Speaker was far too busy congratulating himself on the passage, in the House, of his latest Contract With America bills—bills that not only had to be passed by the Senate if they were to become legislation, but had then to survive the president's axe.

Totally Remaking the Federal Government

That Newt Gingrich did not read the president's speech was evident the following day when he told reporters in Washington that he didn't think the president of the United States "gets it. I don't think the president should let himself get trapped into being a defender of an obsolete, out-of-touch, old-fashioned, bureaucratic, centralized government."

For himself, the Grinch had given his own televised speech—on cable, since none of the national networks accepted his claim to a State of the Union-style audience in which he could boast of his success in the House. "AND on the [ninety-third] day he rested: for Newt had completed his 100-day Contract With America ahead of schedule," one typical columnist mocked in the next day's paper, "and was releasing his minions to their families and constituents for their Easter and Passover vacations. And he saw all that he had made, and behold, it was very good. Or was it?"

As a firebrand and "bombthrower" in Congress, Gingrich had achieved a Rush Limbaugh-like reputation. As a national leader, second in line to the presidency if the president were assassinated or removed, however, he looked and sounded . . . strange. Speaking on local and cable TV from his office on the Hill, the Speaker had begun by boasting of the various Contract With America items he'd managed to get his cohort of revolutionary House members to adopt. When Gingrich explained them on camera, however, they suddenly sounded rather small, even pathetic. His number one contract item, for example, ran: "First, upon signing this declaration, we average Americans will cut the size of our personal and committee staffs. We will cast no more proxy votes on important national issues. . . ."

The Speaker's attempt to clone Clinton techniques by using show-and-tell props fared no better. As Speaker he wanted, he reminded cable viewers, to reform a moribund American government that desperately needed to be slashed—despite the fact that the vice president's reinventing government project was already doing this very thing. As an example of what he meant, the Speaker mentioned "vacuum tubes."

"The United States government is the largest purchaser of vacuum tubes in the Western world," Speaker Gingrich explained. "This is a Federal Aviation Administration vacuum tube," he said, and then held up a vacuum tube, in the manner of a brush salesman. "Good, solid 1895 technology."

Viewers were astonished as the Speaker continued. "This is the updated mid-1950s version. When you fly in America, vacuum tubes in the air traffic control system keep you safe. Our purchasing rules are so complicated and so wasteful that our government has not been able in seven years to figure out how to replace vacuum tubes with . . . a microchip that has the computing power of three million vacuum tubes." And the Speaker held up a microchip.

In elementary school, as part of a science and technology lesson, such show-and-tell might have interested children, but adult viewers expecting rhetoric worthy of the nation's great chamber of political debate were stunned. Not only did the Speaker's nine items and their props sound and look lame, but his agenda for the next eighteen months of the 104th Congress, though ostensibly designed to make America a land of opportunity rather than of dependency and street crime, rang all too hollow, given as it was on the very same day that his Republican colleagues introduced legislation to repeal the assault weapons ban and allow automatic weapons *back* onto America's sidewalks. "All of us together—Republicans and Democrats alike—must totally remake the federal government," the revolutionary firebrand urged nevertheless, "to change the very way it thinks, the way it does business, the way it treats its citizens. After all, the purpose of changing government is to improve the lives of our citizens, strengthen the future of our children, make our neighborhoods safe, and to build a better country."

How, though, would that be possible with less government and *more* weapons on the streets? viewers asked themselves, thinking back to America of the Wild West.

The answer, several weeks later, would show that it wasn't.

OKLAHOMA CITY

CHAPTER FIFTY-FIVE

THE PLOT AGAINST AMERICA

Expect Heavy Casualties

President Clinton had just begun a meeting at the White House with the Turkish prime minister, Tansu Ciller, when, at 9:02 Central Standard Time on Wednesday morning, April 19, 1995, a note was handed to him, written with a blue felt-tip pen in Leon Panetta's distinctive hand. It read: "Half of federal building in OK City blown up. Expect heavy casualties. Janet Reno has dispatched FBI."

Terrorism was already very much on both President Clinton's and Prime Minister Ciller's agendas. Twenty-one people had recently been arrested for the attempted assassination of Ciller, who, backed by President Clinton, was moving Turkey towards possible inclusion in the European Union rather than allowing his nation to become "separated from Europe"—a direction that would otherwise mean "that fundamentalism would have moved up to the borders of Europe," as the president put it.

Was the blast in Oklahoma an expression, though, of Islamic fundamentalism? As further reports of American loss of life came in to the White House, the question arose: why *Oklahoma City*?

There had been a convention of Islamic scholars in the midwestern city not long before, it was true. The metropolis boasted three mosques, yet the actual Muslim population in the state was small, and the target seemed somehow unlikely as a religious, anti-infidel, fundamentalist choice—at least when compared with the 1993 attack on the World Trade Center as the symbol of Western mammon.

On the other hand, it had to be admitted that there were distinct stylistic similarities between the two bombings, and in fact with a third: the American Embassy in Beirut had been flattened by a massive truck bomb ten years prior to the WTC explosion. Witnesses in Oklahoma reported seeing a truck drive up in front of the Murrah Federal Building, and two men leaving it there and driving off in a brown Chevrolet pickup truck, minutes before the blast—the two of them "Middle Eastern" in appearance.

The force of the bomb was certainly stunning—it had been felt as far away as thirty miles. In the city itself it left a crater thirty feet wide and eight feet deep, blowing out the entire glass front of the Murrah Building as well as the structure behind. Shorn of their supports, the nine stories simply fell on top of each other, like pancakes or a house of cards, crushing the men, women, and children who were caught between them. It would take more than a week to dig out the bodies.

All Wednesday the death toll rose—with hundreds missing. As television footage of a firefighter carrying out the body of a dying child was broadcast, the entire nation went into shock. All 8,300 federal buildings in the country closed down. Teams of FBI and other law-enforcement agencies who had handled the World Trade Center bombing were flown by military transport planes to the city and got to work immediately, sifting and analyzing the evidence.

These People Are Killers

Though technically reminiscent of the World Trade Center attack—a truck-bomb explosion of massive power—the federal nature of the target suggested more an anti-government agenda than an anti-American one. Moreover, the date of the incident suggested the anniversary of something home-grown and government-related: the storming of the Randall Weaver home at Ruby Ridge, Idaho, in 1992, and then of the Branch Davidian complex at Waco, Texas, exactly two years before, *to the day*.

Further reflection on the date of the bombing threw up yet another pause for thought: the day of the Oklahoma City bombing was notable for the scheduled execution of a white supremacist murderer in Arkansas, Richard Wayne Snell. Snell had been convicted eight years previously of the murder of a pawnshop owner he thought was Jewish. He was due to be put to death at Varner, seventy-five miles from Little Rock, by lethal injection—Bill Clinton, as governor of Arkansas, having long ago signed the death warrant. A group related to the Michigan Militia, the Militia of Montana, had denounced the impending execution as a "grand climax" orchestrated by the U.S. government.

Climax to what? Rumors swirled, and it was in this situation that the president demonstrated how much he had learned from his earlier failure of leadership. Appearing before the cameras in the White House Briefing Room that afternoon, he looked—and was—angry. Newt Gingrich and others might rail against the federal government, but the people now looked to that same federal government to deal with something that was clearly much more than a state or city problem. "The bombing in Oklahoma City was an attack on innocent children and defenseless citizens," the president declared, flanked by his attorney general, Janet Reno, reading from the notes he had written out shortly before, in longhand. "It was an act of cowardice, and it was evil. The United States will not tolerate it. And I will not allow the people of this country to be intimidated by evil cowards."

Weighing his words carefully, the president explained what the federal government was doing, sending the "the world's finest investigators" to Oklahoma "to solve these murders." He not only had put together a team of government investigators, but had dispatched also the director of the Federal Emergency Management Agency, FEMA, to the city, having declared, under the Stafford Act, the bombing to be a federal emergency (since the Murrah Building contained a federally owned courthouse), and having ordered precautions taken at all federal facilities in the entire nation. "Let there be no room for doubt," he stated. "We will find the people who did this. When we do, justice will be swift, certain, and severe. These people are killers, and they must be treated like killers."

The president paused a moment at the lectern. "Finally, " he added, "let me say that I ask all Americans tonight to pray—to pray for the people who have lost their lives, to pray for the families and the friends of the dead and the wounded, to pray for the people of Oklahoma City. May God's grace be with them.

"Meanwhile, we will be about our work."

A Salutary Caution

Formally welcoming the president of Brazil the next day, the president—having ordered flags to be flown at half-mast throughout the country—reiterated his determination to find the perpetrators of the Oklahoma City bombing. "Let me say again, those responsible will be brought to justice," he declared. "They will be tried, convicted, and punished. We will never let the forces of inhumanity prevail in the United States." When reporters pressed him over assumptions that the bombing was the work of Middle Eastern terrorists, the president warned them not to jump to conclusions, but to wait until the investigatory work—currently being carried out by some two hundred federal agents on the scene as well as other experts across America—clarified and confirmed who had been responsible. Three Arab-American organizations had already condemned the taking of so many innocent lives. "This is not a question of anybody's country of origin. This is not a question of anybody's religion. This was murder. This was evil. This was wrong. Human beings everywhere, all over the world, will condemn this out of their own religious convictions. And we should not stereotype anybody. What we need to do is to find out who did this and punish them harshly. . . . The American people should know that the best investigators in the world are working to find the truth. Let us support search and rescue and investigation and deal with the facts as we find them."

Given the emerging facts, it was a salutary caution. Another journalist, attempting to blame the United States government for "meddling in the affairs of others" around the world, was slapped down by the president. "I would hope the American people would draw exactly the opposite conclusion from this," Clinton responded. "Our future lies in an open society, a free economy, and the free interchange of people, of ideas, and goods. In that kind of world, we cannot withdraw from the world, nor can we hide. Look at what happened in Argentina," he pointed out, referring to the recent bombing of an Israeli embassy. "No one thinks the Argentines are out there meddling in the affairs of people throughout the world. No great country can hide. We have to stand up, fight this kind of madness, and take appropriate steps. Moreover, I will say again we do not know who the perpetrator is. Technology gives power to people to do this sort of thing. Look at what happened in Japan, where there was no outside influence." There the Tokyo subway system had been twice attacked by "a radical group within Japan able to take a little vial of gas and kill large numbers of people."

While media suspicion in New York and the eastern seaboard of the United States fell on Islamic militants, local police and FBI agents were tending towards an even more sickening hypothesis: that America was now witnessing a home-grown hate crime—indeed, the worst hate crime in its history, carried out by American white supremacists.

CHAPTER FIFTY-SIX

HIS FINEST HOUR

The Children of America

As in New York's WTC bombing, the VIN number of the vehicle that had contained the explosives was found amid the rubble—this time not in four days but in sixteen hours. Via an open line to the Ford Motor Co. in Detroit, which had manufactured the van, the truck was traced to Elliott's Body Shop in Junction City, Kansas. Within hours, detailed descriptions of two white men who had rented the vehicle were being broadcast by television stations across the country and around the world. A former co-worker who saw one of the composites on television called immediately and identified him as Timothy McVeigh, a twenty-seven-year-old Desert Storm veteran who had become obsessed by Waco and, with his army buddy Terry Nichols, had joined the so-called Michigan Militia, a paramilitary organization said to number ten thousand adherents.

As an interstate dragnet was cast to catch McVeigh, the murderer was found to be already in police custody in Noble County, about sixty miles from Oklahoma City, having been stopped by a traffic cop only thirty minutes after the bombing, driving a lime-colored Mercury Marquis without plates. He also had an unregistered Glock semiautomatic pistol peeking out of a shoulder holster, loaded with armor-piercing "cop killer" bullets. Incarcerated in the county jail, he was just about to be released when it was realized he resembled the composite image being broadcast, and might indeed be the bombing suspect.

Though McVeigh still refused to talk, the dim but daunting pattern of mass murder in Oklahoma City and its white supremacist militia-cult

441

backdrop was elsewhere becoming clearer every hour. The bombing, involving upwards of fifteen hundred pounds of ammonium nitrate and fuel explosive (later estimated to be forty-five hundred pounds), had been a deliberate, symbolic assault on the federal government.

Shock became anger as Americans faced up to the possibility that they harbored, in their own midst, a Christian-raised terrorist no less fanatical and murderous than the Muslim extremists denouncing America abroad.

Stabilizing the Country

Responding to this, the president grew a foot taller as he began to fulfill his new role on the American stage: no longer the inexperienced commander-in-chief, but the father of a young daughter: as shocked as every parent in the nation, and as determined to find the murderers of American children and see them punished. In an interview with Wolf Blitzer and Judy Woodruff of CNN the week before the bombing, Ms. Woodruff had pointed to a "common, increasingly common, perception out there" that the president was now "less relevant" in American life "because of the successes of the center-stage role that Newt Gingrich and the House Republicans have played." As Woodruff harried the president again and again on the topic of his "relevance," Clinton had been driven almost to exasperation. "Well, I'm not responsible—I can't control the perception," he had replied, aware that his Capitol armory was now empty save for vetoes. "All I can do is show up for work every day."

In the aftermath of the mass murder in Oklahoma this work suddenly took on new import, as the president directed the federal agencies in their hunt for the killers, and the whole nation suddenly looked to the White House for its cue.

Many Americans had been "left wondering, if it can happen in the nation's heartland, can it happen in their hometown? What can you say to calm these fears?" one reporter asked the president on April 20, the day before McVeigh was identified as the bomber. "And what can you say to the nation's children, who have been terrified by seeing other children killed?"

The president's reply—discouraging any premature speculation, drawing attention to the increased efforts of the FBI and CIA, as well as tougher legislation he had already, two months before, sent to Congress to cut off funding to terrorist organizations, track explosives and weapons movements, and extradite wanted terrorists from havens abroad—showed a leader with a clear, calm agenda in countering the growing threat to America, at home and abroad. As for the terror being experienced by young kids, the president added, "I would say to the children of this country, what happened was a bad thing, an evil thing, but we will find the people who did it, and we will bring them to justice. This is a law-abiding country. And neither the leaders nor the citizens of this country will permit it to be paralyzed by this kind of behavior."

The next day, as hopes for more survivors dwindled, the body count mounted, and the numbers of dead children rose, the president went further. The children of America, he declared in an interview at the White House, "need to know that almost all the adults in this country are good people who love their children and love other children, and we're going to get through this. . . . I don't want our children to believe something terrible about life and the future and grownups in general because of this awful thing. Most adults are good people who want to protect our children in their childhood, and we are going to get through this."

To help the young, the president and the first lady then did something unprecedented: they invited some of the children of White House staff to join them in the Oval Office for a question-and-answer session that would be broadcast on radio and television. "Our family has been struggling to make sense of this tragedy, and I know that families all over America have as well," President Clinton explained, before leaving for Oklahoma City to lead a national memorial service for those who had died. "We know that what happened in Oklahoma is very frightening, and we want children to know that it's okay to be frightened by something as bad as this," the president said, opening the meeting, as seemingly comfortable with the children as with adults: a born teacher, at once caring and curious, intelligent and firm, understanding and determined. "Your parents understand. Your teachers understand it. And we're all there for you, and we're working hard to make sure that this makes sense to you and that you can overcome your fears and go on with your lives." He introduced the first lady, and after she too had spoken, the president addressed, via the cameras and microphones, "the parents of America."

I know it always—or at least, it's often difficult to talk to children about things that are this painful. But at times like this, nothing is more important for parents to do than to simply explain what has happened to the children and then to reassure your own children about their future. . . . This is a frightening and troubling time. But we cannot let the actions of a few terrible people frighten us any more than they already have. So reach out to one another and come together. We will triumph over those who would divide us. And we will overcome them by doing it together, putting our children first.

In the history of his presidency, these would be his finest hours as he guided the nation away from premature assumptions and accusations, and helped his fellow countrymen to confront the bitter truth: that this plot against America was the work of fellow Americans.

Before the crowds of mourners assembled the next day in the Oklahoma State Fair Arena, alongside Governor Frank Keating and the Reverend Billy Graham, the president then gave a speech that marked a sea change in his presidency.

Today our nation joins with you in grief, [the president said to his fellow mourners.] We share your hope against hope that some may still survive. We thank all who have worked so heroically to save lives and to solve this crime, those here in Oklahoma and those who are all across this great land and many who left their own lives to come here to work hand in hand with you. We pledge to do all we can to help you heal the injured, to rebuild this city, and to bring to justice those who did this evil.

This terrible sin took the lives of our American family: innocent children, in that building only because their parents were trying to be good parents as well as good workers; citizens in the building going about their business; and many who served the rest of us, who worked to help the elderly and the disabled, who worked to support our farmers and our veterans, who worked to enforce our laws and to protect us. Let us say clearly, they served us well, and we are grateful. But for so many of you they were also neighbors and friends. You saw them at church or the PTA meetings, at the civic clubs, at the ball park. You know them in ways that all the rest of America could not.

And to all the members of the families here present who have suffered loss, though we share your grief, your pain is unimaginable, and we know that, we cannot undo it. That is God's work.

Searching for words of comfort, the president explained with what emotion he had read the letter that a bereaved wife of one of the two hundred murdered passengers aboard Pan Am Flight 103, destroyed by a bomb in 1988, had sent him.

Here is what that woman said, and I should say to you today: "The anger you feel is valid, but you must not allow yourselves to be consumed by it. The hurt you feel must not be allowed to turn into hate but instead into the search for justice. The loss you feel must not paralyze your own lives. Instead, you must try to pay tribute to your loved ones by continuing to do all the things they left undone, thus ensuring they did not die in vain." Wise words [the president commented] from one who also knows.

He had his own words of comfort, however—words that would never be forgotten by those who heard them that day.

You have lost too much, but you have not lost everything. And you have certainly not lost America, for we will stand with you for as many tomorrows as it takes.

If ever we needed evidence of that, I could only recall the words of Governor and Mrs. Keating. If anybody thinks that Americans are mostly mean and selfish, they ought to come to Oklahoma. If anybody thinks Americans have lost the capacity for love and caring and courage they ought to come to Oklahoma.

To all my fellow Americans beyond this hall, I say: one thing we owe those who have sacrificed is the duty to purge ourselves of the dark forces which gave rise to this evil. They are forces that threaten our common peace, our freedom, our way of life.

Let us teach our children that the God of comfort is also the God of righteousness. Those who trouble their own house will inherit the wind. Justice will prevail.

Let us let our own children know that we will stand against the forces of fear. When there is talk of hatred, let us stand up and talk against it. When there is talk of violence, let us stand up and talk against it. In the face of death, let us honor life. As St. Paul admonished us, let us not be overcome by evil but overcome evil with good.

Yesterday Hillary and I had the privilege of speaking with some children of other federal employees, children like the ones who were lost here. And one little girl said something we will never forget. She said we should all plant a tree in memory of the children. So this morning, before we got on the plane to come here, at the White House, we planted that tree in honor of the children of Oklahoma. It was a dogwood with its wonderful spring flower and its deep, enduring roots. It embodies the lesson of the Psalms that the life of a good person is like a tree whose leaf does not wither.

My fellow Americans, a tree takes a long time to grow, and wounds take a long time to heal. But we must begin. Those who are lost now belong to God. Some day we will be with them. But until that happens, their legacy must be our lives.

At Last, the President of the United States

Simple, sincere, elegiac, and compassionate, the memorial speech helped a shocked nation to recover.

Never had the still-young president, at forty-nine, looked more like his admired predecessor JFK, or sounded more like President Reagan, the revered master of homey, heartfelt rhetoric. In a matter of days, President Clinton's federal team had solved the heinous crime while demonstrating to Congress and to the nation the importance of responsible and responsive *government* in a democracy. "So often criticized for bumbling, botching and indecisiveness, the Clinton White House has established a record little remarked on for decisiveness in the face of crises," it was noted in the press, as reporters reviewed the Clinton administration record—citing the way it had responded during the midwestern floods in 1993 and the Los Angeles earthquake half a year later. "In the immediate aftermath of Oklahoma City, the president was doing it again, aides say. Orders were issued, lines of command were made clear. . . . More important, says a former aide, crises free Clinton from having to balance the competing claims of interest groups. Freed from his congenital compromising, he can be decisive."

Bill Clinton was, at last, president of the United States of America, in word and in deed.

CHAPTER FIFTY-SEVEN

IN THE AFTERMATH
OF OKLAHOMA

A Defining Moment

"Let us turn away from the fanatics of the far left and the far right," the president's plea ran, "from the apostles of bitterness and bigotry, from those defiant of law, and those who pour venom into the nation's bloodstream." Those words had been spoken by Lyndon B. Johnson, after the assassination of President Kennedy. In the aftermath of Oklahoma City, they had become President Clinton's plea, too.

For neither president was healing a matter of rhetoric alone. Just as President Johnson, former master of the Senate and vice president, was impelled by the Kennedy assassination to create the sort of Great Society he had dreamed of in his youth, so Bill Clinton was impelled by the Oklahoma bombing to return to the bedrock principles of compassion that had marked his own youth—and as a Democratic centrist leader of his nation, to seize and hold the high ground, against the forces of evil.

"As horrible as it was, it was a moment he was born to be president for," George Stephanopoulos said later. "This sounds so clichéd, but it's true—he immediately felt what happened in Oklahoma City and was able to articulate it." Donna Shalala saw the Oklahoma emergency also as "the real test of leadership," for which, in the end, a president is elected—"and that's what I've seen in Bill Clinton," she recalled. "He can step up at a moment when everyone's devastated around him, and say the right thing to the American people. . . . Oklahoma City, for many of us, was the most devastating thing that happened during the course of the Clinton presidency. Nothing like that had ever happened before, and the president brought us together."

Leon Panetta, as White House chief of staff, thought it was "a real turning point. And I felt it even at that point, because up to then it was a political give and take. There was a lot of mudslinging going on. You just had no sense that the president was able to establish any traction with the American people about who he was." Oklahoma showed them. "People really, for the first time in a long time, connected with the president and what he was trying to be and who he was."

Henry Cisneros—whose maternal grandfather had fought in the Mexican Revolution—saw Oklahoma as undoubtedly the supreme moment of Bill Clinton's career so far: the final coming-of-age of the young president, in the same way as Cuba had been for JFK. "Oklahoma City was the moment when Bill Clinton grew up and into the presidency. Because it was no longer abstract initiatives, policy, fashionable policy, interesting political gamesmanship. People talk about the weight of the presidency. I think it was fun—until that moment." Cisneros paused, reflecting on his own words. Until Oklahoma "it was kind of fun—we'd got through a lot. But it still had aspects of a game, an adult game. A serious game—but a game. After Oklahoma City it wasn't a game. It was life and death."

He had traveled with the president to Oklahoma City, and was devastated by the sight. "I lost more people in my department than any other department—we had a HUD office on the seventh floor of that building: thirty-five people were killed. Very scary. But you know, you grow up. It was for him something like what the *Challenger* disaster was for Reagan: to show your healing and spiritual powers before the whole country. You can't fake it. He did his duty as president at that moment. He was sober and I think it changed him. People asked me later on, what was the most important moment of the first four years. And that's the one I cited: Oklahoma City."

Robert Reich, as labor secretary, was also awed by the president's instinctive leadership at this moment of crisis. "The president has an extraordinary capacity to empathize and also to preach," he remarked later. "I don't mean preach in terms of telling people what to do, or in a self-righteous way. I mean in terms of making people aware that the cosmos sometimes works in strange ways, in almost a religious aspect. Now, that may seem strange in the wake of Monica Lewinsky and all of that, and the moral turpitude that the president has displayed. But he comes from a Southern Baptist tradition, and he is extraordinarily able to feel the emotions in a situation, and to express those emotions in a very articulate way. The time of that bombing was one of his most eloquent times. He really did express the feelings of the nation."

As a young White House presidential aide, Rahm Emanuel also felt Oklahoma was a landmark in Bill Clinton's journey as president, but more than that, was a turning point in the history of America. The Oklahoma City bombing was, after all, not an isolated event, but a culmination of anti-government rhetoric that had, as Clinton's speechwriter Michael Waldman put it, "swirled" around Washington in the spring of 1995. For Emanuel and Waldman, as for millions of Americans who had listened to the rising cacophony of negative radio broadcasting, "there was no doubt that the intense anti-government sentiment was expressed through Timothy McVeigh and that bomb."

The snowball of American anti-government sentiment had grown larger and larger in recent years. There were, by the spring of 1995, militias active in a dozen states, and more units sprouting every day, openly espousing an anti-government agenda. President Abraham Lincoln, a Republican, had warned that those who have "ever regarded Government as their deadliest bane" could destroy America if they went unchecked. The "operation of this mobocratic spirit," Lincoln had warned, would undermine "the strongest bulwark of any Government, and particularly of those constituted like ours—I mean the attachment of the People."

The time, then, had come for the president, like Lincoln, to challenge the "mobocratic spirit" threatening the nation.

Words Can Have Consequences

Flying to Minneapolis for a national convention of community college administrators on April 24, 1995, the president seemed still visibly upset, especially by the tears of the bereaved—wives, mothers, husbands, fiancés, children, each with his or her own charged story of an innocent life extinguished mercilessly. Without real hope of finding anyone alive, rescue workers were still continuing to dig through the rubble in Oklahoma, fighting as they did so the sickening stench of the decomposing bodies they could not reach—dreading the moment they would finally come to the children's day care center, on what had once been the second floor.

Asked, after meeting with the children in the White House, whether "the general atmosphere of anti-government statements" had contributed to the "growth of groups" such as the Michigan Militia, the president had recalled times in Arkansas when "the venom, the hatred" had gotten out of hand and had led to the killing of innocents, but said that as the state's economy had improved, things had subsequently improved. Now that the national economy was picking up so fast, might one hope the same would happen—or was there a new evil burgeoning in the further reaches of America, fanned by anti-governmental rhetoric coming out of Washington? He wasn't sure, but he abhorred the "demonization" of those who worked for the government. "They are, after all, our friends and neighbors. We go to school with their children. We go to church with them. We go to civic clubs with them. This is—this is not necessary, this is *wrong*."

As the days had gone by, the question had been raised again and again, until he could avoid it no longer.

America, the president felt, was in danger of coming apart, not only economically as a result of globalization and technology, with a wider and wider disparity between the haves and have-nots, but culturally too, in the wake of that disparity. The rise of talk radio and the Internet had licensed the purveyors of simplified, hateful rhetoric in a new way, threatening a breakdown of civil discourse. "In this country we cherish and guard the right of free speech," Clinton acknowledged, proud to tolerate people saying even "things we absolutely deplore. And we must always be willing to defend their right to say the things we deplore to the ultimate degree. But we hear so many loud and angry voices in America today whose sole goal seems to be to try to keep some people as paranoid as possible and the rest of us all torn up and upset with each other. They spread hate. They leave the impression that, by their very words, that violence is acceptable." Referring to transcripts that were circulating of certain FM and AM radio shows, he remarked: "You ought to see—I'm sure you are now seeing the reports of some things that are regularly said over the airwaves in America today.

"Well, people like that who want to share our freedoms must know that their bitter words can have consequences and that freedom has endured in this country for more than two centuries because it was coupled with an enormous sense of responsibility on the part of the American people. . . .

"Our country, our future, our way of life is at stake. I never want to look into the faces of another set of family members like I saw yesterday," he declared, "and you can help to stop it."

Promoters of Paranoia

Watching the news wires, staffers back at the White House became anxious over the new direction in which the nation's preacher-in-chief was going. His presidential poll ratings had broken back into the fifties for the first time in a year, indeed had moved up to 58 percent; approval for his handling of the Oklahoma bombing remained in the upper eighties. They hoped therefore that such talk of "purveyors of hatred and division" and "promoters of paranoia" would not lead to a Republican talk-radio backlash. They were therefore appalled when, disregarding the dangers, the president flew to Ames the next day to address several thousand students at Iowa State University.

"Words have consequences," the president said, hammering home his message. "To pretend that they do not is idle." Quoting the Continental Congress firebrand Patrick Henry and President Thomas Jefferson, after whom he himself had been named, the president insisted that "even as we defend the right of people to speak freely and to say things with which we devoutly disagree, we must stand up and speak against reckless speech that can push people over the edge, beyond the boundaries of civilized conduct, to take this country into a dark place.

"I say that, no matter where it comes from, people are encouraging violence and lawlessness and hatred. If people are encouraging conduct that will undermine the fabric of this country, it should be spoken against whether it comes from the left or the right, whether it comes on radio, television or the movies, whether it comes in the schoolyard, or, yes, even on the college campus. The answer to hateful speech is to speak out against it in the American spirit, to speak up for freedom and responsibility."

To whom was the president referring? many students asked each other. Reporters, though, knew exactly. As the president's words raced around the country they, too, had consequences. While the presses rolled and newscasters reported the president's admonition, it became clear he had stirred a hornet's nest. Right-wing talk show hosts became apopleptic with rage, their programs—unnamed by the president—awash in self-righteous indignation.

Rush Limbaugh now accused liberals of trying to foment a "national hysteria" against the conservative movement, and called the president's remarks "irresponsible and fatuous." "Make no mistake about it: Liberals intend to use this tragedy for their own political gain," Limbaugh warned as a national debate began over the source and content of so much unregulated and unbridled negativism towards U.S. government departments and individuals. He blamed "many in the mainstream media" for "irresponsible attempts to categorize and demonize those who had nothing to do with this."

Limbaugh's colleague G. Gordon Liddy, one of Richard Nixon's infamous Watergate "plumbers," hosted a similar talk radio program aired on more than two hundred fifty American stations; he too had hitherto traded in insults and the wildest, most reckless rhetoric, breezily talking about taking rifle practice at stick figures named Bill and Hillary. If the authorities such as the Bureau of Alcohol, Tobacco, and Firearms came to take away their weapons, Liddy had advised his ten million listeners, "resist them with arms. Go for a head shot; they're gonna be wearing bulletproof vests. . . . Head shots, head shots." Questioned about this on CNN's *Crossfire*, he too refused to face up to the consequences of his radio hate. His new prescription for bringing down Treasury agents was, he corrected himself: "You shoot twice to the body, center of mass, and if that does not work, then shoot to the groin area." Reminded that the president was calling for an end to just such irresponsible rhetoric, in the wake of Oklahoma, Liddy told viewers, "I don't feel that I am fueling the lunatic fringe."

No Connection with Mainstream Conservatism

Not only Rush Limbaugh but the Speaker of the House fumed at the suggestion that his hate-filled attacks on the government had helped create a climate conducive to the Oklahoma City bombing. The "bombthrower" affected outrage. "It is grotesque to suggest that anybody in this country who raises legitimate questions about the size and scope of the federal government has any implication in this," he said. Besieged by NRA gun lobbyists fearful lest Congress now drop as a hot potato the assault weapon repeal movement, Gingrich issued a historic dare. "I challenge the news media," he declared, "to go add up the number of people killed by those [assault] guns this year and come back with a list. And then compare the bombing in Oklahoma City."

To Gingrich's chagrin the media did just that. According to the *Wall Street Journal*, some 229 homicides had been committed by assault weapons during the latest year of record, 1992—exceeding the death toll of Oklahoma City.

Though Gingrich was again publicly shamed, White House communications staffers nevertheless remained anxious over the president's new tack, scrambling to double-check the president's exact remarks and assure Rush Limbaugh the president had not singled out him—or Gingrich—by name. Targeting influential broadcasters could only backfire, politically, they felt. And when the president's polls began to slip again in the South, they felt vindicated in their concern.

For himself, however, Bill Clinton was glad he'd spoken his mind. For the first two years of his presidency he had, through inexperience and in an attempt not to make enemies, failed to transmit a clear set of principles by which he could be recognized and judged as president of the United States. For that he had been criticized by even his closest colleagues. Now, at the moment of America's biggest internal challenge since the Civil Rights era, he was at last able to show moral backbone, standing up for the principles in which he believed: freedom *and* responsibility in the advancement of America's "great experiment" in democracy.

Suddenly, far from being labeled irrelevant, the president looked essential, and the whole landscape of American politics looked different. Even Republicans in Congress expressed a newfound admiration for Mr. Clinton—especially those from Oklahoma. First-term representative J. C. Watts declared that "the president, from day one, has set the proper tone." The Republican governor, Frank Keating, expressed unalloyed gratitude. "Our president was swift to act," he said in a special radio address. "He sent us the resources to solve this terrible crime, he offered condolences and heartfelt assistance of a grieving nation." Even the rarely charitable Robert Novak called the president "decisive and in command." And the Senate, in a special vote, unanimously congratulated the president.

From arrant congressional ascendancy the Republican Party was now put on the defensive, their angry-white-male supporters tainted not by a rogue element, a single, crazed assassin, but—as FBI and media investigations were revealing—a mass-murderer thrown up by a subculture of government-hating Americans behaving not very differently from Ernst Roehm's brownshirts during the Weimar Republic. "They are convinced the U.S. Government is trying to disarm U.S. citizens," one Australian journalist reported in an article entitled "America in the Grip of Militia Madness." Australia was noted for its outback white individualists, the journalist wrote, but the Oklahoma bombing was true craziness—sponsored by militias that threatened the very fabric of American society. "They are convinced the U.S. Government is doing so because it is conspiring to destroy the American Way Of Life. They are convinced the U.S. Government is in cahoots with the United Nations to carry out this conspiracy. They are convinced the UN has an enormous fleet of jet black military helicopters hidden in the U.S. midwest. Soon these will be deployed to every big town and city in the U.S. and UN troops will take over. They are convinced this will be the second stage of the New World Order and New World Government conspiracy initiated by former president George Bush. They believe also in countless more looney accusations. They are convinced they are right, and they are convinced only they, citizens' militias, can stop this. 'Families are going to be split up,' said one member on *Dateline* as he shot at a human shaped target. 'They're going to be taken to these concentration camps and locked up. You'd better believe it, because it's true.'"

Mr. Crackdown

The bombing was the very worst thing that could have happened to Speaker Gingrich and his Contract With America. However hard he and Senator Dole now attempted to separate themselves from the individuals responsible for the bombing, the arsenals of ammonium nitrate barrels, the handguns and automatic weapons, and the sheer volume of militia firepower located by the FBI in its nationwide series of raids were undeniable.

Even the normally conservative *Boston Herald* warned that Senator Dole's public vow to repeal the assault weapons ban "could strike the general electorate as a foul sop to a freakish fringe whose most evil adherents are Public Enemy No. 1." The president's counterterrorism package, which had languished in the Republican-controlled Congress since the beginning of the year while Gingrich had pushed through his Contract With America measures, would surely now have to be passed without delay. As Lou DiNatale, another political pundit in Boston, predicted in his Bay State idiom, "even Joe Bag-of-Donuts is looking at this tragedy as a side effect of nasty rhetoric. If he's clever enough, Clinton can look like Mr. Crackdown, picking a nice spat with the ACLU, while Bob Dole and the NRA types look like creampuffs on crime."

DiNatale was right. The Speaker objected to the president's anti-terrorism legislation, which included the creation of an FBI-led domestic counterterrorism center, a thousand more anti-terrorist officers, and new powers for federal law enforcement officers. These would permit officers to infiltrate suspected terrorist groups and be given access to motel registers, phone logs, and credit card records. Such powers smacked of "internal espionage," Gingrich complained, but his tactic won little traction in the nation. McVeigh was found to have carried out a reconnaissance first in Omaha, Nebraska, with a view to planting a massive bomb there, but decided that the driveway was too far from its federal building to achieve the size of bomb blast he planned. Across the country, government officials reviewed their security arrangements—and with each day's revelation about the spread of America's brownshirt brigades, congressionally approved internal espionage to avoid another Oklahoma seemed more urgent.

Militia spokesmen might accuse the FBI of planting the bomb at the Murrah Building to make the armies of the right look bad, and Michael Reagan, a talk show host in California and the former president's son, might accuse Mr. Clinton of having prepared his anti-hate media speech *before* the bombing, but as the rubble was finally cleared and the last of the 186 dead were brought in—the children and adults unrecognizable even in gender, so crushed were their bodies—it was clear the nation had come to a crossroads. The president, the vast majority of Americans felt, was right to crack down on extremists and to warn of the dangers of irresponsible negativism, if the republic was to be preserved.

To the chagrin of the militias and NRA lobbyists, both Dole and Gingrich formally agreed to drop the idea of repealing the assault weapons ban—and proposed, instead, to pass the president's stalled Omnibus Counterterrorism Act within a month.

TURNING
THE BATTLESHIP

CHAPTER FIFTY-EIGHT

TRIANGULATING MORRIS

Tax Cuts No Lure

For the Republicans the Oklahoma City tragedy was not only a national disaster, it was—thanks to the party's poor response to the bombing, its insistence on repealing the assault weapons ban, its opposition to anti-terrorism measures in Congress, and its anti-government rhetoric—a *political* disaster. Conservative pundits assured those who would listen that the fickle nation would soon forget the president's "pitch-perfect" performance, and voters would be lured back to the Republican Party by promises of across-the-board tax cuts. They proved wrong. Not only Morris's polls but Republican surveys, too, showed that most Americans, when asked if they would like a tax cut, responded positively; but if the question was phrased differently, the majority favored dealing with the national deficit first, and taking tax cuts later. The Reagan lure was proving, for the moment, a dud.

There were other problems for Republicans, too. Gingrich might think himself prime minister of America, but versions of his bills had also to go before an American House of Lords, the Senate, before they could go to the president for his signature—or veto. Gingrich had prided himself on passing nine of his ten Contract With America items in the House in less than a hundred days, but hopes that the Republican-controlled Senate would follow suit had been smashed by the Senate majority leader, Bob Dole.

Senator Dole's concern was that the passing of Congressman Gingrich's Contract could only add to Gingrich's glory, not his own. He therefore had little interest in pressing his fellow senators to follow Gingrich's suit—indeed, the opposite seemed to be the case. While this strategy might serve to fell Gingrich as a potential rival for the 1996 Republican presidential nomination, however, it overlooked the fact that, if the much-vaunted Contract With America failed, then the president would look stronger, and thus be harder for Dole to beat.

Movement in the Senate to match Gringich's Contract items with Senate bills thus became turgid, leading radicals to call for Senator Dole to step aside and resign his leadership or even his seat, the better to concentrate on the presidential nomination and thereby allow his feistier Republican colleagues to push through the Gingrich revolution. As Gingrich later admitted, "the force and passion of the House freshman class of 1994" was a problem the aging senator had not come across before: members of Congress "who were not so much politicians as dedicated reformers full of moral certainty."

Dole declined for the moment to step down in the Senate, however. He had waited more than twenty years to occupy Lyndon Johnson's spacious old majority leader's office, and had no desire to surrender it after such short tenure, however much he aspired to Johnson's ultimate goal. Power was sweet, and gave Dole's candidacy early teeth in comparison with other Republican contenders. Moreover, it guaranteed him a Senate hearth if, in fact, he lost the nomination race. Suppose, for example, General Powell decided to run, or was drafted by the party as General Eisenhower had been? Or what if one of the younger Republican contenders were to beat Dole in the primaries? Former governor Lamar Alexander of Tennessee was only fifty-five, and despite having been secretary of education under President Bush, had not only signed on, in February 1995, as a challenger for the nomination, but had called for the abolition of the department of government he had headed, in a cynical move to fly the banner of states' rights against those of the federal government.

Thus the almost seventy-two-year-old majority leader sat tight in his Senate office, hoping his passivity would help flush out the extremists like Senator Phil Gramm and Steve Forbes, the editor of *Forbes* magazine, whom he could hopefully then trounce for the presidential nomination with the gravitas of his leader's robes—leaving Newt Gingrich to rough up the supposedly lame-duck Democratic president.

Unfortunately for both Dole and Gingrich, the president, after Oklahoma City, was looking suspiciously like a spring chicken.

Who Will Be the James Carville
of the 1996 Campaign?

Several weeks before the Oklahoma bombing the president had decided to come clean with the rest of his senior advisers: "Charlie," his mysterious, anonymous "adviser," was none other than Dick Morris, a Republican.

Morris was furnishing the president with excellent polling data and policy ideas, Clinton had early on confessed to the vice president, Al Gore—recommending that Gore meet Morris, and that they work out a plan for Morris's eventual integration into White House operations. With Gore's assent it had thus been agreed that Morris's existence should be kept from the rank and file of the White House staff for the moment, but in terms of strategic planning—policy, and the communication of that policy—he should be taken on board demi-officially. From March 1995 he would be permitted, Gore had agreed, to take part in the weekly Wednesday, top-level post-meltdown strategy meetings in the White House residence, and his suggestions and ideas would be discussed openly in front of the White House chief of staff, the vice president, the vice president's chief of staff (Jack Quinn), and Panetta's two deputies, Erskine Bowles and Harold Ickes, instead of continuing to arrive via mysterious unsigned faxes and memoranda.

It had not taken long for word to leak out, however—and on April 14, 1995, Ann Devroy of the *Washington Post* had slipped Morris's name into a page-9 piece about the opening, that day, of the Clinton-Gore 1996 campaign office at 2100 M Street NW, Washington, D.C., on the seventh floor, not far from the White House—raising the question "Who will be the James Carville of the 1996 campaign?"

The cat was peeping out of the bag, and by the time of the Oklahoma City bombing even the conservative columnist Robert Novak was forced to consider the political implications of a Republican Carville to guide the president's hand. Novak had gloated over Clinton's backs-to-the wall assertion that "the president is relevant"—which had, Novak pointed out, "brought back memories of Richard Nixon saying, 'I am not a crook.' " Yet the news that Dick Morris was now working for the president spelled, in the wake of Oklahoma, real trouble for Republicans, Novak admitted.

Novak was right. Several weeks later even the sleepy *New York Times* began to pick up on the difference in the president's handling of himself—and of his handlers. "A bill to reshape the nation's legal system is on the ropes in the Senate," the newspaper reported on May 7. "The president, so lately accepted as weak—or worse, irrelevant—brands it the 'Drunk Drivers Protection Act' and it dies that afternoon." In other words, the president had no need to heap up a pile of vetoes: the very *threat* of veto was now enough to kill a Gingrich bill. "From the cornfields of Iowa, where he staked out his ground on farm policy, to the hotel ballrooms of New York and Washington, where he has delivered rousing red-meat speeches on Mideast terrorism (to Jewish groups), abortion rights (to women) and Medicare (to the elderly), the president has adroitly moved to rally the traditional Democratic voter groups, whose support he must not lose. Mr. Clinton has also taken actions that were nothing more or less than presidential, but that seemed unusually decisive and rhetorically charged for him," the *Times* commented. Mr. Crackdown was also moving more swiftly than the Republicans in Congress could keep up with—"Indeed, Mr. Dole and Speaker Newt Gingrich found themselves in the unusual position of defending the First Amendment lest the White House move too fast." As the newspaper added, "The Oklahoma City bombing galvanized national attention on the man in the Oval Office in a way that was routine during the Cold War but is rarer now. A president comfortable from childhood with the liturgical idiom has flourished as pastor and choirmaster."

Forming a Team

The success of the president's ministering, pundits had also begun to notice, had been enabled by his new, more efficient and effective White House operation, under Chief of Staff Leon Panetta. His reorganization of the once-rickety White House staff operation was at last beginning to pay off—"the result of patient, grinding work by a staff reorganized months ago," the *Times* acknowledged, "to reduce the number of presidential appearances, give Mr. Clinton more quiet time each afternoon to think and read and make phone calls and to focus on the things that matter most."

Ironically, "to some extent what saved Bill Clinton's presidency the second two years—and in the end probably saved his re-election—was the Republican capture of Congress," Panetta later reflected. "Because in many ways it helped define who Bill Clinton was. Particularly after the [midterm] election he saw the role that money played, he saw how the Republicans were able to package their message—particularly in the Contract With America. . . ."

Initially, following the election, Clinton had felt miserable about the Democratic senators and congressmen who'd lost their seats—"it hurt him," Panetta recalled. "He felt that he had to bear some responsibility for what happened to those guys. I mean, he did make them walk the line on gun control . . .

"I think Clinton will always try to find that there was somebody else who was responsible—so it was real hard for him to say it was totally his fault. I think what he really thought was that it wasn't that he was so much to blame for what he'd tried to do. It was really that he'd never developed the kind of PR ability, message ability, to get it across to the American people. That for all of the good things he was trying to do for the country, that he couldn't just bring it together, and really sell it to the American people. And I think that's probably why in the end, when he brought in Dick Morris, he reached back into his past. And brought this guy in who was . . . I mean, he's totally amoral!

"Harold Ickes had dealt with Dick Morris [before], and when he found out he was involved in some polling for the president, it drove him crazy! But Clinton was now trying to figure out, from a political point of view: what is it that I've got to do? Where are the American people? Where's the head? And Morris was obviously able to do that—from the time in Arkansas, when he lost the governorship.

"Was there a struggle for the *soul* of Bill Clinton? No—I mean, he would never concede that. But there was a lot of soul searching. I think Clinton knew what he wanted to do for the country, he knew what he wanted to accomplish; I mean he knew the areas that he wanted to achieve in—I think that part of it was O.K. I just think he always felt ambivalent about *how* could he put this together, so that you can then sell it to the country?"

The Black Hole

It was in the context of the president's soul searching that all the president's men reared in fury at the prospect that Dick Morris be allowed not only to come *aboard* the Good Ship Clinton, but to *pilot* it!

The long, deliberate concealment over the identity of "Charlie" and the influence the anonymous consultant was clearly already exerting on the president was bad enough. As Stephanopoulos later put it, the months of working "with a parallel black hole White House that you couldn't fight openly" had been depressing for the staff: the feeling "that you never knew when its influence was going to be brought to bear. . . . And you'd be in a situation where the entire administration would be sent down a path for a certain speech or a certain initiative, and then late at night it gets upended in a phone call with Dick Morris. It's just an incredibly unproductive and just dispiriting way to work." The revelation, then, that the "black hole" was none other than Republican consultant Dick Morris, currently working for the Republican opposition, was even *more* dispiriting. "The problem, the concern we had," Panetta recalled, "was that Morris was basically doing polling work for Trent Lott, who was deputy senate majority leader! Morris was a double agent, or spy. I said [to the president]: 'Aren't you a little nervous?'"

"Resentful" was George Stephanopoulos's characterization of the White House staff's reaction to Morris's influence on the president, once his identity was exposed. "They despised him. We all despised him, and more than that," Stephanopoulos confessed, since it "certainly seemed to a lot of us that his views unfiltered were simply just accepting the Republican ideas and claiming them as our own—abandoning everything we had fought for, everything we had fought for in the election and everything we had fought for in the first two years in the White House."

The Oklahoma City bombing on April 19 (though left unmentioned in Morris's self-laudatory memoirs) had certainly permitted the president to seize the high ground in terms of American values, but it did not resolve the further, more specific question: exactly what Republican legislation would the "triangulating" president (a word Morris had invented for the president's new choose-from-both-plates policy) countenance, and what not? What policy initiatives should he promote, as an independent president—and what (if he wished to be nominated as Democratic Party candidate the following summer) could he *not* allow to pass?

On May 16, 1995, finally, matters came to a head.

Morris's Pulled Teeth

"There are too many pulled teeth," Morris groaned, in despair at the waste of so many of his "brilliant" ideas. His every bold proposal had either been shot down, he claimed, or rejected by a government department (such as Justice), or been leaked to the media so that the press could pre-trash it. In his view, Panetta's team was simply mouthing the "obsolete orthodoxies of the Democratic congressional leadership," and recycling Congressman

Gephardt's "leftover speeches." "Why hurry?" Morris asked sarcastically. "Just because we are below forty percent in vote share and under fifty percent in approval, why have any sense of urgency at all?"

Panetta was outraged. He could listen no longer; he refused to, as he put it, "turn the White House"—and thus the executive command post of the nation—"over to a political consultant." Undeterred, Morris countered by saying they would lose the White House in 1996 *unless* they did so.

"The president said little as the argument intensified," Morris recalled of one meeting, but merely "brought the combat to a close by saying he would address the conflict 'later on.'"

The altercation with Panetta early in the evening, proved, however, only the beginning. Morris remained behind with the president and vice president, and then launched into a tirade the like of which had seldom been heard in the history of the Treaty Room (named, as it was, for a peace agreement—the one ending the Spanish-American War). Intent on using the room as his private study, former professor Clinton had employed Kaki Hockersmith, his and Hillary's Arkansas designer friend, to transform the Treaty Room into a private "club library" for the bookworm president—a place where he could consult the past. In it he had filled the new shelves with his biography and history book collection. He had also requested General Grant's eight-drawer walnut conference table on which to mount his framed photographs of his family and of JFK. "Think plush Victorian velvet," a reporter had described the Treaty Room after its makeover: "voluptuously swagged fabrics and dark woods." (For its part, the Lincoln Sitting Room, nearby, was "now dressed up like a 'Gone With the Wind' belle in her best frou-frou silk, velvet and gold," the reporter described.) To achieve the sense of warm coziness the president wanted, Hockersmith—who had redecorated the Governor's Mansion in Little Rock for the Clintons—had used crimson fabric with gold Napeolonic wreaths on the wing chairs, deep red drapes, and mottled burgundy walls. There was an eighteenth century royal blue Chippendale sofa, and an ornate deep-pile Persian carpet in shades of pink, cream, and blue.

However much other interior designers sniffed—"Kaki's taste is horrible; mixed metaphors in everything," one was heard to comment—Bill Clinton loved Hockersmith's transformation. But on this evening the president was still suffering jet lag after his four-day visit to Moscow with Hillary for the fiftieth anniversary of the end of World War II in Europe—VE Day. He had therefore dreaded a fight between his own advisers.

Though he'd avoided a fistfight between Panetta and Morris, he was in for a fight himself, he now realized, with the New Jersey triangulator—a fight he could not escape. Compared with the previous month he was, he believed, looking good in terms of re-election; in fact, the various strands of his presidency were, he felt, finally coming together in a remarkable way—foreign affairs, domestic, legal, and personal. Hillary had begun to overcome her sense of guilt over health care reform failure, and was, he thought, successfully refashioning herself as first lady—just as she had when she dropped her surname, Rodham, after Bill's defeat as governor of Arkansas in 1980. Kenneth Starr, the Whitewater investigator, had been to the White House with his three top deputies, a few days after the Oklahoma bombing, and they had all been very civil with one another—indeed, following the meeting, the president had asked one of the White House lawyers, Jane Sherburne, to show the prosecutor and his men the Lincoln Bedroom, with its copy of the Gettysburg address, copied in Lincoln's very own hand so that the original could be auctioned on behalf of war veterans. It was the gesture of a president who loved history, but "Hillary thought I was being too nice to them," he recalled later. In his own mind he was, however, "just behaving as I'd been raised to do, and I hadn't yet given up all my illusions that the inquiry would, in the end, follow a legitimate course."

Hillary had fumed at such largesse towards their enemies. "The idea of hard-core Republican partisans rummaging through our lives, looking at every check we had written in twenty years, and harassing our friends on the flimsiest of excuses infuriated me," she admitted later—disregarding the way she had earlier ordered just such a probe of the White House's longtime travel staffers. As she acknowledged, though, "This was only the first illustration of the differences between Bill's way of dealing with Starr and mine. We were both in the eye of the storm, but I seemed to be buffeted by every gust of wind, while Bill just sailed along."

The president certainly seemed to have picked himself up after the midterm catastrophe with extraordinary resilience. An eternal optimist, he had continued to do his duty as he saw it—saving the Mexican peso, improving the American economy, healing the nation in its time of shock over the Oklahoma City bombing. Ignoring protests at home over the barbarous Russian invasion of Chechnya, he had, in return for voicing no U.S. objection to the largely indiscriminate Russian devastation of the secessionary state, also gotten President Boris Yeltsin, after conclusion of the official VE

Day anniversary celebrations, to agree to Russia joining the Partnership for Peace—thereby accepting, on behalf of the Russian Federation, a deferred but inevitable enlargement of NATO, after the Russian presidential elections in 1997 (thus bolstering Yeltsin's prospects in his 1996 reelection battle). "We're completely agreed on this, Boris, completely?" Clinton had asked, double-checking Yeltsin's undertaking, also, *not* to supply centrifuges to Iran and thereby "give the new Ayatollah an A-bomb." Strobe Talbott, as deputy secretary of state, was summoned to witness the international gentleman's agreement, which Vice President Gore and Russian Prime Minister Viktor Chernomyrdin could translate into a formal agreement at a meeting of foreign ministers of NATO at the end of the month. "I think we got a big *da*," Clinton then summarized for his old Rhodie friend. "You can go have a drink. I assure you *he's* had a few."

Dealing with the mercurial Morris, however, was far more difficult than dealing with the Russian bear. Furious that his great Republican ideas—especially on immigration—were being·shot down by Panetta, the son of Italian immigrants, Morris blamed the president. "You're the biggest problem," Morris shouted at the commander-in-chief. "You've lost your nerve. You're not the same man I worked for in Arkansas. That guy took risks. That guy took on issues. That guy knew that a good fight with a good enemy would build him a political base. That guy tested teachers. That guy took on the utilities. Where is that guy? He's the one I signed on to work for. I'd follow him to the ends of the earth and back. I'd bet on him any day. Where in the hell is he?" Morris screeched.

Vice President Gore put his finger to his lips, to quieten Morris's tirade. The president himself, attempting to defuse the tension with a joke, pointed to the door and said that if Morris shouted any louder the Secret Service might appear, guns at the ready, anxious lest Morris was threatening the president's life.

Morris—a maverick among political marketing strategists, and with an artist's often manic ego—lowered his voice. Like Salome, Morris then demanded the head of Panetta, claiming the president's chief of staff was continuing to crush his best proposals, however extremist. "I don't care whether he's liberal or he's part of the establishment or he's a bureaucrat or he's just contrary. I don't care what the reason is; he just keeps blocking the stuff I develop—at your behest—to move you to the center."

Vainly, the president pointed out that Panetta *was* a centrist, like himself—the architect of deficit reduction. The New Jersey dynamo, however, was having none of it. He wanted Panetta fired, and was prepared to risk his own neck to achieve it. "I know you got the living daylights beaten out of you on health care. And I know that you got killed for raising taxes. And I know all about gays in the military, but Goddamn it, we have to have fights—the right fights. You have to take new positions—the right positions, the ones you believe in. You have to act boldly. You have to reposition yourself. Or it won't work."

Vice President Gore defended the chief of staff, whom he'd urged the president to appoint in place of McLarty. The president finally spoke up for Panetta, too. Panetta had, after all, brought order to White House operations. "There used to be chaos around here," the president confessed. "Every day we would have three, four meetings lasting hours and hours," he confided. "I'd sit in them, and we'd make decisions like a committee. And every day I'd read about them in the papers. It got so that the public had an impression that I was indecisive. I wasn't. I just didn't have the luxury of making my decisions in private. Every step, every stage, every word was leaked."

This was true (as Elizabeth Drew's and Bob Woodward's accounts of his first eighteen months had demonstrated, to the president and first lady's extreme discomfort). The admission avoided, however, the president's own responsibility for permitting such bull sessions, indeed his patent love of such chaos. In any event, Panetta had been a godsend, the president now insisted—though perhaps he was, as chief of staff, keeping too tight a rein on new ideas, he allowed. "I've been worrying about terrorism and Oklahoma City, I've been up all night working on Bosnia. I haven't been sleeping well," Clinton excused himself, saying he would nevertheless "get it done."

Dismiss Panetta? Allow a Republican pipsqueak, a man incapable of even delegating business to a secretary, to have free rein in the White House, to become an American *Rasputin?* Gore was horrified, but wisely chose to leave the room. The president had brought Morris in, and the president must decide whether to sling him out—or accede to his demands.

No sooner had the vice president quitted the room than Morris struck up again, peppering the president with a hail of bullet-like accusations. Then, reaching up to grab the president's flabby biceps, he squeezed tight, and through clenched teeth, snarled: "Get your nerve back. Get your fucking nerve back"—and went home to his hotel room, walking on air.

Triangulating Not Strangulating

Was Morris's version of the gunfight, published two years afterwards, accurate? Loath to admit to Morris's role in his supposed move to the center, Bill Clinton declined to mention it in his memoirs, a decade later. But he did not deny it.

Morris had referred to him, Clinton knew, as "passive." This was not how the president saw himself, however. He was not aggressive by nature, he accepted. But he *was* competitive: deeply competitive. Where others used fists, however, he had always used his brain. He was, he believed, almost supernaturally patient, right up to the point where his patience snapped and he erupted in anger, lashing out at his staff and conferring blame in brief storms of abuse, which then subsided.

Why had he not felled Morris, as he had once slugged him in Little Rock, when Morris pulled a tantrum and resigned from his team? Why did he allow Morris to leave the Treaty Room with that smug smirk of self-satisfaction on his face—having spoken to the president in a manner no other U.S. citizen, however senior, would dare employ?

Why? The president himself didn't know, beyond jet lag, and the allergies that flared up whenever he stayed at Camp David (where he'd spent the past weekend). And yet, in his heart of hearts, Bill Clinton *did* know. Knew that the diminutive Dick Morris, with his crazy rat-a-tat-tat agenda of ideas, held the key to the enemy's castle: to the cynical, self-centered, brazen, often hypocritical Republican ethos of the eighties that seemed to have embedded itself in the American psyche in a way that European conservative movements had not quite managed. Conservative prime minister Margaret Thatcher had become an exemplary mentor and ally to Ronald Reagan, but her day was over and her successor, John Major, was hanging on to power in Britain by a thread, facing overthrow by voters by 1997, the latest point at which he had to call an election. By contrast, in the United States, Newt Gingrich and other conservatives had created an alliance of anti-everything-to-do-with-government: anti-tax, anti-abortion, anti-welfare, anti-national health care reform, anti-evolution teaching, anti-weapons ban, anti-environmental protection, anti-public broadcasting, anti-civil rights, anti-immigrant, anti-UN, anti-international voters. . . .

Could a more forceful Democratic leader have better countered the Republican tide sweeping America in the 1990s? In Britain, the leader of the opposition Labour Party, Neil Kinnock, had failed to unseat the Conservatives at the post-Thatcher election—and Tony Blair, his successor as parliamentary leader of the Labour Party, was now crafting his election strategy, after sixteen years of Conservative Party rule, on a centrist platform that rolled back very little, if any, Conservative legislation. In Russia, Boris Yeltsin had been forced to surrender his tough economic reforms and even embark on a tragic war in Chechnya to hold on to a popular base—and even so, Yeltsin's chances of winning the 1996 Russian presidential election looked slight. If Bill Clinton was portrayed as a chameleon, changing his color to suit his environment, it was not necessarily a pejorative description. Chameleons changed color in order to survive in the brutal world of nature—just as politicians needed to do at times: the "shifting of the battleship in a new direction," as his political campaign director, Doug Sosnik, called it.

The chameleon was therefore unwilling to slug Dick Morris, let alone expel him from the re-election team. In fact, it was in this reflective rather than reflexive nocturnal moment that the president realized it was not only sensible to continue to use Morris as an adviser, but that it was crucial for him to do so. He must, he recognized wearily, continue to triangulate Morris and his White House team of Democrats—rather than strangulate the little bastard, as he would happily have done after Morris's latest act of insolence—if he was to go on beating Republicans at their own game.

CHAPTER FIFTY-NINE

FIRST VETO

Gingrich Is Devastated

Whether or not Morris's Treaty Room challenge tipped the scales in Clinton's forever-calculating mind, the president announced the very next day after his combative session, on May 17, that he would use his presidential veto for the first time in his presidency.

This first veto would be employed, the president declared, to sink Congress's proposed "rescission bill": a special bill to permit the use of money already appropriated by Congress for 1995 but unspent, in order to cover not only emergency funding but other projects Gingrich now wished to fund, including items of his Contract With America.

The president's announcement winded Gingrich. The Speaker had already suffered one self-inflicted disaster, in March, when insisting not only that a balanced budget resolution bill be passed in Congress, but that it be made permanent as a *constitutional amendment*—thus forever tying the hands of the Treasury, the Congress, and the president. (The bill, though it passed the House, hadn't got through the Senate—thanks to a brave Republican, Mark Hatfield of Oregon, chairman of the Senate Appropriations Committee.)

Gingrich had been livid—but had still not gotten the message. Indeed, it had only hardened the Speaker's determination to force a showdown with the "irrelevant" president. Now, several months later, Gingrich had again stuck out his neck. "I just don't get it," Gingrich wailed as he saw his Republican rescission bill now sink beneath the water. "It's the first chance the president has had to sign a bill that moves us to a [Republican] balanced budget."

What part of the defeat of the Republican proposal didn't Gingrich get? the *St. Petersburg Times* asked in an editorial. The president was vetoing Gingrich's bill because it savaged $1.5 billion from job training, national service, summer employment, and anti-drug programs, the newspaper pointed out—cuts that Republican lawmakers wanted made not in order to reduce the deficit, but to provide whole slabs of Federal "pork" for Republican members' constituencies, including "$438 million for new federal offices, $450 million for highway construction, $474 million for government travel and $60 million in tax breaks for billionaires who renounce their American citizenship." The president, in other words, looked moral, Gingrich looked corrupt.

It was in this context that the balked Speaker first raised the possibility of blackmail—warning for the first time of a "train wreck" he would engineer in the fall if the president would not co-operate. For, as the missile launcher threatened, the Republican-controlled Congress could simply refuse to authorize the current annual deficit by refusing to pay government salaries—indeed, if necessary, by defaulting on U.S. government loans. In other words, the Speaker would shut down the U.S. government.

An Opening Salvo

A *deliberate train wreck? Default? Shut down the government?* "We were relying on our belief that the majority of Americans wanted a balanced budget," Gingrich later said of his error. "If he would not bend to our will," the Speaker wrote of the president, "and we would not bend to his, there would be stalemate. The stalemate would in turn lead to a very public and much publicized fight"—a fight in which public opinion would help force "the president to agree to our program of cutting taxes, reforming welfare, and balancing the budget." His political troops and his lieutenants were "all gung ho for a brutal fight over spending and taxes"—enthusiasm that the Grinch "mistook," he himself later confessed, for the "views of the American people."

However significant symbolically, the rescissions bill veto battle was, in retrospect, only a skirmish, involving only a tiny fragment of the national budget—a small opening salvo in what Gingrich himself described later as the Republicans' long-planned "grand showdown over [federal] spending."

As Gingrich prepared the next battle of his Barbarossa strategy, leading inexorably towards Moscow, the president now prepared his defenses, in anticipation of the "grand" assault. He could continue to give battle via Democratic Party members of Congress, but would these be enough? Thanks to his poor early presidential performance, these members were now in the minority, and were in danger of being overcome by the very fierceness of the Republican siege.

Que faire? The president's constitutional power, on domestic issues, lay only in his veto—which could be overruled by a two-thirds majority on the Hill. Yet his greatest authority, he knew, was *moral*: namely, his role as elected president not of Congress but of the American *people*—and with this in mind Clinton declared, in an interview with New Hampshire Public Radio on May 19, that he was not intrinsically against balancing the U.S. budget. He had, after all, always had to balance the state budget when governor of Arkansas. "Well, I'm—first of all I'm not, certainly not at odds with those who are determined to balance the budget by a date certain," he had told Peter Malof. "For two years, for two years," he emphasized, "they said no to all my efforts to get them to work with me" over deficit reduction. "So we reduced the deficit three years in a row for the first time since Harry Truman, with *nobody* helping us in the other party, none of them. And they were saying we were going to have a big recession, and it would wreck the economy." Those predictions had proved idle, he reminded listeners. "New Hampshire had a 7.6 percent unemployment rate when I became president, and it's 4 1/2 percent today," he pointed out. "You've got forty thousand new jobs, and in the previous four years you lost forty thousand jobs. So they were wrong."

The president, as steward of a now burgeoning economy that Republicans had done everything to ruin, was clearly in his element. Newt Gingrich's belated recognition of the need to tackle the deficit, and his new target of achieving a federal budget balance within seven years, however, seemed unnecessarily arbitrary. Why *seven*, particularly? Though the details of the Republican bill had still not been announced, it was clearly going to be based on huge, ideologically inspired tax cuts for the rich that could only be paid for by massive cuts in federal services for the ordinary middle class and the poor, especially in Medicare and Medicaid. "So my answer is, if we have a targeted tax cut that focuses on [helping] the middle class and rewards education and childrearing, we can do that in the context of deficit reduction. But we cannot afford a big, broad-based huge tax cut in the magnitude that the House passed and balance this budget without doing severe damage to the elderly of this country, including the elderly people in New Hampshire."

It was at that moment, as the interview came to an end, that the president let slip his own bombshell. Asked to confirm that he was at this point against setting an arbitrary date by which to balance the federal budget, Clinton reiterated that the budget *could* be balanced in seven years—but that it would entail cutting too many important federal programs, and thus tear the fabric of American society in an unfortunate way. There was, however, an alternative timetable. "I think it clearly can be done in less than ten years. I think we can get there by a certain date."

Sneaking Off the Bench

The president's statement—whether deliberate or inadvertent—soon not only had pundits in the media buzzing, but the president's own staff. Caught off balance, the White House staff at first refused to supply journalists with a transcript of the president's interview. Surely it must have been a slip of the tongue, an inadvertent speculation, even a trick of the microphone? Or was it, as Stephanopoulos and others portrayed it within the West Wing, a presidential *betrayal*? Was the president now unilaterally reneging on the agreed White House and Democratic Party Congressional Caucus strategy of fighting Gingrich's Republican attacks, as and when they were launched—as they had successfully done over the "pork-laden" Republican rescission bill—forcing the Republicans to declare first what specific federal cuts they were proposing, and then each time hitting them out of the ballpark?

The morning assembly of senior White House staffers held in the Oval Office immediately after Memorial Day, on May 23, 1995, had therefore become a crisis meeting of economic advisers, prior to the president's planned Rose Garden press conference that afternoon. Withdrawing his interview remark, the president sounded sheepish before his team, giving the impression that he'd been caught "sneaking off the bench," as Stephanopoulos later put it—especially as Democrats in Congress were reported to be "apopleptic," according to the vice president.

Senate Minority Leader Tom Daschle and House Minority Leader Dick Gephardt visited the White House to protest. Yet the proverbial writing on the wall was now there for all those with eyes to see. Armed with his power of veto, the president was *not* going to follow the battle plan of his party in Congress. He was going to produce his own!

The Need for a Positive Vision

Liberals such as George Stephanopoulos and Gene Sperling, Clinton's economic adviser, understandably viewed the president's *faux pas,* as they saw it, with horror. Not only had his offer to balance the budget in under ten years not been rehearsed or discussed prior to broadcast, but, they claimed, it was a sign of weakness at such an early stage of the battle—a tactical mistake that would merely embolden Gingrich's ideological standard bearers in their march on Washington and the federal government.

The president was embarrassed but unrepentant. "You guys want me to go out and criticize the Republicans, and when they say, 'Where's your plan?' you want me to say, 'Well, who am I? I'm just the president of the United States. I don't have a plan,' " he said, mocking his critics. That was not *his* idea of presidential leadership, the president explained. He had spent a lifetime working out the intricacies of budgeted governmental programs at a state level, and since late 1992 a national one. As a modern president, he had at hand his own White House Office of Management and Budget. There was no reason why he should not propose his own long-term American balanced budget plan. Once prepared, and once their respective long-term budget balancing declarations were announced (ten years, say, against seven), the armies could then meet on the field of battle, and fight it out. Moreover, he was not yet a sitting president in his second term, defending the measures of his first. Standing for re-election to office, he would soon be joining Republicans in his own electoral battle, in hand-to-hand combat—not in Congress, but across the nation. For that campaign he needed a positive plan, a vision, a program he could put forward as he had done in 1992, and for which he could ask his campaign troops to fight.

As Doug Sosnik, the newly appointed political director for the 1996 campaign, recalled, elections are about people's expectations of the future, not the past. "Obviously, we had a bad midterm election. Clinton spent ninety to a hundred and twenty days trying to sort out what it all meant and how he was going to proceed. Then he told me in February or March how he was 'looking forward' to the campaign."

Looking forward? Sosnik was surprised. "I mean, at that point, if you were to look at newspapers in this country, they were basically saying he was a lame-duck president. Gingrich was running the country! Gingrich was the most powerful—he was the 'it' guy there, for a while. For the first hundred and twenty days of '95 he was a bigger story than we were." Sosnik laughed at the painful recollection. "Why are you looking forward to it?" he'd therefore asked the president.

Clinton, in a thoughtful mood, had confided: "Well, I'm going to move into a period now where I'm going to be compared against somebody who's going to be running against me—not just against some idealized version. I don't know if I'm going to win re-election or not. I think I can, I think I will, but I'm not sure. But I tell you, what I don't want to do is run for re-election and not have the kind of presidency for the next two years the way *I* want to do it." "And so, in March of '95," Sosnik recalled, "we started putting together the campaign, what it would look like."

The notion of merely fighting the Republican army with negative vetoes was fatuous, in Clinton's view. Had not President Bush failed to win re-election because, after Desert Storm, he had no domestic vision or plan? How then did staffers like Stephanopoulos imagine he could sit still and wait for the enemy to attack, as the French had waited in the Maginot Line in 1940? However misguided his Contract, Newt Gingrich had won control of the House by putting forward a positive-sounding agenda, not a defense line. Besides, as Sosnik saw firsthand, the president was by nature an optimist, a doer, a believer in improvement, both personal and communitarian improvement—not a rear guard.

"So really," Sosnik recalled, "with no support on Capitol Hill outside of a few Democrats in the Senate—certainly none of the House Democratic leadership—[and no support from] virtually the entire West Wing staff: against all of that, Clinton went out and put his own ten-year plan down!"

Stephanopoulos was aghast. "*Putting People Last*," he mocked openly at the May 23 meeting, and *sotto voce* ribbed Sperling (the same age as himself) as to which of them had seniority if one of them were to run against the president as a *real* Democrat in the '96 primaries.

A Volatile Atmosphere

Even Robert Rubin, as Treasury secretary, had hitherto opposed the notion of a time-framed balanced budget, since there "wasn't any real economic difference between small deficits that continued to decline as a share of GDP and actual balance." The president's determination, on May 23, to go for a budget to be balanced within ten years—or less—however, changed Rubin's mind. "Basically, I knew what he was saying was right," Rubin later confessed. "We advisers were all sitting there telling him there was no economic difference between a few billion dollars and zero, which is true as an analytical point. But there was a much bigger point, the one Clinton was making: if we wanted to talk about spending money on education and programs for the inner city, people weren't going to listen to us unless we talked about these problems in the context of a balanced budget," once Gingrich had made it such a feature of his Republican Contract.

This was the crux: that to save and improve vital social programs in a nation in which, thanks to white flight, there was less and less support of President Johnson's Great Society, the majority of voters would listen only if the administration placed the value of those programs within a larger, *feel-right* context: balancing the budget. As Rubin belatedly recognized, "Balancing the federal government's books did resonate and was a goal that voters could relate to and rally around. In that meeting the president was pretty much alone in what really was an extraordinarily perceptive insight about what was needed to make his agenda work with the public"—a "threshold issue, because it was a precondition for getting people to listen to us and hence for doing almost everything else the administration cared about."

For the Treasury secretary the meeting was, in its personal way, epochal. "Working in the White House, I had already come to understand that if you want people to listen to you, you have to express yourself in a way that connects with them. But sometimes even that isn't enough. On some subjects, people simply won't listen to you unless you say or do something that opens the door first—which was Clinton's point about the [ten-year] balanced-budget proposal."

Reluctantly, even Stephanopoulos gave way. The next morning Erskine Bowles, Panetta's deputy, exploded when Stephanopoulos again questioned the president's strategy. "Damn it, George, the president has made a decision. He wants a ten-year budget. Let's just give it to him," Bowles urged, "and make sure he has a balanced presentation." Under the hawkish eyes of Panetta's successor at OMB, Alice Rivlin, the president's ten-year plan was to be drawn up over the succeeding weeks—with the onus on the White House team to now convince their party colleagues in Congress: a prerequisite to joining battle with Gingrich's army.

With Dick Morris delighted by the president's stand and gung-ho for an immediate national announcement, there was another explosion at the weekly strategy meeting held at the White House residence on May 25. Urging the president to make an instant television broadcast before Panetta and his staff were ready, Morris took on airs less of Rasputin than of Rumpelstiltskin now—stamping his feet, and in danger, it was said, of going through the floor rather than the roof. Insisting that Clinton's polls showed a 10 percent drop in the president's current approval rating, he demanded that the president give his ten-year budget address the following Tuesday, May 31—"it has to be next week or never."

Panetta not only disagreed with the rush, but was appalled that his president could allow a political consultant with no understanding of Congress, let alone White House operations, to speak so rudely—"the double indignity," as Stephanopoulos recalled Panetta's lament the next day, "of being insulted by a charlatan and hearing no defense from the president in return." So upset was Panetta by the president's behavior that he talked of resigning, along with Rubin's successor as chair of the National Economic Council, Laura Tyson. It was in this volatile atmosphere that the president now convened, on May 30, a meeting of his entire economic team—without Morris's incendiary presence.

On Ground of His Own Choosing

Though Morris was not allowed to attend the convocation, his gravitational pull was evident to all: "the black hole," as Reich called him.

"Mr. President," Reich pleaded, "the Republicans have given you a *gift*. Their [seven-year] budget is a moral *outrage*. It demonstrates who they're for and who they're against. It's a perfect platform for fighting on behalf of hard-working people and the poor."

Clinton, determined to get into the fight with Gingrich but on ground of his own choosing, remained adamant that he still wanted an announcement of his own ten-year balanced budget, if possible the next day. "I *must* propose a way to balance the budget," he explained to his distinguished economic cabal. "I *want* a balanced-budget plan. The voters *care* about this." But why the next day, his advisers asked?

It was now that Robert Rubin, the Treasury secretary, added his voice to those arguing against a premature announcement—and with that the vice president spoke up. "Mr. President, you're in a different place from your advisers," Al Gore summarized, regarding the matter of timing. By the end of the day, Stephanopoulos remembered proudly, the president "had agreed to put off any announcement for a week—a good day's work for our side." The broadcast would now be delayed until the whole team was ready with OMB-backed facts, figures, and, above all, a proper communications plan to support it.

Meanwhile, half a world away, another confrontation was taking place that would have equally momentous ramifications—for on May 25 NATO bombers had struck at the Bosnian Serbs, at a town called Sarajevo.

CHAPTER SIXTY

ENDGAME

The Problem from Hell

Intent upon promoting his Contract With America program at home, Newt Gingrich had called for huge cuts in U.S. foreign aid spending but had largely deferred to the president over U.S. security issues—hoping such largesse would make the president more amenable to the Republicans' revolutionary domestic program.

There was a second reason, however: the intractable mess in the Balkans. For Gingrich as much as for the Clinton administration, Bosnia was the "problem from hell," as the secretary of state, Warren Christopher, called it—the graveyard not just of former Yugoslavs, but of anyone who attempted to mediate or enforce a solution.

The first attempt, after Haiti, to use American offensive military power in southern Europe, over Thanksgiving 1994, had proved a complete failure. U.S./NATO airplanes had been authorized to bomb airfields that were openly being used to support the Serb counter-assault on the UN "safe haven" at Bihac. "I thought they [the U.S. bomber aircraft] were going to crack the hell out of them," Anthony Lake recalled. "And the next morning woke up to discover—because of the UN influence, largely—they waited until there were no [Serb] planes on the runway! So I threw up my hands there for a while."

The Serbs had responded, as Lord Owen and other European diplomats had predicted, by blockading two hundred UN peacekeepers guarding the weapons-collections sites around Sarajevo, and by taking fifty Canadian troops captive. They had also shut down the free movement of UN military observers in Bosnia—making a U.S. military strike even less promising. And President Radovan Karadzic warned that one more NATO strike would mean war—"because we would have to treat you as enemies. All United Nations Protection Force personnel as well as NATO personnel would be treated as our enemies."

Lake's impulse had been to accept the challenge. But how? The UN-NATO dual key restriction agreement on air strikes had proven a calamity; the UN-declared "safe-havens" were, as a result, nothing of the sort—neither safe nor havens. Thanks to the failed Bihac air strike, the United Nations Protection Force—though helping to keep alive many hundreds of thousands of largely defenseless Muslim civilians—had essentially become, as Lord Owen had predicted, a UN hostage force for the Bosnian Serb leader, Radovan Karadzic, and the situation was threatening to spill over into neighboring Kosovo and Macedonia. It was no longer a problem from hell; it became a nightmare.

Lake, who had to brief the president every day, came to feel he had "a B engraved on my forehead—scar tissue from banging my head against the issue all that time."

"Everybody is saying there's nothing we can do," Lake recalled. The State Department, under its anodyne secretary, Warren Christopher, had argued for "containment, 'just don't let the Bosnian issue infect everything else—it's NATO or Bosnia. We've gotta choose NATO,' et cetera. And I didn't see any way out," Lake later confessed. "I finally decided, maybe the folks in the State Department were right. And we weren't going to make the case with the Europeans. . . . And so to my great regret, I agreed. And sent a memo to Clinton saying, 'We all agree that we've got to back off.'"

As the president had gotten his second wind in the early months of 1995, however, working secretly with Dick Morris, so too had Lake, working with *his* staff: the National Security Council. He'd been warned by General Colin Powell—who had himself been national security adviser from 1987 to 1989—that the initial Clinton administration team responsible for defense and diplomacy was a calamity. One staffer recalled Powell comparing the national security adviser to the driver of a horse team—"and you don't have the horses," Powell had warned Lake. "So you'll have to start pulling it yourself."

Lake's reluctance to do so had stemmed from his own experience with too-powerful advisers such as Henry Kissinger, whose egomaniacal drives had improperly influenced President Nixon. Lake had resigned from Kissinger's NSC staff over the U.S. invasion of Cambodia, and had thereafter become a firm believer that the role of national security adviser was that of broker between the president, the State Department, and the military. By appointing Christopher and Aspin to State and Defense, however, the president had simply ensured that he had no clear and forceful foreign policy team to broker.

Once Secretary Aspin's place had finally been taken by William Perry, matters had improved, but though Lake had attempted to be more robust in advising the president, the Bosnian cancer had not been successfully treated. Instead it had returned in all its ugliness at Bihac. As in Somalia, the great force for potential humanitarian good represented by U.S. air power had been revealed to be a hollow stick. "I was very frustrated," Lake recalled—though he was in retrospect aware, a decade later, that the Bihac humiliation was, in its awful way, a turning point. "The irony of Bihac is that on the one hand it discouraged us. But on the other hand, it showed how bad things were getting, so we had to concentrate. . . . "

Doing nothing would not, Lake knew, address the malignancy. Once the 1994/5 winter ceasefire (negotiated by former president Jimmy Carter) ended on April 30, 1995, violence on a massive scale would return to Bosnia—Sarajevo and the three remaining eastern Muslim "safe havens" of Srebrenica, Zepa, and Gorazde being seen by Serbs as thorns in the side of Greater Serbian quest for more territory.

It was in this context, therefore, that in the early spring of 1995, while the Bosnian Serbs prepared their own Final Solution, Lake had ordered a review of American diplomatic and military options. Just as Bob Rubin had, as national economic adviser to the president, marshaled the different economic departments and advisers into a cohesive team to promote deficit reduction, so belatedly Lake would have to do the same in terms of U.S. foreign policy over Bosnia—but with a still reluctant Pentagon and a deeply ambivalent State Department, headed by Warren Christopher.

Bosnia had become Lake's obsession—"to try and figure it out." Working together with his European desk director, Sandy Vershbow, Lake had thus come to his own conclusion: one that would go down in modern humanitarian history as The Endgame.

Human Shields

"It's a chess concept," Lake later recounted. "Instead of thinking, 'We're here; what's the next step to get to somewhere where we want to be?' we should *start* with: 'What's the *end* state that we want to achieve? And what are the decisions that will get you there? And if we make *those* decisions— primarily about military force—can we use that then to leverage a diplomatic solution? And what are the key barriers to it?' "

Lake's conclusion was that a key barrier to being able to put force behind our diplomacy was UNPROFOR—the United Nations Protection Force, which the Serbs saw as easy hostages. The force had been doing "good work," Lake recalled. "And the Europeans were so invested in it. And if you collapse UNPROFOR, then what happens to the humanitarian supplies? And will the Europeans agree—which they didn't before?"

Through the spring of 1995, then, Lake's NSC team had worked on the notion of a new, post-United Nations Protection Force strategy, which boiled down to an American-led strategy. The end objective was a negotiated peace settlement. To achieve it, muscular international force would have to be threatened, and if necessary used. To relieve the besieged cities of Bosnia, it would probably be necessary for the arms embargo to be lifted. Muslim forces would then be armed and trained; the threat of U.S. air strikes would protect them while this happened. If the Serbs did not withdraw, the Western allies would strike.

Before such a policy could be enacted, however, the State Department's *status quo* supporters would have to be convinced, and also the European governments and the United Nations. It was in this context that, in the same way as Newt Gingrich's Republican army would overreach by shutting the entire government and defaulting on U.S. loans, the Serbs made a massive miscalculation of world opinion—thus doing Lake's work for him, in innocent blood.

On May 7, 1995, the Serbs lobbed shells into the civilian heart of Sarajevo, deliberately killing eleven people. The UN refused the UNPROFOR commander's request for a NATO air retaliation, and two weeks later, on May 22, the emboldened Serbs then entered the twenty-kilometer exclusion zone around Sarajevo to seize back their impounded heavy artillery weapons stored there.

This time, after a forty-eight-hour ultimatum, NATO bombers *were* authorized by the UN to strike: targeting two ammunition bunkers outside Pale, the "capital" of the Bosnian Serb state.

In a tit-for-tat response, the Serbs counter-retaliated by shelling all six UN safe havens, including Tuzla, in the north, where they killed seventy-one young people in an outdoor café, and wounded two hundred fifty others.

NATO planes responded by bombing six *more* Serbian ammunition dumps, at which point the Serbs took more than three hundred fifty UN peacekeepers hostage, as they had at Bihac—this time declaring them "human shields."

UN Surrender

The situation was fast becoming a fiasco; the world watched French troops surrendering with white flags, and Canadian peacekeepers being handcuffed to a Serb ammunition dump.

Using stolen French uniforms, Serb forces then seized the UN checkpoint on the Vrbanja Bridge into Sarajevo on May 27—causing the UN commander, on direct orders of an outraged new French president Jacques Chirac, to seize it back, at the cost of two French soldiers' lives. On June 9 Lt. General Bernard Janvier, commander-in-chief of all UN forces in the former Yugoslavia, then held a secret meeting with the Serb commander, Ratko Mladic, to obtain the release of the UN peacekeeper-hostages—by allegedly promising, as UN C-in-C, not to order any more NATO air strikes. It appeared to be an abject surrender by the Western allies—indeed, the way was now open for Serbs to seize *all* the lightly protected safe havens.

The European insistence on the lightly armed UN Protection Force and Warren Christopher's long appeasement policy were now utterly confounded: paving the way either for another Mogadishu or for Lake's accelerated Endgame.

High Noon

The summer of 1995 now became the test of Bill Clinton's resolve to be an affirmative, not negative, president. Wrestling with his staff already over the ten-year budget balance declaration—as well as a new Supreme Court decision (*Adarand Constructors, Inc. v. Peña*) that put affirmative action in jeopardy—he had to decide how to handle the Bosnian crisis. First, however, he would have to face the music on the domestic front.

On June 13, the day after the Supreme Court's ruling, having ordered his staff to draw up a comprehensive new report on affirmative action in the light of the justices' decision, the president gave his brief, delayed ten-year balanced budget speech. Robert Reich hated it.

"B's cave-in brings us halfway down the slippery slope," the Labor secretary wrote in his diary. "B has thrown in the towel. I'm sure Morris is behind this."

Morris was—though not in the way that Reich, who had still not met him, imagined. On Sunday, June 4, Morris had been summoned from his holiday in Maine to meet with the president and Leon Panetta, in the Treaty Room. Sitting in wing chairs on opposing sides of the coffee table, with the vice president on one couch and Panetta on the other, the quartet had tackled the question of how to meld policy initiatives for the president's re-election campaign into the business of the presidential day. Morris read out a memo his colleague had prepared, outlining the controversies thrown up by recent re-election campaigns, Democrat and Republican. "I'm bringing Dick in to throw long," Clinton had explained to Panetta, "and I need you to help him do it."

Panetta, sickened at the prospect of Morris's extreme ideas (especially on immigration) becoming campaign rhetoric, warned: "Mr. President, you can have my resignation before I will allow half-baked ideas to make it out of this building, before experts who have spent their lives working in these areas have a chance to review them and modify them to make them work. We cannot just turn the White House staff and the cabinet over to a political consultant."

It was High Noon (though nearly midnight) in the Treaty Room, and a truce was desperately needed. Al Gore backed Leon Panetta, saying there could only be one chief of staff. As he looked at the president's face, Morris realized that he had, like Gingrich, finally overreached. Recalling the moment vividly in his memoirs, Morris was brutally candid. The president's unspoken instruction to him was, he remembered, all too clear: "The president was telling me to fold my hand and get out of the meeting alive." Apologizing for his inexperience in top-flight management ("There's nothing like learning at the top," he tried to joke), Morris agreed to a set of new rules outlined by the vice president to satisfy the chief of staff. "I would not go to the West Wing offices unless specifically invited to a meeting there. Before I saw any government official," Morris recalled, abjectly, "the meeting had to be cleared by Leon or Erskine Bowles." Rumpelstiltskin had been denied the queen's baby; the president would continue to triangulate, on his own terms, not Morris's.

The president's new ten-year proposal for a balanced budget, delivered before the cameras in the Oval Office on June 13, then ensured that the Clinton-Gore electoral campaign got off to a brilliant start. The new administration plan, the president explained to viewers on national television, "does not raise taxes," and would not be easy, "but elected leaders of both parties agree with me that we must do this, and we will."

It was 9:05 P.M. and in a mere five minutes, before sixty million Americans watching on all four major TV networks, the president of the United States had seized back the domestic initiative. The national project of balancing the federal budget was now the president's plan, not the Republicans'.

COMMANDER-IN-CHIEF

CHAPTER SIXTY-ONE

SREBRENICA

The Threat of Armageddon

Liberal commentators in the press were surprisingly slow to see the merit of the president's strategy. With opinion polls still showing Dole more likely than Clinton to win the 1996 presidential election, many Democrats hated to see Clinton bending so far backward to make a budget deal with Republicans in Congress. Only E.J. Dionne in the *Washington Post* seemed to get the point, writing that although congressional Democrats felt the president had removed the bullets from their guns, "the move could also be Clinton's way of strengthening his hand for the big breakdown that will take place in the fall if the Republicans insist on cutting more than Clinton decides he can accept."

In this scenario, the train wreck being threatened by the Republicans could give the president and the Democrats a *cause célèbre*. "If there is going to be Armageddon on October 1," one administration official told Dionne, the president wanted to be in a position "to lay the predicate. He wants to use these four months to do everything he can to show he's reasonable." As Dionne warned readers, "the really important choice has yet to be made." Indeed, he predicted, "the real issue here is whether Clinton decides that he is willing to pay the Republicans a very high price for budget peace, or whether he will risk Armageddon and take on their view of government. Clinton hasn't decided that yet, and there will be a lot of fighting for his soul before he does."

Kicking the Can

Armageddon, meanwhile, seemed much closer in Bosnia than in Washington. The Bosnian Serbs released their UN hostages, then began massing for an attack on the remaining UN safe areas.

The great Balkan showdown was approaching. In 1992 some 130,000 people had lost their lives in the former Yugoslavia; in 1994 "only" 3,000, President Clinton had pointed out on June 16, defending his administration's and the UN's efforts. Yet General Janvier's capitulation to Serb demands, though it secured the final release of all remaining UN hostages, opened up Bosnia to a tragic denouement. If mass murder was to be avoided, action would have to be quick.

"We have to get the policy straight," President Clinton complained at a "pre-brief" with his national security team, the morning after his budget-balancing broadcast, "or we're just going to be kicking the can down the road again." President Chirac was due to visit him on his way to the G–7 meeting in Halifax, Canada, and was sure to raise the Bosnian crisis. "Right now," Clinton said bluntly, "we've got no clear mission, no one's in control of events."

The humiliation of the peacekeepers brought back painful memories of Mogadishu. "I never would have put forces on the ground in such a situation," the president said, criticizing the UN. "The rules of engagement are crazy." An American F–16 fighter pilot, Captain Scott O'Grady, enforcing the UN no-fly zone over Bosnia, had been shot down by Serb anti-aircraft missiles, and after six days' hiding had been plucked from potential captivity by marine helicopters operating behind the Serb positions. In an emotional ceremony at the Pentagon on June 12, the president had welcomed O'Grady home—but rescuing downed American fliers was scarcely the way to put pressure on the president of Serbia, Slobodan Milosevic, or on the Bosnian Serbs in Pale to negotiate withdrawal from the Muslim territories they had seized, let alone stop them from committing more atrocities.

Fortunately, compared with his predecessor, Francois Mitterand, the new French president proved a breath of fresh air, indeed a new dynamic in the Bosnian drama. His proposal was to form a UN Rapid Reaction Force—an idea that had been mooted as far back as 1993. But who would pay for it?

Determined to simply arm the Muslims and let the Bosnians fight out their Armageddon, and skeptical of UN competence in military matters, Senator Dole and Speaker Gingrich were steadfastly refusing to fund

American participation in any proposed RRF. Arranging for Chirac to visit Dole and Gingrich on Capitol Hill, Clinton attempted to get Chirac to help break the American stonewall. With Dole eyeing the presidency and Gingrich eyeing the budget-balancing fight, neither was willing to back Chirac's initiative, however—and the ten-thousand-strong RRF, consisting of French, British, and Dutch troops, was eventually deployed the next month without American soldiery. By then, however, the tin can was no longer a can. It was an international disgrace, and a human catastrophe.

Srebrenica

In the early hours of July 6, 1995, heavily armed Bosnian Serb forces launched a concerted attack on the Muslim city and supposedly "safe area" of Srebrenica, lightly protected by Dutch UN peacekeepers—resulting in the worst war crimes in Europe since World War II, enacted by radical Serbs in cold blood.

Under their commander, General Ratko Mladic, Serb forces herded twenty-three thousand women (many of whom were to be raped in transit) and children out of the Srebrenica enclave and moved them to the Tuzla area, while almost eight thousand unarmed Muslim males (men and boys) were callously executed. Babi Yar, the site of which Clinton had so recently visited on his way back from Moscow, was being reenacted before the disbelieving eyes of a stunned world.

Europeans and Americans alike were aghast. Madeleine Albright had ignored the terrible genocide in Rwanda until it was too late, but as U.S. ambassador to the UN—the very body that had guaranteed the disarming and military protection of Muslims in Srebrenica—she now had a duty to demand action. She tried. As each day more and more newspaper and television reports emerged of the merciless killing, and the U.S. State Department contented itself with Serb denials, she urged the CIA to seek corroboration in the field.

Meanwhile, at the White House, Clinton's stomach turned at the accounts of ongoing Serb atrocities. Congress and public opinion had, since the disaster at Mogadishu, tied his hands as commander in chief except within the Americas, permitting genocide in Rwanda on a scale that was, in retrospect, unimaginable in its brutality. That had been in black Africa, however. Now the same inhumanity was being visited in southern Europe, bringing back images of the Nazis in Poland, Russia, and elsewhere. Even the commitment of twenty-thousand American troops to a NATO plan to cover the possible withdrawal of the UN Protection Force had been damned in Congress, forcing the president to give a humiliating assurance that, if American troops were committed, no American life would be endangered. The situation was becoming catastrophic. With the Western allies still powerless to stop them, thanks to American pusillanimity, the Bosnian Serbs were indulging in homicidal mass mania.

To Fight Back, or Not to Fight

On July 13, President Chirac personally telephoned the president. "We must do something," he implored—suggesting the French fight their way back into Srebrenica with ground forces, supported by American helicopters. But *where then*? Clinton asked. An escalating land war in Europe?

The question facing the United States was how to act within a long-term strategy, a true endgame—not merely react. The next evening, on the putting green of the White House garden, the president nearly became hysterical. "This can't continue," he screamed at Sandy Berger and Nancy Soderberg, as Berger confirmed further emerging details of Serb atrocities—and the powerlessness of the Dutch UN forces in the city to stop it. "We have to seize control of this. I'm getting creamed!"

Swearing with frustration, the president rehearsed, for three-quarters of an hour, the humiliation of the UN's peacekeeping mission, and the damage it was doing to American prestige as the world's last superpower.

Thus, finally, in the tragic, criminal end to the UN "safe area" of Srebrenica, Tony Lake's Endgame was given the green light.

Genocide at Srebrenica

Years later Serbian apologists would continue to deny, in the manner of Holocaust deniers, the deliberate murder of the eight *thousand* men and boys they took captive in Srebrenica—hoping to muddy the deliberate atrocity by parlaying it within the context of other ethnic violence in the war-torn Adriatic peninsula. But the horror of Srebrenica in July 1995 was not only unerasable, it symbolized the ultimate, inescapable truth in Bosnia: that the Serbs, at bottom, had no fear or respect for the Western European nations. Neither the arms embargo nor the economic embargo had proven effective, while the presence of limited numbers of lightly armed

UN peacekeepers, as potential hostages, had made NATO threats of aerial bombardment hollow. The only threat of intervention that the Serbs feared was that of the United States—and without that, the Serbs would not negotiate, or let go their ill-gotten gains.

On Monday, July 17, with more and more reports coming out of Srebrenica, Lake put his Endgame proposal before the principals meeting at the White House, in front of Madeleine Albright, General Shalikashvili, William Perry, Sandy Berger, and Secretary Christopher. Mladic's forces would, unless stopped, now move on to "cleanse" other UN "safe havens." The Europeans could not handle the worsening crisis without provoking war; ergo, the United States would have to take charge, unilaterally if necessary, and force the Serbs to the negotiating table by the use of force—air force.

As Warren Christopher attempted to derail Tony Lake's assumption of his role as secretary of state, the president—by arrangement with Lake— entered. Two and a half years of American heckling from the sidelines of Bosnia had resulted in UN impotence, NATO emasculation, Serb impunity—and the nightmare stories emerging from the "safe haven" of Srebrenica, which the UN was supposed to have protected. "This policy is doing enormous damage to the United States and to our standing in the world," the president reiterated. "We look weak. And it can only get worse. The only time we've ever made any real progress is when we geared up NATO to pose a real threat to the Serbs." But what to do? "We have a war by CNN. Our position is unsustainable; it's killing the U.S. position of strength in the world."

Ambassador Albright, humiliated by the dishonor the UN was suffering in Srebrenica, was at least glad to see that the president now saw Bosnia as a test of American resolve in world affairs. As Lake put it, Bosnia had become "the symbol of U.S. foreign policy"—and the time had now come to assert that symbol, as they had done in Haiti the previous fall: with military determination, based upon humanitarian and security concerns. It was thus agreed that the next day, July 18, the team would reassemble in the Oval Office, as they had before Haiti.

Like the Europeans, they had dithered too long—but while no European nation had the power to force a settlement, America had. And with the images of Serbian atrocity on every TV screen in America, the refuseniks in Congress were temporarily silenced, for shame. It was imperative, then, to move swiftly. And this time, to make an American solution stick.

CHAPTER SIXTY-TWO

OPERATION DELIBERATE FORCE

How to Think

"Think about the date on which Bill Clinton became president of the United States: January 20, 1993," *Washington Post* reporter Tom Lippman reflected, a decade later. "We really are in a period where it's only just vaguely dawning on people that the world is going to have to be managed in a whole new way now, after the implosion of the Soviet Union and the end of the Cold War. People understood it intellectually, but that whole premise had never been tested on the ground really, by the time Bill Clinton came to power. The idea that it would become the mission of the United States to undertake invasions for humanitarian reasons, or that you would put out brush fires that were becoming forest fires for the sake of doing it, was really a very alien concept to the United States. And it was not one that Bill Clinton brought with him to office. And so these events took place in an intellectual vacuum—there was no construct, no framework, by which these atrocities could be evaluated as they occurred. 'What does this truly mean for the national interests of the United States of America, and for our friends?' There was no way to calculate that. I mean, all these years later, you can see: 'Who cares about Somalia? Completely irrelevant!' And so: 'We should be out of there!' But the way in which it was handled looked terrible at the time. And in fairness to Clinton and his team, I think that part of the learning process of those first couple of years was to say, 'We have to think about this in a different way.' And the theme of the meeting has to be a different theme now. 'What are the stakes in each of these episodes?' In Haiti, in 1994, it was: 'Democracy in the Americas'—which was a consistent theme, for better or worse, in the Clinton administration. But in Bosnia it was much different.

"George Bush had talked about the New World order—but no one had any idea what it was going to look like. Meanwhile, the infamous Chinese Communists are suddenly buying Buicks, and taking on the mantle of a manufacturing state driven by money. All the eternal verities of managing the world vaporized, almost overnight! At the same time, you had a new generation of military officers who were not traumatized by Vietnam.

"And so I think it would be fair to say, there was a very steep learning curve—not just about how to run the government or how to administer foreign policy, but about *how to think about the world*. And even now it's still going on. What is the global mission of NATO, for example?" Lippman shrugged. "But we're much more comfortable with the idea that—for better or for worse—we're going to go over there and kick butt, even if they're not Communists.

"And so this kind of use of American power for objectives that previously would not have been considered sort of intellectually valid was something they had to learn to do. And how to pick their spots. And why to do it in place A and not place B . . . "

Now, finally, there was a chance to show how effective the world's last superpower could be, once it fully charged itself with a mission.

At the meeting on July 18, 1995, Vice President Gore led the discussion—a discussion that mirrored similar ones taking place across the United States, as ordinary Americans confronted the wanton rape, mass eviction, and merciless mass murder of civilians in Bosnia.

Almost sixty years before, similar feelings had been experienced by American citizens over stories leaking from Czechoslovakia and Poland following Hitler's invasions, and then the Blitzkrieg spring of 1940—with America Firsters forcing the United States president to stay out of European affairs, lest he face defeat at the November 1940 presidential election.

Senator Dole and Speaker Gingrich, on behalf of Congress, had remained adamant: no American ground forces should be deployed. Yet the situation could not be allowed to continue if the United States was to have the right to call itself the world's leading power. A photograph of a Muslim girl, the same age as Gore's daughter, had been published across the world; she had hung herself by her belt and habib from a tree. "My twenty-one year-old daughter asked about that picture," Gore confided. "What am I supposed to tell her? Why is this happening and we're not doing anything? My daughter is surprised the world is allowing this to happen," the vice president acknowledged. "I am too."

The Serb conquerors had, in medieval fashion, even singled out any Muslim females known or found to be related to the local Muslim commanders to be *gang* raped: a deliberately symbolic, dishonoring act that the Serbs wanted all Muslims to be aware of. The cost for everyone, the vice president warned, would be paid over decades to come. America must act. "It goes to what kind of people we are. Acquiescence is the worst alternative."

Ignoring the ever-anxious Warren Christopher, the president summed up. They agreed, he said, that "the status quo is untenable"—with the murderous Bosnian Serb commander, Mladic, openly boasting that the Serbs would next seize the UN-protected safe havens of Zepa, Gorazde, and Bihac. And "in the end Sarajevo and we'll finish the war," the president paraphrased the genocidal Serb agenda.

Such a Final Solution was a challenge that the UN and the community of civilized nations—especially the United States, housing the headquarters of the UN—could not turn away from. "The United States," Clinton declared, "can't be a punching bag in the world anymore." It had to act.

The London Conference

In anticipation of the outcome of the president's July 18 crisis meeting, General Shalikashvili, the chairman of the Joint Chiefs of Staff, had in fact already been sent to London to confer with his British, French, and other NATO military counterparts, as well as contributors to the twenty-three-thousand-strong UNPROFOR units in Bosnia.

Christopher and his new assistant secretary of state for European Affairs, Richard Holbrooke, were skeptical whether the French and British would sign up to a clear, unified strategy, for the British were against air strikes that would lead to yet more hostage taking, particularly the three hundred Welsh Fusiliers "protecting" Gorazde. Meanwhile, the French wanted to rush more troops into Gorazde, using American helicopters, under NATO air cover.

Journalists, too, were cynical. "The latest test of wills between the Bosnian Serbs and the West has followed a familiar pattern," the *Washington Post* reported. "In military terms, the Bosnian Serb army is no match for

NATO. Unlike the West, however, the Serbs have the advantage of strong leadership, a clear idea of their territorial goals and a strategy for achieving it. The Western alliance has been hamstrung by constant bickering between troop-contributing countries such as France and Britain, which are vulnerable to hostage-taking, and the United States, which has sought the moral high ground without risking the lives of American soldiers."

Aware of such skepticism, Secretary of Defense William Perry accompanied Warren Christopher to the London Conference convened by Prime Minister John Major that week, to put metal in the secretary of state's spine. It was just as well. Over four days they managed to bring the Western allies, together with Russia, one more step towards Tony Lake's Endgame: deciding to use massive American airpower not only to protect the remaining safe haven enclaves over the ensuing months but, in carefully targeted punitive attacks elsewhere, to bomb the Serbs back to the negotiation table, and put an end to the civil war.

Operation Deliberate Force, as the plan was called, would begin in five weeks' time, on August 30.

CHAPTER SIXTY-THREE

AFFIRMATIVE ACTIONS

A Day in the Life of the White House

The entire world now waited to see how the Western powers would react to the atrocities in Srebrenica. While NATO's military commanders readied their combat echelons in secret for Operation Deliberate Force, the president of the United States masked such preparations by addressing three areas of concern at home: the future of the FBI, of the CIA, and of civil rights.

That Bill Clinton, in the midst of one of the biggest crises in Western allied military-political relations, could focus not only on the resolution of that crisis but simultaneously on the crucial issues of counterterrorism and civil society in America was a significant testament to his chief of staff, Leon Panetta.

Panetta's effect on the nature of the White House and thus the presidency had been transformative. "The typical day began at, usually, 6 o'clock," he recalled later. "You get up, you go to the office. Sometimes you had to do television at 7, the morning shows. We did the 7:30 closed staff meeting, which included the very key people: the national security adviser, the press secretary, the vice president, the first lady, the OMB director. Bob Rubin also came to that, even after he went to Treasury. So it was a close-knit, high-level group. And . . . what I would do is walk through the day, talk about what was going on on the Hill, talk about what was happening in foreign affairs, talk about economic policy. And then I talked about other key issues that were going on": in sum, the president's agenda.

"Then I would have a broader staff meeting with all the larger staff at 8:30 in the Roosevelt Room, to brief them on what was going on—because I really felt that was a way to make sure they felt part of the team—and I would get additional information from that group, as well.

"Then with the president right after that, to brief him on what was going on. And hear any concerns he had.

"Then the usual CIA briefing . . . "

Instead of McLarty's free-for-all, with competing cabals of influence, there was now a coherent, structured order to the day—indeed, each day would include an "event," which helped focus the staff and provided clear programming for the news media.

"There were three things I wanted to do as chief of staff that I felt were important," Panetta recounted. "One was to clearly develop a chain of command, and better discipline. Secondly, to create a focus as to what are the key things to do. Instead of trying to do a thousand things a day, what's the one thing? And thereby use the 'bully pulpit' of the presidency as effectively as possible. And thirdly, to develop long-term scheduling, so that it wasn't just day-to-day, but was over six months—three to six months ahead.

"And those were the pieces. So when I was with the president, we would do that, we would do the 'event of the day.' I tried to block out time for him to have time to read, the time to do letters, the time to make the calls that he had to do. So we tried to find a period between 12 to 2 P.M., or 12 to 3 P.M. Then we would do briefings in the afternoon.

"During that time I'd be up on the Hill, negotiating issues. But we'd do briefings some time after that on issues that he had to deal with. He had receptions in the evening. So I wouldn't get out of there till some time between 8 and 9 P.M., and probably sometimes as late as 12 to 1 A.M. Long days."

Panetta chuckled—glad such days were long over, for him. Following in the footsteps of Napoleon's Berthier, of Eisenhower's Bedell Smith, and Montgomery's Freddie de Guingand, the chief of staff had made it possible for his boss, finally, to lead—and he was proud of his selfless work.

Panetta's new command of White House operations had certainly freed the president to become president, at last. He and his staff, indeed the nation, were still saddled, however, with the other grave mistakes he had made in the transition and his freshman year. Two of these were now proving headaches of the first magnitude: the FBI and the CIA.

The Choice of Freeh

The director of the FBI is appointed for ten years, and can only be dismissed with due cause. Only when the unsatisfactory director, William Sessions, was found by the attorney general to have abused the perquisites of office had he been formally fired in July 1993. Still struggling to understand the changing nature of the post-Cold War world, and still monumentally deficient in his ability to appoint good subordinates to whom he could delegate power and responsibility, the president had asked the advice of Bernie Nussbaum, his wife's former boss and legal counsel to the president, to suggest a replacement.

Nussbaum had already made a near-catastrophic bungle over the selection of Hillary's nominee for attorney general, Zoë Baird, and would become such a problem over Whitewater that he himself would have to be fired. In the meantime, in July 1993, the president had listened to his advice—or misadvice. There had thus resulted one of the most disastrous, yet irremediable, choices of his entire presidency. He had chosen a young Republican judge and former FBI officer, Louis B. Freeh, whom he had never previously met, to stand in J. Edgar Hoover's shoes as director of the FBI.

Nussbaum was initially delighted with his nominee. So was Webb Hubbell, the number three at the Justice Department. As Hubbell wrote, "Freeh looked like the perfect candidate," given his years investigating and prosecuting Mafia criminals—until Hubbell learned, firsthand, the McCarthy-like tactics Freeh would employ in his pursuit of Whitewater.

Whitewater completely turned the head of the young Republican. Meanwhile, before Whitewater investigations even began, Freeh gave notice, as director of the FBI, that he was not going to participate with the White House in national security in any but the most alienated way. Within a week of his confirmation, he returned the White House pass sent to him by Mack McLarty—saying that he did not want any visit he might make to the building, six months before the first Whitewater investigator was appointed, to be anything less than formal, official, and logged.

Poor Bill Clinton, receiving news of this insult from the latest recruit to his administration, realized immediately that he had made a mistake; he had been warned, he later confided, by a retired FBI agent. The agent called Nancy Hernreich at the Oval Office to warn the president that Freeh was a narrow-minded, dangerous Republican bigot—"too political and self-serving" for the job of FBI director. "It gave me pause," Clinton later confessed, "but I sent word back that it was too late; the offer had been extended and accepted."

Impressed by the way Freeh had answered his questions over the FBI decision to use premature force at Waco ("They get paid to wait"), Clinton had merely rubber-stamped Nussbaum's recommendation—and was then stuck with him, for the rest of his presidency.

Not only had Freeh declined to participate in the attempt by the Clinton administration to do its job as the government of the United States, but he had failed to grow in the post of director of the FBI in a time of monumental cultural, technological, and world-political change. As Joshua Micah Marshall later commented, "Freeh ran the bureau from the rise of al-Qaeda in the early 1990s until just two months before bin Laden landed his roundhouse blow on the United States. Under his leadership, the FBI made many mistakes and missed many opportunities that paved the way for 9/11. He presided over a bureau that fell almost laughably behind in information technology. On his watch, the counterterrorism division languished as a career-killing backwater. As David Plotz noted in *Slate* more than a year ago, Freeh's chief accomplishment as FBI director was to oversee an almost endless litany of fiascos while successfully ducking responsibility for all of them."

Chief among Freeh's failures of vision was his utter inability to see that counterterrorism, in the new age of the 1990s, must be the FBI's new priority.

Freeh Blocks Counterterrorism

The Oklahoma City bombing on April 19 taught Freeh nothing beyond FBI procedures. Thus, while the president attempted to focus the entire nation's attention on the danger of terrorism as the new challenge of the 1990s, Freeh and fellow Republicans in Congress did everything possible to thwart presidential measures for increased surveillance and anti-terrorist action.

Richard Clarke had already been made head of the president's Counterterrorism Security Group—encompassing the leaders of each of the nation's counterterrorism and security organizations—late in 1992. The World Trade center attack in 1993 had turned all eyes to the growing problem of Islamic jihadism, and by 1995 counterterrorism had become the number one national security priority to all but Louis Freeh—who in turn helped persuade

Republican senators and congressmen *not* to support the president's counter-terrorist measures. Thus, when in January 1995 the president issued an executive order making it a felony to give money to designated terrorist groups or their front organizations, Freeh refused to act on the order for fear of legal or even constitutional challenge. In consequence, Clarke had sought a new law to force Freeh's hand—but, as he later wrote, this was not approved by the Republican Congress in 1995.

"I had thought these issues were bipartisan," Clarke recalled, "but the distrust and animosity between the Democratic White House and Republicans in the Congress was strong and boiled over into counter-terrorism policy. The World Trade Center attack had happened, the New York landmarks and Pacific 747 attacks had almost happened, sarin had been sprayed in the Tokyo subway, buses were blown up on Israeli streets, a federal building in downtown Oklahoma City had been smashed to bits, but many in Congress opposed the counterterrorism bill. Republicans in the Senate, such as Orrin Hatch, opposed expanding organized crime wiretap provisions to terrorists. Tom DeLay and other Republicans in the House agreed with the National Rifle Association that the proposed restrictions on bomb making infringed on the right to bear arms."

Later, sexual wrongdoing in the White House would become far more important to Freeh as a former Boy Scout and father of four than the threat to America from terrorism. Still more vexing, however, was the fact that the president's first choice for director of the CIA had proven just as disastrous as the choice for director of the FBI.

Paying a Steep Price

The president's choice of James Woolsey for the CIA in December 1992 had impressed no one, and with the rise of terrorist operations abroad, the need for a smarter, more effective CIA director had become paramount. Woolsey had been made to resign, but the man the president wanted to replace him, General Michael Carns, proved to have unexpected legal problems with a legal Filipino immigrant servant, and was forced to withdraw his candidacy for the post in March 1995, amidst Republican mudslinging. So important was the job, the president felt, however, that he had switched the deputy secretary of defense, John Deutch, to the post, temporarily.

The president—and the nation—were paying a steep price for the president's own early incompetence in selecting senior personnel. He himself had the ability to grow: to learn from his mistakes, and become a potentially great leader of his nation. But did the nation—as represented by its elected leaders, the majority of whom were now Republican—have an equal ability to grow, in a period of tabloid infotainment reminiscent of the fall of Rome? Would the batteries of the right, recharged by their congressional triumph in November 1994, become more and more determined to humiliate, even oust, a president they had stereotyped as weak and ineffective, ignoring his growing skill in leading the nation through the perilous challenges it was facing?

Why, observers abroad wondered, had the culture of America become so divided, so partisan, so bitter, so tabloid, so religiously ideological, so *fundamentalist* in its political demonizations? Was it a case of the *nation*, not Nero, now fiddling while Rome burned? And if so—with the Speaker threatening a national "train wreck" unless the president accepted Republican tax cuts for the wealthy and the destruction of educational, housing, medical, and social services—where would it end?

Addressing the CIA

Somehow President Bill Clinton, who had begun his first term of office so poorly, now had to find a way of leading the nation into the twenty-first century as a democratic, reasonably unified society, tolerating dissent but accepting its responsible role as the world's last superpower following the fall of communism—and in the face of mounting new threats at home and abroad. Though idle tongues—especially on right-wing hate radio—still claimed the president was anti-military and anti-CIA, it became quite clear to most people that the reverse was true: that in reality the president was far ahead of the majority of Republicans in his concern for American safety and security. Certainly those who heard him speak to a thousand CIA employees in the central courtyard at Langley, Virginia, on the sweltering morning of July 14—Bastille Day—were converted.

"We are living at a moment of hope," the president said, in explaining his world view at Langley. "Our nation is at peace; our economy is growing all right. All around the world, democracy and free markets are on the march. But none of these developments are inevitable or irreversible," he warned, "and every single study of human psychology or the human spirit, every single religious tract tells us there will be troubles, wars, and rumors of war until the end of time."

His own job, the president declared, was to direct the organs of government to meet the multiple challenges of the new age. Far from the CIA being redundant in the post-Cold War world, as some had claimed after the recent arrest of Aldrich Ames, accused of spying for Russia, the Central Intelligence Agency was needed more than ever. Soviet Communism might no longer be the problem, but other threats were taking its place. "Now, instead of a single enemy, we face a host of scattered and dangerous challenges, but they are quite profound and difficult to understand," the president admitted. "There are ethnic and regional tensions that threaten to flare into full-scale war in more than thirty nations. Two dozen countries are trying to get their hands on nuclear, chemical, and biological weapons. As these terrible tools of destruction spread, so too spreads the potential for terrorism and for criminals to acquire them."

In his new directive to the CIA, the president wanted the agency to concentrate first on providing the U.S. military with the intelligence it needed for its operations. Then he wanted the CIA to provide accurate military, political, and economic intelligence on countries hostile to the U.S.—especially those with weapons of mass destruction. Finally there was the trafficking in terrorism, weapons, and drugs—trafficking that was and would remain the object of U.S. surveillance: work that "is hidden from the headlines" but vital to U.S. security in saving American lives and promoting the nation's prosperity. Technology was helping, but "no matter how good our technology, we'll always rely on human intelligence to tell us what an adversary has in mind," he declared, together with "good analysts to make a clean and clear picture out of the fragments of what our spies and satellites put on the table." And for that to happen, there had to be more cooperation and streamlining between American intelligence agencies, including the CIA and the FBI.

All this the more thoughtful of CIA officers knew—but it was important they should know that the president knew it also, indeed valued it no less highly than his predecessor, who had once been CIA director. In the aftermath of the discovery of Aldrich Ames's treason, it was a significant marker of the president's continuing belief in the importance of American intelligence.

Tradition would not be sufficient to survive in the modern world. To maintain "our edge," the president urged, "you have to deliver timely, unique information that focuses on real threats to the security of our people on the basis of information not otherwise available"—and this meant, inevitably, being selective. "We can't possibly have in a world with so many diverse threats and tight budgets the resources to collect everything. You need and deserve clear priorities from me and our national security team," he acknowledged, and he promised to deliver "public support and confidence" in the integrity and competence of the CIA and other intelligence services.

A Favorite Football of the Republican Right

The Langley speech was given by a president who had, finally, found his feet—and it was the more remarkable for being given at a time when the president was under enormous stress on other fronts. In order to give the imminent air war, not civil war, a chance in Bosnia he was holding off the threat of a Senate move, under Bob Dole, to pre-emptively lift the multilateral arms embargo—indeed, several weeks later he would have to veto it—but he was simultaneously facing the forces of the cultural right in his own country, forces determined to end special treatment of minorities. In that respect, too, the time had come for the president to make a major presidential decision.

Pushed through Congress by President Johnson as part of his Great Society initiative, the 1964 Civil Rights Act had outlawed negative employment discrimination. The act had then been followed by a presidential executive order (number 11246), instructing federal employees and contractors to help minorities—to "take affirmative action to ensure that applicants are employed, and that employees are treated during employment, without regard to their race, creed, color, or national origin."

Over the years LBJ's executive order had opened the economic doors to hundreds of thousands of blacks and other victims of discrimination—but it had, inevitably, spawned cases of reverse discrimination, favoring less qualified minority employees over more qualified whites.

Of late the issue had become a favorite football of the Republican right, which delighted in pinpointing its excesses, making them the tabloid *causes célèbres* for a revoking of the executive order. Newt Gingrich, unable to resist temptation, openly warned a group of black journalists, for example, that he intended as Speaker to halt the legal pressure on institutions and businesses to hire blacks, minorities, and women. Rather, he proposed making available extra congressional funding for poor people "provided they were willing to work extra hard," as the Associated Press reported him. "The Speaker said: 'I am prepared to say to the poor, 'You have to learn new habits. The habits of being poor don't work.'" There was, Gingrich claimed, "a growing consensus" against helping people because of their race or sex, rather than their poverty. The flaw with affirmative action, the Speaker maintained, was that it was "built on lawsuits, a structure encouraged by civil rights advocates who used the courts to break down segregation during the 1960s. 'When you create that kind of backward-looking, grievance-looking system, you teach people exactly the wrong habits,' he said. 'They end up spending their lives waiting for the lawsuit, instead of spending their lives seeking opportunity.'"

Morris's Counsel

Was Gingrich right? For Bill Clinton the Republican move to axe affirmative action posed an interesting, symbolic conundrum.

Backed by massive television and radio advertising, Republicans had created a political hurricane over the issue, which had been given extra wind in June 1995 by the *Adarand* v. *Peña* Supreme Court ruling that affirmative action *was* unconstitutional, save in cases where it was "narrowly tailored" to achieve a compelling antidiscriminatory interest.

Dick Morris therefore counseled the president to bow to such Republican pressure, to appease Republicans, and to demonstrate his independence from fusty old Democratic positions by withdrawing President Johnson's famous executive order.

Morris's enthusiasm for the overthrow of affirmative action was fueled by a more Machiavellian consideration: that if the president gave in to such Republican pressure on a race issue, it would lure Jesse Jackson into running against the president as a candidate for the 1996 Democratic Party presidential nomination. Although this would dent the president's popularity in the black community, and hobble him in terms of the black vote in the subsequent presidential race, there was, Morris argued, a counterbalancing electoral advantage. From his polling surveys he had become certain there were many *millions* of white swing voters who would turn out and cast their votes for Clinton if he were to take such a step—outnumbering those black votes he would lose. As Nixon had captured the votes of white Democrats in the South who objected to civil rights, so Democrats would recapture them, Morris argued, by the president's axing of affirmative action.

Clinton's July 19 speech, given at the National Archives building on Constitution Avenue, a few hundred yards from the White House, was thus the president's chance to show his new colors, over a litmus-test issue that went to the very heart of American society.

Stopping the Silver Bullet

For months Stephanopoulos had felt the president to be "equivocating" in their weekly meetings over the subject.

"The Republicans think this is a silver bullet to destroy Democrats," Clinton told Stephanopoulos, "a bird's nest on the ground." Even centrist Democratic senators like Joe Lieberman felt that racial preferences were "patently unfair." "Preferences we lose," Clinton had told Stephanopoulos, but "affirmative action we win."

Would they, though? The president was torn over the best way to deal with it. In the end, with the help of Christopher Edley, a black Harvard professor who was associate director of OMB under Alice Rivlin, the president had found the answer. The growing terrorist threats to American security had convinced Clinton that a partisan, divided America, inflamed by Gingrichian anti-government rhetoric, would mean a more vulnerable, less secure, less internationally effective America. Therefore, he must give his all to maintain the cohesiveness of American society, not allow it to be further divided.

The president's epiphany, born of his daily intelligence briefings and his discussions with Tony Lake and Richard Clarke, was a simple yet profoundly important insight, at once intuitive and intellectual. Seeing the crucial importance of national unity as a war-winning tool in the struggle against terrorism—at home and abroad—placed him in a different league from advisers such as Stephanopoulos and Ickes, who *relished* domestic partisan struggle. Only if the United States, with its great melting pot of races and traditions, could be held together in a common endeavor, the president reasoned, would America be strong enough and capable of fulfilling its manifest destiny. Dumping affirmative action and singling out minorities, especially blacks and the poor, as Gingrich had done, as malingerers, was socially divisive—and could only help America's enemies.

By appointing Stephanopoulos to head up a committee to review the issue, the president showed that he had learned the lesson of gays in the military—

not to act precipitately over an issue that burned so deep in the national political conscience. Coming to his realization, he not only stood above the issue,
as the father of the nation, but recognized in it the key to the presidency—to
his presidency—in the 1990s. It was no longer a question of whether to follow Morris's polling path to more votes over a controversial, seminal issue: it
was a question of how best to hold and weave together the moral fabric of the
nation. In times of war, this was straightforward, as presidents from Lincoln
to Roosevelt had shown. In peace, it was more difficult—yet no less important if the nation was to survive and face the challenges of the twenty-first
century as a unified, coherent, educated, and confident society. Unity, in other
words, was everything.

Triangulating between Morris's and Stephanopoulos's views, the president therefore proceeded to give what columnist Mary McGrory considered the best presidential speech on race since 1965.

The Rocky but Righteous Journey

"In recent weeks," the president started his address on July 19, "I have begun a conversation with the American people about our fate and our duty to
prepare our nation not only to meet the new century but to live and lead in a
world transformed to a degree seldom seen in all of our history. Much of
this change is good, but it is not all good, and all of us are affected by it.
Therefore, we must reach beyond our fears and our divisions to a new time
of great and common purpose. Our challenge is twofold: first, to restore the
American dream of opportunity and the American value of responsibility;
and second, to bring our country together amid all our diversity into a
stronger community so that we can find common ground and move forward
as one.

"More than ever," the president averred, "these two endeavors are insep-
arable. I am absolutely convinced we cannot restore economic opportunity
or solve our social problems unless we find a way to bring the American
people together. To bring our people together we must openly and honestly
deal with the issues that divide us. So let us today trace the roots of affirmative action in our never-ending search for equal opportunity. Let us determine what it is and what it isn't." And after paying tribute to Supreme Court
Justice Thurgood Marshall, grandson of a slave, he went on in words that
suggested a second inaugural: "Emancipation, women's suffrage, civil

rights, voting rights, equal rights, the struggle for the rights of the disabled, all these and other struggles are milestones on America's often rocky but fundamentally righteous journey"—a journey "to close the gap between the ideals enshrined in these treasures here in the National Archives and the reality of our daily lives."

In some ways it was the most personal speech Bill Clinton would ever make as president, recalling his first time in Washington as a Boys Nation delegate, his grandparents' grocery store in Hope, his experience of segregation, the day he listened—and wept—to hear Martin Luther King's "I Have a Dream" speech, his own attempts to create a racially diverse administration as governor of Arkansas, and subsequently as president.

Slavery, segregation, discrimination, and racial hate had proved difficult hurdles in American history—but they were finally being overcome, the president claimed, not simply because they were morally wrong, but because economically they made no sense. In 1960, the city of Atlanta, Georgia, he pointed out, "in reaction to all the things that were going on all across the South," had adopted the motto "The City Too Busy To Hate." "And however imperfectly over the years," he noted, "they tried to live by it. I am convinced that Atlanta's success—it now is home to more foreign corporations than any other American city, and one year from today it will begin to host the Olympics—began when people got too busy to hate.

"The lesson we learned was a hard one," President Clinton acknowledged on behalf of his fellow Americans. "When we allow people to pit us against one another or spend energy denying opportunity based on our differences, everyone is held back. But when we give all Americans a chance to develop and use their talents, to be full partners in our common enterprise, then everybody is pushed forward."

Taking issue with Newt Gingrich's recent assertion that those "conservatives who knew how to create wealth" had failed to get involved in the movement towards integration thanks to government programs, the president pointed out that the very *opposite* had happened:

Thirty years ago in this city [Washington], you didn't see many people of color or women making their way to work in the morning in business clothes, or serving in substantial numbers in powerful positions in Congress or at the White House, or making executive decisions every day in businesses.

A lot has changed, and it did not happen as some sort of random, evolutionary drift. It took hard work and sacrifices and countless acts of courage and conscience.

Women have become a major force in business and political life, and far more able to contribute to their families' incomes. A true and growing black middle class has emerged. Higher education has literally been revolutionized with women and racial and ethnic minorities attending once overwhelmingly white and sometimes all-male schools.

Police departments now better reflect the makeup of those whom they protect. A generation of professionals now serve as role models for young women and minority youth.

Hispanics and newer immigrant populations are succeeding in making America stronger.

Our search to find ways to move more quickly to equal opportunity led to the development of what we now call affirmative action. The purpose of affirmative action is to give our nation a way to finally address the systemic exclusion of individuals of talent, on the basis of their gender or race, from opportunities to develop, perform, achieve, and contribute.

To be sure, the president allowed, there were people who were "honestly concerned about the times affirmative action doesn't work, when it's done in the wrong way. And I know there are times when some employers don't use it in the right way. They may allow a different kind of discrimination." When this happened, it was wrong, "but it isn't affirmative action," the president emphasized, "and it is not legal. So when our administration finds cases of that sort, we will enforce the law aggressively. We should have a simple slogan," he suggested, offering a phrase that would, in its way, define the modernized liberal Democrat centrism of the 1990s: "Mend it, but don't end it." One day, perhaps, discrimination would be a thing of the past. "I am resolved," the president concluded, "that that day will come, but the evidence suggests—indeed, screams—that that day has not come. The job of ending discrimination in this country is not over."

And with that, he let President Johnson's order stand.

CHAPTER SIXTY-FOUR

PEACE IN BOSNIA

Foreign Reporting

Black Americans, especially, breathed a sigh of relief after the president's decision on affirmative action. Others, too, were impressed—both in America and abroad. "It looks now as if the Hamlet president has thrown off the shackles of indecision and determined to himself be true," wrote John Carlin for the London *Independent*. "First of all, he has taken a position on affirmative action that flies in the face of conventional political wisdom. The Republicans won the last congressional election, and hope to win the next presidential one, to a large degree because of the vigour with which they have peddled the argument that employment policies favouring women and blacks have discriminated against white American males. Last month, after long prevarication, Mr. Clinton discarded the customary fudge and declared that affirmative action was a good and necessary thing. Then last Thursday he grasped the cigarette nettle, speaking forthrightly as he revealed plans to curb advertising aimed at the susceptible teenage market. Mr. Clinton took his stand in the full knowledge that the powerful tobacco lobby could be expected to redouble its campaign contributions to next year's Republican candidate and that, in the view of the Washington chatterers, he has written the redneck South out of his re-election plans. The following day he announced, to the dismay of America's Cold Warrior constituency and the embarrassment of Britain and France, that the U.S. would henceforth put a stop to all nuclear testing.

"On Bosnia Mr. Clinton has been warily hesitant, aware that the prevailing view in Middle America is, 'what the hell's it got to do with us?' During the last two months of unrelenting crisis he has been happy to take a back seat to his European allies. Suddenly, in the last week, the U.S. has emerged as a more visible player, urging a peace initiative which, however flawed, displays a new American determination to play an active role."

This was foreign reporting that Speaker Gingrich, who had spent half his childhood in Europe, would have done well to read. As it was, Gingrich had already decided to back off his call for line-item voting on finance bills rather than omnibus bills that contained endless "pork"—for the measure would have given the Democratic president veto-power over each line, and threatened Gingrich's blackmail: that if the president did not sign off on the entire balanced budget bill, the Speaker would turn off the signals and deliberately cause a national train wreck.

The president was disappointed in Gingrich—especially when the Speaker also backed off another notion he had publicly espoused, in New Hampshire, of a bipartisan committee to cut back lobbying on K Street in Washington, where upwards of thirty thousand lobbyists, many of them ex-congressmen, earned fortunes pressuring legislators on behalf of rich interests. "When you shake hands with someone in broad daylight and say you're going to do something, you ought to at least act like you're going to do it," the president had declared as he packed to go away for a short summer vacation in Wyoming. "Where I come from, you know, if kids did that, their mamas wouldn't let them have dinner. . . . They got spanked when I was growing up."

Clearly, the president was at the top of his form, but on August 19—the president's birthday, still eleven days before the projected launch of Operation Deliberate Force in Bosnia, and the day after Chelsea arrived in Wyoming—there was more terrible news from the Adriatic. This time it concerned Americans: senior Americans of the Clinton administration.

The Administration Never Learns

Refused permission by Bosnian Serb commanders to fly into the still besieged city of Sarajevo, Dick Holbrooke and a team of American plenipotentiaries appointed by the president had been forced to drive along a treacherous rain-soaked mountain road—off of which one of the armored vehicles had slipped when the road itself collapsed. Careering three hundred feet down the sheer slope, the vehicle had burst into flame. Three of Holbrooke's senior deputies—Deputy Assistant Secretary of State Robert

Frasure, Deputy Assistant Secretary of Defense Joseph Kruzel, and Colonel Nelson Drew, a National Security Council officer—were engulfed, and died.

Holbrooke, heartbroken, insisted on bringing back their bodies to America, where a funeral service was held at Arlington Cemetery. "One of the most touching tributes I have seen in 20 years of observing Washington came from 16-year-old Sarah Frasure after the tragic death of her respected diplomat father in Bosnia," wrote columnist Georgie Anne Geyer, who quoted Sarah's tearful words by the coffin: "I took him for granted. I never told him I loved him. One question I will always ask myself is, 'Why?' I know I will never have the answer to my question."

Geyer, deeply upset, gave her own answer: that "the administration your father served so loyally never, ever learns"—an administration "still unable to grasp the fact that you build for peace on military victory and military victory alone, and so, instead of using American power to defeat the Serbs, they continued to try to woo those same Serbs with hapless 'peace programs' and to partition the Bosnia of the victims. But they themselves didn't go; they sent your father." Ms. Geyer had covered the Croatian and Bosnian wars for six years, and she was convinced the Serbs would *only* respond to military power—American military power. Unaware of the impending military operation, Geyer was dismissive of the Clinton administration, which "cannot decide which diplomatic or military waters it wants to ford—in Bosnia or, for that matter, anywhere. It is characterized by a utopian, pseudo-therapeutic and essentially reactive view of the uses of American power. And so it puts its men and women in unnecessary danger in a world in which others will gladly use their power. And that, Sarah, is 'why.' "

Fiddling While Sarajevo Burns

Arriving by air from Wyoming the next day to lead the memorial service at Fort Myer and to decide on a new team to go out with Holbrooke, the president met and spoke to Sarah Frasure and other members of the grieving families. His elegaic address ("Today we gather to honor three peacemakers who gave their lives seeking for others the blessings we Americans hold dear and too often take for granted, the opportunity to work and to dream, to raise our children to live and to love in a land of peace") had struck the appropriate tone for the occasion—but two former State Department officials who had resigned over his Bosnia policy had also written a scathing indictment, published in the *New York Times*, accusing the Clinton administration of wanting to get Bosnia "off the front pages" and thereby "clean the president's slate for the 1996 elections" by cynically giving in to Serbian aggression. Both the House and the Senate had now passed a bill for presidential signature, calling for the arms embargo to be lifted—which could only lead to more bloodshed. If Lake's Endgame strategy was to be followed, it was more imperative than ever that the president not react, but continue to work backwards from the desired end result: a settlement negotiated under American auspices, backed by American force and troops.

Several days later, when the Serbs callously shelled Sarajevo yet again—this time killing thirty-seven civilians, and wounding eighty more, in a crowded market area of the city—Holbrooke's patience broke. By refusing air access to the city, the Serbs had been responsible for three of his colleagues' deaths; now, with this latest massacre of civilians, they had gone too far. Their leaders were claiming to be ready to talk, but Holbrooke was not—at least not until NATO forces gave their promised demonstration of who was really in charge now, in the war-torn peninsula.

The military targets for Operation Deliberate Force had been drawn up, the coordinates prepared. The three and a half years of fiddling while Sarajevo burned were over.

Operation Deliberate Force

In Jackson Hole, Wyoming, the president had already given his prior approval to retaliatory military action in such a circumstance; nevertheless it was imperative to ensure that other contributing NATO nations back the mission, without alienating the Russian Federation, which for historical and domestic political reasons backed the Serbs. Everything was therefore done to damp down speculation or administration comment until the planes were fuelled and took off.

When the news reached the mobile communications center in Jackson Hole on August 30 that the first wave of some sixty NATO warplanes—American, British, French, Dutch, and Spanish—were in flight from military airbases in Italy, from the flight deck of HMS *Glasgow* in the Adriatic, and from the decks of the U.S. aircraft carrier *Theodore Roosevelt* as it steamed back from Rhodes, the president closed his eyes and whispered "Whooopppeee!" Nothing could bring back the three American peacemakers, or the ten thousand dead in Sarajevo, or the nearly eight thousand Muslim men and boys murdered in cold blood in Srebrenica, or the hundreds of thousands of other Muslims the Serbs had "cleansed" in Bosnia over the past three years, but a line had at last been drawn in the sand—and the United States military was in action.

Jumping with Joy

At 2:00 A.M. U.S. Navy F–18 and F–14 fighters roared over Sarajevo, all but the last several UN peacekeepers having this time been withdrawn from behind the Bosnian Serb lines lest they be taken hostage in retaliation.

"A Joyous Cry of 'At Last' " was the *Washington Post* headline given to Stacy Sullivan's report from inside the besieged city of Sarajevo on August 31. "Worn down by more than 3 1/2 years of warfare in which thousands of their neighbors had died, most people here went to bed certain that NATO and the United Nations would not respond forcefully to a Serb mortar attack Monday that killed 37 people and wounded scores more at a crowded Sarajevo marketplace. But when it was clear that the planes were pounding Serb forces surrounding the city in a mighty show of force, shouts of joy could be heard from balconies all over Sarajevo. Even as window panes in the heart of the city's old quarter rattled with the shock of bomb blasts, jubilant figures could be seen jumping up and down in silhouette against candle-lit interiors. 'We were so sure NATO wasn't going to do anything,' said Nermina Hajric, a 33-year-old mother of two who works just 50 yards from the site of Monday's market carnage. 'When I heard the explosions, I thought, "My God, the Serbs are bombing us." When I realized it was NATO, I was literally jumping through my flat with joy.' "

Bosnian Prime Minister Haris Silajdzic called the NATO airstrikes an "operation that restored credibility to the world." Edhem Bicakcic, vice president of the Party of Democratic Action, said simply, "The West has found its soul." "As the Muslim call to prayer wafted over the old city at dawn," Sullivan reported, "and the bombing campaign showed no signs of letting up, celebration spread to the streets with impromptu demonstrations of joy and relief."

While NATO planes took out Serbian air defense sites, missile sites, radar sites, and communications facilities, French medium and heavy artillery of the new Rapid Reaction Force pounded the Serb guns still deliberately firing into the civilian quarters of Sarajevo. Refuelling and re-arming their aircraft, NATO's commanders sent in more and more waves of NATO bombers, in what became the largest military combat operation ever undertaken in NATO history.

After three years of wrangling impotence, the European nations had swung behind American leadership, and soon commentators became aware that the NATO blitz wasn't just the opening salvo in America's bid to end the conflict in Bosnia, but was evidence of a recreation of the post–Cold War rationale of NATO itself. Originally formed as the Western European bulwark against the threat of Soviet expansion, it had finally found a new role and a new cohesion, as it prepared to expand its membership under the Partnership For Peace. Within twelve hours some two hundred NATO sorties had been flown—and by September 1, some five hundred.

"Transatlantic squabbling had given way," the *Financial Times* noted, "to the appearance, at least, of rock-solid unity."

Snatching Defeat from the Jaws of Victory

In Hawaii, meanwhile, following the end of his Wyoming holiday, President Clinton honored the fiftieth anniversary of the ending of another war: World War II in the Pacific.

Fifty years before, General Douglas MacArthur had taken the surrender of Japan after almost four years of bitter struggle, and though Bosnian Serb leader Radovan Karadzic still claimed, "They'll never crush us. Never!" the signs that Richard Holbrooke saw suggested the opposite. In the Krajina region, Croatian forces were pushing back the Bosnian Serbs, and in a frosty meeting with General Mladic, General Janvier, on behalf of the UN, delivered the new NATO ultimatum: Withdraw all heavy weapons beyond a twelve-mile radius of Sarajevo, stop shelling Sarajevo and other safe havens, and join talks on the U.S. peace plan.

"No one should doubt NATO's resolve to prevent the further slaughter of innocent civilians in Sarajevo, and in other safe areas in Bosnia," President Clinton declared at the Honolulu ceremonies, as he paid tribute to those veterans who had fought for freedom—yet to the consternation of NATO commanders, Janvier did just that: withdrawing his ultimatum to Mladic, and suggesting the NATO bombing be stopped in favor of a simple cease-fire, as before!

Clinton, Lake, Holbrooke, and others were aghast. One military source commented that Janvier's climbdown—at a moment when the Serbs were still deliberately lobbing shells into the residential streets of Sarajevo—was "snatching defeat out of the jaws of victory." At President Clinton's urging, the NATO secretary-general overrode his southern commander-in-chief, Admiral Leighton Smith, and NATO bombers took off once again on September 5. As Holbrooke wrote later, there seemed to be but one language the Bosnian Serbs spoke, and respected—superior force.

A further nine days of bombing were required, including the use of American cruise missiles, before Karadzic and Mladic gave in—but at last, on September 13, 1995, the Serbian guns firing into civilian communities went silent, and were withdrawn from the vicinity of Sarajevo.

The secretary-general of the UN, Boutros Boutros-Ghali, had proved a broken reed; the United Nations, the world's supposed bulwark of peace-making, would therefore have to be virtually frozen out of Holbrooke's difficult next mission, after the lifting of the thirty-month siege of Sarajevo: a general ceasefire (announced by President Clinton on October 5) and a peace conference to be held under American aegis and American rules, in America, and at an American military airbase—in fact, in the very town in which the Wright brothers, the fathers of aviation, had been born: Dayton, Ohio.

Dayton, Ohio

As the world watched anxiously, the plenipotentiaries of Serbia, Croatia, and Bosnia flew in to negotiate a 51–49 percent assignment of Bosnian territory between the Muslim-Croat federation on the one hand and a Serbian republic on the other.

As the UN observer Carl Bildt recorded, the annual budget of the Wright-Patterson Air Force Base in Ohio, which employed over twenty-three thousand people, was "far larger than the total economy of all Bosnia." The negotiations proved tortuous, with the Serbian president, Slobodan Milosevic, acting as negotiator on behalf of his puppet regime in Bosnia, the Bosnian Serbian assembly in Pale. Dick Holbrooke, the American chief negotiator, often despaired. Many times the conference came close to collapsing—the Muslims, in particular, loath to see the Serbs rewarded for military conquest, rape, pillage, and crimes against humanity. Tony Lake, Sandy Vershbow (Lake's aide on Bosnia), Sandy Berger, the State Department's Peter Tarnoff, Madeleine Albright, Strobe Talbott, William Perry, and General Wesley Clark all played crucial roles. Several times President Clinton became directly involved, as the process teetered backwards and forwards. After twenty days and twenty nights the negotiations came to a climax. Though "things went backwards" whenever the weak-willed Warren Christopher appeared, according to Bildt, even the American secretary of state had eventually shown backbone—in fact, it was Christopher who was personally authorized by President Clinton to deliver to the Bosnian president, Alija Izetbegovic, the final ultimatum: sign within the next sixty-two minutes, or the Dayton conference will be closed down.

On November 21, 1995, Izetbegovic—reluctant to reward a Serbian holocaust—reached for his pen. A compromise peace was better than endless continuing slaughter. It had snowed in the night. "It is not a just peace," he stated. Then, after pausing for a few heartstopping seconds, he added: "But my people need peace." He initialed the accord.

After four long years of bloodshed, there would be peace in Bosnia— guaranteed by America.

CHAPTER SIXTY-FIVE

A HISTORIC
POWER STRUGGLE

Gingrich Says No

Ironically, as the U.S. government struggled to bring lasting peace in Europe, Newt Gingrich was simultaneously doing his best to incite civil war at home—by closing down the U.S. government.

Not even Bill Clinton, with his famed sensory receptors capable of detecting the slightest shift of political wind, could believe it. Yet, as the November days of 1995 shortened, the wrecking ball grew closer. Advisers like Stephanopoulos—who neglected to record the Bosnian crisis or Dayton Accords in his memoirs—had actually hoped the peace conference would fail, given the commitment to send in twenty thousand U.S. troops to police the agreement in Bosnia and the financial contribution promised towards reconstruction.

Stephanopoulos had ample reason to be so blinkered, however, for at midnight on November 13, while the negotiators in Dayton toiled to achieve a peaceful resolution of the war in Bosnia, Speaker Gingrich listened to the president's last proposals for political compromise—having once again threatened total shutdown of the U.S. government if he did not get his way.

"We had kept offering different compromises, and it was never enough," Leon Panetta recalled. "And it finally came down to that meeting. We had offered one last compromise. . . . I presented it in the Oval Office—to cut Medicare. It wasn't the decision to balance the budget so much as how much we were willing to cut Medicare, in order to cut a deal. . . . And it was Bob Dole, Dick Armey, Newt Gingrich, Dick Gephardt, Tom Daschle, the vice president, the president, and myself. That was pretty much it. And I made the presentation. It was a paper chart, one of those boards. I think Bob Dole pretty much thought it was a good deal, and they should accept it.

"And Gingrich said, 'No, I can't do it.' "

Was Gingrich's refusal to sign a reflection of his fear of radical Republican Dick Armey and the army of revolutionary ideologues who were pressing the Speaker in Congress? "Well, that was never clear," Panetta reflected. "I'd like to believe that Gingrich understood that it was a good deal, but that he felt he had created this revolution, and didn't—that they were saying, 'This is your chance to win it all!' "

So Gingrich in the end refused to go along with a compromise, and demanded that the president accept Republican cuts. "And that's when Clinton made that comment, 'I just can't do this.' He said it to them, directly. There had been all this very nice give and take—and as I said, one of the things that always drove me crazy was that neither he nor Gore nor anybody sort of said, 'Well, this is madness!' Or, you know: 'We're not gonna do this!' It was always, 'Well, how about *this?*' "

"And finally, after going through this, Clinton said: 'I just can't do what you want me to do.'

"And, he added, 'I know it may cost me the election. But I'm not going to do this.' And they talked a little of the politics of it—the shutdown. But it was just that kind of very clear moment in which I thought: 'He *does* get it! There is a point at which that line *has* to be drawn.' "

For Panetta, it was an unforgettable memory.

"From that," Panetta pointed out, "obviously there were other things that followed. But I do think that it kind of gave him the ability, at last, to kind of say, '*This* is what we're about. And it does contrast with what *they're* about. And this is the message that we have for the American people—that, in many ways, this is the kind of America we want, and *that* is what they want.' "

The President Says No

"Dole tried to calm things, saying that he didn't want the government to shut down," President Clinton later recalled. Gingrich's deputy, Congressman Dick Armey, interrupted Senator Dole, however, to say that the senator did not speak for Republican congressmen in the House of Representatives—upon which there was a verbal shootout between Armey and the president.

Congressman Armey complained of Morris's latest TV ads sewing anxiety among old folk over Medicare cuts, then threatened that the government would be shut down *that very night*, warning that Clinton's presidency would be finished. The president, stung by such a direct threat, responded that he would *never* allow the Republican budget, with its savage cuts in Medicare, Medicaid, education, and other federal programs, to become law. Even were his approval polls to drop to 5 percent across the country, he would *never* sign such a draconian measure. "If you want your budget," he had warned, "you'll have to get someone else to sit in this chair"—and by that declaration he now stuck.

As the president himself later noted, Senator Daschle, Congressman Gephardt, and the White House team "were elated by my confrontation with Armey," after the Republican delegation left. "Al Gore said he wished everyone in America had heard my declaration"—especially, Gore added, the president's insistence on standing firm, even if his approval polls fell to 5 percent.

"No, Al," the president corrected him. "If we drop to 4 percent, I'm caving."

They all laughed, but as Clinton recalled, "our insides were still in knots"—as well they might be.

Never in U.S. history had the government completely shut down, or defaulted on its loans. War, however, had been declared—and was about to begin.

At noon the next day, November 14, all offices of the U.S. government were compelled by Congress to shut down—sending almost a million workers home, and stunning countless millions more who depended on federal institutions. United States embassies and consulates across the world went into crisis mode. Washington museums and monuments locked their doors. Even the national parks closed.

This was the moment the president's advisers and supporters had dreamed of. The Republican capture of Congress had backed the president up against the wall—and forced him to "define who he was," as his chief of staff recalled.

Despite his brave remark about his polls, the president worried, lest the people blame him for the shutdown. It was the president, after all, who was vetoing the Republicans' punitive continuing resolution bill, which would at least keep the government funded at the previous year's level until there was agreement on a new budget. Whatever his advisers said in lauding his stand, Clinton was not convinced, at this stage, that he would not be the one who was blamed, rather than the Republicans. "I was afraid they'd get away with it," he later confessed, "given their success at blaming me for the partisan divide in the '94 election."

With the Dayton negotiations pivoting on a knife-edge—indeed, looking as if they were going to fail—it was wholly understandable that the president should be nervous, and make others nervous lest he lose his nerve.

Napoleon's question in asking about a potential commander, 'Is he lucky?' was never so apposite as now, in the wake of his stand over Gingrich's cuts to Medicare—for to the president's amazement, the Speaker now shot himself in the foot.

The Death of Yitzhak Rabin

On November 4, 1995, Yitzhak Rabin, the prime minister of Israel, was assassinated as he left a peace rally in Tel Aviv.

For the president, who had formed an extraordinary filial relationship to the prime minister, the news of the attempt on Rabin's life—confirmed as fatal by an ashen-faced Tony Lake—had been different from the death of Vince Foster. Foster's mind had been disturbed, and suicide his personal, if tragic, choice. By contrast the Israeli prime minister died at the hand of an aggrieved Israeli, a fanatical Zionist who opposed the restitution of land occupied by Jewish settlers to their original Palestinian owners.

Flying on Air Force One to the funeral in Tel Aviv on November 5, and accompanied by the first lady, the president had not only taken with him a delegation of America's most senior lawmakers, but had given a memorable oration the next day, ending with words that had already become a healing valediction across the world: *Shalom, chaver*—farewell, faithful friend.

On the plane, returning to Washington and grieving for his lost ally who had turned from terrorist to peacemaker, the president had paid only perfunctory attention to the self-appointed prime minister of America, Newt Gingrich. In the Speaker's mind, this was a snub Gingrich—the only member of Congress to have been permitted to take his then-wife—could not stomach. After smoldering for a full week, he threw a child-like tantrum that suddenly gave the White House communications team the opportunity of a lifetime in the midst of the first full shutdown of the U.S. government in its history.

At a press conference on November 15, two days after his White House showdown with the president, with millions of working Americans sent home without pay at his behest, Gingrich complained that he had been insulted by the president. The matter sounded trivial, he acknowledged, "but you land at Andrews [Air Force Base] and you've been on the plane for twenty-five hours and nobody has talked to you and they ask you to get off the plane by the back ramp. You just wonder, where is their sense of manners? Where is their sense of courtesy?" And the Speaker added, referring to the temporary spending bill the president had just vetoed: "I think, by the way, that is part of why you ended up with us sending down a tougher continuing resolution," which made a re-opening of government operations impossible.

Within minutes the Speaker's remark hit the news wires.

The president's press secretary, Mike McCurry, affected disbelief at the White House daily press briefing. The Speaker had, after all, been the sole member of the congressional delegation to the Rabin funeral who was permitted to take his spouse; there were photos of the president (though not the first lady) talking with the couple, amiably. "Until someone shows me these words in black and white," McCurry responded to the reports, "I will refuse to believe that the Speaker said anything that, as you described it, is so petty."

When shown that the words had appeared in the *New York Times* and the *Washington Post*—as they had in most newspapers in the nation—McCurry shrugged. "Maybe," he said, twisting the blade, "we can send him some of those little M&Ms with the presidential seal on it."

And the press conference broke up in helpless laughter.

Eight hundred thousand government employees had been sent home, millions more were out of work as a consequence, the functions of the most powerful nation on earth had been shut down—and the Speaker of the House was blaming the president for snubbing him? The front page of the *New York Daily News* had published a cartoon showing the Speaker in the throes of a tantrum. He was dressed in diapers and above it ran the simple headline: "CRY BABY."

By mid-morning, after the newspaper had been held aloft on the floor of the House of Representatives, Republicans were pushing a bill—which passed 231 to 173—barring any display of the offending tabloid in the chamber. This did not stop the flow of mockery, however. Representative

Patricia Schroeder of Colorado held up, instead, a model Oscar statuette. Speaker Gingrich, she explained, had "sewn up the category of best performance by a child actor this year." As Democrats roared, Schroeder went on: "There's only one problem. This Speaker is not a child."

By the following day it was clear that any tide of support for the Republican blackmail in shutting down the U.S. government's operations unless the president signed their bill had turned.

"Let's take it into the next election [and] let the American people decide," President Clinton told CBS News. "If the American people want the budget that they [Republicans] propose . . . they're entitled to another president. That's the only way they're going to get it."

As the *Montreal Gazette* commented, "More by good fortune than design, this week's shutdown of government not only gives the beleaguered Democratic president an opportunity to demonstrate his often-missing backbone, but also provides a platform on which to fight the GOP in 1996."

A Dilemma

Behind the scenes, President Clinton berated his press secretary for his M&M remark. "Mike, why did you do it?" the president yelled at McCurry—who was rather proud of his ad lib humiliation of the Speaker.

"Don't kick him when he's down," the president warned. "We can't. We have to be very conscious of Gingrich's standing. He's the only one that can pull it together. If we get something, and we put it together, he's got to be able to sell it."

The president, in other words, was not actually seeking a standoff, but a negotiated settlement.

Here, once again, was a dilemma—both the president's and the nation's. Ever since the Oklahoma City bombing and his address to the CIA in June, the president had worried about the "fabric" of American society: how to maintain national unity in the face of increasing terrorism—homegrown and foreign. Prime Minister Rabin's assassination had only strengthened Clinton's conviction that America, indeed the West, could survive the growing clash of civilizations—and the terrorism which that clash engendered—only by unity of purpose, not disunity. But how to create and maintain that national unity? His response to Oklahoma had been a model. Now, once again, the government was under attack, this time from "revolutionaries" in Congress who were indifferent to the suffering their ideological agenda imposed on millions of others. How deal with such home-grown political revolutionaries?

The partisanship that had led to the current shutdown of the government was to Bill Clinton anathema, in this respect. Rather than gloating over Gingrich's mistake, he kicked himself for not having taken the time to talk quietly with Senator Dole and the Speaker about a further compromise that might have avoided the shutdown—and berated his advisers for now making a possible compromise more difficult, not easier.

Among his advisers the president's conciliatory approach met with consternation. The national tide was turning, the Republicans were losing the battle of ideas. Why deliver them from their self-made abyss?

Tormented, the president tied himself in knots—his heart saying one thing, his brain another. And his advisers yet another.

Like his predecessor Democratic president, Jimmy Carter, Bill Clinton was by nature and childhood traumas a healer of divisions rather than a warrior. Moreover, the healer in him had an uncommon ability to read the minds and psyches of his opponents.

Despite his wild mouth the Speaker certainly was not the worst of the Republican junta. Dick Armey was far worse—and there were many other congressional Republicans standing to the ideological, even messianic, right even of Armey! How to defuse their anger, even hate, in the quest for national unison? What would happen if terrorists attacked America while the government was shut down, government loans were not paid, and Congress was divided?

Thus, while his White House staff gloried in the "Cry Baby" discomfort of the Speaker, the president himself remained troubled—as he did over the latest Republican candidates fighting for the Republican presidential nomination. Suppose Senator Dole was beaten in the primaries by one of his more outspoken conservative colleagues, frothing in the same hateful and polarizing manner as Gingrich and Armey? In the Florida straw poll on November 18, Dole had been expected to sweep up 40 percent of the vote; in the event, he was lucky to get 33, with Lamar Alexander only 7 percent behind.

Can national unity be forged without attack, war, or suffering? the president wondered. Appeasing Newt Gingrich and his revolutionaries, however, would be like Neville Chamberlain's attempt to placate the Führer. Gingrich was clearly on the ideological and political warpath—determined to railroad through Congress a right-wing agenda that demanded radical cuts in the federal government, fewer social programs, and fewer taxes on the rich, as the way to achieve deficit reduction and a balanced budget.

To successfully counter that revolutionary agenda it had become necessary to take off the gloves, and to show rock-solid determination. The U.S. government was shut down, its employees unpaid and shut out. Would this lead to national unity, Clinton worried, or to disunity in ongoing domestic partisan struggle? As Leon Panetta recalled, with battle joined *both* sides were spurring on their chiefs, lest they waver.

Going Off a Cliff

"I kept, we kept, offering these compromises," Panetta recalled of his negotiations during the shutdown. "And it was never enough." Republicans did not dispute this. "I don't think they understand how resolute our members are," the second-ranking Republican on the House Budget Committee, David L. Hobson, told reporters at the time. "There are people who would go off a cliff before they would go away from a seven-year balanced budget."

The need for national consensus or unity was therefore irrelevant to the Republican stance. As Gingrich put it, the seven-year ultimatum, reducing entitlement programs while giving tax breaks for the wealthy as an incentive to entrepreneurship, was not even Republican economics. It was a symbolic act designed to hold a sword over Congress, and compel balancing of the budget, however much it enriched the rich and hit the poor as it did so. "Seven [years] is the longest period in which you can maintain the discipline to insist on it happening," the Speaker explained. "Ten [years] allows you to avoid all the decisions that get you to a balanced budget."

When asked on what basis he could say this, Gingrich gave a one-word answer: "Intuition."

Intuition? Was this the basis on which the Speaker of the House of Representatives was willing to shut down the U.S. government? To default on America's loans—dividing the country and stunning the world community?

As Bill Clinton made frantic telephone call after telephone call to Gingrich, attempting to inveigle him into a less ideological commitment to the savaging of government programs, the White House team attempted to stop its leader from committing what it saw as hara-kiri, at the moment when they were winning—for their latest polls showed public approval for the president's stand over the government shutdown running two-to-one in his favor, over Gingrich's.

The Republicans were clearly digging their own grave. The president's injunction to his staff to hold their fire thus made no sense; it was similar to Hitler's halting of his Panzers outside Dunkirk in May 1940, instead of delivering the *coup de grâce*. The Republicans were boxed in by their own ideological insistence on making this a "historic" partisan confrontation instead of listening to the majority of American people. Why then allow them to escape? Stephanopoulos and others asked.

Unplanned, unanticipated, Gingrich's "train wreck" was making it more and more likely that the Republican Contract With America would be wrecked, while the forty-second president—written off as irrelevant only six months before—would be re-elected by an American public dismayed by the Republican leaders' antics.

THE FULL CLINTON

CHAPTER SIXTY-SIX

IN THE PINCHING CAVE

Cell of Ignorance

Why? Why now, on the cusp of presidential greatness, did Bill Clinton give in to his age-old weakness?

In a hidden cave in the Welsh mountains Shakespeare's Lord Belarius, we may recall, rears the kidnapped sons of the British king Cymbeline. He talks disparagingly to the boys of the vice and corruption of the royal palace—of "courts, of princes," and men and women "rustling in unpaid-for silk." The sons listen respectfully. He tells them of the "tricks of war." He rails against the treacherous slope of such ambition, "whose top to climb / Is certain falling, or so slippery that / The fear's as bad as falling . . . "

The sons listen.

Belarius tells them of courage and public service that seem only to earn "a slanderous epitaph / As record of fair act." Many times, Belarius relates, a public servant "Doth ill deserve by doing well; what's worse, / Must court'sy at the censure."

The sons, living in their "cell of ignorance," remain unconvinced. Indeed Arviragus, the younger son, puts the problem hauntingly. "What should we speak of / When we are old as you? when we shall hear / The rain and wind beat dark December, how, / In this our pinching cave, shall we discourse / The freezing hours away? We have seen nothing . . . "

Like Prince Alviragus in his guardian's cave, we who have never experienced or witnessed power at its apex have seen nothing. Moreover, the lens of our biographical telescope is far less finely ground than Shakespeare's. We will address the much-debated social, judicial, and political ethics of the tragedy later, at a time in Bill Clinton's life course when the saga became public and caused the whole nation to descend into an orgy of self-destructive moralizing seldom, if ever, witnessed in American history: a fractious performance that, sadly, could only encourage fanatics in the United States and abroad to despise the presidency and the country, even to attack it again. Would that the president had then resigned—as President Nixon had resigned—to spare his nation such self-rending torment! But that account must come in its proper chronological place. For now, let us simply record the fateful relationship in *its* proper place—that is to say, starting on November 15, 1995, during Gingrich's first government shutdown. For it was because of the furloughing of all but essential government workers that an unpaid intern, aged twenty-two, was able, uniquely, to go into the inner sanctum of the West Wing, and seduce the all-too-sexually-available president of the United States.

Had the intern been an enemy spy—as had been the case earlier, when Ellen Rometsch seduced President Kennedy—the security fallout could have been critical. As it happened, the intern was not a spy, but her seduction, and the political capital Clinton's enemies would make from it, would turn out to be far more damaging to the ultimate security and well-being of the nation.

How?

How? How could an unknown twenty-two-year-old intern—a Californian college graduate intent on retaking the college courses in which she had received low grades in order to improve her prospects for attaining a master's degree, or even a Ph.D., in psychology—have gotten continual access, sexual access, to the leader of the world's last superpower?

Monica Lewinsky's penetration of the nation's highest palace, within three months of working in a subsidiary building, defies retrospective belief, as does so much in American culture before 9/11: the tragic wake-up call America would experience one-and-a-half years into the following millennium.

As part of her college coursework in 1993 Monica had, as a junior, worked briefly with the mentally ill—her only genuinely adult experience of life outside *her* cave, the classroom. More to the point, however, she'd conducted a fateful sexual relationship with a theater technician working at her Beverley Hills high school, Andy Bleiler: a man seven years her senior, who in turn was secretly engaged to marry Kate, a divorcée eight years *his* senior, with whom he already had a son. Monica's low self-esteem as the daughter of a divorced couple—made worse by compulsive, emotional overeating that made her, she felt, less attractive still—seemed straight out of central casting for a California suburban soap opera: Monica agreeing to have sex with Andy after he married Kate and, once she graduated from Santa Monica College, encouraging him to follow her to Oregon, where she attended the tiny Lewis & Clark College in Portland for her final two undergraduate years, even forging a letter from the head of the college theater department offering Andy contract work, to allay Kate Bleiler's suspicions. "A piece of garbage" was how Monica's mother described the technician, yet she failed to halt her daughter's adulterous "obsession"—or the technician's abusive relationship with her daughter. As Monica herself reflected later, "I came to learn with married men that they feel guilty, say they want to stop it and then succumb to temptation anyway. So they always come back."

Addictive Personality

If this was Lewis & Clark's best contribution to human insight by its smart psychology major, it was of little use to Monica's mother, since weaning her away from Bleiler, as an older, married, and promiscuous man, proved as difficult, Monica's mother considered, as "trying to bring her off drugs."

Addictive personality was certainly a part of the problem—the self-described "fat" psychology major was as big, loud, hot, and potentially self-destructive, in her way, as the president of the United States was in his. Like the president, Monica had struggled with potential obesity throughout her childhood, and still fought with her weight. Crowned by a fountain of jet-black hair, and boasting a curvaceous figure and full lips, she had obtained her White House internship through her well-connected, divorced mother, who had moved to Washington, D.C., and who believed that the internship, though unpaid and irrelevant to her daughter's career path (given Monica's complete lack of interest in politics), would, at least, help put the married Bleiler behind her.

In August 1995 it did. To Monica's chagrin, Andy took yet another extramarital lover—prompting Monica almost immediately to set her cap for the married president: recognizing that he was a flirt and, like most men, a weak vessel when struggling with lust. Winning his attention, and if possible his sexual attention, became her new challenge. On November 15, 1995, in the midst of the government shutdown, she got her way.

An Easy Target

Despite a world-class security team protecting him from assassination, the president, nearing fifty, was a surprisingly easy target for seduction. The sixties had been good to the high school band player—too good. Avoiding Vietnam and service in the military as a student, he had devoted himself to politics and, after marrying his highly motivated, highly intellectual, highly disciplined college sweetheart from Yale Law School, had enjoyed a cornucopia of extramarital sex in Arkansas. He had enjoyed, in effect, the best of both modern worlds: an intellectually brilliant companion as wife and an endless succession of liberated girlfriends.

Born and brought up a Baptist, however, the president forever struggled with what he later saw as his dark side: his shame at being so vulnerable to temptation and sin. Thus, beyond his select group of long-term mistresses, his promiscuity in the seventies and eighties he confined largely to brief oral sex.

Like LBJ in his time, Bill Clinton was not handsome in the conventional sense, yet he radiated intelligent energy and a curiosity about the people he encountered that could swing from compassion to predatory interest at will—and was difficult for the victim to deflect. His personality—his aura of power, his vigor, sheer intellect, instant empathy, blue eyes, strong chin, six-foot-three frame, southern sense of humor, and "eye for the gals"—had proven a veritable light to the moths of Arkansas: an illumination further brightened by his travels as the young, dynamic representative of his small state.

The White House, by contrast, had proved in every way a challenge, given his sexual indiscipline and surprising lack of team leadership and executive skills after twelve years in a gubernatorial chair. After his party's midterm melt-down, however, he'd at last been able to put his high intelligence and prodigious speaking skills to more effective use—not only helping to heal the nation's wounds over Oklahoma City, but demonstrating new American purpose in foreign affairs, while attempting to mitigate by his presidential veto the worst of congressional "revolutionary" Republicanism on the home front.

William Jefferson Clinton was coming of age as president—though not, as it turned out on November 15, as a faithful married man.

CHAPTER SIXTY-SEVEN

ACHILLES' HEEL

Gambling with Destiny

When asked years later whether President Clinton "grew" in character while in office, former Treasury Secretary Larry Summers reflected for a moment, then shook his head.

Larry Summers had become involved in the '92 campaign, and would serve in the Clinton administration until the end. In his admiring estimation Bill Clinton never really changed: was as brilliant a politician at the beginning of his presidential tenure as at the end. Neither his personality nor his character really altered, essentially. What changed was his game, as the hard knocks of failure, scandal, and opposition taught him he must alter his style of political combat if he was to outwit the forces ranged against him. He became, in other words, *cleverer*—a fact that Newt Gringrich, for one, simply missed, until it was too late.

This lack of change in essential character, combined with a growing ability to outwit the opposition, was in 1995 promising to be successful in a way that most domestic observers could scarcely credit in comparison with the year before. Yet, as in the third law of motion, there had been an equal and opposite Newtonian reaction to such positive energy: this most brilliant and dynamic of presidents remained not only temptable sexually, if his security detail failed to fend off predatory females, but temptable by something more than lust—namely, the urge to gamble with destiny, and see whether he could not only get what was forbidden, but get away with it.

The Biggest Fish

Cleverness in outwitting the opposition, as in the case of JFK, thus meant for Bill Clinton the outwitting not only of political opponents but of his *protectors*, too—especially his loyal and wonderfully effective chief of staff, Leon Panetta.

Panetta had struggled to create a military-style White House hierarchy in which each staffer answered to his or her superior, not to the president, unless specifically authorized. The president was thus deliberately accorded time to be by himself—time in which he could reflect, telephone, and share his thoughts in privacy, not in public, as in his first two years. The historic government shutdown by Gingrich's revolutionary Republicans, however, had not only furloughed all but a skeleton staff, but was keeping Panetta himself, as the linchpin of the White House operation, deeply involved in the critical negotiations with Republican leaders on Capitol Hill, on the one hand, while communications with the Dayton team preoccupied remaining senior staffers.

With so many of his critical personnel furloughed, Panetta was temporarily unable to police access to the president as, say, Betsey Wright had once policed access to Governor Clinton in Arkansas, before she was made to resign. Thus when, on November 15, 1995, an unpaid intern—and thus *non*-government employee—who had been brought over from Panetta's second office in the Eisenhower Building next door to answer West Wing phones in the chief of staff's office, saw her chance, she seized it. Casting her heavily baited line, she was stunned to find the biggest fish in the entire world struggling upon her hook.

Why did the president respond to Monica Lewinsky's flirtatious signals? Again and again, often without real purpose, the president returned to the chief of staff's office that day to ogle the plump intern. The president's own later explanation—that he had simply given in to abused-childhood temptation because he could—fails to do justice (let alone justify) the choices he made that day, and repeatedly, in the ensuing months.

The truth was that at some perhaps unconscious level, the gladiator in Bill Clinton—winner, like Commodus, of a thousand bouts in the colisseum of American political life—needed constantly to test the bounds of restraint: to see what he could get away with. JFK had done so, flagrantly, in his short lifetime—leading Bill Clinton to say of his predecessor in the

Oval Office that he "obviously was a man who thought he was ill, was in a hurry in life, grew up in a different time, was raised in a home where the rules were apparently different than most of us believe they should be now, and where the role of women in society was different than it is now."

It was the question of where the rules, not the roles, were now that the sexually addicted, dynamic president found himself driven to test, despite—or to spite—his better judgment. On the evening of November 15 he *again* returned to Panetta's office, this time to attend the farewell party for staffer Jennifer Palmieri.

"There was continued flirtation," Monica would later confess to the grand jury—which promised her immunity only as long as she told the much-garnished, lascivious truth. Monica's flirtation climaxed when, standing by the doorway, out of sight of any colleagues but the president, she turned her back, and lifting her jacket, showed her thong and her ample, naked upper cheeks, like a chimpanzee—an act of primal teasing and a promise of sexual submission the president could not ignore.

Unable to Resist

To act, or not to act? To remonstrate—or acknowledge the signal? For a president already fighting a major lawsuit over his own sexual exhibitionism and thus harassment in the workplace, it was a question he was to wrestle with for several hours, up in the Residence—where news of Newt Gingrich's childish reaction to his treatment aboard Air Force One was playing on the television.

Later, after dinner, the president returned to the chief of staff's office. Had Panetta been there, history might possibly have turned out differently, but he wasn't. Monica was—and was too tempting to refuse. It was "around 8:00 in the evening," Monica later told the grand jury. "I was in the hallway going to the restroom, passing Mr. Stephanopoulos's office, and he [the president] was in the hall and invited me into Mr. Stephanopoulos's office, and from there invited me back into his study."

Monica had been reading Gennifer Flowers's new book, *Passion and Betrayal*. She had no illusions—indeed, one of the first things she did to assure the president he could count on her compliance and loyalty was to assure him that despite her young age, she had already been in a relationship with an older, married man.

The president, equally, had no illusions. Paula Jones's lawyers were still contesting Judge Wright's ruling that a president cannot be brought to trial during his term of office. Casting denial and discretion to the four winds, the president led the plump intern into his den—to see not so much if he could do it "because he could," as he later explained his actions, but to see if he could do it *and get away with it.*

CHAPTER SIXTY-EIGHT

STANDARDS OF BEHAVIOR

An Accident Waiting to Happen

The president ought, in fact, to have been in Japan, for the Osaka summit of Asian-Pacific leaders, but had decided not to go, owing to the shutdown of the U.S. government.

Without those two misfortunes—the latter not only emptying the West Wing of its normal staff but requiring the chief of staff's presence on the Hill—could the catastrophic liaison between the president of the United States and the intern possibly have developed as it did?

Probably. Monica Lewinsky had made "intense eye contact" on numerous occasions since her internship first began in August, and had had physical contact in shaking hands with the president several times. "He exudes sexual energy," she would say later—his handshake soft and sensual, the gaze deliberately predatory. The old phrase "the Full Monty"—meaning the real and whole shebang—was soon to be (in 1997) recast to signify total male nudity before mobs of eager, liberated women. The phrase "the Full Clinton," likewise, would be coined by Monica to describe the deliberately denuding gaze of the forty-second president. "It was this look," she later explained, "it's the way he flirts with women. When it was time to shake my hand, the smile disappeared, the rest of the crowd disappeared and we shared an intense but brief sexual exchange. He undressed me with his eyes." The second time he shook hands with Monica in public—at a White House forty-ninth pre-birthday bash, to which interns were invited—he even "accidentally" brushed his arm against her ample breast.

Applying for a second internship and then a full-time post in the White House, Monica Lewinsky had been star-struck. Not only did she openly tell fellow interns she had a crush on the president (whom she'd first scorned as "an old guy," replete with "big red nose and coarse, wiry-looking gray hair"), she had even written a poem in September for him on National Bosses Day, which she got her fellow interns to sign.

For a flirtatious president, Monica was an accident waiting to happen—and on November 15 it happened. After she had shown her bare backside, the president was hooked; once she told him, in Stephanopoulos's empty office, that she had "a big crush" on him, there was no way the middle-aged leader of the free world could escape. In his "back office" he put his arms round her and pulled her tight against his chest. It was not harassment or abuse, at this point, but wholly consensual: two office workers acknowledging not only the chemistry of hothouse attraction but also the swirl of excitement and escapism that accompanies such illicit liaisons. The president's eyes were "soul-searching, very wanting, very needing and very loving," Monica related. "There was a sadness about him that I hadn't expected to see." He even *asked* if he might kiss her, to which she consented. She remembered thinking, "I can't believe this is happening," and, once it happened, "What an incredible, sensual kisser."

"I knew that one day I would kiss you," the president later confided to Monica—each aware that, given the intense sexual charge between them, it was almost inevitable their planets would collide. In order to avoid suspicion they went back to work, but then, around 10 P.M. the president reappeared yet again. Anticipating this, Monica had already written down her name and phone number, which she handed him surreptitiously, but he was reluctant to wait or defer an assignation. He suggested they meet in Stephanopoulos's empty office a few minutes later. There in the dark he kissed her passionately, and they "licensed" each other's roving hands to explore one another physically—culminating in oral sex.

In a sexual sense, the president had chosen unerringly. "We clicked at an incredible level. People have made it seem so demeaning for me but it wasn't, it was exciting, and the irony is," Monica later confided, "that I had the first orgasm of the relationship."

Friendship with Benefits

Monica Lewinsky felt no personal shame, either at the time or later. For millions of American girls in their teens oral sex was already becoming the sexual exchange of choice, given the dangers of pregnancy and sexual disease, encapsulated in the phrases "hooking up" and "friendship with benefits."

Talking with the ebullient, plump, and well-endowed twenty-two-year-old, and brushing away the thick black hair from her wide, friendly face, the forty-nine-year-old president was grateful for such a promising friendship. As he would later confess to the grand jury, on his own account, he was fully aware how inappropriate was the relationship and how much he was playing with fire in acting upon his attraction. But with Monica telling him she had already had a similar relationship with an older man, he persuaded himself she was older than her years, and would discreetly join his stable of beneficent relationships, formed over the previous twenty years—if temporarily expunging, in his excitement, the fact that he'd suffered grave consequences over the years from such dangerous liaisons. Monica, however, was like a luscious fruit in the Garden of Eden, eager to be plucked: and he could not simply say no.

The Oldest of Adult Sins

Eventually the president returned to the Residence and to Hillary—feeling guilty but aroused, too (he had not allowed Monica to overexcite him). The government was shut down, the Dayton negotiations were reaching make-or-break stage, the ramifications of sending American troops to Bosnia had yet to be handled with allies, NATO, Congress, and the United Nations, but he felt as President Kennedy had so often felt after being with "Fiddle" and "Faddle," his own White House interns in their early twenties: a rush of masculine adrenaline.

While Monica excitedly woke up her mother and aunt in the famous Watergate complex, where she was living, to tell them the fairy-tale news that the president had kissed her, Bill Clinton was hardly in a position to wake up Hillary with the same news, and he didn't. Nevertheless, he'd had a rejuvenating experience. He'd found a new partner in the oldest of his adult sins—adultery—yet one with whom, by virtue of not "having sex," he could, like millions of young adults, claim he was not committing adultery, since he was not having "real sex" with her.

It was a distinction others would not find so easy to make—or forgive—in terms of the dignity of the presidency.

The High Road, Not the Low

Negotiations on the Hill over the government shutdown were not easy. Each side now feared the other might win; the game became one of brinkmanship. For the moment, the president held firm, however. "Today the Republicans in the House of Representatives voted to enact the biggest Medicare and Medicaid cuts in history," the president said on November 17, in a bill that required "unprecedented cuts in education and the environment, and steep tax increases on working families. I will veto this bill." Their proposed budget called for a reduction of $32.5 billion in earned income tax credit to low income workers, but a $35.6 billion tax break for investors in stocks and property, as well as tax cuts for heirs of wealth that would deprive the Treasury of $12 billion—in order to benefit only twenty-five thousand American families. "I am determined to balance the budget, but I will not go along with a plan that cuts care for disabled children, reduces educational opportunity by cutting college scholarships, denies preschool to thousands of poor children, slashes enforcement of environmental laws, and doubles Medicare premiums for the elderly. We should balance the budget in a way that reflects our values," the president ended—the high road, in other words, not the low.

Yet that same evening the president—who had attempted via body-language to indicate to Monica that their intimacy had been a one-off aberration—was lying in wait by the door of his secretary's office when Monica emerged from the restroom, after cleaning off some spilled pizza sauce. He told her she could go out through the Oval Office.

A Jewish Name

A fellow intern had said to Monica, "I think the president has a crush on you"—causing Monica, now, to be alarmed. "Oh my goodness," she thought as he led her through the famed room to his back office. "This is so unbelievable."

It was—at the very heart of America's Kremlin. Discussing her telephone number, after they had kissed, Monica reassured the president she had her own line at home—though teased him, too, by suggesting he didn't even remember her name. "Lewinsky," he responded, culling his extraordinary memory. "What sort of a name," he then asked, "is that?"

"Jewish."

It was the most reassuring answer the president could have gotten. Monica had already indicated she was not a virgin; that she was no stranger to adulterous activity with an older man; that she had her own phone line at home. And now that she was neither a Muslim nor a Russian, but Californian Jewish: honored and safe. They were home free to renew their dangerous liaison as a "hookup."

The president then asked if Monica would fetch him a vegetarian pizza. To keep his secretary, Betty Currie, on board, Monica relayed to her the president's instructions that she was following.

Bad Pornography

"Sir, the girl's here with the pizza," Betty called in to the president, when Monica returned, bearing the box like a French maid.

If Ken Starr's later investigation read at times like a bad pornographic script, that was because, in certain respects, it was.

"Okay, and what happened in the back study area?" Karin Immergut [in German, literally, *always good*], a U.S. attorney, later asked on behalf of the grand jury.

"We were in the—well, we talked and then we were physically intimate again."

"Okay," Ms. Immergut said, taking a deep breath, not wanting to upset her victim's outrageous testimony: that Monica had been intimate with a serving president in the hallowed sanctum of the Oval Office. "And was there oral sex performed on that occasion?"

"Yes."

"Okay," Ms. Immergut repeated—knowing this was historical, political, and social dynamite. Her questions were utterly outrageous in their quest for sexual detail; in the history of divorce there probably had never been as forensic an investigation of the sexual act as part of a lawsuit. Yet the lawyer was not just a lawyer; she was one of a small army of self-righteous peeping Toms, licensed by a Republican Congress to try to entrap a serving president by showing that he had—as with Paula Jones—abused his power as an employer. As a lawyer she must get it right, so that the wicked president or *his* lawyers could not wiggle out of the revelation, as they had so far with Paula Jones. "And that would be you performing oral sex on him?"

In the history of the presidency, certainly, no such investigation into the sexual behavior of a serving chief executive had ever taken place—yet the fact was, the situation, in Bill Clinton's case, had been predicted by a hundred historians and observers, of both sexes. With the opening of presidential archives, the "institutionalization of gossip" (as one writer called it), and the frankness with which historians addressed the subject of the president in a candid society, it was now well known that adultery was as common among American presidents as among the general population—especially among younger, more active presidents.

Ten years older than Bill Clinton when he became president, Dr. Woodrow Wilson, for example, had had an affair with Mrs. Mary Allen Peck, a wealthy socialite from the Midwest, who had taken a house in Bermuda and one in New York, several years before Wilson ran for office. What had saved Woodrow Wilson in the presidential election of 1912 was not only the era—one in which sex-smearing had become temporarily taboo in politics—but the inherent unlikelihood of an egghead, a deeply serious academic, indulging in such adventurous extramarital activity. As former president Theodore Roosevelt, the "Bull Moose Party" candidate, remarked, "You can't cast a man as a Romeo who looks and acts so much like an apothecary's clerk." Nevertheless, the rumors were true, and Wilson went so far as to prepare a public admission of his "passage of folly," for which the candidate was "deeply ashamed and repentant." In the event, however, the confession had proved unnecessary. Dean West, Wilson's bitterest foe, dismissed any hint of indiscretion as "nonsense, simply not in character," and even Wilson's devoted wife, Ellen, privately forgave him his misbehavior—"the only unhappiness during our whole married life," she confided to her doctor before her death, while first lady. Discretion, by all, had proven the better part of political valor.

Discretion had long since departed from American presidential politics, however. In a situation in which Jerry Springer was now broadcasting a daily television diet of revelatory sexual exhibitionism, literally exposing real Americans to their fellow Americans (and the rest of the world, once his *Jerry Springer Show* was sold abroad), it seemed almost perverse to expect presidents to be miraculously above temptation. Yet such was the case, however illogical—and Bill Clinton knew and accepted this. Whether he could tailor his sexual behavior—or his cover-ups—to the expectations of the public, however, was another matter.

Historians and observers had thus had every reason to be anxious—especially after Troopergate and the Paula Jones lawsuit. Understandably, Hillary had denounced the Arkansas troopers' stories as politically motivated lies. Better than anyone, however, she knew that they were, for the most part, a fairly accurate record of her husband's Achilles' heel—indeed, in an unusually reckless moment in 1992 she had pretty much admitted this. "When it was suggested during an interview last week," one journalist had noted in 1992, "that, after Gary Hart [whose political career was wrecked by charges of infidelity], a candidate who ran around while running for the presidency would have to be psychotic, Hillary Clinton burst out laughing. 'That's a pretty fair estimate,'" she said.

Mary McGrory, a nationally syndicated journalist, had put the matter very well before Clinton even became president. Marital infidelity might be considered by most women to be of secondary importance to the task of fixing the American economy in 1992, but it had to be said, too, that "women who wish to be modern and sophisticated about the Sixth Commandment still wonder if their husbands might misread their enlightenment," as McGrory put it, "for a generalized tolerance for roaming"—whereupon she gave as example a typical young wife thinking: "I certainly wouldn't want Tom to get any idea that it would be okay for him."

The potentially roaming tomcat might, in other words, be an acceptable cause for fantasy, yet it raised, too, alarm bells among female voters. McGrory was certainly not alone. As a woman Sally Quinn had found herself just as worried about the politico-cultural ramifications of this new post-feminist situation when applied to the White House. In the media-frenzied aftermath of the Gennifer Flowers revelations, Quinn had written that America "is a country with a residual puritan ethic. In our hearts, we know adultery is not right. It doesn't make us feel good about the person doing it. And we believe the person doing it doesn't feel good about himself. In all the agonizing we did about Hart and the press, our declarations that adultery was not the issue were not entirely true. It just didn't seem 'modern' somehow, or sophisticated or open-minded to say that adultery made us squirm. Americans do think there are certain standards of behavior, character and morality that a president must maintain," Quinn declared, "and women, in general, seem to care more about the issue of presidential character than men. That doesn't give people the right to know every detail about a person's private life, but. . . ."

These warnings—published even before Bill Clinton won the White House, or Paula Jones appeared on the national radar—proved uncannily prescient. "There are endless questions," Ms. Quinn—married to Ben Bradlee, former journalist-pal of President Kennedy—acknowledged. Yet what was the alternative to a dynamic, but adulterous, president? An unmarried president? "Do we want a bachelor like Bob Kerrey or Jerry Brown in the White House?" Quinn had asked—rehearsing the nightmare "logistics" of a presidential date in such singleton circumstances: "An entourage of 40-odd people, including sharpshooters, communications specialists, doctors, decoy limousines. *For a date*? Wouldn't gossip about the president's love life detract from the agenda? What if the president got AIDS? Or fell in love? People in love can be crazy. Do we want to chance that?"

Wanting a safely married man in the White House—at least currently safe—seemed, ultimately, to most Americans a sensible thing, and a matter about which the candidate, in speech after speech mentioning his wife and his daughter, had sought to reassure the public.

Yet of all wise counselors, Quinn's own, previously divorced husband could have told her the simple truth with regard to virile young men in positions of power: that such married men are *never* safe.

CHAPTER SIXTY-NINE

CEASE-FIRE

Something to Work With

The budget showdown was permitting the president's somewhat blurry presidential image to become clear—at last. "Bill Clinton had not come into sharp focus for most Americans," even his press secretary, Mike McCurry, later admitted. "Who is this guy? Where is he on the political spectrum? How does he relate to me and my needs? That was the moment in which they finally said, 'He's fighting for things that I care about. He's standing up to these Republicans in Congress that want to take the country in a direction I don't believe in.'"

Dick Morris, as the polling genius who had masterminded the president's below-radar advertising campaign throughout the fall, was now hoist on his own petard. A coward by nature, he hated the shutdown of the government, which he feared might backfire, politically. Yet Morris's own polls suggested the president should hold firm rather than give in. Day by day the president's approval rating improved as those of Republican leaders dropped. By mid-November Bill Clinton's overall approval rating as president was higher than 52 percent—his highest for eighteen months.

Gingrich's favorability rating, by contrast, dropped to 25 percent. Gingrich's *un*favorable poll rating, by the same token, had soared—to 56 percent. Yet Morris (who had been wrong on Haiti, but right on Bosnia) still felt it vital for the president's re-election as a centrist "do-er" to agree to Gingrich's seven-year budget and get the government open again.

More and more, then, it became Leon Panetta's job, as chief of staff, to ensure cohesion in the Clinton camp—to go on showing White House willingness to be reasonable, while the president refused on moral grounds to accept a budget that would hurt children, the elderly, and the poor.

Hillary's back seat, ever since the midterm meltdown, had empowered Panetta in a way that had been impossible until catastrophe forced her hand. "It was interesting," Panetta later recalled, for he had always felt Hillary's interventions had been a misguided attempt to compensate for poor White House management. Once she'd finally witnessed the White House machine working well, she had become content to stand back for the most part, and did not interfere. "I had made the decision to meet with her once a week to brief her on what was going on—just to make sure she was aware of that," he explained. "And there was a moment about six months into it when she said, 'We don't need to meet.' I sensed that at that point that she had a certain confidence that things were on track. I had a good relationship with her—she never came into my office to pound the table or anything like that. It worked out."

With the government still shut down, triangulation once again produced a synthesis. On Sunday, November 19, the president went as far as accepting a "goal" of balancing the budget in seven years, subject to ring-fencing Medicare, Medicaid, education, and the environment—and signs came back that the Republicans were softening, and would accept such a compromise. "God, this is something to work with," Panetta exclaimed as Gingrich's agreement came through by fax. That night, after six days of almost complete U.S. government shutdown—the longest in U.S. history—the Senate voted in a continuing resolution to re-open the government for one month, during which, it was hoped, a balanced budget could be agreed.

Rewritten by Republicans, Panetta's draft compromise was an agreement whereby the president and the Congress promised to negotiate a budget that would reach balance by the seventh year—2002—but one that "must protect future generations, ensure Medicare solvency, reform welfare and provide adequate funding for Medicaid, education, national defense, veterans, agriculture, and the environment." In addition, the budget had to include "tax policies to help working families." "This is a tremendous achievement," Speaker Newt Gingrich was quoted saying, while Leon Panetta was equally hopeful. "We've established a framework for negotiations," he declared, though he warned that "Nothing is agreed to until everything is agreed to."

The next day, Monday, November 20, the House duly passed a one-month continuation bill, re-opening the government until December 15. Peace, suddenly, was in the air—especially when, on Tuesday, November 21, word came through that Assistant Secretary Holbrooke had got his Bosnian agreement in Dayton, after all. Following last-minute touch-and-go disagreements, and a call from President Clinton to the Croation president, Franjo Tudjman, the treaty had been initialed by all the parties. President Clinton was then able to give the long-awaited address in the Rose Garden, at 11 A.M.

It was a historic moment. The Europeans having failed, the United States had taken charge—and had won peace in Bosnia. After congratulating his negotiating team for their selfless devotion to a settlement, and the parties who had agreed the treaty, the president moved on to the future. "We are at a decisive moment. The parties have chosen peace," he began. "America must choose peace as well."

What the president meant was that America must undertake a firm congressional and public commitment to make Dayton work. This would be easier said than done, however.

An Address to the Nation

A third of the sixty-thousand-strong NATO peacekeeping contingent would be American soldiers, the president declared, the remaining two-thirds coming from NATO partners and from other nations around the world. "I am satisfied that the NATO implementation plan is clear, limited, and achievable and that the risks to our troops are minimized. I will promptly consult with Congress when I receive this plan, and if I am fully satisfied with it when I see it in its final form, I will ask Congress to support American participation." Thereupon he asked all Americans "in this Thanksgiving week to take some time to say a simple prayer of thanksgiving that this peace has been reached, that our nation was able to play an important part in stopping the suffering and the slaughter. May God bless the peace and the United States."

Once America had consumed its millions of turkeys, however, the wrangling and hand-wringing began. Having failed to bulldoze the president into a right-wing budget, Republicans were reluctant to accord him victory at Dayton. American isolationism had precluded the use of American ground forces in Bosnia from the start of the conflict. The notion of now sending twenty thousand American sons into possible harm's way, in a far-off, ethnically and religiously torn country, seemed, well, unpopular. Why couldn't the Europeans do it all?

In Europe, there was equal concern lest American isolationists sunder the agreement their own government had so notably won. In Barcelona the European Union's chief negotiator was clear that murderous Serbs, in particular, had no respect or fear for anyone save Americans. "There will be no peace in Bosnia without U.S. troops," Carl Bildt warned after briefing officials of the fifteen EU governments. The agreement signed at the Dayton peace talks was but "a pile of paper," he said, echoing Holbrooke's view. "Judging by the *Dayton Daily News*"—his only contact with the outside media world during the peace negotiations—"there is great hesitancy on the part of American public opinion to go into Bosnia." As he candidly acknowledged, "President Clinton will have to fight that battle."

Bildt was confident that President Clinton, with his command of rhetoric, would win the communications battle. But what if he didn't? "If he loses it," the veteran Swedish diplomat asked, "how can you ever speak about America's leadership role in the future? Then it's a leadership role in word and not in practice. I don't expect that to happen. And if it were to happen it would of course have very serious repercussions for peace in Bosnia [and] for the trans-Atlantic relationship."

"If he can't persuade the American people, it's going to be very difficult to persuade the Congress," even Senator Dole warned. American pilots had risked their lives, American negotiators had lost theirs, and American diplomats had pulled out every stop to halt the ethnic killing—but Dayton as an agreement could not work unless Bill Clinton swayed the hearts and minds of the American public, thereby licensing Congress to back his implementation plan.

From the Oval Office on November 27 President Clinton therefore gave a special twenty-minute television address to the nation, to explain how the Dayton Accords would be applied in Bosnia. Opposed by Senator Phil Gramm, publisher Steve Forbes, and isolationist Patrick Buchanan, as well as polls showing that the majority of Americans were still against sending in American ground troops, Clinton's speech "was considered by his aides to be among Clinton's most critical," the *Washington Post* noted, "testing both his ability to persuade the nation to stand behind him in a risky venture and his credibility as commander in chief in pushing for and overseeing such a complicated, no-guarantees commitment in an area that polls suggest few Americans see as being of vital U.S. interest."

Oil had, in 1991, persuaded even the most skeptical that America had to respond to Saddam Hussein's invasion of Kuwait. This time there was no oil to secure; there was only the humanitarian, moral goal of ending sectarian genocide in Europe—and keeping the NATO alliance intact.

No one else in America, it appeared, as the eyes of Congress and the nation turned to the White House, could do it. The hour of the wolf was over, dawn was breaking, and the president must pull from his rhetorical quiver the words and conviction that could sway the majority from isolationism to the proud implementation of peace.

"He doesn't have to convince them that he's 100 percent right," Newt Gingrich declared as, like Senator Dole, he clung to the president's coattails, "but he has to win the benefit of the doubt."

From an empty desk—speaking to the hearts as well as minds of his nation—President Clinton thus set about making one of the most crucial cases of his presidency. The eyes of the world were literally upon him. "Generations of Americans have understood that Europe's freedom and Europe's stability is vital to our own national security. That's why we fought two wars in Europe," he explained. "That's why we launched the Marshall Plan to restore Europe. That's why we created NATO and waged the Cold War. And that's why we must help the nations of Europe to end their worst nightmare since World War II, now."

Those who'd heard the freshman president give his first television address from the Oval Office on February 15, 1993, calling for economic patriotism, could hardly credit the transformation as the president spoke with what was called, in the *New York Times*, a mesmerizing display of "political artistry and human drama."

Even skeptical Republican senators and congressmen were impressed by the president's historical *tour d'horizon*, as the commander in chief emphasized: "The only force capable of getting this job done is NATO, the powerful military alliance of democracies that has guaranteed our security for half a century now. And as NATO's leader and the primary broker in the peace agreement, the United States must be an essential part of the mission. If we're not there, NATO will not be there; the peace will collapse; the war will reignite; the slaughter of innocents will begin again. A conflict that already has claimed many victims could spread like poison throughout the region, eat away at Europe's stability, and erode our partnership with our European allies."

From rationale, the president turned to practicalities—accepting that "no deployment of American troops is risk-free." "As president," he explained, "my most difficult duty is to put the men and women who volunteer to serve our nation in harm's way when our interests and values demand it. I assume responsibility for any harm that may come to them. But anyone contemplating any action that would endanger our troops should know this: America protects it own. Anyone, anyone who takes on our troops will suffer the consequences. We will fight fire with fire and then some."

It was, all agreed, a *tour de force* on behalf of force, but for a humanitarian mission: perhaps the finest such speech ever delivered from the Oval Office. Single-handedly, emerging as the greatest orator of his generation, Bill Clinton had turned the skeptical tide of the country.

That night some 30 percent of those polled *changed their view*—declaring, as a result of the president's speech, their support of U.S. troop involvement in Bosnia. Over half now believed the United States had a "moral obligation to keep the peace in Bosnia." Almost two-thirds reported that they were "very confident" or "somewhat confident" in the president's ability to handle the situation.

The next afternoon, fifty lawmakers of both parties were invited to the White House, and over subsequent days a huge campaign was launched to win support in Congress for the president's message of pride, hope, power, and military-humanitarian purpose—with some thirty-seven thousand American troops now designated for the task inside Bosnia and on its borders. "We cannot stop all war for all time," the president had said in his address to the nation, borrowing from Winston Churchill's cadences, "but we can stop some wars. We cannot save all women and all children, but we can save many of them. We can't do everything, but we must do what we can."

CHAPTER SEVENTY

KING BILLY

A Leader Who Delivers

Two days later, rising in the Royal Gallery of the House of Lords, on his first official trip to the U.K., it was clear the former Yank at Oxford had, like Dwight Eisenhower before him, earned the respect and even adulation of a country not his own.

Addressing the joint session of the British Parliament, Clinton began with a self-deprecating joke, confessing his envy of a system in which senior parliamentarians from the House of Commons were by tradition made Lords—"not a bad place to be after a long and troublesome political career," he joked, recounting how, from the time he was a lowly student he had often visited, and always "felt the power of this place, where the voices of free people who love liberty, believe in reason, and struggle for truth have for centuries kept your great nation a beacon of hope for all the world and a very special model for your former colonies which became the United States of America."

The president congratulated the British and Irish prime ministers for their latest agreement to an American-sponsored "twin-track" process to achieve peace in Northern Ireland—a process that the U.S. would fortify by contributing an American to chair the committee negotiating and overseeing the decommissioning of arms by the IRA: former Senate majority leader George Mitchell. Then, recalling the World War II alliance of President Franklin Roosevelt and British Prime Minister Winston Churchill, he turned to the challenge of Bosnia and the need for Western nations to concert their efforts if they were to defeat the forces of evil threatening the post–Cold War world.

"After so much success together, we know that our relationship with the United Kingdom must be at the heart of our striving in this new era," he declared. American isolationism, he stated frankly, had not helped end World War I or II, and was no recipe for peace or even safety. "We have gone down that road before. We must never go down that road again. We *will* never go down that road again."

This was not the president who had addressed the UN in mealy-mouthed language in 1993, nor the president who had allowed the killing of eighty-seven American soldiers in Somalia thereafter to cause his State Department to turn a blind eye to the swiftest mass killing in human history in Rwanda. There was a new resolve in his voice. "For nearly four years, a terrible war has torn Bosnia apart, bringing horrors we prayed had vanished from the face of Europe forever: the mass killings, the endless columns of refugees, the campaigns of deliberate rape, the skeletal persons imprisoned in concentration camps," he stated. "Those crimes did violence to the conscience of Britons and Americans. Now we have a chance to make sure they don't return. And we must seize it."

Clinton's speech—given from the same gallery from which President Reagan had once forecast that it would be communism's fate to end up in the "dustbin of history"—marked "an important evolution in his thinking on foreign policy," American newspaper correspondents now noted. "For almost three years, administration officials have struggled without much success to define a 'Clinton Doctrine' in foreign policy, a theme to bind together their responses to a confusing post–Cold War world—and, just as important, to rally public support behind U.S. activism abroad. Now they think they may have it—by describing the sources of global instability as a new enemy that threatens the American way of life just as Nazi Germany and the Soviet Union did in earlier decades."

"We must help peace to take hold in Bosnia because so long as that fire rages at the heart of the European continent—so long as the emerging democracies and our allies are threatened by fighting in Bosnia—there will be no stable, undivided, free Europe," the president declared.

Members of Parliament burst into applause. Bill Clinton, the former Rhodes Scholar, had finally harnessed the words, the policies, and the *forces* that might well, as JFK had once promised, make the world safe for democracy.

Winning the Peace

From London the president and first lady flew to Northern Ireland, where they were mobbed, and thence to Dublin and the Republic of Ireland—"two of the best days of my presidency," as Clinton recalled, later.

The reception in the Emerald Isle was both energizing and humbling—the crowds larger than those who had welcomed John F. Kennedy in the 1960s. Feted and honored, Bill Clinton was in his element: humble when recalling his student years, nostalgic when recalling his delight in reading the literatures of the island people, inspiring when speaking of the challenges and hopes of his baby boom generation. "My friends, we have stood together in the darkest moments of our century," he had said in London. "Our forebears won the war. Let us now win the peace." And with every fiber of his charismatic personality, his gift for rhetoric, and his determination to look forwards rather than backwards, he was willing to lead the fight.

"America," he declared in Belfast, as a nine-year-old Catholic girl held hands with a Protestant boy, "salutes all the people of Northern Ireland who have shown the world in concrete ways that here the will for peace is now stronger than the weapons of war." The eighteen-month-old cease-fire and increasing interdenominational activities were signs that the people, not the terrorists, would now triumph. It would not be straightforward. "For just as peace has its pioneers, peace will always have its rivals. Even when children stand up and say what these children said today, there will always be people who, deep down inside, will never be able to give up the past. . . . The greatest struggle you face," he repeated, after three years of listening to the views of both sides, "is between those who deep down inside are inclined to be peacemakers and those who deep down inside cannot yet embrace the cause of peace, between those who are in the ship of peace and those who are trying to sink it. Old habits die hard. . . . But you, the vast majority, Protestant and Catholic alike, must not allow the ship of peace to sink on the rocks of old habits and hard grudges. You must stand firm against terror. You must say to those who would still use violence for political objectives, 'You are the past. Your day is over. Violence has no place at the table of democracy and no role in the future of this land.' "

Then, as a heckler screamed "Never!" the president added—thinking of the Muslim negotiators who had had to swallow their grief and anger to negotiate with mass-murderers of their people—"By the same token, you must also be willing to say to those who renounce violence and who take their own risks for peace that they are entitled to be full participants in the democratic process. Those who do show courage to break with the past are entitled to their stake in the future." And with this, his high tenor voice straining, he urged his listeners to "summon the strength to keep moving forward. After all, you have come so far already. You have braved so many dangers. You have endured so many sacrifices. Surely there can be no turning back. But peace must be waged with a warrior's resolve, bravely, proudly, and relentlessly, secure in the knowledge of the single greatest difference between war and peace: In peace, everybody can win."

King Billy

Even Protestants whose hearts had turned to stone after so many IRA bombing outrages, and murder of innocent civilians, were stirred.

After the president spoke the next day to a crowd of eighty thousand on Dublin's College Green, the *Irish Times* dubbed him "The Patron Saint of Hopeful Causes." "Bosnia, Palestine and now Northern Ireland have yielded to his magic touch. Is there no stopping this guy?" its reporter asked—and answered it with the old Dublin refrain: "Bill, you're elected!"

Anne Simpson was but one of the many hundreds of newspaper correspondents touched by the Clintons' visit to the heartland of sectarian violence—the first president and first lady ever to go to Northern Ireland. As she wrote in the *Scotsman*, "the American President and First Lady have come closer than anyone to snapping shut the door on a brutal past. This was the day when history reasserted itself with a brighter face. A day when, by simply stating the obvious, the world's most powerful citizen turned mundanity into magic."

Would Americans see their own president in such a way, though? To Anne Simpson he was "an extraordinary peace-broker, a man who in one year of gambles in foreign policy has pulled off the Arab-Israeli accord, the Bosnian peace agreement, and now is articulating with such potency the ordinary people's desire for a settlement in Northern Ireland. It cannot be disregarded by those who hesitate and see it as the opportunism of an upstart outsider."

Cynics in Britain might still question whether the president had "gone south" and, by his meetings with Sinn Fein leader Gerry Adams, was tacitly permitting the IRA to fundraise in the U.S. to the tune of $1 million. The president had, however, committed his administration to contribute twenty times that figure to the International Fund for Ireland in 1995, and had promised a further $60 million over the next two years. "What President Clinton is doing is nudging the key political players, north, south, and over the water, towards a permanent and stable peace, stripped of triumphalism for anyone. To view his actions simply as an exercise in gathering votes back home recklessly misreads the dynamics of what is happening," Simpson warned. She, at least, was certain of the future. "And when they come to recall Big Bill tomorrow and the day after, and the day after that," she predicted, "it will be as a man who arrived as a conciliator, but one of forthright vision."

"It was the presidency Bill Clinton had dreamed of, but never experienced," Maureen Dowd remarked in the *New York Times*. "In Ireland, the prodigal son of the Cassidy clan was celebrated as a statesman, a saint, an angel of peace, a ruddy handsome devil 'with a bottomless bucket of charm,' the most powerful man on earth and 'King Billy.'"

THEATER
OF THE ABSURD

CHAPTER SEVENTY-ONE

A GIFT FROM HEAVEN

The Key to the Future

In Europe and the wider world, Bill Clinton was now seen as a visionary president, a man who had at last found a key to the future of modern liberal democracy. His earlier fumblings were forgiven, while his dynamic commitment to reconciliation and collective security brought back memories of JFK at his most inspiring.

Among Republicans in the United States, however, there was no such forgiveness. The president's faltering, immature grasp of leadership in his first years had left an indelible impression in the minds of millions of Americans that he was incapable of change. In *Saturday Night Live* skits he was still portrayed, Maureen Dowd noted, "as gluttonous and insecure." Those sketches were at least comic. More worrying, in terms of the cohesion and collective will of the American nation, was the continuing poison spewing from right-wing radio shows, pivoting on age-old relish for cynicism, contempt, and even hate, but writ larger in an age of such mass and swift communication. In Ireland prosperity at last encouraged Protestants and Catholics to rhyme hope and history, in the words Clinton kept quoting from the poet Seamus Heaney, but in America, curiously, reviving prosperity seemed to do the opposite: making many people more, not less, self-centered. Thus, as "the Emerald Isle disappeared in a gray mist, like Brigadoon, the president found himself facing a crowd more resentful than grateful," Dowd noted, accompanying the presidential party. They landed at the U.S. Army base at Baumholder, Germany, where the president had arranged to talk to young soldiers who would be going to Bosnia, and their families. "As he explained why America must send troops to that muddy, snowy, murderous terrain, Melissa Gammage, the twenty-one-year-old wife of a soldier who clears land mines, offered a mordant running commentary. When the president said the division had trained long and hard, she objected, 'Not for this.' When he said the mission would be clearly defined, she called softly, 'Boo.' When he said that the task force was ready to roll, she muttered, 'That's a bald-faced lie.' When he said that the soldiers were about to do 'something very important for the world,' she snapped, 'I don't want to be a twenty-one-year-old widow with two kids.' "

"In Ireland," Dowd ended her report, "Mr. Clinton discovered the joys of being a foreign policy president." At U.S. Army bases in Germany the next day the presidential motorcade passed people holding signs that read "Draft Dodger Go Home" and "The President Who Stole Christmas." It was, Maureen Dowd warned, "a taste of the perils" to come, from his own countrymen, as the rain and wind beat in dark December 1995.

A Gift from Heaven

Lighting the lights on the Christmas tree outside Belfast City Hall before a crowd of fifty thousand, Clinton had quoted Jesus' words "Blessed are the peacemakers, for they shall inherit the earth." Rallying behind Newt Gingrich's banner, however, Republican congressmen seemed more than ever determined the president should inherit nothing. There would be no compromise, let alone surrender, on the budget, they were adamant—even if this led to the darkening of the city lights in Washington in a second U.S. government shutdown.

The mood was mean.

Later, in the aftermath, Gingrich could not believe his own tactical stupidity, however. "Our decision to go ahead and freeze the Medicare premium merely on the assumption that he would agree," Gingrich said, berating himself, "must have seemed to him a gift from heaven"—"a painful self-inflicted wound to the Republicans," and "an unexpected boon to a president who was at that time," Gingrich claimed, "in pretty bad political shape."

The president was far, far from being in bad political shape, however. On the contrary, his trip to Europe had strengthened his moral determination. More and more he saw himself as a guide, charged not simply with the duties of a centrist politician in public service but as a leader called upon to handle extremists. Getting men like Gerry Adams, Slobodan Milosevic, and Yasser Arafat to renounce violence in favor of democratic political means was, it seemed to him, a moral purpose worth pursuing—and, as he kept repeating in Ireland, a model to the rest of the world in postmodern, multi-ethnic times.

What Gingrich took for weakness was thus the opposite: a president willing to fly into the eye of the sectarian storm in Ireland—as he would soon do again in flying to Bosnia proper, the following month. Convinced that a compromise resolution of the budget crisis could and would be achieved before the December 15 deadline, the president could not credit that Gingrich would once again shut down the entire American government and default on its loans—without popular support. But he was wrong.

A Second Government Shutdown

Just how confident Bill Clinton was becoming in his own leadership skills was demonstrated on December 7, when the president rounded on his Republican adviser, "the little shit" (as Leon Panetta called him), Dick Morris.

Morris had, once again, been whining about the president's White House staff. At a special event in the Oval Office the day before, Clinton had taken President Johnson's pen, originally used to sign Medicare into law, to veto Congress's latest seven-year budget bill, which would castrate Medicare, Medicaid, education programs, and environmental protection—but promising, as he did so, that he would offer his *own* seven-year balanced budget the next day, which he did. Furious that Morris was yet again getting ideas above his station, Clinton—who was smarting over accusations that he was giving in to Gingrich's blackmail—yelled at Morris: "*You* are the cause of the factionalism around here. *You* are." His face red with anger, he repeatedly pointed his finger at the cowering adviser. "*You* are the one creating factions and friction around here. *You* are"— and stormed off.

Morris, who was under press siege for supposedly fiddling his expense account to include alcohol and pornographic movies, resigned that night— only to answer the telephone once the president called him in Connecticut at 11 P.M. to apologize.

Aware that Clinton was now almost twenty polling points ahead of Bob Dole, his most likely presidential contender, Morris was advised by his wife to go back to Washington and swallow the bitter pill. The president no longer needed him to get re-elected. What he wanted was merely his advice, in order to triangulate it with his official White House staff.

Returning to the capital with his tail between his legs, Morris now recognized how much Clinton had changed. No longer was he the gregarious, garrulous team member: he was the president. "Normally he is extroverted and talkative," he recounted. But in the White House, Morris now noted, the president had clearly taught himself "to be introverted, like a southpaw who has taught himself to throw right-handed. He made himself elusive. At meetings he would often say nothing. Nothing. He would let others talk, keep a poker face, and leave his visitors with no impression at all of the decision he intended to make. The blank stare."

Nowhere was this transformation better seen than in the way the balanced budget negotiation was handled. Morris assumed the president's blankness was because he "trusted no one," but in truth the president trusted his chief of staff—and to the consternation of Republicans, Bill Clinton flew off to Paris on December 14 to witness the signing of the Dayton Accords at the Elysee Palace, flanked by President Chirac, Chancellor Helmut Kohl, Prime Minister Major, Prime Minister Chernomyrdin, and the three Balkan presidents.

Republican isolationists had predicted mayhem and American casualties for the U.S. military contingent designated to police the Dayton Accords. Even the Pentagon had planned for significant numbers. But as General Wes Clark reassured the president on the way home, such official estimates had to err on the side of possibility, not probability. Holbrooke agreed—though even he was to be amazed at the result: "zero American forces killed or wounded from hostile action in the first three years after Dayton."

This was an extraordinary achievement, and a great tribute to Tony Lake, Wesley Clark, Holbrooke, and the U.S. negotiating team that had brought peace to Bosnia.

Getting peace in Washington was to prove even more difficult, however.

In the Theater of the Absurd

Not only had it proven a tough struggle to get members of Congress to back the major U.S. peacekeeping force but the budget stalemate was becoming almost a farce.

"Enough is enough in the theater of the absurd," one presidential aide exclaimed at the refusal of the Republicans to accept the president's compromise proposal—yet the absurdity was real. From being king of the Capitol castle at the start of the year, Speaker Gingrich—who had been found guilty by Congress of ethics violations over his book contract with Rupert Murdoch, his lecture course, and re-election funding, which had resulted in the appointment of a special prosecutor—was now fearful of losing his Speakership. "The revolution will continue even if they brought him down," his chief whip, Congressman Tom DeLay, was heard to say. By December 15, when the one-month continuing resolution ran out, it had become clear the Speaker no longer spoke for his troops. Though Bob Dole favored acceptance of the president's budget compromise, Gingrich's revolutionaries favored *another* shutdown. Thus when Gingrich sat down that afternoon in Room H 227 he was told that even a week's extension of the continuing resolution was impermissible. "You've got to understand," Congressman DeLay had tried to make clear to anyone who imagined Republicans were merely old-fashioned libertarians, "we are ideologues. We have an agenda. We have a philosophy." And he had given an example: environmental protection. "I want to repeal the Clean Air Act," DeLay had admitted—with pride. Young John Boehner, serving only his third year in Congress and already elected to a leadership position, was equally adamant. "Newt, this isn't going to work," Boehner now told the Speaker when he heard that Gingrich had made tentative plans with Senator Dole to keep the government open. There would be no more continuing resolutions, Boehner made clear. The government would be shut down at midnight that night. "You've fought the battle this far. You can't cave," Republican governor John Engler harangued the House Republican leadership meeting. "A new CR [continuing resolution] would be seen as capitulation."

Seldom had such bad advice been given by elected representatives of the people, affecting the entire American government. The Republican leaders were now hopelessly out of sync with the electorate. At 6 P.M. the president, informed that negotiations had been terminated, spoke to newspaper reporters and broadcasters in the Oval Office, announcing the sad news. "As all of you know," he began, "today the Republicans in Congress broke off our negotiations on how best to balance the budget in seven years. They said they would not even continue to talk unless we agreed right now to make deep and unconscionable cuts in Medicare and Medicaid. That's unacceptable. The cuts they propose would deprive millions of people of health care: poor children, pregnant women, the disabled, seniors in nursing homes. They would let Medicare wither on the vine into a second-class system. And these things are simply not necessary to balance the budget . . . "

The president was sincere and impressive: no longer the over-eager, activist freshman trying to reform health care in America, but the patient, avuncular family man attempting to save it. Whatever Gingrich might then or later claim, the president had not wanted the shutdown and had not planned for it, indeed had bent over backwards to accommodate the Republican deficit reduction agenda, because it had been, since the very start of his presidency, his own agenda too—but one that Republicans had virulently opposed, because of their ideological aversion to new taxes. The Republicans had now insisted upon still more cuts in government funding as their own way to cut further the deficit, ignoring public opinion. As Dick Morris put it: "Most people don't commit suicide twice, but Gingrich did."

The decision was thus made by the Speaker, on behalf of his revolutionary ideologues. The federal capital, and all federal operations, would be closed down again.

CHAPTER SEVENTY-TWO

THE SECOND SUICIDE

A Wonderful Experience

Scott Fleming, director of congressional affairs in the Department of Education at the time, well remembered the crisis. The Clinton administration had, as part of the vice president's REGO initiative, already slimmed down the department from its level under President Bush, but to Gingrich's young ideologues, bent on complete abolition, this had not been enough. They argued that, as with HUD and the Department of Commerce, power should be devolved onto the states and local communities.

Having spent twenty-two years on the Hill in congressional work, Fleming was amazed not only at Republican ignorance about what the Education Department did, from PELL grants to school funding, but at the political dynamite of what they were proposing. "They made a huge mistake. The Department of Education was the smallest cabinet level department"—but after Medicare, perhaps the most emotive in the public's mind. Was it really possible that, in a new information age, with education the nation's priority in raising competitiveness and living standards, Republican revolutionaries were really proposing that its national offices—employing five thousand people—should be vaporized?

Voters, generally, might have little notion of the work of HUD or even the Department of Commerce. Education, however, was clear, simple, and important to every parent in America: the pathway to the next generation and the future, in a global economy. "People get it! We weren't talking about something amorphous, we were talking about something very real and very practical in their communities"—with a brilliant spokesman not only in the crusading education secretary, former governor Richard Riley, who insisted on national standards of student-testing, but in the president himself. The mood in the department, when all but a few members of a skeleton staff were furloughed, was one of pride in the chief executive. "It was a wonderful experience," Fleming recalled. "You knew that Bill Clinton cared about education. He'd been the education governor. You knew that, under his presidency and in that department, you were going to be at the cutting edge of policy debates"—a role the Republicans now insisted be abolished to make way for tax cuts for the wealthy.

The Clinton advertising machine thus had little to do but pick the juiciest targets. "Belle is doing fine. But Medicare could be cut. Nicholas is going to college—but his scholarship could be gone. The stakes in the budget debate. Joshua's doing well—but help for his disability could be cut. President Clinton. Standing firm to protect people . . . "

The Bus of Fools

Night after night, from December 16, 1995, the television ads hammered the Republicans in Congress—and Gingrich in particular. Indeed, just as in the previous year Republican PR consultants had designed television ads morphing local candidates with cut-out versions of the president, so now Democrats did the same in reverse, using Gingrich as the morphing target. Even the right-wing *Washington Times* warned that Gingrich now "risks being portrayed as the grumpy Republican leader who stole everyone's Christmas."

Time magazine might put Gingrich on its cover as its Man of the Year, but as *Time*'s own columnist Margaret Carlson told CNN, "Hitler was on the cover twice. Stalin was on the cover." The picture itself was certainly unflattering: it showed Gingrich in Richard Nixon mode, set against a neon-green-and-yellow background, his jowls prominent, with dark stubble and deep wrinkles creasing his skin, which had an orange glow. A purple splotch made its way from his right eye to the bottom of his nose. "He may be *Time*'s Man of the Year," the *Washington Post*'s Howard Kurz remarked, "but he looks like the thug of the week."

The Speaker had started the year a new household name, with the possibility he might even run for president as the successful architect of the GOP's Contract With America. He was ending it in a cloud of ethics questions, plummeting popularity, and sheer ridicule. He had thrown Congress into turmoil, and after boasting he would make the House more family-friendly in its hours, was ruining family Christmases owing to the shut-down of the government, even causing some Republican members to explode, for "frustration is increasing everywhere," as one commentator noted.

At the 1995 convention of the Florida state Democratic Party, the party chairwoman, Terrie Brady, remarked on the difference a year made. "I get a warm feeling inside every time Newt opens his mouth," Brady told a cheer-ing crowd. "He's done more single-handedly than anyone to strengthen our party." "Nuck Fewt" buttons were everywhere, trashing the Republican Speaker. Others portrayed a green-faced image of "The Gingrich who stole Christmas," complete with holly and a red bow.

In the *Boston Globe* Mike Barnicle described the year's "bus of fools"— the biggest of whom was the Speaker. "The Georgia porker" was the desig-nated Republican driver, "now that he has returned from outpatient shock therapy treatment that became necessary after Clinton didn't give him an Air Force One coloring book complete with crayons as a memento. What a dope. Grab a doughnut, flab-face."

Boxing Himself In

"If we postpone it, if we cave, if we walk off," Gingrich kept up his dooms-day rhetoric to the press, "you'll see interest rates skyrocket and the stock market crash." Such apocalyptic predictions, when the president had al-ready agreed to a seven-year balanced budget, only made the Speaker sound loonier.

The shutdown itself was even more farcical, since this time—in a bid to look less draconian in making workers pay the price of his antics— Gingrich had agreed that federal employees' pay would be withheld, not axed. Almost three hundred thousand workers were furloughed, but hun-dreds of thousands who were allowed to go to work had no work and were sent home, as the agencies they were working for were not permitted to in-cur extra expenses. In other words, the federal government would be shut, yet be paid for doing no work.

With the U.S. passport office closed, parks closed, museums closed, and even foreign consulates and embassies closed, it seemed incredible that Gingrich would refuse to authorize a continuing resolution while talks went on. The president, all honey and sweetness, played him as a large cat might a small, fat mouse—Gingrich admitting that when in the presence of the president he was so overwhelmed by Clinton's intelligence and charm that he needed to "go through detox" for several hours afterwards until he came back to reality.

The reality was that, whatever revolutionaries in the House might demand, the White House wouldn't go below its bottom line, and that, by creating a Speaker's Advisory Group as a quasi-cabinet to his quasi-prime ministership, Gingrich had boxed himself in—unable to persuade or order his colleagues to lift the embargo while talks continued. "I think you're wrong," he told them at one point, only to find himself overruled. He'd lost control, but with the vice president and Leon Panetta stiffening the president's spine at the White House each time Clinton looked like weakening, there was nowhere for the Republicans to go but into captivity.

Panetta flew back to California for Christmas, the Clintons flew to Hilton Head for their New Year's Renaissance Weekend, and the people of America watched the Washington spat with near disbelief.

The Senate Votes for the President

On January 2, 1996, Gingrich once again urged his colleagues to permit a continuing resolution and reopen the government. They were all exhausted, he said—and exhaustion makes for poor decisions. "We made a mistake. We miscalculated the effect our pressure would have on Clinton in December," he admitted. And he confessed to his own error—that he'd ignored the Republicans' plummeting polls in the mistaken belief they would go up again, once they won the battle. But they hadn't won, and the polls were sinking still further. "We didn't calculate that a surge in Clinton's numbers," he added, "would cause him to dig in even more."

The response, among the revolutionaries, was merely adamant refusal to concede defeat in the House.

In the Senate the mood was different. The Christmas holidays had been ruined—and without visible reason, since the president had offered a seven-year balanced budget, as Republicans had demanded. With seven hundred sixty thousand federal employees either furloughed or having to work on the promise of eventual remuneration, Senator Dole therefore declared, "Enough is enough," and dragooned his fellow senators into voting to re-open the government for at least a week.

The battle was now turning into a fight between Republicans in the House and Republicans in the Senate, with Gingrich's diehards refusing to harken to reason. The next day, however, even the diehards became aware that support in the House was slipping—indeed, a mutiny was in the offing. At a Republican conference meeting some fifty-four congressmen voted to end their shutdown immediately.

The writing was on the wall. Congressman David McIntosh, a freshman, recommended a resolution that would allow federal workers to go back to work, but with no funding for their agencies, and no back pay to cover the period they were furloughed. Gingrich looked at him. The penny had finally dropped. He had listened to his own fanatics too long.

"There aren't going to be any questions or comments," the Speaker declared. "This is what our strategy is going to be, and why. We're going to get the shutdown off the front page and get back to the balanced budget. You don't like the job I'm doing as Speaker, run against me," he challenged.

It was January 3, 1996. On Friday, January 5, the Republican leadership accepted the president's version of a seven-year budget, and in consequence a continuing resolution, which was duly signed by the president.

The longest shutdown of government in U.S. history had ended, after twenty-one days, in anticipation of an agreed balanced budget compromise that safeguarded Medicare, Medicaid, education, and the environment, as the president wished.

The president had won.

The Speaker, by contrast, had lost—indeed, in the days that followed the re-opening of the U.S. government it became clear to the White House team that they no longer even needed to agree an arbitrary seven-year balanced budget, in their negotiations. The Republicans would not dare shut down the government a third time.

On January 9, 1996, after more than fifty hours of further, futile talks, accompanied by snow and blizzards, Gingrich got the picture—and it was bleak. His patience, never very pronounced, snapped. Panetta had got the parties to agree to disagree, and to take a week's "recess," lest the markets be affected. "Why are we wasting our time and saying we are recessing for a week?" Gingrich exploded, once Panetta left him alone with Senator Dole in the Roosevelt Room. "We should suspend the discussions, as we originally agreed. I don't see any reason to be down here in a week. We agreed to suspend. Why are we talking about a recess? We're wasting our fucking time down here dealing with the White House." With that, Gingrich flounced out—and the entire balanced budget, once the linchpin of his Contract With America, was cast to the four winds: another victim of ideological overreach.

"Numbers, numbers, numbers!" Senator Dole later lamented. The president, a self-confessed policy wonk to his fingertips, had beaten them down with numbers. "It got to be an endurance test," Dole said, explaining why, in the end, the Republicans walked away from a settlement. "Meet, meet, meet. Snowstorm! Meet! Blizzard! Meet! Snowstorm!"

The old warrior now left winter-clad Washington to try to resuscitate his presidential campaign—knowing that he might still win his party's nomination, but he would never now beat the president of the United States, whose State of the Union speech would give him a platform to trumpet his victory over the shutdown.

CHAPTER SEVENTY-THREE

A WINNER EMERGES

The First Debate

On January 23, 1996, fifty million Americans prepared to watch the president's State of the Union Address, to be followed by the majority leader's response—the "first debate" of the presidential election, as journalists soon dubbed it.

The president had just flown to Bosnia to visit American troops—and to the astonishment of those who'd predicted a sullen reception, he'd received a hero's welcome. "The vast majority of soldiers Clinton dispatched at Christmas to this unlovely corner of the world have come to accept him first and foremost as their commander in chief," Rick Atkinson reported for the *Washington Post*. "His visit is widely viewed as an act of good faith, further strengthening the bond between leader and led. Conversations with dozens of soldiers, from private to general, suggest that they have come to view him—sometimes grudgingly—as their rightful leader, the boss. They admire the risk he's taking to fly here; anticipation has been building all week."

Major-General William L. Nash, commander of U.S. forces in Bosnia, had been in Germany when Clinton visited the Smith barracks—and was impressed. "The president came to Baumholder, looked the soldiers in the eye, said, 'I'm sending you to Bosnia and here are the rules, this is why I'm doing it and this is what I expect.' From a commander in chief, it doesn't get any better than that."

General Nash was right. Switching from the luxury of Air Force One to a C–17 cargo plane, escorted by Apache helicopters, and emerging in khakis and a brown leather bomber jacket bearing the insignia of "Old

Ironsides"—the patch of the 1ˢᵗ Armored Division, the main force in Tuzla—the president gave an address to a group of eight hundred fifty U.S. soldiers that was transformational in terms of his relationship with the military. Telling them they were "warriors for peace" in their bid to implement and enforce the Dayton Accords, he'd thanked them and wished them well on their mission. Together with their NATO comrades, they were "raising the torch of a new undivided Europe." He went on, "Step by steady step, you are making history here in Bosnia. Don't ever forget it, even when this extraordinary mission may seem routine. Your country is very proud of you. The Bosnian people have chosen peace, but they cannot do it alone. The Bosnian people are exhausted by war; you can give them the strength they need for peace."

After "what was admittedly a fairly rocky start," the White House press secretary acknowledged on the plane home, the president "feels like their commander-in-chief now"—and it had shown.

State of the Union

Back in Washington, reading a pre-delivery transcript of the response Senator Dole would be giving to the president's State of the Union speech, the president's aides were anxious. On paper, Dole's words read so much better than Clinton's.

They need not have worried. Before the cameras on the podium in the House of Representatives on January 23, 1996, the president's body language reflected a man completely at ease and at one with himself. Newt Gingrich had said mockingly, in advance, that he wanted to hear just four words from the president: "Thank you and goodnight." Shaking hands with the Speaker, who had introduced him to the packed chamber, the president passed Gingrich a slip of paper—containing the four words.

If Gingrich thought for a moment the president was intending to be brief, however, he was mistaken. Clinton talked for over an hour, interrupted eighty times by applause, and at one point, towards the end, slowed his delivery of a couple of remarks that—given Gingrich's threat to close the government yet again, once the latest continuing resolution ran out that Saturday—made Gingrich's face go ashen.

"The president set the Republicans up the way Mike Tyson sets up bum fighters," columnist Carl Rowan described with awe the next day, "when he introduced Richard Dean, a Vietnam veteran who entered the bombed federal building in Oklahoma City four times to save the lives of three women. Republicans who had sat in grim silence all evening suddenly were on their feet, cheering a great American hero. Before they sat, Clinton hit them with a Reaganesque sucker punch. He said Dean had been 'forced out of his office' in the Social Security Administration in November when the government shut down. 'I challenge all of you in this chamber,' Clinton said. 'Never—ever—shut the federal government down again.' "

Even Republican observers agreed the speech was a "masterly" accomplishment at the start of an election year—in part because the president stole virtually the entire Republican thunder. Sentence after sentence, minute after minute, segment after segment the president co-opted their concerns, from teenage pregnancy to new welfare rules—and added his own. The state of the economy was excellent, he declared proudly: unemployment and inflation rates the lowest in twenty-seven years, new businesses starting up at record rates, American carmakers selling more cars than Japan for the first time since the 1970s.

Declaring that "the era of big government is over," the president conceded that people wanted leaner federal organizations to keep their taxes from rising—but then set out specifics for government programs that he thought important for a just, safe, well-educated, entrepreneurial, and vibrant American society: television screening chips for concerned parents, cessation of tobacco advertising to minors, time limits on welfare and work requirements, Internet-access computers in every classroom and library in the U.S. within five years, national educational standards upheld under Goals 2000, parental school choice, charter schools—even school uniforms! Student loans, the national service program AmeriCorps, work study, merit scholarships: initiative after initiative the president orchestrated his practical as well as moral commitment to the American family as the "foundation of American life. If we have stronger families, we have a stronger America."

Though some sat stony-faced and sullen, it was difficult for most congressmen and senators not to be swept along by the president's sheer vision of a better society: improvements that seemed for the most part worthy and doable, given that the U.S. economy was now back on track.

In a mere three years his administration had already cut the deficit in half, and had a realistic plan to balance the budget completely in another seven—why then was Congress insisting upon yet another train wreck, starting on Saturday, by its fanatic insistence on ideologically targeting

Medicare, Medicaid, education, and the environment, knowing that the president would veto such bills? Surely, Clinton pointed out, it was in America's interest as a nation that there be social cohesion and unity of purpose at the approach of a new millennium?

The truth was, in the wake of the Oklahoma City bombing President Bill Clinton had seized the high ground of American values—the vague yet profound consensus in the country over the importance of family, respect, responsibility, and compassion.

Viewers across the country now watched, awed, as the president articulated those democratic values, with telling examples and with the same easy sincerity that Ronald Reagan had employed. Indicating his wife in the gallery, and with tears in his eyes, he paid tribute to "the person who has taught me more than anyone else over twenty-five years about the importance of families and children, a wonderful wife, a magnificent mother, and a great first lady. Thank you, Hillary."

"Unfortunately," wrote Tom Shales, the television critic of the *Washington Post*, the next day, Hillary "returned his beaming and loving look with a rather chilly gaze. But his gesture was gallant and touching. It had the appearance of being damn fine behavior."

In the Record Books

Never one to show emotion in public, Hillary was feeling especially hostile to the Republican-dominated Congress, whose independent counsel, Judge Ken Starr, had insisted that she, and her legal counsel, appear before a grand jury the next day—the first time in American history that a first lady had been subpoenaed. (She was required to explain why, in the investigation of Whitewater malfeasance, her billing records at the Rose Law Firm and other documents were secretly removed from Vince Foster's office after his death, were withheld, and then had "accidentally" surfaced two years later in the White House private residence.)

If the president was affected by such politically driven investigations, he simply refused to show it. As his recent staff secretary John Podesta pointed out in the *New York Times*, President Bush had withheld his diary from Iran-contra investigator Lawrence E. Walsh for *five* years, before it was "found" in the president's safe—and only handed it over when he had lost the 1992 election! The president's job was to govern, and at long last, this was what the forty-second president was doing.

The president's sheer energy and intelligence seemed boundless. "Clinton appeared robust, youthful and forceful, qualities people like in a leader, and delivered the speech with virtual flawlessness," Shales commented, noting how "Visually, speeches from the House keep looking better and better, largely because Gingrich opened the door to more cameras, including the hand-held kind. There was a Busby Berkeley style overhead shot of the entire chamber that was just about breathtaking. The president himself was better framed than usual so that viewers didn't constantly see Gingrich and Vice President Gore as they sat behind him. Instead, most shots of Clinton showed him against the red and white stripes of the flag. The presentation was terrific. And with television, presentation is content, so it's hard to imagine that this Clinton speech won't go down in the record books as a winner."

Dole's Disaster

"He's a much stronger figure than he was a year ago," admitted Eddie Mahe, a Republican consultant. "He finally figured out that he was president. He stopped carrying on like some out-of-work hippie. The American people want a president, not a tennis mate, and Clinton has learned that."

Republicans in the audience, however, "looked as if they had been forced to sit through a long banquet speech—and then had dinner snatched out of their mouths," another reporter described. "The president certainly took words right out of the Republicans' mouths. From V-chips to beefed-up prison sentences, he stole so many items off the Republicans' plate that they were left with little more than the bitter gruel served up by Bob Dole in his response."

Delivered before the camera in his deserted office, without an audience and with terrible lighting, Dole's response proved a disaster. The president had paid tribute, in his address, to the majority leader for his World War II service. Responding, the seventy-two-year-old senator grumpily trotted out negatives, stumbling over sentences that he read on the teleprompter, and offering no specific policies whatever in ten long minutes.

Was this the man who would be president? Even Rush Limbaugh called the Senate majority leader "lackluster." "It was an absolute disaster," Roger Linn, the Republican chairman for Sioux City, Iowa, was quoted saying. "By God, he had a week or two to prepare and he couldn't even read it. If this is the beginning of the campaign, Clinton could quit right now, because he's got it."

Clinton certainly seemed in a different league. "I'm in awe of the guy," said Florida GOP Representative Joe Scarborough. "He's moving so quickly, it's really hard to nail him down. He's a great television presence and I think Dole's going to have a hard time."

Old, Wooden, and Partisan

Though Senator Dole had responded to the president's address, the two men had still not appeared face-to-face—prompting former governor Lamar Alexander to ask listeners to imagine presidential debates in the fall, where Clinton would "walk out from behind the podium and over to the questioners and he'll look them in the eye and he'll feel their pain and he'll give a very good answer." If the other contestant is Dole, Alexander maintained, "the response is about OMB and CBO and Washington and getting a bill out of subcommittee." In that case, "We've got President Clinton for four more years," Governor Alexander predicted, "and we've got a Democratic Congress for four more years."

Inevitably, because Dole now had to fight his own Republican colleagues for the Republican nomination, such candor was replicated across the nation.

"Any Republican who watched the two speeches last night must be thinking the same thing," Governor Alexander told another audience, the Omaha Rotary Club. "President Clinton can fake a compelling vision, while Senator Dole is too decent to try to fake a vision he does not have."

Alexander's campaign director in Florida was equally frank. "Bob Dole doesn't stack up very well to Bill Clinton. My kid would say Dole hit an air ball last night. He's old, wooden, not engaged, too partisan."

It was difficult for Dole not to be partisan, however, when rivals in his own party were now intent upon stealing his seemingly promised crown. Steve Forbes, the magazine publishing heir and tax-reform aficianado, was seen closing to within striking distance of Dole in New Hampshire, where the first Republican primaries would be held.

Dole's response to the president seemed better suited "for a rubber chicken dinner crowd in Manchester" than a national audience, Forbes sneered—his caustic remarks not only making headlines, but helping him gain ground on his rival. The latest Pew Research Center poll soon showed Forbes at 29 percent and Dole at 24 percent among Republicans and independents who were likely to vote in New Hampshire's February 20 primary. Stumping in Des Moines, the multi-millionaire mogul said he wished the

Senate majority leader could have provided the nation "more of a vivid contrast" with Clinton. "The key is the message. The message must be one of high ground, of getting America moving again, removing obstacles to progress." But how could Dole, or any other Republican contender, do that when President Clinton so utterly and completely dominated that high ground?

Seizing the ball, the president had made an end-run that left Republicans gaping.

Forging Ahead in the Polls

The financial markets had gone up after the State of the Union speech, as had the president's poll ratings. Those of Dole dipped. Hillary's did also, though.

At the time of the inauguration the first lady had enjoyed an almost 70 percent favorability rating. Now she was down to 43 percent, and slipping further—the lowest of any postwar first lady. Her positive influence on the administration had been polled in the spring of 1993 at 65 percent; now it was down to 40 percent, while 52 percent felt she was not telling the truth over Whitewater: a "growing skepticism of the first lady and her honesty," as *USA Today* reported.

It was an extraordinary reversal of their fortunes, commentators observed. Just four years previously, Hillary had saved her husband's presidential candidacy during the adultery scandals that had surfaced in the midst of the New Hampshire primary. Now White House press secretary Mike McCurry was detailing for the media how the president was prepping and encouraging his beloved wife. He had spent time with the first lady and their daughter, Chelsea, McCurry explained to White House correspondents, before Hillary headed to the courthouse—indeed, McCurry told how the president visited yet again with his wife privately in their White House residence before her departure. He did so, McCurry said, as a concerned husband, "to reassure her and tell her that he loves her and that she'll do a good job and that the grand jury will see that she's telling the truth, just as she has been telling the truth."

With the president's own favorability rating soaring, it was noted with relief, Hillary's poor showing had no damaging effect; in fact, a *Newsweek* poll soon showed 66 percent of respondents saying that the controversies surrounding the first lady, ranging from her involvement in the White

House travel office to investments in Whitewater in the 1970s, would not make them less likely to vote to re-elect Clinton. Not only that, but President Clinton would easily defeat both Senator Dole and Steve Forbes in head-to-head competition if the election were held in January 1996.

The president had confounded his critics and made a mockery of those who had questioned his relevance only months before. He was, or seemed, unbeatable now: a commanding presence on the political stage domestically and internationally; a man so far ahead of his political rivals, commentators reflected, that only scandal—financial or sexual—could now bring him down.

MONICA, ACT II

CHAPTER SEVENTY-FOUR

DOLE'S FAUSTIAN BARGAIN

Driven Off a Cliff

There was only one possible contender the president feared, early in 1996: The General.

No one else on Pennsylvania Avenue seemed worried. Did the president, with his x-ray political eyes, see what his White House staff could not see? Or did the staff see what the president could not see?

"I think there was some concern he [Powell] might run," Doug Sosnik later acknowledged, "but I didn't have it." Indeed Sosnik recalled how the president telephoned him late one evening. "He called me one night at midnight, at home. It was a Sunday night. And he asked if I had read the Colin Powell profile that day in the *Post*. Asked whether he was going to run or not. And I said, 'Mr. President, I didn't read any articles on Colin Powell, because I don't think he's running; I never have, and I'm not wasting my time!' My wife was watching me talk to the president of the United States like that—and started to laugh!"

Sosnik was right. In the wake of the Bosnian peace accords and Gingrich's defeat, the president's ever-rising polls meant that Powell was now too late. The freshman president had finally, in his fourth year, become a senior: a leader, a conciliator-in-chief—taking Powell's wind as the political armada rounded the final mark and turned into the home straight. Powell could now only hope to get in the political game as a running mate—which, as journalists discovered, would be music to Senator Dole's ears, but not necessarily to Powell's, given the "perception," as Sosnik put it, "at the time Dole was looking for a vice president, that Dole probably was not going to win."

As the majority leader of the Senate, Bob Dole was widely seen as having brought the Republican shutdown of the government to an end in a statesmanlike manner, yet he gave little evidence he had ended the warring of the factions in his party across the nation. The Republican tide in the country, backed by the Christian Coalition, was still running strong—but it was dividing Republicans into libertarians and radicals. By uniting the party, Dole could harness a growing mass of voters, but would still have to be seen to be able to match the fleet footwork of the president. If he were chained to Gingrich's revolutionary agenda, this would make his task all the harder.

"Bob Dole had the ultimate Faustian bargain," Sosnik reflected later, "as the leader of the Senate with a right-of-center party. He knew he couldn't have any daylight between himself and Gingrich and the right-wingers to get the nomination. But he also knew that Gingrich was driving him off a cliff."

In New Hampshire, Dole lost.

The President as Charlemagne

The president, now in his fourth year in office, had six superlative teams running under his aegis: the White House, under Leon Panetta; the economic team, under Treasury Secretary Bob Rubin; the national security team, under Tony Lake; the communications team, under Mike McCurry; the re-election team, under Doug Sosnik; and the foreign team—under himself.

Throughout January, February, March, and April 1996, while the Republicans beat up on each other in their primaries, the president built upon his burgeoning peacemaking/world trade record—agreeing to meet with Sinn Fein leader Gerry Adams, as well as David Trimble and the Rev. Ian Paisley from Northern Ireland; conversing with Boris Yeltsin; traveling to meet with President Mubarak of Egypt, PLO leader Yasser Arafat, prime ministers Simon Peres and John Major; and visiting South Korea, Japan, St. Petersburg, and Moscow. Terrorism was emerging, everywhere, as the number one threat in the post–Cold War world; it could only be confronted successfully, leaders agreed, by vigilant international security, and by demonstrating peaceful cooperation between democratic, multi-ethnic, and religiously diverse and pluralistic nations. In this way the extremism of fanatics would be exposed, as it had been in Oklahoma City, at home in the United States.

In Dick Morris's eyes international statesmanship had not been enough for George H. W. Bush to win re-election, and would not be, he warned, enough for President Clinton. Obsessed with getting a budget deal between the president and Congress, Morris even sent a White House poll and memo on the subject direct to a Republican pollster working for Senator Dole.

The president did not fire Morris, despite all his double-dealing, subversion, alleged expense fiddling, megalomania, and outright lying. As Karl Rove would be to Clinton's successor, the truth was that Dick Morris had become too valuable to the president's fifth team: his re-election team.

Though he didn't like Morris any more than did the rest of his White House colleagues, Doug Sosnik was in awe of Morris's contribution. The "little shit" might be a conniver, disloyal, and dark, but it was Morris who had seen the opening in campaign finance strategy whereby funding could legitimately be channeled not to Clinton but to the Democratic National Committee to spend—on Clinton's reelection. Tens of millions of dollars were thus raised for the DNC, leaving the president free to raise tens more millions for his own campaign.

Morris's prize results would not only go into the DNC coffers and television advertising on behalf of the president, they would go into American campaign history. Instead of waiting for the spring or summer of 1996 for the incumbent president to kick off, as incumbent presidents usually do, Morris had insisted they start a television and radio advertising campaign already in the fall of 1995, more than a year before the election—buying spots in cities that fell under the Washington radar, across the country. Designed to confirm the president's growing status as a leader and highlight the issues for which the Democrats were rooting, they were meant to be seedbed ads. The darkening budget war and government shutdown then played straight into the team's hands—allowing them, to their own surprise, to be able to paint President Clinton as Charlemagne, the Republicans as barbarian hordes.

Something Could Happen

Mercilessly, in his advance advertising campaign, Morris had exploited the unexpected gift Gingrich's extremists had handed the president. Moreover, because the Republican frontrunners were "otherwise engaged," thanks to their divisive primary battles, Morris's ads went unanswered, month after month.

Publicly, the president stood above this provincial media-blitz fray, but privately, in the White House, he oversaw every DNC-paid ad and every message. His ability to use Morris's best ideas and discard the worst, Doug Sosnik later reflected, was uncanny—not only in immediate terms, but for the long term. He wanted the aging Senator Dole as his adversary in the presidential election; therefore, he must not knock the senator personally, or even Gingrich, whatever stupidities the Speaker uttered, but allow them to dig their own political graves. He refused to allow Morris to flash Dole and Gingrich's faces when attacking proposed Republican budget cuts. When Morris's colleague Bob Squier protested, the president was adamant. "That's the way it's going to be, and you do what I tell you to do."

McCurry, as communications standard bearer, was puzzled. "Why do you care so much about what Dole's position in the primaries is going to be?" he asked the president. Clinton claimed it was because Dole's rivals were "a bunch of nitwits," and that as president he wanted, if he lost, "to have some confidence in the person I hand the keys over to."

McCurry swallowed. The president's answer was strangely pious for a humble Arkansan who normally avoided false piety. Bill Clinton seemed well on his way to becoming a great leader—why would he suddenly be saying to his own press secretary that "Something could happen to me" and the public "might throw me out on my rear end"? What did the president know that McCurry didn't—yet?

CHAPTER SEVENTY-FIVE

INQUISITION

Letters to Sign

When embarking on his foolishness with Monica Lewinsky, the president knew he was under investigation, both by Kenneth Starr and by the Office of Independent Counsel over Whitewater, and by Paula Jones's lawyers over sexual harassment. To give in to momentary lust was one thing—a lapse of self-control. But for the president of the United States, throughout the winter and spring of 1996, to have pursued his compliant intern (who had by then been appointed to a full-time clerical job in the Eisenhower Building) was folly. It not only raised the stakes in terms of risk, it transformed the lapse into a *relationship*.

With each act of sexual hubris, the now middle-aged president grew more embroiled, more aroused, more unable to fight temptation. Guilt, fantasy, escapism, and excitement struggled in a heady combination—a cocktail the most powerful citizen in the world could not resist. He had told Monica the West Wing was relatively unmanned at the weekends; he began to call her at home to tell her when the coast was clear, so that she could invent excuses to bring over "letters" for the president to see and to sign. The very illicitness no doubt added to the potency—deliberately tempting fate.

Starr's Quasi-pornographic Drive

JFK had been reckless, but had fallen to an assassin's bullets before his philandering could become a matter of national voyeurism. Bill Clinton, however, would still be alive and still the president when Kenneth Starr decided, having failed to indict him over prior financial impropriety, to switch his Whitewater spotlight to the president's private behavior. Presented and published, with pseudo-academic footnotes, while the president was still leading the nation and the world, the Starr report would be, deliberately, the most scandalous and salacious document of its kind in American presidential history.

Thanks to Starr's obsessive stalking, historians and biographers would, thereby, become privy to the most intimate details of a president's sexual behavior in a manner that was unique in American annals—for Starr would leave no stone unturned, no detail of the psycho-sexual tangle unrecorded, in his search to find witnesses to the moral turpitude of the Democratic president, on the one hand, and satisfy his quasi-pornographic drive on the other—regardless of how much it subverted the dignity of the office of president, or that of the nation's professional confidence in its elected leader.

As Harvard law professor Alan Dershowitz later protested, Starr's inquisition would become an odious example of "sexual McCarthyism" in America—one that intimidated and bankrupted a swath of White House staff, Clinton administration officials, and innocent Clinton friends, former associates, lovers—and haters. Starr's motives had been politically suspect since the moment he offered to help Paula Jones's lawsuit in 1993, but his documentary erotica would go down in history as the most egregious, unmerited, salacious, and deliberate misuse of public money (over $60 million) ever sanctioned by Congress, or funded by ordinary taxpayers. But Starr didn't care—for the genius-IQ president was, in the jealous eyes of the paragon of judicial mediocrity, all too invitingly human.

"According to Ms. Lewinsky," Starr later informed Congress of the December 31, 1995, assignation between the president and the intern, "they moved to his study." He then quoted Ms. Lewinsky verbatim: "'And then . . . we were kissing and he lifted my sweater and exposed my breasts and was fondling them with his hands and with his mouth.'" And so on.

Visit by visit, Starr chronicled the escapades of the president, deliberately blind to the national security implications or indeed any implications other than those of successful snooping on the president's sex life. What did Starr hope to achieve by such a report on the serving president of the United States, made public to Congress and the nation?

On a Sunday afternoon in January 1996, as the president worked on his State of the Union address, the undress encounter was repeated, and though

Monica willingly entered into the spirit, she was uncertain where all this was going—"I didn't know if this was sort of developing into some kind of longer-term relationship than what I thought it initially might have been, that maybe he had some regular girlfriend who was furloughed. . . ."

Why was this any of Kenneth Starr's business? Was he the Spanish Inquisition, suddenly the guardian of private morality in America? Oblivious of the history of intimacy in the White House, and indifferent to the sad but not criminal midlife folly he was exposing, Starr became hell-bent on *creating* a crime: a wrongdoing that would justify a political lynching, and thus bring down the president. By overreaching, as Gingrich had done with the shutdown of the American government, Starr would ultimately self-destruct and become the most reviled lawyer in America—and his Republican efforts would profoundly compromise American standing and security in the world.

CHAPTER SEVENTY-SIX

BOUND TO BLAB

Basically a Good Girl

The literature of adultery is immense. Although the relationship between President Clinton and the White House intern Monica Lewinsky stopped short of adultery in the biblical sense, it exhibited many of the hallmarks of an adulterous affair; an affair that, given the gender situation and media evolution of the 1990s, was doomed to end badly.

"I formed an opinion early in 1996," the president would admit two years later, "once I got into this unfortunate and wrong conduct, that when I stopped it, which I knew I'd have to do and which I should have done a long time before I did, that she would talk about it. Not because Monica Lewinsky is a bad person," he was at pains to emphasize. "She's basically a good girl. She's a good young woman with a good heart and a good mind. I think she is burdened by some unfortunate conditions of her, her upbringing. But she's a good person."

A good person, unfortunately, who was bound to blab.

Since the nineteenth century, gender relations had been changing dramatically in the Western world—and were still changing in the late twentieth. Tolstoy's great fictional exploration of adultery, *Anna Karenina*, opens with a scene in the house of Prince "Stiva" Oblonsky. Evicted from his wife's bedroom for "carrying on an intrigue with a French girl, who had been a governess in their family," Stiva is in a state of despair. Of *that* adultery we never hear more, or indeed of the French girl; all too quickly the prince's married sister Anna Karenina, submitting to the love of conquest of handsome Count Vronsky, dominates the story.

Over a century later, however, Monica Lewinsky had no intention of being the forgotten "French girl." Brought up in California by middle-class divorced parents, she had every reason to demand more. Her mistreatment at the hands of her former lover Andy Bleiler only made her more determined to want better. The president might wish, like Prince Oblonsky, to gratify his flirtatious ego and lust with a compliant family servant, but Monica was a late twentieth-century, college-educated young woman with an irrepressible if emotionally oscillating personality. When she "met" the president, therefore, on January 21, 1996, she was "determined to have a showdown with him," as she confided to her biographer, "and where better than the Oval Office?" She was suffering a "bad hair day," and was wearing a black beret that the president found charming, framing her "cute little face," and which he complimented her on. Che Guevera in a skirt?

The president smiled and pushed away some of the hair from her forehead as she complained that "Handsome" hadn't contacted her for two long weeks. If he wanted her to be a formal employee, she said, she would behave so—i.e., she would give him no more free favors. If he wanted her to treat him as a man, however, he should treat her as a woman.

What could a twenty-two-year-old secretarial assistant in the correspondence section of the Office of Legislative Affairs of the White House possibly mean by her challenge? The president was taken aback by Monica's accusation—and assured her, as she afterwards recalled, he "cherishes the time that he had with me."

The president doubtless did—but despite his mega-intelligence he completely failed to see, in reassuring Monica that he was sincere in liking her as a young woman and a person, what the effect of such an assurance would be on the former intern, still extricating herself emotionally from her abusive affair with the California theater technician.

Monica wanted not physical attention so much as emotional connection, validation, affection—even a little *love*. And looking into her big, willing, and appealing eyes, the middle-aged political genius, the smartest president ever to occupy the Oval Office in the twentieth century, was overcome by the same muddled motives that characterized the follies of hundreds of thousands of ordinary men in America, and millions in history in every nation across the world: erotic thrill at the sensual power he was exerting over a voluptuous, open-hearted female; gratitude to the young woman for offering herself to him sexually;

electric excitement at the illicitness of their encounters (supposedly avoiding detection or the knowledge of his staff and Secret Service detail); delight in finding a liberated post-adolescent with whom to share the sheer fun of unbridled sex talk.

Never in his wildest dreams did the president imagine that each gesture, each consensual touch would be deposed by Kenneth Starr, leaked, and *published* for the world to read. But since the publication of Gennifer Flowers's *Passion and Betrayal* the year before had given ample enough warning, how did the president imagine he could get away with his sexual dalliance with Ms. Lewinsky—or avoid having his wife learn of the affair?

Saying No

As voices in the corridors of the White House whispered, the president was clearly *infatuated*. In such a state, could even a herd of elephants have caused the baby boomer now to pull back? Yet the president *did* pull back: twice.

On President's Day, Monday, February 19, 1996, the president issued a statement lamenting the latest IRA terrorist bomb that had exploded on a London bus, one week after the IRA had also exploded a massive bomb in London's docklands area. The eighteen-month IRA cease-fire seemed, effectively, over—testing the faith and patience of men of peace.

An American army sergeant had also been killed, prodding for mines in an off-limit area in Bosnia. Though the death had been ruled an accident the previous day, it weighed on the commander-in-chief who had ordered the peacekeeping mission. With a heavy heart, the president picked up the phone and called Monica, not for phone sex but to try to nip his infatuation in the bud.

Monica could tell something was up, for the president hadn't called her since a February 7 tryst, even on Valentine's Day. She suggested coming in from the Watergate, but he was non-committal. She therefore went to the Oval Office uninvited. There the president told her they must cease and desist.

He felt guilty, the president said. He was concerned for his daughter, Chelsea. He wanted to work at his marriage, he did not want to be "like that schmuck" Andy Bleiler, manipulating her affections for his own gratification when he was a married man and there could be no future for them as a couple. He had said, earlier, that she made him feel twenty-five. But he was not, he now reminded her. "You know, if I were twenty-five years old and not married," he boasted, thinking back to his days at Oxford and Yale, "I would have you on the floor back there in three seconds right now. But you will understand when you get older."

The office "affair," as so often happens, had accelerated from explosive consensual chemistry to something potentially more profound—and then overload. "In the beginning it was this very raw, sexual connection," Monica later recalled, "which had now developed into romance and tenderness as well." But once it did, it had frightened even the president. His heart had gone out to her, hearing of her unhappy relationship with Bleiler. His joy at finding a young woman so feisty, so plump, and even more anxious to please than himself, was unfeigned—yet it was his very affection and gratitude that made him ashamed at expecting her to pleasure him, when he knew he was never going to consummate the relationship sexually, and would thus leave her in ultimate sexual as well as romantic limbo. He therefore hugged her and said they could remain friends, but that there should be no more physical intimacy.

A Terrible Secret to Bear

At home Monica broke into tears—to the great relief of her mother. "I felt it was wrong," her mother later stated sagely, in recalling the moment, "not so much in the biblical sense, but wrong for her as a young woman. It was such a dead-end relationship and it frightened me because of the enormity of it. It was a terrible secret to bear."

The secret, however, was already leaching. As the president confessed later to Starr's inquisition, "I frankly, from 1996 on, always felt that if I severed inappropriate contact with Ms. Lewinsky, sooner or later it would get public"—not because Monica wanted money or to be punitive, but because "I did believe she would talk about it." She was, he reiterated, a good person, but she was Californian—from a state where people talked about their feelings, incessantly. "I knew that the minute there was no longer any contact, she would talk about this. She would have to. She couldn't help it. It was, it was a part of her psyche," the president reflected. "So I had put myself at risk, sir."

Recognizing the risk, Bill Clinton had tried his very best to end the business. It had proved a losing battle, however. Monica reminded him of his irreverent, uninhibited, often outlandish mother: Virginia Cassidy Clinton, with her fountain of hair, her love of make-up (her "war paint"), her penchant for glitter and costume jewelry, her appetite for *life*. Behind the façade of sexual courage, moreover, a lonely young woman was seeking to make sense of the world, and to matter to someone. Monica needed him: needed his legendary compassion and intelligent listening. She'd told him her secrets—how and where she'd grown up, how she'd lost her virginity, her favorite things—and that he, her idol, was "like rays of sunshine, but sunshine that made plants grow faster and made colors more vibrant." Reciprocating, he had told her of his loneliness, and the weight of his responsibility—as when the young American soldier had died in Bosnia. How could he now sever that cord? How could she be made to understand it was not only for his family they must desist, but in *her* best interests, too: that he was *not* sunshine, but was radioactive—and that his rays would be ineradicable, in terms of her life?

Back in Lewd Business

A week after ending his physical relationship with Monica, the president called her. The world was crazy. Paula Jones's appeal had succeeded—her lawyers were free to bring the president of the United States to trial. Meanwhile, he himself, the president of the United States, had been subpoenaed by Starr to testify in the defense of Susan McDougal, his penniless former Whitewater partner from *decades* before. In Britain, Princess Diana had agreed, under pressure of Buckingham Palace, to divorce Prince Charles. Palestinian suicide bombers were committing mass murder in Jerusalem, the IRA was planting more cowardly bombs in London, a sheep in Scotland had been successfully cloned, while in the same Scotland a former Boy Scout had entered a primary school gym in Dunblane village to murder the teacher and *sixteen* children in cold blood before killing himself.

Life was too short. Monica represented youth, vitality, fleshliness, self-consciousness, affection, fun. They began conversing on the phone once more, and on March 31, 1996, while Hillary was in Athens, they resumed their intimacy.

They were back in business. It was lewd business, to be sure—but it was mutually agreed, consensual intimacy, at this stage. It was none of Starr's business, nor that of the vicious Paula Jones and her lawyers. Nor was it criminal. *Their* business as Republicans, the president knew, however, was to blackmail and ruin him if they could—in whatever way they could. Therefore, he was crazy to chance discovery, or add to his travails.

CHAPTER SEVENTY-SEVEN

BEATING REPUBLICANS
AT THEIR OWN GAME

Jack Kemp As VP

Though Senator Dole had lost the primary in New Hampshire—as Bill Clinton had done in 1992—no other Republican contender could match Dole's national standing, or his personal story of military service and courage in overcoming his war wounds: courage that reminded people of FDR. By March 26, 1996, following victory in the California primary, the senator found he'd secured sufficient primary pledges to guarantee him the Republican nomination in August. Unfortunately, he had not won sufficient popularity among ordinary voters to give him a real chance of beating the incumbent, despite the trend towards voting Republican nationwide. And since General Powell did not believe in reinforcing failure, the chance of his accepting the role of vice president was zero.

The result was that Senator Dole was compelled to take as his vice presidential nominee former congressman Jack Kemp—a little-known former professional football quarterback, who had backed Forbes in the primaries, and who acknowledged to friends he was not smart enough to be president, if called upon *in extremis*. When Dole also surrendered not only his position as Senate majority leader, a move that people expected, but his Senate seat also, which nobody had expected, it was clear the aging Kansan had lost his once-legendary good judgment. Intending to look stronger by being willing to risk all in his bid for the presidency (after two failed attempts), and also to look less of a long-term Washington insider, Dole merely looked a presidential outsider, an elderly man without a title: a has-been.

The Coast Is Clear

For Bill Clinton, suddenly, the 1996 coast was now not only clear, it was so sunlit he became anxious lest his staff become complacent. On February 27, he had attended a performance of *Les Misérables* at the National Theater, and the image of Inspector Javert, relentlessly pursuing his quarry, haunted him. His only recourse, however, was to move forward, not look back.

Campaigns had always energized Clinton, especially the business of stump speaking: retail politics, where he could sense, feel, and hear the response he incited (or did not incite) among voters. And now he was in top form.

In addition, the government shutdown by the Republicans had played into the president's hands at a deeper level than Newt Gingrich, whose whole professional career as a politician had been spent in the House of Representatives, ever realized.

As a matter of conservative ideology the anti-federalist from Georgia had insisted upon ever more devolution, involving the transfer of power and funding responsibility to the states. But Bill Clinton had been governor of one of those states for *twelve* years. If anyone knew and understood the intricacies and problems of state-and-federal responsibility in budgeting, it was Bill Clinton. The budget resolution battle was thus "an area that he already knew; he knew its *substance*," Doug Sosnik recalled. "They spent over fifty hours—Daschle and Gephardt and Clinton and Armey and Gingrich and Dole, together. That was one area that the president really *knew*. And out of that experience he became even *more* confident."

For Gingrich to have fought to the death on that territory, when the president was already proving so much more of a leader and statesman on the larger stage, was therefore a grave mistake. The picture that emerged of a centrist president seeking a fair compromise, but struggling against ideologues interested only in getting their own way, was not inaccurate, Sosnik affirmed. "I never thought they were crazy enough to shut the government down," Sosnik remarked of Gingrich's Praetorian Guard. Bill Clinton's positive-minded DNA and his experience in working with the legislature in

Arkansas meant that he was by nature and political training a conciliator, a leader who genuinely wanted a fair resolution—an objective that his Svengali, Dick Morris, was just as keen to reach.

"Morris had all that stuff going on of back-channeling to Trent Lott," Sosnik remembered. "And he was doing polling, and trying to use polls, to get to Dole—he was *everywhere*." The government shutdown had never been a part of Morris's strategy—indeed, the reverse had been the case. Morris "didn't drive this thing. He was looking for a deal, from early on. He was late to the party on this one." Nor was Morris infallible on smaller issues—"for every good idea, he truly had three or four really bad ideas. So you had to have filters.

"Having said this," Sosnik continued his reflections on Morris, "he's a big thinker. He thinks outside the box, you know—he's strategic, he's thinking: *our* move, *their* move, *our* move, *their* move—three stages ahead of their move." His constant tactical strategy, at a time of increasing Republicanism in the country, was to beat the Republicans at their own game, by co-opting as many as possible of their issues ahead of them. "You know, the tobacco stuff, the drug czar . . .

"Remember, elections are always about the future, not the past," Sosnik remarked. To beat Dole, the president had to be *more* positive, *more* constructive, *more* confident, *more* specific, *more* values-centered than his opponent—and, in Morris's view, the president must therefore swallow and sign a new Republican welfare bill, not continue to veto it.

EXIT MONICA

CHAPTER SEVENTY-EIGHT

GETTING RID
OF THE CLUTCH

For the President to Decide

For many older Democrats, signing a Republican-drafted welfare bill would mark the president's betrayal of his party, after a brilliant stonewalling defense of Medicare, Medicaid, education, and the environment. Moreover, signing a Republican version of welfare reform was—in their eyes—unnecessary, since the president was, from the moment the government shutdown had failed to win Republican support, way ahead of Dole.

As Robert Reich would say to himself in July 1996, when the cabinet met to discuss the latest version of the Republicans' welfare bill and whether the president should sign it, "You're twenty points ahead in the polls, for chrissake. You don't need to hurt people this way. You don't need to settle for this piece of shit. Veto it, and explain to the public why you did. Explain that you want to get poor people into jobs, and that to do so requires money."

But Reich held his tongue, lest his passionate objections become counterproductive. It was up to the president, after all, to decide.

The Hungry Lion

The Clinton administration's original idea, in 1992, had been to fund a massive overhaul of welfare with $2 billion, to help move the unemployed from welfare entitlement to work. Putting Hillary's health care reform bill first on the agenda, they had lost control of Congress—and thus now had to face a Republican version of the welfare bill.

The Republican version, it turned out, would cut welfare entitlement by $9 billion but provide *no* compensatory funding for training, child care, or jobs. With such a fair political wind behind him since the government shutdown, Reich argued, why did the president not use Keynesian economic theory to fund new public-sector jobs, to finance skill training, and to pay for child care in a way that would counter growing income and opportunity inequality in America?

Reich blamed Morris rather than Congress. There were lies, damned lies, and Morris's polling statistics, he railed in his diary—heartbroken at being accused of being "off reservation" for criticizing his own administration for not demanding corporate responsibility along with personal responsibility on the part of the unemployed.

Years later, in the wake of MCI, Enron, and other corporate scandals, Reich would be proved right—but at a very personal level he would learn how hard it is to build a constituency, when failing dismally in his bid to be nominated for the governorship of his state, Massachusetts. He would be respected for his theory, but humiliated in terms of political reality. The fact was, the United States was becoming relentlessly more conservative in its overall voting patterns in the religious mid-West and South—and with a Congress already controlled by the Republicans, the president's ability to read his nation's political tea leaves was remarkable.

Tirelessly Clinton criss-crossed the country. Tirelessly he cross-examined political leaders and voters. His curiosity was insatiable, as Panetta recalled. "This guy is like a hungry lion who searches for every morsel of information he can get."

While relentless critical application of intelligence was required behind the scenes, in public the president now wanted only Democratic optimism. He would lead the charge for a long-overdue increase in the minimum wage—which passed the Republican Congress finally in July, to universal surprise—but he did not like members of the administration talking doom if more federal funding was not found for investment in the poor, as part of welfare reform. The Senate and the House had in large part been lost to Democrats in 1994 because, despite the administration's success in tackling "the economy, stupid," that success had not yet translated into tangible benefits for voters. Now, with the American economy clearly booming, the president understandably wanted to trumpet that success—and deny it to the Republicans, who had predicted economic disaster. And the best man to mastermind the trumpet, he felt, was Dick Morris, however despised he was by the staff.

Morris's Genius

Morris's genius was to see, as a Republican, the Republicans' likely strategy—and to counter it. Also to get in under the Republicans' national radar, by pursuing a regional strategy. Sosnik was frankly amazed at its success. "I never thought the Republicans would let those ads go unmatched," Sosnik confessed. "I mean, we were going at it every few weeks, we didn't have a long-range plan—but Morris did."

Sosnik was skeptical as to whether the early ads, as Morris claimed, won the election for the president, but they certainly ensured that, with Clinton's polls having risen as a result of Gingrich's nefarious government shutdown, they never fell back. Bill Clinton's '92 election had been pitched to be a platform of change; now it was being pitched as a platform of *success in making those changes*—especially with regard to the economy—as the basis for a positive Clinton program in a second term.

Nor was this all. In order to beat off any Republican attempt to seize back the high ground by trashing the president as a liberal, as had been done in '94, there was a concerted effort to garble and obscure certain issues. Morris "drove a strategy of, effectively, 'get a handful of areas where we're vulnerable, let's muddy it up'—and if you muddy it up," Sosnik explained, "they can't put him in that box, and we're gonna win."

Suddenly, by the spring of 1996, it was almost as if it was all over but the shouting—for if the president chose to accept the punitive Republican welfare bill, the last hope of a Republican comeback would be cauterized.

Old Democrats held their breath, aghast at the prospect—but New Democrats, especially those who had watched the president's cautious approach to the reform of affirmative action, were convinced he would sign, once he had won the safeguards he wanted for mothers and children.

"You have to weigh it all out," Sosnik reflected later. "I think he believed—whether he believed it because he wanted to believe it, or he believed he believed it, however he got out of it—I think he believed it was right." Clinton was a New Democrat, whose "coin of the realm was the notion that at the end of the day, what made us a little different than the New Deal Democrats, or Johnson's Great Society Democrats, was, ultimately *the individual has got to take responsibility.*"

Should the president therefore refuse to sign the Republican welfare reform legislation, if he did *not* get the safeguards he wanted, though? Or was it more important to remove the issue from Bob Dole's armory, and assure himself re-election in November?

It was a difficult decision, and one that had a personal component for the president. If he wanted people on welfare to stop seeing federal entitlements as their right, and to start accepting their personal, individual responsibility to change, and to seek employment—especially in a burgeoning economy in which there was no shortage of available jobs—he had to accept individual responsibility in his own life. Therefore, Monica must go.

The Mission to Save the President

Whether or not Bill Clinton himself was the mover behind the effort to move Ms. Lewinsky out of temptation's way, across the Potomac River, was not something Kenneth Starr or any of the president's myriad investigators—official, media, legal—ever determined. Or, for that matter, whether Hillary, too, was involved. But both the president's and the first lady's staffs certainly were involved. Indeed, the record would suggest the staffs were on a desperate mission to save the president, who was performing so well as the nation's leader, from himself, and from Monica.

The president's new deputy chief of staff, Evelyn Lieberman, was close to Hillary—"closer to Hillary than anyone," according to Dick Morris. Lieberman had become Hillary's communications director when Hillary had been chair of the Children's Defense Fund, and then assistant to Hillary's loyal chief of staff, Maggie Williams, at the White House. After this, Lieberman had been promoted to deputy White House press secretary under Mike McCurry, and had finally succeeded Erskine Bowles as deputy to Leon Panetta. A former high school teacher from Long Beach, New York, Lieberman was charged with ending any residual factional fighting in the White House in the run-up to the election, as the president had explained to her. Known as "Mother Superior," she was a no-nonsense White House "enforcer." It was therefore upon her that the responsibility for axing Monica would fall.

Evelyn Lieberman had already accused Monica, late in 1995, of being a "clutch"—one of the women "trafficking" the vicinity of the West Wing in hopes of flirting with the notoriously "sexy" president—and had even forbidden Monica access to the inner sanctum as a mere intern without a proper pass. Monica's job as a correspondence assistant in the Office of Legislative Affairs thereafter, however, entitled her to the prized Blue Pass. Thus, having "scampered off" with her tail between her legs after being challenged by Lieberman, Monica had summoned her courage and returned to the West Wing, where she informed the deputy chief of staff that she was legit.

To set herself against "the enforcer" was not wise, however, and, knowing that Lieberman was her potential enemy, Monica had made every effort to avoid her when going to the West Wing. Given Lieberman's position, this was not easy. Not only was Monica seen "loitering" some five to ten times by an increasingly annoyed "Mother Superior," but in the hothouse, gossipy atmosphere of the palace, with its retinue of courtiers and guards, it was impossible to keep her assignations with the president quiet. Rumors of the intrigue had proliferated.

Seeing her again and again in the West Wing with no good reason, Lieberman had become more and more irritated, worried by the prospect of a scandal that might taint the office of the president. She later explained to Starr that "the president was vulnerable to these kind of rumors . . . yes, yes, that was one of the reasons" for transferring Monica. "I decided to get rid of her," Lieberman further explained, not simply because Monica was a poor secretarial assistant—often away from her desk—but because she was becoming a public menace. "I talked to her supervisor," Lieberman recalled. "And I said—I think I asked about how she was doing. And he or she—I can't remember who I talked to—said not very well; correspondence is not in great shape. And I said, 'Get her out of here.'"

Overfamiliarity

Leon Panetta, as chief of staff, agreed with his deputy. So did Hillary's fixer, Patsy Thomasson, who—having helped remove Hillary's private papers from Vince Foster's office before it could be sealed—had become director of the Office of Administration. Lieberman put Thomasson in charge of finding Monica a job well away from Pennsylvania Avenue. She quickly found one for her across the Potomac River, in the Pentagon, where Monica would, Thomasson felt, be properly guarded. Her salary would be doubled, to sweeten the pill, but she would be deprived of her all-important Blue Pass to the White House *instanter*—a pass that her boss, Tim Keating, asked her on April 5 to hand over.

For Monica, who was well-aware how unpopular she was becoming in the White House (the butt of rude jokes and sneering references by "The Meanies," as she called them), the interview with Keating and the news of her transfer were humiliating, however much dressed up as promotion. Pride, vanity, a sense of victimization, and childhood insecurity welled up. She burst into tears in front of Keating (who had been told by Lieberman that Monica was being moved for the crime of "overfamiliarity" with the president). After that she returned home to her mother's apartment at the Watergate, where she cried herself to sleep. "I was hysterical all weekend," she later remembered. "All I did was cry and eat pizzas and sweets."

Pizzas and sweets? Could the president of the United States really have put his career as leader of the free world in the hands of such an "obsessional, jealous and hysterical" girl, as her authorized biographer called her? Seemingly uninformed of the transfer, the president called Monica two days later, on Sunday, April 7. His friend and commerce secretary, Ron Brown, had been reported killed in a plane crash in eastern Europe, and the White House was in mourning. When Monica told him of her dismissal, he affected innocence, indeed anger, at the decision. "I bet this has something to do with me," he responded. "O.K., come over."

Why? Why, when knowing or deducing that Monica had been transferred to prevent a sex scandal, did the president invite her yet again to his office?

In his memoirs, President Clinton, understandably, did not explain. Knowing as we do the extent to which Monica had made it her mission to seduce the president of the United States (according to Andy Bleiler's embittered wife, Monica had boasted that she was going to go to Washington with "presidential kneepads"), we must assume that the president was (as with the Arkansas troopers) simply concerned to make absolutely sure she would not talk, and thus sully his almost certain chance of re-election in November. Yet there was probably more to it than this: the complicated mix of arrogance, calculation, and compassion that, by this point in his life chronicle, we must acknowledge as typically Clintonesque. The president wanted to ensure her silence, yes—understandably. He wanted to console the weeping former intern, yes—compassionately, and through his legendary charm. But he wanted, too—as he heard her sobbing—self-gratification.

"Why did they have to take you away from me?" he asked, rhetorically, once she got to the White House that afternoon. He had just been speaking to Hillary on the internal line to the Residence, ending, "I love you, too"—which did not make Monica feel at all comforted. It was Easter Sunday. "I trust you so much. I promise if I win in November I will bring you back here," he assured Monica, snapping his long fingers—"just like that."

The meeting was, however, more than a farewell, as Starr intended his account to reveal. It was grotesque—as all illicit sex tends to be in the eyes of outsiders. Disturbed by a phone call in the back study, the president used the opportunity to further assert his sexual power over his employee, in Starr's account. "The president indicated that Ms. Lewinsky should perform oral sex while he talked on the phone, and she obliged."

Dick Morris was the caller, from Paris. After subpoenaing the White House telephone logs, Starr was even able to prove to Congress (and the world) the exact duration of oral intimacy between the president and Ms. Lewinsky (nine minutes). No sooner was the call over, however, than it was followed by the unmistakable voice of Harold Ickes, hollering "Mr. President!"

Pulling away, Clinton shot to his feet, did up his pants, and rushed into the Oval Office, while Monica stole out via the dining room door. It would be their last physical contact for a year. The Protectors had won.

CHAPTER SEVENTY-NINE

THE DEATH OF RON BROWN

Clinton's Alter Ego

The deaths in Croatia of Ron Brown, the commerce secretary, and of a thirty-five-person trade delegation from the U.S. weighed heavily on the president, as Doug Sosnik recalled—even more deeply, Sosnik felt, than the death of his childhood friend Vince Foster, three years before. Foster had *chosen* his death, however sadly; Brown had not.

It was Richard Holbrooke who had begged Brown to visit Croatia and Bosnia, to encourage U.S. investment in the rebuilding of the region. In Dubrovkik, however, the Serbs had seized and removed the city airport's bad-weather navigational equipment. In heavy rain and fog, Brown's official Boeing 737 had slammed into a Dalmatian hillside at 158 miles per hour without anyone being able to warn the pilot.

With his big dark eyes, his infectious grin, his black mustache, the always nattily dressed former director of the Democratic National Committee had not only helped Clinton become the Democratic Party nominee in 1992, but had shared human as well as political traits with the president. He was Clinton's alter ego, in a dark skin—carrying on an affair with one of his employees at the Commerce Department, a beautiful young woman who had worked on Clinton's 1992 campaign, and who died in the plane crash also. Brown, too, was being investigated, at Republican behest, by a so-called independent counsel for irregularities in some of his past business dealings. Brown, too, had been labeled "irrelevant" when, after the midterm elections, Republicans called for the dissolution of his Commerce

Department, but he had courageously defended it, and had backed the president throughout the government shutdown.

Stunned by the relentless McCarthy-like interviewing of his colleagues, friends, and even fellow golf club members, Brown had confided to Clinton his sense of a racist conspiracy to bring him down, both for helping Clinton to win in 1992 and for being a successful black (Mike Espy having already been forced to resign). Clinton had comforted his friend—and now grieved the more at his cruel death halfway across the world, in the president's service. Without hesitating, Clinton had ordered a state funeral, complete with a service in Washington Cathedral: Brown's body to be born there by the same catafalque that had carried John F. Kennedy's flag-draped casket.

A Funeral Oration

"The Bible tells us," the president declared in his personal eulogy—perhaps the finest he had ever given in his life, because it came straight from his heart—" 'though we weep through the night, joy will come in the morning.'

"Ron Brown's incredible life force brought us all joy in the morning. No dark night could ever defeat him. And as we remember him, may we always be able to recover his joy. For this man loved life and all the things in it. He loved the big things: his family, his friends, his country, his work, his African-American heritage. He loved the difference he was making in the world, this new and exciting world after the Cold War.

"And he loved life's little things: the Redskins and basketball and golf, even when it was bad, and McDonald's and clothes. And I'm telling you, folks, he would have loved this deal today. I mean, here we are for Ron Brown in the National Cathedral with full military honors, filled with the distinguished citizenry of this country and leaders from around the world in a tribute to him. And as I look around, I see that all of us are dressed almost as well as he would be today."

As laughter subsided, the president went on. "Ron Brown enjoyed a lot of success. He proved you could do well and do good. He also proved you could do good and have a good time. And he also proved that you could do all that and, at the same time, still take time to help other people.

"With his passion and determination, his loves and his joys, his going beyond the stereotypes of his time, he lived a truly American life. He lived his life for America, and when the time came, he was found laying down his life for America . . . "

Those who knew Brown well, sobbed. Those who knew the president well, understood that Bill Clinton was, in the strangest of ways, speaking of himself as much as of Ron Brown: a "force of nature," as he called him. It was, too, a sort of invocation *to* himself. "In his letter to the Galatians, St. Paul said, 'Let us not grow weary in doing good. For in due season we shall reap if we do not lose heart.' Our friend never grew weary; he never lost heart. He did so much good, and he is now reaping his reward. He left us sooner than we wanted him to leave, but what a legacy of love and life he left behind.

"Now he's in a place where he doesn't even have to worry about how good he looks," the president ended. "He will always look good. He's in a place where there's always joy in the morning. He's in a place where every good quality he ever had has been rendered perfect. He's in a place he deserves to be because of the way he lived and what he left to those of us who loved him. Let there always be joy in the morning for Ron Brown."

THE SUMMER OF '96

CHAPTER EIGHTY

A DARKER CHALLENGE

Oklahoma Anniversary

The first anniversary of the Oklahoma City bombing was now approaching. At the School of Education at the University of Central Oklahoma, Clinton reiterated that every classroom and every library in America should have computers accessing the Internet, thereby offering digitized knowledge from across the world. This meant, however, "that terrorist networks can get information about how to build bombs and how to wreak mischief if you just know how to find the right home page." The good news was that "we are reducing the traditional threats to your security and your future. Communism has failed. The Cold War is over. We have agreed to treaties that will reduce by two-thirds the number of nuclear weapons that existed when the Cold War was at its height. And for the first time in the history of nuclear weapons, for the last two years there's not a single nuclear weapon pointed at any American citizen.

"That is the good news," he repeated. The bad news was that "in an open world of easy information, quick technology, and rapid movements, we are all more vulnerable than we used to be to terrorism," together with its "interconnected allies, organized crime, drug-running, and the spread of nuclear weapons." Addressing himself to students, he declared: "What we have to do now is to fight back these organized forces of destruction so all the opportunities that await you young people will be there and so you can pursue them without fear; so that if you're willing to work hard and obey the law and make the most of your own lives, you will be able to live out your dreams."

Few Republicans, at the time, took such issues seriously, nor did those issues garner votes, particularly. Bill Clinton would not have been Bill Clinton, however, had he not wished to share his presidential concerns. Four years before, he had traveled the country with a message of optimism and higher social and economic responsibility. Now, four years into his presidency, he was looking into a crystal ball with eyes seared with the images of the innocent dead.

"The lessons we have to take out of what happened to us at the World Trade Center, what happened to us in Oklahoma City, what we were able to avoid when we stopped terrorist attacks in the last two years on our own soil and against our airplanes as they were flying over the oceans," he exhorted the assembled students and their educators, "*those* are the things we have to learn." He himself would not be in Oklahoma for the anniversary, which was why he was visiting the city early, he explained; he would be in Russia at a nuclear summit—both to reduce the stockpile of nuclear weapons and to secure it against theft. "The United States has to be part of that. And that's an important thing, but we also have to recognize that there are things that we have to do here at home.

"Last year I asked people in other parts of the world to stand with the United States because we took a tough stand against the countries that support terrorism, against Iran and Iraq and Sudan and Libya. And I get frustrated when they don't help. But when those bombs blew up in Israel," he remarked, "it sobered a lot of countries up, and in three days the president of Egypt and I were able to persuade twenty-nine countries to send high-level leaders, including heads of state, to Egypt to meet to stand up to terrorism in Israel for the first time. So we've got—we're getting in a position now where the people are willing to say we can't let terrorism pay. We can't let terrorism pay. We've got to make sure that terrorists pay for what they're doing. We have to make sure that's true here and around the world.

"When I was in Israel—and I suppose they have about as much experience with terrorism as anybody—I talked to leaders of both political parties. And they hardly agree on anything over there; they fight just like we do. [*Laughter*] But you know what? They were both agreed on one thing. They said, 'You have got to continue to take the lead in the fight against terrorism, and you need to pass the legislation that you're trying to pass to crack down on the forces of terrorism in the United States and enable us to stand against them when they invade our country.'

"It's been almost a year since I was pledged [by Congress] that terrorism bill, and it's still not in the shape it needs to be," the president went on. "But let me just tell you three things that I think ought to be in it. . . .

"We know what kind of bomb blew up the federal building. We propose that we be able to have markers that go into explosives when people buy them. Contractors don't have a thing in the world to fear. People need to buy explosives, you can't do a lot of work without them. But if explosives are used to kill innocent civilians, we ought to be able to find out where they came from and who bought them. That's what I believe, and I hope you do, too.

"We ought to have explicit authority that permits the attorney general of the United States to stop terrorist groups like Hamas from raising money in America. And if we catch people doing it, we ought to be able to throw them out of the country immediately—immediately, not after some long, drawn-out process.

"We ought to have the technology available to our law enforcement officials to keep up with these terrorists that move around in a hurry, and they're very sophisticated and very hard to catch. And we can do that without violating the civil liberties of the American people, without undermining the constitutional rights of criminal defendants. But I'm telling you, folks, these people are smart. They understand computers. They understand information. They understand how to hide. They understand how to doctor bank records. They understand how to launder money.

"And when it comes down to it, just think what would happen if Oklahoma City had happened five or six or seven times within a month or two. Think what it would have done if three thousand people had been killed at Oklahoma City," he urged, in one of the most prescient warnings of his entire presidency, "and every American had felt like these people were within fifty miles of them."

It had happened, and was happening in Israel—and would surely happen in America unless people in the United States woke up to the danger. "I am not saying these things to frighten any Americans," he emphasized.

"I am just telling you I have been around the world representing you; I've talked to people all over the world. I do not believe that you will have to worry about nuclear weapons wiping out a whole American community or killing lots of Americans in the way that our parents worried about us when I was growing up. But I do not believe you can fulfill your dreams and be totally free until we have taken the strongest possible stand against terrorism, organized crime, drug running, and weapons sales. And they are all related.

"So I ask you, I ask you because you will have more weight than most people—this state has suffered, this state has felt it, this state understands the human dimension of people killing people for perverted, allegedly political reasons—to say in clear, simple terms, this is not a political issue; this is not a partisan issue; this is not an ideological issue. This is a matter of getting America ready for the future and guaranteeing our young people the opportunities that they deserve to live out their God-given dream and destiny. Thank you, and God bless you."

Industrial Society and Its Future

Abroad, leaders marveled at President Clinton's articulate grasp of the issues confronting the modern world. In America, sadly, legions of ideologues and anti-patriots still remained hatefully hostile—even set upon violence.

On April 3, 1996, the FBI had arrested a Harvard-educated Polish-American hermit with a Ph.D. in math, Ted Kaczynski—universally known as the Unabomber. The Unabomber's arrest and conviction, after a seventeen-year manhunt, said little for the FBI's counterterrorism abilities or priorities in an age when terrorism was becoming the single biggest threat to national security. All too often it seemed as if the new director of the FBI, Louis Freeh, was more interested, along with Ken Starr, in bringing down the president of the United States and those who knew him than in pursuing terrorists operating against America.

In Japan, President Clinton signed with the Japanese prime minister the "Alliance for the 21ˢᵗ Century," pledging almost fifty thousand troops to maintain, with Japan, regional security. No sooner was the president back in Washington, however, than he was subpoenaed to testify for the defense of his old partner's wife, Susan McDougal, in Judge Starr's *still* ongoing Whitewater investigation—an investigation that Starr's predecessor had recommended be terminated, but that Starr had insisted upon pursuing and broadening, and that, in March 1996, had seen the start of a sensational trial of no lesser figure than the serving governor of Arkansas, Bill Clinton's successor, Jim Guy Tucker, along with both McDougals, who were all found guilty of making illegal loans and were, in due course, imprisoned.

No Republican, it was noted in Arkansas, was ever jailed by Starr.

America's Madness

For the president, this politically-driven vendetta against his gubernatorial successor and against his penniless former Whitewater real estate partner (who was ill, and subsequently died in the penitentiary) was a constant nightmare.

Starr's investigation had been supposed, by Senate ruling, to end that February, but in deference to the chair of the Whitewater hearings and chairman of the Senate Banking Committee, Republican senator Alfonse D'Amato, it had been extended—involving thousands of innocent people in its Kafkaesque wake. As Haynes Johnson would lament in his ironically titled *The Best of Times* in 2001, "To a degree not appreciated by the public, the entire Scandal Times era wreaks extraordinary damage internally on those who work in government, and particularly in the White House." Indeed, seen a decade later, the tens of millions of dollars of taxpayers' money spent by D'Amato on Whitewater and the Starr investigation as a "fishing expedition" to embarrass and possibly bring down the Democratic—and democratically elected—president, at a time when the police and security forces of the United States were urgently needed to combat the growth in terrorist networks and plots, would appear beyond rational comprehension. Foreign observers watched in disbelief as, on June 18, 1996, the Senate Whitewater Committee issued a scathing report in which the first lady was portrayed as the central figure in a "pattern of deception and arrogance," and D'Amato came close to accusing both Clintons of criminal wrongdoing—while the Republican Senate completely ignored terrorism.

Had America gone raving mad? such journalists asked.

Terror Strikes Again

In the meantime, in the early summer of 1996 there was nothing Clinton could do, save, like Ron Brown, go on doing his job: leading America to the best of his considerable ability. In May his lawyers appealed to the Supreme Court to rule against the appeals judge in the Paula Jones case—

pleading again that the chief executive must, in accordance with the Constitution, be granted immunity until his job was over.

Ms. Jones's right-wing financed lawyers counterpleaded, however, that despite the fact that Jones had happily waited three long years before bringing her suit, the president's trial for sexual harassment should go ahead immediately.

By agreeing, on June 24, that they would take on the president's immunity issue only in their 2005–2006 term, the judges of the Supreme Court saved the president from having to submit to an immediate trial, in the run up to the party convention in New York and the November elections. By the same token, however, their decision was merely a deferral. If the president lost the November election, they would be spared from having to make a judgment at all. But if the president won, they would be required to rule definitively on the constitutionality of such a civil lawsuit against a sitting president, in an era of bitter political partisanship and growing terrorism that required the president's undivided attention.

As if to emphasize the importance of the president's case, on June 25, 1996, terror struck again—this time in Saudi Arabia.

The Khobar Towers

The massive truck bomb that exploded in Khobar was little different from the one in Oklahoma—only this time an alert sentry had spotted the suspicious approach of the vehicle and sounded the alarm in Building 131 of the American military compound, housing more than 3,000 air force personnel. In contrast to Oklahoma City, the Jersey barriers deflected the main force of the 3,000- to 5,000-pound bomb blast as it blew a crater 85-feet wide and 35-feet deep outside the building. McVeigh's mass murder had ended the lives of 189 Americans; in the Khobar Towers "only" 19 were killed, with some 378 wounded.

As the president had warned, terrorists were clearly the number one enemy of the United States, posing a threat from which no one was safe, in the U.S. or abroad.

Richard Clarke, the president's anti-terrorism czar, quickly determined to the satisfaction of his anti-terrorism committee that a Saudi wing of the Iranian-backed group Hezbollah had been responsible for this latest mass murder, but getting the Republican Congress to pass the president's year-long-delayed anti-terrorism measures, and the Republican director of the FBI to upgrade the agency to tackle international terrorism effectively, proved an uphill battle. Freeh was, as Clarke later recalled, sold a bill of goods by the Saudis—who adhered to their tradition of secrecy by beheading all those whom they caught, in order to avoid publicity. When one of the suspects, Hani el-Sayegh, escaped to Canada, Freeh arranged that he be extradited to the U.S., where he could testify to the Iranian plot. No sooner was el-Sayegh on American soil, however, than el-Sayegh refused to cooperate, claiming the right to silence and American political asylum.

As Clarke later wrote, "Freeh should have spent his time fixing the mess that the FBI had become, an organization of fifty-six princedoms (the fifty-six very independent field offices) without any modern information technology to support them. He might have spent some time hunting for terrorists in the United States, where al Qaeda and its affiliates had put down roots, where many terrorist organizations were illegally raising money." Instead, Freeh threw himself behind high-profile cases in the vain hope of stardom—"cases going down dark alleys, empty wells," as Clarke put it. "His back channels to Republicans in Congress and to supporters in the media made it impossible for the president to dismiss him without running the risk of making him a martyr of the Republican right and his firing a cause célèbre."

America, in other words, was paying a terrible price for the president's misjudgment in appointing a Republican "Boy Scout" (as Clinton was heard to call Freeh) to direct the FBI, and for his loss of the Democratically controlled Congress in 1994.

TWA Flight 800

Would Islamic terrorists seek to disrupt the Olympic Games in Atlanta now? After the Khobar Towers bombing, this became the next great White House concern—with Vice President Gore backing Clarke in assembling an army of security personnel in the city and the Olympic arenas. How to ensure a successful "family" event, yet screen many hundreds of thousands of daily visitors, was clearly a daunting task that made everyone, including the president, jittery. Thus when, a few days before the opening ceremonies, news came in of a Trans World Airlines commercial jetliner exploding in mid-air off Long Island on the night of July 17, it was hard not to see the hand of yet more Islamic terrorists.

The Boeing 747 bound for Paris was only minutes into its flight when it broke into two fireballs, killing all two hundred thirty passengers and crew instantly, at fifteen thousand feet, and fell into the ocean.

The president had been examining, with his national security chiefs, punitive steps to be taken against Iran in order that it rein in its Hezbollah allies—he'd declared, in fact, that he didn't want any "half-pissant measures, but a full-scale operation"—when TWA Flight 800 exploded. It was a mark of his increasing maturity as a leader, then, that he made an instant public appeal for patience ("Let's wait until we get the facts, and let's remember the families," he declared) in determining the cause of the explosion before rushing to premature judgment. For the families of the victims, however, this proved a terrible trial as they impatiently waited for the wreckage to be retrieved from the Atlantic waters, and the bodies to be identified.

As the days dragged out, frustrations rose. The president insisted that immediate, significant new airport security measures to be introduced, as Clarke wished, but also insisted he wanted to meet with the grieving families in person—as Clarke did *not* wish. "That did not seem the best idea I had ever heard," Clarke later described, given the frenetic rumor mill about the causes of the disaster—especially those of a friendly-fire cover-up by the U.S. Navy, which had been carrying out surface-to-air exercises in the area at the very time the airliner exploded. "The families," Clarke recounted, "were looking to lynch someone."

The president, however, was adamant, and flew with Hillary to Kennedy International Airport, where they made their way to the Ramada Plaza Hotel. There the president gave a short speech, which was translated into French and Italian for relatives of the dead who had come over, and then Clinton, "to my chagrin and to the horror of the Secret Service, stepped into the crowd," Clarke recalled. "He began to gather them in small groups hugging them, taking pictures with them, looking at the pictures of their now dead loved ones, and listening intently. I thought he was about to cry. I know I was." Seeking sanctuary in a makeshift chapel next door, Clarke found the first lady there, praying.

For Clarke, who did not suffer fools gladly, the president's compassion was exemplary. As the New York *Daily News* reported, "fed up with the slow pace of the search for bodies and angered by conflicting reports from government officials, many of the relatives had reached their breaking points." The hotel was a "madhouse rife with conspiracy theorists," said the brother of one of the victims. In that atmosphere, the president's words "had a calming effect on all the frustrated people. Nobody was the slightest bit disrespectful. Another man, who had lost a brother, spoke for all the families: 'We're very grateful to see the president. You could see the decency of the man. He and Mrs. Clinton talked to everyone who wanted. He would hold your hand and ask you about your loved one. . . . '"

From JFK the president then flew to open the Olympic Games in Atlanta. There, to Clarke's chagrin, yet *another* deadly explosion took place. Seven days into the Centennial Summer Olympic Games in Atlanta, with over ten thousand athletes competing, an estimated two million spectators attending in person, and 3.5 billion following the games on television around the world, a 911 emergency call was received, saying there was a bomb in the Centennial Olympic Park. This was a twenty-one-acre area where a free open-air rock concert was taking place before an estimated seventy thousand people—and where a suspicious green military-style backpack, or ALICE pack, had just been found, beneath a bench below the five-story NBC light and sound tower. Summoned by a security guard, FBI bomb expert Bill Forsythe examined the bag with a sickening feeling. Later he recalled the moment after he peeled back the top flap and looked inside, and saw "three large pipes, about fourteen inches long and two and a half inches wide with end caps. I saw the wires. I saw what looked like a box, like a plastic sandwich container. I could see the side of a Big Ben clock."

Immediate evacuation of the site was ordered and, with the nearest people some forty feet away, the bomb—packed with twenty-four pounds of explosives, nails, screws, and other shrapnel—suddenly went off, killing two people and wounding a hundred and eleven others. Had evacuation not commenced, mayhem would have resulted, and the games would have been closed.

The Two Starrs

A group of skinheads had been seen by the bench, before the backpack was found. Given that FBI agents had uncovered a plot by a militia group in Georgia to set off bombs at Olympic sites prior to the games, the explosion, at 1:20 A.M. on July 27, was perhaps inevitable. The Georgia Republic Militia group, numbering eleven to fifteen members, had been raided in May. Ten bombs had been confiscated—bombs constructed, the arrested men explained, "in case of government invasion." One of the men was called, ironically, Starr—a bankrupt self-employed electrician.

At 10:06 A.M. the president, from the Oval Office, expressed his condolences on behalf of "all Americans" to the families of the killed and injured. The bombing was, he said, "an evil act of terror," aimed at the "innocent people who were participating in the Olympic Games and at the spirit of the Olympics. It was an act of cowardice that stands in sharp contrast to the courage of the Olympic athletes." The government would, he promised, track down and bring to justice those responsible. Meanwhile, however, the games would go on—for "an act of vicious terror like this is clearly directed at the spirit of our own democracy"—and "we cannot let terror win; that is not the American way."

CHAPTER EIGHTY-ONE

OUTFLANKING DOLE

Republican Desperation

The games did continue—but the FBI director, Louis Freeh, did not track down the perpetrators. He became, instead, convinced that the security guard who had found the ALICE pack and raised the alarm had staged the incident to win publicity and a full-time job! Ruining Richard Jewell's life, Freeh ignored the real murderer, Eric Rudolph—an anti-government, anti-gay, anti-abortion fundamentalist who went on, after Atlanta, to murder a security guard at an abortion clinic in Birmingham, and was only apprehended by local police *nine years* later, in 2003.

Freeh's myopia, sadly, replicated that of Ken Starr, whose investigation of Whitewater continued unabated—funded still further by a Republican-controlled Congress indifferent to the threat of terrorism, and asleep at the switch. Awaiting sentencing in August 1996, both McDougals were asked by Starr's team to lie, and to claim, in return for a reduced sentence, that Governor Clinton had pressured David Hale, a former head of an investment company chartered by the Small Business Administration, to give the McDougals' company, Madison Guaranty, a three-hundred-thousand-dollar SBA loan. Although Hale was exposed as an unmitigated liar, out to save his corrupt skin, and the president and the first lady were exonerated, the stories of Starr's witness-tampering, bribery, and intimidation in his efforts to bring down the Clintons were lamentable. Indeed, they smacked of treason. The whole iniquitous saga, in which the arch-fraudster Hale got off with only twenty-eight months in jail by offering to Starr to slander the president in public, would be told in Joe Conason and Gene Lyons' *The Hunting of the President* in 2001—but by then the damage had been done, the Republican obsession with Whitewater having turned the nation into an object of ridicule the world over.

Why Governor Bill Clinton, who was personally unavaricious and did not even own a home of his own, would have bothered to induce David Hale to give a loan to McDougal was never a matter that concerned Starr. But Jim McDougal, mortally sick and facing a sentence of twenty years that Starr was demanding, gave in to Starr's pressure. Susan, his ex-wife, did not—and went to jail.

Bill Clinton, hearing the news, was mortified, as he was by the sentencing of Governor Jim Guy Tucker, his successor. Terrorists were getting closer, while the Republicans were so desperate to unseat the elected president of the United States that Jim McDougal was even encouraged to beg his ex-wife to admit, at least, to having had an affair with Governor Clinton, after she refused to lie about Hale. "You don't have to say that Clinton pressured David Hale to make the loan," McDougal urged. "You can just say you had a sexual affair with him. The election is coming up. That would be enough to destroy him. It would be enough to win the election"—for the Republicans. "There's a man named Hickman Ewing who works in the independent counsel's office, and he believes he can get Clinton on a sex charge before the election. If you will come in and do this, you can write your own ticket."

Was *this* the American way—at least the conservative way of the nineties? Again Susan refused—saving, as she saw it, the president of the United States from terrorists of another dimension: fanatical Republicans made even more livid by the failure of Bob Dole, the candidate whose nomination they unanimously welcomed at their convention in San Diego in mid-August, to make any headway in public opinion polls. Thus when in late August, as the Democratic Party's own convention came to its climax in Chicago, news spread of a new sex scandal erupting, the hearts of Clinton aides and supporters sank once again.

Would the Republicans and the increasingly tabloidized press *never* let go? Why could they not allow the president—whose popularity polls were now reaching record levels with the public—to just lead the nation, now that he had mastered the business?

Then, almost with relief, they realized it was not the president's head on the chopping block, but—in a supreme historical irony—that of his Svengali, Dick Morris.

Signing Welfare Reform

There was good reason why Democrats reveled in the fall of Dick Morris, at the climax of the Democratic National Convention on August 29: Morris's insidious influence in having gotten the president to sign the Personal Responsibility and Work Opportunity Reconciliation Act of 1996, or the Republican welfare reform bill, several days before.

The night he'd signed the punitive act, the president had poured forth his own agony and his bile in language Morris would never forget. "I had given him to believe that Lott would produce a somewhat better bill than finally emerged," Morris later candidly admitted. "I was wrong. The final bill did grant Medicaid to legal immigrants, but other cutoffs remained."

The president's fury had been undisguised. "He *loved* cutting off children," Clinton shouted at Morris—referring to Senate Majority Leader Trent Lott. "You should have seen his face. He was *delighted* that he could savage them, *delighted*." Then the president had switched to Morris's role. "You've given me biased polling on this bill. Did you ever ask if they want me to sign or veto a bill that would let three-year-old children starve, go hungry in the street, because their mother was cut off? You didn't ask that, did you? You didn't want to know the answer, did you? Did you ask if they wanted a father who waits his turn, waits for years to come here, works hard, is always employed, and suddenly gets hit by a truck? Did you ask if they wanted me to cut off benefits to his six-month-old baby now that he can't work? Did you ask that?" And the president answered for himself, "I bet you didn't."

Morris hadn't. But it didn't help. It was too late. The president had signed the bill, instead of holding out for better terms in the way that he had done over the government shutdown. George Stephanopoulos had warned that "signing the bill will cut the legs out from Democrats running against the extreme Gingrich Congress"; it might even lose Democrats the chance of winning back Congress—and *for what*? To follow the prescription of a Republican maverick who was still working with Senate Majority Leader Trent Lott? It was small wonder the president had felt ashamed and angry.

Peter Edelman, Clinton's assistant secretary of Health and Human Services, was gutted and resigned from the Clinton administration, later confiding that he saw the president's decision to sign the Republican version of the welfare bill as a mark of Clinton's "inveterate caution—that he wanted to make absolutely sure of re-election" by seizing Dole's last major possible weapon from his hands. Others, however, blamed Morris's gray and evil eminence, saying that Morris had become central to Clinton's re-election campaign, like James Carville in 1992, and that the president had not dared go against his advice.

"President Bill Clinton deprived the American poor of a sixty-one-year-old safety net Thursday when he signed into law a radical overhaul of the United States welfare system," the London *Guardian*'s Washington correspondent, Jonathan Freedland, had reported on August 23. "It was condemned by trade unions, women's groups, ethnic minorities and immigrant organizations as a betrayal of the Democratic Party's heritage and a shameless attempt by Clinton to outflank his Republican rival, Bob Dole." Moreover, Freedland predicted, "The law will antagonize the Democratic Party's traditional supporters, and is likely to provoke angry protests at next week's convention in Chicago."

It hadn't, in fact. Day after day the president had announced new programs and signed laws that demonstrated his right to a second crown. As he proclaimed on his whistle-stop train tour through the Midwest, with Chelsea his companion (while Hillary addressed the convention in Chicago), he'd halved the national deficit, had overseen an economic resurgence that had added ten million new jobs, had gotten the minimum wage increased to $4.75 per hour, had signed a bill guaranteeing the portability of medical insurance from one job to another, and was campaigning against teenage smoking and for school uniforms, as well as V-chips to enable parents to censor children's television-watching. He was proposing job retraining for workers and a $110 million middle class tax cut to help families save for education.

The president's charisma was undiminished, his charm overwhelming, his grasp of international issues now as strong as his grasp of domestic issues. There was no one in the country to match either his rhetoric or his energy. His train trip confirmed his star status: the big Arkansan who had shown such a feeble command of presidential power in his first two years now towered head and shoulders over his rivals. Newt Gingrich had barely been seen at the Republican convention, and Ross Perot's reemergence frightened only Dole. Nonetheless, Clinton's signing of the Republican welfare bill stuck in almost every Democratic craw—a bone that, like the presence of Dick Morris in the White House, could not be got out. Or so it seemed.

CHAPTER EIGHTY-TWO

THE FALL OF MORRIS

Dick Goes Bad

For some time Dick Morris's arrogance had made people anxious about his sanity. As the president continued his whistle-stop trip aboard what was called the *Twenty-first Century Express* (though using President Harry Truman's 1948 Pullman) and pressed the flesh of every human being at every stop (even remarking favorably on their dogs), Morris's arrogance had allowed the *Wall Street Journal*, no lover of the president, to headline a front page story "TOP STRATEGIST LOSES HIS GRIP ON CAMPAIGN."

Morris had clashed with Vice President Gore's chief of staff over the speech that disabled actor Christopher Reeve was scheduled to give to the Democratic Party National Convention in Chicago, and had tangled so angrily with adman Bob Squier over Indiana governor Evan Bayh's keynote address that Squier had stopped speaking to him. "I'm not arguing what I think," Morris had begun saying when challenged, "I'm arguing what I *know*." At his dentist's office Morris had brazenly pushed to the head of the line, saying he needed to be seen immediately, because he was "running the country." Morris had proposed that the first lady say of children's issues: "Bloom, little ones, wherever you are planted." Even Harry Thomason had shaken his head and remarked, "Dick's gone bad. Someone's gonna have to put him down." Not even Thomason—a Hollywood producer—could have dreamed how the put-down would happen, however.

Perhaps the most worrying evidence of Morris's Napoleonic posturing was his reaction to George Stephanopoulos's latest news. Material from a meteorite from Mars indicated the possibility, Stephanopoulos told him, of life on that planet. "This is huge. Huge," *Newsweek* reported Morris saying to Stephanopoulos. Life on Mars was "futuristic, millennial, spiritual—just the story for the man to lead the nation into the 21st century. It was so obvious: Clinton = future, Dole = past. Mars could be Clinton's New Frontier," as Stephanopoulos recalled the train of Morris's high-priced consultancy-thought. "I've got it," Morris blurted to Stephanopoulos after a couple of seconds: "We announce a manned mission to Mars." Invoking the summer's hit movie *Independence Day*, about a president who fights off space invaders, life on Mars was for Morris the ultimate triangulation: "Clinton as leader of the Earthlings, boldly going where no Democrat had ever gone before."

It was small wonder, in the circumstances, that Morris's latest dalliance, Sherry Rowlands, had begun to question the New Jersey pollster's sanity, after a rendezvous in a six-hundred-dollar-a-night suite at the Jefferson Hotel on Sixteenth Street in Washington, D.C.

The suite had been kept reserved for Morris's trips to the White House, and was paid for out of Clinton campaign funds. That Morris was a control freak who needed a woman to discipline him in the role of dominatrix Rowlands accepted, for two hundred dollars per hour. But Morris's growing megalomania, as well as his stories of the power he wielded over the president, worried her. Morris insisted that she listen in to his live telephone conversations with the president, and even revealed state secrets to her. Suppose she were to be threatened, or even rubbed out, for knowing too much? Rowlands had started, therefore, to keep a diary, as well as the tapes of Morris's messages setting up their trysts, in the same manner as Gennifer Flowers. Eventually, early in August 1996, she went to the same tabloid Gennifer Flowers had used to protect herself, *Star*. Sherry Rowlands would not be rubbed out. Rather, she would rub out the megalomaniac.

Handling the News

Photographed standing naked but for bath towels with Rowlands on the Jefferson hotel balcony, Morris was slated to be the latest star victim of *Star* magazine, which wrote up her sensational account and scheduled it to appear in the September 10 issue, after the convention. The *New York Post*, however, got wind of the *Star* report early. Checking first to ascertain that the story was not a hoax, the *Post* telephoned Morris on the afternoon of August 28 for his response. Their story would run the next day, they said:

the day on which the president was scheduled to accept his presidential renomination in Chicago.

Morris denied the allegations—skeptical that any newspaper, even a tabloid, could publish such a story without proof. But when told there was "documentation"—including a diary, tapes, and even a cashed check from him to Rowlands—Morris dialled the president.

Mike McCurry took the call.

"How should we handle this?" Morris asked, innocently.

"We?" McCurry replied. When Morris then attempted to fill McCurry in on the details, the press secretary stopped him in mid-sentence—not out of prudery, but because, in the long sorry saga of Starr's investigation of Whitewater, it was becoming apparent that the Republican prosecutor would subpoena anyone known to have known anything, at any stage, however secondhand, about anything that caught his interest. Moreover, given the swiftness with which bad news leaked—or was leaked—to the press, McCurry would all too soon be called to tell what he knew about it.

The president, meanwhile, was speaking to a large crowd at the Old Lighthouse in Washington Park, Michigan City, Indiana—energized by such renewed contact with ordinary people, of all generations. He was proud of his administration's accomplishments, and he could justly take pride in his efforts—efforts he promised to continue over the next four years so that "when the year 2000 comes around we will go roaring into the twenty-first century as the greatest nation in the world, with our best days before us." In Chicago, Al Gore was preparing to give one of the best speeches of his life—as Hillary, the night before, had given the best of hers, and Christopher Reeve, the night before that, of his. (Speaking slowly and quietly, the paralyzed Reeve had compelled everyone to listen carefully to a message "almost unbearably poignant," *USA Today* had reported.)

As the president got into the limousine that would take him to the helicopter pad from which he would be whisked to Chicago to give his own speech to the Democratic convention, he was told by Evelyn Lieberman of Morris's dilemma.

The president swallowed, at once furious and alarmed. Morris was his electoral talisman, the guarantor of his re-election—the man who, with Betsey Wright, had put him back in the Governor's Mansion after his defeat in 1980. It seemed so unfair, the night before his grand acceptance speech, on the cusp of becoming, as Morris's polls predicted, only the fourth Democrat in American history to serve two elected terms—and the first since Franklin D. Roosevelt.

Clinton recalled his own crisis, in New Hampshire in January 1992, after *Star* magazine's publication of the Gennifer Flowers story. Should Morris brazen it out? Or could the president do without him: the genius of the polling process, the great triangulator, the man who allowed him to peer into the dark soul of Republicanism in America?

Shrugging, the president gave his decision: that no one should jump to conclusions, until the truth was verified. If it was true, however, it was, as he put it, "not tolerable."

Morris Refuses to Go

Who would tell Morris he must go? It was Clinton's familiar nightmare. Morris had begged to speak with him personally, but the president couldn't bring himself to take the call—any more than he'd been able, until forced, to give the bad news to Surgeon General Elders. Once again, then, the horrid business of dismissal would have to be handled by someone else. Thus, as Morris became more and more distraught, asking why he had not heard from the president, Leon Panetta got White House counsel Jack Quinn to call and tell the "little shit" he should resign. Morris refused.

In his suite at the Sheraton Towers, Morris had invited his closest aides to a private dinner. "This thing will blow over," he had assured them. "The president and I have never been closer."

"Waiters proffered platters of shrimp and flutes of champagne," *Newsweek* afterwards wrote of the surreal tableau. "Morris played the benevolent pasha, presenting a young assistant with a chocolate-mousse birthday cake. At 8:30, he showed his guests the door. The vice president was speaking in an hour and a half. 'Folks, there's a show tonight,' Morris exclaimed. 'Go to the convention. Have a great time.'" He himself would watch it on television, with Eileen, his wife of twenty years.

Around 10 P.M. the president's second emissary knocked on the door—his former assistant Erskine Bowles, who was no longer in the administration and could talk the business through with Morris "off the record."

Bowles—whose wife had been to college with Eileen Morris—stayed almost all night. He suggested that Morris take a leave of absence until the matter blew over. Morris had already in recent weeks seemed to White

House staffers to be disturbed and not entirely capable of rational thought. "Why am I not hearing from the president on this matter?" he kept asking.

At 1:30 A.M. Jack Quinn, a tough Irish-American, appeared in person. Quinn demanded to know whether Morris thought he had a right to cast such a dark shadow over an otherwise triumphant convention. Morris countered by asking what right yellow journalists had to destroy him. "Morris seemed convinced he could talk his way out of the jam," *Newsweek* reported.

Eventually Morris agreed to resign—but only on his own terms. He must be paid his hundred-thousand-dollar cut on the August advertising budget that he considered was owed to him as chief consultant for the campaign; he should be spirited away on an aircraft so that Eileen would be spared the media frenzy that would ensue; he should be allowed to write, alone and without interference, his own resignation statement.

Only the last of these demands was feasible, at this moment—and even over this, Morris behaved like a crazy person, describing himself as similar to a Christian being thrown to the lions in Roman times. His friend and co-consultant Hank Sheinkopf reminded him that he was a Jew. Morris therefore removed the phrase—but refused to alter the line that he had been "deeply honored to help this president come back from being buried in a landslide."

All decorum seemed to go out the window as, at 7:30 A.M., Morris finally summoned his aides. "Eileen, standing amid the suitcases, talked to the early arrivals," *Newsweek* reported. "A professional litigator, she seemed more furious than sad. 'Clinton gets away with this s—t all the time,' she said. 'Why should Dick have to go?' [She was apparently unaware of a second bombshell, which would be revealed that day and featured in the next edition of *Star*: that Morris had yet another mistress, Barbara Jean Pfafflin, of Austin, Texas, with whom he'd conducted a fifteen-year-long affair, and by whom he had a love child.] Morris was still despondent over Clinton's silence. 'I would have hoped my friend would have at least called me,' he said."

Clinton never did call. Unable to speak for fury and emotion, Morris typed a farewell message on his laptop and projected it onto a screen. It thanked his staff for their loyal service, hoped they would continue to work with other White House consultants in his absence—though not with the "wolves"—and last, but not least, promised "to treat each of you generously and fairly in anything I might say or write." For, true to character, the political consultant had already secretly negotiated, in advance, a multi-million dollar book contract with Random House to write his White House story.

And with that, Morris stumbled into the corridor—and into Chelsea.

Svengali's Demise

Upstairs, on the thirty-first floor, Bill Clinton was fuming. "Do I need this today?" the president asked rhetorically, as he drew up, with his staff, a statement that would be released to the press once Morris had safely departed.

The president's words—unlike Morris's self-congratulation and tirade against "yellow journalism"—were remarkably gracious, and grateful. Clinton knew what he owed the New Jersey cad—and what he shared with him. They were both political warriors, one a battlefield chieftain, the other a shaman. They had courted similar demises.

Though neither the president nor Hillary had yet called Morris, Hillary did ask the White House staff not to gloat or rub in the Svengali's demise— indeed, she expressed anxiety lest Morris, if further humiliated, become suicidal. "Dick Morris is my friend, and he is a superb political strategist," the president wrote in the statement he proposed to make. "I am, and always will be, grateful for the great contributions he has made to my campaigns, and for the invaluable work he has done over the past two years."

Informed of Morris's departure from Chicago, in ignominy, the president then reflected on his own good fortune. There, but for the grace of God, he himself might have been exiting the convention, he reflected. And thousands, perhaps tens of thousands, also breathed a sigh of relief that it was Morris, not the president, who had been caught *in flagrante*.

THE DEBATES

CHAPTER EIGHTY-THREE

DOLE'S PRAYERS
ARE NOT ANSWERED

Life Without Morris

A few weeks before his fall from grace Dick Morris had discussed the business of presidential greatness with the president, and had given his own view: that without a war, Bill Clinton could not hope to be considered in the top tier of presidents, from George Washington and Abraham Lincoln to FDR. Nevertheless, he could hope to rise from the third rank and be included in the second tier of presidential "greats," if he continued his popular, centrist stewardship in his second term—under Morris's guidance.

Without Morris, now, Clinton recognized that he would have to face the election alone. Had he not triumphed in 1992 without Morris, though? As the president and first lady boarded the same election bus that had taken them across America after the 1992 New York convention, all the signs pointed to victory by an overwhelming margin in November—as long as the presidential debates led to no unexpected tumble.

It had been intended that there be four presidential debates, starting on September 26 in St. Louis, Missouri. Fearful that Ross Perot would eat into his ailing popular support, however, Bob Dole had contested Perot's right to participate as an independent in the debates. The Presidential Debate Commission, composed of six Democrats and six Republicans, had declared Perot had "no reasonable chance" of winning and had accepted Dole's argument that Perot be excluded, along with twenty-one other independent presidential candidates (from socialists to prohibitionists) on ballots across the country. In other words, at Dole's insistence, it would be one-on-one combat in the presidential debates arena.

The president's preference for just two debates between the two main candidates, plus one vice presidential debate, was then accepted by Donald Rumsfeld on behalf of Dole: the first debate to be held on October 6, 1996, in the Bushnell Theater in Hartford, Connecticut—after renewed but vain legal attempts by Perot to be allowed to join in, or have the debates stopped.

Former senator Dole was now the undisputed underdog. Under the "no reasonable chance" rule, the nominee of the Natural Law Party, John Hagelin, was heard to say, mockingly: "I would exclude Bob Dole"—for in Hagelin's view Dole had no more hope of beating Clinton than he himself did.

Republican Party chairman Haley Barbour was equally pessimistic: "Bob Dole is a plainspoken, humorous man. He is not the television performer Bill Clinton is and never will be. Bill Clinton could sell Fords to Chevrolet dealers. He is the first politician in history who has perfected the ability to cry in just one eye. So there is nobody that can expect theatrical talent comparable to Clinton. . . . "

Most impartial journalists, in truth, had already written off the Republican contender and his vice presidential candidate, Jack Kemp. In sum, "it will take an improbable Dole Exocet against the fast-moving Clinton battleship," the *Financial Times* correspondent Jurek Martin reported, "to prevent the incumbent from sailing back home to the White House on November 5."

On the debates, therefore, rested Dole's last hope of victory.

Weariness Sets In

Weariness in the Clinton camp was setting in, however—with growing accusations of campaign contribution unfairness, even malfeasance, including rumors that nights in the Lincoln Bedroom in the White House had been used to drum up funds. Doug Sosnik recalled how, without Morris's warnings of doom, "We just kind of played out the clock. We're kinda outta gas. The campaign finance stuff started to dribble its way into the press. The press was bored"—and beginning to sympathize with Dole's predicament.

"It was hard getting Clinton ready for those debates," Sosnik remembered. "First of all, it requires a tremendous amount of discipline. And it's like doing your homework—who needs it? Fortunately, we got Senator Mitchell in there, who really worked him over—gave him his wake-up call, that he had to take this seriously, or he could lose. So we did mock debates, on mock sets, staffed up—hunkering down, doing run-throughs for two or three days in advance."

Thanks to the president's intensive training and rehearsal, Dole—whose forté in the Senate was his cutting one-liner—had but one chance to fire an Exocet in the first debate, when the questioner, Public Broadcasting anchorman Jim Lehrer, asked the challenger to comment on the president's ethics. As the Clinton team trembled in their control booth, Dole declined to do so; there would be no Exocet, at least in terms of an attack on the president's character, or White House ethics, in Connecticut. Though younger voters seemed tempted by Dole's promise of a 15 percent income tax cut and a steep reduction in capital gains tax (the former senator failed to explain how this could be reconciled with budget deficit reduction), older voters and "soccer moms" were overwhelmingly supportive of the president's references to his efforts to fight crime, tobacco use, and violence on TV, and his promises to protect Medicare.

Worst of all for Dole, some 20 percent *fewer* viewers watched the debates than in 1992—the lowest figure for thirty years. Among those who did, however, the president scored a 5–3 slam. By excluding Perot, Dole had, unintentionally, removed the very lure that might have guaranteed high viewing figures. As a result, Clinton's lead, in a number of polls, now topped twenty points. "Is It Over?" *Newsweek* headlined its cover, on its next edition. Inside, the headline asked: "Does Dole Have a Prayer?"

Wonkism at Its Best

Three days later, Al Gore trounced vice presidential contender Jack Kemp almost 2–1, in another substantive but non-theatrical debate in St. Petersburg, Florida.

"It may have been too elevated for casual citizens," one reporter concluded, but for policy junkies "it was Washington wonkism at its best: 90 minutes of tax policy, enterprise zones, Mexican peso devaluations, more tax policy"—the vice president looking distinctly presidential, if wooden, in his grasp not only of finance but of the other issues facing America.

Which left the final presidential debate, in San Diego, California—its format a town-hall style that favored, as viewers recalled, the big Arkansan whose ability to engage directly with people had made him legendary among twentieth-century presidents.

Dole had been urged by his advisers that he could no longer afford to be gentlemanly. He had, they urged, to turn aggressive—and wound his adversary. "We're going to tear his face off," the Dole campaign manager, Scott Reed, boasted. Tension rose, with wild predictions being made, "as often happens with prize boxing matches," the *New York Times* reported—leaving viewers expecting more than the elderly Bob Dole could possibly deliver.

Below the Belt

Warned in advance of the likely Republican tactics in the final debate, the president went into purdah in preparation for appearing in the University of San Diego ring on the evening of October 16, 1996. With Senator Mitchell again in the role of Bob Dole, the president rehearsed himself for Dole's likely bombardment. He did not have long to wait.

Having introduced himself as a good middle-class family man, the former Senate majority leader took the first swing, as expected. It went straight below the belt. The town hall question, from Jim Lehrer, was a mild one, concerning children, but the former senator transformed it into a withering attack. "There's no doubt about it that many American people have lost their faith in the government. They see scandals almost on a daily basis. They see ethical problems in the White House today. When you're the president of the United States, you have a public trust, and you have to keep that public trust. And I think now that trust is being violated."

Clinton's aides, in their viewing booth, held their breath. "I was praying for the hatchet man," Paul Begala related afterwards. "Soccer moms don't like hatchet men." Again and again they had coached the president to roll with the punch, not show anger. "I thought he [the president] was going to blow—he was seething," Dole's campaign manager said describing afterwards the president's body language in the first fifteen minutes of the ninety-minute debate. Asked if that was what he'd wanted, Reed replied, "Of course."

"The temptation was to go tit for tat—they wanted some drama, they wanted a circuit breaker," Doug Sosnik afterwards remarked. "But the polling is clear, the dial groups are clear, the focus groups are clear: people aren't interested in politicians going negative against one another." Saying he did not "want to respond in kind for all of these things," the president insisted he wanted to keep the focus on his administration's record and plans for the future. "No attack ever created a job or educated a child or helped a family make ends meet," he commented with presidential gravitas—and "no insult ever cleaned up a toxic waste dump or helped an elderly person."

Stung, the elderly contender claimed the president had presided over the "worst economy in a century"—a claim so outrageous that the president could only shake his head, sadly. In February, the president reminded the audience, Dole had said the opposite: that the country was experiencing the "best economy in thirty years." Then, when Dole complained that Clinton had tried to scare senior citizens with ads accusing Republicans of wanting to cut Medicare drastically, the president brushed aside the complaint and concentrated on the issue. "We need to reform it," he remarked of Medicare, "not wreck it."

With each jab and the president's blocking action, Dole looked more exhausted. Asked by a voter how he could relate to young people, the seventy-three-year-old said, "Wisdom comes from age, experience, and intelligence." To which the president responded that he didn't think the venerable Senator Dole was necessarily too old to be president, but he questioned, as he put it gently, "the age of his ideas."

The clock was ticking towards the end of this, the final presidential debate of 1996. It had been Bob Dole's last chance to turn the tables, and the president had simply outboxed him. Phone surveys quickly gave the viewing public's verdict: a 2–1 victory for the president.

Bad News for Dole

There were only eighteen days to go now.

"Poll after poll / points to bad news for Dole," one newspaper rhymed the darkening picture for the former senator. Dole confessed that he and his wife, Elizabeth, had prayed before the last debate and had agreed that whatever happened, it was God's will. Dole sounded brave but resigned.

A *Newsweek* pre-election survey, in the aftermath of the final debate, found the president at 52 percent, Dole at 29 percent, and Perot, the Reform Party candidate, at a mere 8 percent. A CNN-*USA Today* poll put Clinton's lead even higher, at 55-to-32—with 59 percent of respondents claiming that Dole was more "negative or nasty" in the campaign.

Without the benefit of Dick Morris, the polls had thus furnished the president with the information he needed to stick to the issues and avoid the trading of "bozo" insults that had soured the last days of President Bush's campaign in 1992.

It was a tremendous achievement.

In a misguided last-ditch effort, Bob Dole then headed to California, where his team had arranged to unleash one of the biggest barrages of negative television advertising ever broadcast in the final two weeks of an election.

The president's team, however, were equally well-funded, and followed a policy of responding to each and every Dole ad. Meanwhile, the president, on the campaign trail, continued to sound positive, optimistic, energetic.

At Dole's insistence the White House had finally released a twelve-page statement on the president's medical history. To Republican disappointment the president had as yet no history of high blood pressure, diabetes, tuberculosis, sexually transmitted disease, cancer, stroke, or heart disease. He'd undergone an HIV test for insurance purposes in 1990, and the result had been negative. He had only just turned fifty on August 19, and appeared to be in rude good health. The nation was at peace. The Olympic Games, despite the as-yet unresolved bombing incident, had proved a huge success in American trophies, viewership, and financial gains. Economic indicators were good, crime statistics down, the deficit slashed in two. Home ownership was up. Gingrich was the most despised politician in the country, his Contract With America a distant and embarrassing memory.

Could the Democrats, on the back of a now popular president, win back the House and the Senate? A net gain of only three seats, after all, would restore the Senate to Democratic control. A mere nineteen would do it in the House.

Finnegan's Wake

Hopes rose—as did the president's morale. Yet at this moment, heading for seemingly certain victory in the 1996 election, Bill Clinton still worried about the relentless predations of the religious right—particularly the Christian Coalition.

Why was the Christian right so opposed to him? He had, after all, stewarded a veritable *Wirtschaftswunder* in which employment had reached record levels, while the national deficit was halved. He had mastered the business of foreign affairs by talking softly but firmly while wielding America's big stick. He had learned to handle Congress effectively, and was holding up a proud, positive, forward-looking, articulate, and compassion-ate vision of America at the cusp of the twenty-first century—a vision that made Robert Dole look small, incoherent, and unimaginative. "Bob Dole's unintelligible campaign—the 'Finnegan's Wake' of presidential politics—was premodern in its indifference to the rhetorical dimension of the mod-ern presidency," wrote conservative columnist George Will on the eve of the election, "and postmodern in its randomness. His contention that the liberal media made matters worse called to mind the sign on the ruins of an ancient British church: 'Anyone damaging these ruins will be prosecuted.'"

Lauding the half-crazed Barry Goldwater, who "lost 44 states but brought conservatism from the fringe to the center of America's political conversation," Will sniffed at Clinton's "low, dishonest campaign" as being "fueled by financial corruption and nourished by immigrants rushed onto voting rolls by naturalization procedures that trashed the idea of citizen-ship"—unable to see a single redeeming feature in the president's steward-ship either of the economy or of international stability.

What, Clinton had cause to wonder, could ever persuade such diehard antagonists that he was doing a reasonable, indeed magnificent job in the White House after a flaky start? He'd learned the vital importance of an effective chief of staff—just as Hillary had learned she could not be co-president. She was now performing her role of first lady with distinction—aware that she could be a committed patron of social causes, but not policy-maker, unless elected. Meanwhile, the president had learned to han-dle major crises with aplomb, and was gaining an appreciation of the dan-ger of religiously inspired jihadists and of terrorism far deeper than the Republicans, who had resisted the Clinton administration's urgent anti-terrorism bill tooth and nail. Moreover, along with his remarkable intelli-gence, did not the president maintain an extraordinary connection with ordinary Americans, despite the isolating nature of the West Wing?

"We now know how to mix drugs in a way that has more than doubled the life expectancy for people with HIV and AIDS in only four years," the president said on the campaign trail, carrying a message of optimism and hope in the progress being made in science, technology, and medicine. "We now know that for the first time in history, laboratory animals with their spines severed have shown movement in their lower limbs because of nerve transplants. . . ." If we can do that for people, we can revolutionize life in America. . . ." Watching him in action, Maureen Dowd was awed again by the president's energy, optimism, knowledge, intellect, and connection with ordinary Americans. "Mr. Clinton treats the rope line like a revival meeting," she wrote. He "gathers impressive testimony in 10 minutes shaking hands: a professor who, thanks to a Bill Clinton grant, says he will cure Parkinson's disease; a man who, thanks to Bill Clinton's family-leave law, can adopt a baby without his wife losing her job. There are moments when you fear the president is about to start laying on hands. After an El Paso rally he was so eager to get close to the faithful that he stepped forward, inside the rope. The Secret Service had to untangle his legs."

Yet for all this the president remained an object of seemingly unmitigated hate among religious conservatives in America—unable, it seemed, to appease their hostility whatever he did, and however well he did it. *Why?*

CHAPTER EIGHTY-FOUR

A QUESTION
OF CHARACTER

The President's Integrity Attacked

As election day approached, most survey polls still showed the president holding on to a double-digit lead over Bob Dole, with Ross Perot, Ralph Nader, and other independents trailing—but there was evidence, also, that Dole's savage attacks on President's Clinton's "character" and the ethics of the White House were having an effect.

Presidential "character" had become a uniquely American feature in election campaigning, as befitted a nation that had overthrown monarchy, declared its independence, and instituted a system of four-year terms for the chief executive and commander-in-chief. Two centuries into its democratic experiment, the symbolic significance of the president's, or potential president's, personality and integrity still counted with many voters, as much as, or more than, his political agenda. And relentlessly, day after day in the final two weeks of the campaign, Bob Dole hammered the president on the subject, dropping all pretense of advancing a Republican agenda in order to cast further suspicion on the president's tangled dealings in Whitewater, the questionable contributions to his campaign by foreign donors, and the numerous scandals that attached to his meteoric career, including the Arkansas troopers' revelations, Paula Jones, and a widespread sense that the fifty-year-old president was not done with women. As John Carlin reported from the Dole campaign rally in California, "In the last days of his campaign, Mr. Dole has hit upon a message that resonates with the Republican faithful. It is 'character,' of which Mr. Dole says he has much and President Clinton has little. Where Mr. Clinton has remained weakest in the campaign was on the question of public trust, mountains of allegations having rained down upon the White House concerning illicit deals of one shape or another. So barely a mention of Mr. Dole's fabled 15 percent tax cut in San Diego or elsewhere on his '96-hour Non-Stop Victory Tour' but lots of suggestions that if Mr. Clinton is re-elected 'shades of Whitewater' will haunt him during his second term. Revealingly, however, when Mr. Dole made that point it sounded more like a prediction than a warning."

Staying Positive

For Bill Clinton and his campaign team, presidential "character" was the hardest issue to deal with, and to their credit, the team remained determined to ignore it while focusing equally relentlessly on their positives, such as a booming American economy, now in its sixty-eighth month of recovery; a raft of small but important legislative achievements at home, from gun control to education grants; peace abroad; and a determination to build "a bridge to the future" rather than harping on the past. Polls showed the president would still win by this strategy, but that Dole's personal attacks were definitely spoiling Clinton's pitch.

Such character-baiting, foreign observers noted, seemed somewhat hypocritical, since Dole was hardly a paragon of virtue. "As for philandering, Mr. Dole is no saint," Carlin explained to readers of the London *Independent*. "Possibly, if the unverified stories are true, Mr. Clinton has been more prolific, but Mr. Dole did have an affair some thirty years ago, towards the end of his first marriage, with a nurse at the hospital where he recovered from his grievous war wounds after the Second World War." That affair had ended his marriage—"Mr. Dole told his first wife it was all over with a typically terse 'I want out' and abandoned her and his teenage daughter, begging the question: what, if anything, can Mr. Dole teach Mr. Clinton about 'family values'?"

Nor was the former Senate majority leader a paragon in terms of campaign funding ethics, for it was "on the record," Carlin pointed out, "that Mr. Dole has been far from immune to the blandishments of big business during his senatorial career. No company has contributed more campaign money to Mr. Dole than the Gallo wine company. In exchange, Mr. Dole went to great lengths to introduce legislation specifically, and successfully, aimed at improving Gallo's profits. Mr. Dole also used his position to bolster the business of Archer Daniels Midland, a giant food company, which reciprocated not only by way of large campaign donations. In 1982, the chief executive of Archer Daniels sold a condominium in Florida—where Mr. Dole spent last night watching the election returns—to him at below market price . . . "

Such realism abroad, however, found little traction in America, where the culture wars of the 1980s still simmered beneath and on the surface of political life. The ever louder, ever more strident conservative Christian right demanded sacrificial victims for what it saw as the lasting corruption of American moral standards in the 1960s. A quintessential baby boomer such as Bill Clinton was thus meat for the hunters, however hypocritical their own candidates for office.

Dole's sell-out to such fundamentalists, therefore, disappointed the president. Clinton genuinely admired Dole for his war service and his courage in surviving his grievous wounds. Had Dick Morris still been his *eminence grise*, Bill Clinton might well have countered Dole's negative campaigning with his own, as he had done in Arkansas when subjected to vicious personal attacks by opponents, but Morris was disgraced and there was no one of Morris's maverick, evil-eyed ilk on the Clinton team. Thus the president held to the high ground and refused to attack Dole personally, grateful at least that Dole seemed too late in his switch in tactics to affect the outcome of the presidential election.

Thinking of the Alamo

Looking back, the president saw his fight for deficit reduction, at the very start of his presidency, as his signature achievement—indeed, at one rally he had said that when he fought Republicans over the budget "I thought of the Alamo."

That he had had to fight his own Democratic Party to achieve that deficit reduction, and without a single Republican vote to assist him, remained a supreme irony, given the now-booming American economy. Dole still talked deficit reduction, but economists both on Wall Street and in academia who put Dole's tax-cut figures through their computerized projections warned that a Dole-Kemp ticket triumph would cost the U.S. Treasury $548 billion in lost revenues in the years 1997–2002, and all pretense of a balanced budget by 2002 would have to be abandoned, whereas the president's more modest middle-class tax cuts could be paid for, and leave the nation in surplus (which they did).

It was small wonder the president therefore shook his head at Republican tactics. By publicly trashing the president's "character" and integrity, Bob Dole was presenting himself as "a man of my word." "Maybe," commented A.M. Rosenthal in the *New York Times*, "but in his case [it is] a frightening thought. That means he would keep his word to fight the right of abortion, keep a cuckoo-land position that tobacco was not really addictive, keep fighting gun control, keep struggling for a deficit-boosting tax policy he once said was like playing football without a helmet, keep an anti-immigrant line so nasty that he would throw little kids out of school unless their parents had the right immigration papers. . . . "

That President Clinton could survive such smear tactics was, thanks to the buoyant economy, never in real doubt at such a late stage; but whether Democrats aspiring to wrest back control of Congress would survive the tsunami of such relentless character-bashing now became increasingly uncertain as, in the closing days of the campaign, Republicans began warning voters that putting Democrats back in control of Congress would give President Clinton a "blank check" in his second term. Huge sums of campaign finance that would ordinarily have gone into Dole's final blitz were now switched to help Republican senatorial and congressional advertising. "Republican despondency was evident yesterday as congressional candidates continued running TV ads warning of a Democrat controlled Congress with Clinton in office—instead of vote-for-Dole rhetoric," foreign journalists noted—with corresponding polls showing a lessening likelihood that either chamber of Congress would change hands. Thus, although Bill Clinton looked set to become the first Democratic president since FDR to win a second term, it seemed all too possible that Republicans would also make history: the first time since 1930 they would hold House and Senate majorities in two successive Congresses.

Rejigging the schedule

The president was all too aware of the problem, and did his best to counteract it. "We are rejigging our whole schedule for these final days of campaigning with the Christian Coalition in mind," Clinton confided to a

British journalist, informing him of a new Democratic Party $2-million-a-day advertising blitz across the Bible Belt, featuring a non-partisan Baptist preacher. "The turnout is going to be the key to this thing," the president explained. "And that puts me in a box," he admitted—for every appearance of the president pulled Democratic Party workers away from their local battles, in which issues were constantly and relentlessly dumbed down to a Christian Coalition hit-list.

The air-waves battle, in sum, had become no longer a battle between the president and the former Senate majority leader. Instead, its thrust had been displaced to fund and press a titanic struggle between activist conservatives and progressives at a congressional level: a fight that would have enormous consequences for the country—and for Bill Clinton. Should the Republicans manage to hold on to their majorities in both the House and the Senate, they would, the president feared, be able to continue to pursue their seemingly unending ethical investigations into Whitewater, while opening new ones into Democratic campaign funding allegations, and possibly even other claims.

A Historic Moment

Flying from New Hampshire, after campaigning in twenty-two states and having that final day stopped in Cleveland, Ohio; in Lexington, Kentucky; in Cedar Rapids, Iowa; and in Sioux Falls, South Dakota, the president found himself exhausted but still not ready for sleep as his plane landed in Little Rock in the very early hours of November 5, 1996. Conscious of the historic moment in his extraordinary life's journey, he left Hillary to sleep and joined Leon Panetta and his political campaign director, Doug Sosnik, in their hotel suite, where they played hearts for four hours till dawn came, and the polling stations opened.

Sosnik won at cards. Despite his legendary dislike of losing, the president wasn't concerned about his loss, or even, it appeared, his likely triumph in the presidential election—where latest surveys suggested he would win a landslide victory. Rather, his nervousness betrayed a mix of historical pride and anxiety over the future.

Aboard Air Force One, Clinton had already mapped out with Leon Panetta (who had told the president he would be stepping down as chief of staff to return to California) his second-term cabinet. It was the "what ifs," however, that still peppered his sleepless brain. A year ago, he'd been trailing

Dole 10 percent in survey polls and among bookmakers. What if Gingrich and Dole hadn't overreached by shutting down the U.S. government? *What if General Colin Powell had run?*

The vagaries of political warfare—its vocabulary studded with military terms—were predictable and yet unpredictable: fair and yet unfair, idealistic and yet steeped in cynicism. . . . Though he would know by nightfall the full extent of his landslide victory, and whether he had achieved his target of a clear majority over Dole, Perot, and other contestants combined, he knew already that a big victory could only inflame his enemies—those who could see no good in him, or in his policies, or in his party. It would, he felt, lead them to redouble their efforts at demonization, regardless of the likely injury to the fabric of American society and to American political discourse. Who knew where the Atwater-molded Republican attack machine might strike? Down what nightmare alleys might a future, Christian-coalition-backed *über*righteous Republican administration lead a future America?

Emerging a few hours later from Little Rock's Precinct 476E, his designated polling station that morning, and looking at the streets and houses of the small capital city of the little southern state that had been his home for most of his adult life, Bill Clinton could not but feel tenderness. Yet also, it had to be admitted, somewhat estranged—not only as a result of his four years' absence in Washington, which had necessarily taken him away from the ordinary people of his state, but because times themselves in Arkansas in the 1990s had changed.

Once, seemingly long ago, Bill Clinton had longed for the comparative security of the landlocked former territory, with its rivers, its Delta plains, its mountains; its hamlets, villages, towns, and small cities; its steamy summers, its twisters and storms; its eccentrics, its characters, its ordinary and extraordinary folks, from farmers to retailers, clerks, and lawyers; its congregations in churches, town halls, legislature. He had felt at times he knew *all* its citizens, the state was so tiny and his recall so prodigious, and that for the most part people wished him well: knowing that he was smart, if perhaps self-indulgent and overly ambitious, and that, in the end, he was sincere in wanting his state to make progress and to prosper in the modern world. In a word, such people—friends and fellow citizens of the state— were, he had always felt, forgiving of his failings and ultimately appreciative of his strengths, to the point where they had elected him five times as their governor.

The initial hostility of Washington, D.C., to his presidency in 1993 and the media's chorus of ridicule at his continuous missteps had thus come as a terrible shock, both to him and to Hillary. It had caused him to desperately miss his fellow Arkansans, whether in the First Baptist Church choir, at Emmanuel Church, or his office in the midst of the Capitol building—the daily interaction with people of all stations in life: people whom he could read as straightforwardly as he could read a book.

Now, however, William Jefferson Clinton was aware as the forty-second president, surrounded by a perpetual retinue of staffers and Secret Service agents, he'd lost some of that forgiving support in his native state. Hard as he'd tried to make his people proud of him—the first Arkansan ever to occupy the Oval Office—and hard as he'd tried to bring people together in a more centrist, less partisan, less ideologically driven approach to modernizing America as a New Democrat, he'd failed in his own home state to an alarming degree. The state now had a Republican governor, in succession to Jim Guy Tucker—a *Baptist minister*. Across the South, generally, the president's personal popularity had risen—even Texas looked like casting its vote for him—but he had also become more than ever a lightning rod, a scapegoat in the struggle of the unforgiving American puritanical soul.

The Troopergate scandal, the Paula Jones lawsuit, the Whitewater investigations: individually they might not amount to what he would later call "a hill of beans," but collectively they bespoke a nagging resentment, at once envious and punitive—and that resentment had, with the very swiftness and openness he had instanced in his inaugural address, been peddled and broadcast across the nation, finding no majority of takers, but a significant groundswell of disaffected voters nevertheless. As the president had finally gotten his bearings, the majority of voters had begun to give credit to his more efficient administration, and his more centrist agenda—especially the president's new epicenter in "American values": that hugely symbolic realm of politics, where "the family" was king. Yet the president's very shift to the center was, among diehard Republicans, also seen as a form of theft: that a wily Arkansas Democrat, with the help of a Republican strategist, had stolen into their camp at night and made off with their traditional weapons, leaving them naked and ridiculous.

Oklahoma City *had* thus marked the pivotal point in Bill Clinton's presidential fortunes. The turnaround in public support had, via the government shutdown, led to an unassailable lead over potential rivals for the presidency in 1996—Republican, Democrat, or independent. As a political leader he had come to tower, literally, over his opposition, and he seemed likely to be remembered not only for winning a second presidential term as a Democrat but for the success he had brought to America, globally and domestically, in the mid-1990s—from technological innovation to the triumph of the Olympic Games in Atlanta.

Yet for all this he had still not stilled the relentless number of religiously backed extremists baying for the president's scalp as a sixties-era scapegoat. The question was: what would the mullahs of Republicanism do next, in their attempt to unseat him as president of the United States?

The most extraordinary feature of the mid-nineties, in a way, was that the more the president learned to do better as chief executive, after his early tribulations and the loss of Congress, and the more respected he became throughout the world, the shriller and more hateful had become the tone of his conservative enemies, and the more poisonous their personal allegations—as if desperate that he *not* become the president of their country he aspired to be. Why, Tabitha Soren of MTV had recently asked him, in a campaign television interview, "do some people dislike you so much?"

Any other president might have found the question disrespectful but, if the president did, he had on camera swallowed his annoyance. "When I was governor of my state, I got elected five times and would regularly get two-thirds of the vote," he said, noting how there would nevertheless "always be a core of people who were intensely opposed to my policies."

Soren was unconvinced. After all, she pointed out, "People didn't necessarily like Reagan's policies, either, but it didn't seem to get personal. Do you think it has to do with your generation?"

"Perhaps. And it may be—"

The president had faltered, unsure how far to take Ms. Soren's question. "It may have more to do with the way people are talked about now," he had said—the tendency, in modern celebrity culture, to either demonize or adore. He himself had "tried so hard—especially since the Oklahoma City bombing, which I say had a profound impact on our country and on me—I have really tried so hard to bring a sense of civility and decency back into public discourse." But it was, he confessed, an uphill struggle. Perhaps it had always been so. Politics "has always been a rough-and-tumble business," he pointed out, "and people have always disagreed. And if you go back to the early 1800s, for example, it's a period of real tumult in our country, what was said and done and how much people had it pretty rough." It was said of his namesake, Thomas Jefferson, that he wanted to "kill religion in America," and that his election "would end godliness in America. So we've always had some of this, but I think we need to resist it."

For himself, the president had made clear, he remained undaunted by the arrows of his Republican enemies. He was, in his way, like Gulliver in Lilliput. He would try to look beyond his tormentors, and take comfort in the difference he was able to make in the lives of ordinary citizens who urged no Christian Coalition to proclaim their righteous bile, but would come up to him quietly on his bus and train journeys and tell him how they had benefited from his policies. "I've got a home because of one of your programs," one might say, or "I've gotten a job since you were here," or "I'm on one of your college loans."

These personal reassurances by ordinary Americans had meant a great deal to him as president, Clinton had explained to Soren with sincerity— for they allowed him to swallow the natural feelings of resentment, even despair, at the hateful things his opponents and enemies said about him. "When you live in a time which is really rough," he'd summed up, philosophically, "with no holds barred, and a lot of people seek personal advantage by what I call the politics of personal destruction, you have to be always, always, always defining yourself and the quality of your life by what is inside. And you can't confuse who you are and the quality of your own life with whatever is going on in the day to-day headlines. It's destructive. Otherwise you shrivel and become little."

As the poet John Milton had put it in *Paradise Regained*, more than three centuries before, leadership was a "wreath of thorns" that "Brings dangers, troubles, cares and sleepless nights/To him who wears the regal Diadem,/When on his shoulders each man's burden lies;/ For therein stands the office of a King,/His Honour, Virtue, Merit and chief Praise,/ That for the Public all this weight he bears."

The past four years in the White House had been an epic journey— vastly more difficult than he had ever imagined as governor of little Arkansas. Agonizingly slowly he had learned to don the mantle of command, without which good policies and noble ideals were useless. Once he'd done that, he'd finally been able to show his skills as a statesman, a commander-in-chief, a careful guardian of his nation's financial fortunes, and—like presidents Kennedy and Reagan—an embodiment of national optimism and hope. Losing control of Congress had woken him to the perils facing America internally and from abroad, expressed in hate-filled rhetoric and acts of homegrown and international terrorism. With their callous indifference to other people's suffering or pain, terrorists like Timothy McVeigh were now the single most potent threat to peace and coexistence in the modern world. Guiding his country forward so that it combated such extremists yet did not become embroiled in wider struggles it could not win was now priority number one. Manfully dealing with Haiti and North Korea and Bosnia, as well as Gingrich's half-crazed assault on the U.S. government, he had shown how American superpower *should* be wielded in the postmodern world.

Against Republican predictions of economic disaster Clinton had restored the United States to prosperity and control of its spiraling deficit; had quietly laid the groundwork for the expansion of NATO in central Europe while keeping Russia friendly, and its prolific arsenal of nuclear weapons under lock and key. America's status in the world, as the last superpower, was now as high as or higher than it had ever been—a tribute to his learning skills, in a perplexing, post-communist world. Civil strife in Northern Ireland was, thanks in large part to his leadership, on the wane, after decades of violence between Protestants and Catholics. In the Middle East, too, there seemed a prospect of eventual reconciliation between Palestinians and Israelis.

More than he realized, he had begun to achieve greatness as president of the United States—the shepherd of his nation in troubling new times. In contrast to his successor's more disciplined start, followed then by a chain of disastrous misjudgments, missteps, and failures, from Iraq to Katrina, Clinton's accomplishments would merit almost universal admiration among historians, as one of the finest performances of an American chief executive in the late twentieth century. He had kept his country prosperous, safe, idealistic, optimistic, and—once having found his feet—out of foreign wars. He had learned to wield a big stick over those who would threaten the peace, while using America's authority to bring warring factions to the negotiating table, and then provide the forces necessary to police the peace. Abroad, such conduct would place him in the pantheon of great leaders, and at home looked set to garner for him re-election as the first Democratic president since Franklin Roosevelt to win a second term.

Not so, however, among extremists and die-hard opponents—those who reveled in sneering rhetoric and malicious character assassination. As the president told Ms. Soren, even in these toughest of times for a leader trying to do his job in the White House while assailed daily by hate-mongers on radio, in the press, and in the pulpits of the right, "the president should always be trying to be bigger than he is and lifting the country up. And you just have to put that [*ad hominen* hostility] out of your mind; you just have to let it go," he'd told Ms. Soren. He had his flaws, like all mortals—and all presidents—but believed the good in him outweighed the bad. "I can't do anything about what happened yesterday or even an hour ago; you just have to let that stuff go and keep trying to lift the country up."

Could he but avoid the poisoned arrows of his opponents, that was what he proposed to do for the next four years if re-elected on November 5, 1996, as the forty-second president of the United States of America.

ACKNOWLEDGMENTS

This sequel to *Bill Clinton, An American Journey*—my account of William Jefferson Clinton's early years up to the White House—has had a somewhat protracted gestation. The initial manuscript was too long for publication, but thanks to the help of my friend the biographer Larry Leamer, I was able to cut it to a more readable size. Mark Booth, my editor at Random House UK, remained committed to the enterprise throughout, as did my English agent, Bruce Hunter. My New York agent, Owen Laster of the William Morris Agency, also remained unwaveringly supportive, as was his successor (on Owen's retirement), Mel Berger. And Peter Osnos, the founder and editor-at-large of PublicAffairs, backed by his distinguished outside editor Bill Whitworth, agreed to publish the much-shortened *Bill Clinton: Mastering the Presidency* in the United States. To them all, I am deeply indebted.

In addition to thanking also my U.S. publisher, Susan Weinberg; my in-house editor, Lindsay Jones; and the whole staff of PublicAffairs for their faith in my Clinton project, I'd like to thank some of the people who assisted me in compiling this second Clinton volume. I was wonderfully supported, as before, by the staff and fellows of the John W. McCormack Graduate School of Policy Studies at UMass Boston, under its provisional dean, Dr. Edmund Beard, and then its founding dean, Steve Crosby, as well as Assistant Dean Sandy Blanchette. To them and to Candyce Bushnell, Jamie Ennis, Mike McPhee, Padraig O'Malley, Sheila Gagnon, Donna Haig Friedman, Carol Hardy-Fanta, Erica White, John McGath, Phyllis Freeman, Margery O'Donnell, Elaine Werby, Erika Kates, Julia Tripp, Pat Peterson, and all my colleagues at MGS, my lasting thanks. To Bill Baer and his wonderful colleagues in the university's Healey Library, my gratitude also, as always.

For the necessary research in Washington, D.C., I was given visiting scholar posts in the history departments of George Washington University and Georgetown University. At Georgetown University I would like to thank Professor David Painter, in the history department, who sponsored me, and Professor Alex Sens, in the classics department, who housed me, as well as Professors Clive Foss, Vicky Pedrick, Charlie McNelis, Cathy Keesling, James O'Donnell, and Maxine Weinstein for their company, support, and encouragement. At George Washington University I'd like to thank Professor Marc Saperstein, who sponsored me, and Professors Ron Spector, Dane Kennedy, Ed Berkowitz, and Hope Harrison, and the history department, who made my time in Washington so fruitful. Senate historian Donald A. Ritchie was also especially helpful.

Contemporary history and biography cannot be written without oral history—especially where the documents relating to a presidency are not available. Declassified White House and Clinton administration documents only became accessible, in part, in 2006, too late for this work. Moreover, the presidential oral history project being conducted by the University of Virginia for the Clinton Presidential Library (and thus, the National Archives) will not be available to scholars before the next decade. I am thus especially indebted, as a historian, to those witnesses, colleagues, friends, foes, and observers who allowed me to interview them for this work, especially former congressman and presidential chief of staff Leon Panetta. I'd like to thank, too, former OMB Director Alice Rivlin, former Treasury secretary Larry Summers, former HUD director Henry Cisneros, former national security adviser Tony Lake, former surgeon general Joycelyn Elders, former army chief of staff General Gordon Sullivan, former deputy transition director and assistant health secretary Judy Feder, former White House personnel director David Watkins, former presidential campaign director Doug Sosnik, former assistant education secretary Scott Fleming, former senior presidential adviser and now congressman Rahm Emanuel, former gubernatorial chief of staff Betsey Wright, former presidential speechwriter David Dreyer, and distinguished journalists Stephen Hess, Tom Lippman, the late David Nyhan, John Brummett, Marvin Kalb, and Dan Moldea, as well as Jim Blair, Ann Henry, Cal Ledbetter, George Fisher, Cliff Jackson, Lynn Davis, Gene Lyons, Roy Reed, Jane Kirschner, Kerry Kirschner, Ernie Dumas, Burl Rotenberry, the late Frank White, Skip Rutherford, Jim Morgan, Joe Purvis, David Leopoulos, Paul Greenberg, Paul Root, John Ferguson, Jim Johnston, Al Witte, Billy Geren, Milt Copeland, and Glenda Cooper. In Arkansas, Becky Moore, George and Gail Hamilton, Audrey Burtrum-Stanley, Griff Stockley, Tom Dillard, and Rod Lorenzen were most helpful during my research trips, as was the late

Kevin Shepard in California. Without their contributions I simply could not have compiled this account—whose errors of understanding, judgment, and detail remain mine alone.

A number of excellent books have been written on aspects of the Clinton presidency, as listed in the bibliography; I am deeply indebted to their authors for their work and insight. I'm indebted also to the journalists whose contemporary reports provided such a vivid and for the most part accurate account of history in the making; their reports are fully footnoted. A special Clinton Conference was held by Hofstra University in November 2005—"William Jefferson Clinton: The 'New Democrat' From Hope." This proved enormously helpful in testing my understanding and account of the Clinton presidency, and I am most grateful to the organizers for the opportunity to meet personally and hear the views of participants such as Douglas Brinkley, Ted Widmer, Shirley Anne Warshaw, Peter Edelman, Richard Riley, Mickey Kantor, John Podesta, Paul Begala, Gene Sperling, and many others. The panels on the UN, presidential elections, Northern Ireland and Middle East peace processes, international economics, terrorism, Latin America and the Caribbean, the environment, Africa, the "New Democrat" direction, the press and media, education, Iraq, Russia and central Europe, liberalism, Congress, the vice presidency, humor and cartoons, speechwriting, Asia, defense and nuclear policy, rhetoric, the first lady, domestic economic policy, civil rights, culture, culture wars, labor, justice, humanitarian intervention, the 1994 midterm congressional election, the commander-in-chief's role, the constitution, welfare reform, family policy, impeachment, and science and technology provided a veritable kaleidoscope of perspectives on the Clinton presidency—as well as a reminder how fleeting and cursory any attempt at presidential biography is bound to be. John Harris and David Maraniss gave particularly interesting perspectives as journalist-chroniclers of the forty-second president in their panel for historians and biographers. Most heated, however, was the panel on failed health care reform, featuring Ira Magaziner and Bruce Vladeck. The conference—a model of its kind—was doubly notable for the appearance, halfway through, of Mr. Clinton himself, taking personal issue, from a raised podium and with jabbing finger, with criticisms made by some of the historians present!

Morale is as important to the biographer-historian as to a soldier. I could not have stayed the research-writing-publishing course without the love and affection of my partner and now wife, Dr. Raynel Shepard; and of my sons, Alexander, Sebastian, Nicholas, and Christian; or without the support of my friends Larry and Vesna Leamer, Mark and Judith Schneider, David and Lisa Chanoff, Paul and Alexandra Hans, David and Emily Polstein, Judy Rosenberg, Ilya and Rachel Schneider, Claudia Liebeskind and Rafe Blaufarb, Carlo and Shirley D'Este, Martin and Jane Brauer, Sam Pitroda, and others too numerous to name. The Washington Writers Group, under the aegis of veteran reporter Dan Moldea, was also unfailingly supportive—especially Dan Rapaport, Bob Merry, Jeff Stein, and David Kaiser. Thanks to George Scialabba I was able to obtain the services of Tara Masih, who helped subedit the first shortened version. No author could ask for more. It remains only to hope that *Bill Clinton: Mastering the Presidency* proves worthy of their collective faith.

NOTES

Page   *Chapter One*

5   "Here at the feet": David Dahl, "Bells ring in Clinton's arrival in D.C.," *St. Petersburg Times* (Florida), January 18, 1993.

5   "polycultural mass": James Ridgeway, Marc Cooper, and Dan Bischoff, "Showtime," *Village Voice*, February 2, 1993.

6   "they had a ball": *Jet*, February 1, 1993.

6   "a run-of-the-mill program": Ibid.

6   "Dylan sounded terrible": Greil Marcus, *Double Trouble: Bill Clinton and Elvis Presley in a Land of No Alternatives*, 2000, 56–57.

7   "kicked out marine": Donna Minkowitz, "High Anxiety," *Village Voice*, February 2, 1993.

7   "got there all by": Christopher Ogden, *Life of the Party: The Biography of Pamela Digby Churchill Hayward Harriman*, 1994, 439.

8   "Bill came up": Bill Turque, *Inventing Al Gore*, 2000, 256.

8   "As a White House FBI agent recalled": Gary Aldrich, *Unlimited Access: An FBI Agent Inside the Clinton White House*, 1996, 11.

8   "was because Vice President": Ibid.

8   "fucking bitch": Joyce Milton, *The First Partner*, 1999, 262.

8   "Sources I consider": Gary Aldrich, *Unlimited Access*, 11.

9   "Topic A": Sally Quinn, "Beware of Washington," *Newsweek*, December 28, 1992.

9   "women lawyers": Ibid.

9   "From the very beginning": *The New York Post*, December 5, 1998.

10   "were startled": Gail Sheehy, *Hillary's Choice*, 1999, 222.

10   "Avoid this crowd": Ibid.

10   "the word was": Ibid.

11   "throughout the transition": Ibid., 220.

11   "the woolly mammoth": Jonathan Alter, "Clinton's Challenge," *Newsweek*, November 30, 1992.

11   "The biggest problem": Ibid.

11   "Whoever managed": George Stephanopoulos, *All Too Human*, 1999, 114.

12   "The result": Elizabeth Drew, *On the Edge*, 1994, 18.

12   "another all-nighter": Stephanopoulos, *All Too Human*, 115.

12   "pattern for his Presidency": Drew, *On the Edge*, 18.

15   "Here on the pulse": Maya Angelou, *On the Pulse of Morning*, 1993.

16   "Bill and Hillary Clinton": Aldrich, *Unlimited Access*, 11.

16   "You fucking asshole": Sheehy, *Hillary's Choice*, 223, quoting "two knowledge-able sources who were present."

16   "Apparently": Aldrich, *Unlimited Access*, 11.

Chapter Two

17   "He'd be a valuable": Robert Reich, *Locked in the Cabinet*, 1997, 17.

18   "intellectual pragmatist": Bob Woodward, *The Agenda*, 1994, 71.

18   "What?": Ibid., 77.

19   "Clearly, budget making": Alice Rivlin, interview with the author, March 10, 2005.

19   "turning point": Larry Summers, interview with the author, January 5, 2005.

19   "all the principal": Robert Rubin, interview with Chris Bury, "The Clinton Years," *Frontline*, PBS television, 2001, accessible at http://www.pbs.org/wgbh/pages/frontline/shows/clinton/interviews and for tapes and transcript: http://www.pbs.org/wgbh/pages/frontline/shows/clinton/etc/tapes.html—hereafter, "The Clinton Years," PBS television.

19   "You all are": Robert E. Rubin and Jacob Weisberg, *In an Uncertain World: Tough Choices from Wall Street to Washington*, 2003, 119.

20   "You mean to": Woodward, *The Agenda*, 84.

20   "Alan Blinder and": Alice Rivlin, interview with the author, March 10, 2005.

20   "Look. There are a lot": Robert Rubin, interview with Chris Bury, "The Clinton Years," PBS television.

21   "I think my view": Larry Summers, interview with the author, January 3, 2005.

21   "There were some": Leon Panetta, interview with the author, January 20, 2005.

21   "Roosevelt was trying": Woodward, *The Agenda*, 91.

21   "The biggest problem": Panetta, interview with the author, January 20, 2005.

21   "I think what happened": Ibid.

22   "If the transition has": Charles O. Jones, *Passages to the Presidency*, 1998, 179.

Chapter Three

23   "I mean": Dee Dee Myers, interview with Chris Bury, "The Clinton Years," PBS television.

23 "He just went": Henry Cisneros, interview with the author, November 29, 2004.

24 "plans for going forward": Ibid.

24 "Mickey just has": Ibid.

24 "The confetti still": Warren Christopher, *Chances of a Lifetime*, 2001, 158.

25 "develop a transition": Ibid.

25 "the weary Clinton": Dan Balz, "Looking Ahead: At Home and Abroad; The Transition: Clinton Sidestepped Planners in Decision on Team Leaders," *Washington Post*, November 8, 1992.

25 "not expected": Linda Diebel, "Clinton tells America: 'We're in this together,'" *Toronto Star*, November 4, 1992.

26 "[t]he degree of squabbling": David Halberstam, *War in a Time of Peace*, 2001, 169.

26 "Unlike President Bush": "Clinton's indoctrination, transformation begins," *St. Petersburg Times* (Florida), November 6, 1992.

26 "We're all in this": Linda Diebel, "Clinton tells America," *Toronto Star*, November 4, 1992.

27 "We're a new": Ibid.

27 "We will ask": Ibid.

27 "a bloody, ugly": Gwen Ifill, "Clinton May Quickly Name Transition Chief in Effort to End Dispute within Staff," *New York Times*, November 6, 1992.

27 a history of transitions: Sally Quinn, "Making Capital Gains; Welcome to Washington, but Play by Our Rules," *Washington Post*, November 15, 1992. Galston would report three golden rules: define your mandate, appoint good people—and work on your "relationships" with power people, from Congress to industry.

27 "My view was": Paul Begala, interview with Chris Bury, "The Clinton Years," PBS television.

27 "he doesn't want": Al Kamen, "Choice for Chief of Staff Offers 'Loyalty and Trust'; McLarty a Clinton Friend Since Childhood," *Washington Post*, December 13, 1992.

28 "I had written": Stephen Hess, interview with the author, February 14, 2005.

28 "the worst transition": Ibid.

28 "Clinton so far": Al Kamen, Ruth Marcus, "Clinton Isn't Rushing on Transition; Little Movement Seen In Selecting Director Of Changeover Team," *Washington Post*, November 6, 1992.

29 "a palace coup": Webb Hubbell, *Friends in High Places*, 1997, 166–167.

29 "The campaign team": Balz, "Looking Ahead," *Washington Post*, November 8, 1992.

29 "devastated": Hubbell, *Friends in High Places*, 166–167.

29 "transition was the worst": Dee Dee Myers, interview with Chris Bury, "The Clinton Years," PBS television.

29   "Since 1987": Hubbell, *Friends in High Places*, 166–167.

30   "we were starting": Christopher, *Chances of a Lifetime*, 159.

30   "Christopher's not": Panetta, interview with the author, January 20, 2005.

30   "He would have been": Ibid.

30   "What they focused on": Ibid.

31   "so much time": Bill Clinton, *My Life*, 2004, 467.

31   "I said, I want": Paul Begala, interview with Chris Bury, "The Clinton Years," PBS television.

32   "Well, that was": Ibid.

32   "getting off that focus": Ibid.

32   "The biggest mistake": Jones, *Passages to the Presidency*, 176.

32   "absurd": Panetta, interview with the author, January 20, 2005.

32   "It's probably": Ibid.

33   "Pretty naïve?": Ibid.

33   "a paradox": Ibid.

33   "many of whom were": Clinton, *My Life*, 448.

34   "White House chief of staff": Anne Devroy, "Clinton Picks Brown for Commerce Post; Friend, 'Outsider' McLarty to Be Chief of Staff," *Washington Post*, December 13, 1992.

34   "the president's policy": Christopher, *Chances of a Lifetime*, 162.

34   "depends in large measure": Ibid.

34   Christopher had coveted: Devroy, "Clinton Picks Brown For Commerce Post," *Washington Post*, December 13, 1992; "the former deputy secretary of state said on Nov. 6 that he was not a 'potential officeholder'"—Michael Kranish, "Clinton appoints Brown to Cabinet, McLarty key aide," *Boston Globe*, December 13, 1992.

34   "the nerve center": Hillary Rodham Clinton, *Living History*, 2003, 117.

34   "put his White House team": David Gergen, interview with Chris Bury, "The Clinton Years," PBS television.

35   "Clinton has remained": Michael Weisskopf, "Clinton Backs Early Military Retirement; Strong Defense, Better Health Care for Vets and POW Action Pledged," *Washington Post*, November 12, 1992.

36   "It was Veteran's Day": Begala, interview with Chris Bury, "The Clinton Years," PBS television.

36   "The incoming administration": Eric Schmitt, "The Transition: News Analysis—Challenging the Military; In Promising to End Ban on Homosexuals, Clinton Is Confronting a Wall of Tradition," *New York Times*, November 12, 1992.

36   "Gays in the military?": Stephen Hess, interview with the author, February 14, 2005.

37   "public official": Title 5, Sec. 3110, a(2), U.S. Code.

37 "relative": Title 5, Sec. 3110, a(3), U.S. Code.

38 "Lady Macbeth of Little Rock": Martha Sherrill, "The Education of Hillary Clinton," *Washington Post*, January 13, 1993.

39 "respected Clinton's intellect": Turque, *Inventing Al Gore*, 248.

39 "He may have sensed it": Ibid.

39 "Clinton received from Gore": Michael Kelly and Maureen Dowd, "The Company He Keeps," *New York Times*, January 17, 1993.

39 "Los Alamos Experiment": Nigel Hamilton, *Bill Clinton, An American Journey: Great Expectations*, 2003, 646–648.

40 "a greedy, avaricious": Balz, "Looking Ahead," *Washington Post*, November 8, 1992.

Chapter Four

41 a succession of other wannabees: Drew, *On the Edge*, 33.

42 "sent a chill": Ibid.

42 "Al Gore hasn't yet": Kelly and Dowd, "The Company He Keeps," *New York Times*, January 17, 1993.

42 "Ultimately": Christopher, *Chances of a Lifetime*, 163–164.

42 "the most diverse cabinet": Warren Christopher (State), Lloyd Bentsen (Treasury), Les Aspin (Defense), Bruce Babbitt (Interior), Mike Espy (Agriculture), Ron Brown (Commerce), Robert Reich (Labor), Donna Shalala (Health), Henry Cisneros (HUD), Frederico Peña (Transportation), Hazel O'Leary (Energy), Richard Riley (Education), Jesse Brown (Veterans), Madeleine Albright (UN), Carol Browner (Environment), Leon Panetta (OMB), Mack McLarty (chief of staff), Laura Tyson (economic adviser), and Lee Brown (drug control).

43 "The nominee's style": Christopher, *Chances of a Lifetime*, 238.

43 "stunning barrage": "Clinton Says He Knew of Baird Error; Hunt for New Nominee Not Limited to Women," *St. Louis Post-Dispatch* (Missouri), January 23, 1993.

43 "phone calls to the Hill": Drew, *On the Edge*, 39.

43 "Majorities of men and women": "Poll finds widespread opposition," *USA Today*, January 22, 1993.

44 "'Well, dub'": George Stephanopoulos, *All Too Human*, 110.

45 "My job that day": Ibid., 108.

45 "wearing a sweatsuit": David Dreyer, interview with the author, October 30, 2004.

Chapter Five

46 "very soon—": Stephanopoulos, *All Too Human*, 110.

46 "the big leagues": Ibid., 109.

46   "I found George": Hubbell, *Friends in High Places*, 178.

46   "In front of": Ibid., 188.

47   "Anyone with an ounce": Panetta, interview with Chris Bury, "The Clinton Years," PBS television.

47   "You know, the thing": Michael Waldman, interview with Chris Bury, "The Clinton Years," PBS television.

47   "it became our priority": Rahm Emanuel, interview with Chris Bury, "The Clinton Years," PBS television.

47   "knowingly allowed": Clinton, *My Life*, 450.

48   "I'm going to meet": "Remarks on the Establishment of the Economic Council and an Exchange With Reporters," January 25, 1993, "Homosexuals in the Military," Bill Clinton, *Public Papers of the Presidents: William J. Clinton* (hereafter, *PPP:WJC*) 1993, Vol. I, 13.

48   "It was the very first": General Gordon Sullivan, interview with the author, April 5, 2005.

49   "Well, he certainly": Tony Lake, interview with the author, May 17, 2005.

49   "I did *not* welcome": Ibid.

50   "When I raised": Clinton, *My Life*, 483.

50   "There was not": Sullivan, interview with the author, April 5, 2005.

50   "And then Colin said": Ibid.

50   "O.K. That's fine": Ibid.

50   matter of a compromise was studied: Seven hundred "administrative separations," or evictions from the U.S. military, had taken place during 1992, and approximately 13,000 men and women cashiered as homosexuals since 1982. As part of the compromise agreement brokered with Senator Sam Nunn (to avoid legislative imposition of a ban), incoming service members were no longer to be questioned about their sexual orientation over the subsequent six months, while current members who declared their homosexuality before July 15, 1993, were to be separated from active duty and placed in the standby reserve.

51   "So it gets": Hess, interview with the author, February 14, 2005.

51   "I think anytime": Panetta, interview with the author, January 20, 2005.

52   "They were confined": Stephanopoulos, *All Too Human*, 111.

52   "*I'm not your problem*": Ibid.

52   "Clinton had an idea": Tom Lippman, interview with the author, April 14, 2005.

Chapter Six

54   "was not well served": Colin Powell, *My American Journey*, 1995, 577.

54   "a bizarre event": Madeleine Albright, *Madam Secretary*, 2003, 194.

55   "If Bill and Hillary": Robert Reich, *Locked in the Cabinet*, 17.

56   $125 billion worse: Drew, *On the Edge*, 59.

56   "the central importance": Reich, *Locked in the Cabinet*, 48.

56   "President Clinton yesterday": Dana Priest, "Clinton Names Wife to Head Health Panel; President Says Plan Is Due at End of May," *Washington Post*, January 26, 1993.

57   "work constantly day and night": Ibid.

57   "which is expected": Ibid.

57   "few on the White House": Hillary Rodham Clinton, *Living History*, 143.

58   "Clinton's advisers": R.A. Zaldivar (Knight-Ridder Newspapers), "Hillary Clinton Gets Health Plan," New Orleans *Times-Picayune*, January 26, 1993.

58   "read me the riot": Judy Feder, interview with the author, March 8, 2005.

58   later confessed: Clinton, *My Life*, 149.

59   "much of his chances": Dick Morris, *Behind the Oval Office*, 1997, 68.

59   "a President had to be": Joyce Milton, *The First Partner*, 248.

59   "Bill wanted to approach": Rodham Clinton, *Living History*, 143.

59   "Capitol Hill veterans": Ibid., 144.

59   "I'm hearing": Ibid.

60   "On January 25": Clinton, *My Life*, 482.

61   "What did you do": Rodham Clinton, *Living History*, 149.

61   "How does a secretary": Quoted in Sally Jacobs, "Hillary Clinton again securely in high profile," *Boston Globe*, January 27, 1993.

61   "They'll be sorry": Mimi Hall, "First lady leading charge on health care," *USA Today*, January 26, 1993.

61   "obvious influence": "Hillary Clinton's qualifications," *St. Petersburg Times*, January 26, 1993.

61   "placeholder": Feder, interview with the author, March 8, 2005.

62   "Was it a bad political": Donna Shalala, interview with Chris Bury, "The Clinton Years," PBS television.

62   send Chelsea, one day, to college: Hamilton, *Bill Clinton*, 364–365. Also see Joe Conason and Gene Lyons, *The Hunting of the President*, 30 et seq.

62   such a profit: Hillary was not alone among lawyers in this respect. "Back when everyone around us seemed to be making so much money," Webb Hubbell later related, "Vince [Foster], Hillary, another Rose partner name Ken Shemin, and I decided to pool our communal 'expertise' to see if we could get rich, too. We called ourselves the Midlife Investment Club, and we were hopeless," he admitted. "Overall we lost money, as our tax records show." Even their five-hundred-share investment in Arkla, Inc., the company that Bill's childhood buddy Mack McLarty came to run, produced a profit of only $3,000—a profit so low that, when concerns were raised that the club had been guilty of insider trading, it made Bernie Nussbaum, the White House counsel, snort with laughter. 'Webb,' he said, 'if you had inside information and only bought five hundred shares and only made three thousand dollars, then you aren't *smart* enough to be associate attorney general.'" Hubbell, *Friends in High Places*, 227.

63   "We've lost track": Woodward, *The Agenda*, 108.

63   "pure oxygen": Albright, *Madam Secretary*, 195.

63   "I want to get this shit": David Brock, "His Cheatin' Heart," *American Spectator*, January 1994.

64   "Bentsen thought": Woodward, *The Agenda*, 104.

64   "got on well with Hillary": Summers, interview with the author, January 3, 2005.

64   "She's moderated": Ibid.

65   "It was, the newspaper stressed": *Washington Post*, January 27, 1993.

65   "Powerful lobbies": Quoted in the *Houston Chronicle*, January 26, 1993.

Chapter Seven

68   "Hillary spoke": Drew, *On the Edge*, 51.

68   "darling of the reform-minded-liberal press": Woodward, *The Agenda*, 110.

68   "In 1983, when": Ibid.

69   "taken on education": Ibid.

70   "Why don't you": Ibid., 111.

70   "The Plan": Ibid., 112.

Chapter Eight

73   had no formal White House job: Begala was retained by the Democratic National Committee, which had to foot his bill.

74   "Bill Clinton has a problem firing": Alice Rivlin, interview with the author, March 10, 2005.

74   "I love Mack": David Dreyer, interview with the author, October 30, 2004.

75   "That's nonsense": Rivlin, interview with the author, March 10, 2005.

Chapter Nine

76   "small, boyish": John Brummett, *Highwire*, 1994, 86.

76   "I ask you that you join": Woodward, *The Agenda*, 115.

76   "Federal deficit has roared": "Address to the Nation on the Economic Program," February 15, 1993, *PPP: WJC, 1993*, Vol. I, 105.

77   "people seemed to hear": Brummett, *Highwire*, 86.

77   "I had hoped to invest": "Address to the Nation on the Economic Program," *PPP: WJC, 1993*, Vol. I, 106.

77   "Waving the old": Brummett, *Highwire*, 86.

78   "Okay": Woodward, *The Agenda*, 136.

78   "I love this": Ibid., 132.

79   "If you believe": Dreyer, interview with the author, October 30, 2004.

81   "fabulous": Woodward, *The Agenda*, 138.

82   "control, some control": Ibid., 140.

Chapter Ten

87   "very heavy hand": *St. Petersburg Times*, March 6, 1993.

87   "sensational confessions": *Chicago Sun Times*, April 2, 1993; and Youssef M. Ibrahim, "Mubarak Says a Suspect in Blast Revealed Details," *New York Times*, April 3, 1993.

88   role models: 10 Downing Street, Press Briefing Wednesday, April 30, 2003, "Evidence document submitted by the British Government: Responsibility For the Terrorist Atrocities in the United States," September 11, 2001—www .number–10.gov.uk/output/page3554.asp. In November 1989, bin Laden had taken control of assassinated Sheik Abdullah Assam's "Office of Services," dedicated to recruiting an Islamic army to fight Soviet forces occupying Afghanistan. Bin Laden had redirected and absorbed the organization into his global terrorist jihad, Al Qaeda. He would be widely suspected of having conspired in the 1993 World Trade Center bombing, as calls were made by the other conspirators to him from a safe house. http://www.pbs.org/wgbh/pages/frontline/shows/knew/etc/ cron.html.

88   "World politics is entering": Samuel P. Huntington, "The Clash of Civilizations?" in *Foreign Affairs*, Summer 1993. As the article pointed out, and Huntington clarified in the following issue of *Foreign Affairs,* "this civilization paradigm accounts for many important developments in international affairs in recent years, including the breakup of the Soviet Union and Yugoslavia, the wars going on in their former territories, the rise of religious fundamentalism throughout the world, the struggles within Russia, Turkey, and Mexico over their identity, the intensity of the trade conflicts between the United States and Japan, the resistance of Islamic states to Western pressure on Iraq and Libya, the efforts of Islamic and Confucian states to acquire nuclear weapons and the means to deliver them, China's continuing role as an 'outsider' great power, the consolidation of new democratic regimes in some countries and not in others, and the escalating arms race in East Asia."

88   "In the modern world": Huntington, "The Clash of Civilizations?," *Foreign Affairs*, Summer 1993.

Chapter Eleven

90   "What about heat?": Mike Clary, "Reno, Revved Up To Fight Crime," *Chicago Sun-Times*, February 13, 1993.

90   "I went through it": Associated Press, July 27, 2000.

91   "I had no idea": Stephanopoulos, *All Too Human*, 142.

92   "The first rule": Ibid.

Chapter Twelve

93   "We're Eisenhower Republicans": Woodward, *The Agenda*, 165.

94   "I don't have a goddamn": Ibid.

94   "We've done the responsible": Rodham Clinton, *Living History*, 166.

96   "basically said": Panetta, interview with the author, January 20, 2005.

96   "Don't look for": Ibid.

96   "offended me": Ibid.

97   "So we knew that": Ibid.

97   "Bill Clinton, he's a very": Ibid.

97   "The part of Bill Clinton": Ibid.

98   "It had nothing to do": Henry Cisneros, interview with the author, November 29, 2004.

Chapter Thirteen

99   "I knew": Haynes Johnson and David Broder, *The System*, 1996, 100.

100   "I'm quite astonished": Leslie Phillips, "Power and image; The first lady, access-limited," *USA Today*, May 24, 1993.

100   "People can't receive": Woodward, *The Agenda*, 151.

101   *"Don't tread on us"*: Ibid., 150.

101   "The criticism of the salute": Stephanopoulos, interview with Chris Bury, "The Clinton Years," PBS television.

102   "I don't talk to": Drew, *On the Edge*, 45.

102   "I've never forgotten my first": Marvin Kalb, interview with the author, February 23, 2005.

103   "lowest poll rating": According to Bob Woodward, "Clinton's approval rating was at 55 percent, the lowest in recent times of any elected president on his [hundredth] day." Kennedy's had been 83, Reagan's 68, and Carter's 63—Woodward, *The Agenda*, 177.

103   "It's just a physical force": Stephanopoulos, interview with Chris Bury, "The Clinton Years," PBS television.

103   "We've just gone too far": Woodward, *The Agenda*, 162.

103   "I wanted to keep": Stephanopoulos, interview with Chris Bury, "The Clinton Years," PBS television.

104   "getting control of the deficit": Woodward, *The Agenda*, 162.

104   "Clinton later said": Rubin and Weisberg, *In an Uncertain World*, 127.

104 "Unlike George Bush": Kalb, interview with the author, February 23, 2005.

105 "He could not let go": Ibid.

105 "president had failed": Woodward, *The Agenda*, 171.

106 "We start shooting": *Congressional Quarterly Almanac*, 103rd Congress, 1st Session, 1993, Vol. XLIX, 1994, 106.

106 "It doesn't take": Ibid.

106 "I know what's wrong": Woodward, *The Agenda*, 172.

107 "the president's plan": Ibid., 179.

108 "Mr. President, this is": Ibid., 182.

108 "If you could help": Ibid., 185.

109 "The key in Congress": Panetta, interview with the author, January 20, 2005.

109 "The way Clinton arrived at": Ibid.

109 "He was not confrontational": Ibid.

110 "What happens in the White House": Drew, *On the Edge*, 98.

110 "those who have the most time": Ibid., 98–99.

110 "convinced more than ever": Brummett, *Highwire*, 44.

111 "politically trained": Ibid., 47.

Chapter Fourteen

116 "Very early, some saw": Drew, *On the Edge*, 108–109.

116 "Two investigative accounts": James B. Stewart, *Blood Sport: The President and His Adversaries*, 1996; Joe Conason and Gene Lyons, *The Hunting of the President: The Ten-year Campaign to Destroy Bill and Hillary Clinton*, 2000.

116 "are continually changing": Matt Ridley, *The Red Queen: Sex and the Evolution of Human Nature*, 1993, 76.

117 "Congress takes its measure": Drew, *On the Edge*, 107.

117 The president's Omnibus Budget: So called because it was designed to bring tax and spending policy into line with deficit reduction goals, involving hundreds of changes in the U.S. tax code and mandatory programs.

117 "If the president failed": *Congressional Quarterly Almanac*, 103rd Congress, 1st Session, 1993, Vol. XLIX, 109.

117 "eagerness to please": Brummett, *Highwire*, 269.

118 "thinking woman's approach": Jeannie Williams, "Getting in Hillary's hair; New York trim triggers a media frenzy," *USA Today*, May 18, 1993.

119 "based on Federal Aviation": Drew, *On the Edge*, 174.

120 "This is not good press": St. Anne V. Hull, "Clinton may pull his hair out next time," *St. Petersburg Times*, May 22, 1993.

120 "It's not your hair": Elizabeth Snead, "Clintons, failing to keep the press out of their hair," *USA Today*, May 24, 1993.

120 "It's stunning to me": Anne Devroy, "Clinton Staff Says Flap Over On-Board Trim Is Splitting Hairs," *Washington Post*, May 21, 1993.

120–121 "It smacks of being": Greg Schneiders, quoted in "Called For Clipping," Cleveland *Plain Dealer*, May 21, 1993.

121 "By filing time": Stephanopoulos, *All Too Human*, 144.

121 "A lot of the press": Drew, *On the Edge*, 176.

121 "George": Stephanopoulos, *All Too Human*, 145.

122 "Charging gross financial": Ann Devroy, Al Kamen, "Longtime Travel Staff Given Walking Papers," *Washington Post*, May 20, 1993.

122 "I'm not sure": Rodham Clinton, *Living History*, 173.

122 "surprised by the reaction": Ibid., 172.

123 "war on the press": Stephanopoulos, *All Too Human*, 144.

123 "trying to ward off": Martin Fletcher, "U.S. officials sacked in cash investigation," *The Times* (London), May 20, 1993.

124 "The whole episode": Stephanopoulos, *All Too Human*, 145.

124 "President Clinton ended": Ian Brodie, "Unkind cut tops Clinton's week of trouble," *The Times* (London), May 22, 1993.

126 "It wasn't policy-making": Drew, *On the Edge*, 150.

126 "You've been a great": Ibid., 156.

127 "We have a serious": Ibid., 157.

127 "turned into an absolute": Halberstam, *War in a Time of Peace*, 224–225.

127 "The president's reputation": Conor O'Clery, "Travails of a President," *The Irish Times*, May 25, 1993.

Chapter Fifteen

129 "Whooosshhhh!!": David Gergen, "Give Clinton a chance," *U.S. News & World Report*, May 10, 1993.

130 "Time and time again": Albright, *Madam Secretary*, 181–182.

131 "planning and training": Sullivan, interview with the author, April 5, 2005.

131 "kept revisiting": Joe Klein, "Slow Motion," *Newsweek*, May 24, 1993.

132 "dropped by to say": Gergen, *Eyewitness to Power*, 265.

132 "Not my happiest": Stephanopoulos, interview with Chris Bury, "The Clinton Years," PBS television.

Chapter Sixteen

135 "No matter how talented": Gergen, *Eyewitness to Power*, 297.

135 "I'm in trouble": Ibid., 265.

135 "Mr. President, I'll make": Drew, *On the Edge*, 205.

136 "You don't have": Ibid., 204.

136 "I'm not going to withdraw": Ibid., 208.

137 "He was really angry": Ibid., 206.

137 "doesn't have much": Ibid., 209.

137 "It's two minutes to": Ibid.

137–138 "soft-core relativists": William Bennett, *The Death of Outrage: Bill Clinton and the Assault on American Ideals*, 1998.

139 "to the question that every discussion": Joe Klein, "Slow Motion," *Newsweek*, May 24, 1993. Author's italics.

140 "he could no longer say": Margaret Carlson and Michael Duffy, "Where is 'my center'?" *Time*, June 14, 1993.

141 "His downward spiral": Ibid.

141 "All three of them": Gergen, *Eyewitness to Power*, 292.

142 "a rolling disaster": Ibid., 293.

Chapter Seventeen

144 "there were some episodes": Dreyer, interview with the author, October 30, 2004.

144 "charismatically challenged": Drew, *On the Edge*, 217.

145 "Partly this was": Ibid., 218–219.

145 "the President tearing-up": Richard Lacayo and Michael D. Lemonick, "Hands have no tears to flow, but presidents do," *Time*, June 28, 1993.

145 "I cannot sleep": Bruce W. Nelan and J. F. O. McAllister, "Do something . . . anything," *Time*, May 3, 1993.

145 "We have no ability": Drew, *On the Edge*, 186.

145 "personnel is policy": Ibid., 184.

146 "THE INCREDIBLE SHRINKING PRESIDENT": *Time*, June 7, 1993.

Chapter Eighteen

148 "Fix it, Vince!": Hubbell, *Friends in High Places*, 212.

148 " 'they' would use": Ibid.

148 "not a perfect": William Jefferson Clinton, "Remarks Announcing the New Policy on Homosexuals in the Military, July 19, 1993," *PPP:WJC*, Vol. I, 1111.

148 "So we're like": Myers, interview with Chris Bury, "The Clinton Years," PBS television.

149 "At first I was irritated": Clinton, *My Life*, 531.

149 "came back down": Myers, interview with Chris Bury, "The Clinton Years," PBS television.

149 "The next day the press": Ibid.

150 "Hillary and I love his wife": "Clinton lawyer dies in apparent suicide; Aide's death stuns, saddens first family," *Houston Chronicle*, July 21, 1993.

150 "of course, once": Myers, interview with Chris Bury, "The Clinton Years," PBS television.

150 liberal criminal reporter Dan Moldea: Dan Moldea, *A Washington Tragedy: How the Death of Vincent Foster Ignited a Political Firestorm*, 1998.

150 "a cosmic kick": Lloyd Grove, "Striking at the Heart of the White House; Death of Clinton Friend Marks a New Low for Staff," *Washington Post*, July 22, 1993.

151 "One of the things": Ibid.

151 "I don't think so": "Clues Scant in Suicide of Clinton Aide," *St. Louis Post-Dispatch*, July 22, 1993.

151 "perplexed like everyone else": " 'Unlike some other people who did know that he had been quite distressed, I was not really aware of that.' Instead, Myers said, Clinton by coincidence called Foster because the president felt 'lonely' for his lifelong friend."—Michael Kranish, "Questions mount over death of aide; White House withheld note," *Boston Globe*, July 30, 1993.

151 "I lived with": "Clues Scant in Suicide of Clinton Aide," *St. Louis Post-Dispatch*, July 22, 1993.

152 "For more years": "Clues Scant in Suicide of Clinton Aide," *St. Louis Post-Dispatch*, July 22, 1993.

152 "Even if you had": Marcus and Devroy, "Clintons Mystified by Aide's Death; Staff Shaken by Apparent Suicide," *Washington Post*, July 22, 1993.

152 "He may have felt": Simon Tisdall, " 'Innocent Hounded To Death' By Ruthless Power-Play," *The Guardian* (London), July 23, 1993.

152 "appeared to be": Myers, interview with Chris Bury, "The Clinton Years," PBS television.

152 "did show him to be": Kranish, "Questions mount over death of aide," *Boston Globe*, July 30, 1993.

153 "I made mistakes": Ibid.

153 "sheer willpower": Rodham Clinton, *Living History*, 179.

153 "too late to save Bill": Hubbell, *Friends in High Places*, 255.

154 "a team specializing": Ibid.

154 "We shouldn't have asked": Ibid., 244–245 and 253.

154 "brutal": Rodham Clinton, *Living History*, 178.

154 Another lost relative: Leon Ritzenthaler. Although the surfacing of a half-brother to the president of the United States created a considerable stir at the time (see, inter alia, Jane Gross, "A First Half-Brother? A Californian Claims Kinship With Clinton," *New York Times*, June 27, 1993), the event quickly passed from memory, and would be excluded from both Bill Clinton's and Hillary Rodham Clinton's memoirs.

155 "being sidelined": Rodham Clinton, *Living History*, 166.

155 "adversity": Ibid., 178.

155 "ready to explode": Ibid., 166–167.

155 "I probably should have": Ibid., 166.

156 "Don't believe a word": Christopher Ruddy, *The Strange Death of Vincent Foster*, 1997, 188.

Chapter Nineteen

159 "near-death experience": *Congressional Quarterly Almanac*, 103rd Congress, 1st Session, 1993, Vol. XLIX, 111.

160 "This is a time": *Congressional Quarterly Almanac*, 103rd Congress, 1st Session, 1993, Vol. XLIX, 111.

160 "BTU is one": Panetta, interview with the author, January 20, 2005.

161 "so that Clinton": Ruth Marcus, "Waiting to Hear the Bottom Line; 'Weird Day' at White House Capped With Word About Senate Holdout," *Washington Post*, August 7, 1993.

161 "Tonight is the time": George Hager and David S. Cloud, "Democrats tie their fate to Clinton's budget bill," *Congressional Quarterly Weekly Report*, August 7, 1993.

162 "For several more moments": Ibid.

162 "House leaders agreed": Phil Reeves, "Senate set for close vote on deficit bill; Defeat of plan to trim the budget despite Democrat majority would deal a body blow to Clinton," *The Independent* (London), August 7, 1993.

162 "She let the fifteen": Bill Turque, "The stitching in the 'plaid' budget; Congress: A freshman is fed to the beast," *Newsweek*, August 16, 1993.

162 "President Clinton's entire": Dave Kaplan, "DeConcini: Clinton's Convert," *Congressional Quarterly Weekly Report*, August 7, 1993.

162 "who could not have": Clinton, *My Life*, 536.

163 "That sealed it": David S. Cloud, "Big risk for Margolies-Mezvinsky," *Congressional Quarterly Weekly Report*, August 7, 1993.

163 "fed to the beast": Turque, "The stitching in the 'plaid' budget," *Newsweek*, August 16, 1993.

163 "I let out a whoop": Clinton, *My Life*, 536.

164 "One poll": R. W. Apple, "Clinton Is Pulled From the Brink. He'll Be Back," *New York Times*, August 8, 1993.

164 "Someone once said": Clinton, *My Life*, 535.

164 "Clinton exploded": Dan Balz, "Kerrey's Odyssey From Rage to Reassurance; Nebraska Senator Reflects On His Shift From 'a Solid No' to a Cliffhanger 'Yes,'" *Washington Post*, August 8, 1993.

164 "Would it help": Ibid.

165   "He listens to his own": Richard L. Berke, "The Budget Battle; A Walk Offstage, Holding Fate of Budget," *New York Times*, August 7, 1993.

165   "Oh, yeah": Panetta, interview with the author, January 20, 2005.

165   *Free Willy*: Ruth Marcus, "Waiting to Hear the Bottom Line; 'Weird Day' at White House Capped With Word About Senate Holdout," *Washington Post*, August 7, 1993.

166   "We've seen this before": Eric Pianin and David S. Hilzenrath, "Senate Passes Clinton Budget Bill, 51–50, After Kerrey Reluctantly Casts 'Yes' Vote; President Hails Victory As Economic 'Beginning,'" *Washington Post*, August 7, 1993.

166   "The markets, Wall Street": Congressional Record—Senate, August 6, 1993, *Congressional Record*, Vol. 139, Part 14, 19813.

168   "Mr. President, I've taken": Ibid.

169   "Oh, you say this plan": "The Budget Struggle; Excerpts from the Senate's Debate on the President's 5-Year Economic Plan," *New York Times*, August 7, 1993.

169   "President Clinton, if you are": Congressional Record—Senate, August 6, 1993, *Congressional Record*, Vol. 139, Part 14, 19813.

170   "loved to joke": Clinton, *My Life*, 536.

171   "When the vote": David E. Rosenbaum, "The Budget Struggle; Clinton Wins Approval of His Budget Plan as Gore Votes to Break Senate Deadlock," *New York Times*, August 7, 1993.

171   "President Clinton's battle": Colin Smith, "He begged, he got laryngitis, he won," *The Observer* (London), August 8, 1993.

171   "A lesser man might have": Ibid.

171   "What we heard tonight": "Kerrey's vote swings budget for Democrats," *St. Petersburg Times*, August 7, 1993.

172   "the largest tax increase": Phil Reeves, "Senate Set for Close Vote on Deficit Bill: Defeat of plan to trim the budget despite Democratic majority would deal a body blow to Clinton," *The Independent* (London), August 7, 1993.

172   "a job-killing recession": George Hager and David S. Cloud, "Democrats tie their fate to Clinton's budget bill," *Congressional Quarterly Weekly Report*, August 7, 1993.

Chapter Twenty

173   claimed he did not want: Barton Gellman and R. Jeffrey Smith, "Hesitant by Design; Aspin's Style at Pentagon Often Leaves Important Decisions in Hands of Others," *Washington Post*, November 14, 1993.

174   "assure Mr Clinton's place": Judy Kean and Judi Hasson, "Democrats to hard-sell health plan," *USA Today*, September 16, 1993.

175   "stepped back out of": Clinton, *My Life*, 544.

175   "Today": William Jefferson Clinton, "Remarks at the Signing for the Israeli-Palestinian Declaration of Principles," September 13, 1993, *PPP:WJC*, Vol. II, 1475.

177   offer to sabotage: Following Hillary's lead, Kantor laid out a possible scenario whereby the Hill (where many Democrats feared for their seats if they supported a trade agreement that might cost union jobs in America), rather than the president, would carry the can.

177   "know the agreements": Tim Golden, "Salinas changes his tune on NAFTA; Mexicans told troubled pact is not 'a panacea' for country," *New York Times*, September 15, 2005.

177   "giant sucking sound": Mary McGrory, *Washington Post*, November 21, 1993.

177   "Yesterday": "Remarks at the Signing Ceremony for the Supplental Agreements to the North American Free Trade Agreement," September 14, 1993, *PPP:WJC*, Vol. II, 1486.

179   "I understand why": Gwen Ifill, "Clinton Recruits 3 Presidents to Promote Trade Pact," *New York Times*, September 15, 1993. Also Drew, *On the Edge*, 299.

180   "One other exception": Rivlin, interview with the author, March 10, 2005.

Chapter Twenty-One

181   "When the President": David Dreyer, interview with the author, October 30, 2004.

182   "And George doesn't": Ibid.

183   "Bill and Hillary Clinton can": Rupert Cornwall, "Clinton to fulfil health pledge; The President proposes 'managed competition' to provide medical care for all Americans," *The Independent* (London), September 20, 1993.

183   "what amounted to a co-presidency": David Gergen, interview with Chris Bury, "The Clinton Years," PBS television.

Chapter Twenty-Two

188   "cast a pall over": James Bone and Wolfgang Munchau, "Somalia setback forces Clinton to rethink peacekeeping role," *The Times* (London), September 27, 1993.

188   "bringing with him into government": Edward Mortimer, "Sights set on a wider world: The imperatives guiding America's hesitant foreign policy," *Financial Times* (London), September 27, 1993.

189   "Amazingly": Halberstam, *War in a Time of Peace*, 258.

190   "It was certainly one": Sandy Berger, interview with Chris Bury, "The Clinton Years," PBS television.

191   "News organizations": Anthony Lake, interview with Chris Bury, "The Clinton Years," PBS television, and interview with the author, March 1, 2005.

191   "It was in all ways": Halberstam, *War in a Time of Peace*, 262.

191 "first reaction was": Lake, interview with Chris Bury, "The Clinton Years," PBS television.

191 "revolted and furious": Berger, interview with Chris Bury, "The Clinton Years," PBS television.

191 "It was absolutely": Lake, interview with Chris Bury, "The Clinton Years," PBS television.

191 "His first meeting with congressional": Lake, interview with the author, May 17, 2005.

192 "I remember arguing": Ibid.

192 "The message would be": Lake, interview with Chris Bury, "The Clinton Years," PBS television.

192 "major league CNN-era": Halberstam, *War in a Time of Peace*, 262.

192 "bin Laden involvement": See U.S Government Indictment of bin Laden (*U.S District Court, Southern District of New York* v. *Usama bin Laden*, Indictment S(10) 98 Cr 1023 (LBS), at http://news.findlaw.com/hdocs/docs/binladen/usbinladen–1a.pdf , and also PBS *Frontline*, "Al Qaeda's Global Context," April 2004. http://www.pbs.org/wgbh/pages/frontline/shows/knew/etc/cron.html.

192 "Somalia wasn't quite": Gergen, interview with Chris Bury, "The Clinton Years," PBS television.

Chapter Twenty-Three

194 "People blame me": Ibid.

194 "one of the most embarrassing": Halberstam, *War in a Time of Peace*, 272.

195 "Looking back on it": Berger, interview with Chris Bury, "The Clinton Years," PBS television.

195 "I remember it vividly": Sullivan, interview with the author, April 5, 2005.

195 "A string of policy failures": Mary Curtius, "Cold War's end puts Clinton on uncertain path; A Democrat in the White House," *Boston Globe*, November 22, 1993.

196 "confirmed the worst suspicions": Halberstam, *War in a Time of Peace*, 264.

196 "It does no good": Lake, *6 Nightmares: Real Threats in a Dangerous World and How America Can Meet Them*, 2000, 128.

196 "We're not inflicting pain": Stephanopoulos, *All Too Human*, 214.

196 "The Reagan people": Ibid., 217.

197 "Americans are basically": Ibid., 214.

197 "would leave the impression": Barton Gellman and R. Jeffrey Smith, "Hesitant by Design; Aspin's Style at Pentagon Often Leaves Important Decisions in Hands of Others," *Washington Post*, November 14, 1993.

197 "Mr. President, you": Stephanopoulos, *All Too Human*, 218.

197 "No one told me about": Drew, *On the Edge*, 317.

197 "I'm never going to": Halberstam, *War in a Time of Peace*, 273.

198 "a huge knock-on effect": Sullivan, interview with the author, April 5, 2005.

Chapter Twenty-Four

201 "*Millions* avoided the draft": Cliff Jackson, interview with the author, July 27, 2002.

202 "Robert Caro's book": Robert Caro, *The Years of Lyndon Johnson: The Path to Power*, Vol. I, 1982.

202 "steppingstones to the end goal": Cliff Jackson, interview with the author, July 27, 2002.

204 "A large segment": Ibid.

205 "We lied for him": Ibid.

205 "I am a trial lawyer": Ibid.

206 "was instructed to stand": Danny Ferguson deposition under oath, *Jones* v. *Clinton*, November 9, 1997. See also Sheehy, *Hillary's Choice*, 1999, 295, and David Brock, "His Cheatin' Heart," *American Spectator*, January 1994.

207 "More than most presidential": Michael Kelly and Maureen Dowd, "The Company He Keeps," *New York Times*, January 17, 1993.

207 historic sums of money: Bill Clinton was paid an advance of $10–12 million by New York publisher Alfred Knopf for his memoirs *My Life*, while Hillary received an $8 million advance for *Living History* from Simon & Schuster.

207 "It was not hate": Lynn Davis, interview with the author, July 28, 2002.

208 "the property and the women": Machiavelli, *The Prince*, 1995, 58.

208 "contemporary experience": Ibid., 56–58.

209 "There are two things": Ibid., 58–59.

209 "To put it briefly": Ibid., 60.

209 "They were terrified": Jackson, interview with the author, July 27, 2002.

210 "Seeing the sure profit": Machiavelli, *The Prince*, 60.

211 "All mad because": Document supplied by kind courtesy of Cliff Jackson.

211 "If you tell me": David Brock, "His Cheatin' Heart," *American Spectator*, January 1994.

212 "I went to a little three-roomed": Jackson, interview with the author, July 27, 2002.

212 "lack of an inner core": Ibid. "Apparently a lot of people who grow up in difficult circumstances subconsciously blame themselves and feel unworthy of a better fate. . . . My internal life was full of uncertainty, anger, and a dread of ever-looming violence."—Clinton, *My Life*, 46–47 and 149.

213 "Apparently a lot": Clinton, *My Life*, 149.

214 "parallel lives": Ibid.

214   "It appears that Clinton": Stanley A. Renshon, "William Jefferson Clinton's Psychology," in Jerrold M. Post, ed., *The Psychological Assessment of Political Leaders*, 2003, 292.

214   "big $ in [it]": Document supplied by kind courtesy of Cliff Jackson.

215   "After all": Betsey Wright, interview with the author, March 23, 2001.

216   "the subject in the Bible": Jackson, interview with the author, July 27, 2002.

216   "That's the way I would": Wright, interview with the author, March 23, 2001.

217   electoral research: Gerald M. Pomper, "The Presidential Election," in Gerald M. Pomper, ed., *The Election of 1996: Reports and Interpretations*, 1997, 179.

217   "Would you mind if": "J. D. W." in Julia Anderson-Miller and Bruce Joshua Miller, eds., *Dreams of Bill: A Collection of Funny, Strange and Downright Peculiar Dreams about Our President, Bill Clinton*, 1994, 2. Once in bed the president, in the dream, had simply applied himself to the *New York Times* crossword puzzle—and when the lady's ten-year-old son (in the dream) walked in with a baseball mitt and ball, the president had "hopped out of bed and played catch and did high fives with him."

217   "what my husband": Tammy Anderson, in Julia Anderson-Miller and Bruce Joshua Miller, eds., *Dreams of Bill*, 6.

Chapter Twenty-Five

219   "I'm here as a mother": Joe Urschel, "The president is clearly in second place," *USA Today*, October 5, 1993.

219   "fundamentally unsound": Reuter report, quoting CNN/USA poll, "Hillary Clinton: 'the greatest challenge of our day,'" *Hobart Mercury* (Tasmania), October 1, 1993.

220   "serious reservations": Judi Hasson, " 'Concerned' first lady pushes health plan," *USA Today*, September 29, 1993.

220   "Let me just make clear": "Remarks on Presenting Proposed Health Care Reform Legislation to the Congress," October 27, 1993, *PPP:WJC*, Vol. II, 1831.

220   "Once we get hold": Quoted by Richard Wolf, "First lady takes her sales pitch to the skeptics," *USA Today*, September 27, 1993.

221   "substantive and profound": Larry Lipman, "Clinton Health Challenge; Congress gets health reform challenge," *Pittsburgh Post-Gazette*, October 28, 1993.

221   "circus": Bennett Roth, "Clinton delivers health care bill to Congress; Some details change, but emphasis still on coverage for all," *Houston Chronicle*, October 28, 1993.

221   "Distracted by overseas": Martin Fletcher, "Critics gird for battle as health care bill reaches Capitol Hill," *The Times* (London), October 28, 1993.

221   "Big Sister": Ibid.

222   "We're going to crack down": Johnson and Broder, *The System*, 203.

222 "impact is not going to be": "Health Care Reform Debate squeezed into TV ads," *Atlanta Journal-Constitution*, October 23, 1993.

222 "be quiet and go out": Johnson and Broder, *The System*, 210.

222 "Rarely, if ever": Ibid.

223 "Mrs. Clinton blamed": "Insurers accused of deception; Mrs. Clinton says firms want to protect profits," *St. Louis Post-Dispatch*, November 2, 1993.

223 "Taking the gloves off": Michael Putzel, "Mrs. Clinton hits at 'lies' by insurers; Industry calls attack unfair as health debate grows testy," *Boston Globe*, November 2, 1993.

223 "Enough is enough": Ibid.

224 "more and more moved": Johnson and Broder, *The System*, 198.

224 "The fault here": Feder, interview with the author, March 8, 2005.

224 "I mean he was absolutely": Johnson and Broder, *The System*, 225.

225 "incomprehensible health plan": Ibid., 234.

225 "I'm saying: Involve": Joycelyn Elders, interview with the author, February 5, 2001.

226 "most people who were working": Ibid.

226 "There was this elaborate": Rivlin, interview with the author, March 10, 2005.

226 "Inevitably it was going": Feder, interview with the author, March 8, 2005.

227 "Doctor Feelgood": Andy Miller, "Health Care Reform; Don't paint us as the villains, insurance industry says; Attacks on Clinton plan are working, conference is told," *Atlanta Journal-Constitution*, November 9, 1993.

Chapter Twenty-Six

228 "shallow, opinionated": Geoffrey Stevens, "NAFTA puts Clinton in a new light; He's shaping up as under-rated freshman president," *The Gazette* (Montreal, Quebec), November 21, 1993.

229 "That 'giant sucking sound'": Mary McGrory, "The Newt Democrat," *Washington Post*, November 21, 1993; "Odd Couple Joins Forces on NAFTA," *Buffalo News*, November 23, 1993.

229 "There was more": Stevens, "NAFTA puts Clinton in a new light," *The Gazette* (Montreal), November 21, 1993.

229 an unexpected pushover: Ibid. In the event, 102 Democrats and 132 Republicans voted for the bill in the House of Representatives, thus giving the president an easy victory, 234–200. It passed even more easily in the Senate. Only 27 Democratic senators dared vote in favor of the bill—with 28 Democrats against it—but with 34 positive Republican votes, the president had more than a sufficiency, and the bill passed 61–38.

229 "To be effective": Anthony Lewis, "Turning Point," New Orleans *Times-Picayune*, November 22, 1993.

Chapter Twenty-Seven

233 "We hosted, on average": Rodham Clinton, *Living History*, 205.

233 "A Holiday Message": *Parade Magazine*, as published with the *Arkansas Democrat-Gazette*, December 19, 1993.

235 "received from the IRS": Conason and Lyons, *The Hunting of the President*, 30–38.

235 "Gerth's front-page allegation": "Bill Clinton and his wife were business partners with the owner of a failing savings and loan association," Gerth began his article, "that was subject to state regulation early in his tenure as Governor of Arkansas, records show." Jeff Gerth, "THE 1992 CAMPAIGN: Personal Finances; Clintons Joined S & L Operator In an Ozark Real-Estate Venture," *New York Times*, March 8, 1992. This was a completely untrue headline and opening implication; the Clintons were never business partners of Jim McDougal's savings and loan company. Clinton defended himself the next day, as reported in the *New York Times*: "The article seems to imply that my wife and I had no financial exposure," Governor Clinton complained while campaigning in Texas. "There's nothing [that] could be further from the truth. We were jointly and severally liable for more than $200,000 worth of debt," Clinton pointed out—a huge exposure for a mere $20,000 investment. "He termed the relationship 'purely private investment' that was 'nothing but a big money loser for me,'" Gwen Ifill reported, in an item the newspaper buried on page 13: Gwen Ifill, "THE 1992 CAMPAIGN: Personal Finances; Clinton Defends Real-Estate Deal," *New York Times*. In the highly political—and politicized—drama of the approaching general election, Clinton's statement did nothing to dissuade or deter his and his wife's detractors, and, indeed, only inflamed them.

235 "RTC criminal referral": The RTC had postponed calls for a criminal investigation of Jim McDougal's S & L bankruptcy (which cost the American taxpayers $50 million) until after the '92 election, lest the referral be seen as a political plot against the Clintons, but the referral had then been revived.

235 "If a genie offered": Stephanopoulos, *All Too Human*, 226.

236 "more appropriate for corporate": Ibid.

236 "the country probably": Ibid., 227.

236 "as if he were a high school": Ibid.

237 "I was negatively impressed": Lynn Davis, telephone interview with the author, July 28, 2002.

237 gay-dance-club cruising lifestyle: David Brock, *Blinded By the Right*, 2002, 162.

238 "Would I do it again": Jackson, interview with the author, July 27, 2002.

238 "This is a misuse": Ibid.

239 "in conservative circles": Brock, *Blinded By the Right*, 146.

239 "hadn't spent three months": Ibid., 153.

239 "I threw in every last titillating": Ibid., 151.

239 "I actually thought": Ibid., 154.

240   "After we saw": Jackson, interview with the author, July 27, 2002.

241   "These people are not": James B. Stewart, *Blood Sport*, 350–351.

242   "Roger, you will not": Ibid., 351–352.

242   "that the Rose firm": Hubbell, *Friends in High Places*, 272.

243   "think about it": Stephanopoulos, *All Too Human*, 228.

243   "I'm sorry": Stewart, *Blood Sport*, 355.

243   "the keeper of all secrets": Michael Isikoff, *Uncovering Clinton: A Reporter's Story*, 1999, 34.

244   "I just want to tell": Stewart, *Blood Sport*, 355.

Chapter Twenty-Eight

245   " 'Hillary,' Kendall said": Rodham Clinton, *Living History*, 206.

245   "the most vile stories": Ibid.

246   "as far as she could tell": Stewart, *Blood Sport*, 356.

246   "Just about everybody": Ibid.

248   "It was too much": Rodham Clinton, *Living History*, 207.

Chapter Twenty-Nine

249   "The President was elected": Ibid.

249   "What the f—": Brock, "His Cheatin' Heart," *American Spectator*, January 1994.

250   "go upstairs with Bill": Rodham Clinton, *Living History*, 207.

250   "bestseller by Richard Reeves": Richard Reeves, *President Kennedy: Profile in Power*, 1993.

250   "I realized that attacks": Rodham Clinton, *Living History*, 208.

251   "nondenial denials": Drew, *On the Edge*, 383.

251   " 'I think,' said Rempel": Stewart, *Blood Sport*, 360.

252   "They did a masterful": Davis, interview with the author, July 28, 2002.

253   "As the President": Letter of December 29, 1993, Papers of Cliff Jackson, by kind permission.

253   "Stephanopoulos was reminded": Stephanopoulos, *All Too Human*, 228.

253   "So none of this": "Clinton Denies Reports; 'We Have Not Done Anything Wrong,'" *St. Louis Post-Dispatch*, December 23, 1993.

254   "stammered and hesitated": Drew, *On the Edge*, 389.

254   "We, we did, if": "Clinton Denies Reports; 'We Have Not Done Anything Wrong,'" *St. Louis Post-Dispatch*, December 23, 1993.

254   "the effect was very": Drew, *On the Edge*, 389.

254   "Without trust and integrity": Letter of December 29, 1993, by kind permission of Cliff Jackson.

255   "distracted": Drew, *On the Edge*, 386.

255   "he is on the verge": Ibid., 388.

255   "I think character": *Arkansas Democrat-Gazette*, December 23, 1993.

255   "fell short of": Ibid.

255   "I can only deal with": Drew, *On the Edge*, 385.

Chapter Thirty

260   "The tide was indeed turning": Lippman, interview with the author, April 14, 2005.

261   "For twenty years": Simon Tisdall, "Clinton Steals Republican Clothes," *The Guardian* (London), January 27, 1994.

261   "I know there are": Marc Sandalow, "Clinton's Ambitious Goals," *San Francisco Chronicle*, January 26, 1994.

262   "Our country has": "Clinton plea to Congress on reforms," *The Advertiser* (Australia), January 27, 1994; and "GOP Response: Clinton Cure May Prove to be Harmful," *St.Louis Post-Dispatch*, July 26, 1994.

262   "We can fix": Sandalow, "Clinton's Ambitious Goals," *San Francisco Chronicle*, January 26, 1994.

262   "dizzyingly detailed flow chart": Grove, "Getting a Second Opinion; GOP's Health Care Maze Doesn't Amuse Democrats," *Washington Post*, January 27, 1994.

262   "The chart, even more": Ibid.

263   "in trouble": Greg McDonald and William E. Clayton, Jr., "Health care comes first, Clinton says; President also stresses welfare, crime reforms," *Houston Chronicle*, January 26, 1994.

263   "At that particular": Grove, "Getting a Second Opinion; GOP's Health Care Maze Doesn't Amuse Democrats," *Washington Post*, January 27, 1994.

263   "We think that chart": Ibid.

263   "What you don't see": Ibid.

264   "sat down at her dining": Ibid.

264   "In the president's absence": Thomas J. Brazaitis and Tom Diemer, "President Took Reagan's Best Lines, GOP Claims," Cleveland *Plain Dealer*, January 27, 1994.

264   "Health care was once": Ibid.

264   "White House aide": Douglas Turner, "Health-Care Battle Lines Drawn; Clinton Threatens Veto if Congress Balks on Coverage," *Buffalo News*, January 26, 1994.

265   "If there's not a recession": Feder, interview with the author, March 8, 2005.

266 "The consensus on Capitol": Keen and Hasson, "Clinton back in the health-care ring," *USA Today*, January 4, 1994.

267 "I have nothing to say": *St. Petersburg Times*, January 4, 1994.

267 "What I should have": Clinton, *My Life*, 574.

Chapter Thirty-One

268 "not to let the tension": Panel discussion entitled "Oh, by the way, Mr. President, may I suggest . . . ," in which about forty people gave advice: John F. Harris, "Letter from the Renaissance; Clinton Doesn't Let Seminars Cut into His Vacation," *Washington Post*, January 2, 1994.

269 "The names of the mistresses": Brock, "His Cheatin' Heart," *American Spectator*, January 1994.

269 "Now, Paula, I got": Stewart, *Blood Sport*, 387.

271 "Again, I did what I did": Jackson, interview with the author, July 27, 2002.

272 "man in Little Rock": Clinton, *My Life*, 596.

272 "We had been through that": Stephanopoulos, interview with Chris Bury, "The Clinton Years," PBS television.

272 "We can't do anything": Stewart, *Blood Sport*, 388. Among voters, *USA Today*'s polls found, Democrats and Independents were most likely to say the sex allegations were "irrelevant. Republicans were more likely to rate them an important indicator of character": Richard Benedetto, "Public is keeping the faith in Clinton," *USA Today*, January 11, 1994.

272 White House's response: Stephanopoulos, interview with Chris Bury, "The Clinton Years," PBS television.

272 "Ladies and gentlemen": Isikoff, *Uncovering Clinton*, 6.

273 "All Clinton had to do": Ibid., 7–8.

273 "There were a bunch of questions": Jackson, interview with the author, July 27, 2002.

273 "Basically we just pointed": Stephanopoulos, interview with Chris Bury, "The Clinton Years," PBS television.

274 "Danny was way over": Jackson, interview with the author, July 27, 2002.

274 "On several occasions": Paragraphs 76 and 77, *Paula Corbin Jones, Plaintiff*, v. *William Jefferson Clinton and Danny Ferguson* in the United States District Court for the Eastern District of Arkansas, Western Division, May 1994, demanding $700,000 plus legal costs.

274 "I was a small little entity": "'It Started With Me': Paula Jones Reacts to Clinton Memoir; Talks About 'Vast Right-Wing Conspiracy,'" ABC News.com, June 30, 2004, pre-reporting ABC *Primetime* interview with Paula Jones airing on July 1, 2004.

275 "conduct of Clinton": *Paula Corbin Jones, Plaintiff*, v. *William Jefferson Clinton and Danny Ferguson, Defendants*, Civil Action No. LR-C–94–290, United States

District Court for the Eastern District of Arkansas, Wetern Division. May 6, 1994, Filed.

275 "old demons": Clinton, *My Life*, 149.

275 "dark alley": Bill Clinton interview, "Oprah and Bill Clinton," *The Oprah Winfrey Show*, June 22, 2004.

275 three full years: A 1993 amendment to the Arkansas Workers Compensation statute had made mental or emotional injury non-compensable unless caused by a physical injury, but the alleged incident predated the amendment.

Chapter Thirty-Two

277 distract the president: Even if impeachment for a serious crime *were* to be voted for by the House of Representatives, impeachment for the alleged misdemeanor had then to be handed over to yet another chamber, the Senate, for actual trial. Only if then convicted in the U.S. Senate could a president be removed from office—whereupon, and only in that special case, would the ex-president become, finally, subject to normal judicious process, namely "Indictment, Trial, Judgment and Punishment, according to Law" (Article 1, Section 3, Clause 7).

278 "'dark alley' secrets": Many of these had been loyally stored by Webb Hubbell in his basement, including "claims by various women": Hubbell, *Friends in High Places,* 267. Among the stored documents was "a pretty big pack of letters from high school, Georgetown, and Oxford days that I thought he should probably have destroyed many years earlier, given the nature of them," Betsey Wright later recalled—Wright, interview with the author, March 23, 2001.

278 "In a desperate attempt": James Adams, "Clinton offers apology over harassment case," *Sunday Times* (London), May 8, 1994.

279 "sexual harassers": "Statement of NOW President Patricia Ireland Calling For a Fair Treatment of Jones' Suit," NOW press release, May 6, 1994, www.now.org/press/05–94/05–06–94.html.

279 "When the case was": "View Point: Feminists Maintain Integrity in *Clinton* v. *Jones* Case," www.now.org/nnt/03–97/clinton.html.

279 "We know that": Angie Cannon and Aaron Epstein, "Suit Puts Clinton Back on Defensive," New Orleans *Times-Picayune*, May 5, 1994.

280 "almost a million black African": Of all the failures of his administration, Rwanda would, along with failure to achieve a peace settlement between Israel and the Palestinians, be the one that most rankled when Clinton later reflected on his career as president of the U.S.—as it did in the case of Madeleine Albright. "I was not among the very few who saw early that the decade's most shocking crime would engulf the small country of Rwanda. My deepest regret from my years in public service is the failure of the United States and the international community to act sooner to halt those crimes"—Madeleine Albright, *Madam Secretary: A Memoir*, 147. According to Samantha Power, director of the Carr Center for Human Rights Policy, not only did the State Department receive constant on-the-spot appraisals of the mass killings sparked by the shooting down of the

Rwandan presidential plane, but two dozen U.S. special forces operatives were sent to Kigali to verify reports of gathering genocide and reported "so many bodies on the streets that you could walk from one body to the other without touching the ground"—Samantha Power, *A Problem From Hell, America and the Age of Genocide,* 2002, 354. By April 22, the *Washington Post* was reporting more than 100,000 Tutsis murdered, and even the pope, five days later, used the word "genocide." Apart from ordering all American nationals to leave Rwanda, the president, White House staff, CIA, U.S. State Department, and Department of Defense, as well as the UN peacekeeping team, simply watched the extermination of Rwandan Tutsis without interference, or even a genuine attempt to rouse American public interest. Warren Christopher's memoirs, *Chances of a Lifetime,* 2001, did not even mention Rwanda. National Security Council official Richard Clarke was the senior American officer assigned to oversee U.S. peacekeeping policy—but Mogadishu, the Harlan County episode, and the failure of the Clinton administration to take any action at all in Bosnia in more than 15 months had reaped its barren harvest. Clarke blocked the deployment of UN peacekeepers until it was too late. "Peacekeeping was almost dead," Clarke later described the place of peacekeeping in American policy in the spring of 1994. "There was no support for it in the U.S. government." A month after the start of the Hutu extermination program in Rwanda, Clarke finally issued President Clinton's sixteen-point presidential directive PDD–25, formally setting out America's isolationism in global humanitarian matters: the many conditions of which had to be met before U.S. peacekeeping forces could be assigned. Congressman David Obey summed them up in a scathing epithet: "zero degree of involvement, and zero degree of risk, and zero degree of pain and confusion." "It may seem strange to you," the president would acknowledge four years later on a pilgrimage to Kilagi—site of some of the worst atrocities—"but all over the world there were people like me sitting in offices, day after day after day, who did not appreciate the depth and speed with which you were engulfed by this unimaginable terror"—James Bennet, "Clinton Declares U.S., with World, Failed Rwandans," *New York Times,* March 26, 1998. "Today, the images of all that, haunt us all: the dead choking the Kigara River, floating to Lake Victoria. In their fate, we are reminded of the capacity everywhere, not just in Rwanda and certainly not just in Africa, but the capacity for people everywhere, to slip into pure evil. . . . We did not act quickly enough after the killing began. We should not have allowed the refugee camps to become safe havens for the killers. We did not immediately call these crimes by their rightful name: genocide."—Bill Clinton, "Remarks to Genocide Survivors in Kigali, Rwanda," March 25, 1998, *PPP:WJC,* Vol. I, 432.

Chapter Thirty-Three

281 "Chekhov's famous character Platonov": Anton Pavlovich Chekhov's *Platonov,* or *Fatherlessness,* or *Don Juan (In The Russian Manner),* was a six-hour play written by Chekhov in 1881 when he was a medical student in Moscow, and never performed in his lifetime. It was discovered among his papers in 1923, without a title page, hence the alternative names given to posthumous produc-

tions. In one instance, its Russian village setting was transposed to the Deep South of the United States as *Firework on the James*.

281 "During the period": "Declaration of Dolly Kyle Browning," executed on March 6, 1998, and released on March 13, 1998, as part of Paula Jones's lawyers' opposition to a motion for summary judgement by President Clinton's lawyers in the *Paula Jones* v. *William Jefferson Clinton* case.

283 "The Secret Service agents": Ibid.

283 "she didn't have much": "Notes attached to this declaration as Exhibit A," par. 5, "Declaration of Dolly Kyle Browning," quoted in Michael Isikoff, *Uncovering Clinton*, 377. "I stood by the president the entire conversation and heard and watched [Browning] the entire time," recorded Marsha Scott, the president's aide who had accompanied him to the class reunion party. "The conversation lasted thirty minutes . . . and at times she [Dolly] was very animated and threatening acting. . . . It was a bizarre conversation because she repeatedly said her [fictional] story was not true but that she was angry and needed money. She would throw out an accusation and then say it was a lie. It was this erratic behavior that made me stay so attentive."

283 "At the end of the conversation": "Declaration of Dolly Kyle Browning." Following the "angry" reunion in July 1994, Dolly didn't, in fact, move to Washington. Instead she made a "deal" via Clinton's amanuensis, Bruce Lindsey, regarding her novel. "The 'deal' was that I agreed not to tell the true story about our relationship if he would not tell any lies about [destroy] me. I agreed not to use, in public, the 'A words' which were defined as 'adultery' and 'affair.' I was allowed to say that we had a thirty-three year relationship that, from time to time, included sex. If I needed to contact Billy, I would call Dorcy [Dolly's sister, an attorney in Little Rock] and she would call Bruce Lindsey. I used this method of communication several times over the years."

Chapter Thirty-Four

286 "The Founders": *Clinton* v. *Jones*, 520 U.S. 681 (1997), J. Breyer, Concurring Opinion, http://www2.law.cornell.edu/cgi-bin/foliocgi.exe.

287 "3.5 million new jobs": When the U.S. economy was seen to reach 7 percent growth in December 1993, inflation fears caused the Federal Reserve Bank to raise interest rates to 7.4 percent in April 1994. This, however, proved to be a blip; long-term interest rates fell from a high of 9 percent in September 1990 to a stable 6 percent in October 1994—Joseph E. Stiglitz, *Globalization and Its Discontents*, 2002, 44.

Chapter Thirty-Five

291 "Jimmy Carter was an officer": Lippman, interview with the author, April 14, 2005.

292 "William Jefferson Blythe III": For an account of Clinton's parents' marriage, his paternity, and Bill Blythe III's death in an automobile accident before Clinton's birth, see Nigel Hamilton, *Bill Clinton: An American Journey*, 2003, 22–35.

292 "to walk the line": Panetta, interview with the author, January 20, 2005.

293 "the fury of an aroused democracy": William Jefferson Clinton, "Interview With Tom Brokaw of NBC News," June 5, 1994, *PPP:WJC*, Vol. I, 1038.

294 "He was cheered wildly": Charles M. Sennott, "Some Clinton backers put the pageantry aside; D-Day; The heroes remembered," *Boston Globe*, June 6, 1994.

Chapter Thirty-Six

295 "The American people": Kenneth R. Bazinet, "U.S., North Korea near war in 1994, Clinton got no-nuke vow," New York *Daily News*, October 18, 2002.

296 "Korea. It never": Sullivan, interview with the author, April 5, 2005.

296 "the door of the room opened": Jamie McIntyre, "Washington was on brink of war with North Korea 5 years ago; Pentagon had predicted up to 1 million deaths," CNN, October 4, 1999, www.cnn.com/US/9910/04/korea.brink.

296 "The president has returned": Godfrey Sperling, "Damage Control Is on the White House 'Agenda,'" *Christian Science Monitor*, June 21, 1994.

297 "Leon, the president is": Panetta, interview with the author, January 20, 2005.

298 "Unless you hijack a helicopter": Roger Simon, "No one gets lost in the shuffle," *Rocky Mountain News* (Denver, CO), July 5, 1994.

298 "a pillar of strength": "Remarks Announcing Changes in the White House Staff and an Exchange with Reporters," June 27, 1994, *PPP:WJC*, Vol. I, 1148.

298 "In an organizational sense": "Clinton's two hits, and his miss," *Boston Globe*, June 29, 1994.

Chapter Thirty-Seven

300 "the three hundred thousand dollars she'd made": Ruth Marcus, "First Lady Defends Business Moves; News Conference Surprises Many Senior White House Staffers," *Washington Post*, April 23, 1994.

301 "More Whitewater stories": Johnson and Broder, *The System*, 275.

301 "We talked about it": Ibid., 278–279.

301 "paranoid. They think": Ibid., 280.

302 "They were men": Ibid., 461–462.

303 "Don't let the fear-mongers": Remarks at a Health Care Rally in Jersey City, New Jersey, August 1, 1994, *PPP:WJC*, Vol. II, 1403.

303 "acid in the stomach": Johnson and Broder, *The System*, 495.

304 "We've lost our compass": Drew, *On the Edge*, 437.

Chapter Thirty-Eight

307 "Moses brought down": "Eye on the Clintons," *Human Events*, September 23, 1994, Vol. 50, Issue 36, 24.

307 "two to four players": Ibid., August 5, 1994.

307 "The Clinton presidency": Ibid., August 19, 1994.

308 "Cowardly Clinton": *American Spectator*, January 1994.

308 "the Clinton case is something": Editorial, "When politics gets personal," *Atlanta Journal-Constitution*, September 1, 1994.

Chapter Thirty-Nine

310 "the lowest it had ever": Stephanopoulos, *All Too Human*, 310.

310 "I was fed up": Clinton, *My Life*, 616.

310 "Republicans were solidly": Ibid.

311 "After those fucking phone": Stephanopoulos, *All Too Human,* 308.

311 "our most unpopular act": Ibid.

312 "to put that psychopath": Halberstam, *War in a Time of Peace*, 279.

312 "reign of terror": Clinton, *My Life*, 616.

313 "solve every problem": "Interview on CNN's 'Global Forum With President Clinton,'" May 3, 1994, *PPP:WJC*, Vol. I, 823.

313 "that the constant flip-flops": Halberstam, *War in a Time of Peace*, 283.

313 "He was obviously angry": Ibid.

313 "no constant flip-flops": "Interview on CNN's 'Global Forum With President Clinton," May 3, 1994, *PPP:WJC*, Vol. I, 825.

314 " 'Haiti had no military capability' ": Clinton, *My Life*, 617.

314 "without hedging or hesitation": Stephanopoulos, *All Too Human*, 306.

Chapter Forty

315 "I think all of us in the military": Sullivan, interview with the author, April 5, 2005.

315 "was not always pretty": Stephanopoulos, *All Too Human*, 308.

315 In a sort of World War II Gallipoli: See Carlo D'Este, *Fatal Decision: Anzio and the Battle for Rome*, 1991, 413.

316 "QUESTION: Dee Dee, on the": Press release by Dee Dee Myers, September 14, 1994.

318 "I can't believe they got me": Stephanopoulos, *All Too Human*, 305.

319 "I'm a merchant of hope": Press release by Dee Dee Myers, September 15, 1994.

320 "MYERS: Well, I think": Ibid.

321 "It's a mistake": Bill Hord, "Dole: Address Won't Change Mood of Public," *Omaha World Herald*, September 16, 1994.

321 "overwhelming aversion": Fletcher, "Clinton credibility tested in TV speech," *The Times* (London), September 16, 1994.

322 "Mr. Clinton is one of": R. W. Apple Jr., "Showdown in Haiti: In Perspective," *New York Times*, September 16, 1994.

322 "The message of the United States": "Address to the Nation on Haiti," September 15, 1994, *PPP:WJC*, Vol. II, 1558.

323 "Defiant even as U.S.": Douglas Farah, "Leaders Defiant as U.S. Warships Mass for Attack," *Washington Post*, September 16, 1994.

323 "If you have a next-door": "Local Callers Oppose Invasion," *Seattle Times*, September 16, 1994.

324 "There is nothing to": "Interview with Wire Service Reporters on Haiti," September 14, 1994, *PPP:WJC*, Vol. II, 1548.

325 "well-fed and well-dressed": Powell, *My American Journey*, 599.

325 "His spirit would": Ibid.

325 "die with American": Ibid., 600.

326 "We used to be the weakest": Ibid., 601.

326 "This is uncomfortable": Jeanne Cummings and Elizabeth Kurylo, "Envoys risked captivity; Haiti talks were chaotic, bizarre," *Atlanta Journal-Constitution*, September 20, 1994.

326 "He just kind of exploded": Ibid.

326 "Not bad intelligence": Powell, *My American Journey*, 601.

326 "We must immediately": Cummings and Kurylo, "Envoys risked captivity," *Atlanta Journal-Constitution*, September 20, 1994.

327 "caused almost a complete": Joan Kirchner, "Shame Over Policy Motivated Carter," *Chicago Sun-Times*, September 20, 1994.

327 "we didn't have time": Cummings and Kurylo, "Envoys risked captivity," *Atlanta Journal-Constitution*, September 20, 1994.

327 "I said I was ashamed": Cummings and Kurylo, "Envoys risked captivity," *Atlanta Journal-Constitution*, September 20, 1994.

328 "Mr. President, I think": Powell, *My American Journey*, 601.

329 "Then resign": Ibid.

329 "We have too many ministers": Ibid.

329 "I thought that was": Cummings and Kurylo, "Envoys risked captivity," *Atlanta Journal-Constitution*, September 20, 1994.

329 "I am going to": Powell, *My American Journey*, 601.

329 "The president's polls": Michael R. Kagay, "Mission to Haiti: Opinion, Occupation Lifts Clinton's Standing in Poll," *New York Times*, September 21, 1994.

330 "premature condemnation": Carl T. Rowan, "Cut Clinton Slack Over Haiti Deal," *Chicago Sun-Times*, September 30, 1994.

330 "Clinton and Carter have chalked up": Jack R. Payton, "Score a victory for Clinton, Carter," *St. Petersburg Times*, September 19, 1994.

330 "By this time, the Europeans": Sullivan, interview with the author, April 5, 2005.

Chapter Forty-One

333 had been brought up: Mel Steely, *The Gentleman from Georgia: The Biography of Newt Gingrich*, 2000, 1–2.

333 "sixteen to thirty-five": Gail Sheehy, "The Inner Quest of Newt Gingrich," *Vanity Fair*, September 1995.

334 "literally couldn't see": Ibid.

334 "No, I don't think": Ibid.

334 "I took him inside": Ibid.

334 "it is hard to be belligerent": Steely, *The Gentleman from Georgia*, 6.

334 "There was no need to shout": Sheehy, "The Inner Quest of Newt Gingrich," *Vanity Fair*, September 1995.

334 "I was a fifty-year-old": Ibid.

335 "Persistent, and persuasive": Jackie Battley to David Osborne, in David Osborne, "Newt Gingrich: shining knight of the post-Reagan Right," *Mother Jones*, November 1, 1984.

335 "He was her little boy": Sheehy, "The Inner Quest of Newt Gingrich," *Vanity Fair*, September 1995.

335 Jack Prince: Jack Prince was beaten in November 1964 by conservative Democrat Zell Miller—a college history teacher turned politician, who later bequeathed his own gubernatorial campaign strategists James Carville and Paul Begala to Bill Clinton for his presidential run, and later still, changed political affiliation, becoming a Republican .

335 "passing his doctoral": Only "one of five to do so in twenty years"—Steely, *The Gentleman from Georgia,* 23.

335 "the most charismatic teacher": Ibid., 30.

336 "six basic rules": Ibid., 44.

337 "He prefers that *modus operandi*": Sheehy, "The Inner Quest of Newt Gingrich," *Vanity Fair*, September 1995.

337 "Newt Gingrich has a tendency": Osborne, "Newt Gingrich," *Mother Jones*, November 1, 1984.

338 "If elected, Virginia": Osborne, "Newt Gingrich," *Mother Jones*, November 1, 1984.

338 "Newt can handle": Ibid.

338 "She isn't young enough": Ibid.

338 "Newt thought, well": Ibid.

339 "'Frankly,' Marianne later": Lloyd Grove, With Beth Berselli, "Marianne and Newt: Kaput?" ("The Reliable Source" column), *Washington Post*, July 15, 1999.

339 a close relationship with Callista Bisek: David Corn, "Gingrich vs. Gingrich: Why has the former speaker of the House chosen to let his dirty linen be brought out for all to see?" www.salon.com/news/feature/1999/11/24/gingrich.

339 "Newt is apparently trying": "Skeleton Closet: *All the Dirt on All the Candidates—Because character DOES matter*," Real People for Real Change, www.realchange.org, 2004. When Gingrich finally filed for divorce from Marianne, in 1999, he was aware she had been diagnosed with possible multiple sclerosis—but this did not stop him, or stop him from calling to tell her his intention while she was visiting her eighty-four-year-old mother in Atlanta on Mother's Day. Marianne's lawyer's Question No. 25 in the discovery process would ask Gingrich, tellingly: "Do you believe that you have conducted your private life in this marriage in accordance with the concept of 'family values' you have espoused politically and professionally?"

339 "Looking back, do you feel": Osborne, "Newt Gingrich," *Mother Jones*, November 1, 1984.

339 "I think you can write a psychological": Sheehy, "The Inner Quest of Newt Gingrich," *Vanity Fair*, September 1995.

Chapter Forty-Two

341 "You have to give them": Osborne, "Newt Gingrich," *Mother Jones*, November 1, 1984.

342 "Congressman 'Tip' O'Neill": "You deliberately stood in that well before an empty House, and challenged these people, and challenged their patriotism, and it is the lowest thing that I've ever seen in my thirty-two years in Congress," Speaker Tip O'Neill exploded over Gingrich's McCarthyite accusations in after-orders broadcasts in 1984, televised on C-Span after members had left the House chamber. O'Neill was forced to withdraw his *ad hominem* remark from the record, but the spat between the Speaker from Massachusetts and the "back bench bomb thrower" from Georgia became a landmark ("the first such rebuke of a Speaker of the House since 1798") in the increasingly bitter partisanship during the Reagan years—Peter J. Boyer, "Good Newt, Bad Newt," *Vanity Fair*, July 1989.

342 "just about the most disliked": *Washington Post* epithet, quoted in Boyer, "Good Newt, Bad Newt."

343 "is only one in a series": Gingrich memo to "various Gingrich staffs," one of a number of handwritten notes and drawings by Speaker Newt Gingrich, shown as document marked Exhibit 51a, March 29, 1993, to U.S. House of Representatives ethics committee by its special counsel, James M. Cole.

343 five immediate tasks: Ibid.

344 "He takes complete possession": Boyer, "Good Newt, Bad Newt."

344 "you *learn* to be an American": Newt Gingrich, *Renewing American Civilization*, "Class One—American Civilization," January 7, 1995, Reinhardt College version.

345 "you have certain long sweeps": Ibid.

347 "This journey is far, far": "Statement on Health Care Reform Legislation," September 26, 1994, *PPP:WJC*, Vol. II, 1632.

347 "This wasn't a person": Irwin Redliner, quoted in Dana Priest, "Democrats Pull the Plug on Health Care Reform," *Washington Post*, September 27, 1994.

347 "a sort of Bill of Rights": Ed Gillespie and Bob Schellhas, eds., *Contract With America: The Bold Plan by Rep. Newt Gingrich, Rep. Dick Armey and the House Republicans to Change the Nation*, 1994.

Chapter Forty-Three

349 "I'm not satisfied": Dick Morris, *Behind the Oval Office*, 8.

350 "lovingly detailed": Ibid., 10.

352 largely secret negotiations: Prime Minister Rabin had begun secret meetings with King Hussein several weeks after the Oslo agreement was signed; when word of one meeting between Hussein and Israel's foreign minister, Shimon Peres, leaked, King Hussein had had to halt negotiations for six months—a measure of how delicate the issues were. In April 1994, however, the U.S. State Department had offered "the moral, political and financial support" necessary for the accord, involving water rights, border definition, debt forgiveness, and modernization of Jordan's military: Christopher, *Chances of a Lifetime*, 308.

353 "Here at the first of many": "Remarks at the Signing Ceremony for the Israel-Jordan Peace Treaty at the Border Between Israel and Jordan," October 26, 1994, *PPP:WJC*, Vol. II, 1878.

354 "Your ratings are up": Morris, *Behind the Oval Office*, 15.

354   "This babykissing": Ibid., 16.

354   "Tax cut fever": Eric Pianin, "GOP 'Contract' Missing Its Price tag, Critics Say," *Washington Post*, September 28, 1994.

354   "a riverboat gamble": Ibid.

354   "melon head and the Cheshire cat": Mary Anne Sharkey, "Republicans Went One Step Too Far," Cleveland *Plain Dealer*, October 23, 1994.

355   "Clinton is in such trouble": Caroline Lochhead, "GOP Trumpets Conservative Agenda, 10-Point Program Calls for Cuts and More Prisons," *San Francisco Chronicle*, September 28, 1994.

355   "government has a very strong": Jill Zuckman, "GOP Musters House Control: Party promises a very different future," *Boston Globe*, September 28, 1994.

355   "Every item in our contract": Ibid.

355   "They laugh, they scoff": Dick Williams, "Gingrich and GOP Take the Initiative," *Atlanta Journal-Constitution*, October 1, 1994.

356   "The chances are two": Kris Jensen, "Newsstand Gingrich Getting Plenty of Ink," *Atlanta Journal-Constitution*, October 18, 1994.

356   "Not the House, no way": Morris, *Behind the Oval Office*, 14.

Chapter Forty-Four

359   "a full-blown disaster": Rodham Clinton, *Living History*, 256.

359   "On November": Clinton, *My Life*, 629 and 631.

360   "a negative referendum": Gergen, *Eyewitness to Power*, 314.

360   "funereal": Rodham Clinton, *Living History*, 257.

360   "I don't know how to": Sheehy, *Hillary's Choice*, 253.

360   "I had forgotten": Clinton, *My Life*, 632.

361   "I was present with him": Henry Cisneros, interview with the author, November 29, 2004.

361   "He crisscrossed the country": Stephanopoulos, *All Too Human*, 317.

361   "I never should have brought": Ibid., 322–323.

362   "In many races": Michael Kranish, "Democrats See Payoff in GOP 'Contract': Some Republicans Play Down Move," *Boston Globe*, October 23, 1994.

362   "a cardboard cutout": Stephanopoulos, *All Too Human*, 316.

363   "You saw I gave": Morris, *Behind the Oval Office*, 17.

363   "President Clinton never, ever": Ibid., 40.

363   "A race track": Jim Morgan, interview with the author, February 1, 2001.

364   "locked in a sort of zero-sum": Morris, *Behind the Oval Office*, 39.

364   "bitter row between": "Clintons in row over party ideals," *The Advertiser* (Australia), November 25, 1994.

365 "If you will agree": Patrick Cockburn, "America set to return to the bunker; The election triumph of the Republicans will reinforce isolationist trends," *The Independent* (London), November 17, 1994.

365 Christian fundamentalist racism: Senator Helms had mobilized the religious right in the 1970s "and built one of the most profitable political fundraising machines ever," wrote Eric Bates in the May 1, 1995, issue of *Mother Jones* ("What you need to know about the not-so-gentleman from North Carolina"). "And long after die-hard segregationists like George Wallace and Strom Thurmond began courting black voters, Helms fueled white fears by opposing a national holiday in honor of Dr. Martin Luther King Jr., whistling 'Dixie' while standing next to Senator Carol Moseley-Braun, and supporting apartheid in South Africa. 'His racial politics are deeply held convictions, not simply politics of convenience,' says Christopher Scott [North Carolina AFL-CIO President]. 'He has a view of a fundamentalist Christian society in which everyone is not welcome. If you could pick up the South Africa of [twenty] years ago and transplant it to America, that's what he would do.' "

366 "You ask an honest": John M. Goshko, "Helms Questions Clinton's Ability to Hold Commander-in-Chief Post; GOP Senator Criticizes U.S. Military Intervention in Haiti," *Washington Post*, November 19, 1994.

366 "Bill Clinton is still": Steven Greenhouse, "The New Congress Confrontation; Helms Voices Doubts on Clinton as Commander," *New York Times*, November 19, 1994.

366 "That's a mistake": Ibid.

367 "I do not share that view": Greenhouse, "Chairman of Joint Chiefs Defends Clinton Against Attack by Helms," *New York Times*, November 20, 1994.

367 "I had some reservations": Juan J. Walte, "Outspoken Helms returns to the fray; GOP hard-liner stirs a new controversy," *USA Today*, November 21, 1994.

367 Panetta was right to be optimistic: " 'Look,' I said, 'from my own experience with Gingrich, there is a silver lining here. Newt Gingrich has never governed. And Republicans have never governed for a long time [in Congress]. And I'm not sure they know *how* to govern. They know how to be a minority. And they know how to throw grenades. But I'm not sure they know how to really *govern*. And my experience is that, in the end, Republicans will always overreach. So I think you need to be able to make use of the opportunity—because there really is one. In having the Republicans now take the House you may be able to contrast them with what you are trying to do for the country.' "—Leon Panetta, interview with the author, January 20, 2005.

Chapter Forty-Five

370 "a great president": Morris, *Inside the Oval Office*, 37 and 40.

371 "a transitional figure": John King, "Clinton Fires Back At Democratic Critics," *Chicago Sun-Times*, December 6, 1994.

371   "spent to promote the health care": Bill Nichols, "President, 'A slip is not a fall,'" *USA Today*, December 7, 1994.

372   "You know, I was trying": "Remarks at the Democratic Leadership Gala," December 6, 1994, *PPP:WJC*, Vol. II, 2152–2158.

376   "We believe the promise": "Where We Stand:The New Orleans Declaration," Statement Endorsed at the Fourth Annual DLC Conference, DLC, Key Document, March 1, 1990, New Democrats Online, www.ndol.org.

376   "It's just as good": "Remarks at the Democratic Leadership Gala," December 6, 1994, *PPP:WJC*, Vol. II, 2152–2158.

377   "As the president sat down": William F. Powers, "The Night the Bubbly Burst; Republicans Party on Cloud Nine, Democrats Come Down to Earth," *Washington Post*, December 7, 1994.

377   "Dump Bill campaign": Jonathan Alter, "Imagine Dumping Bill," *Newsweek*, December 5, 1994.

377   "a political cripple": Todd S. Purdum, "White House Memo; A Wounded President Strives Not to Become a Lame Duck," *New York Times*, December 8, 1994.

378   "an awful lot of meetings": Ann Devroy, "Clinton Revs Up, Steers to the Center; DLC Speech Reveals New Attempt to Reach Out to Middle Class," *Washington Post*, December 8, 1994.

Chapter Forty-Six

379   "He's Speaker of the House of Representatives": Robin Toner, "Charge of illegal drug use by White House staff has Democrats fuming; Accusations part of smear tactics, official responds," *Ottawa Citizen*, December 6, 1994.

380   "Either I have to close": Ceci Connolly, "House Speaker not one to pull punches," *St. Petersburg Times*, December 9, 1994.

380   "I think there's a big": Dowd, "Gingrich, Now a Round Peg, Seeks to Smooth the Edges," *New York Times*, December 9, 1994.

380   fewer than one in five: Richard Wolf, "Gingrich is gaining in influence, poll finds," *USA Today*, December 20, 1994.

380   "have to be met unless": Elizabeth Shogren, "First lady: Gingrich's orphanage idea 'absurd,'" *USA Today*, December 1, 1994.

381   "I'd ask her to go to": Mark Wilson, "Gingrich Alleges Past Use of Drugs by Clinton Staff," *Chicago Sun-Times*, December 5, 1994.

381   "regularly referred to me": Rodham Clinton, *Living History*, 263.

382   "Shaking hands with Bill Clinton": "1994 Perspectives," *Newsweek*, December 26, 1994 and January 2, 1995.

Chapter Forty-Seven

383   "Christopher had already tendered": Halberstam, *War in a Time of Peace*, 299.

384 "My ideas have been": John Schwartz, "Blunt Talk, Sudden Exit; Surgeon General Outspoken From the Start," *Washington Post*, December 10, 1994.

385 "This is the little lady": "Elders Quits U.S. Surgeon General," *Chicago Sun-Times*, December 9, 1994; Schwartz, "Blunt Talk, Sudden Exit," *Washington Post*, December 10, 1994.

385 "I think that is something that is a part": "Comments After Speech at the U.N.," *Washington Post*, December 10, 1994.

385 "Dr. Elders, I don't": Joycelyn Elders and David Chanoff, *Joycelyn Elders, MD*, 1996, 333.

386 "Joycelyn, I'm sorry": Ibid., 334.

386 "has basically taken positions": Quoted in Schwartz, "Blunt Talk, Sudden Exit," *Washington Post*, December 10, 1994.

386 "Yes, they told me": Elders and Chanoff, *Joycelyn Elders, MD,* 334.

386 "spread further, faster": Kofi Annan, quoted in Lawrence K. Altman, "U.N. Urges Tripling of Funds by '08 to Halt AIDS," *New York Times*, June 2, 2006.

387 "I never got the impression": Elders, interview with the author, February 5, 2001.

387 "This is the wisest decision": Schwartz, "Blunt Talk, Sudden Exit," *Washington Post*, December 10, 1994.

387-388 "This outspoken woman": Ellen Goodman, "Unprotected sex talk," *Boston Globe*, December 15, 1994.

388 "Bill Clinton could have flogged": Anna Quindlen, "Excerpts from newspaper columns. Thanks to the angels," *Atlanta Journal-Constitution*, December 15, 1994.

388 "a man whose libidometer": Patricia Smith, "Elders' sin: delivering us from ignorance," *Boston Globe*, December 14, 1994.

388 "she would have been terminated": "Top U.S. official fired for remark on masturbation," *Toronto Star*, December 10, 1994.

389 a more muscular NATO air approach: A so-called Contact Group had been established in April 1994, consisting of representatives of the U.S., Russia, Britain, France, and Germany. The Group put forward a sort of Vance-Owen II peace proposal on July 6, 1994, but although it was accepted by both Muslims and Croats, it was rejected by the Serbs. When, in desperation, Bosnian Muslims attempted an offensive from the Bihac "safe area" in October, the Serbs felt licensed to restart the war. President Clinton announced the lifting of the Bosnian arms embargo on November 10, 1994, but the strike element—a NATO air attack on a Serb-Croatian airfield—resulted in an utter debacle for the UN and NATO, for the Serbs merely blocked and blockaded all UN humanitarian, peacekeeping, and observer forces in Bosnia. With President Clinton refusing to commit ground troops, the NATO allies dropped all attempts at an air strike strategy for forcing peace. "By the end of 1994, the Clinton administration's policy toward Bosnia had reached a virtual dead end," Ivo Daalder chronicled—with containment and unenforceable negotiation the only option, duly carried out by former president

Jimmy Carter, who obtained a four-month cease-fire, beginning on January 1, 1995—Ivo H. Daalder, *Getting to Dayton: The Making of America's Bosnia Policy*, 2000, 31–37.

389 acceleration of global free trade: In Miami, in the second week in December 1994, the leaders of thirty-four countries from Canada to Uruguay had, at their first "Summit of the Americas," agreed to a "Free Trade Area of the Americas" linking more than 850 million people in a single tariff-free zone over the following ten years. Flanked by the prime ministers and presidents of all the nations of the hemisphere (except Cuba), President Clinton had called the agreement a "historic step" ensuring more jobs and "solid, lasting prosperity for our peoples," which committed the nations to "the observance and promotion of workers' rights. In less than a decade, if current trends continue," he had added, "this hemisphere will be the world's largest market: more than 850 million consumers buying $13 trillion worth of goods and services"—"Remarks Following the First Session of the Summit of the Americas in Miami," December 10, 1994, *PPP:WJC*, Vol. II, 2171.

Chapter Forty-Eight

395 "This idea that there's some battle": Bob Cohn and Bill Turque, "I Know What I Believe," interview with Bill Clinton, *Newsweek*, January 9, 1995.

396 "I'm actually in a very good humor": Ibid.

Chapter Forty-Nine

401 "he seemed off stride": Robert E. Rubin and Jacob Weisberg, *In an Uncertain World*, 154.

401 "Often, when I've heard criticism": Ibid., 24.

402 "This is a cynical age": Robert Reich, *Locked in the Cabinet*, 1997, 225.

403 "You all have to *help* me": Ibid.

403 "really going to hurt Democrats": Rubin and Weisberg, *In an Uncertain World*, 154.

404 no *Jones* v. *Clinton* trial: Fact-finding procedures such as sworn statements would, Judge Wright ruled, be permitted in the meantime. Any such fact-finding was immediately postponed when, in February 1995, Jones's lawyers appealed Judge Wright's decision, and the entire matter was delayed until the appeal could be heard that fall.

404 "I would have preferred": Woodward, *The Choice*, 65.

405 "I miss every inch": Quoted in James D. Retter, *Anatomy of a Scandal*, 1998, 71.

Chapter Fifty

406 "Today the House of Representatives": David Dahl, "Gingrich holds the cards in Congress," *St. Petersburg Times,* January 4, 1995.

407 "Gingrich's book deal": In October 1990, Murdoch had secretly met with the British prime minister to discuss his plan to merge his Sky Television with British Satellite Broadcasting, five days before the deal was publicly announced. Mrs. Thatcher had been bitterly attacked for failing to tell broadcasting regulators of a possible breach of the new law on regulating media ownership. A year later, she had received a reported $5.25 million advance for her memoirs—from Murdoch's HarperCollins.

408 "I think a strategy": Drew, *Showdown,* 53.

408 "Damnit, every day": Ibid., 54.

408 "narrow in hate, his face": Howard Fineman, "Gingrich Goes Ballistic," *Newsweek,* January 30, 1995. Steven Thomma (Knight-Ridder News Service), "Speaker rages at his critics; Gingrich calls capital 'mean,' then faults first lady, ex-speaker, Democrat foes, media," *Pittsburgh Post-Gazette,* January 21, 1995.

408 "Gingrich denounced": David Streitfeld, "$4 Million Book Deal For Gingrich; Political Opponents Decry Windfall From Murdoch Firm," *Washington Post,* December 22, 1994.

409 "If you live by the sword": Bennett Roth, "Gingrich returns fire—everywhere; Speaker defends his ethics, lashes Democrats and media," *Houston Chronicle,* January 21, 1995.

Chapter Fifty-One

411 "I'm looking for another": Woodward, *The Choice,* 73.

Chapter Fifty-Two

413 "to run a covert operation": Stephanopoulos, *All Too Human,* 229–330.

414 "You can stop lobbying": Reich, *Locked in the Cabinet,* 227.

415 "Medicare cuts": Morris, *Behind the Oval Office,* 93.

415 "You're right": Reich, *Locked in the Cabinet,* 227–228.

Chapter Fifty-Three

417 "Panetta was sick and disgusted": Woodward, *The Choice,* 77.

417 "opportunity-responsibility" centrist agenda: Itself a reprise of Governor Clinton's "New Democratic" agenda from the late 1980s.

417 "thirty minute self-indulgent": Morris, *Behind the Oval Office,* 95.

419 "the values and voices": "Address Before a Joint Session of the Congress on the State of the Union," January 24, 1995, *PPP:WJC*, Vol. I, 75–86.

421 "He's a comeback": Todd S. Purdum, "White House Memo; A Wounded President Strives Not to Become a Lame Duck," *New York Times*, December 8, 1994.

421 "I always get the impression": Clinton, "Interview with Tom Brokaw of *NBC Nightly News*," January 26, 1995, *PPP:WJC*, Vol. I, 95–102.

423 "IT WAS CLINTON'S": David Broder, "An Opportunity Missed," *Washington Post*, January 26, 1995; and "IT WAS CLINTON'S BIG CHANCE, AND HE BLEW IT," *Plain Dealer*, January 26, 1995.

424 "the best possible response": Hamish McRae, "Wisdom from a sheepish liberal; Bill Clinton's State of the Union speech had a pragmatic tone that Europe's leaders should head," *The Independent* (London), January 26, 1995.

424 "to let Gingrich": Panetta, interview with the author, January 20, 2005.

424 "February and March": Morris, *Behind the Oval Office*, 96.

425 "She ought to stay:" Margo Hammond, "No ordinary people in 'No Ordinary Time,'" *St. Petersburg Times*, September 27, 1994.

425 "In contrast Hillary has chosen": Donnie Radcliffe, "For Roosevelt Biographer, Clinton Role Is Unwritten, Historian Has Ideas for First Lady," *Washington Post*, November 24, 1994.

426 "when Hillary is stung": Morris, *Behind the Oval Office*, 111.

426 "the few portions": David Maraniss, *The Clinton Enigma*, 1998, 20.

427 "An awkward question": "Interview With Religious Affairs Journalists," February 2, 1995, *PPP:WJC*, Vol. I, 147.

428 *"The Clinton Chronicles"*: Falwell's decision to fund and promote the deliberately defamatory, largely paranoid video *The Clinton Chronicles* on national television made it hard to believe Falwell was an ordained Christian minister. The video, advertised as "Jerry Falwell Presents Bill Clinton's Circle of Power," was an outrageously snide, one-sided narrative of supposed decadence and evil on the part of the United States president, strung together with doom-laden music and a voice-over worthy—as Joe Conason and Gene Lyons later wrote, in *The Hunting of the President* (2001)—of the *Bride of Frankenstein*.

428 "I think there have been": "Interview With Religious Affairs Journalists," February 2, 1995, *PPP:WJC*, Vol. I, 149.

Chapter Fifty-Four

430 "I'm not going to take": Woodward, *The Choice*, 140.

430 "Leon, I want to do it": Morris, *Behind the Oval Office*, 119.

431 "We have entered": "Remarks and a Question-and-Answer Session with the American Society of Newspaper Editors in Dallas, Texas," April 7, 1995, *PPP:WJC*, Vol. I, 474–487.

433   "gets it. I don't think": Bill Nichols, "Clinton refocuses, sets a new agenda," *USA Today*, April 10, 1995.

433   "AND on the [ninety-third] day": I. Stelzer, "Right on Target," *Courier-Mail* (Australia), April 8, 1995.

434   "The United States government is the largest": " 'All of Us Together . . . Must Totally Remake the Federal Government,' " *Washington Post*, April 8, 1995.

Chapter Fifty-Five

437   "Half of federal building": Brian Duffy et al., "Oklahoma City: April 19, 1995; The end of innocence," *U.S. News & World Report*, May 1, 1995.

439   impending execution: April 19, 1995, Snell was executed and at 9:16 P.M. and pronounced dead by prison doctors at the state prison.

439   "The bombing in Oklahoma City": "Remarks on the Bombing of the Alfred P. Murrah Federal Building in Oklahoma City, Oklahoma," April 19, 1995, *PPP:WJC*, Vol. I, 552.

440   "Let me say again": "The President's News Conference with President Fernando Cardoso of Brazil," April 20, 1995, *PPP:WJC*, Vol. I, 557–558.

Chapter Fifty-Six

442   "common, increasingly common": "Interview with Wolf Blitzer and Judy Woodruff," CNN, April 13, 1995, *PPP:WJC*, Vol. I, 527–528.

442   "left wondering, if it": Ibid.

443   "I would say to the children": "The President's News Conference with President Fernando Cardoso of Brazil," April 20, 1995, *PPP:WJC*, Vol. I, 557.

443   "need to know that": "Remarks and an Exchange with Reporters on the Oklahoma City Bombing," April 21, 1995, *PPP:WJC*, Vol. I, 568.

443   "Our family has been struggling": "Remarks by the President and Hillary Clinton to Children on the Oklahoma City Bombing," April 22, 1995, *PPP:WJC*, Vol. I, 569–572.

444   "Today our nation joins": "Remarks at a Memorial Service for the Bombing Victims in Oklahoma City, Oklahoma," April 23, 1995, *PPP:WJC*, Vol. I, 573.

446   "So often criticized": Brian Duffy and Gordon Witkin, "The End of Innocence," *U.S. News & World Report*, May 1, 1995.

Chapter Fifty-Seven

447   "As horrible as it was": Stephanopoulos, interview with Chris Bury, "The Clinton Years," PBS television.

447 "the real test of leadership": Donna Shalala, interview with Chris Bury, "The Clinton Years," PBS television.

448 "a real turning point": Panetta, interview with Chris Bury, "The Clinton Years," PBS television.

448 "Oklahoma City was the moment": Henry Cisneros, interview with the author, November 29, 2005.

448 "The president has an extraordinary": Reich, interview with Chris Bury, "The Clinton Years," PBS television.

449 "there was no doubt": Michael Waldman, interview with Chris Bury, "The Clinton Years," PBS television.

449 "the general atmosphere": "Remarks by the President and Hillary Clinton to Children on the Oklahoma City Bombing," April 22, 1995, *PPP:WJC*, Vol. I, 572.

450 "In this country we cherish": "Remarks to the American Association of Community Colleges in Minneapolis," April 24, 1995, *PPP:WJC*, Vol. I, 579–585.

451 "Words have consequences": Ibid.

451 "Make no mistake": Howard Kurtz and Dan Balz, "Clinton Assails Spread of Hate Through Media; Americans Urged to Stand Against 'Reckless Speech'; Conservatives Take Offense," *Washington Post*, April 25, 1995.

452 "resist them with arms": "Talk radio's tough talkers; The Oklahoma City Bombing," *Boston Globe*, April 29, 1995.

452 "You shoot twice to the body": "Liddy: Hate radio? Aim for the groin," *St. Petersburg Times*, April 26, 1995.

452 "It is grotesque to suggest": "Query Gets Angry Response From Gingrich," *Washington Post*, April 23, 1995.

452 "I challenge the news media": "Sorrow and Suspicion; Anti-terror bills zoom down pike; Gingrich seeks repeal of assault weapon ban," *Atlanta Journal-Constitution*, April 25, 1995.

452 some 229 homicides: Dalton Camp, "U.S. right wingers line up to defend guns," *Toronto Star*, April 30, 1995.

453 "The president, from day one": Ann Devroy, "Clinton Praised for Responding to Disaster Swiftly and Strongly," *Washington Post*, April 24, 1995.

453 "decisive and in command": "Oklahoma City Horror Tests Clinton Leadership," *Buffalo News*, April 26, 1995.

453 "They are convinced the U.S. Government": M. Casey, "America in the Grip of Madness," *Herald Sun* (Australia), April 29, 1995.

454 "could strike the general electorate": Tom Mashberg, "Clinton shows strength in crisis; Issues being debated on his political turf," *Boston Herald*, April 25, 1995.

455 "internal espionage": Ibid.

Chapter Fifty-Eight

460 "the force and passion": Gingrich, *Lessons Learned the Hard Way*, 1998, 61.

461 "who will be the James Carville": "Clear signs that a dissatisfied Clinton is looking for what one official called 'fresh new blood' in his political operation have
been evident the past several weeks," Ms. Devroy—famed for her ability to ferret
out information—reported. And she added: "Republican pollster Dick Morris, a
longtime Clinton occasional adviser" had recommended that the president take
on new pollsters, Penn & Schoen. "Morris is a friend of Donald Schoen"—Ann
Devroy, "Clinton in '96: The Check Request Is in the Mail; As List of Would-Be
GOP Opponents Grows, President Prepares to Open Reelection Office," *Washington Post*, April 14, 1995.

462 "A bill to reshape": Todd S. Purdum, "Desperately in Need of Winning Streak,
Clinton Finds One," *New York Times*, May 7, 1995.

462 "to some extent": Panetta, interview with the author, January 20, 2005.

463 "with a parallel black hole": Stephanopoulos, interview with Chris Bury, "The
Clinton Years," PBS television.

464 "The problem, the concern": Panetta, interview with the author, January 20,
2005.

464 "Resentful": Stephanopoulos, interview with Chris Bury, "The Clinton Years,"
PBS television.

464 "triangulating": It was at the April 5 strategy meeting, Morris recalled, that the
president, backed by the vice president, had decided not to seek a two-way fight
with Gingrich and the Republican congressional agenda on behalf of the Democratic Party, but to "triangulate"—to chart an independent presidential course
"that accommodates the needs [that] the Republicans address," as Morris put it to
the president, "but does it in a way that is uniquely yours"—Morris, *Behind the
Oval Office*, 80.

464 "There are too many": Ibid., 122–123.

465 "Think plush Victorian": Jura Koncius, "An Air of History; Clintons' White
House Redecoration looks to Past," *Washington Post*, November 27, 1993.

466 "Hillary thought": Clinton, *My Life*, 653.

466 "The idea of hard-core Republican": Rodham Clinton, *Living History*, 297.

466 Russian invasion of Chechnya: In 1991 Dzokhar Dudayev, president of the
Chechen Republic, had declared its independence from Russia. Russian troops,
meeting Chechen armed resistence, withdrew, leading to complete anarchy in the
country. In 1994, President Yeltsin had ordered the Russian invasion, with 40,000
troops, but the expected quick solution did not materialize, and the situation soon
resembled that of the earlier Russian invasion of Afghanistan. In February, Russian forces finally occupied Grozny, the capital. By the following year, when a
cease-fire agreement was reached, over 100,000 Chechens and Russians had lost
their lives in what was called the First Chechen War.

467 "We're completely agreed": Strobe Talbott, *The Russia Hand*, 2002, 160.

467 "I think we got": Ibid., 164.

467 "You're the biggest problem": Morris, *Behind the Oval Office*, 124–126.

469 facing overthrow by voters: Tony Blair, conversation with the author, May 8, 1995.

470 "shifting of the battleship": Sosnik, interview with the author, May 23, 2005.

Chapter Fifty-Nine

471 Mark Hatfield of Oregon: So passionately had Senator Hatfield felt about Gingrich's "gimmick" (as he called it) that, on March 2, when the bill had come up for its final vote, he'd offered Bob Dole his resignation from the Senate rather than having to cast the all-offending vote that would smash his party's "linchpin" bill in the much-vaunted Contract With America. Senator Dole had been mortified, yet in his literally war-torn bones the new Senate majority leader had known his longstanding Republican colleague was right—and had told him to vote according to his conscience, dooming the bill.

471 "I just don't get it": Editorial, "Prime cuts of pork," *St. Petersburg Times*, May 20, 1995.

472 "If he would not bend": Gingrich, *Lessons Learned the Hard Way*, 49–50.

473 "Well, I'm—first of all": "Interview with Peter Malof of New Hampshire Public Radio," May 19, 1995, *PPP:WJC*, Vol. I, 715–716.

474 "sneaking off the bench": Stephanopoulos, *All Too Human*, 345.

474 "apopleptic": Woodward, *The Choice*, 208.

475 "You guys want me": Stephanopoulos, *All Too Human*, 345–346.

475 "Obviously, we had a bad": Sosnik, interview with the author, May 23, 2005.

476 "wasn't any real economic": Rubin and Weisberg, *In an Uncertain World*, 164.

477 "Damnit, George, the president": Stephanopoulos, *All Too Human*, 348.

478 "it has to be next week": Ibid., 354.

478 "the double indignity": Ibid., 351.

478 "Mr. President": Reich, *Locked in the Cabinet*, 262.

478 "Mr. President, you're in": Ibid., 260.

479 "had agreed to put off": Stephanopoulos, *All Too Human*, 354.

Chapter Sixty

480 "I thought they": Lake, interview with the author, May 17, 2005.

481 "because we would have to": Roger Cohen, "Fighting Rages as NATO Debates How to Protect Bosnian Enclave," *New York Times*, November 25, 1994.

481 "a B engraved": Lake, interview with the author, May 17, 2005.

481 "and you don't have": Interview with senior Clinton administration official, April, 2005.

482   "I was very frustrated": Lake, interview with the author, May 17, 2005.

482   "to try and figure it out": Lake, interview with the author, May 17, 2005.

485   "B's cave-in": Reich, *Locked in the Cabinet*, 264.

485   "I'm bringing Dick in": Morris, *Behind the Oval Office*, 128.

486   "does not raise taxes": Clinton, "Address to the Nation on the Plan to Balance the Budget," June 13, 1995, *PPP:WJC*, Vol. I, 878.

Chapter Sixty-One

489   "If there is going to be Armageddon": E. J. Dionne Jr., "Peace or Armageddon," *Washington Post*, June 20, 1995.

490   "only" 3,000: Clinton, "The President's News Conference in Halifax," June 16, 1995, *PPP:WJC*, Vol. I, 897.

490   "We have to get the policy straight": Woodward, *The Choice*, 255.

492   "We must do something": Ibid., 260.

492   "This can't continue": Ibid.

493   "This policy is doing enormous": Ibid., 262.

493   "the symbol of U.S.": Lake, interview with the author, May 17, 2005.

Chapter Sixty-Two

494   "Think about the date": Lippman, interview with the author, May 3, 2005.

495–496   "My twenty-one-year-old": Quoted in Woodward, *The Choice*, 262.

496   "in the end Sarajevo": Quoted in Daalder, *Getting to Dayton*, 68.

496   "The United States": Woodward, *The Choice*, 263.

496   "The latest test of wills": Michael Dobbs, "After Another Week of Bosnia Rhetoric, West Is at Square One," *Washington Post*, July 23, 1995.

Chapter Sixty-Three

498   "The typical day began": Panetta, interview with the author, January 20, 2005.

500   "Freeh looked like": Hubbell, *Friends in High Places*, 236.

500   saying that he did not want: Louis Freeh, interview with Mike Wallace, *60 Minutes*, CBS Television, September 9, 2005.

500   "too political and self-serving": Clinton, *My Life*, 530.

501   "Freeh ran the bureau": Joshua Micah Marshall, "The Man Who Wasn't There: How Louis Freeh escaped responsibility for 9/11," *Slate*, July 9, 2002.

502   "I had thought these issues": Richard A. Clarke, *Against All Enemies*, 2004, 98–99.

503 "We are living at": Clinton, "Remarks at the Central Intelligence Agency in Langley, Virginia," July 14, 1995, *PPP:WJC*, Vol. II, 1093.

504 "is hidden from the headlines": Ibid.

505 "provided they were willing to work": Associated Press report, "Affirmative Action Should Focus On Poor People, Gingrich Says," *New York Times*, June 17, 1995.

507 "The Republicans think": Stephanopoulos, *All Too Human*, 365.

508 "In recent weeks": Clinton, "Remarks on Affirmative Action at the National Archives and Records Administration," July 19, 1995, *PPP:WJC*, Vol. II, 1106.

Chapter Sixty-Four

511 "It looks now as if the Hamlet": John Carlin, "Clinton finds a natural touch at last," *The Independent* (London), August 17, 1995.

512 "When you shake hands": Bill Nichols, "Hiking to Horsing Around," *USA Today*, August 16, 1995.

513 "One of the most touching": Georgie Anne Geyer, "Peace Plan Policy Endangered Diplomats in Bosnia," New Orleans *Times-Picayune*, August 29, 1995.

514 "off the front pages": Marshall Freeman Harris and Stephen W. Walker, "Will the U.S. Sell Out the Bosnians?" *New York Times*, August 23, 1995.

515 murdered in cold blood: Even ten years later, Karadzic and Mladic, though indicted *in absentia* for major war crimes, had not been apprehended—while the grisly work of identifying the bodies of their victims had been made immeasurably more difficult by the Serbs' decision to dig up and, wherever possible, destroy evidence of the massacre. "Investigators have identified numerous other places where prisoners were assembled and killed: a soccer field, a warehouse and a school in Bratunac, a warehouse in Konjevic Polje, a riverside at Drinjaca, a bend in the road at Nova Kasaba, and a school and nearby dam at Petkovci," Daniel Williams wrote on the tenth anniversary of the murders. "One of the worst mass executions occurred at a place called Branjevo farm, where more than 1,200 men and boys were shot down in a field. Using aerial photographs, tribunal investigators have uncovered numerous grave sites filled with hundreds of bodies. Some of the bodies had been buried first at other sites, then dug up and moved in an attempt to hide evidence after the war ended. Many victims had their hands manacled or were blindfolded. In addition to the 2,000 corpses buried at the cemetery at Potocari, about 3,500 bodies remain in storage in Tuzla, Bosnia, where forensic experts are trying to identify them."—Daniel Williams, "10 Years After Bosnia Massacre, Justice Not Yet Served; Experts Doubt Top Suspects Will Be Tried Before U.N. Court Is Scheduled to Expire," *Washington Post*, June 30, 2005.

515 "A Joyous Cry": Stacy Sullivan, "From Sarajevo, A Joyous Cry Of 'At Last,'" *Washington Post*, August 31, 1995.

515 "operation that restored": Ibid.

516   "Transatlantic squabbling": Bruce Clark, "NATO Strikes In Bosnia: Jets spearhead new Balkans policy; Bombing raids mark important change in Nato's approach to Bosnia crisis," *Financial Times* (London) August 31, 1995.

516   "No one should doubt": "Remarks at the Joint Service Review at Wheeler Airfield in Honolulu," Septemebr 1, 1995, *PPP:WJC*, Vol. II, 1276.

517   was "snatching defeat out of the jaws": Ed Vulliamy, "NATO Sets Deadline for Serb Pull-out," *The Observer* (London), September 3, 1995.

517   "far larger than the total": Carl Bildt, *Peace Journey: The Struggle for Peace in Bosnia*, 1998, 122.

518   "things went backwards": Ibid., 143.

518   "It is not a just peace": Richard Holbrooke, *To End a War*, 1998, 309.

Chapter Sixty-Five

519   "We had kept offering different": Panetta, interview with the author, January 20, 2005.

520   "Dole tried to calm things": Clinton, *My Life*, 682.

521   "If you want": Ibid.; Woodward, *The Choice*, 316 (though Woodward dates this meeting as November 1, 1995).

521   "were elated by": Clinton, *My Life*, 682–683.

521   "define who he was": Panetta, interview with the author, January 20, 2005.

522   "I was afraid": Clinton, *My Life*, 683.

522   from terrorist to peacemaker: Aged 73, Prime Minister Rabin had been a terrorist in the Haganah underground, the Palmach. On the founding of Israel he had been made chief of the General Staff of the army at thirty-two, and had developed the Israeli blitzkrieg doctrine that won the 1967 Six-Day War. Appointed Ambassador to the United States, he had then been elected a member of the Knesset for over twenty years. He had had to resign as leader of the Labor Party when it was found his wife Leah had an illegal American bank account, but in 1994, having become prime minister for a second time, and having secured recognition of Israel by Jordan and signed the Oslo Declaration of Principles at the White House, he had won the Nobel Peace Prize. Terrorists, he had told President Clinton as an ex-terrorist, should not be permitted to derail peace negotiations—terror should be fought, he felt, as if there were no negotiations, and negotiations should be conducted as if there were no terrorists.

523   "but you land at Andrews": Katharine Q. Seelye, "Battle Over the Budget: the Leader; Snub on Clinton Plane Had Consequences, Gingrich Says," *New York Times*, November 16, 1995.

523   "Until someone shows me": John E. Yang, "Underlying Gingrich's Stance Is His Pique About President," *Washington Post*, November 16, 1995.

524   "sewn up the category": Todd S. Purdum, "Battle Over the Budget: The Flight; A Washington Potboiler Steals Budget's Thunder," *New York Times*, November 17, 1995.

524 "Let's take it into": Julian Beltrame, "U.S. government crackup has lots of echoes for Canadians," *The Gazette* (Montreal), November 17, 1995.

524 "More by good fortune": Ibid.

524 "Mike, why did you": Woodward, *The Choice*, 323.

526 "I kept, we kept": Panetta, interview with the author, January 20, 2005.

526 "I don't think they understand": Roger, K. Lowe, "Voters Need Program Notes to Follow This Political Grand Opera," *Columbus Dispatch* (Ohio), November 19, 1995.

526 "Seven [years] is the longest": John E. Yang, "Underlying Gingrich's Stance Is His Pique About President," *Washington Post*, November 16, 1995.

Chapter Sixty-Six

531 "courts, of princes": William Shakespeare, *Cymbeline*, Act III, Scene iii.

532 "Ellen Rometsch": Laurence Leamer, *The Kennedy Men, 1901–1963, The Laws of the Father*, 691. See also Robert Dallek, *An Unfinished Life*, 2003, 636–638.

533 "A piece of garbage": Andrew Morton, *Monica's Story*, 1999, 41.

533 "trying to bring her off": Ibid.

Chapter Sixty-Seven

537 "obviously was a man": Sally Quinn, "Tabloid Politics, the Clintons and the Way We Now Scrutinize Our Potential Presidents," *Washington Post*, January 26, 1992.

537 "There was continued flirtation": Phil Kuntz, ed., *The Starr Report: The Evidence*, 1998, 124.

Chapter Sixty-Eight

539 "He exudes sexual energy": Morton, *Monica's Story*, 57.

539 "the Full Clinton": Ibid., 58.

540 "whom she'd first scorned": Ibid., 57.

540 "a big crush": Ibid., 63.

540 "I knew that one day": Ibid., 58.

540 culminating in oral sex: Kuntz, ed., *The Starr Report*, 125.

540 "We clicked at an incredible": Morton, *Monica's Story*, 65.

541 "hooking up": "The term itself is vague—covering everything from kissing to intercourse—though it is sometimes a euphemism for oral sex, performed by a girl on a boy," Benoit Denizet-Lewis would later write in a survey for the *New York Times*. He noted how "many teenagers opt for hookups after a romantic relationship has

soured." He warned, however, that "underneath the teenage bravado I heard so often are mixed feelings about an activity that can leave them feeling depressed, confused, and guilty." For all the promised emotional safety of "friendship with benefits," girls especially found themselves hurt when dumped—Benoit Denizet-Lewis, "Friends, Friends With Benefits and the Benefits of the Local Mall," *New York Times*, May 30, 2004.

542   "This is the craziest zoo": Holbrooke, *To End a War*, 282.

542   "Today the Republicans": "Statement on House of Representatives Action on Budget Reconciliation Legislation, November 17, 1995, *PPP:WJC*, Vol. II, 1771.

543   "I think the President": Morton, *Monica's Story*, 65.

543   "Lewinsky": Ibid., 66.

543   "Sir, the girl's here": Kuntz, ed., *The Starr Report*, 126.

544   "institutionalization of gossip": Gail Collins, *Scorpion Tongues*, 1998, 209–232.

544   "You can't cast a man": Betty Boyd Caroli, *First Ladies*, 1955, 355. Also August Heckscher, *Woodrow Wilson*, 1991, 185–188, and Jeffrey D. Schultz, *Presidential Scandals*, 2000, 232.

545   "When it was suggested": Quinn, "Tabloid Politics, the Clintons and the Way We Now Scrutinize Our Potential Presidents," *Washington Post*, January 26, 1992.

545   "women who wish to be": Mary McGrory, "The Front-Runner Stumbles," *Washington Post*, February 11, 1992.

546   "is a country with a residual": Quinn, "Tabloid Politics, the Clintons and the Way We Now Scrutinize Our Potential Presidents," *Washington Post*, January 26, 1992.

546   "There are endless questions": Ibid.

Chapter Sixty-Nine

547   "Bill Clinton had not": McCurry, interview with Chris Bury, "The Clinton Years," PBS television.

548   "It was interesting": Panetta, interview with the author, January 20, 2005.

548   "God, this is something": Ann Devroy and Eric Pianin, "Clinton and Congress Agree on Outlines of Budget Goals; Workers Return Today," *Washington Post*, November 20, 1995.

548   "This is a tremendous achievement": William M. Welch, "Now the real budget battle begins; Entitlements, tax cuts still sticking points," *USA Today*, November 20, 1995.

549   "We are at a decisive moment": Clinton, "Remarks Announcing the Bosnia-Herzegovina Peace Agreement and an Exchange with Reporters," *PPP:WJC*, Vol. II, 1777.

549   "I am satisfied that the NATO": Ibid.

550   "There will be no peace": Peter Benesh, "Europe says U.S. role is essential in Bosnia," *Pittsburgh Post-Gazette*, November 28, 1995.

550 "If he can't persuade": Holly Yeager (Hearst News Service), "President takes political risks in force dispatch," *Pittsburgh Post-Gazette*, November 28, 1995.

550 "was considered by his aides": Ann Devroy and Helen Dewar, "U.S. Troops Crucial to Bosnia Peace, Clinton Says," *Washington Post*, November 28, 1995.

551 "He doesn't have to convince": Jon Sawyer, "Lawmakers Question Clinton's Bosnia Policy," *St. Louis Post-Dispatch*, November 28, 1995.

551 "From an empty desk": Clinton, "Address to the Nation on the Implementation of the Peace Agreement in Bosnia-Herzogovina," November 27, 1995, *PPP:WJC*, Vol. II, 1784–1787.

551 "political artistry": Susan Page and Jim Hoagland, "Accidental Peacemaker," *Washington Post*, November 29, 1995.

551 "The only force capable": "Address to the Nation on the Implementation of the Peace Agreement in Bosnia-Herzogovina," November 27, 1995, *PPP:WJC*, Vol. II, 1784–1787.

552 "moral obligation": Susan Page, "Clinton putting his leadership on the line," *USA Today*, November 28, 1995.

552 "We cannot stop all war": "Address to the Nation on the Implementation of the Peace Agreement in Bosnia-Herzogovina," November 27, 1995, *PPP:WJC*, Vol. II, 1784–1787.

Chapter Seventy

553 "not be a bad place": "Remarks to the Parliament of the United Kingdom in London," November 29, 1995, *PPP:WJC*, Vol. II, 1795–1799.

554 "an important evolution": Doyle McManus and William D. Montalbano (Associated Press), "Clinton in Pitch to Parliament; Touts Bosnia Plan, Blasts Isolationists," *Chicago Sun-Times*, November 30, 1995.

554 "We must help peace": "Remarks to the Parliament of the United Kingdom in London," November 29, 1995, *PPP:WJC*, Vol. II, 1795–1799.

555 "two of the best days": Clinton, *My Life*, 686.

555 "My friends, we have stood": "Remarks to the Parliament of the United Kingdom in London," November 29, 1995, *PPP:WJC*, Vol. II, 1795–1799.

555 "America": "Remarks to Mackie International Employees in Belfast, Northern Ireland," November 30, 1995, *PPP:WJC*, Vol. II, 1804–1807.

556 "The Patron Saint": Deaglan de Breadun, " 'Bill, you're elected' is the verdict of Dublin crowds on patron saint of hopeful causes," *Irish Times*, December 2, 1995.

556 "the American President and First Lady": Anne Simpson, "The United States will stand by those who take risks for peace in Northern Ireland; Clinton promises prosperity for peace," *The Herald* (Glasgow), December 1, 1995.

557 "It was the presidency Bill Clinton": Dowd, "Liberties; Peacemaker's Perils," *New York Times*, December 3, 1995.

Chapter Seventy-One

562 "Our decision to go ahead": Gingrich, *Lessons Learned the Hard Way*, 51.

563 *"You* are the cause": Morris, *Behind the Oval Office*, 190.

564 "Normally he is extroverted": Ibid., 199.

564 "zero American forces": Holbrooke, *To End a War*, 323.

564 "Enough is enough": Christopher Parkes, "Clinton vetoes budget bill," *Financial Times* (London), December 7, 1995.

565 "The revolution will continue": Drew, *Showdown*, 344.

565 "You've got to understand": Ibid., 116.

565 "Newt, this isn't going to": Ibid., 350.

565 "As all of you know": Clinton, "Remarks on Budget Negotiations," December 15, 1995, *PPP:WJC*, Vol. II, 1892.

566 "Most people don't commit": Morris, *Behind the Oval Office*, 187.

Chapter Seventy-Two

567 "They made a huge mistake": Scott Fleming, interview with the author, May 26, 2005.

568 "risks being portrayed": *The Washington Times* national weekly edition, December 25–31, 1995.

568 "He may be *Time's* Man": Howard Kurtz, of *Washington Post*, "Time's Man of the Year is Newt of a different color; Dispute arises over magazine cover portrait," *Houston Chronicle*, December 20, 1995.

569 "frustration is increasing": Roger, K. Lowe, "Reality Scuttles Plan to Make House 'Family Friendly,' " *Columbus Dispatch* (Ohio), December 17, 1995.

569 "I get a warm feeling": Lucy Morgan, "Democrats go from the divine to ridicule," *St. Petersburg Times*, December 11, 1995.

569 "The Georgia porker": Mike Barnicle, "Bus of fools filling up fast," *Boston Globe*, December 10, 1995.

569 "If we postpone it": William Goldschlag, et. al., "Newt's Bear Facts Says Market May Crash," New York *Daily News*, December 6, 1995.

570 "go through detox": Ibid.

570 "We made a mistake": Drew, *Showdown*, 360.

571 "There aren't going to be any": Ibid., 367.

571 "Why are we wasting our time": Ibid., 373.

572 "Numbers, numbers": Woodward, *The Choice*, 353.

Chapter Seventy-Three

573 "The vast majority of soldiers": Rick Atkinson, "GIs on Clinton's Bosnia Visit: 'He's Coming. . . . It's Great,'" *Washington Post*, January 12, 1996.

574 "raising the torch": Reuters, AFP, "Clinton barnstorms the Balkans," *The Australian*, January 15, 1996.

574 "what was admittedly": Steve Komarow, "Clinton on good footing in Bosnia; Boosts image with troops on Tuzla trip," *USA Today*, January 15, 1996.

574 "The president set the Republicans": Carl Rowan, "Clinton on the Ropes—Or a Knockout? He was masterful in making Gingrich and Dole look like ideologues willing to ruin America if they can't rule it their way," *Chicago Sun-Times*, January 25, 1996.

575 "the era of big government": "Address Before a Joint Session of the Congress on the State of the Union," January 23, 1996, *PPP:WJC*, Vol. I, 79–87.

576 "Unfortunately": Tom Shales, "Bill Clinton's Picture-Perfect State of the Union," *Washington Post*, January 24, 1996.

577 it was "found": Beth Nolan and John Podesta,"Missing Records, The Prequel," *New York Times*, January 28, 1996.

577 "Clinton appeared robust": Shales, "Bill Clinton's Picture-Perfect State of the Union," *Washington Post*, January 24, 1996.

577 "He's a much stronger figure": David M. Shribman, "The president as maestro; State of the Union address," *Boston Globe*, January 24, 1996.

577 "The president certainly took words": Editorial, "The president's state," *St. Petersburg Times*, January 25, 1996.

577 "It was an absolute disaster": Patti Waldmeir, "Pomp helps to push Clinton's message," *Financial Times* (London), January 25, 1996.

578 "I'm in awe of the guy": David Dahl, "Clinton borrows Reagan's playbook," *St. Petersburg Times*, January 25, 1996.

578 "walk out from behind": David S. Broder, "A Preview of the 1996 Campaign? President Shows Strength in His Rhetorical Matchup With Dole," *Washington Post*, January 24, 1996.

578 "Any Republican who": Michael Wines, "Dole's Response Gets a Response of Its Own, and It's Fairly Underwhelming," *New York Times*, January 25, 1996.

578 "Bob Dole doesn't stack up": Dahl, *St. Petersburg Times*, January 25, 1996.

578 The latest Pew Research Center poll: John King, "Poll Shows Forbes, Dole Even in N.H.," *Chicago Sun-Times*, January 29, 1996.

579 52 percent felt: Susan Page, "First lady: Behind the numbers; Voters' views shaped by several factors," *USA Today*, January 26, 1996.

579   "growing skepticism": Page, "Embattled first lady launches book tour; Ark. crowd friendlier than poll numbers," *USA Today*, January 17, 1996.

579   "to reassure her and": Timothy Clifford, "Carefully Setting The Stage," New York *Daily News*, January 27, 1996.

580   wouldn't make them less likely: Paul Nyhan, Bloomberg Business News, "Poll: Clinton tops Dole, Forbes," *Pittsburgh Post-Gazette*, January 29, 1996.

580   head-to-head competition: If Dole was the Republican nominee, Clinton would capture 52 percent of the vote, while Dole would get 43 percent, according to the poll. Forbes would fare about the same, with Clinton capturing 49 percent of the vote to Forbes's 42 percent.

Chapter Seventy-Four

583   "I think there was some concern": Sosnik, interview with the author, May 23, 2005.

585   "Morris even sent": Woodward, *The Choice*, 368–370.

586   "That's the way": Woodward, *The Choice*, 354.

586   "a bunch of nitwits": Ibid., 366–367.

Chapter Seventy-Five

587   "unable to fight temptation": Clinton, *My Life*, 811.

588   "According to Ms. Lewinsky": Starr, *The Starr Report*, 86.

589   "I didn't know if": Ibid., 90.

Chapter Seventy-Six

590   "I formed an opinion": President Clinton's videotaped Grand Jury testimony, August 17, 1998, in Phil Kuntz, ed., *The Starr Report: The Evidence*, 399.

591   "determined to have a showdown": Starr, *The Starr Report*, 90.

593   "You know, if I": Morton, *Monica's Story*, 74.

593   "In the beginning": Ibid., 73.

593   "I felt it was wrong": Ibid., 75.

593   "I frankly, from 1996": "President Clinton's Videotaped Grand Jury Testimony," August 17, 1998, in Kuntz, ed., *The Starr Report: The Evidence*, 403.

593   "I did believe she would": Ibid.

593   "I knew that the minute": Ibid., 399.

594   "like rays of sunshine": Morton, *Monica's Story*, 70.

Chapter Seventy-Seven

597 "an area that he already": Sosnik, interview with the author, May 23, 2005.

Chapter Seventy-Eight

601 "You're twenty points": Reich, *Locked in the Cabinet*, 321.

601 "relentlessly more conservative": See, inter alia, Marjorie Randon Herschey, "The Congressional Elections," in Gerald M. Pomper, ed., *The Election of 1996*, 219 et seq.

602 "This guy is like a hungry lion": Woodward, *The Choice*, 417.

603 "I never thought the Republicans": Sosnik, interview with the author, May 23, 2005.

603 "drove a strategy": Ibid.

603 "You have to weigh": Ibid.

605 a "clutch": "It's a slightly derisive term for somebody who, whenever he or she sees the president—or any of the principals, let's put it that way, not even the president, any of the principals [i.e., the first lady or vice president] would want to be around, or would hover, or be close"—Evelyn Lieberman, testimony to the Grand Jury, January 30, 1998, in Kuntz, ed., *The Starr Report: The Evidence*, 37.

605 "the president was vulnerable": Starr, *The Starr Report: The Official Report*, 98.

605 agreed with his deputy: Ibid.

606 crime of "overfamiliarity": Morton, *Monica's Story*, 80.

606 "I was hysterical": Ibid.

606 "obsessional, jealous, and hysterical": Ibid., 83.

606 "I bet this has": Ibid., 81.

607 "Why did they have to": Starr, *The Starr Report*, 101.

607 "The president indicated": Ibid., 102.

607 "Mr. President!": Ibid.; and Kuntz, ed., *The Starr Report: The Evidence*, 25.

Chapter Seventy-Nine

608 slammed into the Dalmatian hillside": Steven A. Holmes, *Ron Brown: An Uncommon Life*, 200, 279–280.

609 courageously defended it: The responsibilities of the Commerce Department would merely have to be added to other departments, saving nothing, Brown argued with senators—who, for the most part, agreed.

609 "The Bible tells us": "Remarks at the funeral of Secretary of Commerce Ronald H. Brown," April 10, 1996, *PPP:WJC*, Vol. I, 562–565.

Chapter Eighty

613 "that terrorist networks": "Remarks at the University of Central Oklahoma in Edmond, Oklahoma," April 5, 1996, *PPP:WJC*, Vol. I, 549–553.

614 "bombs blew up in Israel": A series of four Hamas-trained Palestinian suicide bombers had wreaked mayhem in Jerusalem and Tel Aviv in March, killing 62 and injuring hundreds.

616 "the Unabomber": Targeting a series of innocent strangers for assassination by mail, Kaczynski had succeeded in killing three of them, and wounding twenty-nine people. Giving up on his teaching job at Berkeley, Kaczynski had bewailed, like jihadists across the world, the evils of modern life—indeed, had penned a 35,000-word manifesto he titled "Industrial Society and Its Future." Kaczynski wanted no part in this society—and deeply resented those who did. Denounced by his older brother—who recognized his handwriting—Kaczynski had been tracked down to a lonely cabin in Montana, where he was assembling his *seventeenth* bomb. He was indicted for deliberate mass murder and found insane. Rejecting that diagnosis, he had pled guilty—thus enabling him to avoid the death penalty and permitting him to live a hermit-like existence in a special penitentiary in Florida for the rest of his life, without parole.

617 "No Republican": Gene Lyons, interview with the author, March 21, 2006.

619 "Freeh should have spent": Clarke, *Against All Enemies,* 116–117.

620 "That did not seem": Ibid., 122.

621 "fed up with": Karen Ball, Ying Chan, and Corky Siemaszko, "Prez Steps in to Ease Anger; Will Huddle with Kin of TWA Victims Today," New York *Daily News,* July 25, 1996.

621 "three large pipes": Terry Bohle Montague, "Bomb Tech," *Meridian Magazine,* November 22, 2003.

622 "the arrested men": Robert Edward Starr III and William James McCarnie Jr., both of Roberta, were charged with conspiracy to possess unregistered explosive devices.

622 "an evil act of terror": "The President's Radio Address and an Exchange with Reporters," July 27, 1996, *PPP: WJC,* Vol. II, 1204–1206.

Chapter Eighty-One

624 "the Republican obsession with Whitewater": Joe Conason and Gene Lyons, *The Hunting of the President,* 2001, 86–97, et seq. Thanks to President Reagan's relaxation of federal fiscal supervision, David Hale, a former municipal judge, had, during the worst Republican years of the savings and loans scandal, deliberately and repeatedly defrauded individuals, companies, federal institutions, and taxpayers of more than $3.5 million through his Capital Management Company. He was sentenced to only twenty-eight months in jail, and three years' supervised

release after promising Starr incriminating testimony and documents against the Clintons, Governor Tucker, and other Democrats. No single item of documentation against the president was ever supplied, but the president was nevertheless forced by Starr to give videotaped testimony from Washington, D.C., in the case, refuting Hale's baseless accusations.

624   "You don't have to say": Conason and Lyons, *The Hunting of the President*, 254.

625   "I had given him to believe": Morris, *Behind the Oval Office*, 300–301.

626   "signing the bill": Stephanopoulos, *All Too Human*, 421.

626   "inveterate caution": Peter Edelman to author, Hofstra University Eleventh Presidential Conference, November 12, 2005. See also Peter Edelman, "The Worst Thing Bill Clinton Has Done," *Atlantic Monthly*, March 1997.

626   "the law will antagonize": Jonathan Freedland (*The Guardian*), "Critics condemn Clinton for signing law to overhaul welfare system: Five-year limit placed on welfare assistance," in *Ottawa Citizen*, August 23, 1996.

Chapter Eighty-Two

628   "I'm not arguing what": Evan Thomas, et al., "Wild Card," *Newsweek*, November 18, 1996.

630   "when the year 2000": "Remarks on Concluding a Whistlestop Tour in Michigan City, Indiana," August 28, 1996, *PPP:WJC*, Vol. II, 1404–1407.

630   "almost unbearably poignant": Jill Lawrence, "Convention winners and losers," *USA Today*, August 30, 1996.

631   "not tolerable": Thomas, et al., "Wild Card," *Newsweek*, November 18, 1996.

631   "This thing will blow": Ibid.

632   a second bombshell: Hugh Davies, "How vanity led to downfall of Clinton's guru," *Daily Telegraph* (London), August 30, 1996.

632   " 'I would have hoped' ": Thomas, et al., "Wild Card," *Newsweek*, November 18, 1996.

632   "to treat each of you generously": Ibid.

633   "Do I need this today?": Ibid.

633   "Dick Morris is my friend": "Statement on the Resignation of Political Consultant Dick Morris," August 29, 1996, *PPP:WJC*, Vol. II, 1408.

Chapter Eighty-Three

638   "I would exclude": Joe Shaulis (Scripps Howard News Service), "Two party tag-team keeps others on ropes. Third party candidates say debates keep ideas from reaching voters," *Rocky Mountain News* (Denver), October 5, 1996.

638   "Bob Dole is a plainspoken": Tom Brazaitis, "Damage Control the Issue in Clinton-Dole Debate," Cleveland *Plain Dealer*, October 6, 1996.

638   "it will take an improbable": Jurek Martin, "To the victor, the spoils: Tomorrow's televised presidential debate may affect other electoral battles in the US," *Financial Times* (London), October 5, 1996.

638   "we just kind of played out": Sosnik, interview with the author, May 23, 2005.

639   substantive but non-theatrical debate: See Marion J. Just, "Candidate Strategies and the Media Campaign," in Gerald M. Pomper, ed., *The Election of 1996*, 90–91.

639   "It may have been too elevated": Steve Berg, "Gore appears the winner of high-minded exchange," Minneapolis *Star Tribune*, October 10, 1996.

640   "We're going to tear his": Richard L. Berke, "For Both Camps in Final Debate, Hopes, Risks and a Few Surprises," *New York Times*, October 18, 1996.

640   "I was praying for": Bill Nichols, "Dole on offense in debate," *USA Today*, October 17, 1996.

640   "The temptation was to go": Berke, "For Both Camps in Final Debate," *New York Times*, October 18, 1996.

641   "No attack ever created a job": "Presidential Debate in San Diego," October 16, 1996, PPP:WJC, Vol. II, 1837–1857.

643   "Bob Dole's unintelligible": George F. Will, "Clinton to Extend his Squalid Presidency Because Dole Waged Unintelligible Campaign," *Buffalo News* (New York), November 5, 1996. (James Joyce's *Finnegans Wake*, by contrast, removed the apostrophe from the traditional Irish ballad. This nineteenth-century comic song recorded the "tipplin'way," and supposed death in falling from a ladder, of one Tim Finnegan.)

643   "We now know that": Dowd, "US Election: Comment: Bill's New Campaign for Immortality," *The Guardian* (London), November 5, 1996.

643   "Mr. Clinton treats the rope line": Ibid.

Chapter Eighty-Four

645–646   "in the last days of his campaign": John Carlin, "US Presidential Elections: How old Dole got pumped up, then burst," *The Independent* (London), November 5, 1996.

647   "I thought of the Alamo": Dowd, "US Election," *The Guardian* (London), November 5, 1996.

648   "Maybe": A. M. Rosenthal, "On My Mind; Am I Better Off?" *New York Times*, November 5, 1996.

648   "Republican despondency": Marcus, "President's opponent tries for a miracle," *Hobart Mercury* (Australia), November 5, 1996.

648   "We are rejigging": Martin Walker, "US Election '96; Clinton: My Fears As Lead Starts To Shrink," *The Guardian* (London), November 4, 1996.

652   "do some people dislike you": Clinton, "Interview with Tabitha Soren of MTV, August 30, 1996, *PPP:WJC*, Vol. II, 1425–1430.

BIBLIOGRAPHY

Works relating to Arkansas and Bill Clinton's pre-presidential career are included in the bibliography in the author's *Bill Clinton, An American Journey: Great Expectations*. The following bibliography is not exhaustive, but gives an overview of the main texts relating to President Bill Clinton's first term in the Oval Office, from a variety of political and cultural perspectives, as the subtitles demonstrate.

Abse, Leo. *Fellatio, Masochism, Politics and Love*. London: Robson Books, 2000.

Albright, Madeleine, with Bill Woodward. *Madam Secretary: A Memoir*. New York: Miramax, 2003.

Aldrich, Gary. *Unlimited Access: An FBI Agent Inside the Clinton White House*. Washington, D.C.: Regnery, 1996.

Anderson-Miller, Julia, and Bruce Joshua Miller. *Dreams of Bill: A Collection of Funny, Strange, and Downright Peculiar Dreams About Our President, Bill Clinton*. New York: Citadel Press, Carol Communications, 1994.

Angelou, Maya. *On the Pulse of Morning*. New York: Random House.

Aron, Leon. *Yeltsin: A Revolutionary Life*. New York: St. Martin's Press, 2000.

Barber, Benjamin R. *The Truth of Power: Intellectual Affairs in the Clinton White House*. New York: W. W. Norton, 2001.

Bartley, Robert L., ed. *Whitewater: A Journal Briefing. From the Editorial Pages of the Wall Street Journal*. New York: Wall Street Journal, 1994.

Beckner, Steven K. *Back from the Brink: The Greenspan Years*. New York: John Wiley, 1996.

Bell, Lauren Cohen. *Warring Factions: Interest Groups, Money, and the New Politics of Senate Confirmation*. Columbus: Ohio State University Press, 2002.

Berlant, Lauren, and Lisa Dugan, eds. *Our Monica, Ourselves: The Clinton Affair and the National Interest*. New York: New York University Press, 2001.

Berlet, Chip, ed. *Eyes Right! Challenging the Right Wing Backlash*. Boston: South End Press, 1995.

Bildt, Carl. *Peace Journey: The Struggle for Peace in Bosnia*. London: Weidenfeld and Nicolson, 1998.

Blumenthal, Sidney. *The Clinton Wars*. New York: Farrar Straus & Giroux, 2003.

Bohn, Michael K. *Nerve Center: Inside the White House Situation Room*. Washington, D.C.: Brassey's, 2003.

Bonnell, Victoria E. and Lynn Hunt, eds. *Beyond the Cultural Turn: New Directions in the Study of Society and Culture*. Berkeley: University of California Press, 1999.

Bovard, James. *"feeling your pain": The Explosion and Abuse of Government Power in the Clinton-Gore Years*. New York: St. Martin's Press, 2000.

Bowden, Mark. *Black Hawk Down: A Story of Modern War.* New York: Atlantic Monthly Press, 1999.

Bradley, Bill. *Time Present, Time Past: A Memoir.* New York: Knopf, 1996.

Brock, David. *Blinded by the Right.* New York: Crown Publishers, 2002.

_____. *The Seduction of Hillary Rodham Clinton.* New York: Free Press, 1996.

Brooks, David. *Bobos in Paradise: The New Upper Class and How They Got There.* New York: Simon & Schuster, 2000.

Brown, Floyd G. *"Slick Willie": Why America Cannot Trust Bill Clinton.* Annapolis, MD: Annapolis Publishing Company, 1992.

Brummett, John. *Highwire: From the Back Roads to the Beltway—The Education of Bill Clinton.* New York: Hyperion, 1994.

Burns, James MacGregor, and Georgia J. Sorenson. *Dead Center: Clinton-Gore Leadership and the Perils of Moderation.* New York: Scribner, 1999.

Busby, Robert. *Defending the Presidency: Clinton and the Lewinsky Scandal.* Basingstoke, UK: Palgrave, 2001.

Campbell, Colin, and Bert A. Rockman, eds. *The Clinton Presidency: First Appraisals.* Chatham, N.J.: Chatham House Publishers, 1996.

Caroli, Betty Boyd. *First Ladies: An Intimate Look at How 38 Women Handled What May Be the Most Demanding, Unpaid, Unelected Job in America.* New York: Oxford University Press, 1995.

Carter, Stephen L. *The Confirmation Mess: Cleaning Up the Federal Appointments Process.* New York: Basic Books, 1994.

Carville, James. *We're Right, They're Wrong: A Handbook for Spirited Progressives.* New York: Random House, 1996.

Christopher, Warren. *Chances of a Lifetime.* New York: Scribner, 2001.

Clark, Wesley K. *Waging Modern War: Bosnia, Kosovo, and the Future of Combat.* New York: PublicAffairs, 2001.

Clarke, Richard A. *Against All Enemies: Inside America's War on Terror.* New York: Free Press, 2004.

Clinton, Bill. *Between Hope and History: Meeting America's Challenges for the 21ˢᵗ Century.* New York: Times Books, 1996.

_____. *My Life.* New York: Knopf, 2004.

_____. *The President's Report to the American People, By the White House Domestic Policy Council, with a Letter from President Clinton, and a Foreword by Hillary Rodham Clinton.* New York: Simon & Schuster, 1993.

_____. *Public Papers of the Presidents of the United States: William J. Clinton.* Washington, D.C.: U.S. Government Printing Office, 1993 (two vols.), 1994 (two vols.), 1995 (two vols.).

Clinton, Bill, and Al Gore. *Putting People First: How We Can All Change America.* New York: Times Books, 1992.

Clinton, Bill, et al. *President Clinton's New Beginning: The Complete Text, with Illustrations, of the Historic Clinton-Gore Economic Conference, Little Rock, Arkansas, December 14–15, 1992.* New York: Donald I. Fine, 1993.

Clinton, Hillary Rodham. *Living History.* New York: Simon & Schuster, 2003.

Coburn, Alexander, and Ken Silversten. *Washington Babylon.* New York: Verso, 1996.

Collins, Gail. *Scorpion Tongues: Gossip, Celebrity and American Politics.* New York: William Morrow, 1998.

Conason, Joe, and Gene Lyons. *The Hunting of the President: The ten-year campaign to destroy Bill and Hillary Clinton*. New York: St. Martin's Press, 2001.

Coulter, Ann. *High Crimes and Misdemeanors: The Case Against Bill Clinton*. Washington, D.C.: Regnery, 1998.

Daalder, Ivo H. *Getting to Dayton: The Making of America's Bosnia Policy*. Washington, D.C: Brookings Institution Press, 2000.

Dallek, Robert. *Hail to the Chief: The Making and Unmaking of American Presidents*. New York: Hyperion, 1996.

Doyle, William. *Inside the Oval Office: The White House Tapes from FDR to Clinton*. New York: Kodansha International, 1999.

Drew, Elizabeth. *The Corruption of American Politics: What Went Wrong and Why*. Woodstock, N.Y.: The Overlook Press, 1999.

_____. *On the Edge: The Clinton Presidency*. New York: Simon & Schuster, 1994.

_____. *Showdown: The Struggle Between the Gingrich Congress and the Clinton White House*. New York: Simon & Schuster, 1996.

_____. *Whatever It Takes: The Real Struggle for Political Power in America*. New York: Viking, 1997.

Dumas, Ernest, ed. *The Clintons of Arkansas: An introduction by those who know them best*. Fayetteville: University of Arkansas Press, 1993.

Elders, Joycelyn, and David Chanoff. *From Sharecropper's Daughter to Surgeon General of the United States*. New York: William Morrow, 1996.

Eszterhas, Joe. *American Rhapsody*. New York: Random House, 2000.

Evans-Pritchard, Ambrose. *The Secret Life of Bill Clinton*. Washington, D.C.: Regnery Publishing, 1997.

Ferguson, Niall. *Colossus: The Price of America's Empire*. New York: Penguin Press, 2004.

Fick, Paul. *The Dysfunctional President: Inside the Mind of Bill Clinton*. Secaucus, N.J.: Carol Publishing, 1995.

_____. *The Dysfunctional President: Understanding the Compulsions of Bill Clinton*. Secaucus, N.J.: Citadel Press/Carol Publishing, 1998.

Flowers, Gennifer. *Passion and Betrayal*. Del Mar, California: Emery Dalton Books, 1995.

Frank, Thomas. *What's the Matter with Kansas: How Conservatives Won the Heart of America*. New York, Metropolitan Books, Henry Holt, 2004.

Freeh, Louis J., with Howard Means. *My FBI: Bringing Down the Mafia, Investigating Bill Clinton, and Fighting the War on Terror*. New York: St. Martin's Press, 2005.

Gallen, David. *Bill Clinton as They Know Him: An Oral Biography*. New York: Gallen Publishing Group, 1994.

Gergen, David. *Eyewitness to Power: The Essence of Leadership, Nixon to Clinton*. New York: Simon & Schuster, 2000.

Gillespie, Ed, and Bob Schellhas, eds. *Contract With America: The Bold Plan by Rep. Newt Gingrich, Rep. Dick Armey and the House Republicans to Change the Nation*. New York: Times Books, 1994.

Gingrich, Newt. *Lessons Learned the Hard Way: A Personal Report*. New York: Harper-Collins, 1998.

_____. *To Renew America*. New York: HarperCollins, 1995.

Gow, James. *Triumph of the Lack of Will: International Diplomacy and the Yugoslav War*. New York: Columbia University Press, 1997.

Gross, Martin L. *The Great Whitewater Fiasco: An American Tale of Money, Power, and Politics.* New York: Ballantine, 1994.

Gurstein, Rochelle. *The Repeal of Innocence: A History of America's Cultural and Legal Struggles over Free Speech, Obscenity, Sexual Liberation, and Modern Art.* New York: Hill and Wang, 1996.

Halberstam, David. *War in a Time of Peace: Bush, Clinton and the Generals.* New York: Scribner, 2001.

Hamilton, Nigel. *JFK: Reckless Youth.* New York: Random House, 1992.

_____. *Bill Clinton, An American Journey: Great Expectations.* New York: Random House, 2003.

Harris, John F. *The Survivor: Bill Clinton in the White House.* New York: Random House 2005.

Hitchens, Christopher. *No One Left to Lie To: The Triangulations of William Jefferson Clinton.* London: Verso, 1990.

Hohenberg. John. *Reelecting Bill Clinton: Why America Chose a "New Democrat."* Syracuse, N.Y.: Syracuse University Press, 1997.

Holbrooke, Richard. *To End a War.* New York: Modern Library (rev. ed.), 1999.

Holmes, Steven A. *Ron Brown: An Uncommon Life.* New York: John Wiley, 2000.

Hersh, Seymour M. *The Dark Side of Camelot.* Boston: Little, Brown, 1997.

Hess, Stephen. *Organizing the Presidency.* Washington, D.C.: Brookings Institution Press, 2002.

Hubbell, Webb. *Friends in High Places: Our Journey from Little Rock to Washington, D.C.* New York: William Morrow, 1997.

Hunter, James Davison. *The Death of Character: Moral Education in an Age Without Good or Evil.* New York: Basic Books, 2000.

Isikoff, Michael. *Uncovering Clinton: A Reporter's Story.* New York: Crown Publishers, 1999.

Jacobs, Lawrence R., and Robert Y. Shapiro. *Politicians Don't Pander: Political Manipulation and the Loss of Democratic Responsiveness.* Chicago: University of Chicago Press, 2000.

Johnson, Haynes. *The Best of Times: America in the Clinton Years.* New York: Harcourt, 2001.

Johnson, Haynes, and David Broder. *The System: The American Way of Politics at the Breaking Point.* Boston: Little Brown, 1996.

Jones, Charles O. *Clinton & Congress, 1993–1996: Risk, Restoration, and Reelection.* Norman: University of Oklahoma, 1999.

_____. *Passages to the Presidency: From Campaigning to Governing.* Washington, D.C.: Brookings Institution, 1998.

_____. *Separate but Equal Branches: Congress and the Presidency.* Chatham, N.J.: Chatham House, 1995.

Kalb, Marvin. *One Scandalous Story: Clinton, Lewinsky, & 13 Days That Tarnished American Journalism.* New York: The Free Press, 2001

Kelley, Virginia, with James Morgan. *Leading with My Heart.* New York: Simon & Schuster, 1994.

Kessler, Ronald. *Inside Congress: The Shocking Scandals, Corruption, and Abuse of Power Behind the Scenes on Capitol Hill.* New York: Pocket Books, 1997.

_____. *Inside the White House: The Hidden Lives of the Modern Presidents and Secrets of the World's Most Powerful Institution.* New York: Pocket Books, 1995.

Klein, Joe. *The Natural: The Misunderstood Presidency of Bill Clinton*. New York: Doubleday, 2002.

_____. (writing as "Anonymous"). *Primary Colors: A Novel of Politics*. New York: Random House, 1996.

Koppel, Ted. *Off Camera: Private Thoughts Made Public*. New York: Knopf, 2000.

Kuntz, Phil, ed. *The Starr Report: The Evidence. The Full Text of President Clinton's Videotaped Grand Jury Testimony*, etc. New York: Pocket Books, 1998.

Kurtz, Howard. *Spin Cycle: Inside the Clinton Propaganda Machine*. New York: The Free Press, 1998.

Lake, Anthony. *6 Nightmares: Real Threats in a Dangerous World and How America Can Meet Them*. Boston: Little, Brown, 2000.

Lewis, Charles, et al. *The Buying of the President: An Inside Look at the Special Interests Behind Clinton, Dole, Gramm, Wilson, Alexander, Buchanan, and Others*. New York: Avon Books, 1996.

Lowi, Theodore J., and Benjamin Ginsberg. *Embattled Democracy: Politics and Policy in the Clinton Era*. New York: W. W. Norton, 1995.

Ludwig, Arnold M. *King of the Mountain: The Nature of Political Leadership*. Lexington: University Press of Kentucky, 2002.

Lyons, Gene. *Fools for Scandal: How the Media Invented Whitewater*. New York: Franklin Square Press, 1996.

Malti-Douglas, Fedwa. *The Starr Report Disrobed*. New York: New York University Press, 2000.

Maraniss, David. *The Clinton Enigma: A Four-and-a-Half-Minute Speech Reveals This President's Entire Life*. New York: Simon & Schuster, 1998.

Maraniss, David, and Ellen Makashima. *The Prince of Tennessee: The Rise of Al Gore*. New York: Simon & Schuster, 2000.

Marcus, Greil. *Double Trouble: Bill Clinton and Elvis Presley in a Land of No Alternatives*. New York: Henry Holt, 2000.

Markovits, Andrei S., and Mark Silverstein, eds. *The Politics of Scandal: Power and Process in Liberal Democracies*. New York: Holmes and Meier, 1988.

Matrisciana, Pat. *The Clinton Chronicles Book*. Hemet, C.A.: Jeremiah Books, 1994.

McDougal, Jim. *Arkansas Mischief: The Birth of a National Scandal*. New York: Henry Holt and Company, 1998.

McDougal, Susan. *The Woman Who Wouldn't Talk*. New York: Carroll & Graf, 2003.

Milkis, Sidney M., and Michael Nelson. *The American Presidency: Origins and Development, 1776–1998*. Washington, D.C.: Congressional Quarterly Press, 1999.

Milton, Joyce. *The First Partner: Hillary Rodham Clinton*. New York: William Morrow, 1999.

Moldea, Dan E. *A Washington Tragedy: How the Death of Vincent Foster Ignited a Political Firestorm*. Washington, D.C.: Regnery, 1998.

Morris, Richard. *Behind the Oval Office: Winning the Presidency in the Nineties*. New York: Random House, 1997.

Morris, Richard, and Eileen McGann. *Because He Could*. New York: Regan Books, 2004

Morris, Roger. *Partners in Power: The Clintons and Their America*. Washington, D.C.: Regnery Publishing, 1996.

Morton, Andrew. *Monica's Story*. New York: St. Martin's Press, 1999.

Nelson, Rex, with Philip Martin. *The Hillary Factor: The Story of America's First Lady.* New York: Gallen Publishing Group, 1993.

Noonan, Peggy. *The Case Against Hillary Clinton.* New York: Regan Books, 2000.

Ogden, Christopher. *Life of the Party: The Biography of Pamela Digby Churchill Hayward Harriman.* Boston: Little, Brown, 1994.

Oppenheimer, Jerry. *State of a Union: Inside the Complex Marriage of Bill and Hillary Clinton.* New York: HarperCollins, 2000.

Owen, David. *Balkan Odyssey.* New York: Harcourt Brace, 1995.

Patterson, Bradley H. Jr. *The White House Staff: Inside the West Wing and Beyond.* Washington, D.C.: Brookings Institution, 2000.

Patterson, Robert B. *Dereliction of Duty: The Eyewitness Account of How Bill Clinton Compromised America's National Security.* Washington, D.C.: Regnery, 2003.

Pomper, Gerald et al. *The Election of 1996: Reports and Interpretations.* Chatham, N.J.: Chatham House, 1997.

Post, Jerrold M., ed. *The Psychological Assessment of Political Leaders, with Profiles of Saddam Hussein and Bill Clinton.* Ann Arbor: University of Michigan Press, 2003.

Powell, Colin, with Joseph E. Persico. *My American Journey.* New York: Random House, 1995.

Power, Samantha. *"A Problem From Hell": America and the Age of Genocide.* New York: Basic Books, 2002.

Pritchard-Evans, Ambrose. *The Secret Life of Bill Clinton: The Unreported Stories.* Washington, D.C.: Regnery Publishing, 1997.

Putnam, Robert D. *Bowling Alone: The Collapse and Revival of American Community.* New York: Simon & Schuster, 2000.

Rauch, Jonathan. *Demosclerosis: The Silent Killer of American Government.* New York: Times Books. 1994.

Reeves, Richard. *President Kennedy: Profile of Power.* New York: Simon & Schuster, 1993.

_____. *Running in Place: How Bill Clinton Disappointed America.* Kansas City: Andrews and McMeel, 1996.

Reich, Robert B. *Locked in the Cabinet.* New York: Knopf, 1997.

Renshon, Stanley A. *High Hopes: The Clinton Presidency and the Politics of Ambition.* New York : New York University Press, 1996, 1998.

Retter, James D. *Anatomy of a Scandal: An Investigation into the Campaign to Undermine the Clinton Presidency.* Los Angeles: General Publishing Group, 1998.

Ridley, Matt. *The Red Queen: Sex and the Evolution of Human Nature.* New York: Macmillan, 1993.

Rieff, David. *Slaughterhouse: Bosnia and the Failure of the West.* New York: Simon & Schuster, 1995.

Rohde, David. *End Game: The Betrayal and Fall of Srebrenica: Europe's Worst Massacre Since World War II.* New York: Farrar Straus & Giroux, 1997.

Rozell, Mark J., and Clyde Wilcox, eds. *The Clinton Scandal and the Future of American Government.* Washington, D.C.: Georgetown University, 2000.

Rubin, Robert E., and Jacob Weisberg. *In an Uncertain World: Tough Choices From Wall Street to Washington.* New York: Random House, 2003.

Ruddy, Christopher. *The Strange Death of Vince Foster: An Investigation.* New York: The Free Press, 1997.

Sabato, Larry, et al. *Peep Show: Media and Politics in an Age of Scandal*. Lanham, M.D.: Rowman and Littlefield Publishers, 2000.

Schmidt, Susan, and Michael Weisskopf. *Truth at Any Cost: Ken Starr and the Unmaking of Bill Clinton*. New York: Harper Collins, 2000.

Jeffrey D. Schultz. *Presidential Scandals*. Washington, D.C.: CQ Press, 2000.

Sheehy, Gail. *Hillary's Choice*. New York: Random House, 1999.

Silber, Laura, and Allan Little. *The Death of Yugoslavia*. London: Penguin Books/BBC Books, 1995.

Simon, Roger. *Showtime: The American Political Circus and the Race for the White House*. New York: Times Books, 1998.

Starr, Kenneth. *The Starr Report: The Findings of Independent Counsel Kenneth W. Starr on President Clinton and the Monica Lewinsky Affair, with Analysis by the staff of the* Washington Post. New York: PublicAffairs, 1998.

_____. *The Starr Report: The Official Report of the Independent Counsel's Investigation of the President*, Rocklin, C.A.: Forum (Prima Publishing), 1998.

Steely, Mel. *The Gentleman from Georgia: The Biography of Newt Gingrich*. Macon, G.A.: Mercer University Press, 2000.

Stiglitz, Joseph E. *Globalization and Its Discontents*. New York: W. W. Norton, 2002.

Stephanopoulos, George. *All Too Human*. Boston: Little, Brown, 1999.

Stone, Deborah J., and Christopher Manion. *"Slick Willie" II: Why America Still Cannot Trust Bill Clinton*. Annapolis, M.D.: Annapolis-Maryland Book Publishers, 1994.

Talbott, Strobe. *The Russia Hand: A Memoir of Presidential Diplomacy*. New York: Random House, 2002.

Timmerman, Kenneth R. *Shakedown: Exposing the Real Jesse Jackson*. Washington, D.C.: Regnery, 2002.

Timperlake, Edward, and William C. Triplett II. *Year of the Rat: How Bill Clinton Compromised U.S. Security for Chinese Cash*. Washington, D.C.: Regnery, 1998.

Tolchin, Martin, and Susan J. Martin. *Glass Houses: Congressional Ethics and the Politics of Venom*. Boulder, CO: Westview Press, 2001.

Toobin, Jeffrey. *A Vast Conspiracy: The Real Story of the Sex Scandal that Nearly Brought Down a President*. New York: Random House, 1999.

Troy, Gil. *Mr. and Mrs. President: From the Trumans to the Clintons*. Lawrence: University of Kansas Press, 2000.

Turque, Bill. *Inventing Al Gore: A Biography*. Boston: Houghton Mifflin, 2000.

Tyrrell, J. Emmett. *Boy Clinton: The Political Biography*. Washington, D.C.: Regnery Publishing, 1996.

Walker, Diana. *Public & Private: Twenty Years Photographing the Presidency*. Washington, D.C.: National Geographic, 2002.

Walker, Martin. *The President We Deserve: Bill Clinton, His Rise, Fall and Comeback*. New York: Crown Publishers, 1996.

Warshaw, Shirley Anne. *The Domestic Presidency: Policy Making in the White House*. Boston: Allyn and Bacon, 1997.

Wickham, Dewayne. *Bill Clinton and Black America*. New York: Ballantine, 2002.

Williams, Rhys H., ed. *Cultural Wars in American Politics: Critical Reviews of a Popular Myth*. New York: Aldine de Gruyter, 1997.

Wilson, Colin, and Damon Wilson. *Scandal! Private Stories of Public Shame*. London: Virgin, 2003.

Wit, Joel S., et. al. *Going Critical: The First North Korean Nuclear Crisis*. Washington, D.C.: Brookings Institution, 2004.

Wittes, Benjamin. *Starr: A Reassessment*. New Haven: Yale University, 2001.

Woodward, Bob. *The Agenda: Inside the Clinton White House*. New York: Simon & Schuster, 1994.

_____. *The Choice*. New York: Simon & Schuster, 1996.

_____. *Shadow: Five Presidents and the Legacy of Watergate*. New York: Simon & Schuster, 1999.

Yeltsin, Boris. *Midnight Diaries*. New York: PublicAffairs, 2000.

Zelnick, Bob. *Gore: A Political Life*. Washington, D.C.: Regnery, 1999.

INDEX

PublicAffairs is a publishing house founded in 1997. It is a tribute to the standards, values, and flair of three persons who have served as mentors to countless reporters, writers, editors, and book people of all kinds, including me.

I.F. Stone, proprietor of *I. F. Stone's Weekly*, combined a commitment to the First Amendment with entrepreneurial zeal and reporting skill and became one of the great independent journalists in American history. At the age of eighty, Izzy published *The Trial of Socrates*, which was a national bestseller. He wrote the book after he taught himself ancient Greek.

Benjamin C. Bradlee was for nearly thirty years the charismatic editorial leader of *The Washington Post*. It was Ben who gave the *Post* the range and courage to pursue such historic issues as Watergate. He supported his reporters with a tenacity that made them fearless and it is no accident that so many became authors of influential, best-selling books.

Robert L. Bernstein, the chief executive of Random House for more than a quarter century, guided one of the nation's premier publishing houses. Bob was personally responsible for many books of political dissent and argument that challenged tyranny around the globe. He is also the founder and longtime chair of Human Rights Watch, one of the most respected human rights organizations in the world.

. . .

For fifty years, the banner of PublicAffairs Press was carried by its owner Morris B. Schnapper, who published Gandhi, Nasser, Toynbee, Truman, and about 1,500 other authors. In 1983, Schnapper was described by *The Washington Post* as "a redoubtable gadfly." His legacy will endure in the books to come.

Peter Osnos, *Founder and Editor-at-Large*